INDUSTRIAL RELATIONS RESEARCH

ASSOCIATION SERIES

# Government Regulation
# of the
# Employment Relationship

EDITED BY

**Bruce E. Kaufman**

First Edition

Library of Congress Catalog Card Number: 50-13564

ISBN 0-913447-70-6

INDUSTRIAL RELATIONS RESEARCH ASSOCIATION SERIES:
Proceedings of the Annual Meeting
Proceedings of the Spring Meeting
Annual Research Volume
Membership Directory (every fourth year)
Newsletter (published quarterly)
Perspectives on Work

Inquiries and other communications regarding membership, meetings, publications,
and general affairs of the Association, as well as notice of address changes should be
addressed to the IRRA national office.

INDUSTRIAL RELATIONS RESEARCH ASSOCIATION
University of Wisconsin–Madison
4233 Social Science Building, 1180 Observatory Drive,
Madison, WI 53706-1393 U.S.A.
Telephone: 608/262-2762    Fax 608/265-4591
irra@macc.wisc.edu

# CONTENTS

Dedicated to

John R. Commons, founder of the field of industrial relations,

and

Richard A. Lester, who took the lead in founding the
Industrial Relations Research Association.

# PREFACE

This volume commemorates the fiftieth anniversary of the Industrial Relations Research Association (IRRA). For a half century the IRRA has provided a unique meeting ground where people interested in the world of work, be they academics, practitioners, third-party neutrals, or policy makers, can discuss and debate the major employment issues of the day. It was the strongly held conviction of the founders of the IRRA that if this debate and discussion are to be most fruitful, they must be based on and enriched by sound, rigorous, and objective *research* from all the academic disciplines related to the employment relationship. To leave no doubt about the centrality of research to the mission of the IRRA, the founders included the word "Research" in the very name of the organization.

The IRRA has promoted research through a variety of forums. Every year since 1949, for example, a large number of the papers presented at the annual winter meeting have been published in a Proceedings volume. Beginning in 1959, a second annual Proceedings volume has been published with papers from the spring meeting. In addition to the Proceedings, the Association has published on a periodic basis a multi-chapter research volume. Each volume is dedicated to a specific topic of current relevance and importance within industrial relations and features analysis and commentary by a wide range of experts of both academic and practitioner backgrounds. The first volume, published in 1949, was *Psychology of Labor-Management Relations*.

This research volume is the forty-second in the series. It is fascinating to look back at the different topics of these volumes, as they chronicle both the enduring themes in industrial relations research, most notably unions and collective bargaining, and the rise to prominence in different historical periods of specific employment problems or issues, such as poverty, manpower programs, and equal rights legislation. It is also instructive to examine the content of the volumes for clearly displayed therein is the steady advance over the years in the rigor and sophistication of academic research and in the breadth and depth of the knowledge base in the field.

This volume exemplifies both of these features. The topic, "Government Regulation of the Employment Relationship," has been one of the core subjects in industrial relations research. Indeed, as noted in the Introduction, government legislation and regulation of the employment relationship has been regarded since the earliest days of the field as one of the three major institutional devices available to society to improve efficiency and equity in the workplace. But in recent years this topic has assumed even greater saliency both in this country and other nations due to a growing scholarly and political debate on the merits of regulation versus deregulation of labor markets. The second feature of past IRRA volumes—the steadily increasing sophistication and rigor of IR research—is also manifest in the chapters of this volume. Readers will find state-of-the art theory and empirical analysis in this volume, yet in keeping with the "pracademic" tradition of the IRRA this discussion is nevertheless accessible and relevant to the association's many non-academic members.

In assembling chapters and authors for this volume I endeavored to include a wide range of topics spanning the employment relationship; achieve a mix of theory, empirical analysis and policy; have academic authors from a variety of IR-related disciplines and schools of thought; and provide an opportunity for representatives of management and labor to express their points of view. All of this is in keeping with long-held IRRA traditions. I might note that not all perspectives on regulation (e.g., critical legal studies) and disciplines (e.g., sociology) are represented in the volume, but this is partly due to space constraints and partly due to an unsuccessful search for willing and able authors.

Special thanks go to the authors of these chapters for laboring long and hard—often through three or more drafts—to produce works of high quality and considerable value-added. Also deserving thanks is Paula Voos, IRRA Editor-in-Chief, who helped develop the topic, assemble the authors, and provide comments on individual chapters. And to Kay Hutchison, Administrator and Managing Editor of the IRRA, goes a special and profuse thanks for all the hours and effort she invested in helping transform this volume from an idea to a finished product. And, finally, thanks goes to Jeanette Zimmerman of the IRRA staff for very capable editing. It was a team effort!

BRUCE E. KAUFMAN

# Government Regulation of the Employment Relationship

BRUCE E. KAUFMAN

*Georgia State University*

Industrial relations as a field of study and area of business practice first appeared in the United States in the early 1920s. The catalyst for the birth of the field was growing public and professional concern over the human and social consequences of what were then called "labor problems." The number one labor problem, most experts agreed, was a growing crescendo of overt, often-times violent conflict between workers and their employers with its accompanying bloodshed, destruction of property, and radicalization of emotions. A plethora of other labor problems also captured the public attention, such as astoundingly high rates of employee turnover, widespread "soldiering" (loafing) on the job, poverty-level wages, excessive work hours, and arbitrary and capricious discipline. All of these were seen as not only a serious impediment to the efficient and equitable operation of the workplace but also a threat to the very foundations of the American economic and social order.

As I have described elsewhere (Kaufman 1993), out of this concern with labor problems was born the field of industrial relations. Labor problems and industrial relations were conceived as opposite sides of the same coin—labor problems were the result of various maladjustments and imperfections in the employment relationship and industrial relations was the academic science and vocational practice that sought to understand the causes of these problems and devise solutions thereto.

Given this orientation, industrial relations attracted into its ranks numerous academics and practitioners with a strong commitment to reformist and progressive principles. While they shared both an aversion to the doctrine of laissez faire and a faith in the ability of purposeful human action to improve social and economic conditions, beyond this intellectual "common denominator" agreement among them tended to fragment. In particular, by the late

1

1920s three different approaches or "solutions" to labor problems had emerged as focal points for research and debate in the field. The first was generally referred to as *employers' solutions*, the second as *workers' solutions*, and the third as *the community's solutions* (Estey 1928). The core part of employers' solution to labor problems was adoption of modern, progressive practices of personnel management, the central principle of workers' solution was trade unionism and collective bargaining, while the main element of the community's solution was government regulation in the form of protective labor legislation and social insurance programs.

Most of the early participants in the field of industrial relations, whether academics, business people, or workers' representatives, recognized the utility of all three approaches to resolving labor problems and saw them, at least within broad limits, as complements rather than substitutes. Considerable disagreement remained, however, over the relative weight to be given to progressive personnel management practices, trade unionism, and government regulation as society's main instrument for promoting increased efficiency and equity in the workplace. Also highly contentious was the question of to what extent the adoption of these "solutions" should be a matter of voluntary choice or social compulsion.

It is interesting to gaze over the near-eight decades of American history that separate us from the early 1920s and examine the twists and turns that policy and public opinion have taken on these issues. During the "welfare capitalism" period of the 1920s, for example, the dominant emphasis in industrial relations and the broader society was on voluntarism and the primacy of employers' solution to workplace problems.

The Great Depression of the 1930s then brought on a complete reversal in course, as the economic calamity seemed to both discredit the regime of welfare capitalism and call for strong state intervention. Out of this sentiment arose the New Deal of the Roosevelt administration, the hallmark of which was skepticism of the efficacy of free markets, a substantial increase in government regulation of business, and a shift toward encouragement of collective bargaining. Suddenly, the personnel management solution to labor problems seemed not only ineffective but all too often duplicitous, while the solutions of trade unionism and government regulation now appeared to have a double virtue—they promised a more effective and broad-based improvement in labor conditions than voluntary actions by employers and, at the same time, were seen as effective instruments for promoting macroeconomic stabilization and growth (Kaufman 1996; Craypo in this volume). To promote the "workers' solution" to labor problems, the Roosevelt administration enacted in 1933 the National Industrial Recovery Act (NIRA) which contained the famous Section

7(a) guarantee of labor's right to organize and collective bargain and, in 1935, the National Labor Relations Act (NLRA) which spelled out these rights and their enforcement in much greater detail. The community's solution to labor problems was considerably strengthened through several other landmark pieces of legislation, including the Social Security Act (unemployment and old age insurance, aid to families with dependent children) and the Fair Labor Standards Act (minimum wages, maximum hours, and abolition of child labor).

Although the New Deal sought to improve employment relations by strengthening both the labor movement and protective labor law, for the next three decades, it was the former that proved the most influential and dynamic in reshaping the American workplace. Over this period union density (proportion of the work force represented) nearly tripled and a host of innovative employment practices were pioneered at the collective bargaining table, such as binding arbitration of contract disputes, cost-of-living allowance clauses, multi-year contracts, and supplemental unemployment benefits. By way of contrast, the new protective labor laws and social insurance programs of the 1930s had a relatively modest impact on existing workplace practices and institutions and, furthermore, were not extended in new directions for the next twenty-five years.

Beginning in the early 1960s, however, the pendulum began to swing back toward direct government intervention in labor markets. Partly this reflected the slowdown in both union membership growth and bargaining innovation, but more important was the growth of public concern over new or long-neglected labor problems that collective bargaining either seemed not well suited to solve or, in one or two cases, seemed to perpetuate. First and foremost was race and gender discrimination, attacked first in 1962 by the Equal Pay Act and then again in 1964 by Title VII of the Civil Rights Act. Other labor problems that gained headlines were technological unemployment, poverty, employment problems of older workers, workplace safety and health, and pension abuse. Each of these was in turn addressed by new legislative initiatives, some of which channeled public investment funds to disadvantaged socioeconomic groups, such as through manpower training programs, while numerous others imposed new regulation on employers (and in some cases unions). Examples include the Age Discrimination Act (1967), Federal Mine Safety and Health Act (1969), Occupational Safety and Health Act (1970), and Employee Retirement and Income Security Act (1974).

Although the relative weight given to collective bargaining versus government labor legislation varied between the late 1930s and late 1970s, a substantial majority of the electorate supported selective intervention in labor markets to reduce or ameliorate pre-existing or newly emergent labor problems and saw unions and government regulation as, on net, effective instruments toward this end. All of this seemingly changed, however, with the election of Ronald Reagan to the office of President in 1980.

President Reagan forcefully argued that the nation's social and economic problems had been exacerbated, not ameliorated, by growing government intervention in the economy and his campaign promise was to "get government off the backs of the people." With regard to labor, Reagan attacked the very philosophical foundation of the post-New Deal political order. The traditional view both within industrial relations and the broader society was that the experience of the 1900s-1930s clearly demonstrated that labor markets contain a number of serious imperfections that cause a range of undesirable employment problems, such as inadequate wages, excessive work hours, unsafe working conditions, and so on. The existence of these labor problems thus provides the rationale for the public support of trade unionism and government regulation of labor markets. Reagan effectively turned public dissatisfaction with high inflation, eroding industrial competitiveness, and declining standards of living into an attack on the New Deal ideology by persuading a substantial portion of the electorate that the best antidote to these problems is greater reliance on free markets and less reliance on government and other forms of employment regulation (e.g., collective bargaining). In terms of the trilogy of employers', workers', and community's solutions to labor problems, the "Reagan revolution" in many ways represented a return to the priorities of the 1920s in which employers' solutions were given primacy of place and the latter two were significantly downgraded in importance.

These new priorities played themselves out during the Reagan and Bush presidencies of the 1980s and early 1990s, although with mixed results. Certainly public policy toward collective bargaining turned hostile, evidenced by the events such as the Reagan administration's hard-line stance in the air controllers' (PATCO) strike, administration opposition to striker replacement legislation, and a series of important pro-management rulings by the National Labor Relations Board. Rhetoric against "big government" also intensified, including attacks on various regulatory programs in the labor area, such as affirmative action, unemployment compensation, the minimum wage, and the Davis-Bacon Act (the setting of "prevailing wages" in government construction projects).

And certainly the business community rose in stature and gained new power and influence during these years. This trend was in part due to a more conservative, pro-business political ideology, while another part probably stemmed from public disenchantment with perceived excesses and/or failures of organized labor and government regulatory programs. But business must also be given considerable credit, for much evidence exists that in recent decades American companies have substantially improved the way they manage and motivate employees. More satisfied employees naturally have a smaller demand for external intervention and protection in the workplace, be it in the form of government legislation or union representation (Farber and Krueger 1993).

These events notwithstanding, other trends and developments emerged during the 1980s and early 1990s that either softened the blow against forms of labor market regulation or actually strengthened it. One aspect is what did *not* happen to government regulation. Although the minimum wage was not raised during the 1980s, neither was it abolished. Likewise, a favorite object of attack by economic and political conservatives—the Occupational Safety and Health Act—suffered from budget cuts and staff reductions but was not eliminated or fundamentally changed. The same applies to another favorite target, the Equal Employment Opportunity Commission. A final example is the National Labor Relations Act, which liberals failed to strengthen in their campaign to promote collective bargaining and labor law reform but which conservatives likewise failed to weaken.

A second aspect of note is that even while public opinion noticeably soured toward government in general, the public still supported a limited number of new interventions in labor markets to resolve specific types of employment problems. Examples include the Worker Adjustment and Retraining Act (1988), Americans with Disabilities Act (1990), and the Civil Rights Act of 1991.

The coming to office of the Clinton administration in 1992 suggested that possibly the federal government would again turn toward a more interventionist and activist approach regarding workplace regulation and public support of collective bargaining. Although the full record of the Clinton administration is not yet written, so far the experience is again decidedly mixed. Certainly the rhetoric of the administration, and particularly that of certain key spokespeople such as first-term Labor Secretary Robert Reich, has been on the side of greater activism. To some extent rhetoric has been matched by deeds, such as raising the minimum wage, passage of the Family and Medical Leave Act, stricter enforcement of the Occupational Safety and Health Act, appointment of more pro-labor (or less pro-management) members to the National Labor Relations Board, and administration support for striker replacement. On the other hand, President Clinton has also antagonized organized labor by strongly supporting the North American Free Trade Agreement, more recently signed what many liberals regard as draconian welfare reform legislation, and has failed to demonstrate more than token support for strengthening the NLRA.

Perhaps emblematic of the quandary and cross-currents afflicting American labor policy at this historical juncture is the fate of the report issued by the Commission on the Future of Worker-Management Relations (a.k.a. Dunlop Commission), appointed by President Clinton in 1993 and chaired by Harvard Professor and former IRRA president and U.S. Labor Secretary John Dunlop. The mission of the commission was to review the nation's labor law and make recommendations for change. During eleven regional hearings the commission members heard a welter of conflicting testimony and opinion, out of which they attempted to craft a compromise set of recommendations that on one hand strengthened the National Labor Relations Act but which on the other sought to reduce litigiousness in employment disputes and promote greater flexibility in the administration of labor regulation. None of the three parties with major influence on the fate of the commission's recommendations (organized labor, the business community, the Clinton administration) expressed more than lukewarm enthusiasm for them, and hence they died rather quickly in the political process.

As the United States approaches the 21st century, national employment policy thus seems caught in the political eddy spawned by a deep-seated public mistrust of government and "big labor" combined with a pragmatic desire that government (possibly in conjunction with organized labor) do something to improve specific workplace hardships and inequities. It is to this public sense of ambivalence and uncertainty about labor market regulation and institutions that this volume seeks to speak.

Assembled herein, in the best IRRA tradition, are outstanding scholars and practitioners drawn from a variety of academic disciplines, business and labor organizations, and policy perspectives who address in clear, understandable prose the major research issues and empirical evidence on this topic. It is not claimed that at the end of this volume the reader will find a consensus program for labor market regulation and reform thereof, for crafting such is probably impossible. What the reader will take away from this volume is a much enhanced perspective on the current corpus of labor market law and regulation, the implications that different theoretical schools of thought have regarding the economic efficiency and social equity of these laws and regulations, the weight of empirical evidence for and against their social utility, and thought-provoking suggestions for the future direction of regulatory reform.

## Contents of the Volume

The volume is composed of eighteen chapters and is divided into four sections. The first section contains three chapters on different theoretical perspectives concerning employment regulation. The first one by Bruce Kaufman examines the "old institutional" perspective of John R. Commons and the Wisconsin School, the second by Gregory Dow examines the "new institutional" perspective pioneered by Oliver Williamson, and the third by Stuart Schwab examines the "law and economics" perspective associated with Richard Posner and others at the University of Chicago.

The second section is devoted to an analysis of empirical evidence on the outcomes and effects of employment regulation, both in terms of the overall economy and as a result of individual programs. In the fourth chapter John Addison and Barry Hirsch begin this section with a comprehensive review and evaluation of past research evidence on the labor market impact of a wide range of regulatory programs. Following this in chapter five, Dale Belman and Michael Belzer examine the theoretical and empirical evidence regarding both the benefits and costs of greater competition in labor markets, particularly as they bear upon employees.

The remaining six chapters in this section take a more in-depth view of particular areas of labor market regulation. Charles Craypo examines labor standards legislation, most particularly the Fair Labor Standards Act and Davis-Bacon Act, from a neoclassical and institutional perspective; John Burton and James Chelius look at the area of safety and health, focusing particularly on the stated rationale for government regulation, the research evidence thereon, and the administration of the Occupational Safety and Health Act; Daphne Taras examines reasons for divergences in the legal and administrative regulation of collective bargaining in Canada versus the United States, giving particular emphasis to historical, political, and cultural factors; Mary Radford analyzes the evolution of American labor policy on affirmative action, with special attention given to the development of case law and judicial interpretation regarding this unsettled and controversial area of regulation; Lamont Stallworth focuses on employment disputes within organizations, the development of regulation in this area of employment policy, and the search for alternative methods of dispute resolution that are less litigious, costly, and time consuming; and, finally, Richard Edwards examines alternative regulatory approaches to protecting employee rights in the workplace, with special emphasis on the development of what he calls "enterprise rights."

The third section of the volume is devoted to issues of regulatory structure, administration, and enforcement. Two chapters are featured. The first by David Weil develops a conceptual framework identifying the three major steps or links in the regulation process which separately and together influence the overall effectiveness of regulation. He then provides a comprehensive review of the research evidence on these issues for a wide variety of employment-related regulatory programs. The second contribution in this section is by

David Levine. He critiques existing "command and control" methods of employment regulation and suggests an alternative model of self-regulation.

The fourth and concluding section of the volume features five chapters that are written as personal "opinion pieces" on employment regulation. Both academics and practitioners are featured, as are people who approach the subject from a management and labor perspective. The first of these chapters is by Ray Marshall, who makes a case for wide-ranging reform of safety and health regulation. The second of these chapters is by Robert Pleasure and Patricia Greenfield. They point out that deregulation of employment relations does not necessarily imply a return to a level legal playing field as relations between employers and workers, and the rights and duties of each, are then governed by the common law which, in reality, invariably tilts toward the interests of employers. Thomas Schneider is author of the third opinion piece. He argues that, while government regulation is an important instrument for promoting socially desirable employment conditions, in many respects the organized labor movement is a superior instrument for this task, and thus he advocates reform of the labor law to facilitate the spread and effectiveness of collective bargaining. The fourth chapter is by Herbert Northrup. Northrup argues that traditional economic pressure tactics by unions have lost much of their effectiveness and, as a result, unions are increasingly using regulatory agencies and processes in illegitimate ways to exert pressure on employers as part of corporate campaigns. Finally, in the fifth opinion piece John Raudabaugh argues that the nation's labor law needs to encourage greater employee involvement and labor-management cooperation, but that the National Labor Relations Act is premised on an adversarial model of employee relations and is hence increasingly counterproductive to the nation's social and economic interests.

## Conclusion

As noted in the beginning of this chapter, industrial relations as a field of study has from its birth in the early 1920s been directed at the task of discovering the causes and solutions to labor problems. Many labor problems that were the focus of attention in the 1910s remain very much a concern in the 1990s, although in most cases notable progress has been made over the course of the century in reducing their extent and severity. Examples include poverty-level wages, workplace injuries, and protection of individual rights. Other labor problems, such as child labor, that were once endemic to the workplace of the 1910s have now largely receded as matters of ongoing social concern, while others (e.g., equal opportunity, AIDS in the workplace) have greatly increased in importance.

I believe it is indisputable that government regulation of labor markets and employer-employee relations has made, on net, a very significant contribution to the remarkable progress made over the course of the 20th century in achieving a more productive and humane workplace. Some may argue that government regulation of employment conditions has not been aggressive enough, while others may argue that it has gone too far. I doubt many informed observers would argue, however, that the nation should return to the days of laissez faire in labor markets as existed eight decades earlier. Seen in this light, the reformers and progressives of the late 1910s-early 1920s who founded the field of industrial relations and pushed the cause of government regulation of employment conditions have had their efforts—then widely viewed as impractical and even subversive—soundly vindicated by the passage of time and events.

It also remains the case, however, that the nature of society and the economy has evolved greatly since the 1920s and, as noted above, so have the labor problems that confront us as we approach the 21st century. Part and parcel of this evolution is an ongoing, sometimes intense debate about the continued efficacy of government regulation of the workplace and the manner in which such regulation should be practiced. This volume does not resolve the debate, but I believe it does provide a significant contribution to framing the issues, developing theory, and providing an objective review of the empirical evidence on the subject. If this research proves of value to fashioning more efficient and effective regulation, then not only is the purpose of the volume achieved, but a fitting tribute is made to the vision of those early industrial relations pioneers who founded the Industrial Relations Research Association fifty years ago.

## References

Estey, J. A. 1928. *The Labor Problem*. New York: McGraw-Hill.

Farber, Henry, and Alan Krueger. 1993. "Union Membership in the United States: The Decline Continues." In Bruce E. Kaufman and Morris M. Kleiner, eds., *Employee Representation: Alternatives and Future Directions*. Madison, WI: Industrial Relations Research Association, pp. 105-34.

Kaufman, Bruce E. 1993. *The Origins and Evolution of the Field of Industrial Relations in the United States*. Ithaca, NY: ILR Press.

_____. 1996. "Why the Wagner Act? Reestablishing Contact with Its Original Purpose." In David Lewin, Bruce Kaufman, and Donna Sockell, eds., *Advances in Industrial and Labor Relations*, Vol. 7. Greenwich, CT: JAI Press, pp. 15-68.

# CHAPTER 1

# Labor Markets and Employment Regulation: The View of the "Old" Institutionalists

BRUCE E. KAUFMAN
*Georgia State University*

The true ideal of society is not *laissez faire*, but economic freedom, and freedom is the child, not the enemy, of law and regulation. Thomas Adams and Helen Sumner, *Labor Problems* (1905:15)

The equilibrium of democracy may not be easy to work out, but what else is there to do? John R. Commons, *Industrial Goodwill* (1919:43)

The first group of academic scholars to extensively study and advocate regulation of the employment relationship was the institutional economists of the Wisconsin school, led by John R. Commons (1862-1945). Their work contributed to enactment of numerous pieces of labor legislation, including workers' compensation, unemployment insurance, minimum wages, maximum hours, civil service reform, prohibitions of child labor, immigration quotas, old age insurance, restrictions on the use of court injunctions in labor disputes, protection of collective bargaining rights, and government commitment to maintenance of full employment. The apogee of their reform program was reached during the New Deal years of the Roosevelt administration when many of these initiatives were first passed into law on a national basis.

Given the pioneering role the Wisconsin school played in the movement for employment regulation, the expansion over this century in the breadth and complexity of such regulation and the growing debate in the country over the merits of regulation versus deregulation of the labor market, it seems appropriate to devote the first chapter of this volume to a review and evaluation of the institutional perspective on this subject. Surprisingly, no previous study known to the author exists that provides an in-depth analysis and evaluation of this important body of literature.

## The "Old" Institutionalists and the Wisconsin School

In this chapter I refer to the economists of the Wisconsin school as the "old" institutionalists. This is to clearly distinguish them from the "new" institutionalists of more recent times, such as Oliver Williamson (1985). The transaction cost theory of Williamson and colleagues is considered in the next chapter (see Dow). The old and new institutional economics share a common focus on explaining the origins and characteristics of economic institutions (e.g., hierarchical firms versus decentralized markets) and, following Commons, Williamson makes the transaction a key part of his theory. Beyond this, however, the two approaches are largely dissimilar in terms of methodology and theoretical orientation (Ramstad 1996), particularly regarding the role of power versus efficiency as the primary motive force in economic affairs.

The old institutional school of economics, of which the Wisconsin school is a major component, emerged in the United States in the 1890s, grew in prominence during the first three decades of the 20th century, reached its apex of influence in the early New Deal years of the 1930s, and since then has experienced a slow but cumulatively significant decline in both influence and number of adherents. The field of labor economics has been no exception to this trend. Beginning in the early 1940s, a new generation of labor economists (e.g., John Dunlop, Clark Kerr, Richard Lester, Charles Myers, Lloyd Reynolds, Arthur Ross) largely unconnected to Commons and the Wisconsin school became the dominant intellectual force in the field, and while they continued the institutional emphasis on an interdisciplinary perspective and the constructive role of collective bargaining and labor legislation, they also made a concerted effort to shift the study of labor to a more analytical, market-based orientation and away from the historical, reformist approach pioneered by Commons and associates (Kaufman 1988). After the early 1960s, this second generation of labor economists was itself largely displaced by the resurgent neoclassical school, spearheaded by economists at the University of Chicago. Under the influence of the Chicago school, labor economics became a branch of applied microeconomic theory with a methodological and policy perspective in many respects the opposite of the Wisconsin school. Today relatively few labor economists identify themselves as "institutionalists," although a diverse but modest-sized group (frequently participants in the allied field of industrial relations) continue to write and do research in the institutional tradition (Kaufman 1993).

The key figure in the birth of the "old" institutional school is Richard T. Ely. Ely, along with a small band of other young scholars (e.g., Henry Carter Adams, Simon Patten), did graduate study in economics in Germany during the 1880s and then came back to America determined to breathe new life into the economics discipline which, they thought, had become largely a sterile, unrealistic exercise in deductive logic (Ely 1938).

The new life they sought to impart to economics was to be supplied by extensive empirical fact gathering and close attention to historical processes, which together would furnish the raw material for construction of theories more attuned to the economic, social, and political realities of the day (Jacoby 1990). Commingled with their dedication to a different approach to economics as a science was an equally strong inclination toward social and political reform, marked by an aversion to doctrines such as laissez faire and Social Darwinism and a concomitant dedication to the idea that advancement of economic efficiency and social justice requires various forms of state regulation and control of the market system.

Although Ely and compatriots started the institutional rebellion, the birth of institutional economics as a bona fide school of thought is generally credited to three economists who followed in Ely's footsteps. They are Thorstein Veblen, Wesley Mitchell, and John Commons (Dorfman 1963). Of these three men, it was Commons who specialized in the study of labor and had by far the biggest impact on labor theory and policy in America in the first three decades of the 20th century. Indicative is the statement of Kenneth Boulding (1957:7) that "Commons was the intellectual origin of the New Deal, of labor legislation, of social security, of the whole movement in the country toward a welfare state."

Ely recruited Commons to join him on the economics faculty at Wisconsin in 1904 and together the two men built a department of national reputation (Cain 1993). Labor was an especially strong area, and numerous students who studied under Ely and Commons went on to make notable contributions in labor scholarship, practice, and policy (Saposs 1960). The core members of the Wisconsin school included Edwin Witte, Helen Sumner, Selig Perlman, Don Lescohier, William Leiserson, John Andrews, Elizabeth Brandeis Raushenbush, John Fitch, and David Saposs. Several other prominent labor economists of the period, such as Sumner Slichter and Harry Millis, studied under Commons before going on for doctoral work elsewhere. The labor theories and policy prescriptions of these economists were sufficiently distinct and unique that Commons and colleagues became known in academic circles as the "Wisconsin School" (Barbash 1994) and as key contributors to what was widely recognized in political circles as the "Wisconsin Idea" (McCarthy 1912).

Commons and colleagues produced monumental works on trade unionism and collective bargaining and took a generally advocatory stance regarding their proper place in the economic system (Commons 1918). Although rarely acknowledged in contemporary accounts of the history of management thought, Commons was also the most influential academic writer in the newly emergent field of personnel administration in the late 1910s-early 1920s (Commons 1919; Kaufman forthcoming). Equally pathbreaking but under-appreciated is the work of Commons and associates in the area of law and economics. Two aspects of this work are of particular relevance for this chapter.

The first is in the area of "high theory" and entailed integration of law and legal analysis into the main corpus of economic theory. Commons' two theoretical treatises, *Legal Foundations of Capitalism* (1924) and *Institutional Economics* (1934a), are the exemplars of this literature. Although today's conventional wisdom is that the field of law and economics is a post-World War II development largely originating at the University of Chicago, in actuality the institutional economists of two generations earlier were the first ones to examine the interface between economic and legal theory (see Hovenkamp 1990 and Commons' 1925 article entitled "Law and Economics"). The key difference is that the institutionalists emphasized the transference of legal concepts and reasoning into economic theory, while the modern day law and economics movement approaches the intellectual interface from the opposite direction (see Schwab's chapter in this volume).

A second area of law and economics pioneered by the institutional economists is with respect to labor and the employment relationship. The institutionalists were the first American economists to systematically develop a theoretical rationale for employment regulation and were among the most active and prominent advocates of such legislation. Ely and Commons, for example, were largely responsible for the founding of the American Association for Labor Legislation (AALL) in 1908, and under the direction of their former student John Andrews (with considerable assistance from his wife, Irene Osgood Andrews), it soon became the most active and influential research and lobbying group in the nation on behalf of employment regulation (Pierce 1953; Chasse 1994; Moss 1996). Its quarterly journal, *The American Labor Legislation Review*, was the leading outlet for progressive thought on methods to improve the conditions of labor. In addition, the text, *Principles of Labor Legislation* (1st edition, 1916; 4th edition 1936), co-authored by Commons and Andrews, was widely recognized at the time as the most authoritative source on employment law.

The economists of the Wisconsin school were part of a broader coalition of progressive liberal reformers who promoted the cause of expanded social welfare legislation during the 1900-1930 period. Within American economics, for example, nearly all labor economists, including leading figures such as Paul Douglas, Sumner Slichter, Harry Millis, were strong advocates of additional employment regulation (Douglas 1934, 1938; Slichter 1928; Millis and Montgomery 1938a, 1938b). The institutionalists also had allies or sympathizers among economic theorists, such as Irving Fisher (an AALL president), Alvin Hansen, John M. Clark, Rexford Tugwell, Edwin Seligman, and Henry Seager. Also influential in the development of institutional thought, though from a distance, were several English economists, notably Sydney and Beatrice Webb and John Hobson.

Outside of academia, numerous social reform groups agitated for strengthened employment regulation, including engineers affiliated with the Taylor Society (e.g., Ordway Tead, Morris Cooke), progressive businessmen (e.g., Edward Filene, Henry Dennison), social workers (e.g., Paul Kellogg, Florence Kelley), liberal Christians affiliated with the "Social Gospelers" (e.g., Josiah Strong), leaders of organized labor (e.g., Samuel Gompers, Sydney Hillman), socialists and radicals (e.g., Eugene Debs, Morris Hillquit), and progressive politicians (e.g., Robert La Follette, Robert Wagner).

## Labor Problems

The beginning point for discussion of the institutional perspective on employment regulation is the concept of *labor problems* (Kaufman 1993). In the Preface to the first edition of their *Principles of Labor Legislation* (1920:xii), for example, Commons and Andrews state that the purpose of the book is "to sketch the historical background of the various labor problems, indicate the nature and extent of each, and describe the *legislative remedies* which have been applied" (emphasis added).

Labor problems, as a concept, were typically defined as a maladjustment or lack of harmonious balance in the employment relationship (Daugherty 1933). This maladjustment or lack of harmonious balance took a number of concrete forms (typically labeled "evils") that adversely affected employers and/or employees. Prominent examples from the early decades of the century are the following (for a general overview, see Fitch 1924; Andrews 1932):

- Employee turnover. Slichter (1918) found the majority of companies in the 1910s experienced annual employee turnover of 100% or more. It was not unusual at a number of companies for average length of job tenure among production workers to be three months or less (Lescohier 1919).
- Long hours. In 1909 three-quarters of employees in manufacturing firms worked 54 or more hours per week (Lauck and Sydenstricker

1917:183). The institutionalists considered the steel industry to be the most egregious case of excessive work hours. Until 1924 most of the industry worked its employees 12 hours a day, 7 days a week (Fitch 1924).

- Industrial accidents. Over 25,000 American workers were killed in workplace accidents each year in the early 1910s, and another 700,000 were disabled for four weeks or more. The industry with one of the worst safety records was coal mining. Each year 1 of every 300 miners was killed in a work-related accident (Lauck and Sydenstricker 1917:195).

- Poverty incomes. It was judged that in the early 1910s the ordinary wage-earning family (two adults and three children) needed an annual family income of $800 for "a reasonable minimum" standard of living. Two-thirds of families earned less than this amount, even though the wife and one or more children often were gainfully employed (Lauch and Sydenstricker 1917:249, 376).

- Excessive work speed. Assembly lines, semiautomatic machine production, and piece rate compensation plans led to a steady increase in the pace of work in a number of industries to the point where many workers were "old before their day" due to the physical and mental strain. Industries such as steel, autos, and meat packing were particularly noted for the grueling pace of work, and many employees were worn-out by the age of 40-45. Often companies used seasonal layoffs as an opportunity to cull older employees from their work force, and it was widely recognized that many companies refused to hire new workers past the age of 40 (Commons and Andrews 1936; Millis and Montgomery 1938a).

- Irregular work. Each year the average worker was unemployed between one-sixth and one-third of the time (Lauck and Sydenstricker 1917:360). Reasons included frequent job changing and haphazard search for work, large seasonal swings in production and employment, large numbers of employee discharges, personal sickness and disability, and generalized unemployment during business downturns.

- Workplace autocracy. The common law of that day termed the relationship between employer and employee as one of "master and servant." The employer (master) had an almost unrestricted right to administer whatever personnel policies were deemed appropriate with regard to hiring, firing, pay, discipline, and work speed. Employment was "at will" and workers could be summarily fired for any reason. Formal grievance systems were nearly nonexistent outside unionized establishments, and thus quitting work was the employee's major source of protection (Fitch 1924).

• Conflict. American society witnessed a growing crescendo of strikes and workplace violence between 1880 and 1920. A number of strikes (e.g., the Pullman Strike, the Ludlow Massacre) turned into large scale "labor wars" with mass destruction of property, pitched battles in which numerous people were killed and injured, and use of federal troops to restore order (Lens 1974). Numerous acts of violence were also practiced by employers and workers in efforts to unionize or remain nonunion, including dynamite bombings, lynchings, and beatings.

## The Cause of Labor Problems: The Orthodox Perspective

Having documented the widespread, serious nature of labor problems in American industry, the second step in the research and policy program of the institutionalists was to diagnose the cause of these problems. Appreciation of the institutional perspective on this matter is facilitated by a brief overview of the tenets of laissez-faire economics and Social Darwinism, which together represented the dominant, "orthodox" school of thought at the turn of the century.

The doctrine of laissez faire originated with the French physiocrat economists of the mid-1700s, but it was Adam Smith's *Wealth of Nations* (1776) that gave the concept its most compelling rationale. After additional elaboration by other members of the British classical school of economics, the doctrine was imported to America after the Civil War and adopted by American economists and businessmen with both less qualification and more zeal. Social Darwinism also had British origins, particularly in the work of Herbert Spencer who took the theories of evolution and "survival of the fittest" propounded by Charles Darwin and applied them to the development of human societies.

Laissez faire and Social Darwinism share four basic assumptions (Fine 1956):

1. The existence of certain fundamental laws of nature, such as competition and survival of the fittest, and inalienable natural rights, such as individual freedom and liberty of contract. The laws are held to be immutable, often God-given, and the rights are held to be sacrosanct.
2. The efficacy of self-interest. As Adam Smith (1776) explained, people's pursuit of their self-interest in earning a living and doing business leads them "as if by an invisible hand" to produce the goods and provide the services that promotes the good of the larger society.
3. The merits of free competition. Competition is desirable because it provides a spur to personal initiative, makes individual success a function of ability and effort, not status or privilege; and efficiently and fairly regulates economic production and distribution.

4. The inefficiency of government and the stultifying effect of legislation on economic and social progress. From the perspective of the late 1800s, it was put forth as self-evident that government is corrupt and manipulated for the advantage of special interests and cannot be entrusted to efficiently manage either enterprise or administration.

The evident conclusion from these assumptions is that the best government is the one that governs least. The role of the state is to protect civil liberties and individual property rights; enforce the laws of contract; and provide certain essential services in the realms of education, health, defense, and public protection. Beyond this, the state must not go.

Proponents of laissez faire and Social Darwinism did not dispute the existence of labor problems, such as those listed above. Their diagnosis of the causes of these problems, however, led them to decry nearly all forms of state intervention (Fine 1956). For example, many forms of labor problems were viewed as largely stemming from the individual's own actions or character defects, such as carelessness in the case of work accidents, or laziness in the case of unemployment. State action on these matters would only abrogate individual responsibility and take resources from the provident and transfer them to the improvident. Alternatively, it was argued that competition rewarded people for the assumption of risk (through higher wage differentials for more dangerous or insecure jobs) and that people taking those jobs thus had no legitimate claim for redress. A third argument rested on liberty of contract—as long as employment contracts are free of fraud and duress, there are no legal or ethical grounds for the state to overturn them, since both parties to the contract voluntarily agreed to the wages, hours, and terms of employment and presumably gained from the exchange. Employment regulation is thus an infringement on personal liberty and a cause of economic inefficiency. Finally, proponents of laissez faire and Social Darwinism frequently rationalized labor problems, such as low wages and long hours, as the price that has to be paid for economic and social progress and saw attempts by workers to form trade unions or to strike over these conditions as the work of radicals and agitators intent on overthrowing the system of private property and individual liberty.

These beliefs held wide sway in America in the latter part of the 19th century. Although government might regulate employment conditions for certain groups that are either incapable of safeguarding their own interests (children, the mentally deficient) or for which a clear public purpose is served (women, since harm to them is a harm to future generations), the prevailing view was that employment regulation was unwise policy that violated constitutional guarantees of individual liberty and freedom of contract (Ely 1907; Commons

1924; McCurdy 1984). Examples of employment laws declared unconstitutional were mandates that workers be paid at fixed intervals, wages be paid in cash, women be paid a minimum wage, employees cannot be fined for imperfect work, overtime pay has to be given for work hours of more than eight per day, and companies cannot discharge employees on account of their membership in a labor union.

Illustrative of the reasoning of the courts and the power of the ideology of laissez faire is the decision of the Pennsylvania Supreme Court in a case decided in 1886 involving a state law requiring that wages be paid in cash rather than scrip. The court declared the law unconstitutional and said:

> The act is an infringement alike of the right of the employer and employee; more than this it is an insulting attempt to put the laborer under a legislative tutelage which is not only degrading to his manhood, but subversive of his rights as a citizen of the U.S. He may sell his labor for what he thinks best, whether money or goods, just as his employer may sell his iron or coal, and any or every law that proposes to prevent him from so doing is an infringement of his constitutional privileges, and consequently vicious and void (Lehrer 1987:49).

## Labor Problems: The Institutional Perspective

Ely, Commons, and the other institutional economists took a very different view of the causes of labor problems. Their effort to articulate this view and give it scientific credence took them down the path of "science building"—the creation of a new corpus of economic theory to replace (or at least substantially modify) the classical model of political economy upon which the theory of laissez faire was based. An overview of their "new political economy" is provided below.

### The End Purpose of Economic Activity

The first place the institutionalists departed from the classical economists is with regard to the end purpose of economic activity (Gonce 1966). In the classical view, the primary objective of economic activity is creation of material wealth and its ultimate purpose is satisfaction of consumer wants (Clark 1926:46). Illustrative is the remark of John Stuart Mill (1874:137) that "Political Economy is concerned with him [man] solely as a being who desires to possess wealth," and Adam Smith's (1776:625) contention that "Consumption is the sole end and purpose of all production; and the interest of the producer ought to be attended to, only so far as necessary for promoting that of the consumer."

The institutionalists took a different view. Economic theory and evaluative judgments of an economy's performance have to be based, says Commons (1924:377), on the *purpose* the economic system is intended to serve. And this purpose, he says (p. 38), is not maximization of consumer satisfaction or material wealth (although these are important) but facilitation of each person's quest for self-development and self-realization. This theme is also struck by Ely (1886:3), who defines the purpose of humanity as "the full and harmonious development in each individual of all human faculties—the faculties of working, perceiving, knowing, loving—the development, in short, of whatever capabilities of good there may be within us."

Shifting the focus of economics from material wealth and consumer satisfaction to individual self-development and self-realization has profound implications for economic theory and the analysis of labor problems. Consider work, for example. In classical and modern neoclassical theory, work is assumed to be an irksome, unpleasant activity (i.e., a source of disutility) and people perform it only to obtain an income to buy consumer goods (Ehrenberg and Smith 1994). Labor, in turn, is usually treated as a commodity-like factor input that derives its value from the goods and services produced. But this view, say the institutionalists, is fundamentally flawed.

Consumption of more goods and services gives people a temporary feeling of greater satisfaction, but over the longer run, happiness with life bears only modest relation to income level or quantity of material possessions. Rather, happiness with life has much more to do with a continuing sense of accomplishment and self-development—that one is learning new things, mastering new challenges, and involved in meaningful activities and relationships (Lane 1991). It is for this reason that Ely (Ely and Bohn 1935:210) says, "Work is the greatest blessing," since work, more than consumption, provides opportunities for self-development and self-realization. In institutional theory, therefore, the activity of work has intrinsic value, and labor is not just a commodity input valued for the output it produces but is embodied in human beings whose welfare as producers is as important as their welfare as consumers (Leiserson 1938:11-18).

This perspective helps illuminate why the institutional economists were more critical of a free market, laissez-faire economic system than their classical and neoclassical colleagues. In orthodox theory, for example, long hours of work or low rates of pay may be regrettable on purely humanitarian terms but do not provide justification per se for government intervention in the market, as competition ensures that employment outcomes are the product of voluntary choice and yield a welfare maximizing level of production. If self-development and self-realization are the end goals, however, numerous reasons exist to doubt that competitive outcomes are optimal.

For example, the most important prerequisite for human self-development, according to Commons (1934a), is security of one's person and livelihood. Without a minimum level of security, people revert to more primitive forms of behavior (e.g., physical violence) and shy away from cooperative enterprise and forward-looking, economically productive investments (Chasse 1986). Will a laissez-faire, free market system provide the necessary minimum level of security for self-development? Definitely not, he thought, since the hallmark of competitive markets is volatile prices (as in stock or grain markets), short-term, "spot" relationships between buyers and sellers, and the constant threat to workers and firms that some rival will underbid them and take away their jobs and business.

Competitive, laissez-faire markets are detrimental to human self-development and self-realization in numerous other ways. For example:

- Self-development requires that each person earn what the institutionalists called a "living wage," meaning the income necessary to purchase the social minimum standard of living (Seager 1913; Lauck 1929). A free market system, however, provides no assurance that workers will receive a wage at least equal to this amount, and indeed, the record of competitive markets is that workers with low skills or from minority groups often earn considerably less.
- Competitive markets can result in extensive child labor or employees working 60, 70, or more hours per week, which may be efficient from a narrow economic perspective but is clearly injurious to the self-development of the worker and the well-being of families and the broader community.
- Competition may make a minute division of labor and authoritarian "command and control" management system the most efficient method of production, but self-realization is not promoted by boring, unchallenging work or jobs with no opportunity for employee participation in decision making (Slichter 1928:652).
- Economic efficiency and personal self-realization are both promoted by ethical, law-abiding behavior and cooperative forms of endeavor, but unrestrained competition induces people to engage in selfish, opportunistic behaviors that undercut ethical standards and cooperation.

### Self-Interest and Competition

The second fundamental respect in which the institutionalists departed company with the classical economists (and their neoclassical successors) is with respect to the virtues of self-interest and competition. In orthodox theory,

pursuit of self-interest and the process of competition are regarded as beneficent forces which should be given as much free rein as possible, subject only
to minimal legal safeguards (e.g., protection of property rights, prohibition of
contracts made through duress or fraud) and the occasional, infrequent need
for regulation due to market failure, such as in the case of natural monopoly
(Clark 1926).

The institutionalists had a more ambivalent view of self-interest and competition. Their basic position was that both forces can promote the social good,
but only if channeled in the appropriate direction by public policy and kept
within well-defined limits by social control mechanisms. One reason, states
Commons, is that people are not the rational, dispassionate beings envisioned
in orthodox theory's "economic man." Rather, the starting point for a model of
the human agent, he claims (Commons 1934a:874), is "passion, stupidity, and
ignorance," or what Herbert Simon (1978) later characterized as "bounded rationality." Choices and actions, Commons says, reflect to varying degrees a reasoned, logical process in which people weigh benefits and costs, but the choice
process is often heavily influenced by underlying emotional states (e.g., anger,
envy, lust, greed) and constrained by people's limited ability to think through
problems and acquire the relevant information to make an informed decision.
The consequence is that human behavior is prone to suboptimization, is heavily
influenced by custom and social comparisons, is driven by desire for power and
control, and can all too easily degenerate into acts of aggression and violence.

Given this model of human behavior, it is not surprising that the institutionalists took a less sanguine view of the social benefits to be had from the
pursuit of individual self-interest and the process of free competition. Commons (1893:61) says of self-interest, for example, "Private self-interest is too
powerful or too ignorant or too immoral to promote the common good without compulsion," while Adams (1886:34) says of competition, "Competition is
neither malevolent nor beneficent but will work malevolence or beneficence
according to the conditions under which it is permitted to act." This same sentiment is voiced by Leiserson (1938:15), "There is nothing inherent in economic laws that makes them necessarily work out to promote human welfare
if allowed free play. They need to be controlled and directed if we want them
to accomplish human purposes." The challenge, then, is to construct institutions and "working rules" so that society obtains the benefits of self-interest
and competition and avoids the evils.

One particular set of institutions and working rules is associated with free
markets and laissez faire, but the institutionalists believed these lead to
numerous labor problems. The reason is that a free market system contains a
variety of defects and imperfections that, when combined with human beings'

bounded rationality, generates conflict, poverty, harsh working conditions, job insecurity, and dynamic instability in the macro economy. The sources of market failure are several.

The most important defect is the inability of competitive markets and the price system to maintain the economy at full employment. Commons identified involuntary unemployment as the single most important labor problem and the Achilles heel of American capitalism (Commons 1934a:804-05; Commons and Andrews 1936:1; also see Clark 1926:144; Slichter 1928:850).

Unemployment in the institutional view is not typically the fault of the person unemployed, nor can market forces of demand and supply be counted on to automatically solve the problem. Indeed, while classical and neoclassical theory points to a reduction in wages as the cure for an excess supply of labor, the institutionalists presaged J. M. Keynes (1936) in their belief that wage cuts are ineffective and often counterproductive (Ely, 1886:116; Clark 1926:410). Like Keynes, the institutionalists instead placed greater emphasis on eliminating unemployment through measures that stabilize and expand purchasing power, such as easier credit conditions and countercylical public works (Whalen 1993; Kaufman 1996a).

Commons and the institutionalists attributed a number of the nation's most grievous labor problems to the effects of unemployment. For example:

- The nation suffers a tremendous waste of economic resources when labor and capital remain idle—a waste that seems all the more irrational and unjust when millions of jobless people suffer from acute privation due to lack of the basic necessities of life.
- Unemployment and the threat of joblessness promotes a consciousness of insecurity in the worker. This undercuts the incentive for employees to exert effort and diligence at work, since they may at any moment lose their job and a return on this investment, and promotes various defensive, protective stratagems on the part of employees to stretch out the work or shield themselves from competition (Commons 1918).
- Workers and their families also suffer considerable financial, physical, and emotional distress from unemployment, including in severe situations destitution, family break-up, and alcoholism.
- Firms react to slack times by cutting wages, layoffs, reduced hours, speed-ups, and heightened, often-times arbitrary discipline, all of which are detrimental to employee well being.
- Unemployment demoralizes its victims and erodes their strength of character, leading to a diminution in the nation's quantity and quality of labor input (Commons and Andrews 1936:3).

- Unemployment stokes conflict between management and labor and between social classes and ethnic groups.

A second important defect of the market system is the failure of price in many economic transactions to fully incorporate social costs and benefits. It is a basic theorem of microeconomics that social welfare is maximized when products are produced or activities pursued to the point where marginal social benefit equals marginal social cost. But externalities, public goods, limited information, and restrictions on factor mobility can cause a divergence between the private benefits and costs as seen by individual economic agents and the costs and benefits experienced by society. The result will be either too much or too little of the product or activity relative to the social optimum.

Several examples of labor problems will illustrate the point. Consider, first, work accidents. According to Adam Smith's theory of compensating differentials, firms with dangerous work processes are forced by competition for labor to pay a wage premium sufficient to compensate workers for the higher risk of injury and attendant financial loss and pain and suffering. This higher wage premium, in turn, motivates firms to be safety conscious, while the costs are in the long run passed on to consumers who, as the ultimate user of the product, are legitimately expected to pay for them.

While fine in theory, the institutionalists maintain that most real life labor markets contain defects that allow firms to shift a portion of the cost of accidents to third parties, be it workers, families, communities, or society at large (Clark 1924:371; Slichter 1928:850; Stabile 1993, 1996; Moss 1996). If the economy is at less than full employment, for example, a slew of available job seekers will undercut the pressure on firms to pay a compensating differential. Likewise, restrictions on worker mobility, such as moving expenses, discriminatory restrictions on hiring, loss of seniority rights or nonportability of pension benefits, will hinder the ability of workers in dangerous jobs to leave and seek work elsewhere. Alternatively, workers may not have adequate information about the extent of danger in the workplace and thus underestimate the true level of risk. Whatever the cause, the private cost of accidents to firms will be less than the social cost, leading to excessive numbers of accidents and additional costs for third parties.

This same analysis applies to numerous other aspects of employment. If firms owned labor, for example, they would have an incentive to wisely manage the health and physical stamina of their human asset in order to maximize its financial return. But when firms can rent labor by the hour or week and the costs of maintenance and training fall upon the worker or community, management's time horizon shortens and the incentives change. Particularly when an excess supply of labor is available, whether from cyclical unemployment, immigration, or some other source, the optimal labor policy is to get the maximum work effort from the employee each and every hour and, when the employee's health or physical stamina cracks, replace him or her with a new worker. The problems from this policy are threefold: some of the nation's labor input is wasted, the cost of the damage and depreciation of the labor input is shifted from the firm to the worker (or family/community), and feelings of rancor and bitterness develop in the work force over a policy employees see as patently exploitative.

A third example concerns human rights and dignity. Most people in advanced, Western countries believe that workers have a basic right to justice, fair dealing, and respect in the workplace. Violation of these rights and obligations is a social cost, albeit of a nonmonetary form. It is probable that labor markets will underproduce the socially optimal level of worker rights and protections, since firms are motivated to provide equity and dignity only to the extent that they add to profit. Not only are relative wage offers and employee quit decisions unable to satisfactorily signal firms the nature of employee preferences on these matters, the combination of scarce jobs, significant costs of mobility, and management's desire to preserve power and control in the workplace ensure that justice and dignity will be undersupplied in a free market system.

Social benefits may also exceed private benefits in a laissez-faire market system, leading firms to underproduce some employment "good." An example is general training. Since general training, such as reading blueprints or learning a software program, provides work skills that several or more companies find valuable, individual firms are reluctant to incur the cost of providing the training, because the worker may quickly be lured away by a more attractive job offer from a competitor. The result is a general undersupply of training and an underskilled work force (Clark 1924:362-63).

These considerations of social cost led the institutionalists to look at labor, not as a commodity, but as a human resource and at labor legislation as a crucial instrument for the conservation and development of this resource. If left to the free market, labor will be wasted and exploited, much as happens with unprotected natural resources. Thus Commons (1918:129) remarks that "Somebody must pay for the conservation of the nation's human resources. If left to demand and supply, the most valuable resources are not conserved"; and the American Association for Labor Legislation emblazoned on the masthead of early publications this statement: "The fundamental purpose of labor legislation is the conservation of the human resources of the nation."

Noncompetitive labor market structures are a third type of market defect and source of labor problems (Douglas 1938). Employers are motivated to provide competitive wages and other conditions of employment by the necessity of recruiting and keeping a qualified work force. However, if other employers are not actively competing in the labor market or workers face significant costs of mobility in moving from one firm to another, competition loses some of its effectiveness as a regulator of employment practices. As a result, firms gain the ability to exploit workers by paying less than competitive, full employment wages or by providing substandard hours, working conditions, and management practices. (Note that the institutionalists define "exploitation" broadly to include any situation where the worker's wage is depressed due to some form of contrived dependency or restriction of opportunity. See Taylor [1977].)

Labor economists of the period were almost unanimous in their opinion that employer competition for labor was highly imperfect (Kaufman 1994). Particularly noteworthy are the statements on this matter by two Chicago labor economists, Harry Millis and Paul Douglas. Millis (Millis and Montgomery 1945:364-65) states, for example, "Industry affords an abundance of evidence that a competitive demand for labor does not go far to protect the workers against long hours, excessive overtime, fines, discharges without sufficient cause, and objectionable working conditions." Douglas (1934:95)—the foremost analytical labor economist of the interwar period—similarly states, "It can thus be said that up to the summer of 1933 the forces which operated against labor receiving its marginal product were stronger than those which tended to prevent capital from securing its margin. An increased activity by the state in behalf of labor, or further unionization on the part of the wage-earners themselves, would have helped to redress this balance."

One reason for lack of employer competition for labor is monopsony in the labor market (only one buyer of labor), such as exists in a one-company town. According to one estimate (MacDonald 1938:77), over two million workers in the 1930s lived in towns dominated by a single employer. The extent of employer power over the work force in these towns was often considerable—as witnessed by Senator Wagner's remark (Huthmacher 1968:64) after visiting a number of coal mining towns in 1928 that "had I not seen it myself, I would not have believed that in the United States there were large areas where civil government was supplanted by a system that can only be compared with ancient feudalism." His allusion to feudalism was prompted by life in the coal camps. They were frequently in isolated, mountainous areas; the company often owned the housing and could evict the miners at will; the company also often owned the store at which the miners purchased the necessities of life, as well as the church and other public buildings; payment for work would sometimes be in scrip that was only of value at that camp; the police and camp guards were on the company payroll; and the entire camp was in a number of cases encircled by fencing so that entrance and exit took place through a single gate controlled by the guards.

Another source of imperfect competition in labor markets was oligopsony (only a few buyers of labor) and collusive activities promoted by employers associations. With regard to the latter, most medium-large cities had an active employers association, as did most major industries and trades (e.g., the National Erectors Association). One of the principal purposes of these associations was to promote employer interests in the labor area. Toward that end, the associations monitored labor market developments, disseminated information to member companies about wages and union activity, and tried to stabilize labor supply through training programs and other means. Relatively little research has been done on the labor activities of these associations (for an illuminating exception, see Harris [1991]), and modern-day economists tend to either ignore them or downgrade their likely effectiveness as agents of collusion. But Millis (1935) in his presidential address to the American Economic Association painted a far different picture when he said, "Even in a city like Chicago, an industry may dominate a large community, and the firms engaged in it may control the situation within rather wide limits. Going beyond this, I would cite a number of instances where associations of manufacturers or merchants have fixed wage scales or, indeed, maximum wages to be paid and have enforced them more successfully than any American state has enforced its minimum wage standards."

A third type of imperfect labor market structure of relevance to this historical era is segmented labor markets, particularly with regard to race, ethnicity, and gender. Discrimination in wages and job assignments was widely practiced by employers and condoned by a significant part of the public in early 20th century America (Millis and Montgomery 1938a; Milkman 1987). Most occupations were strictly segregated by gender, women ordinarily earned only one-half to two-thirds the wage of men, and it was common for members of particular ethnic and racial groups to be hired for only one set of jobs in a plant or mill. Although one version of neoclassical theory (Becker 1957) predicts that competition should undermine and eventually eliminate these types of employer discrimination (because nondiscriminating firms can get equally qualified minority workers at a lower wage, thus earning more profit), this process worked only very imperfectly and slowly in the pre-New Deal years and, in some cases, had counterproductive results (e.g., greater competition sometimes fueled outbreaks of racial violence against blacks and orientals).

The institutionalists (Commons 1907, 1934a:844; Ely and Bohn 1935:236-37) flatly rejected the contention in the Declaration of Independence that "all men are created equal." It was taken as an accepted fact that races and ethnic groups coming from countries closer to the equator lag behind those from countries in the mid-latitudes in terms of the strength and development of their intellect, character, and culture. Likewise, men were thought to be superior to women in most lines of work due to their stronger physiques and more disciplined emotional temperaments, while it was also accepted that women more than men needed to be at home to raise children and manage the household.

A portion of the disparity of rewards and treatment given native white men versus other groups (circa the early 1900s) could thus be rationalized by the institutionalists as a legitimate reflection of differences in genetic and cultural "endowments." They also recognized, however, that another significant portion of the differential in rewards and treatment at work reflected plain and simple discrimination (Commons and Andrews 1936:47-48, 319; Millis and Montgomery 1938a; Lehrer 1987). This discrimination arose from several sources, such as race prejudice, fear of labor market competition from minorities, social custom regarding appropriate gender and ethnic roles, and the desire of native white men to maintain their economic and social hegemony. These motives interacted with market imperfections, such as involuntary unemployment, employer market power, and worker collusion (solidarity), to initiate and maintain segmented markets and discriminatory differentials.

Although imperfect forms of competition in labor markets were believed to be widespread by the institutionalists, they did *not* form the central or most important part of their argument in favor of employment regulation and collective bargaining, despite numerous statements to this effect (e.g., Reynolds 1984; Cain 1993). Rather, it was *excessive competition*, not lack of competition, that was deemed a far more serious cause of labor problems (Ely 1907; Seager 1913; Commons 1918:28-29; Commons and Andrews 1936:47-48, 372-74). The terms usually used by the institutionalists to describe this situation were "destructive" or "cutthroat" competition.

The Wisconsin school institutionalists tended to use these terms loosely and did not give them precise definition. The institutionally sympathetic economist J.M. Clark of Columbia University, however, devoted several chapters of his path-breaking book, *Studies in the Economics of Overhead Costs* (1924), to this subject. He describes three conditions that are conducive to destructive competition: fixed costs are a large proportion of total cost of supply, substantial excess productive capacity exists in the market, and factor mobility is costly. The outcome of these three conditions is likely to be a sea of red ink for producers and a decline in prices far below the break-even point of average total cost (as in railroad rate wars) until enough firms go bankrupt that a balance between production capacity and sales is restored.

The innovation of the institutionalists was to apply the model of destructive competition to labor markets. A person's marginal cost of supplying an extra hour of labor, particularly in terms of direct money outlay, is quite small, but the fixed cost of supplying that labor (e.g., food, shelter, clothes, health care) is large. In a situation of excess labor supply (either due to generalized unemployment or low mobility out of depressed areas due to financial and family constraints), the dearth of jobs, the continuing pressure of fixed costs (particularly for breadwinners who have a family to support), and the fact that workers cannot inventory labor hours and sell them at a future date soon results in a bidding down of wage rates to very low levels as the most financially desperate workers undercut their rivals in an effort to obtain employment. This process is described by Commons and Andrews (1936:48) thus:

> Another reason for the low wage scale, largely the result of the first [extensive immigration], is the cutthroat competition of the workers for work. Among the unskilled, unorganized workers, the wage that the cheapest laborer—such as the partially supported woman, the immigrant with low standards of living, or the workman oppressed by extreme need—is willing to take, very largely fixes the wage level for the whole group.

In orthodox economic theory the low wage described above by Commons and Andrews is not a labor problem but a labor *solution*, since a low(er) wage is what must happen in the labor market if a situation of excess labor supply is to be corrected and an equilibrium restored where jobs are available for all those who desire work (Reynolds 1991). But from an institutional perspective this neglects the fixed cost of labor. If the quantity and quality of the nation's work force is to be maintained, workers must earn a wage at least equal to the minimum amount of money required for ongoing (fixed) costs of food, shelter, clothing, education, etc., for themselves *and* all dependent family members. Earnings less than this amount mean that workers and their families suffer a gradual erosion in their physical health and human capital, while firms are "parasitic" in that their existence is subsidized by shifting part of the costs of production to the community at large.

## Property Rights and Inequality in Power

Another source of labor problems, according to the institutionalists, lies outside the market mechanism. This is the unequal distribution of property rights and power in society.

Standard microeconomic theory typically takes the institutional structure of the economy, such as the distribution of property and wealth and the provisions of constitutional and contract law, as a "given" and proceeds to analyze how market forces determine an equilibrium level of prices, production, and allocation of resources. From Commons' point of view, however, it is these "givens" in orthodox theory that are the ultimate determinant of prices and outputs because they determine each trader's endowment of resources and bargaining power. Indeed, the reason why Commons' economics is "institutional" economics is because it is, at a fundamental level, these institutional "givens," not the mechanistic operation of supply and demand per se, that determine price and quantity in the market.

Since property rights, contract law, etc., are determined through the political process, it is not surprising that the "rules of the game" are set up to promote the interests of the rich and powerful. In *Legal Foundations of Capitalism*, Commons described a process of conflict and struggle dating from the Norman invasion of England to early 20th century America in which one disenfranchised group after another (e.g., feudal lords, town merchants, American colonists, black slaves) fought wars, staged revolutions, formed new political parties, etc., in a quest to gain entrance to the polity and use their newly gained political power to change the "rules of the game" in ways that better protected and advanced their interests. Institutional economics is thus "political economy" in that it explicitly recognizes the interaction between political power and market outcomes.

When Commons and fellow institutionalists looked at political government in America, they saw considerable, albeit imperfect, progress in the direction of decentralized power and democratic control. The unlimited power of English kings had given way to representative democracy in which the laws of the land require the consent of the governed, and the arbitrary use of power and privilege was checked by the Bill of Rights and policed by an independent judiciary culminating in a Supreme Court. But when the institutionalists looked at American industry at the turn of the century, they saw a retrogression in security, liberty, and equality of workers as a class. The source of this retrogression was a skewed system of property rights and power that overwhelmingly favored employers, leading to exploitation of labor, injustice in the workplace, and growing labor conflict and social unrest.

The presumption of both law and orthodox economics at the turn of the century was that the individual worker and individual employer have equal liberty to agree or not agree to an employment contract. Furthermore, the worker may quit at any time, just as the employer can fire the worker at any time. This reciprocal freedom, combined with competitive markets, was thought to create an ideal institutional arrangement in which power is highly dispersed and balanced among individual workers and firms with neither party having an ability to coerce or exploit the other.

The reality, said Commons (1924), is quite different. A half century earlier when America was still a country of small shops and farms, a rough equality of power existed between workers and employers. With the rise of large-scale industry and giant trusts in the last part of the 19th century, however, the balance of power tipped substantially in favor of employers. Now the employer, though treated in the law as a fictional person, was a large corporation with numerous plants, thousands of employees, and a multimillion dollar pool of capital drawn from thousands of individuals. The worker, on the other hand, was likely to be a poorly educated, semiskilled or unskilled male breadwinner with a family to support and little if any financial reserve. In the rare situation when the economy was at full employment, the scarcity of labor gave the individual worker a semblance of equal bargaining power. But in normal times, employers had an excess supply of job seekers and the bargaining power of the individual worker, unless skilled or strategically placed, was minimal. "Take it or leave it" became the labor relations philosophy of most firms, and many workers quickly had to take it given their scant resources, dependency on earnings from work, and near complete lack of what is today called a social safety net. Conditions of monopsony, segmented markets, and other market defects only exacerbated the imbalance in power.

For the institutionalists, the inequality of bargaining power between the individual worker and employer was *the* fundamental source of labor problems. While the tendency in modern economic analysis is to dismiss inequality of bargaining power as a vacuous concept (see Reynolds 1991 and Schwab in this volume; an exception is Bowles and Gintis 1993), to the institutionalists it was transparent that the individual worker did not compete on anything close to a level playing field with individual firms; that this tilted playing field results in very low wages, long hours, and harsh working conditions for many employees; and that these conditions are neither preordained by the laws of supply and demand (reflecting as they do socially determined property rights and wealth endowments) nor are they efficiency maximizing (because the sense of inequity that accompanies low wages and harsh treatment leads to a concomitant withdrawal of employee "goodwill" [Commons 1919] and thus motivation to work). Likewise, instead of promoting a harmony of interests, competition with unequal bargaining power degenerates into a cutthroat struggle of "survival of the fittest" in which the more liberal, progressive employers are forced to lower labor standards to the level of their most grasping rival. Inside firms, the inequality of power was manifested in the master-servant relationship that existed between employer and employee. Employers had almost unfettered authority in all areas of personnel policy and practice, including the right to fire employees for any reason. Because employees had little avenue for redress of grievances, quitting, striking, and physical violence were the principal means of resolving disputes.

Seen as a totality, therefore, industrial government at the turn of the century was far more despotic and authoritarian than political government, and the operation of labor markets, rather than making the worker a free man, forced him through economic coercion to accept wages and conditions of employment that were often injurious and unjust. Thus laissez faire was naturally endorsed and labor unions and labor legislation condemned by the ruling elites since they were looking to protect their power and privileged position. The institutionalists, on the other hand, saw unions and labor legislation as essential instruments for balancing power and democratizing industry (Commons and Andrews 1936:502-34).

## Solutions to Labor Problems

Having diagnosed the cause of labor problems, the institutionalists next turned to a search for solutions. What they came up with encompassed an overall policy strategy toward labor problems as well as a number of specific proposals regarding the resolution of individual problems.

The strategy of the institutionalists is captured in the comment by Commons (1934b:143) that his goal was "to save capitalism by making it good." The point to note about this comment is that the goal is to reform capitalism, not replace it. Ely, Commons, and most other institutionalists were political progressives (an American version of European social democrats with respect to social legislation and the welfare state, but much less so with regard to the role and purpose of the labor movement) who accepted the basic institutions of private property, a market-organized system of production and exchange, and representative democracy but thought these needed greater social control and shared governance.

The essential problem, the institutionalists thought, was that the institutional structure within which the profit motive and competition functioned and the dominant economic and social philosophy that guided public policy were by the late 1800s seriously out of date. Laissez faire and limited government were appropriate in the early part of the 19th century in a largely agricultural economy but were increasingly dysfunctional in an economy of huge corporations, national and international trade, and a large urban working class dependent on wages for the necessities of life.

According to Commons (1934a:876-903), the first and most important strategic goal is stabilization of the economy. The jagged ups and downs of production and employment and the persistence of substantial involuntary unemployment in most years were the single greatest source of labor problems. During the entire 1920s, therefore, he devoted his attention to methods of macroeconomic stabilization (Whalen 1993). Policies he advocated included use of open market operations by the Federal Reserve to maintain a stable price level (he was a pioneer in this effort and worked closely with noted monetary economist Irving Fisher), countercyclical spending on public works, a system of unemployment insurance in order to stabilize consumer income during recessions, expansion of collective bargaining in order to prevent destabilizing wage deflation and augment household purchasing power, and public employment exchanges to facilitate adjustment of labor demand and supply. It is noteworthy that J. M. Keynes wrote Commons a personal letter in 1927 and stated (Skidelsky 1992:229), "There seems to be no other economist with whose general way of thinking I feel myself in such general accord."

The next part of the strategy involved a three-pronged effort to improve employment practices. The first prong focused on improvements in the organization and practice of management, particularly in the personnel and employee relations areas. Commons (1918, 1921) was particularly impressed with the progressive personnel management practices of the nation's leading-edge employers and thought that these practices set a benchmark for others to follow. He stated that this group of firms represented between 10% to 25% of employers and were so advanced that unionization had nothing to offer their workers. Although initially skeptical of the new employee representation or "industrial democracy" plans that firms introduced in the late 1910s and early 1920s, by the end of the decade institutionalists such as William Leiserson (1929) admitted that many of these plans were a net plus for the employees (an attitude that soured, however, during the Depression). The institutionalists did not propose direct government intervention in business to promote adoption of improved personnel management practices. They did believe, however, that the spread of such practices would be materially aided by, first, macroeconomic stabilization efforts (because labor scarcity motivates good management practices) and, second, the extension of collective bargaining and protective labor legislation as a means to shield progressive employers from competitive underbidding by unscrupulous or financially distressed rivals who used low labor standards to gain a cost advantage.

The second prong was extension of collective bargaining. The institutionalists recognized that trade unions are imperfect instruments to accomplish the social good, as they often engage in restrictive practices, sometimes boost wages far above market rates, and occasionally are as authoritarian or corrupt as the firms they are attempting to organize (Commons 1913:120-48). Nonetheless, trade unions perform four functions that the institutionalists believed are vital to the public interest.

1.  The introduction of industrial democracy or "constitutional government in industry" into the workplace (Leiserson 1922). Commons and associates saw the bloody labor strikes, voluminous labor turnover, and widespread employee disaffection of the late 1800s/early 1900s as the inevitable outcome of an autocratic form of industrial government in which employers had unchecked power and workers were denied elementary rights and dignities of due process and respect. Although the individual worker was powerless to change the system, trade unions through the power of collective action could do so. In particular, trade unions checked the arbitrary exercise of management power, introduced bilateral methods of dispute resolution, and gave workers a voice in the determination of the system of workplace rules they worked under.

2.  The equalization of bargaining power between labor and capital in the determination of wages and other conditions of employment. Commons and Andrew (1936:373) state it thus: "The need for collective bargaining arises from the serious discrepancy in 'withholding power' between the individual employer and the individual wage earner, a discrepancy which tends to result in terms of employment highly oppressive to the worker and injurious to society in general. . . . The employer is usually a corporation, which is itself a combination of capital; but the disadvantage of the laborer is even more fundamental. Being propertyless, he has no opportunity to make a living except by working on the property of others. Having no resources to fall back upon, he cannot wait until he can drive the most favorable bargain. It is a case of the necessities of the laborer pitted against the resources of the employer." The additional requirement for effective power balancing, they thought, is that collective bargaining must cover all or most of the firms in a product market in order to take labor cost out of competition. In the short run, the standard rate serves as a floor preventing the downward nibbling of wages and working conditions due to cutthroat competition. In the longer run, trade unions gradually increase the standard rate, thereby redistributing income from profit to wages. This, it was thought by many, would help maintain consumer purchasing power and thus help stabilize the economy at full employment (see Kaufman 1996a).

3.  An offset to market failures associated with externalities, public goods, imperfect information, and so on. For example, the institutionalists

thought free markets would lead to plant-level working conditions, such as safety, sanitary conditions, and equitable dispute resolutions, that are substantially below the socially optimal level (Slichter 1928:651-64). The reason is that many working conditions are "public goods"—once provided no person can be excluded from consuming them. It is well known that free markets will underproduce a public good, since each employee has an incentive to remain silent and "free ride" in the hope that some other worker will take the initiative (and risk of management displeasure) and speak up. Collective bargaining, however, can overcome the free-rider problem because workers have an incentive to voice their demands to leaders of the union, and the leaders, in turn, are far more willing than individual workers to present these demands to management.

4. A counterbalance to the business class' otherwise preponderant power in the political system. Veblen (1904:286) observed that "representative government means, chiefly, representation of business interests." Without unions and the influence they exert through lobbying and political endorsements, the rights and interests of the average working person are likely to be underrepresented in legislatures and executive offices. The court system also is likely to become dominated by judges that cater to business interests.

The third prong of the institutional strategy to improve employment conditions is legal enactment. Legal enactment involves use of the sovereign power of the state to prohibit or limit certain practices deemed injurious to the public interest. Legal enactment was seen as the strategy of last resort. Wherever possible, the institutionalists sought social control mechanisms that achieved their purpose through voluntary agreements and the give and take of negotiation. This method, they thought, was far more likely to achieve workable results and be obeyed by those affected. Accordingly, the institutionalists were philosophically opposed to binding arbitration and government intervention in labor disputes. They were also well aware of the dangers of relying on state power, as it is easily manipulated by special interests and can quickly become a tyranny. Nonetheless, the inequality of bargaining power and authoritarian master-servant relationship that were the root cause of so many labor problems are, in the final analysis, legal phenomena (since law establishes the structure of property rights and the permissible methods of competition) and thus have to be corrected through changes in the law.

The institutionalists advocated two basic types of employment law. The first is protective labor legislation. Examples include minimum wages, maximum hours, prohibition of child labor, immigration quotas, and abolition of payment in scrip. Legislation such as antidiscrimination laws also fall in this category. The presumption of protective labor legislation is that competition in labor markets results in certain practices or outcomes that are antisocial, that workers so affected have no reasonable prospect of remedying the situation through individual action, and thus collective action in the form of legislation is necessary to establish minimum standards or to prohibit the practice outright (Seager 1913).

The second major category of labor law is social insurance. Examples include unemployment insurance, workmen's compensation, state-operated health insurance, and old age insurance (Social Security). The rationale for insurance is that individuals generally cannot save enough to provide back-up funds in case of a financial calamity (e.g., a house fire) but that by making contributions to a common fund, money will be available to compensate those few who are struck by disaster. For most people, one form of disaster is loss of livelihood, be it from ill health, the infirmities of old age, a disabling accident, or prolonged unemployment. Social insurance, in turn, is made necessary by the fact that private markets do not provide adequate protection at a reasonable cost for many types of employment-related risks. The reason is due to two market failures (Millis and Montgomery; 1938b:121-22) known today as "moral hazard" (people have an incentive to purposely engage in the risky behavior in order to qualify for benefits) and "adverse selection" (the people most likely to suffer the risk are the ones most likely to buy coverage). If workers are to have access to employment-related insurance, then, it falls on government to establish and operate the program (Moss 1996).

Having stabilized the economy and promoted improved employment practices through the three mechanisms described above, the next part of the institutional strategy is to use collective bargaining and legal enactment to gradually raise what they called the "plane of competition." The plane of competition, first articulated by Henry Carter Adams (1886), connotes the minimum level of employment practices and standards that at any one time all competitors must meet. The object of social policy, and a fundamental prerequisite for social and economic progress, is to first establish a minimum floor of labor standards and then gradually increase these standards over time. Progressive, liberal employers typically chart the way through voluntarily adopted improvements in wages and other labor standards, and then unions and government pressure the remainder to follow by gradually increasing minimum labor conditions through the "stick" of collective bargaining and legal enactment.

The institutionalists subscribed to a labor market version of "Gresham's law"—just as bad money drives out good without government regulation of the money supply, so too bad employment practices drive out good without government- or union-enforced minimum standards. Commons stated (1913:411) with regard to safety regulation, for example, "It is an application of the well-recognized principle of political economy that the competition of the worst employers tends to drag down the best employers to their level." They are able to do this by practicing ethically and economically unfair trade practices, such as skimping on safety or sanitary expenditures, and/or by undercutting established standards through the use of "lower forms of competition," such as impoverished immigrants or child labor. The inability of high-standard employers to resist the forces of unfair competition was called by Ely (1913:405) the "problem of the twentieth man"—nineteen employers would like to increase the safety in their plants but are prevented from doing so by the recalcitrant twentieth employer who refuses to go along and thus threatens the competitive position of the rest. The problem of the twentieth man was vividly illustrated to the institutionalists by the failure of employers in the match industry to eliminate the use of phosphorus (a cause of a grotesquely disfiguring disease among match workers) without government compulsion (see Moss 1996).

From a strategic policy point of view, establishing an appropriate plane of competition through employment regulation is thus vital, for it prevents labor standards from sinking to socially unacceptable levels and also shields progressive, high-standard employers from the competitive pressure of firms less well managed or less socially responsible (Linder 1989; Craypo in this volume). Over time, employment regulation and collective bargaining should be used to then gradually raise the minimum level of employment standards. Although doing so is generally opposed by companies because of the higher cost, it nevertheless serves the public interest by acting as a spur to greater technological innovation, capital investment, employee training and development, and more efficient work organization and management practices (see Filene [1923] for testimony to this effect by a progressive businessman). In the long run, these factors, not low wages and poor working conditions, are the key ingredients to higher living standards and competitive advantage (Marshall and Tucker 1992).

Another useful social purpose of setting a marketwide plane of competition is to eliminate "unfair" methods of competition. The institutionalists support free trade in product and labor markets only as long as it is also *fair* trade. Fair trade, in turn, requires that competition take place on a reasonably level playing field, traders fully incorporate social cost into their prices and wages, and no one uses unscrupulous or unethical trade practices to gain an advantage. For this reason, the old institutionalists believed white, male, native American wage earners at the turn of the century needed protection from newly arrived immigrants, dependent women, convict labor, foreign Third World labor, and other "substandard" groups.

Since workers in these groups have a much lower standard of living, are (in the case of immigrants and foreign labor) often far more necessitous of a job at any price, and have living costs that are in many cases subsidized (e.g., convict labor, married women), these workers will undercut the plane of competition for white-male labor and thus force down their wages and employment conditions (Perlman 1928). Employment regulations that restrict the terms and conditions these workers can accept (e.g., a minimum wage law) or that outlaw such competition altogether (e.g., prohibition of child labor) are thus justified on the grounds that they not only protect substandard groups from exploitation but also protect the most advanced group of workers from unfair competition. Similar reasoning was used to support tariffs on imported goods from low-wage countries (Ramstad 1987). The old institutionalists recognized that these types of restrictions on trade in product and labor markets, while socially beneficial in principle, could in practice become instruments of privilege and monopoly rents for industrialists and other politically powerful groups (as envisioned in theories of regulatory capture), but they were relatively sanguine (probably overly so) that the influence of special interests could be kept at bay through devices such as civil service reform; creation of independent, professionally staffed regulatory agencies; and countervailing organizations of consumers and other "weak" or disorganized bargainers.

Critics object that establishing a plane of competition through collective bargaining and legal enactment raises the price of labor and causes some members of these groups to lose their jobs (Stigler 1946; Reynolds 1991). Then gradually raising the plane of competition only exacerbates the problem. The institutionalists respond, however, that keeping marginal, low-productivity jobs is myopic social policy (Filene 1923). The better approach is to accept that companies will reduce employment in marginal jobs, use private and social forms of investment (e.g., education and training programs) to raise the productivity of the majority of the displaced workers who are employable, and accept that a minority of the displaced are unemployable at reasonable wages and must be supported through state welfare programs (Seager 1913). In effect, the institutionalists see raising the plane of competition as a method to promote continuous quality improvement in the nation's work force. Toward this end, they promoted employer "Americanization" programs in the 1920s as a way to upgrade the social and work skills of immigrants. They also favored prohibition of child labor on grounds that increased length of schooling will increase their productivity as future workers, prohibition of night work for women as a means to improve family life and the "quality" of children, and public employment programs for the able bodied who cannot otherwise find work (Lehrer 1987; Ely and Bohn 1935:256-64).

The final part of the institutional strategy for employment reform was development of a new economic and legal theory of the employment relationship. The institutionalists quickly discovered that newly enacted pieces of labor legislation, such as minimum wage and maximum hour laws, were frequently declared unconstitutional by the courts. The justification was typically that such legislation violated the U.S. Constitution's 14th amendment and, in particular, its stricture that no person's property can be taken without "due process of law" (Commons and Andrews 1936). The institutionalists sought to convince the court that a different standard should be adopted. They argued that while individual male workers confronted the employer on a legal plane of equality, the economic plane of competition was so tilted against the unskilled worker that many adult males were themselves in a dependent position and, thus, open to exploitation (Commons and Andrews 1936:373-74). Since contracts can be ruled null and void when consummated under the pressure of coercion, labor legislation was for this reason constitutional. He further argued that labor of all types was invested in a public interest, since the conditions of labor materially affect the development and character of every worker-citizen and, in addition, the health of the overall economy. Labor, he thought, should be treated as a "public utility" and thus regulated for the benefit of the community (Commons 1918:30).

## Administration and Enforcement of Employment Regulation

Many economists regard the administration and enforcement of employment regulations as "institutional details" and accordingly give them short shrift. Not so the institutionalists. They not only devote considerable attention in their writings to issues of administration and enforcement but also put forth innovative proposals on how these processes should best be implemented. It is symbolic in this regard that Commons had two offices—one at the university and the other at the state capitol.

The importance given to administration and enforcement is indicated in this statement of Commons and Andrews (1936:448): "More important than the hasty enactment of additional laws is the adoption of methods of administration that will enforce them. It is easy for politicians or reformers or trade union officials to boast of the laws which they have secured for labor, and it is just as easy to overlook details or appropriations or competent officials that are needed to make them enforceable." With this general admonition they then proceed to develop a number of specific points.

The starting place is reiteration of the general principle that "free contract must rule" (Ely 1914:731). Wherever possible, the institutionalists want to preserve individual bargaining and responsibility. But adherence to the doctrine of freedom of contract is a qualified one—it is "toleration within limits" (Commons and Andrews 1936:196). Determining the boundaries or limits of freedom of contract occupied Commons for many years and led to one of his major theoretical concepts—"reasonable value" (Commons 1934a:860; Barbash 1976).

Reasonable value, in essence, is an ethical/legal judgement that the terms of a contract are the product of a "reasonable" use of bargaining power by each party and the outcome is likewise "reasonable" in the sense it does not violate the average person's sense of justice and fair dealing. Contracts that are not reasonable fall outside the "limits of toleration" and provide a rationale for regulation. Since "reasonableness" is inherently a subjective, socially determined judgment, public and judicial opinion regarding the need for and merits of regulation necessarily varies over time and across people. It also means that ethics is necessarily a part of the discipline of economics, contrary to standard neoclassical thought.

If regulation is deemed necessary, the second principle is that it should be accomplished with as little coercion as possible. Commons' preferred method to accomplish this end is to enlist the profit motive in pursuit of social goals (Commons 1934a:875). Thus Commons drafted the first Wisconsin worker's compensation statute so that employer insurance premiums rise in tandem with the number of accident claims. This procedure, he thought, was far more effective than the traditional method of state safety inspections and punitive fines for safety violations. The former appeals to employer self-interest to be safety conscious, while the latter provides employers an incentive to be litigious and evasive. Experience rating in unemployment insurance has a similar rationale.

The third principle of administration and enforcement is that the parties affected should whenever possible be represented in the regulatory process (Commons 1913:382-424; Wunderlin 1992). As already mentioned, this consideration predisposed Commons to favor collective bargaining over legal enactment. When legal enactment is necessary, he advocated that the legislature pass broad enabling legislation and then delegate to an independent commission the responsibility for establishing the precise regulatory standards and procedures. Further, the commission should include representatives of employers, workers, and the public so that all interests and points of view are heard. In effect, he proposed that employment regulation be developed and administered through much the same structure and process as used in collective bargaining. Not only will the parties be more likely to obey the regulatory standards if they have a voice in their development, the standards are also more likely to be practical and cost effective.

Certain institutionalists, primarily from the "Veblenian" wing, advocated a further extension of the tripartite representation of interests to include agencies responsible for some form of economic planning at the industry and national level. The Wisconsin school of institutionalists, however, saw this as an engine for fascism and opposed it (Commons 1934a:876-903). During the New Deal these divergent viewpoints often came into conflict within the Roosevelt administration (Barber 1994).

The fourth principle put forward to guide the implementation of regulation is that "reasonable" regulatory standards should be defined in practice as those equal to the standards currently practiced on a voluntary basis by "best practice" employers (Commons 1934a:860). Thus regulation avoids on one hand setting an impractical high standard, yet on the other, it accomplishes a significant upgrading in employment conditions. As the "best practice" standards of employers rise over time, regulatory standards should move in tandem.

The fifth principle of regulation is that effective administration and enforcement requires significant social investment to recruit and train a competent, professional cadre of administrators and to provide them with the human and physical capital necessary to carry out their responsibilities. Effective regulation cannot be done "on the cheap." Commons was pessimistic about the willingness of Americans to make this investment and their ability to effectively implement it. He characterized Americans as "excessively individualistic, politically diverted, and administratively incompetent" (Commons 1934a:846).

## Implications

As noted in the introduction, many of the employment laws and regulations advocated by the old institutionalists were enacted into law on a national basis during the New Deal years of the 1930s. None of the old institutional economists would be surprised to learn that sixty years later these laws, even as subsequently amended, may well need further, perhaps substantial revision. Change and adaptation are, after all, the essence of evolution.

What in our current system of employment law and regulation should be preserved, what parts should be revised or eliminated, and what new parts added?

If the old institutionalists first stopped to consult the academic literature in labor economics, they would be pleasantly surprised to learn that labor problems have largely disappeared from the American workplace. Not only is the term no longer mentioned, but most labor market phenomena, such as wage rates, hours of work, and even unemployment, tend to be portrayed as efficient, welfare-maximizing outcomes arising from rational, optimizing choices made in a system of competitive markets (Ehrenberg and Smith 1994; Dow and Schwab in this volume). Their impression on this matter would then be further reinforced when they find next to nothing in the academic litera- ture that recommends additional employment laws or regulation and a great body of research that argues for considerably less. The reasons, they learn, are that many scholars dismiss inequality of bargaining power as having neither conceptual nor practical significance; that many others maintain that competi- tion in labor markets necessarily results in efficient, welfare-enhancing out- comes (competition spurs workers and firms to search out contract terms that exhaust all gains from trade); and equity is a metaphysical concept that is now held to be outside the realm of economic theory.

After leaving the library, the old institutionalists would discover quite a different world when they visit with managers and workers in real life work- places. Their first reaction would probably be amazement at the advanced technology of production; the much cleaner, safer, and more pleasant condi- tions of work; the number of dual-earner couples; and the extensive pay and benefits. They would conclude, no doubt, that the workplace of today is vastly superior to that of their day. They would also quickly discover, however, that even in today's workplace there exist numerous, sometimes widespread labor problems.

A number of these labor problems appear quite similar to those of the early 1900s, while others are new. Insecurity of employment, though not as severe, remains pervasive and affects even the white-collar and executive ranks. Large pockets of the work force are also employed in menial, low-pay- ing jobs that provide few benefits and even smaller opportunities for self- development, while millions of other adults don't work at all and survive on welfare. Work-related injuries and fatalities also remain unexpectedly high, and equally surprising are the millions of Americans working two or more jobs to make ends meet. Surprise would turn to shock when the institutionalists learn that 35 million Americans do not have health insurance (the AALL began a nationwide campaign for national health insurance in the mid-1910s).

The distinct trend toward greater income inequality would also worry the old institutionalists, as would the decade-long stagnation in real family income. Inside the workplace, they would encounter a number of serious social ills, such as drug abuse, AIDS, sexual harassment, violent behavior, and discrimination of all kinds. As shocking as the lack of health insurance would be the survival of the employment-at-will doctrine in many states and, only slightly less disturbing, the lack of well-defined workplace rights and dispute resolution procedures. Finally, the old institutionalists would also encounter many situations where employers flout the rights and protections given workers to join trade unions and bargain collectively. They would conclude, I think, that while much has changed, much hasn't.

The economics literature, much of the business community, and a majority of elected government officials claim that the economic and social problems of the country stem from too much government paternalism and regulation. The solution is getting government out of people's lives through deregulation and a return to competitive markets.

The old institutionalists would, I think, give this position qualified support in certain areas. In other areas of employment, however, they would advocate either maintaining or increasing the scope of regulation, albeit in ways that promote greater flexibility and consensus.

One rationale for decreased and/or more flexible employment regulation, for example, is the diminution over time in the scope and severity of employer power over wages and other terms and conditions of employment (Kaufman 1989, 1991). For example, the most significant source of employer power— large scale, persistent involuntary unemployment—is considerably reduced relative to pre-World War II years. Contributing factors include Keynesian-inspired countercyclical monetary and fiscal policies, the "automatic stabilizer" effect of social insurance and income transfer programs, and the shift from a manufacturing to a service economy. Also, less unemployment causes individual labor markets to operate in a more competitive manner, such as with respect to the size of compensating wage differentials and inclusion of social costs of production in price.

Other developments have also reduced the need for employment regulation. Certainly the extent of monopsony and collusion on the part of employer associations has declined significantly, for example, due to improved worker mobility and economic development in rural areas. Labor problems have also been substantially reduced due to significant improvements in work organization, personnel practices, and the quality and social responsibility of modern management. Finally, American society has become more egalitarian over time due to reduced class barriers, broader access to higher education, and a higher social consciousness on the part of the American people.

These considerations suggest that the inequality of bargaining power between individual workers and firms in today's labor markets has been reduced, but not eliminated, in both scope and severity. The greatest source of employer power over the worker—the threat of job loss and the availability of numerous desperate job seekers willing to replace him—is certainly still present in a number of industries and occupations, but less so than in the early 20th century. Not only does the economy operate closer to full employment, but the social safety net provided by the modern welfare state, the much greater number of dual-earner families, the greater wealth of households, and the greater proportion of skilled, highly educated employees in the work force all reduce the financial vulnerability of the typical worker and, thus, increase his/her bargaining power in wage determination. (These conclusions are sensitive to the date of comparison—relative to the early 1900s they are certainly true, but a net retrogression may have occurred if attention is restricted to the post-1970s.)

With respect to unions, this analysis suggests that legislation like the National Labor Relations Act still serves the public interest but that it needs revision. Some workers still suffer exploitation and unjust treatment, and the law does not adequately protect their rights to obtain union representation. Collective bargaining also helps maintain a socially acceptable plane of competition in the labor market. For these reasons, the penalties for antiunion discrimination and refusal to bargain first contracts should be strengthened. The definition of the set of employees covered under the act should also be expanded to reflect today's more diverse types of employer-employee relationships (e.g., leased employees, members of self-managing work teams).

On the other hand, the public must have guarantees that unions will exhibit both greater restraint in the use of their collective bargaining power and more interest in promoting the economic performance of the firm than has been typically demonstrated in past years (Kaufman 1996b). In effect, society needs to strengthen the "monopsony-reducing" function of unions (where monopsony is defined broadly to cover all sources of employer power) but place stronger curbs on the "monopoly creating" face of unions. Although not ideal, the most effective device for curbing union power is the threat of striker replacement. In exchange for stronger guarantees of the right to organize, either the legality of striker replacement must be written in the NLRA (with certain restrictions to prevent blatant union busting) or some other safeguard must be devised, such as mandatory profit sharing so that union members have greater incentive to accept wage moderation and flexible work rules. Also, the ban on company-dominated labor organizations ("company unions") is overly restrictive and should be relaxed in order to facilitate employee involvement programs in nonunion companies. The availability of the union election process (particularly in strengthened form) will prevent the more egregious forms of management domination, as occurred in the pre-NLRA days.

Because the playing field in today's labor market is more balanced than in the days of the institutional economists, there is also a case for reducing the amount of countervailing power contained in other labor laws, such as the minimum wage. Allowing the minimum wage to decline from the traditional one-half of the average manufacturing wage to, say, one-third as in more recent years is consonant with this idea. As long as some unorganized workers suffer from a bargaining disadvantage, however, the minimum wage should be retained. Similar reasoning (i.e., maintaining the legislation but making the standards less restrictive) applies to other protective labor legislation, such as overtime laws and prevailing wage standards in construction.

Employer power is not the only rationale for employment regulation, however, and other considerations must also be examined. Employment security, for example, is considered by the institutionalists to be a vital social concern, both because of its intrinsic value to workers and the important part it plays in fostering productive attitudes (e.g., employee commitment) and employment practices (e.g., training). The bulk of the evidence strongly suggests that employment security (or the perception of such security) in the American workplace has declined significantly in the last two decades due to factors such as downsizing, reengineering, outsourcing, and greater global competition.

While the decline in employment security carries with it some socially beneficial results in the form of greater organizational flexibility, reduced cost, and an end to an initiative-killing entitlement mentality, there are numerous other consequences that are inimical to the social interest and warrant improved or additional regulation. Too many companies, for example, use downsizing as a pretext for laying off older employees in order to save money on salaries, pensions, and benefits. Strengthened protections against age discrimination are thus appropriate. Likewise, in many states, particularly those adhering closely to the doctrine of employment at will, employees lack basic legal protections against arbitrary, unfair dismissal. Strengthened termination procedures and requirement that "just cause" be demonstrated in dismissals are thus desirable. As a third example, the recently enacted plant closing legislation (the WARN Act), while good in intent, has proven mediocre in accomplishment due to overly broad exemptions and lack of enforcement (see Addison and Hirsch in this volume). All of these issues can also effectively be dealt with through collective bargaining, thus providing an additional rationale for strengthened protections of the right to organize.

These types of regulation address the negative consequences of employment insecurity, but they do not deal with the underlying causes. Here, too, regulation has a role to play. Part of the motive for downsizing, reengineering, and other such initiatives is the desire of companies to shift part of the cost of labor to third parties. Using temporary workers or part-time employees, for example, allows firms to avoid various employee benefits costs, such as health insurance. This practice, while good for short-run profits, imposes substantial social costs on the workers and community that are more nearly a legitimate charge against production. Some type of universal health insurance, therefore, not only serves the public interest but helps strengthen income security for workers.

Another contributing factor to employment insecurity in today's economy is intensified international competition in product markets. In his masterful article "American Shoemakers," Commons (1909) described how the extension of markets brought successive rounds of pressure upon shoe manufacturers to reduce wages and speed up the work. The same process is at work today, only the extension of markets has proceeded to every corner of the world economy. Thus American workers and companies find themselves in competition with workers and firms in China and Mexico where wages and benefits are a fraction of the American level. And just as with the shoemakers of the 19th century, firms of today find themselves under considerable pressure to reduce cost to stay competitive, be it through wage reductions, greater work speed, replacement of permanent employees with contingent workers, movement of production abroad, domestic plant closings, and other such methods.

The institutionalists recognized that no state or country can isolate itself behind a wall of protection. But equally blind is a public policy that allows free trade to undermine minimum social standards of employment or that subjects American workers to the destructive effects of unfair foreign competition. While reduced trade barriers, as accomplished in the North American Free Trade Act (NAFTA), are thus in the public interest, American companies cannot be allowed (or forced) to compete by paying less than living wages or by shifting the social cost of labor to the community. (The same applies reciprocally to Mexico and other trading partners.) Likewise, it is against the public interest to allow unfettered free trade when countries such as China gain competitive advantage through convict labor and theft of intellectual property rights. From an institutional perspective, therefore, it is critical that employment regulation and selective use of tariffs and other trade weapons be used to both maintain labor standards in this country and promote fair trade practices in others.

The discussion has already touched on the issue of social cost in several places, but it has numerous other implications for contemporary employment regulation. The old institutional economists, for example, would strongly support legislation such as the Family and Medical Leave Act. It requires firms to internalize a portion of the costs associated with employees' childbirth and childrearing activities on the grounds that this is both elementary justice (it is unfair for a woman to lose her job because she requires several weeks maternity leave) and is an ongoing expense associated with production (as with sick leave, firms should bear the cost, not workers or the community). Looked at from another perspective, such expenditures are a form of social investment in the next generation of the work force. Institutionalists would use similar arguments in support of new legislation requiring firms to finance a portion of child care expenses for working parents.

Another area of regulation that the old institutional economists would give a higher priority than their neoclassical colleagues is workplace governance, such as protection of worker rights and institutional methods for employee voice. From an institutional point of view, workers rights and voice in industry are both means to an end (greater efficiency and equity) and a valuable end in themselves. These considerations again provide a rationale for strengthened protections of the right to organize and bargain collectively. Given the small share of the work force that belongs to labor unions, however, the institutionalists would also support legislation that provides alternative forms of representation and due process, such as nonunion employee involvement committees (with some appropriate safeguards to prevent undue management domination) and a provision requiring nonunion firms to have an employee handbook that is enforceable in courts of law (Edwards 1993 and in this volume).

The old institutionalists would also support strong legislation and regulation combatting all forms of discrimination and harassment. They also believed, however, that a portion of the unequal outcomes among race and gender groups arises from innate differences among them. They would thus support equality of opportunity, but not equality of results. Quotas and minority set-asides in affirmative action programs would thus be viewed with considerable concern. They would also support substantial social investment in programs aimed at strengthening the social and human capital of disadvantaged groups in an effort to reduce intergroup disparities in human and social capital.

Another area of employment policy deserving attention from an institutional perspective is the interface between the labor market and macroeconomic stability and growth. As previously noted, Commons thought the greatest threat to reasonable employment conditions is the presence in normal times of an excess supply of labor. The single greatest accomplishment government can make to reasonable employment standards, therefore, is maintenance of a full employment macroeconomy. The old institutionalists were thus active supporters of the Employment Act of 1946 and would continue to lobby today for measures to move the economy closer to full employment. Among these would be public training and employment programs to reduce structural unemployment and tighter immigration laws to stanch the flow of low-skill labor into the United States.

The final area of employment policy deserving comment is the administration and enforcement of regulation. The old institutionalists would no doubt look at contemporary programs, such as the Occupational Safety and Health Act (OSHA), and shake their heads in disbelief that Americans have not learned that "command and control" methods of regulation coupled with punitive sanctions are rarely effective. They would counsel a more voluntary, participative approach where workers and firms are given incentives to meet certain targets and responsibility to jointly fashion a solution.

They would also suggest, I think, that a good deal of the criticism directed against workplace regulation has less to do with the merits of the regulation than the ineffective, sometimes incompetent way the programs are designed and administered. They would see this, in part, as an outcome of the excessive individualism and "ready, fire, aim" approach to organization that permeates American culture (Zuckerman and Hatala 1992). Finally, they would remind us that effective enforcement and administration of labor law requires well-paid and respected civil servants. A social ethos that disparages government, regulatory programs, and the people who administer them makes it difficult to have anything other than a self-fulfilling prophecy.

## Conclusions

Although the old institutionalists of the Wisconsin school were the first group of academics to do significant research on the operation of labor markets and the rationale for employment regulation, this work has languished in relative obscurity in recent years. Given the vigorous debate in the nation over the merits of regulation versus deregulation of labor markets, a fresh look at this body of literature seems both appropriate and overdue.

Out of this review emerges a number of conclusions and implications regarding both research and policy on employment regulation. With regard to research, for example, a clear lesson is the power of assumptions in theoretical models. It is not surprising, for example, that neoclassical economists find scant justification for collective bargaining and most employment regulation, when the model they use assumes individuals are highly rational and dispassionate people, markets are highly competitive, the distribution of property rights and wealth is frequently taken as a "given," and concepts such as Pareto optimality are used to evaluate the welfare effects of a policy change. It is almost axiomatic that tinkering with a near-perfect world is likely to do more harm than good.

If one starts with different assumptions, different conclusions inevitably flow. A case in point is the work of the old institutionalists. They assume much the opposite—a model of the human agent in which emotion, ignorance, and stupidity create conditions of bounded rationality; markets are often characterized by extremes of competition—either too little or too much; the distribution of property rights and wealth are skewed in favor of the rich and powerful; and concepts of justice and commonweal are used to evaluate the efficacy of public policy. Not unexpectedly, they conclude that unregulated labor markets and unabridged freedom of contract often result in outcomes that are both highly inefficient and unjust. Regulation, per the quote at the beginning of the chapter, is thus regarded as the friend, not the enemy, of personal freedom and well being.

Which of these two models best explains the operation and outcomes of modern labor markets and employment relationships is an open question. My conjecture is that both have validity and capture a portion of reality. Unfortunately, an ecumenical perspective and disinterested testing of hypotheses is not always the hallmark of modern research in labor economics. Rather, many labor economists take it as their professional mission to demonstrate that models of rational behavior and competitive markets can explain any and all forms of behavior and that the resulting outcomes are efficient and welfare maximizing. Other explanations and conclusions are either ignored, ruled out of court on procedural grounds (e.g., fairness is a metaphysical concept), or reinterpreted to be consistent with orthodoxy. Also, standard microeconomic models of labor markets almost always implicitly assume conditions of full employment. For these reasons, mainstream contemporary labor economics has much to say about the pros and cons of employment regulation, but the nature of the theory and the way it is used inevitably places the emphasis on the "con" part and very little on the "pro" part. As this chapter has suggested, such a conclusion is neither foreordained by objective economic analysis nor the best solution to many of the nation's pressing labor problems.

With regard to policy, this chapter offers a mixed assessment of the efficacy of current employment law and regulation. In certain respects, labor markets have become more competitive in recent decades (e.g., a decline in monopsony and discrimination). This trend suggests that the amount of protective, countervailing power that needs to be provided to individual employees through law and collective bargaining can be correspondingly reduced (or made more flexible). This conclusion, however, is contingent on the ability of policymakers to keep the macroeconomy near full employment. As unemployment increases, so too does the optimal amount of countervailing power law should give employees.

Employment regulation can be justified on many other grounds besides as an offset to employer market power. Most of these, it is concluded, point in the direction of either maintaining or expanding the sphere of employment regulation. Some of these rationales include promoting higher quality of worklife for employees, providing reasonable levels of job and income security for workers, ensuring that firms pay the full social cost of labor, preventing unfair competition, protecting workers' rights and promoting employee voice in work force governance, motivating companies to devote more resources and attention to technological innovation, capital investment, and new or improved work organization and human resource management methods, and promoting increased stability and growth in the macroeconomy.

Although it is today's conventional wisdom that the institutional economists sought employment regulation to protect wages and labor conditions from *lack* of employer competition for labor (as in monopsony), in truth they considered the greater evil to be *excessive* competition. Excessive competition, in the form of such things as substantial involuntary unemployment, large-scale immigration of low-skill workers, child labor, or low-wage foreign competition in product markets, leads to a cutthroat competitive struggle with substantial downward pressure upon wages and labor standards—particularly in the low end of the labor market (see Belman and Belzer in this volume).

This phenomenon appears to have reemerged in the last two decades in many American labor markets (and European labor markets, per extensive concern over "social dumping" and a "race to the bottom"). Principal causes are a much-expanded flow of low-skill immigrants into the country, a large-scale trade imbalance due to America's relatively open markets and the more restricted markets of some of our trading partners (particularly in Asia), a skill-twist in technological change that has wiped out many low-wage jobs, and the continuing presence of a reserve army of the unemployed and underemployed. The result has been a pronounced widening in income inequality, stagnant real income growth, a loss in job security for tens of millions of American workers, longer and more intense work hours, reduced benefits or cost shifting to workers, a phenomenal growth in part-time and contingent work, a movement of jobs offshore, and a marked increase in antisocial attitudes and behaviors, such as cynicism, greed, violence, and drug abuse.

Combatting these problems is difficult, per the quote of Commons at the beginning of the chapter, but steps must be taken nonetheless if the social and economic progress of previous decades is to be preserved. Certainly the position of many conservative economists—that there is no problem or free markets will take care of it—is untenable. No one, including the old institutional economists, will deny that regulation brings with it significant costs. But they will also claim that the costs of ignoring our social problems or relying on the blind, Darwinian forces of free competition to solve them are even greater.

Were the old institutional economists alive today, they would no doubt be disappointed to learn how little impact their research has had on contemporary economics. They would be able to look with considerable satisfaction, however, on the enduring nature of their contribution to policy. Few economists in this century have had the impact on the lives of working people as have Commons and colleagues. Today the public takes for granted minimum wages, overtime pay after forty hours, unemployment insurance, Social Security, and the right of workers to join unions; but a century ago these ideas were radical, and Ely and Commons were nearly driven out of academe for espousing them.

Although with the passage of time these measures now seem in principle relatively noncontroversial, when attention is turned to solving contemporary labor problems, suddenly the path is not clear at all. More regulation? Less regulation? What kind? I have attempted to deduce what Commons and the other old institutionalists might say to these questions, based on their writings and major precepts, but this is informed conjecture. The one thing we can say with certainty, however, is that they would insist on certain key principles— that people come before things, all interests must be represented, power must be balanced, and outcomes must pass the test of reasonableness. In many ways these remain radical ideas.

## References

Adams, Henry Carter. 1886. "Relation of the State to Industrial Action." *Publications of the American Economic Association*, Vol. 1, no. 6, pp. 7-85.

Adams, Thomas, and Helen Sumner. 1905. *Labor Problems*. New York: MacMillan.

Andrews, John. 1932. *Labor Problems and Labor Legislation*. 4th ed. New York: American Association for Labor Legislation.

Barbash, Jack. 1976. "The Legal Foundations of Capitalism and the Labor Problem." *Journal of Economic Issues*, Vol. 10 (December), pp. 799-810.

_____. 1994. "Americanizing the Labor Problem: The Wisconsin School." In Clark Kerr and Paul Staudohar, eds., *Labor Economics and Industrial Relations: Markets and Institutions*. Cambridge, MA: Harvard University Press, pp. 41-65.

Barber, William. 1994. "The Divergent Fates of Two Strands of "Institutionalist" Doctrine during the New Deal Years." *History of Political Economy*, Vol. 26, no. 4, pp. 569-87.

Becker, Gary. 1957. *The Economics of Discrimination*. Chicago: University of Chicago Press.

Boulding, Kenneth. 1957. "A New Look at Institutionalism." *American Economic Review*, Vol. 47 (May), pp. 1-12.

Bowles, Samuel, and Herbert Gintis. 1993. "The Revenge of *Homo Economicus*: Contested Exchanges and the Revival of Political Economy." *Journal of Economic Perspectives*, Vol. 7 (Spring), pp. 83-102.

Cain, Glen. 1993. "Labor Economics." In Robert Lampman, ed., *Economists at Wisconsin: 1892-1992*. Madison, WI: Department of Economics, University of Wisconsin, pp. 234-46.

Chasse, Dennis. 1986. "John R. Commons and the Democratic State." *Journal of Economic Issues*, Vol. 20 (September), pp. 759-84.

_____. 1994. "The American Association for Labor Legislation and the Institutionalist Tradition in National Health Insurance." *Journal of Economic Issues*, Vol. 28 (December), pp. 1063-90.

Clark, John M. 1924. *Studies in the Economics of Overhead Costs.* Chicago: University of Chicago Press.

_____. 1926. *Social Control of Business.* New York: McGraw-Hill.

Commons, John R. 1893. *The Distribution of Wealth.* New York: MacMillan.

_____. 1907. *Races and Immigrants in America.* New York: MacMillan.

_____. 1909. "American Shoemakers, 1648-1895." *Quarterly Journal of Economics*, Vol. 24 (November), pp. 39-83.

_____. 1913. *Labor and Administration.* New York: MacMillan.

_____. 1918. *History of Labor in the United States*, 4 vols. New York: MacMillan.

_____. 1919. *Industrial Goodwill.* New York: McGraw-Hill.

_____. 1921. *Industrial Government.* New York: MacMillan.

_____. 1924. *Legal Foundations of Capitalism.* New York: MacMillan.

_____. 1925. "Law and Economics." *Yale Law Journal*, Vol. 34 (February), pp. 371-82.

_____. 1934a. *Institutional Economics: Its Place in Political Economy.* New York: MacMillan.

_____. 1934b. *Myself.* Madison, WI: University of Wisconsin Press.

Commons, John R., and John Andrews. 1916. *Principles of Labor Legislation* (2d ed., 1920, 4th ed., 1936). New York: Harper & Bros.

Daugherty, Carroll. 1933. *Labor Problems in American Industry.* Cambridge, MA: Riverside Press.

Dorfman, Joseph. 1963. "The Background of Institutional Economics." In *Institutional Economics: Veblen, Commons, and Mitchell Reconsidered.* Berkeley, CA: University of California Press, pp. 1-44.

Douglas, Paul. 1934. *The Theory of Wages.* New York: MacMillan.

_____. 1938. "The Economic Theory of Wage Regulation." *University of Chicago Law Review*, Vol. 5 (February), pp. 184-218.

Edwards, Richard. 1993. *Rights at Work: Employment Relations in the Post-Union Era.* Washington, DC: The Brookings Institution.

Ehrenberg, Ronald, and Robert Smith. 1994. *Modern Labor Economics.* 5th ed. New York: Harper Collins.

Ely, Richard. 1886. *The Labor Movement in America.* New York: Thomas Crowell.

_____. 1907. "Economic Theory and Labor Legislation." *Proceedings of the First Annual Meeting, American Association for Labor Legislation.*

_____. 1913. *Studies in the Evolution of Industrial Society.* New York: MacMillan.

_____. 1914. *Property and Contract in Their Relations to the Distribution of Wealth*, Vols. 1, 2. New York: MacMillan.

_____. 1938. *Ground Under Our Feet: An Autobiography.* New York: MacMillan.

Ely, Richard, and Frank Bohn. 1935. *The Great Change.* New York: Thomas Nelson.

Filene, Edward. 1923. "The Minimum Wage and Efficiency." *American Economic Review*, Vol. 13 (September), pp. 411-15.

Fine, Sidney. 1956. *Laissez Faire and the General Welfare State: A Study of Conflict in American Thought, 1865-1901.* Ann Arbor, MI: University of Michigan Press.

Fitch, John. 1924. *Causes of Industrial Unrest.* New York: Harper.

Gonce, Richard. 1966. *The Development of John R. Commons' System of Thought.* Unpublished Ph.D. Dissertation, University of Wisconsin.

Harris, Howell. 1991. "Getting It Together: The Metal Manufacturers Association of Philadelphia, c. 1900-1930." In Sanford Jacoby, ed., *Masters to Managers: Historical and Comparative Perspectives on American Employers*. New York: Columbia University Press, pp. 111-31.

Hovenkamp, Herbert. 1990. "The First Great Law and Economics Movement." *Stanford University Law Review*, Vol. 42 (April), pp. 993-1058.

Huthmacher, J. Joseph. 1968. *Senator Robert F. Wagner and the Rise of Urban Liberalism*. New York: Atheneum.

Jacoby, Sanford. 1990. "The New Institutionalism: What Can It Learn from the Old?" *Industrial Relations*, Vol. 29 (Spring), pp. 316-40.

Kaufman, Bruce. 1988. *How Labor Markets Work: Reflections on Theory and Practice by John Dunlop, Clark Kerr, Richard Lester, and Lloyd Reynolds*. Lexington, MA: Lexington Books.

_____. 1989. "Labor's Inequality of Bargaining Power: Changes over Time and Implications for Public Policy." *Journal of Labor Research*. Vol. 10 (Summer), pp. 285-97.

_____. 1991. "Labor's Inequality of Bargaining Power: Myth or Reality?" *Journal of Labor Research*, Vol. 12 (Spring), pp. 151-66.

_____. 1993. *The Origins and Evolution of the Field of Industrial Relations in the United States*. Ithaca, NY: ILR Press.

_____. 1994. "The Evolution of Thought on the Competitive Nature of Labor Markets." In Clark Kerr and Paul Staudohar, eds., *Labor Economics and Industrial Relations: Markets and Institutions*. Cambridge, MA: Harvard University Press, pp. 145-88.

_____. 1996a. "Why the Wagner Act?: Reestablishing Contact with Its Original Purpose." In David Lewin, Bruce Kaufman, and Donna Sockell, eds., *Advances in Industrial and Labor Relations*. Greenwich, CT: JAI Press, pp. 15-68.

_____. 1996b. "A New Paradigm: Deregulating Labor Relations—Comment on Reynolds." *Journal of Labor Research*, Vol. 17 (Winter), pp. 129-34.

_____. Forthcoming. "John R. Commons: Father of Personnel/HRM?" *Proceedings of the Fiftieth Annual Meeting* (Chicago, January 1998). Madison, WI: Industrial Relations Research Association.

Keynes, John. 1936. *The General Theory of Employment, Interest, and Money*. New York: Harcourt Brace.

Lane, Robert. 1991. *The Market Experience*. New York: Cambridge University Press.

Lauck, W. Jett. 1929. *The New Industrial Revolution and Wages*. New York: Funk & Wagnalls.

Lauck, W. Jett, and Edgar Sydenstricker. 1917. *Conditions of Labor in American Industries*. New York: Funk & Wagnalls.

Lehrer, Susan. 1987. *Origins of Protective Labor Legislation for Women, 1905-1925*. Albany, NY: State University of New York Press.

Leiserson, William. 1922. "Constitutional Government in American Industry." *American Economic Review*, Vol. 12 (1 Supplement), pp. 56-79.

_____. 1929. "Contributions of Personnel Management to Improved Labor Relations." In *Wertheim Lectures in Industrial Relations*. Cambridge, MA: Harvard University Press, pp. 125-64.

_____. 1938. *Right and Wrong in Labor Relations*. Berkeley, CA: University of California Press.

Lens, Signey. 1974. *The Labor Wars*. New York: Anchor Books.

Lescohier, Don. 1919. *The Labor Market*. New York: MacMillan.

Linder, Marc. 1989. "The Minimum Wage as Industrial Policy: A Forgotten Role." *Journal of Legislation*, Vol. 16, no. 1, pp. 151-71.

MacDonald, Lois. 1938. *Labor Problems and the American Scene*. New York: Harper & Bros.

Marshall, Ray, and Marc Tucker. 1992. *Thinking for a Living: Education and the Wealth of Nations*. New York: Basic Books.

McCarthy, Charles. 1912. *The Wisconsin Idea*. New York: MacMillan.

McCurdy, Charles. 1984. "The Roots of 'Liberty of Contract' Reconsidered: Major Premises in the Law of Employment, 1867-1937." *Yearbook 1984*. Washington, DC: Supreme Court Historical Society.

Milkman, Ruth. 1987. *Gender at Work*. Urbana, IL: University of Illinois Press.

Mill, John S. 1874. *Essays on Some Unsettled Questions of Political Economy*, 2nd ed. London: Longman, Green, Reader and Dyer.

Millis, Harry. 1935. "The Union in Industry: Some Observations of the Theory of Collective Bargaining." *American Economic Review*, Vol. 25 (March), pp. 1-13.

Millis, Harry, and Royal Montgomery. 1938a. *Labor's Progress and Some Basic Labor Problems*. New York: McGraw-Hill.

_____. 1938b. *Labor's Risks and Social Insurance*. New York: McGraw-Hill.

_____. 1945. *Organized Labor*. New York: McGraw-Hill.

Moss, David. 1996. *Socializing Security: Progressive-Era Economists and the Origins of American Social Policy*. Cambridge, MA: Harvard University Press.

Perlman, Selig. 1928. *A Theory of the Labor Movement*. New York: MacMillan.

Pierce, Lloyd. 1953. "The Activities of the American Association for Labor Legislation on Behalf of Social Security and Protective Labor Legislation." Unpublished dissertation, University of Wisconsin.

Ramstad, Yngve. 1987. "Free Trade versus Fair Trade: Import Barriers as a Problem of Reasonable Value." *Journal of Economic Issues*, Vol. 21 (March), pp. 5-32.

_____. 1996. "Is a Transaction a Transaction?" *Journal of Economic Issues*. Vol. 30 (June), pp. 413-25.

Reynolds, Morgan. 1984. *Power and Privilege: Labor Unions in America*. New York: Universe Books.

_____. 1991. "The Myth of Labor's Inequality of Bargaining Power." *Journal of Labor Research*, Vol. 12 (Spring), pp. 167-83.

Saposs, David. 1960. "The Wisconsin Heritage and the Study of Labor—Works and Deeds of John R. Commons." *School for Workers 35th Anniversary Papers*. Madison, WI: University of Wisconsin School for Workers.

Schlabach, Theron. 1969. *Edwin E. Witte: Cautious Reformer*. Madison, WI: State Historical Society of Wisconsin.

Seager, Henry. 1913. "The Theory of the Minimum Wage." *American Labor Legislation Review*, Vol. 3, no. 3, pp. 81-91.

Simon, Herbert. 1978. "Rationality as a Process and Product of Thought." *American Economic Review*, Vol. 68 (June), pp. 1-16.

Skidelsky, Robert. 1992. *John Maynard Keynes: The Economist as Savior, 1920-37*, Vol. 2. New York: Penguin.

Slichter, Sumner. 1919. *The Turnover of Factory Labor*. New York: D. Appleton and Co.

_____. 1928. *Modern Economic Society*. New York: Henry Holt.

Smith, Adam. 1776. *An Inquiry into the Nature and Causes of the Wealth of Nations* (1937 reprint). New York: Random House.

Stabile, Donald. 1993. *Activist Unionism: The Institutional Economics of Solomon Barkin.* Armonk, NY: M.E. Sharpe.

_____. 1996. *Work and Welfare: The Social Cost of Labor in the History of Economic Thought.* Westport, CT: Greenwood Press.

Stigler, George. 1946. "The Economics of Minimum Wage Legislation." *American Economic Review*, Vol. 36 (June), pp. 358-65.

Taylor, James. 1977. "Exploitation Through Contrived Dependence." *Journal of Economic Issues.* Vol. 11 (March), pp. 51-59.

Veblen, Thorstein. 1904. *The Theory of Business Enterprise.* New York: Scribner's.

Whalen, Charles. 1993. "Saving Capitalism by Making It Good: The Monetary Economics of John R. Commons." *Journal of Economic Issues*, Vol. 27 (December), pp. 1155-79.

Williamson, Oliver. 1985. *The Economic Institutions of Capitalism.* New York: The Free Press.

Wunderlin, Clarence. 1992. *Visions of a New Industrial Order: Social Science and Labor Theory in America's Progressive Era.* New York: Columbia University Press.

Zuckerman, Marilyn, and Lewis Hatala. 1992. *Incredibly American: Releasing the Heart of Quality.* Milwaukee, WI: ASQC Quality Press.

# CHAPTER 2

# The New Institutional Economics and Employment Regulation

GREGORY K. DOW
*Simon Fraser University*

The new institutional economics (NIE) is a large and unruly beast. A wide variety of definitions has been suggested, but the simplest defines the NIE as the study of social, economic, and political institutions using the tools of contemporary microeconomic theory. This definition highlights the fact that microeconomics has moved beyond its roots in price theory (roughly speaking, the study of competitive markets and monopoly) and now sees institutions through more subtle lenses. The analytic methods used by the NIE range from the sophisticated mathematical techniques found in game theory and principal-agent theory to rigorous and systematic verbal reasoning about economic history, property rights, public choice, and the evolution of social conventions.

For our purposes, the most important area of the NIE is the new theory of the firm, understood broadly to include the relationships linking the firm to surrounding markets for labor and capital. By the "new theory of the firm" I mean a line of research developed over the last two decades which tries to expose the inner workings of enterprise organization in order to show how firms cope with problems of coordination, incentives, and bargaining. In this introduction I will sketch out the NIE's conceptual apparatus, scrutinize some key intellectual premises (especially the NIE's reliance on efficiency explanations), and indicate possible rationales for regulatory policy within the NIE framework. The themes of coordination, incentives, and bargaining will also be addressed. In each case I identify some regulatory issues on which the NIE may shed new light. Finally, the NIE's contribution to the analysis of employment regulation is summarized.

## Firms, Markets, and Contracting

In traditional microeconomic theory the firm is modeled as a set of technological possibilities with a profit-maximizing entrepreneur attached. The

NIE has sought to open up this black box and look at what is going on inside. Coase (1937), who is generally credited with initiating this line of inquiry, posed some deep questions early on: What is the nature of the firm? Why do firms exist? What determines the boundaries of the firm? When will transactions be organized within firms rather than by market exchange? Readers interested in the roots of the new theory of the firm and Coase's role in its development should consult Williamson and Winter (1991) as well as Coase's Nobel lecture (1992).

With few exceptions (e.g., Simon 1951; Coase 1960), there was little further work along these lines until the 1970s, when a turning point was reached with two publications: an article on team production and effort incentives by Alchian and Demsetz (1972) and a book entitled *Markets and Hierarchies* by Williamson (1975). Williamson in particular resurrected Coase's earlier agenda of specifying the relative advantages and disadvantages of firm organization in comparison with the alternative of market exchange. The following two decades saw an explosion of related analysis as economists began to apply technical tools drawn from game theory and informational economics to incentive, bargaining, and coordination issues within the firm. An overview of these developments is provided in the anthology edited by Putterman and Kroszner (1996), which reprints many classic NIE articles on firm organization. Other surveys that will guide the novice toward the large NIE literature on the firm include Milgrom and Roberts (1992) and Miller (1992).

The NIE has now reached a consensus on some basic points about employment. Most NIE writers agree on the need to distinguish employment per se, which is regarded as an intrafirm phenomenon, from independent contracting, regarded as a relationship of market exchange. There are various ways to draw this line depending on one's theoretical predilections. For instance, one could define employment by the mode of payment (flat wage for broadly defined labor services rather than payment for a well-specified finished product), by asset ownership (ownership of tools by the employer rather than the worker), or by the identity of the person directing the production process (a boss rather than the worker). Clearly, these features of employment are correlated empirically, but none taken in isolation appears to provide a fully satisfactory definition of the employment relationship.

Whichever definition one may adopt, NIE writers agree that employment would be uninteresting from an institutional perspective if labor contracts were complete. A complete contract fully specifies all of the obligations of each party in advance and is costlessly enforced by third parties such as the courts if necessary. If labor were bought and sold using complete contracts, labor services would become just another market commodity, no different from apples or toothpaste. Firms would buy whatever services were required at the moment and pay the going market price for these services. In such a world, employees would be indistinguishable from contractors: everyone would in effect be self-employed.

The interesting questions for the NIE only arise after some source of contractual incompleteness has been identified. Contracts might be incomplete, for instance, if it is hard to anticipate all future contingencies, if negotiation is costly, or if enforcement of some provisions would require expensive monitoring. Such costs are generally called *transaction costs*. It then becomes necessary to have some decision process that determines the actions of each party as events unfold in circumstances where the original contract is silent. I will adopt Williamson's (1985) terminology and refer to the decision-making process that fills in contractual gaps over time as a *governance structure*. The key question for the NIE is then to explain why specific governance structures tend to be used in particular situations.

As a rule, NIE authors also tend to assume that product, capital, and labor markets are competitive in the sense that there are many alternative trading partners when any given contractual relationship is first established. However, this proposition must be treated with considerable care in a setting of contractual incompleteness. It is *not* assumed in general that the informational requirements of traditional competitive markets are met: there may be informational asymmetries at the time contracts are negotiated (*adverse selection*), or such asymmetries may arise after the contractual relationship begins (*moral hazard*). There may be problems of bilateral monopoly that unfold over time as the parties make investments that are specialized to the relationship and of little value to outside agents (*asset specificity*). It is also possible that employees may be paid more than their next best market alternative, either for incentive reasons (see the discussion of efficiency wage theory below), or for bargaining reasons (see the discussion of asset specificity below). Hence many of the ideas derived from the traditional theory of competitive labor markets (for instance, the notion that employees are paid compensating wage differentials for jobs having unusually severe risks of injury) may apply only in attenuated form, or not at all.

*Economic Efficiency and the New Institutional Economics*

The NIE has both strengths and weaknesses as a device for evaluating regulatory policy toward the employment relationship. On the positive side of the ledger, the NIE has placed the structure of employment contracts under very close analytic scrutiny and has brought a powerful and eclectic set of modeling tools to bear on the problem. However, on the negative side there are two important gaps. First, precisely because the NIE sought to open up the black box of the firm, it has often downplayed the relationship between internal enterprise organization and the external market environment. The effects of outside labor or capital markets are often captured in summary form by specifying an exogenously given "next best alternative" for each participant in the firm. The NIE does not yet possess a well-developed theory where firm organization is determined simultaneously with market prices.

The second gap in the NIE is that its proponents have tended to see their job as one of explanation rather than prescription. A great deal of intellectual effort has gone into the construction of economic rationales for existing organizational practices, while much less time and energy has been devoted to the assessment of policy proposals aimed at changing those practices. This reflects a tendency among most NIE writers to assume, at least prima facie, that actual employment practices represent efficient solutions to complex contracting problems. This efficiency assumption is useful in generating explanatory hypotheses of a functionalist kind (employment practice X exists because it satisfies efficiency criterion Y under environmental conditions Z). However, it also places a heavy burden of proof on advocates of labor market regulation by obliging them to identify specific market failures that warrant governmental intervention. One must often read between the lines (and squint hard) in order to discover a rationale for regulatory policy in the NIE.

The confidence of the NIE in the efficiency of market solutions is puzzling at first glance, because in a world of incomplete contracts one can no longer appeal to the standard result that a perfectly competitive equilibrium is Pareto efficient (Mas-Colell, Whinston and Green 1995:Ch. 16). It is also odd that a theoretical framework seeking to explain why market exchange is displaced by hierarchical organization within firms would at the same time claim that market competition brings about efficient governance structures. Or to put the same point a bit differently, why doesn't the very existence of positive transaction costs become an obstacle to transaction cost minimization? Some circularity is apparent. It is worth taking time to unravel these puzzles, because the NIE's focus on economic efficiency is closely related to its view of regulation. The NIE justifies its efficiency assumptions in two ways: by arguing that rational economic agents have a common interest in designing an efficient governance structure (the ex ante rationale) or by arguing that inefficient modes of governance will be displaced over time by more efficient ones through a process of market competition (the ex post rationale). We examine each of these propositions in turn.

First, consider the argument that economic agents (e.g., employers and employees) are rational and therefore design governance structures that are in their mutual interest. By definition, it is true that all individuals involved in a collective endeavor would be at least as well off, and some would be better off, if efficient contractual arrangements were adopted rather than inefficient ones. This idea places natural theoretical restrictions on the kinds of contracts or governance structures we expect to observe empirically: inefficient structures can be ruled out because there will always be some feasible alternative that is unanimously preferred (Eggertsson 1990; Milgrom and Roberts 1992:Ch. 2). The idea of feasibility is a bit subtle here, since informational and incentive constraints must be taken into account in defining what is feasible. For example, a governance structure where all employees are required to report their own effort levels truthfully could violate incentive constraints with respect to information transmission. But the principle is clear: governance structures are predicted to be Pareto efficient in a *second best* sense, taking such incentive constraints into account. To the extent that there is a conflict over the distribution of the benefits derived from a governance structure, the parties would still adopt an efficient structure in order to maximize the size of the overall pie and settle the distributional conflict by bargaining at the start of the relationship over the size of the side payments to be transferred from one party to another. Efficient arrangements should thus prevail regardless of initial property rights or the relative bargaining power of the parties to the contract, a proposition that has been enshrined in the literature as the *Coase Theorem* (see Coase 1960).

Despite the commonsense appeal of this idea, it is problematic in several respects. First, it may be hard to separate efficiency issues from distributional ones if there are limits on the capacity of some parties (e.g., employees) to pay in advance for benefit streams that will arise later (Dow 1993a, 1993b). Such problems occur, for example, if an efficient governance structure would provide workers with considerable bargaining power after it is implemented, but workers are unable to "bribe" an employer up front to accept this structure due to their limited wealth. Second, even if wealth constraints are not binding, bargaining processes often fall short of Pareto efficiency when the parties have private information about their own preferences or resources (Milgrom and Roberts 1992:140-49; Miller 1992:Ch. 2; Kennan and Wilson 1993). If governance structures are the result of such bargaining processes, then there cannot be any general presumption that such governance structures are efficient. By the same token, labor market equilibria need not be efficient if there are adverse selection problems where firms are uncertain about the true characteristics of job applicants (Greenwald and Stiglitz 1986; Stiglitz 1987; Mas-Colell, Whinston and Green 1995:Ch. 13). The NIE usually finesses these problems by assuming (artificially) that informational asymmetries only emerge *after* a governance structure is established and that such structures do not need to be renegotiated later once private information does exist.

A third set of difficulties stems from the fact that multilateral bargaining is unlikely to be practical when large groups are involved (consider what would happen if pollution problems involving millions of people had to be resolved by direct multilateral negotiation among all affected parties rather than through government regulation). According to the NIE itself (Coase 1937), this is one key reason why firms typically have a central owner who makes bilateral contracts with other input suppliers. The NIE has also acknowledged in other ways that large employee coalitions face difficult collective action problems. For instance, Klein (1991) has argued that this is why groups of employees with firm-specific skills cannot easily seize quasi rents from their employers, and Hansmann (1996) identifies problems of collective choice among workers as the central reason why workers do not usually run their own firms. If we accept these arguments, then we must also conclude that the collective interests of employees as a group are unlikely to be fully represented either at the stage where governance structures are initially designed or in the ongoing management of the enterprise itself. The literature on the "collective voice" role of unions (Freeman and Medoff 1984) is concerned with precisely these problems.

Finally, claims that efficient governance structures arise through conscious ex ante design should meet with skepticism in contexts where bounded rationality is also assumed. This dilemma arises for Williamson's (1985) transaction cost theory, which assumes that comprehensive long-term contracts are infeasible due to the limitations on human cognitive capabilities. At the same time, Williamson argues that efficiency, and in particular the desire to economize on transaction costs, drives the choice among governance structures. This is puzzling because the very limits on rationality that thwart comprehensive contracting might be expected to obstruct a comprehensive assessment of the transaction costs associated with alternative governance systems (Dow 1987; Williamson 1987).

If efficient governance cannot be guaranteed by appealing to ex ante design, we are left with the natural selection analogy: governance structures revealed to be inefficient ex post will be driven out in the long run through competition from more efficient structures. Again, this proposition is debatable (for a thorough dissection of the relationship between evolutionary economics and neoclassical orthodoxy, see Nelson and Winter 1982). First, the assumption of a competitive market environment must now be taken seriously. When firms with differing employment practices compete in an oligopolistic product market, for example, inefficient firms may not be driven out if there are substantial entry barriers facing new competitors. Even if the product market is characterized by free entry, there are cases where the evolutionary selection criterion (profit) diverges from the appropriate efficiency measure (e.g., total surplus). Suppose, for instance, that firm survival or growth depends on profit, but employees receive wages in excess of their outside market opportunities for efficiency wage or bargaining reasons (discussed later in this paper). The wage premium is clearly part of the aggregate social surplus generated by a firm, but firms paying higher wages may be at a competitive disadvantage in the product market because wages are seen by the firm as a cost item. Whenever there is a wedge between the profit captured by firm owners and the aggregate surplus generated by the firm as a whole, differences in rates of investment can lead to the dominance of inefficient organizational structures (Dow 1993c).

There may also be spillover or externality effects where the profitability of a given practice in an individual firm is directly affected by the practices adopted in other firms. For instance, Weitzman (1984) has argued that profit sharing could be unattractive to an individual firm if no other firm adopts it but might be quite attractive in a world where all other firms have profit-sharing plans. Along similar lines, Levine and Parkin (1994) argue that employers may provide too little training if workers are likely to move subsequently to some other firm. Due to this spillover, all firms might benefit by increasing their training expenditures simultaneously, even though no firm would gain by doing so in isolation.

Finally, there are typically multiple equilibria in repeated game models of the labor market (Carmichael 1989; MacLeod and Malcomson 1989, 1993). Two issues then arise: some equilibria will be superior to others on efficiency grounds, and the efficient equilibria will differ in their distributional implications for the players in the game. Although the implications for the theory of firm organization have not been adequately developed, three broad lessons emerge from this literature. First, history matters, because the nature of the currently prevailing labor market equilibrium may be determined in large part by social convention or random drift. Second, it can be misleading to examine firms or employment contracts in isolation from the larger market environment where they emerge and persist. Third, we again have reason to doubt the proposition that competitive markets generate efficient modes of organization, because market-wide coordination problems can arise.

## Rationales for Regulatory Intervention

We have now sketched various difficulties with the ex ante (rational design) and ex post (natural selection) arguments commonly used to justify the efficiency of prevailing governance structures. These difficulties indicate that the scope for efficiency-enhancing policy intervention may be broader than a superficial reading of the NIE would suggest. In the remainder of this introductory section, I will briefly summarize some possible sources of market failure that might justify regulation of employment. In each case I distinguish failures arising ex ante (before a specific governance structure has been adopted) and ex post (after a governance structure is already in place). It should be kept in mind, however, that this distinction is a bit contrived since governance systems may need to be renegotiated periodically in order to track a shifting external environment.

*Informational asymmetries.* The ex ante problem is that agents who will participate in a governance structure have unknown characteristics. This may lead to adverse selection in the labor market or to bargaining inefficiencies at the design stage. The ex post problem is one of enforcement or moral hazard. The enforcement tools available to private parties are usually confined to internal monitoring and incentive systems, along with reputational forces in the external market. These tools may fail because the parties are unable to commit themselves in advance to particular actions, because the future is discounted too heavily, or because information flows are thin.

*Market power.* Although the NIE usually assumes "large numbers" at the ex ante stage, this assumption can fail if market search for alternative partners is costly, since then there will be some degree of bilateral monopoly even at the design stage. This is particularly likely if prospective partners are heterogeneous, so that a match between a firm and worker may be "good" or "bad." The ex post issue is that of bilateral bargaining, which can lead to costs or rigidities when information is not complete. The Coase Theorem then fails and it may not be possible to alter existing governance structures in a way that efficiently tracks the external environment.

*Collective action.* Ex ante, the problem is twofold. Because numerous employees are usually hired by a single firm using bilateral contracts, it is highly unlikely that collective worker interests regarding local public goods such as working conditions will be well-represented at the design stage. For similar reasons, bargaining power is unequally distributed ex ante, because firms can deal with one worker at a time in designing a governance structure rather than with workers as an organized group. At the ex post stage, workers need to overcome preference aggregation and free rider problems, both in articulating their interests and in enforcing agreements.

*Exit costs.* The mechanism of compensating wage differentials requires that labor markets function in a frictionless manner, so that the overall compensation package for each job leaves an employee indifferent between taking that job or instead taking the next best market alternative. But for either informational or bargaining reasons, workers may negotiate compensation exceeding their outside opportunities and thus the labor market may not clear. In this situation there is no guarantee that wages will adequately compensate for unsafe or otherwise unattractive working conditions. At the ex post stage, workers will not generally be indifferent toward losing their jobs, and this provides the employer with some power that can potentially be abused in a self-interested way. Private safeguards devised by the parties themselves may fail to restrain such opportunistic behavior.

*Externalities and multiple equilibria.* Two issues arise ex ante. First, governance structures adopted by some firms may have spillover effects on other firms, so that unaided market forces do not ensure overall efficiency. Second, in a repeated game setting there can be many possible market equilibria which differ in their efficiency and distributional features. At the ex post stage, related indeterminacies give rise to multiple equilibria inside firms, perhaps leading to social conventions about work effort, working conditions, wage structures, or career paths that have more to do with historical accident than with overarching equity or efficiency criteria.

With these preliminary ideas in hand, we next turn to three key themes in the new theory of the firm: coordination, incentives, and bargaining. In each case we will first consider some relevant theoretical literature and then identify regulatory implications.

## Coordination

By far the most popular way of characterizing the difference between firms and markets involves the idea that firms use *authority structures* rather than prices to allocate resources (Menard 1994; Flannigan 1995; Dow 1996). This distinction was emphasized by Coase (1937), and Simon (1951) took a similar view in his theory of employment. Williamson (1975, 1985, 1991, 1996) has repeatedly highlighted the authoritative or "fiat" aspects of hierarchy in firms. Milgrom and Roberts (1990a) characterize the firm by "the substitution of centralized authority for the relatively unfettered negotiations that characterize market transactions." Finally, there is an extensive literature in business history that interprets the firm as an authority structure (see Chandler 1992).

### Theoretical Background

What are the advantages of central authority in relation to the price system? It has been recognized at least since Adam Smith (1994:Ch. 1-3) that the division of labor can increase productivity. Modern writers have emphasized that these gains from specialization can only be realized if there is some way to coordinate the complementary tasks performed by individual members of a production team (Milgrom and Roberts 1990b; Becker and Murphy 1992). This coordinating job could be performed in principle either by market prices or by an authority relationship within a firm (Coase 1937; Arrow 1974). We thus need to explain when each coordinating mechanism will be used and why.

Markets are rather good at solving coordination problems involving large numbers of traders and the equalization of supply and demand for homogeneous goods. But markets seem ill-suited to coordination problems that involve small groups of individuals interacting in complex ways (Richardson 1972). Tasks within production teams must be coordinated both in time (*synchronization*) and in space (*localization*). Intermediate goods often have idiosyncratic features that are of little importance in their own right but which must be made compatible to facilitate final assembly or use (*standardization*). It may make no difference who performs which job, but every job must be assigned to someone without duplication (*assignment*). In cases of this sort, the price system is likely to be displaced by an authority structure as the main mechanism for coordination (Milgrom and Roberts 1992:Ch. 4).

Central authority entails some degree of power over subordinates, at least in cases where subordinates would be tempted not to comply. Numerous regulatory issues turn on the question of whether such managerial power is a source of social concern. This debate was especially sharp in the early 1970s. At one pole, Alchian and Demsetz (1972) rejected the view that firms have power over employees by pointing to the voluntary nature of the employment contract. At the other pole, New Left writers saw the firm as an arena where capitalists use hierarchy to dominate and exploit workers (Marglin 1974; Edwards 1979).

More recently there has been some convergence between the mainstream and radical perspectives. Bowles and Gintis (1990, 1993), for example, argue for the centrality of the power idea but overlap in various other ways with mainstream NIE. Williamson (1980, 1993, 1996) argues for the primacy of efficiency goals but is willing to entertain power as an auxiliary factor. Other points of contact between the two camps have been identified by Goldberg (1980), Rebitzer (1993), and Stiglitz (1993). A reasonable synthesis might be (a) to accept the theoretical possibility that coordination problems could motivate the use of hierarchy even when all parties have identical objectives but (b) to recognize the ubiquity of conflict between peak coordinators and their subordinates (Dow 1987). Or as Milgrom and Roberts (1990a) put it, "The authority to intervene inevitably implies the authority to intervene inefficiently. Yet such interventions, even if they are inefficient overall, can be highly beneficial for particular individuals and groups. Thus either inefficient interventions will be made and resources will be expended to bring them about or to prevent them, or else the authority to intervene must be restricted."

How might authority be abused within firms? Among other things, employers may try to extract more effort than workers are willing to offer at current wages; assign tasks or working conditions in ways counter to worker interests; shift surpluses away from workers by cutting wages, withholding promised bonuses, appropriating pension funds, or shutting down plants; or discriminate on the basis of race, sex, and other irrelevant characteristics. Apart from discrimination, these dangers from employer discretion would disappear if the labor contracts involved were complete and competitive. Bosses who wanted employees to work faster or at more dangerous jobs would have to offer higher wages to attract or retain workers (Rosen 1986), and workers displaced by plant shutdowns would quickly obtain equivalent jobs at some other firm. No employer would be able to cut wages or withhold pensions because the relevant contracts would be enforceable at zero cost. But when contracts for labor are incomplete or costly to enforce, authority is a more dangerous tool.

In theory, the danger would be minimal if employees were paid a wage equal to their next best market alternative, because then worker interests would be adequately protected by the option of exit to an external labor market. But for various reasons the labor market may not clear and employees may enjoy *rents* or *quasi rents* (wage payments exceeding the minimum needed to keep workers in their current jobs). Casual observation indicates that this phenomenon is widespread, since workers are seldom indifferent toward dismissal or layoff. The existence of rents or quasi rents can derive from incentive problems (discussed below), specialized worker skills (also discussed below), adverse selection problems (Weiss 1990), or the search costs incurred to obtain good matches between workers and firms (Rosen 1991). In each case, workers prefer not to leave their current employers, and employers will count the wage premium flowing to workers as a part of total cost. Because the firm does not properly internalize the costs borne by workers, we may see excessive output demands (Dow 1993a), inefficient task assignments (Garvey 1993), or premature plant shutdown decisions (Miceli and Minkler 1995).

*Regulatory Implications*

The capacity of private parties to overcome these hazards is limited. One possibility is that direct bargaining within the firm may ensure efficiency for Coase Theorem reasons. However, if bargaining processes worked smoothly, there would be no reason to rely upon hierarchical allocation mechanisms in the first place (Milgrom and Roberts 1990a; see also below). There is also a fundamental asymmetry derived from the fact that hierarchical firms have a single central authority but many subordinates. Hence efforts by subordinates to forestall or penalize harmful managerial decisions run up against the standard free-rider problems associated with the provision of any public good.

Apart from bargaining within the firm, the greatest protection furnished through the private market is provided by reputational mechanisms. Such mechanisms can operate both within the firm and in the broader labor market. If there is sufficient solidarity among the work force, for example, a firm could find that abusing one employee would provoke costly retaliation from other employees. The recruiting or training costs associated with replacing all employees simultaneously may be prohibitive, so that the firm is effectively deterred. A firm which routinely breaks its promises may also have to offer higher wages in the labor market in order to attract new employees. Depreciating one's reputation can thus be costly.

Unfortunately, reputational mechanisms can be ineffective because new employees may be easy to hire, the firm may not place enough weight on future payoffs relative to the present gains from cheating, or outsiders may lack information about events inside the firm. Hence it can be hard for a firm to credibly commit itself to keep promises, even when a credible commitment would be in the interest of all parties. For instance, a firm might want to promise that a plant will remain open if its employees agree to wage concessions. However, both the firm and its work force know that the firm will be free to demand further concessions later and that promises to the contrary are not credible. Hence no agreement is reached and the plant is closed, contrary to the mutual interests of the parties involved.

Regulation can address these problems in a variety of ways. First, regulation can indirectly facilitate private enforcement. Reducing the obstacles to union organization, for instance, helps workers to overcome the free-rider problems associated with monitoring or punishing opportunistic behavior. Regulation can also overcome precommitment problems by assuring both parties that promises about safety, pensions, and similar matters will be kept or by taking the relevant decisions out of the hands of private parties altogether. Blair (1995), for instance, argues for greater portability of employee benefits across firms, in part to reduce the incentive for firms to renege on implicit agreements with their employees. The reality of such concerns is suggested by Shleifer and Summers (1988), who show that hostile takeovers can be motivated at least in part by the financial windfalls resulting from the abrogation of implicit contracts concerning wages or benefits.

More far-reaching policies to curb employer opportunism have also been proposed, including expanded employee representation on boards of directors.

For example, Levine (1995) suggests that tax subsidies be offered for employee stock ownership plans (ESOPs) holding more than 5% of company stock. To qualify, a firm would have to allow workers to vote all shares held by the ESOP and elect a proportional share of the board of directors and implement a profit-sharing or gainsharing plan. Similarly, Blair (1995:Ch. 9) argues that all stakeholders of the firm should be represented on the board of directors and that employees should exercise full voting rights over shares held for them in ESOPs or profit-sharing plans. Finally, both Blair and Levine recommend changes in U.S. labor law to permit greater employee participation in day-to-day management activities.

Such proposals amount to a form of co-determination, and resemble policies that have already been implemented in Germany and other European countries (Smith 1991). Some potential advantages are readily identified. First, there are the productivity benefits that may be associated with profit-sharing. Second, board representation, even in a minority capacity, may provide employees with access to credible accounting data. Third, to the extent that worker voting power suffices to block decisions detrimental to the interests of employees, such as plant shutdowns, employees would be able either to prevent such actions altogether or secure adequate compensation in advance.

Proposals for employee board representation raise a wide range of issues. For the sake of brevity, I will focus here on a specific theoretical problem involving the aggregation of individual preferences. It is well known that majority voting can exhibit pathologies, including problems of indeterminacy where no proposal commands a majority of votes against all feasible alternatives (Plott 1967). At a more general level, Arrow's Impossibility Theorem shows that individual preferences cannot be aggregated to yield a social preference ordering even under relatively weak requirements on the properties of the social ordering (e.g., Pareto efficiency and nondictatorship; for details, see Miller 1992:Ch. 3). These pathologies are unlikely to be severe when boards of directors represent the interests of a relatively homogeneous group such as shareholders, though even here there are sometimes serious conflicts over merger offers and other forms of corporate restructuring. But under most proposals for employee representation, the board would need to reconcile a far wider range of conflicting interests. Hansmann (1996) argues that collective choice problems are the central reason why more firms are not managed by employees rather than by investors. Furthermore, Skillman and Dow (1996) show that worker-owned firms where preferences are heterogeneous will be vulnerable to takeover by investor-owned firms. This is not to say that employees cannot successfully run firms but just that the obstacles to preference aggregation in worker-owned firms must be faced squarely and overcome

(Benham and Keefer 1991). For more on the topic of worker control, see Dow and Putterman (1996).

## Incentives

Measured by sheer volume, the greatest contribution of the NIE to the theory of the firm during the past two decades is surely in the area of effort incentives. The key premise of this literature is that workers view income as a good and effort as a bad. Employees will accordingly shirk unless employers provide appropriate work incentives. Of course, there would be no shirking problem if employment contracts were complete since then employers could simply specify a desired type and level of effort and pay the corresponding market wage. However, it is usually impossible to write sufficiently detailed contracts or to prove in court that an employee has shirked, and thus firms must rely on other incentive systems.

### Theoretical Background

The classic NIE piece on incentives is by Alchian and Demsetz (1972). They begin with the idea that teamwork is often more productive than work by an equal number of isolated individuals (due for example to gains from a division of labor). But production in teams makes it difficult to assess individual efforts. Unless rewards are tied closely to individual contributions, the productivity gains from team production will be lost because each worker will shirk. In the view of Alchian and Demsetz, the solution is to appoint a specialist who monitors the effort levels of team members and pays wages as a function of estimated effort contributions. One difficulty with this proposal is immediate: why wouldn't the monitor shirk? They handle this objection by pointing out that the monitor can also be the *residual claimant*. That is, the monitor keeps the difference between firm revenues and costs (including wage payments to team members directly engaged in production tasks). In this case any shirking by the monitor implies that wage payments will not be properly aligned with individual efforts, and thus the residual income available to the monitor will fall.

Several standard criticisms of Alchian and Demsetz can now be reviewed (see also Putterman 1984). First, they one-sidedly emphasize shirking by production workers, without appreciating the potential for opportunistic behavior on the part of the monitor. There is a clear incentive for the monitor to understate the true effort inputs, because as the residual claimant the monitor gains a dollar of income for every dollar not paid in wages. Second, it may not be true that monitoring can only be accomplished through vertical supervision by a specialist. One could imagine instead that a team might share profits among its members and rely on horizontal monitoring, where each team member's contribution is reviewed by colleagues. Finally, the Alchian and Demsetz story has been criticized for overplaying the need to monitor effort inputs rather than overall team output. Even if one cannot measure the contributions of individual workers, incentive schemes involving group rewards and penalties have been proposed that could potentially avoid the need for costly monitoring (Holmstrom 1982).

An alternative approach to the incentive problem is provided by *principal-agent theory* (for a survey see Sappington 1991 or Milgrom and Roberts 1992:Chs. 7 and 10-13). Imagine first that output is easily measured for an individual employee, where output depends not just on effort but also on random events. The firm keeps the worker's output and pays the worker a wage that could depend upon output. However, the wage cannot depend on effort, which is unobservable. In standard models the firm is risk neutral and the employee is risk averse. The task is to design an efficient contract between the firm and employee. Due to employee risk aversion, efficiency considerations suggest that all risks should be borne by the firm. Unfortunately, the only way to do this is to have the worker receive a flat wage regardless of output, which would eliminate effort incentives. An optimal contract thus involves some dependence of wages on output (to deal with the incentive problem), but not too much dependence (to deal with the risk aversion problem). In a generalization termed *multi-task principal-agent theory*, Holmstrom and Milgrom (1991) have shown that firms should be cautious about rewarding employees for easily measured aspects of performance, because this induces workers to allocate time and effort toward such dimensions at the expense of other tasks. For instance, sales agents who are paid large commissions will spend less time helping colleagues establish valuable contacts (Holmstrom and Milgrom 1994), and teachers who are rewarded when their students achieve higher scores on standardized tests will spend less time teaching hard-to-test but qualitatively important skills (Milgrom and Roberts 1992:230-31).

Another variation on the basic principal-agent model is to reward workers based on their performance relative to similar colleagues. Such incentive schemes are widely used by firms in making promotion decisions and have come to be known as *tournaments* in the economic literature (Carmichael 1989). A detailed case study illustrating how promotion tournaments are actually used has been provided by Baker, Gibbs, and Holmstrom (1994a, 1994b), who find for a medium-sized U.S. firm in a service industry that there is a simple and well-defined hierarchy of job titles and that employees have standard career paths involving movements from one hierarchical level to the next. This system simultaneously addresses incentive issues as well as the problem of matching employees to jobs: as the firm accumulates internal information about its employees over time, it promotes those who are identified as having higher ability into upper-level jobs that require broader competence.

Tournaments have a number of attractive features. Because rewards are based on relative rather than absolute performance, sources of uncertainty that affect all workers jointly are eliminated. Contests of this kind also reduce temptations for the firm to cheat because promotions must be given to someone, unlike a promised bonus payment that may be withheld by the firm. But on the negative side, tournaments undermine incentives for competitors to help one another in a team setting and could trigger acts of sabotage against rivals. Collusion by contestants to withhold effort is also a danger. And as with standard principal-agent contracts, the employer must possess measures of individual performance, at least of a comparative kind, in order to conduct a tournament in the first place. Some amount of costly individual monitoring is therefore likely to be needed in a team setting.

Yet another approach to the problem of effort incentives is provided by *efficiency wage theory* (for surveys, see Akerlof and Yellen 1986; Weiss 1990; Carmichael 1990; and Lang and Kahn 1990). In this framework, firms offer a wage above the going market rate and threaten to fire anyone who is caught shirking. The dismissal threat must be taken seriously by employees, because their only recourse is to accept a lower wage from some other firm. Of course, if all firms raise wages simultaneously, this is no longer true, but as the market wage increases, the quantity of labor demanded falls while the quantity supplied rises. This generates unemployment so that fired workers cannot quickly find other jobs. In equilibrium, the prospect of prolonged unemployment serves as the penalty for shirking. Models of this kind have been developed by many authors over the last two decades; two of the most influential examples are Shapiro and Stiglitz (1984) and Bowles (1985).

The efficiency wage approach to the effort problem leads naturally to repeated game models, because a long-term relationship between firms and employees must be assumed: if an employee plans to quit in the near future anyway, the firing threat carries little weight. In particular, it has long been recognized that team production has the same structure as the famous prisoner's dilemma game. If output or profit is shared among the members of the team, there is an incentive to withhold effort because effort is costly to individual workers, while its benefits are spread across the entire group. But it has also been recognized that cooperation can sometimes be achieved when such prisoner's dilemma games are played repeatedly (Axelrod 1984). The key idea is that shirking by a worker in the current round of the game can be punished by having other team members engage in retaliatory shirking in future rounds.

When each worker places enough weight on payoffs anticipated in future periods, the transitory gain from shirking now is smaller than the expected losses resulting from retaliation in all future periods. In principle, this mechanism can sustain efficient effort levels even in large teams. Such repeated game equilibria have been studied extensively in the context of partnerships (MacLeod 1984, 1988; Putterman and Skillman 1992; Dong and Dow 1993). A similar mechanism can be used in repeated interactions between a firm and its employees. Here employee shirking is punished not by retaliatory shirking from other team members but by wage cuts or dismissal as in the efficiency wage model.

This research has led to several significant conclusions. First, it is vital to consider the incentives of the firm as well as the employee, since firms can always dismiss or cut the wages of nonshirkers if this happens to be profitable. Such firm-side opportunism may sometimes be restrained by the firm's concern for its reputation in the outside labor market, but reputational forces are limited for the reasons mentioned previously. Second, efficient effort levels may be sustainable even when each individual employee works for a finite period of time in a given firm and the employee's date of retirement is known in advance. At first glance this is surprising, since a finitely repeated prisoner's dilemma normally leads to cheating in the last round, hence also in the next to the last round, and so on back to the initial round. But cooperation nevertheless remains feasible if there is no terminal date for the firm itself and employee cohorts are overlapping (Cremer 1986; Bull 1987). A third conclusion is that efficient effort levels can only be viable if some surplus is generated within the employment relationship, so that either the firm or the employee (or both) prefers to preserve the relationship rather than end it. Carmichael (1989), MacLeod and Malcomson (1993), and Dow (1995) demonstrate that this surplus can be appropriated by either party, depending on whether the labor market is characterized by excess supply or excess demand. But in general, the labor market will not clear, and if employed workers appropriate some of the surplus, they may well face significant exit costs.

Finally, in models of this kind there are multiple equilibria, including an inefficient equilibrium where everyone shirks. The potential for inefficiency is easy to see: if firms expect employees to shirk, they may as well dismiss them, and if the employees expect to be fired, they may as well shirk. The prevalence of multiple equilibria is a standard problem in the analysis of repeated games. A result called the Folk Theorem shows that any individually rational outcome can arise in an infinitely repeated game if the players put enough weight on future payoffs (see Rasmusen 1994:Ch. 5; Fudenberg and Tirole 1991:Ch. 5). Thus there is no guarantee that high-effort solutions must occur, and scope remains for an active managerial role in achieving superior organizational equilibria (Miller 1992:Chs. 9-11). This multiplicity of equilibria carries over to the labor market as a whole, contrary to the usual expectation that market discipline imposes efficient behavior on individual firms and workers. Indeed, it can be shown that labor market equilibria vary not only in their efficiency but also in the way that surpluses are distributed between firms and workers (Carmichael 1989; MacLeod and Malcomson 1989, 1993; Dow 1995).

Given the inability of game-theoretic models to predict a unique effort equilibrium and the mixed track record of principal-agent theory in explaining observed compensation systems (Baker, Jensen, and Murphy 1988), various writers have turned their attention to the organizational and sociological sources of effort incentives. Akerlof and Yellen (1990) argue that workers supply high effort to firms as a gift in exchange for reciprocal gifts offered by their employers (generous wages, job security, respectful treatment). Related ideas have been advanced by Leibenstein (1987). Indeed, game theorists themselves have emphasized the importance of a corporate culture conducive to mutual trust (Kreps 1990). A major task for the NIE is to identify conditions under which such high-trust equilibria are likely to evolve and persist (see Miller 1992:Chs. 9-11, and Ghoshal and Moran 1996).

*Regulatory Implications*

Much recent discussion has emphasized the value of maintaining continuity in the employment relationship. This concern coincides with fears in the 1990s about the effect of corporate downsizing not only on laid-off workers themselves but also on the morale and productivity of the survivors. A related element in such policy discussions has been greater awareness of the merits of Japanese employment practices, which provide large segments of the work force with an expectation of lifetime employment (Aoki 1990). Levine (1995:Ch. 8) recommends a number of policy changes inspired in part by the Japanese example, including just cause dismissal rules and measures to discourage labor turnover.

The NIE provides some support for such ideas, but not of an unqualified kind. The theory of repeated games does establish that high-effort equilibria are more likely to prove viable when workers have long-term attachments to their employers. Indeed, if exit were costless, workers could simply shirk and then quit. But on the other hand, when exit is too costly for employees, there is a serious risk that managerial authority will be abused and that the labor market will no longer function effectively as a mechanism for resource allocation. It can also be argued that if the benefits from continuity of employment are understood, the parties themselves will take steps to reduce labor turnover. Henry Ford's decision to adopt the $5 day in 1913-14 can be explained in this way (Raff and Summers 1987) and modern parallels are easy to find: for example, the Starbuck's coffee chain offers stock options to part-time employees in order to limit labor turnover and reduce training costs.

Unfortunately, firms may find it profitable to renege on promises of job security if demand declines in the product market, if replacement workers can be hired at low wages, if information about firm cheating becomes more difficult to obtain, or if takeovers lead to the breaking of prior implicit agreements. Thus it is possible that regulatory assurances of greater job security could facilitate more commitment to long-term relationships than market forces alone can provide. These could come in the form of tax incentives rather than direct administrative controls: for example, the employer contribution to unemployment insurance might involve more experience rating, with higher taxes for firms with frequent layoffs.

Levine (1995) also advocates abandonment of the doctrine of at-will employment (Epstein 1984) in favor of a rule allowing dismissal only for cause. While such a shift would no doubt promote continuity of employment, as well as providing some protection from employer opportunism, it also raises problems from the standpoint of efficiency wage theory. A policy of just cause dismissal would shift the burden of proof to firms to show that an employee shirked rather than permitting the firm to dismiss shirkers unilaterally. Precisely because it is hard to write legally binding contracts governing effort contributions (if such contracts were feasible, incentives would be redundant), it is also hard to show in court that shirking has actually occurred. Hence a just cause standard might force firms to switch to more costly or less effective incentive devices, such as output-based performance contracts or promotion tournaments.

Another regulatory policy that may be illuminated by the use of NIE concepts is the encouragement of profit-sharing plans through tax benefits to firms which adopt such plans, as has occurred in the U.S. and the U.K. There is now a good deal of econometric evidence indicating that firms which implement profit sharing have a small but nontrivial (4%-5%) increase in labor productivity (for the U.S., see Kruse 1993; for the U.K., see Wadhwani and Wall 1990; and for related Japanese results, see Jones and Kato 1995). This is prima facie evidence against the Alchian and Demsetz (1972) shirking model, which argues for the importance of a single residual claimant who monitors employees. In a more tentative vein, it may be taken as evidence supporting the repeated game idea that shared profit claims facilitate the emergence of cooperative, high-trust equilibria within firms (Weitzman and Kruse 1990). Here, however, we want to focus on a different question: Does this empirical evidence provide a justification for subsidies to firms that share profits?

A believer in market efficiency would say no, for a plausible reason: firms that will benefit from profit sharing already have incentives to implement such plans and require no governmental assistance to do so. The main effect of a subsidy program is to induce profit sharing in firms where it is not particularly beneficial, perhaps because employees already have strong effort incentives and want to avoid further risks to their income (as suggested by the principal-agent framework). The presumption in this view should be that firms and workers will implement on their own whatever employment contract is ex ante efficient in the sense of maximizing the total surplus from the relationship, because then the aggregate gain to be divided between the two parties is as large as possible.

Is this reasoning decisive? Perhaps not. One line of counterargument involves the idea that compensation plans adopted within individual firms have spillover effects on other firms, generating macroeconomic externalities and calling the efficiency of market solutions into question (Weitzman 1984; Levine 1995). An alternative story that invokes adverse selection in the labor market runs as follows. Suppose employers have private information about the financial prospects of their firms. Workers will then wonder whether an offer of profit sharing signals anything about the firm's true prospects. At any specified wage rate, perhaps firms anticipating future financial difficulties are more inclined to propose profit sharing because they want to transfer some downside risk to their employees. If there are enough fly-by-night firms of this type, workers will understandably reject compensation packages that include profit sharing. Unfortunately, financially healthy firms attempting to use profit sharing to raise productivity will also have their proposals rejected by workers. Hence firms that *should* adopt profit sharing will not do so in equilibrium. Under these conditions it may be possible to construct a subsidy that makes profit sharing attractive to workers despite adverse selection problems, where the subsidy pays for itself by increasing labor productivity and thus the tax revenues of government (Greenwald and Stiglitz 1986).

It is impossible to assess the merits of this story here. As pointed out previously, the key point is simply that information or bargaining problems at the ex ante design stage can undermine the efficiency of governance structures and may thus open the door to efficiency-enhancing policy interventions. Whether or not this is true in particular instances cannot be settled through armchair theorizing: careful empirical investigation guided by a relevant body of theory is needed. But the theory used should not directly postulate, as the NIE often does, that market forces lead automatically to efficient employment contracts.

I close this section by looking at a rather different role for regulation, one suggested by the potential for multiple equilibria in repeated game models and by the importance of custom, history, and random drift in evolutionary versions of game theory (Weibull 1995). In this context, regulation may provide a means for recoordinating markets around socially preferred equilibria. Within the firm, for instance, comparable worth or affirmative action programs may provoke reconsideration of traditional and unexamined assumptions about the criteria by which wages are attached to jobs. When implemented by many employers simultaneously (such as large private firms or local and state governments), such programs may also have some impact on the social conventions prevailing in an entire labor market. The same is true for laws prohibiting discrimination based on race, gender, age, disability, or sexual orientation. In effect, regulation identifies a new focal point (Schelling 1960) around which the expectations and practices of private agents can begin to converge.

## Bargaining

We have now considered two themes in the new theory of the firm: coordination and incentives. A third theme in the NIE is that of bargaining. NIE writers often see the firm as an institution that enables private agents to avoid costly bargaining across a market. Others, however, regard the firm itself as an arena where bargaining processes are played out. One's view of the efficiency of firm organization, as well as the costs and benefits of regulatory intervention, depends to a large degree on which of these ideas is emphasized.

*Theoretical Background*

The literature on transaction cost economics originating with Coase (1937) poses a basic question: Why is it that some transactions are organized within a firm, while other transactions are carried out across a market interface? The paradigm application is to vertical integration. Firms buy many inputs from external suppliers, but they also generally produce some of their own components or inputs. What forces govern this make-or-buy decision? One answer advanced by transaction cost economics (Williamson 1975, 1979; Klein, Crawford, and Alchian 1978) is that transactions requiring investments in specialized assets are likely to be carried on within a firm, while transactions that do not require such investments will be conducted via market exchange. For example, a coal mine located next to an electric generating plant is likely to be owned by the electric utility (Joskow 1985). Similarly, Masten (1984) establishes that aerospace companies are more likely to produce specialized components in-house, especially when they are technically complex. But on the other hand, few companies find it necessary or desirable to produce their own paper clips.

To understand these ideas, we need to develop the concept of quasi rent. A quasi rent is defined to be any flow of payments in excess of what is required to keep an asset in its current use after the investment expenditures to create the

asset are sunk.  For example, suppose it costs $1 million to build a widget fac-
tory; but after this ex ante expenditure has been incurred, the factory owner
would be able to get at best $500 per month by putting the factory to an alter-
native use (it is only designed to produce widgets, cannot be operated by anyone else, and would be very expensive to retrofit). At the ex post stage, once the
factory exists, any net revenue to the factory owner beyond $500 per month is a
quasi rent.  Similarly, a worker who has invested time and effort to learn a particular job may be able to get at most $5 per hour by taking the next best avail-
able job.  In this case any payment on the current job that exceeds $5 per hour
would be a quasi rent. Notice that a quasi rent can be viewed as the return on
the portion of the initial investment that is sunk. More specialized assets tend to
have a higher sunk component and thus yield larger quasi rents. A rent is also a
payment exceeding what is needed to keep an input in its current use, but ordinary rents do not represent returns on earlier investments (consider the financial rewards derived from Wayne Gretzky's genetic talent for playing hockey).

Once an asset has been put in place and its cost is sunk, there is a danger
of ex post opportunism because other parties can gain by reducing the existing
flow of payments to the asset owner. More generally, we can expect owners of
related assets to engage in ex post bargaining over the available pool of quasi
rents. Bargaining occurs because after the initial investment expenditures are
sunk, the various parties find themselves in a situation of bilateral or multilateral monopoly where it would be expensive to transact with an outsider who
has not already made the required investments. Such bargaining can be very
costly if the parties have private information (Kennan and Wilson 1990, 1993).
Bargaining costs can take many forms: lawyers may be hired, agreements may
be delayed, unnecessary risks may be incurred, or expensive precautions may
be taken. The clearest example arises during a strike or lockout, where the
value of lost production becomes painfully obvious.

For the generating plant and the coal mine, the need for repeated hag-
gling can be eliminated in a simple way: the owner of one firm can buy the
other. Once all the assets are in the same hands, there is only one profit
stream, namely, the profit going to the owner of the combined firm. A large
amount of NIE analysis has been motivated by the idea that the costs of
opportunistic bargaining can be eliminated by means of integrated asset ownership (Williamson 1975, 1979, 1985; Klein, Crawford, and Alchian 1978;
Grossman and Hart 1986; Hart and Moore 1990; Hart 1989, 1991). But this
solution only circumvents bargaining problems associated with *physical* assets.
Specialized skills present a more intractable problem because it is impossible
to own someone else's *human capital* (that is, a person's accumulated stock of
productive knowledge, skill, and experience).

Therefore, we now consider a firm where (a) employees have specialized skills that are valuable to the firm, (b) it is costly for the firm to train replacement workers, and (c) the skills of the employees would be less valuable in other firms. Such skills are firm-specific, and constitute a specialized asset on which quasi rents can be earned. But after employees have acquired their skills, the firm would like to push wages down to the lowest level that would be compatible with retention of its employees, while employees would like to push wages up until the firm is just indifferent toward continuing their employment.

Several problems arise in this situation. First, there are the usual bargaining costs due to bilateral monopoly, perhaps aggravated by the costs of overcoming collective action problems on the employee side. Second, there is the issue of who pays for worker training ex ante, and whether investments in specialized assets of this sort will even occur. If the employees expect to receive a low wage because the employer will have most of the ex post bargaining power, they have little incentive to invest in costly training (e.g., by sacrificing time that could have been used for other purposes). On the other hand, if the firm expects to be "held up" by opportunistic workers once the specific human capital is in place, it will not have much interest in financing the training either. Ideally, each party will bear a share of the up-front cost equal to its expected share in the ex post quasi rent, since this will lead to efficient contributions by each party. However, this may be difficult or impossible to arrange when the true costs (such as the opportunity cost of a worker's time or the cost to the firm of reduced production during the training period) are private information. A third issue is the possible waste of resources on strategic moves aimed at strengthening one's ex post bargaining position. For instance, employers may adopt new production methods in order to appropriate quasi rents from workers by reducing the level of firm-specific skill required from the work force (Dow 1985, 1988, 1989; Skillman and Ryder 1993).

Many NIE authors claim that such difficulties have motivated the creation of internal labor markets within firms. The ILM idea dates back to Doeringer and Piore (1971) and earlier institutionally oriented labor economists. Rock and Wachter (1996) summarize ILM norms in the following way: "Wages increase with seniority; a business downturn results in employee layoffs rather than wage reductions; if layoffs occur, junior workers lose their jobs before senior workers; discharges are for cause; if an employer catches an employee shirking, the employer will discharge the employee rather than reduce his wages; and if firms discharge older workers before younger workers, they do so through voluntary retirement mechanisms in which the firm buys out the 'contract' of the older worker."

The first explicit application of the new institutional economics to internal labor markets was by Williamson, Wachter, and Harris (1975). These authors argued that ILMs represent an efficient response to two problems: the existence of firm-specific human capital acquired through on-the-job training, and informational asymmetries between the firm and its employees. To diminish costs associated with opportunistic bargaining, the ILM attaches wages to jobs or hierarchical levels rather than individuals and offers an arbitration or grievance apparatus to resolve conflicts. Reliance on internal promotion not only preserves the continuity of the employment relationship (and hence the quasi rents associated with specialized skills), but also helps to overcome informational asymmetries in two respects. First, as the firm learns more about the true abilities of its employees, it can promote higher productivity people into more responsible positions. Second, the internal promotion system motivates effort through a tournament process where high performance is rewarded over time through rapid career advancement. For this system to work, outside hiring must be confined to specified ports of entry near the bottom of the career ladder. Otherwise, firms would fail to take full advantage of the information they accumulate about internal candidates and would dampen work incentives by reducing the pool of prizes in the promotion tournament. These ideas have subsequently been elaborated by Wachter and Wright (1990) and Rock and Wachter (1996); for an empirical assessment in the context of a detailed case study, see Baker, Gibbs, and Holmstrom (1994a, 1994b).

*Regulatory Implications*

What policy implications emerge from the literature on intrafirm bargaining and internal labor markets? Here I will focus on the continuity of the employment relationship and extend the previous discussion on regulatory implications of incentives above. Clearly there can be efficiency losses if valuable skills are sacrificed through layoffs or plant shutdowns. One might think that complementarities between the physical assets owned by the firm and the human assets of employees would motivate both parties to preserve the relationship (Williamson, Wachter, and Harris 1975). However, the quasi rents from such investments are typically shared through bargaining, so that firms and employees both appropriate ex post returns above their next-best market alternatives. Proximately, therefore, a wage premium that is paid to an employee with specialized knowledge or experience is a cost item from the standpoint of the firm; or to put it another way, the private cost to the firm of retaining such an employee is higher than the true social cost. Because the firm does not take into account the quasi rent losses that layoffs inflict on employees, it may be tempted to jettison workers with specific skills prematurely.

Empirically, these costs appear to be large: Hamermesh (1987) estimates that laid-off or displaced workers lose between $4,700 and $15,700 in present value terms (using 1980 dollars) and provides evidence that these losses were unexpected for the individuals involved. These figures do not include losses associated with spells of unemployment between jobs or the value of lost skills that are specific to an occupation or industry rather than a firm. There is also little indication that workers are paid significant compensation up front for the risk of layoff (Murphy and Topel 1987).

According to the Coase Theorem, inefficient layoffs will not occur if workers are prepared to bribe firms in order to retain their jobs, because such a bribe (if equal to the full employee share of the quasi rent on firm-specific skills) would lead the firm to take account of employee losses in making its layoff or plant shutdown decisions. Thus, if the losses to workers from a shutdown were severe, the workers would offer large concessions to their employer to keep the plant open, and if maintaining operations were the efficient solution, then the employee bribe would be sufficiently large to persuade the employer to continue operations. In practice, this process is unlikely to function smoothly due to informational asymmetries, wealth constraints, collective action difficulties facing worker teams, and the firm's inability to commit not to extort further bribes in the future. Indeed, the transaction cost framework identifies such bargaining rigidities as a central rationale for internal labor markets where wages are attached to jobs rather than individuals. More fundamentally still, if short-term bargaining were frictionless, there would be no need for authority structures to coordinate production in the first place (Milgrom and Roberts 1990a). A corollary is that layoff and shutdown decisions by management may be inefficient from a social standpoint.

One response in the U.S. has been legislation mandating advance notice for large plant closures. Another approach would be to expand public insurance against the risk of layoff, either through ordinary unemployment insurance or by subsidizing the retraining of displaced workers. Both advance notice and UI can lead to incentive problems. In the case of advance notice, effort incentives can drop off sharply once all players realize that they are now in the last round of a prisoner's dilemma game; and in the case of UI, unemployed workers may defer serious job search until near the end of the eligibility period. But on the positive side, both measures may improve the quality of matches between laid-off workers and subsequent employers by increasing the average duration of job search. Both policies also help to cushion the blow of unemployment itself either by allowing more precautionary saving after advance notice is given or through UI payments and retraining opportunities. However, neither policy directly addresses the underlying problem, which is the failure of employers to internalize the costs of job loss that layoff or shutdown decisions impose on employees. From a social standpoint, it would be better to discourage inefficient layoffs in the first place, rather than shifting their costs to society at large.

As noted previously, Levine (1995) has suggested an alternative approach where long-time employees can be fired only for cause. This policy would effectively transfer property rights from firm owners to workers, since employees would have to be bribed to leave, rather than needing to bribe the firm in order to stay. One could argue that legislated protections against unjustified dismissal represent an extension to the nonunion sector of provisions already found in existing collective agreements and that such protections would merely codify existing norms in internal labor markets (Rock and Wachter 1996). It is also true that Western European countries have generally adopted public policies providing more job security than is available in North America (although the value of such rigidities has been under active debate in Europe itself). Finally, one can argue that the U.S. and Canada are already moving implicitly toward such a system through the growing number of court decisions where employees are awarded damages for wrongful dismissal.

Does this clinch the case for ending employment at will? Probably not. It remains unclear how just cause requirements would be enforced in sectors that lack the monitoring and enforcement capabilities of unions or the firm-side reputational mechanisms that help to keep internal labor markets viable. The practical result would probably be a shift in the burden of proof toward the employer in civil litigation (although mandatory arbitration by a third party might be used to provide a better informed, faster, and lower cost method of dispute settlement). It is also far from clear how workers with high levels of firm-specific human capital, who are often the chief intended beneficiaries of such proposals, could be distinguished from workers who have made little investment in such skills (by length of service? occupation? degree of responsibility?). Indeed, it might not be desirable to make such distinctions at all. Even if their skills are not firm-specific, employees could be paid a premium for incentive reasons; they might capture some production surpluses through bargaining (Osborne and Rubinstein 1990); or they might capture part of the value from an especially good job match (Rosen 1991). A case could be made that workers who derive wage premiums from any of these other sources are also inadequately protected by the option of exit to an outside labor market. Thus it is not obvious how one should define the employee constituency to be targeted for regulatory or judicial protection.

There are other labor market implications to be considered as well, not least whether employers will insist on lowering wages in order to offset the reduced ex post flexibility associated with constraints on dismissal. As noted above, dismissal threats might have to be replaced with less effective ways of eliciting effort from workers. And finally, if employers must bribe employees to leave by proposing a mutually acceptable severance payment, bargaining costs might make it difficult to end a bad match between a firm and worker and could give employees incentives to shirk or even sabotage production in order to support demands for better severance packages. It is impossible to evaluate all of these issues here, but this short discussion should give some idea of the questions that would be posed by the NIE with regard to modifications in the rule of employment at will.

## Conclusion: What Does the NIE Have to Say about Employment Regulation?

In our tour through the topics of coordination, incentives, and bargaining, we have seen how the NIE can help to shed some light on regulatory issues involving employment. While the NIE framework rarely provides a sharp policy conclusion, it does spotlight some questions that need to be addressed when regulatory proposals are evaluated.

As I emphasized previously, the NIE generally starts from a presumption that individual rationality and competitive market forces can be counted upon to induce efficient governance responses from private agents. At the same time, we noted a tension between the NIE's stress on market failures as the rationale for firm organization and its belief that competitive markets will bring about an efficient set of governance structures. In contrast, we argued that there is a second-order efficiency problem: market failures similar to those motivating the creation of hierarchical firms may prevent private parties from arriving at efficient governance systems and so may justify regulatory intervention. In this closing section I will briefly review the major forms of market failure that can lead to inefficient private governance and summarize the ways in which regulation might be of assistance.

*Informational asymmetries.* The most direct remedy for informational problems will often be disclosure requirements, if these can be enforced successfully. Other remedies include tax and subsidy systems designed to offset the distortions from adverse selection or moral hazard in the labor market. Unemployment insurance is a prominent example, and subsidies to promote profit sharing might be justified in a similar way.

*Market power.* Monopsonistic distortions can arise if job search is costly and firms or workers are heterogeneous. Depending on the situation, possible solutions might be to legislate restrictions on the outcome of wage bargaining (a minimum wage), to diminish search costs through information dissemination (public data banks on job openings), or to strengthen worker bargaining power (unionization). Bilateral monopoly combined with informational asymmetries can lead to bargaining rigidities, which may warrant policies to enhance job security or to ensure a larger employee voice in firm governance.

*Collective action.* Free-rider issues in negotiating and enforcing agreements involving many workers simultaneously are usually addressed through legal recognition of the right to bargain collectively. Other frictions resulting from inadequate representation of worker interests might be handled by requiring employee representation on the board of directors or by subsidizing worker buyouts of conventional capitalist firms.

*Exit costs.* For reasons involving search costs, firm-specific investments, or efficiency wages, it may be costly for workers to exit from firms. Possible restraints on the abuse of managerial authority in such situations include direct regulatory controls (to prevent raids on employee pension funds or limit exposure to toxic materials), guarantees of job security (dismissal for cause), mechanisms through which workers can discipline firms (grievance procedures, arbitration, strikes), and direct employee participation in corporate governance.

*Externalities and multiple market equilibria.* Externalities across firms (e.g., with respect to worker training) could be addressed by suitable incentive schemes (such as a subsidy to training) or other controls (such as mandatory provision of training opportunities). Labor market conventions where wages are governed in part by social custom or historical accident could be altered by antidiscrimination rules, comparable worth programs, or by other regulatory policies that provide new focal points for private sector practice.

It is far beyond the scope of this chapter to comment on the practical merits of any of these policy suggestions. A serious examination would require competent theoretical analysis, detailed empirical knowledge, and a sober assessment of unintended side effects. The main lesson to be drawn is a more general one. The NIE can offer at least two kinds of insights that might aid in the process of policy evaluation. First, it forces advocates of regulatory intervention to explain in a clear and rigorous way why there is a market failure at all, given the incentives of private agents to reach mutually beneficial agreements. This is an important form of intellectual discipline that should help to forestall well-intentioned but misguided interventions. Second, it provides some clues about the kinds of failure one might want to watch out for. As we have seen, a central concern of the NIE is to identify a set of market failures serious enough to motivate the creation of firms. But many of the same frictions that make it attractive to suspend market forces within the firm can reappear elsewhere as reasons to question the market's own judgment about privately established governance systems. Indirectly, therefore, the NIE identifies some important grounds for regulatory intervention in the labor market. One can only hope that future work in this field will begin to address these questions in a more explicit and systematic way.

## Acknowledgments

I am grateful to Gil Skillman and Bruce Kaufman for comments on an earlier draft and to the Social Sciences and Humanities Research Council of Canada for its financial support. All opinions expressed are those of the author.

## References

Akerlof, George A., and Janet L. Yellen, eds. 1986. *Efficiency Wage Models of the Labor Market*. New York: Cambridge University Press.

_____. 1990. "The Fair Wage-Effort Hypothesis and Unemployment." *Quarterly Journal of Economics*, Vol. 105, no. 2 (May), pp. 255-83.

Alchian, Armen A., and Harold Demsetz. 1972. "Production, Information Costs, and Economic Organization." *American Economic Review*, Vol. 62 (December), pp. 777-95.

Aoki, Masahiko. 1990. "Toward an Economic Model of the Japanese Firm." *Journal of Economic Literature*, Vol. 28 (March), pp. 1-27.

Arrow, Kenneth J. 1974. *The Limits of Organization*. New York: Norton.

Axelrod, Robert. 1984. *The Evolution of Cooperation*. New York: Basic Books.

Baker, George, Michael Gibbs, and Bengt Holmstrom. 1994a. "The Internal Economics of the Firm: Evidence from Personnel Data." *Quarterly Journal of Economics*, Vol. 109, no. 4 (November), pp. 881-919.

_____. 1994b. "The Wage Policy of a Firm." *Quarterly Journal of Economics*, Vol. 109, no. 4 (November), pp. 921-55.

Baker, George P., Michael C. Jensen, and Kevin J. Murphy. 1988. "Compensation and Incentives: Practice vs. Theory." *Journal of Finance*, Vol. 43, no. 3 (July), pp. 593-616.

Becker, Gary S., and Kevin M. Murphy. 1992. "The Division of Labor, Coordination Costs, and Knowledge." *Quarterly Journal of Economics*, Vol. 107, no. 4 (November), pp. 1137-60.

Benham, Lee, and Philip Keefer. 1991. "Voting in Firms: The Role of Agenda Control, Size and Voter Homogeneity." *Economic Inquiry*, Vol. 29 (October), pp. 706-19.

Blair, Margaret. 1995. *Ownership and Control: Rethinking Corporate Governance for the Twenty-First Century*. Washington, DC: Brookings.

Bowles, Samuel. 1985. "The Production Process in a Competitive Economy: Walrasian, Neo-Hobbesian, and Marxian Models." *American Economic Review*, Vol. 75 (March), pp. 16-36.

Bowles, Samuel, and Herbert Gintis. 1990. "Contested Exchange: New Microfoundations for the Political Economy of Capitalism." *Politics and Society*, Vol. 18, no. 2 (June), pp. 165-222.

_____. 1993. "The Revenge of Homo Economicus: Contested Exchange and the Revival of Political Economy." *Journal of Economic Perspectives*, Vol. 7, no. 1 (Winter), pp. 83-102.

Bull, Clive. 1987. "The Existence of Self-Enforcing Implicit Contracts." *Quarterly Journal of Economics*, Vol. 102 (February), pp. 147-59.

Carmichael, H. Lorne. 1989. "Self-Enforcing Contracts, Shirking, and Life Cycle Incentives." *Journal of Economic Perspectives*, Vol. 3, no. 4 (Fall), pp. 65-83.

_____. 1990. "Efficiency Wage Models of Unemployment—One View." *Economic Inquiry*, Vol. 28 (April), pp. 269-95.

Chandler, Alfred D. 1992. "Organizational Capabilities and the Economic History of the Industrial Enterprise." *Journal of Economic Perspectives*, Vol. 6, no. 3 (Summer), pp. 79-100.

Coase, Ronald H. 1937. "The Nature of the Firm." *Economica*, Vol. 4 (November), pp. 386-405.

_____. 1960. "The Problem of Social Cost." *Journal of Law and Economics*, Vol. 3 (October), pp. 1-44.

_____. 1992. "The Institutional Structure of Production." *American Economic Review*, Vol. 82, no. 4 (September), pp. 713-19.

Cremer, Jacques. 1986. "Cooperation in Ongoing Organizations." *Quarterly Journal of Economics*, Vol. 101, no. 1 (February), pp. 33-49.

Doeringer, Peter, and Michael Piore. 1971. *Internal Labor Markets and Manpower Analysis*. Lexington, MA: D.C. Heath and Company.

Dong, Xiao-yuan, and Greg Dow. 1993. "Does Free Exit Reduce Shirking in Production Teams?" *Journal of Comparative Economics*, Vol. 17 (June), pp. 472-84.

Dow, Greg. 1985. "Internal Bargaining and Strategic Innovation in the Theory of the Firm." *Journal of Economic Behavior and Organization*, Vol. 6 (September), pp. 301-20.

_____. 1987. "The Function of Authority in Transaction Cost Economics." *Journal of Economic Behavior and Organization*, Vol. 8, no. 1 (March), pp. 13-38.

_____. 1988. "Information, Production Decisions, and Intra-Firm Bargaining." *International Economic Review*, Vol. 29 (February), pp. 57-79.

_____. 1989. "Knowledge Is Power: Informational Precommitment in the Capitalist Firm." *European Journal of Political Economy*, Vol. 5, pp. 161-76.

_____. 1993a. "Why Capital Hires Labor: A Bargaining Perspective." *American Economic Review*, Vol. 83, no. 1 (March), pp. 118-34.

_____. 1993b. "The Appropriability Critique of Transaction Cost Economics." In C. Pitelis, ed., *Transaction Costs, Markets and Hierarchies*. Oxford: Blackwell.

_____. 1993c. "Democracy versus Appropriability: Can Labor-Managed Firms Flourish in a Capitalist World?" In S. Bowles, H. Gintis, and B. Gustafsson, eds., *Markets and Democracy: Participation, Accountability and Efficiency*. New York: Cambridge University Press.

_____. 1995. "Organization, Incentives, and Surplus Appropriation." Unpublished manuscript, Department of Economics, Simon Fraser University.

_____. 1996. "Authority Relations in the Firm: Review and Agenda for Research." In J. Groenewegen, ed., *Transaction Cost Economics and Beyond*. Boston: Kluwer.

Dow, Greg, and Louis Putterman. 1996. "Why Capital (Usually) Hires Labor: An Assessment of Proposed Explanations." Unpublished manuscript, Department of Economics, Simon Fraser University.

Edwards, Richard C. 1979. *Contested Terrain*. New York: Basic Books.

Eggertsson, Thrainn. 1990. *Economic Behavior and Institutions*. New York: Cambridge University Press.

Epstein, Richard A. 1984. "In Defense of the Contract at Will." *University of Chicago Law Review*, Vol. 51, no. 4 (Fall), pp. 947-82.

Flannigan, Robert. 1995. "The Economic Structure of the Firm." *Osgoode Hall Law Journal*, Vol. 33, no. 1, pp. 105-50.

Freeman, Richard B., and James L. Medoff. 1984. *What Do Unions Do?* New York: Basic Books.

Fudenberg, Drew, and Jean Tirole. 1991. *Game Theory*. Cambridge, MA: MIT Press.

Garvey, Gerald. 1993. "Does Hierarchical Governance Facilitate Adaptation to Changed Circumstances?" *Journal of Economic Behavior and Organization*, Vol. 20, pp. 187-211.

Ghoshal, Sumantra, and Peter Moran. 1996. "Bad for Practice: A Critique of the Transaction Cost Theory." *Academy of Management Review*, Vol. 21, no. 1 (January), pp. 13-47.

Goldberg, Victor P. 1980. "Bridges over Contested Terrain: Exploring the Radical Account of the Employment Relationship." *Journal of Economic Behavior and Organization*, Vol. 1, pp. 249-74.

Greenwald, Bruce, and Joseph Stiglitz. 1986. "Externalities in Economies with Imperfect Information and Incomplete Markets." *Quarterly Journal of Economics*, Vol. 101, pp. 229-64.

Grossman, Sanford, and Oliver Hart. 1986. "The Costs and Benefits of Ownership: A Theory of Vertical and Lateral Integration." *Journal of Political Economy*, Vol. 94, pp. 691-719.

Hamermesh, Daniel S. 1987. "The Costs of Worker Displacement." *Quarterly Journal of Economics*, Vol. 102 (February), pp. 51-75.

Hansmann, Henry. 1996. *The Ownership of Enterprise*. Cambridge, MA: The Belknap Press of Harvard University Press.

Hart, Oliver. 1989. "An Economist's Perspective on the Theory of the Firm." *Columbia Law Review*, Vol. 89 (November), pp. 1757-74.

_____. 1991. "Incomplete Contracts and the Theory of the Firm." In O. Williamson and S. Winter, eds., *The Nature of the Firm: Origins, Evolution, and Development*. New York: Oxford University Press, pp. 138-58.

Hart, Oliver, and John Moore. 1990. "Property Rights and the Nature of the Firm." *Journal of Political Economy*, Vol. 98 (December), pp. 1119-158.

Holmstrom, Bengt. 1982. "Moral Hazard in Teams." *Bell Journal of Economics*, Vol. 13, no. 2 (Autumn), pp. 324-40.

Holmstrom, Bengt, and Paul Milgrom. 1991. "Multitask Principal-Agent Analyses: Incentive Contracts, Asset Ownership, and Job Design." Vol. 7 (Special Issue), pp. 24-52.

_____. 1994. "The Firm as an Incentive System." *American Economic Review*, Vol. 84, no. 4 (September), pp. 972-91.

Jones, Derek C., and Takao Kato. 1995. "The Productivity Effects of Employee Stock-Ownership Plans and Bonuses: Evidence from Japanese Panel Data." *American Economic Review*, Vol. 85, no. 3 (June), pp. 391-414.

Joskow, Paul. 1985. "Vertical Integration and Long-term Contracts: The Case of Coal-Burning Electric Generating Plants." *Journal of Law, Economics, and Organization*, Vol. 1, pp. 33-80.

Kennan, John, and Robert Wilson. 1990. "Theories of Bargaining Delays." *Science*, Vol. 249 (September 7), pp. 1124-128.

_____. 1993. "Bargaining with Private Information." *Journal of Economic Literature*, Vol. 31 (March), pp. 45-104.

Klein, Benjamin. 1991. "Vertical Integration as Organizational Ownership." In O. Williamson and S. Winter, eds., *The Nature of the Firm: Origins, Evolution, and Development*. New York: Oxford University Press, pp. 213-26.

Klein, Benjamin, Robert Crawford, and Armen Alchian. 1978. "Vertical Integration, Appropriable Rents, and the Competitive Contracting Process." *Journal of Law and Economics*, Vol. 21 (October), pp. 297-326.

Kreps, David M. 1990. "Corporate Culture and Economic Theory." In J. Alt and K. Shepsle, eds., *Perspectives on Positive Political Economy*. New York: Cambridge University Press.

Kruse, Douglas. 1993. *Profit Sharing: Does It Make a Difference?* Kalamazoo, MI: W.E. Upjohn Institute for Employment Research.

Lang, Kevin, and Shulamit Kahn. 1990. "Efficiency Wage Models of Unemployment: A Second View." *Economic Inquiry*, Vol. 28 (April), pp. 296-306.

Leibenstein, Harvey. 1987. *Inside the Firm: The Inefficiencies of Hierarchy*. Cambridge, MA: Harvard University Press.

Levine, David I. 1995. *Reinventing the Workplace: How Business and Employees Can Both Win*. Washington, DC: Brookings.

Levine, David I., and Richard J. Parkin. 1994. "Work Organization, Employment Security, and Macroeconomic Stability." *Journal of Economic Behavior and Organization*, Vol. 24, no. 3 (August), pp. 251-71.

MacLeod, W. Bentley. 1984. "A Theory of Cooperative Teams." CORE Discussion Paper No. 8441, Universite Catholique de Louvain.

_____. 1988. "Equity, Efficiency, and Incentives in Cooperative Teams." *Advances in the Economic Analysis of Participatory and Labor-Managed Firms*, Vol. 3. JAI Press, Inc., pp. 5-23.

MacLeod, W. Bentley, and James M. Malcomson. 1989. "Implicit Contracts, Incentive Compatibility, and Involuntary Unemployment." *Econometrica*, Vol. 57, no. 2 (March), pp. 447-80.

_____. 1993. "Wage Premiums and Profit Maximization in Efficiency Wage Models." *European Economic Review*, Vol. 37, no. 6 (August), pp. 1223-49.

Marglin, Stephen A. 1974. "What Do Bosses Do? The Origins and Functions of Hierarchy in Capitalist Production." *Review of Radical Political Economy*, Vol. 6, no. 2 (Summer), pp. 60-112.

Mas-Colell, Andreu, Michael D. Whinston, and Jerry R. Green. 1995. *Microeconomic Theory*. New York: Oxford University Press.

Masten, Scott E. 1984. "The Organization of Production: Evidence from the Aerospace Industry." *Journal of Law and Economics*, Vol. 27, pp. 402-17.

Menard, Claude. 1994. "Organizations as Coordinating Devices." *Metroeconomica*, Vol. 45, no. 3, pp. 224-47.

Miceli, Thomas J., and Alanson P. Minkler. 1995. "Transfer Uncertainty and Organizational Choice." *Advances in the Economic Analysis of Participatory and Labor-Managed Firms*, pp. 121-37.

Milgrom, Paul, and John Roberts. 1990a. "Bargaining Costs, Influence Costs, and the Organization of Economic Activity." In James E. Alt and Kenneth A. Shepsle, eds., *Perspectives on Positive Political Economy*. New York: Cambridge University Press.

_____. 1990b. "The Economics of Modern Manufacturing: Technology, Strategy, and Organization." *American Economic Review*, Vol. 80, no. 3 (June), pp. 511-28.

_____. 1992. *Economics, Organization, and Management*. Englewood Cliffs, NJ: Prentice-Hall.

Miller, Gary J. 1992. *Managerial Dilemmas: The Political Economy of Hierarchy*. New York: Cambridge University Press.

Murphy, Kevin M., and Robert H. Topel. 1987. "Unemployment, Risk, and Earnings: Testing for Equalizing Wage Differences in the Labor Market." In K. Lang and J. S. Leonard, eds., *Unemployment and the Structure of Labor Markets*. New York: Basil Blackwell, pp. 103-40.

Nelson, Richard, and Sidney G. Winter. 1982. *An Evolutionary Theory of Economic Change*. Cambridge, MA: Harvard University Press.

Osborne, Martin, and Ariel Rubinstein. 1990. *Bargaining and Markets*. New York: Academic Press.

Plott, Charles. 1967. "A Notion of Equilibrium and Its Possibility under Majority Rule." *American Economic Review*, Vol. 57 (September), pp. 787-806.

Putterman, Louis. 1984. "On Some Recent Explanations of Why Capital Hires Labor." *Economic Inquiry*, Vol. 22 (April), pp. 171-87.

Putterman, Louis, and Randall S. Kroszner, eds. 1996. *The Economic Nature of the Firm: A Reader*. 2d ed. New York: Cambridge University Press.

Putterman, Louis, and Gilbert Skillman. 1992. "The Role of Exit in the Theory of Cooperative Teams." *Journal of Comparative Economics*, Vol. 16, pp. 596-618.

Raff, Daniel M. G., and Lawrence H. Summers. 1987. "Did Henry Ford Pay Efficiency Wages?" *Journal of Labor Economics*, Vol 5, no. 4, part 2, pp. S57-S86.

Rasmusen, Eric. 1994. *Games and Information*. 2d ed. Oxford: Blackwell.

Rebitzer, James B. 1993. "Radical Political Economy and the Economics of Labor Markets." *Journal of Economic Literature*, Vol. 31, no. 3 (September), pp. 1394-1434.

Richardson, G. B. 1972. "The Organization of Industry." *Economic Journal*, Vol. 82, pp. 883-96.

Rock, Edward B., and Michael L. Wachter. 1996. "The Enforceability of Norms and the Employment Relationship." *University of Pennsylvania Law Review*, Vol. 144, no. 1, pp. 1-40.

Rosen, Sherwin. 1986. "The Theory of Equalizing Differences." In O. Ashenfelter and R. Layard, eds., *Handbook of Labor Economics*. Vol. 1. New York: North-Holland.

_____. 1991. "Transactions Costs and Internal Labor Markets." In O. Williamson and S. Winter, eds., *The Nature of the Firm: Origins, Evolution, and Development*. New York: Oxford University Press, pp. 75-89.

Sappington, David E. M. 1991. "Incentives in Principal-Agent Relationships." *Journal of Economic Perspectives*, Vol. 5, no. 2 (Spring), pp. 45-66.

Schelling, Thomas C. 1960. *The Strategy of Conflict*. Cambridge, MA: Harvard University Press.

Shapiro, Carl, and Joseph E. Stiglitz. 1984. "Equilibrium Unemployment as a Worker Discipline Device." *American Economic Review*, Vol. 74, no. 4 (September), pp. 433-44.

Shleifer, Andrei, and Lawrence Summers. 1988. "Breach of Trust in Hostile Takeovers." In A. Auerbach, ed., *Corporate Takeovers: Causes and Consequences*. Chicago: University of Chicago Press.

Simon, Herbert. 1951. "A Formal Theory of the Employment Relationship." *Econometrica*, Vol. 19 (July), pp. 293-305.

Skillman, Gilbert, and Greg Dow. 1996. "Collective Choice and Equilibrium Firm Ownership." Unpublished manuscript, Department of Economics, Wesleyan University.

Skillman, Gilbert, and Harl E. Ryder. 1993. "Wage Bargaining and the Choice of Technique in Capitalist Firms." In S. Bowles, H. Gintis, and B. Gustafsson, eds., *Markets and Democracy: Participation, Accountability and Efficiency*. New York: Cambridge University Press, pp. 217-27.

Smith, Adam. 1994. *The Wealth of Nations*. New York: Modern Library Edition.

Smith, Stephen C. 1991. "On the Economic Rationale for Codetermination Law." *Journal of Economic Behavior and Organization*, Vol. 1, pp. 261-81.

Stiglitz, Joseph E. 1987. "The Causes and Consequences of the Dependence of Quality on Price." *Journal of Economic Literature*, Vol. 25 (March), pp. 1-48.

_____. 1993. "Post Walrasian and Post Marxian Economics." *Journal of Economic Perspectives*, Vol. 7, no. 1 (Winter), pp. 109-14.

Wachter, Michael L., and Randall D. Wright. 1990. "The Economics of Internal Labor Markets." *Industrial Relations*, Vol. 29, no. 2 (Spring), pp. 240-62.

Wadhwani, Sushil B., and Martin Wall. 1990. "The Effects of Profit Sharing on Employment, Wages, Stock Returns and Productivity: Evidence from U.K. Micro Data." *Economic Journal*, Vol. 100 (March), pp. 1-17.

Weibull, Jorgen W. 1995. *Evolutionary Game Theory*. Cambridge, MA: MIT Press.

Weiss, Andrew. 1990. *Efficiency Wages*. Princeton, NJ: Princeton University Press.

Weitzman, Martin L. 1984. *The Share Economy: Conquering Stagflation*. Cambridge, MA: Harvard University Press.

Weitzman, Martin, and Douglas Kruse. 1990. "Profit Sharing and Productivity." In A. Blinder, ed., *Paying for Productivity*. Washington, DC: Brookings Institution.

Williamson, Oliver E. 1975. *Markets and Hierarchies*. New York: Free Press.

_____. 1979. "Transaction-Cost Economics: The Governance of Contractual Relations." *Journal of Law and Economics*, Vol. 22 (October), pp. 233-61.

_____. 1980. "The Organization of Work: A Comparative Institutional Assessment." *Journal of Economic Behavior and Organization*, Vol. 1, pp. 5-38.

_____. 1985. *The Economic Institutions of Capitalism*. New York: Free Press.

_____. 1987. "Transaction Cost Economics: The Comparative Contracting Perspective." *Journal of Economic Behavior and Organization*, Vol. 8 (December), pp. 617-25.

_____. 1991. "Comparative Economic Organization: The Analysis of Discrete Structural Alternatives." *Administrative Science Quarterly*, Vol. 36, no. 2 (June), pp. 269-96.

_____. 1993. "Contested Exchange versus the Governance of Contractual Relations." *Journal of Economic Perspectives*, Vol. 7, no. 1 (Winter), pp. 103-08.

_____. 1996. "Efficiency, Power, Authority and Economic Organization." In J. Groenewegen, ed., *Transaction Cost Economics and Beyond*. Boston: Kluwer Academic Publishers, pp. 11-42.

Williamson, Oliver E., Michael Wachter, and Jeffrey Harris. 1975. "Understanding the Employment Relation." *Bell Journal of Economics*, Vol. 6 (Spring), pp. 250-78.

Williamson, Oliver E., and Sidney G. Winter, eds. 1991. *The Nature of the Firm: Origins, Evolution, and Development*. New York: Oxford University Press.

# Chapter 3

# The Law and Economics Approach to Workplace Regulation

Stewart J. Schwab
*Cornell University*

The economics invasion of labor law scholarship began over a decade ago. (See Posner 1984, noting the paucity of labor law and economics scholarship; Schwab 1989, warning of the invasion.) The last decade has seen economics claim more and more territory, particularly in the distinct field of nonunion "employment law." Indeed, the current critical mass of labor law and economics scholars enables them to fight their own civil wars about the proper law and economics approach to various issues. This chapter attempts to survey the current landscape. (For an earlier survey of labor law and economics scholarship, see Moore 1991.)

I will not comprehensively survey all labor law articles that arguably could be labeled law and economics (L&E). That might demonstrate the growing size of the field, but not much else. Instead, I will be selective. My goal is to show how a L&E approach can help us understand, evaluate, and reform labor and employment policy. Law and economics has matured and is no longer viewed as weird or esoteric. Its terminology and conceptions (such as transaction costs, cheapest cost avoider, and the like) are part of general legal discourse. The acculturation is slower in labor and employment law than in common law fields but is clearly visible. Judges and Board officials deciding labor cases, perhaps more attuned to the costs as well as the benefits of policies than they were a couple of decades ago, are reflecting the approach of law and economics in their decisions. So the L&E approach has its "real-world" impact on labor law.

Let me make a quick note on terminology at the outset. I will discuss the L&E approach both to labor law, meaning the laws regulating trade unions, and to employment law, which covers all other regulation of the workplace. Much of the discussion can be done together, for the L&E methodology is similar for both fields. For convenience I will sometimes use the term "labor law" to include "employment law" as well, relying on context to make my meaning clear.

## A Quick Intellectual History of Law and Economics

Economic analysis of law has been around for more than a century. Jeremy Bentham's utilitarian analysis of law, advocating laws that maximize pleasure over pain, is a clear antecedent. (For a comparison of Bentham and modern L&E, see Posner 1981:Ch. 2.) More recently than Bentham, but still a long while ago, Justice Oliver Wendell Holmes, Jr. made future L&E scholars happy with his famous aphorism on the importance of economics to the study of law: "For the rational study of the law the black-letter man may be the man of the present, but the man of the future is the man of statistics and the master of economics" (Holmes 1897:469). For the first half of this century, however, economic analysis of law was largely relegated to antitrust and regulated industries, legal areas that invited an economics approach. Those laws were explicitly concerned with promoting or regulating competition. Some knowledge of competition, price theory, efficiency, and the like naturally provided insights into law. This is the old law and economics.

The new law and economics, by contrast, analyzes areas of law that do not, on their face, acknowledge the relevance of economics concepts. The traditional dating of the new law and economics comes with the famous articles by Coase (1960) and Calabresi (1961). Both explored whether the common law promotes an efficient allocation of resources. Law and economics blossomed a decade later when Richard Posner began systematically applying economic analysis to many detailed doctrines of the common law. The first edition of Posner's book, *An Economic Analysis of Law*, appeared in 1972. It demonstrated the power and reach of the new approach. Posner unflinchingly applied economic analysis to family law and corporate law and everything in between.

In the beginning, most traditional legal scholars were skeptical that the common law either promoted efficiency or should try to do so. Law and economics was one of several trendy movements in the 1970s applying insights from other disciplines to law. Critical legal studies received much attention as well. CLS scholars, applying insights from German philosophy, declared that embedded within law were "fundamental contradictions" and that the dominant legal paradigms reflected the power of elite groups in society. "Law is politics" became a famous if over-simplified embodiment of CLS thinking. (For an excellent synthesis of CLS thinking and its relationship to the L&E approach, see Kelman 1987.) Feminist legal theory arose a little later. That approach emphasizes that many assumptions of law embody, more or less openly, a male-centered approach to problems. A quick employment-law example comes from the requirements needed to qualify for unemployment insurance benefits. A prime-age worker with steady, full-time work who is suddenly discharged without his fault clearly qualifies for unemployment benefits.

This describes a typical male worker. His spouse who quits work to follow him in his new job, or who is a part-time worker, or who is fired or quits because of child-care problems, has much greater difficulties qualifying for benefits. Unemployment insurance law was not designed with her problems in mind. (For a review of the problems, see Willborn et al. 1993.)

All these various approaches to legal issues give insights. But today, L&E ideas have become integrated, far more than the other schools, into mainstream legal analysis. It is no longer exceptional to have L&E scholars on a law faculty, and fewer academics are concerned with whether a scholar is a card-carrying L&E scholar (I suppose the card might be membership in the American Law and Economics Association or its Canadian, European or South American counterparts), a fellow traveler, or merely a dabbler. Awareness of and interest in L&E issues is increasing for all scholars interested in law, of whatever discipline or label.

Of course, economic analysis has progressed further in some fields than others. No corporate lawyer, for example, could be up to date without considerable familiarity with such L&E ideas as principal-agent problems and the market for corporate control. Every tort lawyer should be familiar with ideas like cheapest cost avoider. Economic analysis in labor law has been slower and remains controversial. Still, the hostility to an economic approach to labor law is lessening as the approach is seen to have practical, real-world applications. In the next section I discuss how basic L&E principles apply to the analysis of labor laws. In the following sections I sketch particular analyses of labor and employment law. Finally, I attempt some general conclusions.

## Basic Principles of Law and Economics as Applied to Labor Law

Law and economics is, as the name suggests, a blend of legal and economic analysis. The L&E research I will describe here is more accurately described as economic analysis of law. It uses economics concepts to examine specific legal doctrines. Metaphorically, it gazes from the land of economics toward the land of law. Often the economic tools are basic or even primitive (binoculars or eyeglasses, if you will), such as the concepts of downward-sloping demand curves and opportunity costs. Fancier concepts (telescopes, to continue the metaphor) such as game theory and asymmetric information can be used as well.

Not all L&E adherents have thought they were using economics to examine law. Founding figure Ronald Coase is the most prominent counter-example. In a well-known statement that puzzled many scholars in law schools, Coase proclaimed that he was not interested in law but only in economics. In his words, "I have no interest in lawyers or legal education. . . . My interest is in economics. . . . I do think some knowledge of legal institutions is essential for economists working in certain areas, but it's what it does to economists that interests me, not what it does to lawyers" (Kitch 1983:192-93 [quoting Coase]). Most L&E figures (certainly those in law schools having to justify their keep, although much of Coase's career also was spent in a law school rather than an economics department) would claim that law rather than economics is their prime focus. Of course, Ronald Coase won his Nobel Prize in economics, not in law. Richard Posner, if he ever wins a Nobel Prize (which I would like to see), will do so for applying economic concepts to law, not the other way around.

Most law and economics analysis follows the general method pioneered by Posner. It describes a rule of law that may seem arbitrary, obscure, or worse and argues that the rule enhances an efficient allocation of resources, compared to other possible legal rules. If an efficiency analysis cannot be tortured into claiming the legal rule is consistent with efficiency, then the rule is criticized on that ground. This L&E methodology differs, in style at least, from the more formal style of economics. An applied microeconomist (including a labor economist) typically creates an economic model to predict behavior (which could include how actors will react to a labor law rule) and then examines whether a data set confirms the predictions. Below I highlight the critical features of L&E analysis.

## Efficient Legal Rules

Many economists use (or say they use) a concept of Pareto efficiency in describing an efficient state of affairs. A state is Pareto efficient if no one would be better off in another state without someone being worse off. As a criterion for legal reform, Pareto efficiency is extremely limiting, because few legal changes can occur without hurting some established interest.

Most law and economics analysts use a looser concept of efficiency known as Kaldor-Hicks efficiency. A law is efficient if it allows resources to be allocated to the person who values them most highly. The highest-valued user is defined as the person willing and able to pay the most for an item. Under this approach, one legal rule is more efficient than another if the gainers under the rule would still be better off after fully compensating the losers. Actual compensation does not have to be made. (If it were, the law would be Pareto superior to the other one, because the move would have no losers.) Kaldor-Hicks efficiency, as I have defined it, is identical to wealth maximization, a term favored by Posner. The key element of this definition is the willingness-and-ability-to-pay criterion. The Kaldor-Hicks, wealth maximization, willingness-and-ability-to-pay definition of efficiency can also be phrased in terms of cost-benefit analysis. Compared to an alternative law, the law under analysis benefits certain people and harms others. If the benefits to some exceed the costs to others, then the law is more efficient than its alternative. Again, all costs and benefits are measured in terms of willingness and ability to pay.

Consider this example. Suppose workers value a new safety law at $3, meaning that they are willing and able to pay up to $3 for the safety (perhaps through a reduction in the wage). The law would cost the firm $2 to implement with no countervailing benefit to the firm in productivity, so the firm is willing and able to pay up to $2 to avoid it. To keep the efficiency discussion simple, let us suppose, counter to fact, that the law would not trigger offsetting changes in wages or number of jobs. The new law is efficient. Workers could compensate employers for the change by accepting a $2 reduction in wages and still be better off. Put in cost-benefit terms, the cost to the firm of the new law is $2 and the benefits to workers is $3, so the benefits outweigh the costs. The cost-benefit calculus becomes more complicated when wage and employment effects are factored in, but the overall question remains the same: Do the overall gains outweigh the overall costs?

Technical problems can arise with this wealth-maximization view of efficiency. Perhaps most problematic is whether value should be measured as the minimum amount someone is willing to accept to give up a right, or the maximum amount someone will pay to obtain a new right. These offer and asking amounts are the same, in economic theory at least, for a profit-maximizing firm that has no budget constraints. But wealth effects for consumers can cause the offer and asking price to diverge. In addition, framing effects and other psychological heuristics can cause offer and asking prices to diverge. In our example, workers were willing and able to pay $3 for a new safety measure, but they may demand $4 to give up the same safety measure once implemented. In many cases, these wealth effects and framing effects will not change the efficiency conclusion: A rule might be efficient under either measurement. But if these effects are great enough, the wealth-maximization criterion may be unable to declare whether the rule is efficient. (For an excellent introduction to various definitions of efficiency, see Coleman 1980.)

## Efficiency and Ethics

More important than the technical problems are the values embedded within the wealth-maximization criterion. As Dworkin (1980) has shown, wealth maximization cannot be an end in itself, but at best is instrumental in achieving other goals. The basic goal of wealth maximization is to further the well being of individuals in society. Wealth maximization thus has important connections with utilitarianism, which for all its faults remains the basic philosophy underlying much of the legal system. The goal of law, from a utilitarian perspective, is to obtain "the greatest good for the greatest number," to use Bentham's phrase. Utilitarianism treats all members of society as equals, in that the utility and disutility of each member (or pleasure and pain of each member, to use the older vocabulary) gets equal weight.

One problem with utilitarianism is the difficulty in determining who gets the most utility from a specific item. (Indeed, the difficulties in interpersonal comparisons spurred the development of the Pareto criterion.) Wealth maximization tries to escape this difficulty by using willingness and ability to pay as a common metric. Anyone can want a benefit in the abstract (or profess to gain utility from it), but the L&E approach requires them to put their money where their mouth is. For example, workers may say they like protection against striker replacements, but only if they will accept a dollar less in wages will such protection be counted as a dollar gain to them. Because of the formal symmetry of the efficiency approach, of course, only if employers are willing to pay for the right to replace strikers with a dollar in wages will striker protection be counted as a dollar loss for employers.

The link between utilitarianism and wealth maximization is close, for generally a wealth-increasing move increases utility as well. People generally are willing to pay more for an item if they get more utility from it. For example, someone willing and able to pay $1,000 for a book probably derives more utility from it than someone willing and able to pay only $2. The wealth-maximizing move would give the first person the book, and this would probably increase utility as well. When the numbers are $3 and $2, the wealth-maximizing principle still awards the book to the first person, but whether this award increases utility is more doubtful. (For a discussion of the links between utilitarianism and wealth maximization, including a debate over these book examples, see Dworkin 1980 and Posner 1981.) The divergence between wealth and utility maximization usually comes from wealth maximization's "ability to pay" test. Someone with limited assets or entitlements is not able to pay for the item, even if he could be said to be willing to pay. Thus wealth maximization seems to favor the wealthy.

Two general responses can reduce the sting of the criticism of wealth maximization. First, as mentioned above the willingness-to-pay criterion can ask how much a person would demand to part with a right. For example, in analyzing the efficiency of safety laws we could ask how much workers would demand to agree to waive their right to safety, rather than ask how much they would pay to obtain a right to safety. This endowment itself ameliorates disparities in wealth.

Second, many legal rules, particularly those outside labor law, have little visible effect on income distribution. If so, a wealth maximization criterion is benign. For example, consider a law that holds strictly liable the rear car in an automobile accident (on the ground that the driver should be able to stop). Imagine that this rule is the wealth-maximizing rule in that, compared to alternative rules, it benefits front drivers more than it harms rear drivers. It matters little that all the benefits of this rule go to front drivers, because sometimes a driver will be the front car and sometimes the rear car. A rule that minimizes the overall costs of accidents is a good rule for all drivers.

Even if the willingness-and-ability-to-pay criterion underlying efficiency analysis is acceptable in other legal fields where winners and losers have less clear identities, it remains controversial for labor law. Unlike car drivers, workers rarely change places with owners (although worker pension funds own much of corporate America). It is harder to defend a rule on the grounds that overall benefits exceed costs, if the benefits go to management and the costs go to workers.

The objection to the willingness-and-ability-to-pay criterion might be articulated this way. Workers are human beings whose welfare is an ultimate value, while the wealth of employers (particularly the reified corporate employer) is at best merely instrumental to the welfare of others. It is inappropriate to evaluate both groups by the same willingness-to-pay test. So what if workers only value a particular law at $2, while the cost to management is $3? Since workers are human and management is not (except in their individual, nonreified role as workers who manage), the law is good even if inefficient.

The law and economics approach offers three ripostes to "only workers matter." First, and least convincing for the skeptic, L&E scholars sometimes put a human face on the corporate employer. They point out that human shareholders ultimately own the corporation and that workers through their pension funds are major shareholders. Thus inflicting costs on the corporate employer is a human cost. Second, corporations and corporate shareholders do not bear all the costs of a legal rule that favors workers. The costs are often passed on to consumers through higher prices. Thus, if a labor rule is inefficient, consumers can suffer large harms while workers gain only a little. This second riposte is unlikely to persuade the skeptic either. Consumers should pay for the costs of, say, preventing workplace injuries, even if they exceed the safety benefits to workers.

The final riposte should be most troubling to skeptics: Workers themselves are the people most often hurt by inefficient legal rules. Wages will fall if a legal rule requires employers to bear additional costs in hiring workers. If the rule is inefficient under the cost-benefit calculus, wages will fall by more than the workers are willing to pay for the rule. Thus, for example, suppose a safety regulation is inefficient because workers would willingly pay only 50 cents for it, but the regulation costs them a dollar in wages. Mandating this safety regulation in order to favor the poor workers, for example, may well harm rather than benefit them. Greater safety regulation can dry up jobs, putting the poor safely out of work. Often, the poor are more likely to benefit from income redistribution through the tax system than from alterations in substantive laws. In summarizing this final riposte, then, the L&E scholar accuses others of being paternalistic toward workers.

## The Neutrality of Labor L&E Analysis

In the prior discussion defending the willingness-and-ability-to-pay criterion, the law and economics approach was on the defensive. But the neutrality of L&E analysis can be put in a more positive light.

Labor law is a polarized field. Labor lawyers are either management side or union side. Their litigation brings victories for management or workers. Labor law scholars applaud or denounce these legal victories depending on their alignment (most scholars, I would say, align with unions). Rarely do traditional labor law scholars self-consciously separate a positive analysis (the law is) from normative analysis (the law should be).

Labor law and economics attempts to rise above this "with us or against us" ideology. The starting point is not "labor should win" or "management should win," as so often seems the case for other types of labor law scholarship. Rather, L&E scholars examine whether a particular labor doctrine promotes efficiency. Do the overall gains to society of the rule outweigh the costs? For example, consider a choice between rule X (e.g., forbid permanent replacements for strikers) and rule not-X (e.g., allow permanent replacements for strikers). If the gains to workers of rule X outweigh the costs to employers, L&E scholars say rule X is positively efficient or normatively good. Conversely, if the costs to employers exceed the gains to workers, rule X is inefficient/bad.

## Positive and Normative Analysis

A well-done law and economics analysis separates its positive and normative analysis in a self-conscious way. A certain law may or may not promote efficiency, compared to its alternatives. This is a positive issue of what the law achieves. In principle, even persons who disagree about whether wealth maximization is a good criterion for evaluating laws can agree on whether a particular law puts legal entitlements in the hands of those willing and able to pay the most for it, thereby maximizing wealth.

One advantage of the law and economics approach to labor law over traditional approaches is that its professed neutrality allows it to engage in a positive analysis of labor law more easily. As a positive description of current labor law, neither management nor labor always wins. For example, while labor law allows employers permanently to replace strikers, it forbids employers from giving super seniority to these replacements. Much of the L&E project attempts to explain this checkered won/loss record as the result of differing conclusions, depending on the particular doctrine at issue, of the cost-benefit balance. Scholars approaching labor law from an avowedly pro-worker perspective (or, more rarely in academics, from an avowedly pro-management perspective) have great difficulty explaining why workers sometimes win cases and sometimes lose. They can only critique the law.

True, many labor law and economics scholars do not accept the positive project as primary. Epstein (1983), for example, does not explain any aspect of current labor law as being pro-efficiency. Indeed, he has urged us to scrap the entire NLRA and return to the common law of union regulation. In part Epstein argues on libertarian grounds (showing he may not be a card-carrying L&E scholar). But he also accepts the basic efficiency or cost-benefit framework outlined above. In his calculus, the costs of the NLRA to workers, employers, and consumers alike outweigh its benefits. (Epstein is more nuanced about current employment law, finding merit in some of the tort actions for wrongful discharge in violation of public policy. See Epstein 1984:952, note 11.)

## Commensurability

As described above, an efficient law allows resources to go to the person willing and able to pay the most for it. This presumes that people are willing and able to set a "price" on legal entitlements. One common but erroneous criticism is that the insistence on a price means that the willingness-to-pay criterion only values money or material goods. The criticism is misplaced. The L&E approach recognizes that workers value job security, healthy working conditions, industrial democracy, and self-fulfillment as well as wages, vacations, health insurance and pensions. What the L&E approach does insist is that all these valued items are commensurable. (See, generally, Sunstein 1995.) Workers can rank these items, at least in principle, on a scale of more important or less important, and they are willing to trade the less important for the more important. In other words, workers want self-fulfillment on the job, but if self-fulfillment becomes too costly they prefer higher wages instead. Additionally, the L&E approach emphasizes that most of these items can be traded on the margin: a little more self-fulfillment for slightly smaller wages.

## The Coase Theorem and Transaction Costs

One of the central points of the law and economics approach is that law should not be viewed as forbidding certain activities but as simply putting a price on them. (Of course, if the price is too high no one will engage in it.)

People willing to pay the penalties set by law (be they fines, imprisonment, damages, injunctions, or whatever) will still engage in an activity. This idea comes from Holmes's "bad man" view of the law. The law states the consequences of a certain action but does not forbid it if someone is willing to pay the price. This conception, which focuses attention on legal remedies, is familiar to many labor scholars. Indeed, the NLRA is regularly criticized for weak remedies so that it remains in an employer's interest, for example, to fire a suspected union organizer despite the legal prohibition. (See Weiler 1983.) Under the L&E approach, this employer is simply weighing the benefits of firing a worker against its costs, as determined by the law against discriminatory dismissals. Moral sermons imploring the employer to obey the law will change nothing, but altering the employer's economic incentives will change behavior. (For a criticism of this "bad man" view of law, see Nonce 1997.)

The modern reformulation of this idea asserts that initial legal rights or entitlements do not affect the efficiency of final outcomes, as long as parties can bargain with each other over these entitlements. If the law does not initially award an entitlement to the highest valued user, the initial entitlement holder will trade it to someone who values it more highly. This insight is the famous Coase Theorem (Coase 1960). In many cases, private bargaining around initial legal entitlements makes the law less powerful or less important than it may initially seem.

Although parties have a strong incentive to bargain around inefficient rules (otherwise, they are jointly throwing away money), they cannot reach efficient bargains if transaction costs are too high. This is the prime message of Coase (1960). In the early days of L&E analysis, the prime bargaining costs were thought to arise from multiple parties. The factory could not bargain with the residents about pollution because of the high transaction costs, including free-rider and holdout problems, of getting lots of residents together. More recently, scholars have emphasized that strategic bargaining problems can prevent deals between two parties stuck with each other. Thus transaction costs can arise with either few or many actors. Today, L&E scholars recognize a wide range of transaction costs that might prevent parties on their own from reaching efficient solutions. These include problems of asymmetric information and collective goods. L&E scholars are skeptical of one concept that scholars from other disciplines emphasize. This is the concept of unequal bargaining power as an explanation for labor and employment law. In a later section, I will explain in some detail the L&E view of unequal bargaining power. For now, I simply say that L&E scholars are skeptical of any claim that unequal bargaining power is a transaction cost that prevents legal entitlements from being traded to the person willing and able to pay the most for it.

*Free Markets*

So far, I have said nothing about the economic approach preferring free markets, a view commonly associated with law and economics. Belief in free markets is not an essential ingredient to labor law and economics. Still, it is fair to say that L&E scholars generally believe that free markets or free bargaining is generally preferable to government mandates. This is not a fundamental result but is derivative of the fact that, in a freely bargained contract, items are likely to go to the party that values them most highly. (Strategic bargaining or other transaction costs can prevent these optimal contracts, but that gets ahead of our story.) For example, suppose a prior collective bargaining agreement called for $10 in wages and (perhaps implicitly) kept the *Mackay Radio* rule allowing the employer to replace strikers. In the next contract the employer explicitly promised not to replace strikers in return for $9 in wages. This trade strongly suggests that workers valued the entitlement at more than a dollar, while it cost the employer less than a dollar. Trading the striker-replacement entitlement to workers, then, was value enhancing (it increased the joint pie). L&E scholars find this convincing because they generally assume that parties rarely agree to something that is not in their best interest. Allowing trade allows value-enhancing bargains.

A major operating assumption of law and economics scholars, then, is that trades embodied in contracts, including collective bargaining contracts or individual employment contracts, generally increase utility for both parties. Labor law should generally allow parties to bargain over any subject. Restated more controversially, labor law should have few inalienable rights or presumptions.

Law and economics scholars recognize two limitations on the free-bargaining-is-good presumption. First, in some situations contracts might not enhance value for one or both sides. For example, misinformed workers might agree to a level of safety that reduces their welfare (even ignoring the regret when things turn out worse than one expected), compared to safety levels mandated by more informed safety experts. The labor L&E project attempts to identify situations where private contracts may not enhance value.

The second major caveat to the belief-in-contracting assumption is that failure to contract does not necessarily imply that a contract would not enhance value. Transactions costs of many types can prevent parties from consummating value-enhancing trades. Return to the *Mackay Radio* example. Suppose the parties bargained, but the employer refused to waive its *Mackay Radio* right to replace strikers permanently. This might imply that the benefits of the *Mackay Radio* rule to the employer exceed the costs to workers. But it might imply only that high transaction costs have prevented the employer from waiving its *Mackay Radio* right. Much of the labor L&E project comes in identifying possible transaction costs that prevent value-enhancing trades. In our example such costs are easy to imagine. In particular, adverse selection problems may prevent parties from correctly determining the relative costs and benefits. Imagine what an employer must wonder when the union demands a promise not to replace strikers. "The union must be seriously contemplating a strike" is the employer's natural suspicion. If so, the employer's cost to waiving its right goes up. A union not contemplating a strike, but simply wanting protection against permanent replacements should the need for a strike unexpectedly arise, cannot easily convince the employer of its benign motives for wanting the clause. When transaction costs prevent bargains, initial legal entitlements become final legal entitlements. The law then affects outcomes in ways that "free markets," because of transaction costs, cannot overcome.

In sum, a law and economics approach does not simplistically denounce all regulation of labor markets. It recognizes that unregulated labor markets are not perfect: imperfect information problems, including adverse selection and moral hazard, are very real; transaction costs are often high; optimal risk sharing is difficult. These are the types of market failure that lead L&E scholars to consider whether regulation might be efficient.

But enough of general frameworks. I turn now to specific works by labor and employment L&E scholars, through which I hope to illustrate some of the common themes and problems of the economics approach to workplace regulation.

## Labor Law and Economics

Law and economics scholars have analyzed a variety of doctrines and policies contained in the National Labor Relations Act. I will discuss the scholarship in three areas, ignoring many other interesting L&E inquiries. First, I discuss the basic goals of Congress in enacting the NLRA and whether efficiency was an important or perhaps even prime goal. Second, I discuss how basic interpretations of the NLRA follow from various visions of unions. Third, I turn to the L&E interpretation of collective bargaining.

### Efficiency as a Goal of the NLRA

One basic question is whether the NLRA has efficiency as a goal. To repeat, the efficiency framework of labor L&E assumes that individual labor doctrines, as a positive matter, can (best) be understood as promoting gains over losses as measured by willingness to pay, and as a normative matter, that labor doctrine should be applauded or denounced by whether it correctly awards entitlements based on this cost-benefit calculus. This efficiency goal is not one clearly articulated (to put it mildly) by the act or by most commentators. Traditional views of the NLRA generally emphasize goals such as industrial peace or the equalization of bargaining power. Behind these goals is the basic policy of supporting unions and collective bargaining, a goal that remains even after the 1947 Taft-Hartley amendments announced a policy of government neutrality in labor relations. None of these goals is self-evidently connected with efficiency. With these as the stated statutory goals, how can L&E scholars get their framework off the ground?

*Macroeconomic efficiency.* One approach emphasizes the Keynesian, macroeconomic goals of the NLRA. Kaufman (1996) reminds us that backers promoted the NLRA as a way of raising workers' wages, thereby increasing aggregate demand and spurring more production in the economy. In other words, supporting unions not only benefitted workers but improved the general economy as well, and thereby was an efficiency-enhancing statute. Other scholars have suggested even more dramatic meta-efficiency effects of the NLRA. By appeasing labor, these scholars suggest, the NLRA may have staved off a violent revolution with all the attending chaos and suffering. Whatever their merits in the 1930s, these macroeconomic or meta-efficiency justifications for the NLRA no longer seem compelling. Central banks and other institutions seem more capable than the NLRA at controlling business cycles; the specter of an American proletariat revolution seems quaint today. To explain how the NLRA might promote efficiency, L&E scholars must turn elsewhere.

*Microeconomic efficiency.* Law and economics scholars have spent more time assessing the doctrinal details of labor law, examining as a positive matter whether they are consistent with efficiency. One puzzle is figuring out what mechanism could drive individual doctrines toward efficiency. If the statute commanded the Board and courts to create efficient rules, perhaps efficient rules could result. But as we just discussed, express efficiency goals are hard to find in the labor laws. Before L&E scholars can convince others that particular labor doctrines promote efficiency, some description of the process leading to efficient rules is necessary.

This challenge is harder for labor L&E scholars than for L&E scholars examining the common law, although the basic problem is similar. Common law judges rarely justify legal doctrine on efficiency grounds, and the claim that judicial decisions enhance efficiency seems implausible at first blush. L&E scholars often claim that efficient rules emerge nevertheless. (See generally Posner 1992.) Labor L&E scholars, however, are under a double bind. Not only is it hard to explain why common law rules promote efficiency, but many L&E scholars sharply distinguish common law from legislative statutes and declare that statutes generally are inefficient wealth transfers.

Hylton (1993) has taken on the challenge most directly. He analyzes the economic models that explain when common law rules have a tendency toward efficiency. (For detailed assessments of mechanisms and situations by which the common law tends toward efficiency, see Rubin 1983; Cooter and Kornhauser 1980.) Hylton argues that NLRB decisions have a similar tendency toward efficiency. Hylton emphasizes that the case-by-case process of NLRB adjudication is structurally similar to common law litigation and thus leads to a similar trend to relitigate inefficient rules until they are overturned and efficient rules take their place. By definition, an inefficient NLRB rule imposes higher costs on the harmed party than it benefits the other side. The party challenging the inefficient rule thus is willing to spend more to overturn the rule than the other side is willing to spend to defend it. Over time, then, more inefficient NLRB rules than efficient rules will be challenged, appealed, and overturned. The resulting "stock" of NLRB rules will tend to be efficient.

## The NLRA and Models of Unions

The Hylton argument—that efficient labor doctrine can occur without an explicit efficiency goal—can only go so far without a belief that some aspects of unions are consistent with efficiency. Without doubt, a major goal of the labor laws is to promote unions. The only debate comes from the extent to which other goals are part of the labor laws as well. Whether labor laws promote efficiency, then, turns to a large degree on whether unions promote efficiency. Scholars who see a large efficiency role for unions are more likely to find labor law doctrines that promote efficiency. The particular conception or model of unions, then, greatly shapes the L&E analysis of labor law.

A basic lesson of modern labor economists is that unions have two faces— a monopoly face and a collective goods face. Legal scholars have incorporated these lessons into their interpretations of the National Labor Relations Act. Indeed, a major leitmotif of labor L&E scholars is that labor laws positively do, and normatively should, enhance the efficiency aspects of unions while minimizing the inefficiencies that unions can cause.

## Union as Monopoly Cartel

Until the last twenty years or so, economists emphasized the monopoly face of unions. L&E scholars following this tradition presume that a central purpose of the labor laws is to foster union monopolies. For example, Posner has asserted that "American labor law is best understood as a device for facilitating, though not to the maximum possible extent, the cartelization of the labor supply by unions" (Posner 1984:990; see also Leslie 1980; Winter 1963). For L&E scholars, this approach presents a methodological puzzle. The general L&E paradigm is to describe positively and advocate normatively the efficiency effects of legal regulation. If the goal of the NLRA is to promote monopoly unions, the scholar following this L&E paradigm can only describe the degree of inefficiency and advocate the law be abolished. Indeed, Posner explains the paucity of labor L&E scholarship (as of 1984) precisely because lawyers committed to economic analysis are unlikely to be attracted to a subject matter founded on a policy that is the opposite of competition and economic efficiency (Posner 1984:990).

Perhaps surprisingly, then, considerable mileage has been achieved by scholars interpreting the NLRA with this monopoly vision at the fore. A leading example comes from Thomas Campbell (1986). Campbell starts with the proposition that Congress "intended a wealth transfer, not merely efficiency enhancement" (p. 995). But this labor-favoring goal does not mean labor should win every disputed issue under the NLRA. The NLRA only allows labor to advance its interests by monopolizing the work force, says Campbell. Labor may not manipulate consumer demand for the final product. Not surprisingly for a theory that focuses on unions as cartels, the interface of antitrust and labor issues provides Campbell with many examples. Still, Campbell comments on many other labor doctrines not usually examined with labor antitrust principles in mind. Thus, suggests Campbell, allowing unions to use an agency shop to prevent free riding by workers is "an entirely correct rule, given the objective of protecting a cartel of laborers from breaking apart" (p. 1013). Similarly, the NLRA appropriately limits competition between unions through its contract bar rules. The money unions would spend fighting each other is socially wasteful, as are all expenditures over economic rents (p. 1014). But many of the NLRA restrictions on secondary boycotts are also appropriate, claims Campbell, because unions here are manipulating product markets. A similarly appropriate line between product markets and labor markets is drawn by the mandatory bargaining rules of the NLRA. Labor can bargain over "issues concerning substitution for labor in production" but should not be allowed to influence how much output a firm produces.

*Union as bargainer over rents (or protector of quasi rents).* Other economists have challenged the central vision of union as a monopolist. Union wage increases are highest in highly concentrated industries. This suggests that the union's role is to grab employer rents or quasi rents created in the product market, rather than to create rents from a labor cartel independent of product market structure. If the prime role of unions is to haggle with employers over the division of rents, then unions do not cause substantial inefficiencies, and government can promote unions without significant loss of efficiency. This rent model of unions has antecedents in the countervailing power model of Galbraith (1952). Galbraith argued that unions bargaining against monopsonistic employers could enhance efficiency by raising wages and employment at the same time. While the countervailing power model focuses on the overall balance of power between union and employer, the more recent bargaining model from law and economics examines more detailed aspects of labor law.

Law and economics scholar Kenneth Dau-Schmidt (1992) has used this rent model of unions, or "bargaining model" as he terms it, to explain a variety of labor law rules. According to Dau-Schmidt, inefficiency occurs when union and management bargain strategically, with each side wasting some of the cooperative surplus in hope of capturing a larger share for itself. A central justification of government regulation, under the bargaining model, is to deter strategic behavior through appropriate regulation of organizing, collective bargaining, and the enforcement of awards. For example, Dau-Schmidt supports the NLRA's prohibitions against discriminatory discharges and plant relocations because these activities are wasteful rent seeking by employers. Dau-Schmidt supports the rule allowing an employer completely to close a plant to avoid unionization, because complete closures cannot be a strategic attempt to gain more in the future. Similarly, Dau-Schmidt's bargaining model justifies the legal regulation of "good faith" bargaining and the mandatory-permissive distinction as attempts to deter strategic bargaining. Even the exclusivity principle, whereby a union with majority support represents all workers, is justified under the bargaining model as a way of limiting the number of actors in the bargaining game and thereby increasing the likelihood of a cooperative solution.

Most of Dau-Schmidt's project justifies existing law as consistent with wealth maximization. This attempt to find efficiency explanations for current law is a common characteristic of L&E scholarship. Dau-Schmidt does urge some legal reform, however. In particular, he argues that, if the main role of labor law is to deter strategic behavior, the penalties against improper behavior should be sharply increased. Dau-Schmidt even tentatively endorses Weiler's (1984) proposal that interest arbitration be an available remedy against parties who bargain in bad faith.

Other law and economics scholars see the union as protecting employee rents rather than grabbing employer rents. Employee quasi rents can arise when employees invest in firm-specific personal skills, or even buy houses near an isolated plant, in order to qualify for a well-paying job. Once the investments are in place, an employer sometimes can threaten to terminate workers, making their investments worthless, unless they agree to wage concessions. Several new institutional economists have proposed a rent-protecting role for unions, whereby unions police implicit contracts to prevent employer opportunism. (See Klein, Crawford, and Alchian 1978; Williamson, Wachter, and Harris 1975.) Alchian (1982) has used this "protect employee rents" model to argue that the NLRA's duty to bargain should be imposed whenever employees have made firm-specific investments that might be expropriated. Applying this model to *First National Maintenance Corporation v. NLRB*, Alchian supports the holding but criticizes the reasoning. In that case, the Supreme Court held that a cleaning company did not have to bargain with the union over a decision to stop servicing one customer. Alchian saw no employee investments in this particular company that the company could expropriate by threatening to close and therefore agreed with the Court's holding that bargaining was unnecessary. But the Court's opinion mentions factors such as whether the employer's proposed action involves "large amounts of capital" or a "substantial change in business." Alchian (1982:245) declares these factors to be "analytically useless and possibly misleading." For example, an employer who threatens a substantial change in the business could be trying to grab the quasi rent from the employees' prior investments. Labor law should not allow an employer "to escape his obligation," says Alchian, through such threats.

Hylton and Hylton (1990) have used the rent-protection model to analyze the successorship doctrine in labor law. The successorship doctrine governs when the buyer of a business is bound by the collective bargaining contract signed by a seller. Without such a doctrine, a seller could opportunistically appropriate promised wages by structuring the deal to make the buyer not bound by the collective bargaining agreement. The Hyltons argue for a simplification of current successorship law. They advocate requiring the new employer to honor the predecessor's contract whenever the transfer of ownership occurs through merger or stock purchase. When the new employer purchases the assets of the predecessor, the Hyltons support much of current law. They argue, however, that the contract should continue in some asset-sale situations even where the successor hires only a minority of the predecessor's work force, in order to police employer opportunism. (For another analysis of the successorship doctrine in the same spirit, see Rock and Wachter 1993.)

*Union as provider of collective goods.* Perhaps most predominant are labor law and economics scholars who emphasize the collective goods aspects of unions. Applying the insights of Freeman and Medoff and others, these scholars argue that the NLRA does and should foster the ability of unions to create collective goods while minimizing the ill effects of monopoly unionism. An early demonstration of this approach was by Leslie (1984). After describing the collective goods view of unions, Leslie used this model to develop criteria for determining the appropriate bargaining unit for a union. The issue of appropriate bargaining units has bedeviled traditional scholars for years, because it seems a highly fact-specific inquiry that resists generalizations. Leslie showed, however, that focusing on the collective goods potential of unions can give workable guidelines to which workers should be included in an appropriate bargaining unit.

## The Law and Economics of Collective Bargaining

Much of labor law governs collective bargaining. Parties must bargain in good faith. They can insist upon and use economic weapons to obtain a particular mandatory term but not a permissive term. When a collective bargaining agreement is silent about a particular item, default rules developed by the NLRB kick in. In recent years, scholars have tried to put the rules governing collective bargaining into a L&E framework.

As an example, let us see how the law and economics approach analyzes the legal doctrine litigated in *NLRB v. J. Weingarten, Inc.* (See Schwab 1987.) At issue there was whether Section 7 of the NLRA (which gives workers the right to organize, bargain collectively, and engage in "other concerted activities . . . for mutual aid or protection") entitles unionized workers to have a representative present at a disciplinary interview. The Supreme Court held that it did.

The central question for a law and economics scholar is whether the *Weingarten* holding is consistent with efficiency. As we said earlier, a legal doctrine is efficient if it allows resources to be allocated to the party who values them most highly, as measured by willingness and ability to pay. If workers would accept, at most, a $1 wage reduction (per worker per pay period, or whatever units make the numbers realistic) for the *Weingarten* right, they value it at $1. As discussed earlier, offer and asking prices sometimes differ, particularly when the right is very important, so we should also determine the minimum amount workers would demand to relinquish their *Weingarten* right. If they would insist on at least $2 to waive the right, they value it at $2. One would expect the offer price to exceed the asking price, but this is not necessarily so, if for example workers have a "grass is greener" mentality about this right. (See Dworkin 1980.) The efficiency calculus compares the value workers place on the right to the value employers place on it. Suppose the cost to employers of giving workers a representative at disciplinary hearings amounts to $3 (per worker per pay period) because of greater delays and hassles. Employers then value the *Weingarten* right at $3.

If we had these precise numbers, we would know that the efficient rule would allow employers to conduct disciplinary interviews without a worker representative (and conversely, if the cost to employers had turned out to be only 50 cents). Of course, only rarely do we have precise numbers. Nevertheless, the cost-benefit calculus is sometimes a helpful exercise if the orders of magnitude differ and can be determined by informal means.

Of greater interest to law and economics scholars than precise valuations is whether the initial legal rule affects final outcomes at all. Traditional labor scholars find this question amazing, because they reflexively assume that legal commands have bite. But L&E scholars are trained to watch out for the Coase Theorem, which states that, as long as transaction costs are low, parties will bargain to the same efficient outcome regardless of the initial legal rule or entitlement. To continue our example, suppose our numbers are correct, but the Supreme Court nevertheless held, as it did, that workers have the *Weingarten* right to a representative at disciplinary interviews. The workers suddenly have a right that they will give up for only $2 and that costs the employer $3. The Coase Theorem predicts that, if bargaining costs are low, workers will waive the *Weingarten* right in the next collective bargaining negotiations in return for a wage increase between $2 and $3.

If transaction costs are low, then, the Coase Theorem argues that legal presumptions or default rules do not affect whether workers end up with a particular substantive right. By the efficiency criteria, then, the critical part of *Weingarten* is not whether workers have a right to a representative at a disciplinary interview, but whether the union was allowed to waive this right. The *Weingarten* majority opinion is silent on the issue, but Justice Powell, concurring, expressly declared that a union could waive the right.

The Coase Theorem does not say the law has no effect under low transaction costs; it only says the law will not affect the efficiency of the bargain. In particular, initial entitlements can affect the distribution of wealth between the bargainers. In other words, the Coase Theorem asserts that, when transaction costs are low, default legal rules will not affect the size of the joint pie but may affect how the parties cut it. Even here, however, legal rules may be less powerful than is commonly thought. Legal rules may not affect wealth in the long run, as wages are raised or lowered to compensate for new entitlements. Coase (1988) himself has recently argued that initial legal entitlements will not even affect wealth distribution in the long run, under a proper interpretation of zero transaction costs.

The central point of the Coase Theorem is that, for an initial legal entitlement to be irrelevant to efficient outcomes, parties must be able to bargain around the law at low cost. The law itself can affect transaction costs. The duty to bargain in good faith can be seen as an attempt to ensure that the parties maximize the joint surplus of bargains. Schwab (1987) argues that, because of the legal apparatus of the labor laws, transaction costs in collective bargaining are often lower than in many other settings. Still, strategic bargaining and imperfect information are problems that can prevent parties from reaching efficient collective bargaining contracts. (See Leslie 1992:422-32.)

Other scholars also emphasize the role the labor laws can play in reducing strategic bargaining. Consider the problem of asymmetric investments. A major source of inefficiency can occur when one side makes irretrievable investments in a relationship (e.g., a plant or skills training) that lock it in. The other side can then exploit the trapped party by expropriating some of the quasi rents due the party. Anticipating this hold-up problem, parties will be reluctant to make such investments, even though they would be profitable if the initial contract terms could be enforced. Labor law can help prevent opportunistic behavior by enforcing the initial terms of the bargain. The problem for the law is that the parties can only reach generally worded bargains because they must cover many contingencies. How should such bargains be interpreted?

Wachter and Cohen (1988) have surveyed the labor cases governing plant relocations and subcontracting, arguing that the implicit rules developed in these cases appropriately deter strategic behavior while allowing flexibility. A basic feature of labor relations is that firms can respond to declining product markets by curtailing production, but that this must be done by laying off workers in reverse seniority rather than cutting wages (the so-called $W°H$ test). Laying off junior workers would be unprofitable if product market conditions were good, while cutting wages would be profitable even if conditions were good. By forcing firms to accept a "sunk cost loss," to use Wachter and Cohen's phrase, workers can be confident that the firm's claim of poor product market conditions is not a fraud designed to capture the gains of the workers' sunk investments. These ideas have been well developed in the new institutional economics by Grossman and Hart, Williamson, Wachter and Harris (1975), and many others. The special L&E contribution of Wachter and Cohen is two-fold. First, the exposition is accessible to a broader audience of policymakers. Second, Wachter and Cohen spend considerable effort connecting their sunk-cost-loss rule and $W°H$ test to a complicated series of Supreme Court cases on plant relocations, arguing that the intuitions of these cases can be rationalized with their model.

## Employment Law and Economics

Employment law and economics scholarship analyzes and critiques the vast array of legal regulation governing the nonunion workplace—or, more precisely, the laws that govern without regard to whether the workplace is unionized or not. The bulk of employment law is stated in terms of worker rights or worker protections. The L&E project attempts positively to explain these rights and normatively to critique them. Many employment law doctrines, the positive explanation runs, can be understood as fostering conditions that maximize the joint gains from the employment relationship. In particular, the positive explanation typically identifies why private contracting will not lead to efficient contracts in certain situations and explains the law as ameliorating that market failure. The reasons for employment market failure include information asymmetries, the prevalence of collective goods in the workplace, the difficulties markets have in assessing preferences of infra-marginal workers, and problems of adverse selection. The normative critique of employment law, by contrast, argues that many employment laws are misguided attempts to protect workers—misguided because the harmful unintended consequences of the laws outweigh the gains.

## Unequal Bargaining Power Cannot Explain Employment Law

Outside the law and economics camp, many scholars justify employment laws as correcting unfair employment relationships caused by workers' lack of bargaining power. Because individual workers lack bargaining power, the justification runs, they are exploited by employers. Government steps in (whether through the courts, the state legislatures, or Congress) to correct this exploitation. Protecting the weaker party to the employment contract becomes the prime positive explanation for employment law. (See Summers 1988:7.) This explanation for employment laws is similar to the correcting-unequal-bargaining-power argument for labor laws. The earlier solution to unequal bargaining power was the labor laws promoting unions. Once unions increased workers' power, it was hoped substantive regulation of employment would be unnecessary. Unions have never fulfilled that hope. Commentators concerned with unequal bargaining power have turned to direct regulation of employment (i.e., employment law to correct the perceived problem).

Law and economics scholars are deeply skeptical of rationalizations based on unequal bargaining power. Those rationalizations fail miserably as a positive explanation, for they cannot explain the many legal doctrines favoring employers regardless of their superior bargaining power (e.g., the right to fire employees at will, the right to give no pension to part-time workers). But even as a normative critique of employment law doctrines that favor employers, unequal bargaining power is unpersuasive because the concept is so malleable and does not justify intervention with private bargains. Duncan Kennedy (1982), a prominent critical legal studies scholar and hardly a L&E enthusiast, disentangles at least five different ideas within the general concept of unequal bargaining power. As applied to compulsory employment-law terms, these would include (1) the subject is public rather than private; (2) the employer drafted the terms and offered them to workers on a take-it-or-leave-it basis; (3) the employer has monopoly power or is bigger than an individual worker; (4) work is a necessity for workers, making them vulnerable to exploitation; and (5) a shortage of work enables employers to exploit workers. None of these tests, explains Kennedy, captures when a mandatory minimum employment term would benefit workers. For example, the big-employer criticism and the take-it-or-leave-it criticism lose their sting when employment-term bargaining is compared to bargaining in a grocery store. No individual customer can bargain with the manager of a big grocery store over price or other terms. This does not make the customer a victim of unequal bargaining power, however, because the customer can shop at rival stores if the terms are not attractive. (For discussions of the grocery customer/employee analogy, see Leslie 1992:29-30; Weiler 1990:17.)

Freed and Polsby (1989) have attacked the monopoly-power variant of unequal bargaining power as applied to employment law. True, a monopsonist employer creates a type of market failure, in that it refuses to hire some workers even though they would willingly work at a wage that would reap extra profits for the monopsonist, but for the fact that the monopsonist must raise wages for other workers. Still, say Freed and Polsby, even a monopsonist will offer an employment benefit if workers value the benefit more highly than it costs the monopsonist to provide—if only to wring even more profits from the workers.

The law and economics position does not suggest that a properly limited concept of unequal bargaining power is meaningless. Indeed, relative bargaining power determines how the parties to a bargain will share the surplus from trade. If employees have little bargaining power, the employer will gain most of the surplus. For example, suppose workers value a particular safety measure at $5 and an employer can provide it at a cost of $4. If the safety measure is provided, the joint gain to the parties is $1. If the employer has great bargaining power, almost all of that $1 surplus will go to the employer. It will offer safety and lower the wage by $4.99. If the employer has less bargaining power, the wage may fall by only $4.50 or less.

The important law and economics point is that unequal bargaining power does not determine whether particular items are traded to their highest valued use. To continue the example above, the degree of bargaining inequality does not affect whether the safety measure will be provided; it only influences how the parties will divide the gains from providing safety. Even an employer monopsonist with complete bargaining power wants to provide a safety measure if workers are willing and able to pay for it. In our example, providing the safety gives the monopsonist another dollar of profit.

The efficient result will occur regardless of bargaining power, unless transaction costs prevent the party from making the deal. Transaction costs include many things, such as strategic behavior, holdouts, or asymmetric information. These are all worthy of serious study. But unequal bargaining power is not a form of transaction costs that will prevent a joint welfare-enhancing contract from being consummated.

Unequal bargaining power can reduce the overall compensation package to workers. This is the central inefficiency that arises from a monopsony employer. (For a debate over whether employers have such bargaining power, see Kaufman 1989, 1991; Reynolds 1991. For a general survey of monopsony models, see Boal and Ransom 1997.) Reduced compensation, in turn, will affect how workers value certain items. To continue the example, workers paid $15 (per hour) may be willing to pay $6 (per month) on a particular safety measure, while workers paid $5 may only be willing to pay $3. In the latter case, the safety measure is no longer efficient and freely bargaining parties will not agree to it. But all this says is that poor workers value things differently than rich workers, and bargaining power influences whether a worker is poor or rich. Unequal bargaining power does not prevent efficient trades over particular items from occurring. Additionally, mandating safety to workers with low bargaining power will not improve their welfare. If the policymaker wishes the workers were richer and so would value safety more highly, the policymaker should attack the monopsony position.

## Mandatory and Waivable Employment Law Rights

Employment law and economics scholars make a basic division between mandatory terms and default provisions that the employer and employee can contract around if they choose. Most employment laws create mandatory minimum terms. Examples include minimum wage laws (the FLSA), workplace safety laws (OSHA), requirements to give advance notice of plant closings (WARN), and unemployment insurance.

Willborn (1988) has clearly articulated the standard economic objection to these mandatory terms (while defending their use in certain situations). In the short run, when employers can lay off workers but cannot lower wages, employers will treat a newly imposed mandatory term like an exogenous wage increase. Facing higher costs with no corresponding change in productivity, employers will lay off workers (or hire fewer new workers) than without the law. A basic point, then, is that the minimum term will benefit some workers (those keeping their jobs) while hurting others (those losing their jobs).

In the longer run, explains Willborn, profit-maximizing employers will avoid the costs of the mandatory term, if possible, by lowering the wage. The long-run unemployment effect of the minimum term may be minimal. Instead, the minimum term will shift the compensation package toward lower wages and more costly terms. The standard economic objection is that this final wage-benefit package makes workers worse off—if not, employers and workers would have bargained for the package without legal compulsion. For workers near the minimum wage (itself a minimum term), the harm from minimum terms might be greater. For low-wage workers, the wage cannot legally be decreased to compensate employers for the increased cost of providing the mandatory term. Greater unemployment may be the result. (See Willborn at 112.)

While traditional legal scholars reject the entire framework in which the standard economic objection to minimum terms is imbedded, many labor law and economics scholars defend particular minimum terms on efficiency grounds. Minimum terms can have an efficiency justification if they mandate collective terms that would be underprovided in a nonregulated workplace, or if they solve information problems workers face, or if they regulate external costs not otherwise felt by employer or workers. An example here would be the costs of workplace smoking, some of which is felt by families of fellow workers or the health insurance system generally. Whether in practice the efficiency gains of a particular minimum term outweigh its costs is an open question. Many L&E scholars are skeptical of minimum terms in practice, although they recognize that under certain conditions they can enhance efficiency. More commonly, minimum terms are justified on distributional grounds for benefitting workers at the expense of employers. Absent some market flaw (the correction of which can be justified on efficiency grounds), the standard economic objection to mandatory terms would be very skeptical that they have a positive distributional impact on workers.

Waivable terms are not subject to the standard economic objection. If transaction costs are low, says the Coase Theorem, parties will write around inefficient waivable terms. Even if the law allows waiver of its minimum terms, however, law and economics scholars worry about the appropriate default rule for two reasons. First, bargaining costs may prevent parties from avoiding the inefficient legal starting point. Second, bargaining around an inefficient rule is itself a cost that a well-functioning legal system should avoid if possible. Employment L&E scholars have debated default rules most extensively in the context of appropriate standards for discharging workers. That is the subject I turn to next.

## Employment at Will

*The appropriate default standard.* Epstein (1984) has powerfully defended employment at will—the traditional American doctrine whereby an employer can lawfully fire a worker for a good reason, a bad reason, or no reason at all. Epstein carefully points out that he advocates employment at will only as a default presumption. Employment contracts can and do call for other standards for discharge. Most union contracts, for example, call for just cause discharge. Still, the vast bulk of nonunion employment contracts have not written around the default at-will rule.

These two empirical points—employment at will is nearly universal in the nonunion sector, while just cause is nearly universal in the unionized sector—have themselves been part of the grist in the debate of law and economics scholars over the appropriate default rule. The most common L&E standard for default rules is that courts should assume that the parties want the clause most parties in that situation would want had they expressly bargained over it. Such a mimic-the-market standard allows most parties to avoid the costs of bargaining over the issue. Epstein argues that "[t]he survival of the contract at will, and the frequency of its use in private markets, might well be taken as a sign of its suitability for employment relations" (Epstein 1984:948). Weiler (1990:78) argues, by contrast, that the prevalence of at-will contracts shows that something is wrong with labor markets. In particular, Weiler emphasizes that established workers locked into their current employer value job protection highly. Nonunion employers seeking to attract new workers who place smaller value on job protection, however, will not respond to the wishes of senior workers. Thus the unionized sector's emphasis on job security may more accurately reflect the values of most workers. Freed and Polsby, refereeing this debate, suggest that references to the union experience "are, at best, inconclusive" (Freed and Polsby 1989:1124).

Schwab (1993) has argued for a more complicated default rule—a life-cycle default. Workers just beginning a career job, if they have quit a prior job or otherwise substantially invested in the career job, should be protected against arbitrary dismissal. Similarly, workers at the end of their career should be protected against opportunistic firings that can arise if their current wage exceeds their current productivity. Courts should presume that mid-career workers, by contrast, are subject to employment at will. These workers are adequately protected by the employer's incentive not to fire good workers; the greater problem at mid-career is employee shirking. Schwab claims as a positive matter that leading court decisions are stumbling toward this life-cycle default, particularly in states like California and Michigan, and normatively defends the default as appropriately curbing opportunism by both employer and employee at different points in the life cycle.

These theoretical debates over employment-at-will are sorely lacking in empirical data (unless discussion of leading court cases can count as empirical testing of theories). Verkerke (1995) has given some empirical discipline to the argument by surveying employers' actual practices. In a random telephone survey of 221 employers with more than twenty employees in five states, Verkerke found that about one-half of all employers (52%) contracted explicitly for an at-will relationship, one-third (33%) use no documents that specify the terms governing discharge, and one in seven (15%) contract explicitly for just cause protection. Small employers (under 50 employees) are significantly more likely to have no documents governing discharge and expressly to adopt just cause rather than at will. Interestingly, Verkerke could detect no contracting differences between the small number of firms that had some unionized employees and those firms with no unionized workers (suggesting no spillover effects between a firm's unionized workforce and its nonunionized work force). Neither could he find any differences between industries. Michigan employers are significantly more likely than others expressly to contract for at-will employment, but otherwise no state differences are apparent.

Verkerke concludes that the survey supports at-will employment as the appropriate legal presumption, under the assumption that default rules should save transaction costs by following what most contracting parties would do. Most employers either explicitly adopt at-will rules or implicitly adopt at-will rules by having no express contract on the issue. Verkerke questions the implications of life-cycle default theory. If California and Michigan courts come closest to a life-cycle default rule, and the life-cycle default makes sense in many contexts, one might expect California and Michigan employers to be relatively reluctant to make express contracts; the survey found, however, that Michigan employers were more likely to give express contracts (especially for at will), and could detect no relative reluctance of California employers to make express contracts. Verkerke's survey is also puzzling for those who think that at will and just cause can each be appropriate in particular circumstances, depending on such factors as whether worker effort is hard to monitor and whether workers are locked into firms by firm-specific investments. While Verkerke found that 15% of employers contracted for just cause employment, he saw no variation by industry, state, or size of employer. Verkerke's survey cannot directly challenge the assertion that the prevalence of just cause in union contracts shows a failure in the nonunion market. But it does seem to indicate that either just cause or at-will employment should be the universal default rule, rather than a rule that varies by type of employment. As Verkerke himself argues, further empirical testing of the theories would be most helpful.

A recent empirical effort is by Kim (1997). She surveys recently terminated workers, finding they are woefully ignorant of their vulnerable legal status under employment at will. Kim argues this ignorance undermines any claim that the prevalence of at-will contracts comes because workers knowingly bargain away job protection. Morriss (1996) also brings data into the analysis. He reports survey data that workers do not value job protection highly, which he argues supports the at-will rule.

*Mandatory just cause rules.* Most traditional advocates of just cause employment propose a mandatory term, with few if any workers being allowed to waive the protection. The Model Employment Termination Act, proposed by the Commissioners on Uniform State Laws, gives the most detailed and concrete proposal of a system of mandatory just cause (although it would allow waiver if the employer promises specified amounts of severance pay). Some L&E scholars have supported mandatory just cause on efficiency grounds. (See Levine 1991; Kamiat 1996.)

Adverse selection may prevent just cause contracts from arising in unregulated markets, even if they are efficient. Two types of workers need just cause protection more than others: First are those workers with marginal skills or work habits for the job; these "shirking" workers, as they have been labeled, are the lemons. Second are good workers who nevertheless want insurance against their employer unreasonably firing them. While all workers want "free" insurance, presumably workers for whom discharge would be particularly harsh would be willing to pay the most for the protection. Such workers might include those with especially great attachment to the community, or who otherwise have made great investments in the particular job or location. This second type of worker would be willing to accept a wage reduction in return for just cause protection large enough to compensate the employer for the additional expected cost of having to prove just cause before it can fire the worker (which is low, because the worker is good). Unfortunately, the shirker worker will also be willing to work at this somewhat lower wage, because the lemon knows he may significantly benefit from the employer's greater inability to fire him. An individual firm offering just cause as a benefit cannot distinguish between the two types of job applicant. It will face a competitive disadvantage if it hires a high percentage of shirkers, because the wage is not low enough to compensate for the greater costs in firing these workers. Individual workers, knowing they are a good worker rather than a shirker, may have difficulty signaling that fact to a skeptical employer. As a result, no firm may offer just cause employment even though certain workers, could they be identified, would be willing to work at a price/benefits package that would be profitable to employers.

If all firms had to offer just cause protection for workers, the adverse selection problem would disappear. No individual firm would be at a competitive disadvantage because all other employers must offer just cause as well. This argument for mandatory just cause is analogous to Akerlof's argument, presented in his original Lemons paper (1970), for mandatory Medicare as a means to solve the adverse selection problem arising as the elderly, knowing their own health better than an insurer does, seek health insurance.

This overcoming adverse-selection argument only demonstrates that mandatory just cause might be efficient; it does not demonstrate that the cure is necessarily preferable to the disease. Several reasons suggest mandatory just cause may not be worth its costs. First, and most basic, the argument depends on the relative size of the two classes of workers. Mandatory just cause exacerbates shirking by the "lemon" workers. (But see Rock and Wachter 1996:1939, note 52, who argue that "[i]n a just cause regime, low productivity employees are no more protected than they are in a norm-governed [at-will] relationship.") Mandatory just cause helps the good workers willing to pay for just cause insurance. Which group is larger is an empirical question. Second, the lemons problem is reduced if, over time, workers can signal their good quality. (See Verkerke 1995:904.) After working on the job for a while, employers can determine worker quality (indeed, this is what probationary periods are for) and tailor just cause offers accordingly. Third, the lemons problem is reduced if employers face penalties for offering at-will contracts. Just as a good worker may lump himself with shirkers if he asks for just cause, an employer may lump itself with opportunistic employers if it insists on at will. (See Verkerke 1995:903.) (But see Kamiat 1996:1962, note 15, who suggests that the two signaling problems simply enhance the contracting problems rather than cancel out.) Finally, as employees are forced to take "arbitrary discharge" insurance, they may try to opt out of the protection by becoming independent contractors or other non-employees, even when (but for the mandatory just cause law) that is not the optimal legal structure for their arrangement.

In sum, theoretical efficiency arguments can be made for and against mandatory just cause. The area is sorely in need of more empirical testing. Unfortunately, empirical testing is not the strength of L&E, and empirical testing of signaling models has proven particularly difficult for labor economists. Verkerke points to the fact that just cause contracts are no more prevalent among experienced workers than among young workers as empirical evidence that signaling problems are not important. Unfortunately, proponents of mandatory just cause remain unconvinced by such evidence, because it may simply show that markets have difficulty reflecting the preferences of older, locked-in, inframarginal workers. (See Kamiat 1996:1963, note 15.)

*Mandatory tort remedies for discharged workers.* More consensus exists among law and economics scholars on the appropriateness of the tort of wrongful discharge. This tort, which is a mandatory term rather than a mere default, protects employees fired for refusing to commit an illegal act, or performing a public duty such as jury duty, or blowing the whistle on illegal company activity. Even where an at-will relationship is the efficient contract between the employer and employee (meaning that the employee is unwilling to pay the greater costs to the employer of offering just cause protection), mandatory tort remedies are needed to protect against unjust discharges that harm third parties not part of the employment contract. (See Schwab 1996.) As Epstein (1984:952, note 11) explains, "just as a contract to commit murder is not enforceable, neither should one to pollute illegally or to commit perjury."

### Future Directions of Employment Law and Economics Scholarship and Policy Approaches

Employment law and economics scholarship will move on two fronts. First, L&E scholars, particularly those located in law schools, will focus more on empirical testing of their models. Labor economics is probably the bastion of empirical testing within economics, and L&E scholars will gradually adopt this empirical work along with the models. Second, employment L&E scholars will gradually take on other areas. So far, the bulk of the literature covers wrongful discharge law (or employment discrimination, which is beyond the scope of this survey). Relatively little has been done to analyze other regulation of the employment relationship, even though labor economists have a voluminous literature here. Preliminary L&E forays have been made into such areas as unemployment insurance (Rappaport 1992), workers' compensation (Hylton and Laymon 1992), and pension law (Fischel and Langbein 1988). But vast areas remain. Unlike wrongful-dismissal law, these areas have extremely complicated statutes and regulations. It is hard to see the forest for all that paper. But the L&E approach is particularly good at spotting general trends and analogies. Once the technical legal mastery is done, the area should be fertile ground for L&E scholars.

As the law and economics analysis matures, its relevance to policymakers will increase. Three general policy tendencies are already apparent. First, the

L&E approach is wary of extensive regulation but recognizes that labor markets are far from perfectly competitive and that government intervention to counter market failure in particular areas is more plausible here than in other markets, such as the securities market. Still, policymakers must avoid assuming that the government should attempt to correct all market failures, for sometimes the cure is worse than the disease. Second, market failure is identified most clearly when the employment contracts harm third parties, or when the parties clearly are unable to assess and allocate risk, perhaps because of asymmetric information. Finally, when intervention is appropriate, the L&E approach generally favors rebuttable presumptions to mandatory rules. The ability of parties to contract around government remedies puts a limit on the possible harm of government intervention, even if it frustrates more elaborate forms of government intervention.

## References

Akerlof, George A. 1970. "The Market for 'Lemons:' Quality Uncertainty and the Market Mechanism." *Quarterly Journal of Economics*, Vol. 84, no. 3 (August), pp. 488-500.

Alchian, Armen A. 1982. "Decision Sharing and Expropriable Specific Quasi-Rents: A Theory of First National Maintenance Corporation v. NLRB." *Supreme Court Economic Review*, Vol. 1, pp. 235-47.

Boal, William M., and Michael R. Ransom. 1997. "Monopsony in the Labor Market." *Journal of Economic Literature*, Vol. 35, no. 1 (March), pp. 86-112.

Calabresi, Guido. 1961. "Some Thoughts on Risk Distribution and the Law of Torts." *Yale Law Journal*, Vol. 70, no. 4 (March), pp. 499-553.

Campbell, Thomas J. 1986. "Labor Law and Economics." *Stanford Law Review*, Vol. 38, no. 4 (April), pp. 991-1064.

Coase, R.H. 1960. "The Problem of Social Cost." *Journal of Law and Economics*, Vol. 3, no. 1 (October), pp. 1-44.

_____. 1988. *The Firm, The Market, and The Law*. Chicago: University of Chicago Press.

Coleman, Jules L. 1980. "Efficiency, Exchange and Auction: Philosophic Aspects of the Economic Approach to Law." *California Law Review*, Vol. 68, no. 1 (January), pp. 221-49.

Cooter, Robert D., and Lewis A. Kornhauser. 1980. "Can Litigation Improve the Law without the Help of Judges?" *Journal of Legal Studies*, Vol. 9, no. 1 (January), pp. 139-63.

Dau-Schmidt, Kenneth G. 1992. "A Bargaining Analysis of American Labor Law and the Search for Bargaining Equity and Industrial Peace." *Michigan Law Review*, Vol. 91, no. 3 (December), pp. 419-514.

Dworkin, Ronald M. 1980. "Is Wealth a Value?" *Journal of Legal Studies*, Vol. 9, no. 2 (March), pp. 191-226.

Epstein, Richard A. 1983. "A Common Law for Labor Relations: A Critique of the New Deal Labor Legislation." *Yale Law Journal*, Vol. 92, no. 8 (July), pp. 1357-1408.

_____. 1984. "In Defense of the Contract at Will." *University of Chicago Law Review*, Vol. 51, no. 4 (Fall), pp. 947-87.

Fischel, Daniel R., and John H. Langbein. 1988. "ERISA's Fundamental Contradiction: The Exclusive Benefit Rule." *University of Chicago Law Review*, Vol. 55, no. 4 (Fall), pp. 1105-60.

Freed, Mayer G., and Daniel D. Polsby. 1989. "Just Cause for Termination Rules and Economic Efficiency." *Emory Law Journal*, Vol. 38, no. 4 (Fall), pp. 1097-1144.

Galbraith, John K. 1952. *American Capitalism: The Concept of Countervailing Power.* 1st ed. Boston: Houghton Mifflin.

Holmes, O. W. 1897. "The Path of the Law." *Harvard Law Review*, Vol. 10, no. 8 (March 25), pp. 457-78.

Hylton, Keith N. 1993. "Efficiency and Labor Law." *Northwestern Law Review*, Vol. 87, no. 2 (Winter), pp. 471-522.

Hylton, Keith N., and Maria O'Brien Hylton. 1990. "Rent Appropriation and the Labor Law Doctrine of Successorship." *Boston University Law Review*, Vol. 70, no. 5 (November), pp. 821-63.

Hylton, Keith N., and Steven E. Laymon. 1992. "The Internalization Paradox and Workers' Compensation." *Hofstra Law Review*, Vol. 21, no. 1 (Fall), pp. 109-82.

Kamiat, Walter. 1996. "Labor and Lemons: Efficient Norms in the Internal Labor Market and the Possible Failures of Individual Contracting." *University of Pennsylvania Law Review*, Vol. 144, no. 5 (May), pp. 1953-70.

Kaufman, Bruce E. 1989. "Labor's Inequality of Bargaining Power: Changes over Time and Implications for Public Policy." *Journal of Labor Research*, Vol. 10, no. 3 (Summer), pp. 285-98.

_____. 1991. "Labor's Inequality of Bargaining Power: Myth or Reality?" *Journal of Labor Research*, Vol. 12, no. 2 (Spring), pp. 151-66.

_____. 1996. "Why the Wagner Act? Reestablishing Contact with Its Original Purpose." In D. Lewin, B. Kaufman and D. Sockell, eds., *Advances in Industrial and Labor Relations*, 15-68. Greenwich, CT: JAI Press.

Kelman, Mark. 1987. *A Guide to Critical Legal Studies.* Cambridge, MA: Harvard University Press.

Kennedy, Duncan. 1982. "Distributive and Paternalist Motives in Contract and Tort Law, with Special Reference to Compulsory Terms and Unequal Bargaining Power." *Maryland Law Review*, Vol. 41, no. 4, pp. 563-658.

Kim, Pauline T. 1997. "Bargaining with Imperfect Information: A Study of Workers' Perceptions of Legal Protection in an At-Will World." *Cornell Law Review*, Vol. 83, no. 1 (November), forthcoming.

Kitch, Edmund W., ed. 1983. "The Fire of Truth: A Remembrance of Law and Economics at Chicago, 1932-1970." *Journal of Law and Economics*, Vol. 26, no. 1, pp. 163-233.

Klein, Benjamin, Robert G. Crawford, and Armen A. Alchian. 1978. "Vertical Integration, Appropriable Rents, and the Competitive Contracting Process." *Journal of Law and Economics*, Vol. 21, no. 2 (October), pp. 297-326.

Leslie, Douglas L. 1980. "Principles of Labor Antitrust." *Virginia Law Review*, Vol. 66, no. 7 (November), pp. 1183-1234.

_____. 1984. "Labor Bargaining Units." *Virginia Law Review*, Vol. 70, no. 3 (April), pp. 353-418.

_____. 1992. *Cases and Materials on Labor Law.* 3d ed. Boston: Little, Brown & Co.

Levine, David I. 1991. "Just Cause Employment Policies in the Presence of Worker Adverse Selection." *Journal of Labor Economics*, Vol. 9, no. 3 (July), pp. 294-305.

Moore, Gary A. 1991. "Economic Efficiency and the Monopoly Legal Status Accorded Labor Unions: Non-Posnerian Approaches." *Journal of Contemporary Law*, Vol. 17, no. 1, pp. 71-89.

Morriss, Andrew P. 1996. "Bad Data, Bad Economics, and Bad Policy: Time to Fire Wrongful Discharge Law." *Texas Law Review*, Vol. 74, no. 7 (June), pp. 1901-41.

Nonce, Dale A. 1997. "Guidance Rules and Enforcement Rules: A Better View of the Cathedral." *Virginia Law Review*, Vol. 83, no. 5 (August), forthcoming.

Posner, Richard A. 1981. *The Economics of Justice.* Cambridge, MA: Harvard University Press.

_____. 1984. "Some Economics of Labor Law." *University of Chicago Law Review*, Vol. 5, no. 4 (Fall), pp. 988-1011.

_____. 1992. *Economic Analysis of Law.* 4th ed. Boston: Little, Brown & Co.

Rappaport, Michael. 1992. "The Private Provision of Unemployment Insurance." *Wisconsin Law Review*, Vol. 1992, no. 1, pp. 61-129.

Reynolds, Morgan O. 1991. "The Myth of Labor's Inequality of Bargaining Power." *Journal of Labor Research*, Vol. 12, no. 2 (Spring), pp. 167-83.

Rock, Edward B., and Michael L. Wachter. 1993. "Labor Law Successorship: A Corporate Law Approach." *Michigan Law Review*, Vol. 92, no. 2 (November), pp. 203-60.

_____. 1996. "The Enforceability of Norms and the Employment Relationship." *University of Pennsylvania Law Review*, Vol. 144, no. 5 (May), pp. 1913-52.

Rubin, Paul H. 1983. *Business Firms and the Common Law: The Evolution of Efficient Rules.* New York: Praeger.

Schwab, Stewart J. 1987. "Collective Bargaining and the Coase Theorem." *Cornell Law Review*, Vol. 72, no. 2 (January), pp. 245-87.

_____. 1989. "The Economics Invasion of Labor Law Scholarship." *Proceedings of the Forty-First Annual Meetings* (New York, Dec. 28-30, 1988). Madison, WI: Industrial Relations Research Association, pp. 236-42.

_____. 1993. "Life-Cycle Justice: Accommodating Just Cause and Employment At Will." *Michigan Law Review*, Vol. 92, no. 1 (October), pp. 8-62.

_____. 1996. "Wrongful Discharge Law and the Search for Third-Party Effects." *Texas Law Review*, Vol. 74, no. 7 (June), pp. 1943-78.

Summers, Clyde W. 1988. "Labor Law as the Century Turns: A Changing of the Guard." *Nebraska Law Review*, Vol. 67, nos. 1 and 2, pp. 7-27.

Sunstein, Cass R. 1994. "Incommensurability and Valuation in Law." *Michigan Law Review*, Vol. 92, no. 4 (February), pp. 779-861.

Verkerke, J. Hoult. 1995. "An Empirical Perspective on Indefinite Term Employment Contracts: Resolving the Just Cause Debate." *Wisconsin Law Review*, Vol. 1994, no. 4, pp. 837-918.

Wachter, Michael L., and George M. Cohen. 1988. "The Law and Economics of Collective Bargaining: An Introduction and Application to the Problems of Subcontracting, Partial Closure, and Relocation." *University of Pennsylvania Law Review*, Vol. 136, no. 5 (May), 1349-1417.

Weiler, Paul C. 1983. "Promises to Keep: Securing Workers' Rights to Self-Organization under the NLRA." *Harvard Law Review*, Vol. 96, no. 8 (June), pp. 1769-1827.

_____. 1984. "Striking a New Balance: Freedom of Contract and the Prospects for Union Representation." *Harvard Law Review*, Vol. 98, no. 2 (December), pp. 351-420.

_____. 1990. *Governing the Workplace: The Future of Labor and Employment Law.* Cambridge, MA: Harvard University Press.

Willborn, Steven L. 1988. "Individual Employment Rights and the Standard Economic Objection: Theory and Empiricism." *Nebraska Law Review*, Vol. 67, no. 1 and 2, pp. 101-39.

Willborn, Steven L., Stewart J. Schwab, and John F. Burton, Jr. 1993. *Employment Law: Cases and Materials*. Charlottesville, VA: Michie Publishing Co.

Williamson, Oliver E., Michael L. Wachter, and Jeffrey F. Harris. 1975. "Understanding the Employment Relation: The Analysis of Idiosyncratic Exchange." *Bell Journal of Economics and Management Science*, Vol. 6, no. 1 (Spring), pp. 250-78.

Winter, Ralph K., Jr. 1963. "Collective Bargaining and Competition: The Application of Antitrust Standards to Union Activities." *Yale Law Journal*, Vol. 73, no. 1 (November), pp. 14-73.

# CHAPTER 4

# The Economic Effects of Employment Regulation: What Are the Limits?

JOHN T. ADDISON
*Washington University–St. Louis and
University of South Carolina*

BARRY T. HIRSCH
*Florida State University*

In this chapter we investigate the controversial topic of government mandates and regulation in the labor market, with emphasis given to empirical evaluation and evidence. We say "controversial" for several reasons. First, at the level of theory, it is not clear that any single framework can accommodate adequately the plethora of labor market interventions in place today, despite the attempt in the literature to categorize and justify mandates according to broad types of market failure. In the second place, there is the critically important issue of fixing the level of a mandate in those circumstances where market failure is identified. Third, it is rare that we have precise estimates of the effects of proposed or adopted policies. And finally, the adoption, interpretation, and implementation of labor market policies are products of the political process, a process that is informed by but not ultimately determined by economic arguments.

In the political and sometimes scholarly debate regarding mandates, the case made by either side is often less than compelling. The more enthusiastic supporters of mandates attempt to justify them with rationale from what are incomplete models, ignore what are unintended although predictable secondary effects of employment regulation, exaggerate benefits and understate costs, and demonstrate little appreciation for market alternatives. Because mandates typically set standards without sufficient knowledge of their effects, proponents sometimes advocate what might be termed a "try-it-and-see" approach—that is, they call for revision of the mandate as required in the light of experience. This is a rather disingenuous response to concerns about lack of knowledge, given the difficulty of subsequently observing and measuring the consequences of mandates and the endogeneity of public policy. Once in place, mandates may be difficult to modify given the constituencies ranged against change.

Excess is no stranger to opponents of mandates either. Benefits are downplayed, costs are overstated, and recognition of the possibility of market failure is often conspicuous in its absence.[1] Such opponents would be better advised to examine the logic of individual mandates, rather than behave as if even qualified support for any one intervention might transform into unqualified support for all interventions. And even in those instances where the case for opposition to mandates is a strong one, opponents should be cognizant of the political economy surrounding policy formation. The alternative to a given mandate may be an even less attractive policy, thus introducing the need to confront what are essentially second-best arguments for particular policies.

We have in these opening remarks rather over accentuated the drama surrounding mandates. Mandates may be less far reaching than was the intention of their proponents or the fear of opponents. Mitigating factors that might pertain here include the development of market escape routes, modification of costly measures during the passage of enabling legislation, adjustments in enforcement and interpretation of the law in response to actual experience, and, in some cases, noncompliance. Nevertheless, it is commonly asserted that the U.S. is today subject to a regulatory morass that may ultimately, if not immediately, bring about death by a thousand possibly small cuts. At the same time, there has been sufficient political support to largely preserve and in some areas expand government's role in the labor market. These seemingly conflicting beliefs underscore the need for an analysis of employment regulation via mandates, an analysis that is necessarily exploratory rather than definitive and that demonstrates what is still a rudimentary understanding of its effects.

In what follows, we will argue that broad allegations of market failure do not in general provide a convincing case for mandates, that some sources of market failure may not be amenable to correction, that the imprecision of the political marketplace augurs ill for the design of efficient policy instruments, and that methodological problems and data limitations cloud measurement of the effects of employment regulations. This is all rather negative, but the positive case for mandates is implicit in our critique. Although a general case for mandates cannot be made, we do not discount the benefits of individual mandates. And where specific mandates may be dominated by politically less feasible mechanisms, second-best arguments for mandates may prevail. Although allocative inefficiencies accompanying employment regulations abound, empirical evidence, albeit hazy, suggests that a number of mandates may pass at least a crude benefit-cost test. The broad scope of this chapter leads us to provide what will be a rather brief treatment of individual mandates, while ignoring altogether some topics addressed elsewhere in this volume (e.g., discrimination).

## Employment Regulation: The Theoretical Framework

The standard competitive model views labor markets as not fundamentally different in kind from product or other markets. To be sure, standard models account to some degree for labor market complexities. In particular, the wage is viewed as just one component of the compensation bundle that also includes fringes and a variety of characteristics that accompany the job. These characteristics include effort, job security, job hazards, and other working conditions, opportunities for advancement, and so on, with such characteristics resulting in market-determined compensating differentials. The costs of varying the components of the payment bundle differ across firms so that there will be variation in the job characteristics offered in the marketplace. Equally important, workers will not value a given mix of job characteristics in the same way. Given the heterogeneity of firm costs and worker tastes, a sorting process takes place. Thus, for example, risk averse workers will gravitate toward firms that can provide stable jobs most cheaply. In these circumstances, wages will still vary with, say, job security, but the gradient will be less steep than would exist absent the matching process that extracts the maximum of worker utility from each unit of labor cost.

If we project on to this distortion-free, full-information scenario a mandate that decrees some fixed or minimum level of a given benefit, it follows unambiguously that welfare—defined as the sum of the joint employer-employee surplus—cannot be increased, given that firms fulfill an arbitraging function for which they are rewarded by lower costs. The simple case can be seen using a demand-supply diagram as shown in Figure 1. The mandate shifts downward both the labor demand and labor supply curves—the demand decrease owing to firms' cost in complying with the mandate and the supply increase owing to employees' valuation of the mandated benefits. Absent distortions or imperfect information, employers will have already provided (i.e., "sold" to workers) all workplace benefits whose value exceeds costs. Hence, a mandated benefit will shift the demand curve downward by more than the supply curve, leading to a decrease in employment and a welfare loss.[2] Were government to mandate a workplace regulation or nonwage benefit that the market fails to produce but that workers value by more than the costs, there may be an efficiency gain (i.e., a larger shift in supply than demand). This is possible if adverse selection/asymmetric information lead to underproduction (see below). Likewise, if benefits accrue to nonworkers, the

FIGURE 1
Effects of Mandates on Labor Demand and Supply

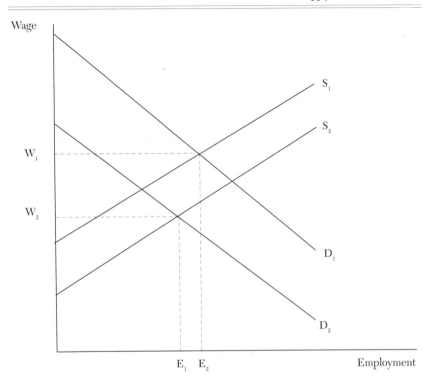

labor supply curve will not shift downward, yet economywide efficiency may nonetheless increase. This is the externality case, also discussed below.

## Market Failure

The conclusion that mandates produce welfare losses need not follow if there exists market failure. Categories of market failures that might permit an efficiency-enhancing mandate are externalities (including public goods), adverse selection/information asymmetries, and imperfectly competitive labor markets. Although economic efficiency will provide the primary basis for much of the analysis that follows, it is not the sole criterion for policy evaluation. Redistribution is an important rationale, as seen, for example, by the income maintenance basis for minimum wages and unemployment insurance. Institutionalists (see Kaufman in this volume) have emphasized that workers should have basic rights in the workplace that parallel those in the broader society—due process, fair treatment, certain freedoms of speech, and the like. And in practice, policy is determined in a political "marketplace" in no small part through the relative strength and efforts of alternative constituencies.

Externalities are spillover (i.e., third-party) benefits or costs not properly accounted for by decision makers. Unlike other market failure arguments, inefficiency resulting from externalities is not normally based on imperfect information, nor is it a product of any irrationality among parties to the employment contract. Rather, imperfectly defined resource rights and high transaction costs result in decision makers basing decisions on socially incorrect prices. When such externalities are present (at the margin), social benefits or costs diverge from private benefits or costs. Allocative inefficiency caused by a mandate, while imposing losses on workers and firms, might pass a social benefit-cost test owing to third-party benefits or reductions in costs.

Examples of externalities often cited in the literature include health insurance, the public goods aspects of certain working conditions, advance notice, severance payments, and parental leave. Taking each in turn, the case for mandatory health insurance may have a basis in the fact that health care benefits are in practice extended by society to indigents so that an uninsured individual who obtains a job with health insurance reduces the costs to others.[3] Similar reasoning can be applied to mandatory pensions and employment protection. Relatedly, the public goods aspects of employment conditions can create underprovision of valued services since individuals may be expected to underinvest in making their preferences known or in investigating, say, whether the use of certain chemicals in the workplace poses a threat that may be remedied by changes in conditions or the establishment of a compensating differential (Krueger 1994:302). Advance notice for its part has been advocated on the grounds that plant closings and mass layoffs impose costs on communities in which the plant is located. The argument often also includes reference to imperfect experience rating so that layoffs at one firm raise the costs of other firms. By interfering with private layoff decisions through advance notice, inter alia, so the argument runs, the distortions introduced through another measure may be counteracted. Exactly the same second-best argument can be applied to severance payments. Finally, parental leave has been advocated on externality grounds, it being argued that the care of children of working mothers leads to healthier and more productive adults, thereby placing lesser strain on government support systems.[4]

The prisoner's dilemma case is a special case of externalities and pertains to a situation in which individually rational behavior is nonetheless inefficient because it generates an outcome that is less preferred by all the parties than a cooperative (but unstable) outcome. This has led a number of observers to argue that it is possible for a government mandate to shepherd them to a preferred solution. The argument has most recently been applied to worker participation (Levine and Tyson 1990; Freeman and Lazear 1995), which we comment on subsequently.

Another source of market failure is adverse selection, typically associated with asymmetric information or an inability to distinguish among heterogeneous parties. Here, private contracting does not maximize the surplus because of the risks associated with worker/firm heterogeneity. Thus, for example, a firm that voluntarily adopts a just cause dismissals policy may be expected to attract a disproportionate share of workers who will supply low effort or shirk but be difficult to dismiss with cause (Levine 1991). Or if private insurance companies sold unemployment insurance to firms, they would attract as clients those firms most prone to unemployment. As with externalities, the identification of adverse selection or other potential examples of market failure does not establish the case for mandates nor suggest the complete absence of markets. For example, private insurance companies do provide medical insurance and firms do provide just cause in nonunion regimes. Given the presence of adverse selection, however, it need not follow that provision levels and mix in private markets are optimal.

In recent years the literature on mandates, in particular, has emphasized the role of asymmetric information (Summers 1989). It is argued that where workers or firms have private information that they may be unwilling or unable to disclose, mandates can facilitate an improvement in efficiency. Addison, Barrett, and Siebert (1995) offer an evaluation of this important argument. The informed party in this case is the worker side. It is confirmed that insurance-type components of the labor contract (e.g., maternity benefits and medical insurance) may be underprovided compared to the full-information contract. In these circumstances, it is shown that mandates that increase the level of insurance offered may permit potential Pareto improvements, irrespective of whether or not the premandate contracts differentiated between high- and low-risk workers (see also Aghion and Hermalin 1990). (Differentiation means a separating equilibrium, whereas non-differentiation implies uniform contracts or a pooling equilibrium.) In the model, the improvement comes as a result of gains to high-risk workers exceeding the losses of the low-risk workers. This redistribution in favor of high-risk workers accords well with equity considerations in the case of unhealthy workers, although this is not true in general. For example, it is not so easy to justify redistribution from high-effort to low-effort workers implied by an employment protection mandate.

Apart from these equity considerations, there is a fly in the theoretical ointment. The model assumes homogeneous firms. If a mandate implies higher costs for some firms than others—maternity leave may be more disruptive to small than to large firms—the conclusions change. If premandate contracts do in fact differentiate between worker types, then the switch in regime (from a premandate separating equilibrium to the pooling equilibrium of the mandate) can be shown to reduce output and no longer guarantee a potential Pareto improvement. The burden of this result is that the designers of mandates have to be concerned with differences between large and small firms and, indeed, other sources of firm heterogeneity that might lead to misallocation. In other words, mandates may need to be carefully targeted rather than uniform in reach. Yet targeted policies introduce their own set of informational, legislative, and administrative requirements.

Needless to say, not all mandates conform to the structure imposed by this model. A case in point is advance notice, which can be modeled as forcing firms to reveal their type—either temporary or permanent employers. Kuhn (1992) argues that a notice mandate can yield actual Pareto improvements. His model assumes that notice contracts are prohibitively costly to write and enforce. Where employers cannot use the wage to signal their type, it is shown that the premandate situation conforms to a pooling equilibrium. Absent valued notice, there is obvious scope for efficiency gains through the better informed quit behavior of workers, abstracting from the thorny problem of the length of notice to be fixed. Of course if one argues to the contrary that firms can commit to give notice, then even in the presence of market failure on the other side (i.e., the fundamental inability of workers to alienate their right to quit), the case for a mandate can be shown to evaporate (Addison and Chilton 1997).

Labor market distortions arising from market structure, in particular the possibility of monopsonistic power among employers, can provide a rationale for at least some forms of regulation (most notably, a minimum wage). Although pure monopsony (i.e., a single employer and the absence of mobility across labor markets) is rare, a violation of the competitive assumption of a perfectly elastic long-run labor supply curve is not. Most firms face upward sloping labor supply curves in all but the very long run, owing to costly mobility among workers and training that is nontransferable across employers, among other reasons. Although upward sloping labor supply curves can indicate a *potential* for the exercise of monopsony power (i.e., through lower employment and wages), evidence for such outcomes is meager. Even in textbook examples of monopsony, such as the employment of registered nurses (RNs) by hospitals, the presence of upward sloping labor supply curves (Sullivan 1989) does not imply monopsonistic outcomes. For example, Hirsch and Schumacher (1995) find that the wages of RNs relative to similar workers within 252 labor markets vary neither with the number or density of hospitals nor with market size. In a comprehensive survey of the theoretical and empirical literature on monopsony, Boal and Ransom (1997) conclude that there is little evidence of long-run monopsony power being exercised in the labor market.

More broadly, the fact that most labor markets are at variance with the textbook characterization of a distortion-free competitive market in and of itself provides no rationale for labor market regulation and mandates. As we have seen, development of such a rationale, as has been done for selected types of mandates in the case of externalities and adverse selection, requires careful analysis. That labor markets need not operate "by the book" simply makes good analysis all the more difficult. Indeed, imperfections elsewhere in the system (e.g., progressive income taxation and imperfectly rated unemployment insurance) in some instances provide a cogent case for mandates if reform of these preexisting distortionary influences is deemed politically infeasible.

Although our focus has been on economic efficiency, we return to the point that equity may figure more largely than efficiency considerations in the design of public policy. Two major questions are posed here. In the first place, measures that may notionally increase earnings equality (e.g., minimum wages) may not do the same for incomes in the presence of disemployment effects. Here the fundamental question is whether the focus should be upon employment mandates that benefit only those in employment. The second question concerns the degree of equality of incomes to be sought. The problem arises in the situation where there is a tradeoff between average income and equality of incomes. Here, efficiency considerations are inextricably linked with redistribution. In this context, we should like to find policies that improve or at least little affect efficiency while redistributing toward the disadvantaged. Yet the disadvantaged are sometimes the victims of measures seeking to place floors under working conditions. Given these problems, the search should perhaps be toward alternative measures for improving the prospects of unskilled and disadvantaged workers.

We would be remiss if we failed to emphasize that policy is determined through the political process and not primarily on the basis of efficiency arguments or benefit-cost calculations. Politicians and, to a lesser extent, regulatory agencies and the courts respond to lobbying by interest groups. Efficiency considerations do matter, to the extent that the benefits and costs associated with employment regulations are transmitted through the political process. In those cases where a particular workplace arrangement provides large social benefits relative to costs, we should see it evolve voluntarily, unless market failure from externalities, asymmetric information, or the like are important. If market failure is present but benefits of a policy are high relative to costs, political opposition should not be strong, although it need not follow there will be an organized constituency lobbying for beneficial policies. In cases where there is not a compelling economic case for a workplace mandate or regulation, its passage and implementation face constraints. Lobbying by business groups (or others) expected to be hurt by legislation lowers the probability of passage or alters legislation in a way that mitigates the costs. Likewise, agency and court interpretation and implementation of legislation are likely to display some sensitivity to costs. For those policies where total benefits and costs move in tandem (e.g., a family leave policy in which few workers participate might entail low costs and benefits, and vice versa), it follows that opposition (and costs) should be substantial in those very cases where benefits are most significant. Legislation that overcomes what is relatively weak opposition may well provide small gains.

An interesting facet of the political debate surrounding employment regulation is that much emphasis appears to be given to effects that economists would expect to be short run. Economic analysis suggests that in circumstances where workers value mandated benefits, a mandate should in the long run result in a substantial wage offset yet have little effect on employment. Even where workers place little value on the benefits, the costs of a universal mandate (i.e., one covering all workplaces) will be borne largely by workers and have few aggregate employment effects, given the low elasticity of aggregate labor supply (but there will be allocative costs, since even universal mandates will not affect all sectors identically). Yet political lobbying by business emphasizes its added costs and the expected deleterious effects on employment, while organized labor and other worker interest groups rarely express concern for the downward wage pressure associated with mandates. The seeming incongruity between the political debate and long-run economic effects may result from an extreme short-run emphasis in policy making or from general economic illiteracy by the public, politicians, and interest groups. Alternatively, standard economic models may fail to explain the effects of workplace mandates. In what follows, we give little credence to the latter view.

Finally, we should mention two opposing views of the political process that impact on the debate over employment mandates. The "foot-in-the-door" view, heard frequently from regulation opponents, asserts that adoption of any new mandate makes future regulation more likely. Hence, even though a particular policy proposal may be unobjectionable or entail minor costs, business groups might nonetheless fight it vigorously to reduce the likelihood of future policies with substantial costs. A very different view, what we term the "try-it-and-see" approach, is that we typically have poor knowledge about the benefits and costs of policies until after they are adopted. Once adopted, policies whose costs are high relative to benefits can be modified or abolished. Neither view is altogether without plausibility. By the same token, neither should be adopted as a general rule.

## Evaluation: Measuring the Effects of Workplace Regulations

A principal argument of our chapter is that the evaluation of employment regulations and workplace mandates should be informed by empirical evidence. In this section we outline in general terms the methodological framework by which employment regulations are assessed, using language popularized in social science literature characterized by quasi-experimental methods (Meyer 1994). This framework is then used in the next section when we review evidence on individual mandates and regulations.

Suppose we are interested in the effect of policy Z on outcome Y, for example, the effect of a mandated family leave policy on employment and/or wage outcomes. The prototypical experiment would randomly assign the treatment in some markets but not in others. One might then measure the treatment effect by taking the simple difference between outcomes in those markets with and without the policy. That is,

$$(1) \qquad E[Y \mid Z = 1] - E[Y \mid Z = 0],$$

where the first term is the mean value of outcome Y for the group receiving treatment Z and the second term is the mean outcome for those not receiving treatment. Alternatively, equation (1) can correspond to differencing over time, where $Z = 0$ represents the pre-treatment and $Z = 1$ the post-treatment period. In this case, we are simply observing changes in outcomes before and after implementation of a universal employment mandate.

We rarely have pure public policy experiments and must assess as best we can the mostly nonexperimental evidence at hand. Typically, we use regression analysis to calculate something of the form

$$(2) \qquad E[Y \mid X,Z = 1] - E[Y \mid X,Z = 0],$$

where X represents a set of measurable control variables intended to account for (at least some of) the differences in the treatment and nontreatment group that are correlated with outcome Y. Or in the case where we are differencing over time, X accounts for changes in Y over time not related to Z.

What are the concerns regarding the single differencing approach described above, in which we either compare outcomes between observations with and without a policy or the change in outcomes among a group before and after a policy? Meyer (1994) identifies factors that threaten the internal and external validity of simple experimental approaches such as (1) or (2). Internal validity refers to whether or not one can draw the inference that measured differences in the outcome variables are in fact *caused* by the treatment, within the context of the particular study. External validity refers to whether or not the results in a specific study can be generalized to different settings, time periods, groups of individuals, and the like.

An important threat to internal validity or, stated alternatively, a major cause of false inference, is *omitted variables*. The failure to account for factors that affect Y and are correlated with Z (or Z and X) will lead to biased estimates of the treatment effect (omitted variables uncorrelated with Z and X will not bias estimates). In the context of parental leave, this would include unmeasured factors that affect employment or wages and are correlated with the presence of a family leave policy across, for example, time, firms, states, or countries. *Treatment endogeneity*, whereby adoption of a treatment or passage of a law requiring treatment is in response to past, present, or expected future outcomes, also may bias estimated treatment effects. For example, the adoption of parental leave policies by companies, states, or countries may be determined in part by the level of (or changes in) wages and employment. Emphasized in the experimental literature are issues of *selectivity* or nonrandomness with respect to assignment to a treatment group. In the context of nonexperimental data, selectivity can be thought of as a form of omitted variable bias—those receiving treatment (e.g., those in companies or locations with family leave) differ in a systematic way from measurably identical individuals not receiving treatment. Bias also can result from a failure to account for underlying trends in outcomes, in effect, a form of omitted variable bias. As discussed subsequently, experimental designs that include (appropriate) nontreatment comparison groups are intended to account for underlying trends.

*Data quality* problems arise from imperfect measurement of variables. Estimates of the effects of family leave may be biased if policies treated as identical in fact differ across time, firms, states, or countries. For example, a single dummy variable denoting presence or absence of maternity leave would not account for whether leave is paid, whether leave is voluntary or mandatory, the length of leave, job retention rights, or a host of issues regarding policy interpretation and implementation. Another potential source of faulty inference is an overly restrictive model specification that does not properly measure the causal effect of explanatory variables. For example, the effects of family leave may differ with respect to other factors (e.g., gender, marital status, or number and age of children), necessitating a specification that interacts the treatment variable with other explanatory variables.

A lack of external validity can arise where the population from which a researcher's data are drawn differs substantially from the larger population to which one seeks to generalize results. Interactions of the treatment with the setting, time period, or the outcome variables often make it inappropriate to generalize results from a specific study or data set to other settings. In this respect, the selectivity and endogeneity concerns discussed above threaten not only internal validity (i.e., the inference of causality) but also external validity or the ability to generalize outside the particular setting. For example, the effects of voluntary family leave measured among companies adopting such policies is not likely to provide an accurate measure of outcomes that would result from those same policies if adopted or mandated among companies not previously adopting them. Likewise, effects observed in the past may not be identical to effects in the future.

In practice, researchers use a number of alternative approaches for measuring the treatment effect associated with a particular policy. As emphasized by Meyer (1994), a goal of the researcher ought to be either to have exogenous variation in the treatment variable or, if not exogenous, to understand the source of its variation. And as emphasized below, it is important that there be appropriate comparison groups with which outcomes from the treatment group can be compared. The key feature of the alternative approaches is that they employ multiple comparison groups and differencing techniques to measure treatment effects.

A common research design is what we refer to as the single *difference* approach, as seen previously in equations (1) and (2). Yet the difference approach is not likely to provide reliable estimates of the treatment effect, unless one is confident that one has controlled for all important factors influencing outcome Y and that treatment Z is exogenous. In order to improve the accuracy of estimates, researchers often employ one or more comparison groups and calculate a *difference-in-differences (DD)* estimator of the treatment effect. For example, if a state (or several states) mandated family leave policies during some period, one can measure the treatment effect by taking the difference between the change in outcomes among companies in the state(s) that adopted family leave policies and the change in outcomes among companies in the comparison state(s) not adopting family leave. One can also include additional control variables reflecting factors that influence employment and wage outcomes but whose influence over the period differ between states adopting and not adopting the policy. Here it is particularly important that the comparison group(s) be similar to the treatment group and, if not, that adequate control variables be included that account for differences. The use of multiple comparison groups provides a check on the robustness of estimates.

Multiple comparison groups also make possible alternative ways of measuring treatment effects if the groups differ in ways likely to influence their response to a policy. For example, suppose we expect women but not men to be affected by a mandated family leave policy. This enables researchers to provide a *difference-in-differences-in-differences (DDD)* estimate of the treatment effect. This estimator might measure the difference between states that did and did not enact family leave policies in the changes over time (the pre- and post-enactment periods) in female-to-male employment (or wages). Whereas the *DD* estimator provides for time period controls by introducing comparable nontreated states during the same years, the *DDD* estimator additionally controls for state-specific effects by introducing a within-state comparison group (i.e., males) assumed not to be affected by the policy. Of course, the quality of an estimator need not be a function of the extent of differencing. In this example, the *DDD* approach may well provide a less accurate measure of the treatment effect than the *DD* approach, if men are significantly affected by family leave and if unmeasured state-specific effects are unimportant. The important point is that policy evaluation may be enhanced by the use of multiple comparison groups. It is important the researcher exercise good judgment as to what questions should be addressed and the appropriateness of alternative research designs.[5]

Additional points regarding research design warrant mention. An advantage of examining changes in rather than levels of outcomes is that one may thereby control for what would otherwise be endogenous policy change. If the adoption of a policy is related to the (past, present, or future) outcome level, treatment effects estimated in levels are likely to be biased. While adoption of a policy is often affected by the outcome level that it in turn is likely to affect, it need not follow that adoption is related to *changes* in outcomes. Also, while the method of analysis is important, it is critical that there be a high degree of signal-to-noise in the data itself. In the example above, reliable estimates are likely only if a number of countries make *substantial* changes in family leave policy during one or more periods and if changes in outcomes occur shortly following the policy change.

The methods described in this section can be used to characterize much of the empirical literature measuring the effects of employment regulations. Three themes warrant emphasis. First, empirical studies cannot be conducted in boilerplate fashion; rather, reliable empirical work requires good judgment, knowledge of the data, and an understanding of the processes that generate both the employment policy and the labor market outcomes under study. Second, it is rare that one has reliable empirical estimates on which to base policy decisions. And third, even were reliable estimates of policy effects available (say, the employment and wage effects from family leave), this would not constitute a full-fledged benefit-cost or welfare analysis of alternative policy proposals. Ideally, it is the latter that might best inform (if not influence) policy decisions.

## Workplace Mandates, Regulations, and Selected Public Policies: An Analysis

### Workers' Compensation

State workers' compensation laws provide for employer-mandated no-fault insurance covering workplace injuries, coupled with limits on liability from lawsuits. The passage of workers' compensation laws in several states during the 1910s constituted one of the earliest and more important government interventions into the workplace. Currently, workers' compensation is compulsory in all but three states (New Jersey, South Carolina, and Texas); even in those states most employers voluntarily choose coverage in order to limit their liability. Total payments from workers' compensation are sizable, amounting to $44.1 billion in 1992. Of this total, 41% was for hospital and medical payments. Payments for workers' compensation exceed those for state and federal unemployment insurance, food stamps, supplemental security income (SSI), veteran programs, or housing programs (U.S. Bureau of the Census 1995:Table 585). Workers are eligible for medical and indemnity (lost wage) benefits when disabled by job-related injury or illness. Employers are liable regardless of fault but may dispute the severity of an injury or illness and challenge whether it is work related. Workers' compensation costs are nominally paid for by employer payroll taxes. A few states require that employers insure through a state-operated insurance system. Many states operate a state system but permit insurance through private insurance companies or self-insurance. In most states, the typical small employer purchases private insurance and large employers self-insure. Insurance companies set rates based on a combination of manual rates, which vary on the basis of rather detailed industry/occupation breakdowns and experience rating (larger established firms have full or close to full experience rating).

Is there a strong economic rationale for workers' compensation? We believe there is. Absent some form of no-fault insurance for workplace injuries, a large number of accidents would be handled by the courts using a negligence standard. The joint costs of determining liability under these circumstances would be large, substantially larger than the indemnity and medical costs of most accidents. Only a minority of workers would be compensated for injuries if it were necessary to prove company (or coworker) negligence, and payment would be received long after most medical expenses occurred and wages were foregone. In principle, workers and firms could enter into employment contracts that include forms of no-fault injury insurance not unlike workers' compensation. Were it not for a mandatory system, it is likely we would see such contracts in some workplaces, assuming adverse selection were not too serious. But contracts of such detail involve considerable transaction costs and are rarely the norm. Workers' compensation systems, in effect, provide a standard contract, albeit one in which the parties cannot bargain away. Indeed, the fact that workers' compensation arose prior to the Depression and New Deal social legislation suggests that there was either business support for or weak opposition to mandatory workers' compensation.[6]

Workers' compensation might be justified by forms of market failure discussed in the previous section. Workers (at the relevant margin) may not have good knowledge about workplace dangers, and employers have little incentive to truthfully reveal such information. This implies that compensating risk differentials would be inefficiently small and workplace safety too low. Mandatory compensation for injuries forces the employer to take account of the cost of workplace injuries (even if the costs are fully shifted to workers in the form of lower wages). Externality arguments might also be made. Absent workers' compensation, much of the medical costs and some of the indemnity costs from workplace injuries will be shifted to others. Indeed, an advantage of having workers' compensation rather than other forms of health insurance pay for the medical cost of workplace injuries is that it shifts costs to parties whose behavior can affect safety.

Although a strong case can be made for some system of mandatory workers' compensation, such a system creates inherent inefficiencies, primarily by reason of moral hazard. Moral hazard here refers to a situation where insurance coverage affects the actions of insured parties; specifically, the probability and extent of injury and illness claims. Moral hazard is inevitable absent symmetric information between insurers and those insured and complete experience rating of premiums. Workers receiving generous compensation for workplace injuries are more likely to make claims for benefits than they would were compensation lower, and time away from work is likely to be longer for any given health limitation. If health care providers and injured workers receive compensation for medical treatment, more treatment is likely to be provided than would otherwise occur.

If the level of safety were suboptimal in an unregulated market, the introduction of workers' compensation should be associated with a safer workplace. Likewise, higher benefit (cost) levels should result in fewer workplace injuries. Yet the empirical evidence unambiguously points to a positive relationship between both injury claims and duration and the level of benefits (for reviews, see Ehrenberg 1988; Krueger 1990; Butler 1994).[7] In contrast, there is a *negative* relationship between workplace *fatalities* and benefit levels. Taken together, this evidence suggests that employers respond to workers' compensation by making the workplace safer, but that moral hazard on the part of workers increases claims from nonfatal accidents. The moral hazard to some extent will take the form of reduced risk avoidance by workers on the job. The more important behavioral effect is that in the event of an injury, absence from work and indemnity claims are more likely the more generous are benefits, the more informed are workers, and the greater protection offered workers to management discouragement of claims (Hirsch, Macpherson, and DuMond 1997; Weil in this volume). There is also evidence that medical costs are higher for workers' compensation patients than for patients with similar medical conditions not resulting from work-related injuries. Although some of the difference may result from higher prices, most of the difference appears to be a greater use of medical services for workers' compensation patients (Durbin, Corro, and Helvacian 1996; Johnson, Baldwin, and Burton 1996).

Although employers nominally pay for workers' compensation, theory suggests that most of the costs should be shifted back to workers in the form of lower wages, given aggregate labor supply curves of close to zero elasticity. Fishback and Kantor (1995) provide evidence on relative wage changes among states enacting and not enacting workers' compensation early in the century and find full or almost full wage offset. Gruber and Krueger (1991), using more recent data, report that wage growth is inversely related to changes in benefit levels.

It is the variation in indemnity benefits across workers that provides the basis for much of the empirical work on workers' compensation. Because provisions vary by state and benefit replacement rates vary with worker earnings within states (owing to benefit ceilings), the standard empirical strategy has been to examine differences in claim rates with respect to benefit levels using industry, state-by-industry, or (less frequently) individual data. An example of a recent study explicitly using a quasi-experimental approach is Meyer, Viscusi, and Durbin (1995), which examines evidence in Michigan and Kentucky following increases in benefits for higher but not lower wage workers. They find evidence that in both states duration of absence from work increased among higher wage workers following the increase in benefit levels, but that there was no change in behavior among lower wage workers.

Workers' compensation provides an important source of insurance to workers for medical costs and indemnity losses arising out of workplace injuries. A system mandating coverage may well be superior to what would exist absent government mandates and regulation, although we cannot describe with confidence what the unregulated counterfactual would be (this would depend in part on the nature of a country's health and unemployment insurance systems). But our current system of state workers' compensation insurance is costly and suffers from no small degree of moral hazard. As evident with other government programs, inefficiencies increase as program generosity expands. It is difficult to provide adequate compensation for workplace injuries in a way that does not entail substantial inefficiency costs.

*The Fair Labor Standards Act: Minimum Wages and the Overtime Premium*

The Fair Labor Standards Act of 1938 (FLSA) introduced, inter alia, two important forms of federal wage regulation—minimum wages and an overtime premium. Because the FLSA is examined elsewhere in this volume, our treatment is brief. The overtime provision requires that overtime wages of at least one and one-half times the straight-time hourly wage be paid for hours worked per week in excess of 40. Although interpretation is not always clear, the provision applies to workers whose pay varies directly with hours worked. Employees are exempt if paid a bona fide salary and if their duties are performed independently of a supervisor or detailed company procedures. Roughly two-thirds of all workers are subject to the overtime pay provision (Ehrenberg and Smith 1994:138; Zachary 1996), with the major categories of excluded employees being executive, administrative, and professional workers, outside salespersons, and agricultural workers, as well as some groups of workers covered by other labor legislation (e.g., truck drivers, airline personnel, and railroad workers).[8]

A principal argument used to support the overtime premium is that it will increase employment. To discourage routine use of overtime and increase employment, proposals were made in Congress during 1979 and 1985 to increase the overtime premium to double time (Ehrenberg and Smith 1994:138n). An overtime premium mandated *economywide* cannot increase employment significantly, however, unless there exists excess unemployment (we ignore the unlikely possibility that an overtime premium attracts individuals into the labor force). If there exists high unemployment, then the argument that an overtime premium increases employment is possible *if the straight-time wage (W) remains fixed.* Firms determine the optimal mix between employment and hours per worker (see Ehrenberg and Smith 1994:136-43); an increase in marginal wage costs from W to 1.5W may shift firms' mix toward employment and away from overtime hours, although this need not follow given the increase in costs faced by employers.

The argument that an overtime premium will increase employment is weakened further by the possibility that as a result of the premium the straight-time wage will *decrease* so that the wage-hours combination is of equivalent value to workers (Trejo 1991). That is, the availability of jobs offering overtime hours may result in an equilibrium straight-time wage that is slightly lower than it would be in the absence of the premium. Trejo refers to this possibility as the "fixed-job" model, as compared to the "fixed-wage" model assumed previously. Trejo attempts to compare these models empirically, testing for wage and employment effects associated with overtime pay. Because the overtime provision is federal, has remained at 1.5W over time, and applies broadly across the labor market, estimating its effects reliably is difficult. Based on occupation and industry of employment, Trejo compares wages and employment of male hourly workers who are likely to be covered by the overtime provision to those for workers not likely to be covered. His evidence is not fully consistent with either the fixed-wage or fixed-job model, leading him to conclude that the overtime provision may cause both small increases in employment and small decreases in straight-time wages.

We know even less about the costs of the FLSA overtime provision resulting from reduced scheduling flexibility. Absent overtime pay regulation, firms requiring workers to regularly or occasionally work long or variable hours would be required to pay a compensating differential only if workers regarded long hours with pay as a disamenity. Labor market sorting would result in what is likely to be a rather modest wage premium for long hours.[9] With the overtime provision in place, firms will often choose to employ existing workers at 1.5W rather than hire additional workers at W, owing to variable product demand and fixed employment and training costs. But the overtime premium does raise the cost to firms of using variable work hours and is likely to increase reliance on temporary workers in positions where firm-specific skills are minimal (for evidence on the use of such workers, see Polivka 1996). Flexibility costs appear to have renewed interest in modifying the FLSA overtime provision, with business groups and the Clinton administration engaged in discussion over legislation providing provisions for compensatory hours or an accounting period longer than a week (Zachary 1996; Stout 1996; Siwolop 1996).[10]

Although empirical evidence on the effects of the overtime mandate is highly limited, theory and available evidence suggest that (a) the effects on aggregate employment are small; (b) utility from the compensation package may change little for workers relative to what would exist absent the mandate, given that compensating premiums might otherwise exist and the straight-time wage would be higher; and (c) there exist efficiency costs from reduced scheduling flexibility for workers and firms, but the magnitude of these costs is unknown. As with other employment mandates, we suspect that both the benefits and costs associated with the FLSA overtime provision are lower than those asserted by proponents and opponents. But unlike the case with other mandates, an argument for market failure in the absence of an overtime provision seems difficult to sustain.[11]

The FLSA also established a minimum wage (MW) for workers, with subsequent legislation periodically raising the (nominal) wage and expanding coverage.[12] As is the case for the overtime standard, the rationale for a minimum wage cannot readily be rooted in market failure arguments. Textbooks routinely show that a minimum wage imposed on a monopsonist can increase wages and employment. Yet employers of low-wage workers rarely fit the standard monopsony model. In an effort to account for what is a weak empirical relationship between the minimum wage and teen employment (see below), theorists recently have proposed models in which small employers in competitive markets face upward-sloping supply curves or behave as if they were monopsonists (see Card and Krueger 1995). It is far too early, however, to evaluate the generality or empirical importance of such models. Despite the absence of a clear efficiency-based rationale for minimum wage laws, public support is widespread, albeit on grounds other than economic efficiency. The most typically stated rationale for the minimum wage is to improve the well-being of workers least well off. Public support may also spring from a belief that fairness dictates some minimum level of compensation for work or some minimum spread in relative wages within the workplace. The principal critique of the minimum wage by employers and economists is that higher labor costs for low-skill workers will decrease employment among those least well off and that the minimum wage does little to reduce poverty or family income inequality.

We will not attempt a thorough analysis of the burgeoning economic literature, much of it focusing on teenage employment effects (see surveys by Brown, Gilroy, and Kohen 1982; Card and Krueger 1995). Rather, we will briefly summarize what we believe can be concluded from the research, focus on the methodological approach used in recent studies, and relate our conclusions regarding minimum wage laws to the larger issue of workplace mandates and regulations.

Most variants of a standard neoclassical model predict that a binding minimum wage will reduce employment (e.g., Card and Krueger 1995:Ch. 11). Until recently, much of the literature estimating the employment effects of MW were based on quarterly time-series data relating changes in the teen employment to population ratio to a prevailing minimum wage measure (typically a coverage-adjusted relative wage), holding constant other determinants of teen employment. An often stated range for the teen elasticity of employment with respect to MW is -.1 to -.3 (Brown, Gilroy, and Kohen 1982), although studies using more recent data produce estimates closer to -.1 (Wellington 1991; Card and Krueger 1995:Ch. 6).[13]

Recent analyses, most notably those authored (or coauthored) by Card or Krueger, have used new methods and touched off a number of new studies.[14] The Card and Krueger studies correspond closely to the quasi-experimental approach described above. For example, Card (1992b) examines the effects of the April 1989 MW increase from $3.35 to $3.80 on teen employment. At the time the new MW went into effect, several high-wage states (including those with state minima exceeding the federal minimum) had as few as 10% of teens that should have been affected by the federal minimum (i.e., with pre-April 1989 wages ranging from $3.35 to $3.80), whereas low-wage states (typically those in the South) had as many as half of their teenagers affected. The expectation from standard theory is that one should observe lower teen employment growth (or a larger reduction) in low-wage states with a high fraction of teens affected than in high-wage states with a low fraction affected. Card finds no significant differences, however, in employment growth based on differences in the fraction of teens affected. One can interpret this as a difference-in-differences (DD) approach, comparing the difference in employment changes between markets most affected and those least affected by the treatment (MW), controlling for other factors affecting teen employment such as demand conditions.

Other studies from Card and Krueger use a similar methodology. Card (1992a) examines the employment effects of an increase in California's MW but finds differences in employment growth to be largely unaffected by the proportion of workers who should be impacted, or relative to comparison states. A study by Katz and Krueger (1992) using self-collected data on Texas fast-food restaurants found differences in employment growth following an increase in the MW that were largely unrelated to the previous wage level in the restaurants. And in one of the more publicized (and disputed) studies, Card and Krueger (1994) collected data on fast-food restaurants in New Jersey and Pennsylvania. Using a DD methodology similar to the Texas study, they found that employment growth among the New Jersey restaurants was unrelated to the proportion of workers affected by the New Jersey state minimum wage law. In addition, they used the Pennsylvania restaurants as an alternative comparison group, comparing changes in employment growth in New Jersey restaurants (the treatment group) to growth in Pennsylvania restaurants, the latter serving as a comparison group not subject to a minimum wage increase. In neither case did they find that MW increases had a negative and significant impact on employment.[15]

The new research on the minimum wage reinforces and strengthens rather considerably prior evidence concluding that employment effects associated with changes in the minimum wage, at least at levels historically adopted in the U.S., are rather small. Our understanding of *why* MW employment effects are so small is on less firm grounds. But the absence of large effects of MW on employment clearly undercuts the case for opposing moderate increases in the minimum.[16] Less encouraging is the fact that the antipoverty effectiveness of minimum wages is limited (see Gramlich 1976; Addison and Blackburn 1996a; for a more positive view, see Card and Krueger 1995:Ch. 9). This is not surprising, given the weak linkage between low-wage workers and family income. MW laws disproportionately affect teenagers, yet teen workers are distributed evenly throughout the family income distribution. Despite Card and Krueger's upbeat evaluation based on the MW effect on "worker" poverty and the distribution of earnings, overall antipoverty effects are not substantial. The MW appears to be a far less effective antipoverty tool than direct income maintenance programs or alternative earnings-related policies such as the earned income tax credit (see Burkhauser, Couch, and Glenn, forthcoming).

Ultimately, one is reduced to making second-best arguments for the minimum wage. Not unlike the conclusion that will be made with respect to other worker mandates or regulations, the often vitriolic debate over minimum wage laws exaggerates its importance. Neither the benefits nor costs match those asserted by its more vocal proponents and opponents.

## Employment-at-Will/Wrongful Discharge

Outside of the union sector, the employment relation in the U.S. is largely governed by the common law employment-at-will doctrine, the legal basis of which rests on notions of freedom of contract and mutuality of obligation or consideration. The at-will principle is often referred to as "fire-at-will," because the employer can legally terminate an individual open-ended contract (i.e., one of indefinite duration) without cause (we ignore for now *implicit* contracts binding workers and firms). The at-will principle, however, has been attenuated over time as a result of incursions of state legislatures and the courts.

Courts in almost all states have recognized some exceptions to the traditional common law. The most commonly recognized exception has been a so-called "public policy exception," designed to protect whistleblowers, those exercising statutory rights, and those refusing to act unlawfully. Secondly, courts in a majority of states have held that company personnel handbooks and oral statements to the employee constitute implied-in-fact contracts that preclude dismissal without proper cause. Thirdly, a minority of states have proceeded well beyond these two exceptions to argue that there is an implied covenant of good faith and fair dealing that governs the employment relation, effectively requiring just cause. Despite this judicial activism, only Montana has thus far enacted just cause legislation per se. Other states have introduced such legislation (for details, see Krueger 1991:650-52).

The case for unjust dismissals legislation may be made on either first- or second-best grounds. The former would typically have a basis in freeing up valuable information possessed by workers and in encouraging consummate as opposed to perfunctory cooperation. Without a mandate, adverse selection would result in "problem workers" (i.e., those who might lose jobs with employment-at-will but could only be dismissed with difficulty under just cause) being attracted to those firms who voluntarily adopt an unjust dismissal policy. Firms, thus, are reluctant to adopt such policies and too little job security is produced absent a mandated policy. The second-best case might be predicated on the argument that such a mandate might offset imperfections in the UI system that encourage too much turnover. Since unjust dismissals legislation raise employment adjustment costs, however, the second-best argument is not altogether a comfortable one.

But as we have indicated there is no national unjust dismissal legislation in the U.S. Empirical analyses have thus been devoted to an examination of the attenuation of hire-at-will by the courts. One irony of this is the suggestion that a mandate might secure a low-cost and predictable alternative solution to the casuistic rulings of the judiciary.[17] Surveys of average awards granted in unjust-dismissal cases point to substantial (and positively skewed) settlements. In successful cases, the median initial award approximates $180,000 (this figure does not account for post-trial actions that may reduce awards) (Dertouzos, Holland, and Ebener 1988; Shepard, Heylman, and Duston 1989). That being said, total costs (including legal fees) to employers would appear to be less than .1% of the total wage bill. But note that one cannot directly infer the effects of the legal system based on total award and legal costs, since high awards and an unfavorable judicial climate will deter businesses from dismissing workers without clear-cut cause, lowering the number of total cases and awards.

Turning to the empirical evidence, Dertouzos and Karoly (1992, 1993) have provided a direct test of the effects of legal incursions, using state-level data for 1980-87. States are distinguished according to which of three (hybrid) wrongful dismissal doctrines their courts have embraced and whether or not the remedies provided for are contractual or tort based. They examine a fixed-effects employment model in which regressors include gross state product, the growth in gross state product, year dummies, and dummies for legal doctrine and type of remedy. The latter are instrumented to account for their nonrandom distribution across states (i.e., adoption of a particular doctrine or remedy may be influenced by unmeasured factors affecting employment).

Dertouzos and Karoly report that aggregate employment is on average 2.9% (1.8%) lower in the years following a state's recognition of tort (contractual) damages for wrongful termination. Regressions run for other combinations of doctrine and remedy confirm that it is the availability of tort remedies rather than type of exception that drives the disemployment result. Recalling that legal costs represent a tiny proportion of the wage bill, the authors conclude that in their employment decisions employers seem to be reacting as if the costs were much greater. Despite this evidence, Dertouzos and Karoly argue that the benefits of unjust dismissal legislation may be worth the employment sacrifice. Among other things, they speculate that a clear legal doctrine limiting unjust dismissal might reduce uncertainty about the enforceability of implicit labor market contracts and allow the parties to more fully reap the benefits of long-term employment relationships.[18]

Other analysts have interpreted court rulings in a rather different sense. For example, Krueger (1991) takes the position that the courts and current legal system are costly, if not yet so costly as to lead to the adoption of legislation. His maintained hypothesis is that the prospects for actual legislation are improved by draft legislation, which in turn is directly linked to the erosion of employment-at-will by the courts. He models the determinants of the likelihood that a state will introduce unjust dismissal *draft* legislation, using state data for 1981-88. His logit estimates suggest that the good faith and public policy exceptions by the courts (he does not examine remedies) are significant determinants of states drafting legislation—the probability that a state legislature will introduce legislation is increased by 6.7% and 8.5% if its court system has recognized good faith and public policy exceptions, respectively. Causality appears to run from legal incursion by the courts to legislation, rather than the converse. Features of the draft legislation he examines include limits on employer liability. Krueger links the success of unjust dismissal legislation in Montana to a substantial prior reduction in employer liability. To repeat, for states that have introduced but not passed legislation, it is suggested that the threat raised by court attenuation is not yet great enough.

The evidence marshalled by Krueger offers some support for the notion that unjust dismissal legislation may come to represent for employers "an acceptable political compromise" (Krueger 1992:799).[19] This interpretation is consistent with the idea expressed elsewhere in this chapter that enabling legislation for mandates may ultimately represent a less radical departure from existing practice than is often alleged.

There has been much debate about employment protection more generally, and invidious comparisons drawn between Europe and the U.S. in this regard. Yet the evidence is both sketchy and contentious. Perhaps the best-known study is that of Lazear (1990), who examines the effect of severance pay on employ-ment and unemployment in twenty nations over the interval 1954-86. His evi-dence suggests that more generous statutory severance pay (and longer advance notice) is associated with lower employment and elevated joblessness. A repli-cation of this study by Addison and Grosso (1996) confirms the directional influence of severance on the two outcome measures but their country fixed-effects estimates show the contribution of severance pay to unemployment is not material. That still leaves intact the adverse impact of severance on employ-ment, although it remains to be seen whether this result survives reestimation with a richer mix of country-level controls. Interestingly, Addison and Grosso also report that advance notice seems to be associated with generally favorable labor market outcomes. One conclusion is, then, that different job protection mandates may have different effects on the outcome indicators. But the broader and more important conclusion from this research is that more sub-stantive progress awaits formal parameterization of individual regulations, recognition of the broader institutional structure in which they are adopted and administered, and, importantly, more widespread (but not universal) adoption so that outcomes can be measured using quasi-experimental methods.

*Unemployment Insurance*

The principal rationale for UI is probably less one of economic efficiency and more one of stabilization and income maintenance. UI acts to stabilize consumer spending and provides incentive to firms to smooth employment and production over the business cycle (Moss 1996). Danziger and Gottschalk (1990) report that UI payments reduce the poverty rate of unemployed indi-viduals by about 20%, although, as with minimum wages, UI benefits are not received disproportionately by the poor (Hutchens 1981). Efficiency argu-ments for UI can also be made. While some workers desire insurance against losses from unemployment, adverse selection coupled with asymmetric infor-mation makes voluntary private insurance markets incomplete at best. Hence a government mandate that employers provide insurance (as with workers' compensation) can be welfare improving. Public *provision* rather than man-dates might be justified on the grounds that unemployment risks are not eas-ily diversifiable for private insurance companies (Anderson and Meyer 1993) or, for that matter, states. Indeed, UI is structured so that more federal funds flow to states with high unemployment.

Much attention has focused on the inefficiencies associated with UI and, in particular, the impact of imperfect experience rating on layoffs and the effects of UI benefits on unemployment duration. On the former question, it is clear that imperfect or incomplete experience rating—firms do not bear the full cost of worker layoffs through higher taxes—increases the level of unemployment by causing excessive use of temporary layoffs (e.g., Topel 1983, 1984). Although there has been no major reform of the system to make UI taxes more closely accord with the layoff risk, we should note that among Western countries the U.S. is an anomaly in having even partial experience rating.

Analysis of the effects of UI on the behavior of the insured unemployed has received close attention. From a theoretical perspective it is clear that subsidizing unemployment should lead to longer joblessness. Both the static labor-leisure model (Moffitt and Nicholson 1982) and the alternative job search model (Mortensen 1970) produce this result. The difference between the models resides in the prediction of the latter that UI may improve the quality of job matches. Empirical research has confirmed the longer unemployment duration of those covered by UI. Although there are acknowledged statistical problems associated with left censoring and accounting for unobserved individual heterogeneity, a typical result from U.S. research is that a 10% increase in the UI replacement rate increases unemployment by between 0.5 and 1 week, with some studies reporting higher estimates (Meyer 1990). Similarly, longer entitlement periods are associated with elevated unemployment (Katz and Meyer 1990). At issue is whether this longer unemployment is productive of income. Unfortunately, the evidence on the effects of UI on subsequent earnings is both sketchy and sufficiently varied in approach and results to lead experienced observers to reach opposing interpretations (cf. Burtless 1990; Cox and Oaxaca 1990). Recent research by Addison and Blackburn (1996b) evaluates this issue and concludes that a modest favorable impact of UI on earnings is evident in the data but only when a comparison is effected between UI recipients and nonrecipients (as opposed to samples consisting of claimants only). These favorable effects, where observed, nevertheless fall well below those reported in earlier studies (e.g., Burgess and Kingston 1976). Furthermore, Addison and Blackburn find no evidence of lesser subsequent job changing among UI recipients than among nonrecipients.

Possible efficiency effects of UI remain empirically elusive and are likely to remain so in the absence of experimental studies. Some such studies have been conducted on the use of reemployment bonuses awarded to those who quickly find jobs. In a survey of evidence from the bonus experiments, Meyer (1995) concludes that bonuses speed up job finding on the part of the insured unemployed, that this does not detract from subsequent earnings growth, and that the benefits and costs of the programs may be roughly equal. Meyer, however, notes the difficulty of proceeding from these experiments to permanent policies. The problem in a nutshell is that a reemployment bonus makes filing for a benefit more valuable, leading those who are eligible for benefits but who currently do not claim them to do so. The empirical suggestion is that this effect could be substantial. The bonus program also acts as an indirect subsidy toward the growth of relatively unstable jobs and industries with short unemployment spells. This pessimistic evaluation does not, however, carry over to experiments involving job search assistance, also reviewed by Meyer. Here the evidence from five programs points to reduced UI benefit receipt, increased earnings, and savings to the UI system and government as a whole. Note that these job search experiments strengthened not only the employment service but also the UI work test (see Johnson and Klepinger 1994).

An overall evaluation of UI cannot ignore the inefficiencies associated with the system as presently constituted. Imperfections of the UI system are often deployed to present a second-best case for a number of other mandates. Improvements made to UI, while welcome, appear marginal from this perspective since they do not tackle incomplete experience rating. And from the perspective of income maintenance, the safety net remains incomplete for those with long durations of joblessness. The potential efficiency improvements to UI from job search assistance and reemployment bonuses only partially address the problems of disadvantaged workers for whom more fundamental changes are likely to be required. Such assistance is not likely to come from changes in the UI system.

*Pensions*

Pensions provide an important mechanism by which employers influence worker selection, turnover, effort, and retirement behavior (for reviews, see Ippolito 1987; Gustman, Mitchell, and Steinmeier 1994). Pensions facilitate a more optimal matching of workers with job slots in the face of asymmetric information. For example, pension contributions by a firm, a high degree of wage tilt (i.e., low initial wages but rapid wage growth), and a lengthy vesting period discourage applications from workers with high discount rates and workers most likely to leave the firm. Such a compensation structure is particularly attractive for companies where turnover is costly. Traditional defined benefit (DB) pension plans are structured in a way that penalizes both early exit or delayed retirement from a firm, with pension value maximized at an optimal retirement age.[20] And as argued by Lazear (1995:Ch. 4) and others, backend loading of compensation through pensions (or wage tilt) may increase effort (i.e., reduce shirking) among workers to avoid dismissal from the firm.

The Employment Retirement Income Security Act of 1974 (ERISA), the Tax Reform Act of 1986, and additional federal regulations have restricted firm discretion with respect to pensions (for a summary of regulations, see Hoopes and Maroney 1992). We will focus on two forms of pension regulation—

vesting provisions and pension insurance. First, beginning in 1986 most private sector pensions were required to be fully vested within five years of employment. Employees leaving after five years must receive either a lump-sum payout or be eligible for future pension benefits, based on *employer* contributions or promises (workers receive their own contributions even if they leave prior to vesting). Second, ERISA created the Pension Benefit Guarantee Corporation (PBGC), which acted to insure at least partial pension payments to workers whose employer terminated a pension plan, while at the same time placing restrictions on firms' ability to terminate plans. Companies with DB plans were required to maintain a minimum level of funding, disclose information to the PBGC, and pay insurance premiums (not risk rated) to the PBGC to cover the cost of failed plans.[21]

What are the possible economic justifications for mandated vesting requirements, information disclosure, pension insurance, and other governmental regulations of pensions? As stated forcefully by Ippolito (1987:459-60):

> On its face, the pension contract is tenuous. In exchange for lower cash wages, the firm promises workers pension payments many years in the future. Yet it can either terminate the plan any time or fire workers prior to retirement; in either case, the firm can impose large capital losses on workers. Because of the complexity of the contract and its long-term nature, informational problems would appear to abound. And, the contract is largely implicit, making it unenforceable in the courts. Moreover, there is a potential for a lemons market; if some firms perpetrate fraud, the expected "quality" of all pensions is reduced. Pensions appear to offer a classic example of a product that could not survive in an unfettered competitive market, one that would require at least some government regulation to ensure its survival.

In short, a case can be made for government regulation on grounds of asymmetric information, adverse selection, and externalities.[22] To this list we would add the goal of increasing savings. Insuring a minimum amount of pension savings can be justified on externality grounds, because without such savings older persons will require greater public support. It might further be argued that individuals might prefer a form of forced savings as a disciplining device, as individuals' short-run behavior is often relatively myopic and inconsistent with long-run discount rates (Thaler 1992:Ch. 8).

How do such arguments apply specifically to vesting requirements and pension insurance? With respect to vesting, it can be argued that workers have inadequate knowledge about pension provisions and firms may default on implicit contract promises. Such arguments appear more convincing for regulating financial practices and mandating information disclosure than for vesting regulations, however, since vesting provisions are relatively easy to understand and reputational effects limit firms' opportunistic short-run behavior. We believe a stronger argument for mandatory vesting is to encourage greater pension savings than would otherwise occur among workers who regularly switch employers. One would expect a five-year cliff vesting provision to be associated with low quit rates just prior to five years of tenure, followed by a spike in quits. We are not aware of strong evidence for a vesting spike in quits, suggesting that young workers are not well informed about pension rules or that they highly discount the accrued pension benefits. Either explanation would lend support to a mandated vesting rule, although not necessarily at five years.

Why mandatory federal pension insurance? Prior to the mandate, private markets did not develop because of adverse selection (firms in poor financial shape are most likely to insure), asymmetric information (companies have better knowledge than insurers), and moral hazard (insured companies may underfund absent minimum financing requirements). Federal insurance pooling across risk classes overcomes some of these difficulties and might be warranted on the grounds of imperfect worker knowledge and a reduction in externalities resulting from terminated pension plans. Mandated federal insurance makes the most sense where firm failure is a possibility and where there are few private market alternatives.

That being said, federal insurance is not without its own set of problems; in particular, adverse selection. Many firms have dropped out of the PBGC insurance pool by phasing out their DB plans, instead making DC plans available to workers. Plans remaining with the PBGC then become more risky and require higher premiums, in turn accelerating the movement out of DB plans. Terminated plans, whose pension liabilities are shifted to the PBGC, primarily have been underfunded plans of union firms. Despite the ability for a union as workers' agent to monitor a firm's pension funding, this has been outweighed by the incentive for union firms to rationally underfund plans (and use debt financing) as a means to moderate future wage demands (Ippolito 1985; Bronars and Deere 1991).

Although there has been much recent theoretical and empirical research on pensions (see Ippolito 1987; Gustman, Mitchell, and Steinmeier 1994), the literature provides insufficient information to assess the benefits and costs associated with federal regulations. We believe that government policies intended to mandate or encourage private savings are appropriate, the principal lever here being the subsidy given pensions through their tax deferral status. Likewise, disclosure and financial regulation of pensions seems justified on information and externality grounds. A case can be made for federal insurance owing to asymmetric information and adverse selection, although the PBGC has not been immune to these same forces. But regulation comes with a cost; in particular, distortions in the value-enhancing contractual arrangements between workers and firms. The magnitude of benefits resulting from government pension policies is largely unknown, while at the same time costs and unintended consequences associated with such policies have been readily apparent.

*Advance Notice*

After many false starts the U.S. now has an advance notice mandate.[23] The Worker Adjustment and Retraining Notification Act (WARN) (Public Law 100-379) was enacted on August 4, 1988, and became effective February 4, 1989. The act requires employers with 100 or more full-time employees to provide 60-days' written notice of a plant closing or mass layoff to workers or their representatives. A plant closing is defined as the shutdown of a single site of employment, or part thereof, involving 50 or more employees. A mass layoff is a layoff with duration of more than six months that affects at least one-third of the work force (but not less than 50 employees) at a single site of employment. If 500 workers or more are involved, the one-third rule does not apply and notification is automatic (for further details, see Addison and Portugal 1991).

Considerable effort has been devoted to analyzing the effects of *voluntary* notice on unemployment and earnings. Less attention has been accorded the effects of WARN, but there have been interesting theoretical developments that might usefully be addressed. In what follows, we briefly review the theoretical work and then note the difficulty of making inferences about the effects of a mandate based on evidence from voluntary notice. We conclude with observations on the practical impact of notice legislation.

The general case for an advance notice mandate is typically predicated on the existence of externalities or preexisting distortions in UI. Recent theoretical work, however, has focused on other considerations. As was noted in our introduction, models based on asymmetric information and prohibitive transactions costs have produced the result that notice, although valued by the parties, will not be provided in equilibrium under freedom of contract (Kuhn 1992). The alternative mechanism of using the wage to signal the temporary or permanent status of the firm provides a solution—with permanent firms offering higher wages that serve to increase their future retention rates and which temporary firms find unprofitable to mimic—but only if firms can reset wages in response to information about the need to lay off workers. Where firms have to fix the wage before they know their type (i.e., viability), there will result a pooling equilibrium characterized by a uniform, noncontingent wage. In these latter circumstances, a mandate can now benefit both sides because of the better informed separation decisions of workers.

It is possible to erect alternative models in which a mix of notice and no notice contracts typify equilibrium under freedom of contract, even in the presence of market failure, once the restrictive notion of prohibitive contracting costs is relaxed. Addison and Chilton (1997) argue that the firm's option of not giving notice substitutes for the inability of the worker to commit by virtue of the prohibition on involuntary servitude. In these circumstances, a no-notice contract (at a sufficiently high wage) is a simple arrangement for retaining the worker and avoiding inefficient quits. Nevertheless, a mix of notice and no-notice contracts will emerge in the equilibrium, their relative frequency being determined by the distribution of firm-specific parameters of the model. It is shown that there is no underprovision of notice under unrestricted contracting, with the result that a notice mandate cannot increase the joint surplus of the employment relation. Indeed, in some cases the mandate will actually reduce the joint surplus by causing excessive quits. Also, although the mandate may be simply redistributive, there are also instances in which workers and not simply firms are adversely affected.

Here, as elsewhere, our discussion points to the sensitivity of expected outcomes to assumptions. The plot thickens somewhat when we come to examine the empirical evidence, most of which is based on the CPS Displaced Worker Surveys (DWS). It can be concluded from evidence on *voluntary* notice that prenotification "works" in the sense that it is associated with reductions in joblessness and perhaps with improved earnings development as well.[24] But it is a large leap from these results to the conclusion that notice should be mandated. After all, opponents of a notice mandate would argue that beneficial effects of voluntary notice are to be expected; if notice is valuable, it will be contracted (and paid) for by the parties.[25] Empirically, the endogeneity of notice is addressed by instrumenting notice or employing Heckman-type selection procedures. In the latter case, we may in principle then use selection coefficients from notified and non-notified worker equations to predict the effect on, say, unemployment of mandating notice (Addison and Portugal 1992b). Unfortunately, it has proved difficult to model the notice endogeneity using available data. Even if it were concluded that notice were exogenous, so that the beneficial effects of notice on, say, unemployment duration obtained from single-equation specifications could be generalized to a regime of mandatory notice, debate would not end. All that is being measured in these studies are benefits from notice. The costs of notice have still to be reckoned with, and we have even less information on these.

What are the costs associated with advance notice? One potential cost for employers is premature quits by notified workers. Indirect evidence in Fallick (1994) suggests that these costs could be substantial. Fallick, who examines the determinants of notice, finds that concerns about early exit reduce significantly the probability that an employer will provide notice. A larger cost may be a plant having to continue operations longer than is privately (and perhaps socially) optimal. Deere and Wiggins (1996) suggest that workers often receive little notice in those firms where the need for closing is known only a short time in advance. The longer the time horizon (proxied by facility obsolescence, for example), the longer the amount of notice given. The considerable variation in the amount of notice across firms may be driven by heterogeneity in firm circumstances. In the Deere and Wiggins sample, actual notice was frequently longer than that contractually required but was also far shorter than the 60 days set under WARN. The legislation does allow for a reduction in the notice period in cases of unforeseeable business circumstances, but Deere and Wiggins caution that this provision is not satisfactory given the potential for legal wrangling and requirements that employers bear the burden of proof.

Enough has been said to indicate that our knowledge of the effects of WARN is rudimentary, particularly on the costs side. Our understanding of the potential benefits is better, but even here, unemployment may not be reduced if the observed gains of notified workers come at the expense of non-notified workers—although there are few concrete signs of this in the (cross-national) data (Addison and Grosso 1996). The evidence is still such that an opponent of legislation might readily accept the evidence that those who have been notified in the past have benefited yet nonetheless believe that the costs of making such notice mandatory exceed the benefits.

Might not the effects of WARN be considerably more muted in practice than opponents and antagonists alike have speculated? To examine this possibility we turn in conclusion to a descriptive statement of the impact of the act on the incidence of notice. In the six-year period prior to WARN, roughly one-half of all (displaced) workers received some form of notice. But this was predominantly informal in nature—three-quarters of those with notice either "expected" to be laid off or received verbal notice. Just 8.6% of workers received written notice of greater than one month (3.9% having between one and two months' written notice and 4.4% having more than two months' written notice).[26] In the three-year period following the act, a rather smaller proportion of workers (8.2%) received written notice of greater than one month.[27] Once we control for observable factors that might be related to the provision of notice (e.g., nature of displacement, predicted eligibility for UI, the state unemployment rate, firm size, union density, etc.), the conclusion that WARN failed to affect receipt of written notice still stands (Addison and Blackburn 1994). One interesting result, however, is that short written notice of less than one month became more prevalent after WARN. This hints at an increased formalization of layoff procedures that may be linked to the act, although such notice is not of the type actually mandated under WARN.

Why did the legislation not lead to greater notice being given workers? The most likely explanation is that usual employer layoff behavior leaves most displacements uncovered by the act. Thus, for example, a recent General Accounting Office (1993) study which investigated 650 layoffs that affected 50 or more workers in facilities employing at least 100 workers found that 49% of these layoffs would anyway have been exempted because they fell below the one-third rule. Another 15% of the cases were also identified as being exempted on other grounds. And it will be recalled that WARN only covers firms with at least 100 workers, thereby excluding at a stroke 35% of the work force from potential entitlement to notice. Given that the act has had no discernible impact on notice—at least for its first three years of operation—it is tempting to conclude that this may have been the intention of its designers in Congress. Politicians simultaneously could claim support from one constituency (workers) in voting for the legislation, while those same politicians could appeal to another constituency (employers) by voting to attenuate the mandate's impact, through the adoption of escape routes in those instances where economic and political costs may be high.

## Maternity Benefits/Family Leave

Maternity and family leave arrangements provide an interesting case because a variety of theoretical arguments can be used to make the case for market failure. The externality argument is that imperfect information on the part of a parent as to the importance of child care, or undervaluation of the welfare of children in the parental utility function, raises costs to society via the subsequent well-being or behavior of their children. More compelling is the argument that asymmetric information, in particular the limited information available to the employer as to high-risk workers (i.e., those likely to become pregnant or access leave), would lead to adverse selection among firms voluntarily adopting maternity benefits or family leave provisions. A mandate may provide a (potential) Pareto improvement in which high-risk workers' gains exceed the low-risk workers' losses (Addison, Barrett, and Siebert 1995). Complications are introduced by firm heterogeneity. Where high-risk workers cause greater difficulties for some firms than others, and if separation has achieved the appropriate allocation of labor to begin with, then it automatically follows that a mandate, which amounts to enforced pooling, must adversely affect the allocation of labor. The benefits provided are group specific, applying disproportionately to younger women (and their families). Mandating higher benefits for this group means that their wages must fall. Where this is constrained by antidiscrimination rules, fair wage laws, or relative-pay norms, there will be disemployment among the target group.

U.S. research on maternity benefits per se has focused on whether the cost of maternity insurance has in fact been shifted. The principal study is that of Gruber (1994) who, as previously noted, employs a DDD methodology. The basis of his inquiry is legislation in selected states during 1975-79 that outlawed treating pregnancy differently from other health insurance benefits. Prior to legislation, there typically was no coverage or pregnancy benefits were treated differently. He seeks to ascertain the effect on earnings from the state laws (inter alia) among a "treatment group" of married women aged 20 to 40. In order to identify this effect, his estimating equation controls for year effects to capture common national trends in earnings, state effects to control for state-specific differences across areas fixed over time, and finally state-by-year effects to control for state-specific shocks correlated with the passage of the laws. The earnings of treatment individuals (married women aged 20-40) in the states passing laws are compared with a set of control individuals in those same states (individuals aged over 40 and single males aged 20-40), and the differences before and after the change in state laws are expressed in relative terms; that is, relative to earnings changes among the same groups in states that did not make changes in the law.

Gruber reports a 5.4% fall in the relative wages of prime-aged married women in states that passed laws compared to the change in relative wages in the nonexperimental states, ignoring other observables that affect earnings, and 4.3% following control for observables. Since the cost of expanding maternity benefits amounted to between 1% and 5% of wages, these estimates (as well as others provided by Gruber) suggest that the full cost of the mandates were shifted back to prime-aged women in the form of lower wages. Although women's hours worked increased, numbers employed fell by almost 2%. The suggestion is that although the mandate is valued by the treatment group, some disadvantage is experienced by part-time workers—not surprising given that pregnancy insurance is a fixed cost with respect to hours. Nevertheless, the main conclusion by Gruber is that efficiency may not have been adversely impacted.

Finally, we turn to a study with a bearing, albeit indirect, on the Family and Medical Leave Act of 1993 (FMLA). Ruhm (1996) provides a cross-national study of 16 European countries during 1969-88, using a DDD methodology much like Gruber's analysis for states, to measure the effects of alternative mandated parental leave provisions on employment, working hours, and wages.[28] He reports that total leave and its paid leave component are on net *positively* related to employment, although the effects ultimately become negative for extended leave provisions (total leave beyond 52 weeks and paid leave after 26 weeks). Ruhm finds rather material reductions in wages at long durations of (paid) time off work, namely, a 3% wage loss associated with paid leave beyond 26 weeks. Provisions with respect to total (as opposed to paid) leave suggest modest wage gains at 27 weeks and minor losses at 52 weeks. Ruhm interprets his evidence as supportive of parental leave of up to three months (the FMLA standard) and as suggesting that employers are able to shift to workers some of the costs, particularly at lengthier durations. We are wary of drawing strong inferences for efficiency from this single study, but nonetheless find it interesting that the research again suggests that the *level* of a mandate appears to affect outcomes. This result underscores the need for caution in designing a mandate, even where the case for market failure is a strong one. The relatively weak standards associated with what are politically feasible mandates may have no small degree of economic justification.

### The National Labor Relations Act: Worker Voice and Economic Consequences

Discussion to this point has centered on what can be considered "direct" mandates, whereby the state requires that covered firms provide specific personnel policies (e.g., family leave, advance notice), employment terms (e.g., minimum wages, an overtime premium), or insurance coverage (e.g., workers' compensation, UI, and ERISA). In this section, we consider what can be considered an "indirect" form of regulation—U.S. labor law. The National Labor Relations Act (NLRA) provides the legal structure for private sector union organizing and collective bargaining. The regulation is "indirect" in the sense that government does not dictate terms of employment but, rather, establishes a framework in which workplace outcomes may be determined locally through collective bargaining.

The principal economic justification offered for the NLRA or Wagner Act at the time of its passage was the need to redress what was widely regarded as a fundamental imbalance of power in the labor market. Important noneconomic arguments for the legislation included the desirability of supporting industrial democracy and due process. The NLRA thus sought to encourage collective bargaining and to prohibit specified unfair labor practices on the part of management. Recent discussion of the NLRA has focused more on its role in maintaining a labor relations system often dominated by confrontation rather than cooperation, and the act's alleged chilling effect on worker participation within nonunion companies.

The sources of unequal bargaining power have been addressed by Kaufman (1989, 1991), who identifies generalized unemployment, monopsony power, and discrimination/labor market segmentation as the chief culprits. The diagnosis of a need for countervailing power during the 1930s remains controversial (see, for example, Reynolds 1991). Kaufman (1996) has recently added an important clarification of the macroeconomic context of his earlier analysis. Drawing on congressional testimony, the language of the act, and Senator Wagner's legislative record and speeches, Kaufman concludes that the ultimate goal of the act was "greater economic stability through better economic balance" and as a component part of a coordinated economic program designed to protect against the downward spiral of wages and labor standards or "destructive competition." Regardless of the validity of these economic arguments, we find Kaufman's historical description compelling. We would also note that the notion of destructive competition is alive and well in Europe, where the justification of mandates establishing a floor of worker rights has often rested on precisely this rationale. Here it is usually also argued that unfettered competition threatens consensus and may call into question the achievement of greater economic integration (Addison and Siebert 1991, 1994, 1997). We would also note that modern-day concerns with widening income inequality, sharpened by an improving environment for profitability, offer political appeal for mandates and other forms of government intervention. In short, many of the same arguments that motivated the Wagner Act still lurk in the contemporary wings and once again signify that distributional concerns may transcend those of efficiency.

With these preliminaries behind us, we now turn toward an examination of the economic effects of the Wagner Act. The principal consideration is of course the effect of labor cartelization. If the monopoly face of unionism were all that occupied us, our narrative would be comparatively straightforward, but as is well known, unions have been endowed in modern research with potentially important offsetting collective voice attributes that dilute the monopoly effects. Moreover, the consequences of a precipitous decline in private sector unionism have to be addressed, issues which much exercised the Dunlop Commission on the Future of Worker-Management Relations (Commission 1994).[29]

Absent widespread monopsony or other distortions, the encouragement given to unions by the Wagner Act can initially be evaluated using the standard on-the-demand curve union monopoly model. The result is allocative inefficiency stemming from the union wage premium. Too few workers will be employed in the union sector and too many in the nonunion sector. Any wage rigidities in the nonunion sector (by reason of minimum wages, the floor of welfare payments, and queuing for union jobs) serve to exacerbate the problem, since output losses from unemployment now have to be factored in. Yet conventional estimates of the efficiency loss are tiny. The crude estimates offered by Rees (1963) amount to just 0.14% of GNP. More sophisticated estimates by DeFina (1983) that allow for corporate income tax distortions—which artificially reduce capital intensity—are even smaller. To be sure, such calculations assume that union gains are effected by means of a costless transfer from the rest of the community, but they do not give tremendous traction to the cartelization argument. (A more serious criticism that centers on the static nature of such empirical applications will be dealt with below.)

Moreover, conventional estimates of the costs of the union rule book and featherbedding do not wildly inflate the output loss. Rees (1963) guesstimates that manning standards, workplace restrictions, and other working practices probably exceed 0.3% of GNP, while Allen's (1986) careful analysis of the construction industry concludes that removal of work rules would reduce staffing levels by 3% and total costs by 2%. These are nontrivial but still modest estimates and may potentially be offset by other union job regulatory practices. Finally, nearly all studies indicate that the prototypical union bugbear, strikes, even if laid at the door of unions—an assumption that is vastly naive (Bertram, Siebert, and Addison 1985)—are unlikely to affect output materially by reason of intertemporal substitution of production and the emergence of bargaining protocols designed to take strikes out of competition (Reder and Neumann 1980; Neumann and Reder 1984).

All of this provides thin gruel for opponents of unionism in general and of the enabling legislation of the NLRA in particular. Developments associated with the notion of collective voice (Freeman 1976) further seem to attenuate the economic case against unions as combinations in restraint of trade. The collective voice argument is, of course, that unions lower turnover and establish more effective governance structures in workplaces characterized by public goods (i.e., shared working conditions), complementarities in production, and long-term contractual relationships. Following Brown and Medoff's (1978) important paper, numerous empirical studies sought to obtain estimates of the effects of unions on productivity using a unions-in-the-production-function test. We have summarized the unions and productivity literature elsewhere (Addison and Hirsch 1989). Our conclusion at that time was that no compelling case existed to support the presence of a statistically or quantitatively significant positive union productivity effect *on average* and that such effects were anyway inconsistent with other pieces of evidence concerning profitability and employment. This conclusion seems to have stood the test of time and the publication of more refined estimates based on firm data (e.g., Clark 1984;

Hirsch 1991a). Although we would not wish to overstate the precision with which union productivity effects can be estimated or deny the existence of substantial positive and negative effects in particular settings, productivity effects appear to be small on average.[30]

This evidence is of course not exactly favorable to the collective voice model. And work on profit effects seemed meantime to further qualify the reach of that model. That is to say, the evidence points rather clearly to negative union effects on firm profitability, irrespective of the particular profit indicator used (rate of return on capital, Tobin's q, price-cost margin, etc.) and level of aggregation. Addison and Hirsch (1989) survey the earlier evidence; more recent studies include Hirsch (1991a, 1991b), Becker and Olson (1992), and Bronars, Deere, and Tracy (1994). One response to the adverse impact of unionism on this aspect of firm performance has been to argue that unions simply tax away monopoly rents (Freeman and Medoff 1984). But there are few signs to indicate that union profits or wage gains stem from *concentration-related* profits (Hirsch and Connolly 1987). This does not deny that unions capture rents, although these are more likely to accrue because of regulatory barriers (e.g., airlines, trucking, railroads, and telecommunications prior to deregulation) or quasi rents associated with long-lived tangible and intangible capital (Hirsch 1991a).

Yet it is entirely possible that these facts, namely, lower profitability in union regimes coupled with little or no effect on productivity, are nonetheless consistent with (static) efficiency. This theoretical point is derived from the so-called "efficient contracts" model (McDonald and Solow 1981), which demonstrates that wage-employment outcomes on the demand curve—the context of the monopoly union model—are inferior from the point of view of the bargaining parties to some alternative combination off that curve with lower wages and higher employment, affording the union higher utility and the firm higher profit. Although efficiency from the perspective of the parties is not in general Pareto optimal from a societal perspective, in the strong efficiency case (i.e., a vertical contract curve) at least the outcome is neutral; that is, output, prices, investment, and employment are identical to the competitive (i.e., union-free case). The parties can thus be envisaged as maximizing the size of the pie and then bargaining over the division of the surplus. The negative effect of unions on firm profitability, noted earlier, may constitute no more than a lump-sum tax.

But the story does not end here because in all of this it is assumed that capital is fixed. Not surprisingly, therefore, recent theoretical and applied research has sought to endogenize capital (on the former, see Hirsch and Prasad 1995; Addison and Chilton 1996). One of the more thorough applied studies is that of

Hirsch (1991a) because of its attempt to link the issues of profit and investment in physical and intangible capital. He is concerned to measure both direct and indirect effects of unions on investment. The direct effect stems from the union tax on the quasi rents to long-lived and relation-specific capital, leading firms to cut back on investment so as to equate the marginal post-tax rate of return with the marginal financing cost. The indirect effect of unions on investment arises from the higher financing costs in the wake of reduced profitability.

Using data for 1968-80 on approximately 500 publicly traded U.S. manufacturing firms, Hirsch first estimates the profit effect for a typical unionized firm relative to a nonunion firm, reporting a reduction in market value of roughly 20% (for a somewhat lower estimate, see Hirsch 1991b). He next estimates a physical capital investment equation in which the independent variables are union coverage, profits, and detailed firm and industry controls. Other things equal, it is found that the typical unionized firm has 6% lower capital investment than its observationally equivalent nonunion counterpart. Allowing for the profit effect increases the estimate to about 13%; that is, about half of the overall impact of unions is an indirect effect. Hirsch repeats the exercise for intangible capital (annual investments in R&D). His findings imply that the average unionized firm has 15% lower R&D, holding constant profitability and the other determinants. Allowing for the indirect effects induced by lower profitability only modestly raises the estimate. These deleterious union effects on capital investment have been confirmed in subsequent studies (e.g., Hirsch 1992; Becker and Olson 1992; Bronars and Deere 1993; Bronars, Deere, and Tracy 1994). Another interesting finding is that debt-equity ratios are higher in unionized firms (Bronars and Deere 1991, 1993). The basic idea is that firms increase debt to reduce opportunistic future union wage demands, especially in the presence of firm-specific capital.

Overall, then, the evidence indicates that union effects are real and distortionary. Whatever the positive benefits of collective voice on firm performance, these seem to have been overshadowed by rent-seeking behavior as reflected in reduced profitability and lower investment. It is not surprising, therefore, that we observe substantial management resistance to unions and slower growth in union than in nonunion employment. Indeed, what is commonly characterized as "deindustrialization" is in no small part "deunionization" (Linneman, Wachter, and Carter 1990). The literature on union organizational strength has of course stressed a number of alternative explanations for private sector union decline. One such theme is the contribution of the growth in unfair labor practices by management (Freeman 1988), which is not unrelated to union effects on wages and profits. Another closely related theme is the apparent shift in the National Labor Relations Board's interpretation and enforcement of labor law (Sockell and Delaney 1987; Allen 1994). Both views suggest that the Wagner Act has been diluted and that labor law now needs to be strengthened (Weiler 1990), whereas the rent-seeking approach, while not condoning flouting of the law by management, would view the erosion of union bargaining power as both natural and not altogether unwelcome, other things being equal.

Other things may not be equal, however. One interesting issue here is raised by the apparent decline in the demand for unionism on the part of workers (Farber and Krueger 1992). A change in worker sentiment could in part reflect changes in the industrial relations environment noted above. It may also be expected to reflect the expanding role of the government (and the courts) in extending worker rights. Causation likely runs in both directions, however, raising the question of whether the decline in union density may have gone too far. This necessarily imprecise argument rests on the problems with mandates identified in this chapter as well as the litigation stemming from laws that rely wholly or in part on individual lawsuits for their enforcement.

Stated bluntly, the decline in private sector unionism (i.e., "indirect" regulation) and absence of a formal mechanism for worker voice in most private sector workplaces might be leading to an undue reliance on costly "direct" mandates and a litigious labor relations environment. The Dunlop Commission was of course much exercised by the impact of law and administrative regulation on the workplace. Implicitly its "solutions" look to unionism. For example, in recommending experimentation with in-house dispute resolution the Commission (1994:29) seems to favor unions in expressing its concern "about the potential for abuse of ADR [alternative dispute resolution] created by the imbalance of power between employer and employee."

A final issue raised by the decline in unionization relates even more directly to the Wagner Act. It is widely felt that worker participation is pro-productive but is likely to be underprovided by the market, especially if the law places constraints on participative arrangements within nonunion regimes. There may thus be first- and second-best arguments favoring a participation mandate. It has also been argued that participation is less effective in nonunion regimes or where employee groups are not largely independent of management control, although employee autonomy also can foster the same type of rent-seeking behavior associated with unions.

As is well known, Section 8(a)(2) of the Wagner Act prohibits employer-sponsored employee involvement schemes from engaging in functions similar to those of independent unions. Although recent legal cases are consistent with a strict interpretation of the law,[31] it has not been established that Section 8(a)(2) has in fact had a chilling effect on the introduction of participation schemes in nonunion regimes (Rundle 1994), despite common assertions to the contrary. There remains the possibility of repealing or modifying it, the latter approach having been adopted in the TEAM (Teamwork for Employment and Management) Act.[32] Potentially more important, then, is the issue of the underprovision of participation in unregulated markets. The general case for a participation mandate is supplied by Levine and Tyson (1990), who offer a prisoners' dilemma argument. They contend that were all firms to adopt participative machinery each would benefit. But participative firms require among other things compressed wage structures to encourage group cohesiveness and dismissals protection to lengthen the time horizon of workers. Unlike the participatory firm, "traditional" firms are said to motivate their work forces through the threat of unemployment and also via sharply differentiated wage structures. The scene is thus set for the emergence of a nonparticipatory equilibrium, since the viability of the single participative firm will be prejudiced by adverse selection such that it will attract the "work-shy," while losing highly productive workers to traditional firms with a less compressed wage structure. In this way, so the argument runs, the market will be systematically biased against participatory workplaces and the economy will be locked in a suboptimal equilibrium. It is also argued by Levine and Tyson that participation works better in unionized regimes because union workers have greater job security (among other reasons), although they downplay rent-seeking insider behavior and provide little more than a caricature of "traditional" firm behavior.

Freeman and Lazear (1995), on the other hand, are alert to the rent-seeking problem. In their model, works councils both increase the joint (shareholder plus worker) surplus, at least over some range of council power, and engage in rent-seeking that reduces shareholder profitability and eventually dissipates the surplus.[33] Because works councils reduce profitability, they are either not established or are given insufficient authority by management; hence an inefficient underprovision of participation absent a mandate. The sources of improved joint surplus identified by Freeman and Lazear are very much those emphasized by the collective voice model, this time underwritten by high quality information exchange and the enhanced job security made possible by a codetermination process which also inculcates in workers a longer-run view of the prospects of the firm. Ultimately, though recommending that participation be mandated, Freeman and Lazear seek to decouple pay from the factors that determine the size of the pie. This explains why they alight on the German institution as an exemplar or template. There is, of course, a certain irony in all of this—if the goal is to decouple issues of production and distribution, the grounds for managerial opposition to works councils are opaque.

But at least we see here an attempt to define the content of a participation mandate. There remains the issue of whether efficient participation can be mandated, as well as the lingering ambiguity over the contribution of independent worker representation to outcomes. Advocates of participation mandates, in general, and German-style mandates, in particular, have rested their arguments on rather partial evidence concerning the efficacy of participation (on the German evidence, often ignored by works council proponents, see Addison, Kraft, and Wagner 1993; Addison, Schnabel, and Wagner 1996). As for the specific contribution of unionism to participative outcomes, the most favorable interpretation of that evidence is that participative programs "work" in both union and nonunion regimes vis-à-vis the nonparticipative nonunion firm (Cooke 1992, 1994). Any such interpretation has to be considered alongside the unfavorable dynamic effects of unions on firm performance noted earlier.

Evidence to the effect that workers would generally welcome greater involvement in their companies and that participation appears to be lower in nonunion regimes (Delaney 1996) might at first blush appear to complement recent theoretical arguments pointing to underprovision in regular markets. Even were it established that there exists a systematic market bias against participation, there is scant knowledge of the type of public policies that might encourage effective worker participation in what is a largely nonunion private sector. More troublesome is the difficulty in disentangling policies that might enhance worker participation from the rather contentious debate over the appropriate role for unions and labor law. The NLRA has undoubtedly strengthened the bargaining power of organized labor in the private sector, with net effects that may well have hastened union decline. This conclusion is of course quite consistent with the argument that certain aspects of the union decline raise legitimate grounds for concern.

Even a crude benefit-cost evaluation of the NLRA is difficult, absent a clear counterfactual. Two possible comparisons are (a) the present NLRA relative to a labor market largely free of direct or indirect regulation and mandates or (b) a strengthened NLRA and union sector as compared to a largely nonunion but heavily regulated labor market (i.e., one with an expanded role for direct mandates). By either standard of comparison, the NLRA (in weak or strengthened form) is arguably superior. Perhaps the more interesting comparison is of the current mix of a relatively weak but rigid NLRA, a diminishing private sector union presence, and a growing albeit limited role for direct mandates versus an alternative regulatory and legal structure that might better facilitate worker voice and participation in union and nonunion companies. Of course, by this comparison our current system does not fare so well.

What is far less certain is that achievable political pathways to a superior system of labor law and regulation can be found. The outline of an ideal system of labor law and regulation lies well beyond the scope of this chapter and our expertise. Such a system, however, must be one that simultaneously offers workers many of the types of organizing rights and legal protections offered by current labor law, while at the same time allowing considerably greater flexibility and enhancing worker participation and cooperation at both union and nonunion workplaces.[34]

## Conclusions

Economic theory can support the case for a number of employment mandates, at least at a general level, based on a variety of market failure arguments. Concerns about equity and worker rights often strengthen the case for state intervention in the workplace. At a more precise level, the predicted effects of mandates depend crucially on assumptions being made and the setting in which regulations are implemented. Policy debate over mandates often accords all too little attention to the milieu of considerable firm and worker heterogeneity in which policies must be implemented, as well as to the market adjustments that evolve in response to mandates. Even where a strong case can be made for a specific workplace mandate, it does not follow that the actual policies adopted and implemented via the political process will be Pareto improving.

The role of economic analysis is potentially important. Theory often provides a good understanding of the qualitative effects of mandates and a reasonable framework for identifying benefits and costs. Empirical evidence, although suggestive, rarely provides information sufficiently specialized for policy makers. Well-designed studies providing internally compelling results need not be generalizable to the policy issue at hand. Much of the evidence reviewed here suggests rather muted benefits and costs resulting from workplace mandates. The effects of mandates are mitigated in part through market escape routes, the shifting of costs, and the mobility of resources, and in part via a political process that shows some sensitivity to both benefits and costs. Politicians in recent years have been unable to devise policies that provide large benefits to their constituencies yet entail low economic costs. This of course comes as little surprise to economists, whose role in all of this has been to cast a rather skeptical eye over governmental intervention. The analytical stance of the economist confronts head on not only the enthusiasm of those who see mandates as a deliverance in a world of pervasive market failure but also those who stubbornly defend the status quo based on equally doctrinaire grounds.

Our analysis has emphasized that workplace mandates face substantial economic limits. Older and larger programs such as workers' compensation and

UI, whose existence can be readily justified on economic grounds, in practice entail no small amount of inefficiency, arising in particular from moral hazard. There is far less evidence of substantial costs or benefits associated with recent programs such as WARN and the FMLA. We are even less sanguine of the role of the NLRA, which on the one hand serves as a less than ideal framework for what is a shrinking and rigid union labor relations system, while on the other hand either restricting or doing little to facilitate worker voice in the mostly nonunion private sector. It seems appropriate that governmental labor law and regulations should better facilitate the development of worker participation and voice. At the same time, it is important that the NLRA not be replaced with a plethora of federal mandates dictating specific terms of employment—outcomes which might better be determined by market forces and decentralized communications and bargaining in union and nonunion workplaces.

## Acknowledgment

We have benefited from discussion with or comments from Kin Blackburn, John Chilton, Sam Estreicher, Dave Macpherson, and Paula Voos.

## Endnotes

[1] There is a logical inconsistency here. Were markets free of distortion, then parties could negotiate around mandates, mitigating negative effects. This argument assumes that mandates do not bestow inalienable rights.

[2] The loss in surplus is seen by the decrease in area of the triangles (the sum of the employer and employee surplus) moving from $W_1$-$E_1$ to $W_2$-$E_2$. With linear demand and supply curves and parallel shifts, this area decreases as long as employment decreases. More generally, the magnitude of the allocative losses depend on the elasticities of demand and supply. See Summers (1989) for a more comprehensive presentation. If wages are inflexible downward by reason of a minimum wage or other constraint, then the allocative costs are even higher.

[3] For a good discussion of the rationale for health care policy, see Cutler (1996).

[4] It is interesting to note that Pigou (1920:87) identified as the "crowning illustration" of negative external effects the work done by women in factories since it threatened injury to the health of their children particularly during the periods immediately preceding and succeeding confinement. Pigou's solution, however, was simply to prohibit such work!

[5] Studies using the *DDD* approach in the context of family leave are Gruber (1994) and Ruhm (1996), described subsequently.

[6] Fishback and Kantor (1994) argue that state workers' compensation was a precursor to the development of the welfare state.

[7] Although benefit elasticities differ considerably across studies, depending on research design, the outcome measure, and data, a ballpark estimate of the average benefit elasticity is .40, implying that, say, a 10% increase in benefits is associated with a 4% increase in claims. Our evaluation of the evidence places the benefit elasticity at the lower end of the range of estimates in the literature, closer to .20 to .30.

[8] Compliance with the overtime provision is not universal. Estimates by Ehrenberg and Schumann (1982) and Trejo (1991) suggest that about 10% of covered employees working in excess of 40 hours do not receive overtime payments. Noncompliance results because of financial incentives to firms to hold down labor costs, legal ambiguities regarding coverage and a poor understanding of the law among many workers and employers, and relatively weak enforcement and low penalties by the Department of Labor (Zachary 1996).

[9] The widespread presence of moonlighting (or dual jobs) is consistent with there being for many workers a constraint on hours and the desire to work longer hours on the primary job (Paxson and Sicherman 1996).

[10] A business-backed bill (the Working Families Flexibility Act) that would allow workers, with employer consent to choose to take compensatory hours rather than pay at time and one-half passed the House on July 30, 1996, with *no* Democratic votes (*St. Louis Post-Dispatch* 1996:5A).

[11] One could make an externality argument. By discouraging long hours of work, one provides parents the opportunity to spend more time with their children, thus enhancing future human and social capital. Otherwise, parents might underinvest in their children either because they are not fully cognizant of the impact of time with their children or because they do not take into account the nonprivate benefits. Even if one were to accept the argument of parental underinvestment, it does not follow that the overtime premium is an effective way to increase investment in children. Many families will circumvent the constraint on work hours through moonlighting or increased hours of work by another family member.

[12] Recent legislation raised the federal minimum wage from $4.25 to $4.75 beginning in October 1996 and to $5.15 in September 1997. Some states require wages in excess of the federal minimum.

[13] The finding that teen MW elasticities are far smaller than standard labor demand elasticity estimates need not be inconsistent, because a relatively small fraction of teens (particularly older teens) are affected by the MW. For example, if one-quarter of teens are affected by the MW, a teen elasticity with respect to the MW of -.2 would correspond roughly to a labor demand elasticity of -.8.

[14] For a description as well as an analysis of prior literature, see Card and Krueger (1995). For a critique of the "revisionist" literature, see the July 1995 *Industrial and Labor Relations Review* symposium.

[15] In fact, Card and Krueger report that employment fell by more in Pennsylvania than in New Jersey. This study received considerable criticism based on measurement error in data collected by their phone survey. In particular, Neumark and Wascher (1995) reexamine the evidence, substituting establishment records provided by restaurants. They find a small but negative MW employment effect based on the New Jersey/Pennsylvania comparison but fail to find a significant MW effect based on the within-state New Jersey data.

[16] It should be noted that weak employment effects from the MW are not a result of low compliance. Evidence from Card and Krueger and others indicates clearly that MW laws do increase wages. Nor does the evidence support the proposition that small employment effects can be explained by a changed mix in the compensation package, with higher wages offset by lower training and fringes. Fringes and training costs are low on most MW jobs. A higher MW does, in fact, increase costs to businesses, some of which are passed forward to

consumers. Card and Krueger (1995:Ch. 10) provide evidence from an events study surrounding the 1989 legislation showing that expectations of a higher MW are associated with lower market values among companies that are low-skill labor intensive.

[17] An analogy can be drawn with workers' compensation laws passed with some support from labor and management.

[18] An indirect test is Hamermesh (1993), who examines the speed of adjustment of employment to output in nine two-digit industries for the period 1973 to 1988. He finds a reduction in the adjustment speed in retail trade and finance and an increase in responsiveness in construction, mining, durable manufacturing, nondurable manufacturing, wholesale trade, and transportation, public utilities, and communications. Since the former group of industries have levels of union density that are low and most of the latter have relatively high union densities, Hamermesh speculates that the observed reduction in flexibility in the former group could well reflect an erosion of hire-at-will, namely, a reduced willingness on the part of nonunion employers to both lay off and hire workers.

[19] But see also Stieber and Block (1992:795), who argue that Montana is simply an outlier. They claim that employers will oppose and continue to oppose such legislation because it "would extend protection against unjust dismissal to a vastly larger number of discharged employees than are now generally involved in court suits." The latter are typically middle- and upper-level management groups rather than hourly workers. Krueger (1992) responds that there are degrees of opposition and that business resistance to legislation will be less fierce in states where the status quo is least attractive.

[20] Defined benefit plans promise workers specific benefits, based on a formula that is typically the product of an earnings base (e.g., earnings averaged over the last several years), years of service and a "generosity factor" (typically about 1% in the private sector and more in the public sector). DB plans discourage early and late exit from the firm. Because the earnings base is in *nominal* terms, workers leaving a firm mid-career suffer a substantial loss in pension wealth since the earnings base will have a low real value at the time of retirement. Pension wealth also declines if an employee works late into life since payment is received for fewer years. In contrast to DB plans, defined contribution (DC) plans (including 401[k] plans) provide a payment by the company into individual worker pension accounts, where funds are then managed largely by workers. DC plans are by definition fully funded, portable (following vesting), and are not structured to penalize early or late retirement. In recent years, there has been a large shift away from DB and toward DC plans.

[21] These provisions do not directly affect DC plans, since they are fully funded. While ERISA provides for minimum funding requirements, Internal Revenue Service (IRS) provisions place *maximum* limits on funding, since company earnings placed in pension funds are not taxed until distributed to workers. Many firms have terminated DB plans and switched to DC plans because they believe IRS limits produce less than optimal funding of future pension liabilities.

[22] Despite the strong a priori case for market failure, Ippolito and others do not believe that there is evidence for widespread market failure and violation of implicit contracts, owing primarily to the disciplinary role reputational effects have on employers.

[23] National plant closing draft legislation dates from 1973 and state legislation from 1971 (see Ehrenberg and Jakubson 1988; Abbey 1989).

[24] The evidence is reviewed in Addison and Portugal (1991). More recent treatments are Addison and Portugal (1992a) and Ruhm (1992, 1994).

[25] Although we note in passing that Ehrenberg and Jakubson (1988) fail to detect any evidence of compensating differentials.

[26] The principal data set available to researchers, the DWS, identifies three lengths of written notice: less than one month, between one and two months, and more than two months. The ambiguity is that WARN grants 60 days' notice, an interval that might be reported by the DWS respondent as either of the two longest categories.

[27] Of the post-WARN sample, 4.4% and 3.8% received between one and two months' notice and more than two months' notice, respectively.

[28] Ruhm (1996; forthcoming) provides a useful, succinct critique of the parental leave literature. He notes that the exemptions and restrictions of the FMLA limit its reach to around 31% of working women. The Clinton administration is expected to propose expansion of family leave to require most employers to grant up to 24 unpaid annual hours of leave for family obligations (e.g., parent-teacher conferences, transporting a parent to a doctor's appointment) (Stout 1996; Siwolop 1996).

[29] Union density among private sector workers declined from 24.2% in 1973 to 10.3% in 1995 (Hirsch and Macpherson 1996:10, Table 1).

[30] For an identical conclusion, see the recent survey by Booth (1995). An evaluation more favorable to the voice interpretation is offered by Belman (1992).

[31] See *Electromation, Inc.*, N.L.R.B., No. 163 (December 16, 1992); *E.I. du Pont de Nemours & Co.*, 311 N.L.R.B., No. 88 (May 28, 1993).

[32] The TEAM Act limits the scope of 8(a)(2) and allows employer-organized and employer-funded worker participation groups in nonunion plants and offices. The measure was passed by the House of Representatives in September 1995 and by the Senate in July 1996. The President vetoed the bill on July 30, 1996, on the grounds that the legislation "would undermine the system of collective bargaining that has served this country so well for many decades" (*St. Louis Post-Dispatch* 1996:5A).

[33] In fact, the authors accept that workers will always demand more than the socially optimal level of power.

[34] For examples of labor law reforms that satisfy these criteria and promote "value-added" unionism, see Estreicher (1994, 1996). Levine (this volume), among others, proposes a system that would lessen direct regulation while maintaining a minimum set of labor standards for firms that voluntarily adopt alternative regulatory systems *with employee oversight and approval*. He would maintain the current system of standards for firms not adopting alternative systems (see, relatedly, Kochan and Osterman 1994). Levine argues that movement in this direction, while weakening workers' de jure rights, would strengthen their rights de facto and produce net welfare gains.

## References

Abbey, Michael. 1989. "State Plant Closing Legislation: A Modern Justification for Use of the Dormant Commerce Clause as a Bulwark of Free Trade." *Virginia Law Review*, Vol. 75 (May), pp. 845-94.

Addison, John T., C. R. Barrett, and W. Stanley Siebert. 1995. "Mandated Benefits, Welfare, and Heterogeneous Firms." Unpublished Paper, University of South Carolina.

Addison, John T., and McKinley L. Blackburn. 1994. "The Worker Adjustment and Retraining Notification Act: Effects on Notice Provision." *Industrial and Labor Relations Review*, Vol. 47, no. 4 (July), pp. 650-62.

_____. 1996a. "Minimum Wages and Poverty." Unpublished Paper, University of South Carolina.

_____. 1996b. "Unemployment Insurance and Postunemployment Wages." Unpublished Paper, University of South Carolina (May).

Addison, John T., and John B. Chilton. 1996. "Self-Enforcing Union Contracts: Efficient Investment and Employment." Unpublished Paper, University of South Carolina.

_____. 1997. "Nondisclosure as a Contractual Remedy: Explaining the Adverse Notice Puzzle." *Journal of Labor Economics*, Vol. 15, no. 1 (January 1997).

Addison, John T., and Jean-Luc Grosso. 1996. "Job Security Provisions and Employment: Revised Estimates." *Industrial Relations*, Vol. 35, no. 4 (October), pp. 585-603.

Addison, John T., and Barry T. Hirsch. 1989. "Union Effects on Productivity, Profits, and Growth: Has the Long Run Arrived?" *Journal of Labor Economics*, Vol. 7, no. 1 (January), pp. 72-105.

Addison, John T., Kornelius Kraft, and Joachim Wagner. 1993. "German Works Councils and Firm Performance." In Bruce E. Kaufman and Morris M. Kleiner, eds., *Employee Representation: Alternatives and Future Directions*. Madison, WI: Industrial Relations Research Association, pp. 305-35.

Addison, John T., and Pedro Portugal. 1991. "Advance Notice." In John T. Addison, ed., *Job Displacement—Consequences and Implications for Policy*. Detroit, MI: Wayne State University Press, pp. 203-43.

_____. 1992a. "Advance Notice and Unemployment: New Evidence from the 1988 Displaced Worker Survey." *Industrial and Labor Relations Review*, Vol. 45, no. 4 (July), pp. 645-64.

_____. 1992b. "Prenotification of Job Loss: From Voluntary Exchange to Mandated Benefits." *Industrial Relations*, Vol. 31, no. 1 (Winter), pp. 159-78.

Addison, John T., Claus Schnabel, and Joachim Wagner. 1996. "German Works Councils and Firm Performance: Evidence from the First Wave of the Hannover Firm Panel." *Kyklos*, Vol. 49, no. 4 (November), pp. 555-82.

Addison, John T., and W. Stanley Siebert. 1991. "The Social Charter of the European Community: Evolution and Controversies." *Industrial and Labor Relations Review*, Vol. 44, no. 4 (July), pp. 597- 625.

_____. 1994. "Recent Developments in Social Policy in the New European Union." *Industrial and Labor Relations Review*, Vol. 48, no. 1 (October), pp. 5-27.

_____ (eds.). 1997. *Labor Markets in Europe: Issues of Harmonization and Regulation*. London: The Dryden Press.

Aghion, Phillipe, and Benjamin Hermalin. 1990. "Legal Restrictions on Private Contracts Can Enhance Efficiency." *Journal of Law, Economics, and Organization*, Vol. 6, no. 2 (Fall), pp. 381-409.

Allen, Steven G. 1986. "Union Work Rules and Efficiency in the Building Trades." *Journal of Labor Economics*, Vol. 4, no. 2 (April), pp. 212-42.

_____. 1994. "Developments in Collective Bargaining in Construction in the 1980s and 1990s." In Paula B. Voos, ed., *Contemporary Collective Bargaining in the Private Sector*. Madison, WI: Industrial Relations Research Association, pp. 411-46.

Anderson, Patricia M., and Bruce D. Meyer. 1993. "Unemployment Insurance in the United States: Layoff Incentives and Cross Subsidies." *Journal of Labor Economics*, Vol. 11, no. 1, pt. 2 (January), pp. S70-S95.

Becker, Brian E., and Craig A. Olson. 1992. "Unionization and Firm Profits." *Industrial Relations*, Vol. 31, no. 3 (Fall), pp. 395-415.

Belman, Dale. 1992. "Unions, the Quality of Labor Relations, and Firm Performance." In Lawrence Mishel and Paula P. Voos, eds., *Unions and Economic Competitiveness*. Armonk, NY: M.E. Sharpe, pp. 41-107.

Bertram, Phillip V., W. Stanley Siebert, and John T. Addison. 1985. "The Political Model of Strikes: A New Twist." *Southern Economic Journal*, Vol. 52, no. 1 (July), pp. 23-33.

Boal, William M., and Michael R. Ransom. 1997. "Monopsony in the Labor Market." *Journal of Economic Literature*, Vol. 35, no. 1 (March), pp. 86-112.

Booth, Alison L. 1995. *The Economics of the Trade Union*. Cambridge: Cambridge University Press.

Bronars, Stephen G., and Donald R. Deere. 1991. "The Threat of Unionization, the Use of Debt, and the Preservation of Shareholder Wealth." *Quarterly Journal of Economics*, Vol. 106, no. 1 (February), pp. 231-54.

_____. 1993. "Unionization, Incomplete Contracting, and Capital Investment." *Journal of Business*, Vol. 66, no. 1 (January), pp. 117-32.

Bronars, Stephen G., Donald R. Deere, and Joseph S. Tracy. 1994. "The Effects of Unions on Firm Behavior: An Empirical Analysis Using Firm-Level Data." *Industrial Relations*, Vol. 33, no. 4 (October), pp. 426-51

Brown, Charles, Curtis Gilroy, and Andrew Kohen. 1982. "The Effect of the Minimum Wage on Employment and Unemployment." *Journal of Economic Literature*, Vol. 20, no. 2 (June), pp. 487-528.

Brown, Charles, and James Medoff. 1978. "Trade Unions in the Production Process." *Journal of Political Economy*, Vol. 86, no. 3 (June), pp. 355-78.

Burgess, Paul L., and Jerry L. Kingston. 1976. "The Impact of Unemployment Insurance Benefits on Reemployment Success." *Industrial and Labor Relations Review*, Vol. 30, no. 1 (October), pp. 25-31.

Burkhauser, Richard, Kenneth Couch, and Andrew Glenn. Forthcoming. "Public Policies for the Working Poor: The Earned Income Tax Credit versus Minimum Wage Legislation." In Solomon Polachek, ed., *Research in Labor Economics*, Vol. 15. Greenwich, CT: JAI Press.

Burtless, Gary. 1990. "Unemployment Insurance and Labor Supply." In W. Lee Hansen and James F. Byers, eds., *Unemployment Insurance: The Second Half Century*. Madison, WI: University of Wisconsin Press, pp. 69-107.

Butler, Richard J. 1994. "Economic Determinants of Workers' Compensation Trends." *Journal of Risk and Insurance*, Vol. 61, no. 3 (September), pp. 383-401.

Card, David. 1992a. "Do Minimum Wages Reduce Employment? A Case Study of California, 1987-1989." *Industrial and Labor Relations Review*, Vol. 46, no. 1 (October), pp. 38-54.

_____. 1992b. "Using Regional Variation in Wages to Measure the Effects of the Federal Minimum Wage." *Industrial and Labor Relations Review*, Vol. 46, no. 1 (October), pp. 22-37.

Card, David, and Alan B. Krueger. 1994. "Minimum Wages and Employment: A Case Study of the Fast-Food Industry in New Jersey and Pennsylvania." *American Economic Review*, Vol. 84, no. 4 (September), pp. 772-93.

_____. 1995. *Myth and Measurement: The New Economics of the Minimum Wage.* Princeton, NJ: Princeton University Press.

Clark, Kim B. 1984. "Unionization and Firm Performance: The Impact on Profits, Growth, and Productivity." *American Economic Review,* Vol. 74, no. 5 (December), pp. 893-919.

Commission on the Future of Labor-Management Relations. 1994. *Report and Recommendations.* Washington, DC: U.S. Department of Commerce/U.S. Department of Labor (December).

Cooke, William N. 1992. "Product Quality Improvement through Employee Participation: The Effects of Unionization and Joint Union-Management Administration." *Industrial and Labor Relations Review,* Vol. 46, no. 1 (October), pp. 119-34.

_____. 1994. "Employee Participation Programs, Group-Based Incentives: A Union-Nonunion Comparison." *Industrial and Labor Relations Review,* Vol. 47, no. 4 (July), pp. 594-609.

Cox, James C., and Ronald L. Oaxaca. 1990. "Unemployment Insurance and Job Search." *Research in Labor Economics,* Vol. 11, pp. 223-40.

Cutler, David M. 1996. "Public Policy for Health Care." National Bureau of Economic Research Working Paper No. 5591.

Danziger, Sheldon, and Peter Gottschalk. 1990. "Unemployment Insurance and the Safety Net for the Unemployed." In W. Lee Hansen and James F. Byers, eds., *Unemployment Insurance: The Second Half Century.* Madison, WI: University of Wisconsin Press.

Deere, Donald R., and Steven N. Wiggins. 1996. "Plant Closings, Large Layoffs, and Advance Notice Provision." Unpublished Paper, Texas A&M University.

DeFina, Robert H. 1983. "Unions, Relative Wages, and Efficiency." *Journal of Labor Economics,* Vol. 1, no. 4 (October), pp. 408-29.

Delaney, John T. 1996. "Workplace Cooperation: Current Problems, New Approaches." *Journal of Labor Research,* Vol. 17, no. 1 (Winter), pp. 45-61.

Dertouzos, James N., Elaine Holland, and Patricia Ebener. 1988. *The Legal and Economic Consequences of Wrongful Termination.* Report No. R-3602-ICJ. Santa Monica, CA: The Rand Corporation.

Dertouzos, James N., and Lynn A. Karoly. 1992. *Labor Market Responses to Employer Liability.* Report No. R 3989-ICJ. Santa Monica, CA: The Rand Corporation.

_____. 1993. "Employment Effects of Worker Protection: Evidence from the United States." In Christoph F. Buechtemann, ed., *Employment Security and Labor Market Behavior—Interdisciplinary Approaches and International Evidence.* Ithaca, NY: ILR Press, pp. 217-27.

Durbin, David L., Daniel Corro, and Nurhan M. Helvacian. 1996. "Workers' Compensation Medical Expenditures: Price vs. Quantity." *Journal of Risk and Insurance,* Vol. 63, no. 1 (March), pp. 13-33.

Ehrenberg, Ronald G. 1988. "Workers' Compensation, Wages, and the Risk of Injury." In John F. Burton, Jr., ed., *New Perspectives in Workers' Compensation.* Ithaca, NY: ILR Press, pp. 71-96.

Ehrenberg, Ronald G., and George H. Jakubson. 1988. *Advance Notice Provisions in Plant Closing Legislation.* Kalamazoo, MI: W.E. Upjohn Institute for Employment Research.

Ehrenberg, Ronald G., and Paul L. Schumann. 1982. "Compliance with the Overtime Pay Provisions of the Fair Labor Standards Act." *Journal of Law and Economics,* Vol. 25, no. 1 (April), pp. 159-81.

Ehrenberg, Ronald G., and Robert S. Smith. 1994. *Modern Labor Economics: Theory and Public Policy,* 5th ed. New York: HarperCollins.

Estreicher, Samuel. 1994. "Employee Involvement and the 'Company Union' Prohibition: The Case for Partial Repeal of Section 8(a)(2) of the NLRA." *New York University Law Review*, Vol. 69, no. 1 (April), pp. 125-61.

_____. 1996. "Freedom of Contract and Labor Law Reform: Opening Up the Possibilities for Value-Added Unionism." *New York University Law Review*, Vol. 71, no. 3 (June), pp. 827-49.

Fallick, Bruce Chelmsky. 1994. "The Endogeneity of Advance Notice and Fear of Destructive Attrition." *Review of Economics and Statistics*, Vol. 76, no. 2 (May), pp. 378-84.

Farber, Henry S., and Alan B. Krueger. 1992. "Union Membership in the United States: The Decline Continues." National Bureau of Economic Research Working Paper No. 4216.

Fishback, Price V., and Shawn Everett Kantor. 1995. "Did Workers Pay for the Passage of Workers' Compensation Laws?" *Quarterly Journal of Economics*, Vol. 110, no. 3 (August), pp. 713-42.

_____. 1994. "A Prelude to the Welfare State: Compulsory State Insurance and Workers' Compensation in Minnesota, Ohio, and Washington, 1911-1919." National Bureau of Economic Research Historical Paper No. 64.

Freeman, Richard B. 1976. "Individual Mobility and Union Voice in the Labor Market." *American Economic Review Papers and Proceedings*, Vol. 66, no. 2 (May), pp. 361-68.

_____. 1988. "Contraction and Expansion: The Divergence of Private Sector and Public Sector Unionism in the United States." *Journal of Economic Perspectives*, Vol. 2, no. 2 (Spring), pp. 63-88.

Freeman, Richard B., and Edward P. Lazear. 1995. "An Economic Analysis of Works Councils." In Joel Rogers and Wolfgang Streeck, eds., *Works Councils: Consultation, Representation, and Cooperation in Industrial Relations*. Chicago: University of Chicago Press.

Freeman, Richard B., and James L. Medoff. 1984. *What Do Unions Do?* New York: Basic Books.

Gramlich, Edward M. 1976. "Impact of Minimum Wages on Other Wages, Employment and Family Incomes." *Brookings Papers on Economic Activity*, Vol. 7, no. 2, pp. 409-51.

Gruber, Jonathan. 1994. "The Incidence of Mandated Maternity Benefits." *American Economic Review*, Vol. 84, no. 3 (June), pp. 622-41.

Gruber, Jonathan, and Alan B. Krueger. 1991. "The Incidence of Mandated Employer-Provided Insurance: Lessons from Workers' Compensation Insurance." In David Bradford, ed., *Tax Policy and the Economy*. Cambridge, MA: MIT Press, pp. 111-44.

Gustman, Alan L., Olivia S. Mitchell, and Thomas S. Steinmeier. 1994. "The Role of Pensions in the Labor Market: A Survey of the Literature." *Industrial and Labor Relations Review*, Vol. 47, no. 3 (April), pp. 417-38.

Hamermesh, Daniel S. 1993. "Employment Protection: Theoretical Implications and Some U.S. Evidence." In Christoph F. Buechtemann, ed., *Employment Security and Labor Market Behavior—Interdisciplinary Approaches and International Evidence*. Ithaca, NY: ILR Press, pp. 126-43.

Hirsch, Barry T. 1991a. *Labor Unions and the Economic Performance of Firms*. Kalamazoo, MI: W.E. Upjohn Institute for Employment Research.

_____. 1991b. "Union Coverage and Profitability among U.S. Firms." *Review of Economics and Statistics*, Vol. 73, no. 1 (February), pp. 69-77.

_____. 1992. "Firm Investment Behavior and Collective Bargaining Strategy." *Industrial Relations*, Vol. 31, no. 1 (Winter), pp. 95-121.

Hirsch, Barry T., and Robert A. Connolly. 1987. "Do Unions Capture Monopoly Profits?" *Industrial and Labor Relations Review*, Vol. 41, no. 1 (October), pp. 118-36.

Hirsch, Barry T., and David A. Macpherson. 1996. *Union Membership and Earnings Data Book: Compilations from the Current Population Survey* (1996 Edition). Washington: Bureau of National Affairs.

Hirsch, Barry T., David A. Macpherson, and J. Michael DuMond. 1997. "Workers' Compensation Recipiency in Union and Nonunion Workplaces." *Industrial and Labor Relations Review*, Vol. 50, no. 2 (January), pp. 213-236.

Hirsch, Barry T., and Kislaya Prasad. 1995. "Wage-Employment Determination and a Union Tax on Capital: Can Theory and Evidence Be Reconciled? *Economics Letters*, Vol. 48, no. 1 (April), pp. 61-71.

Hirsch, Barry T., and Edward J. Schumacher. 1995. "Monopsony Power and Relative Wages in the Labor Market for Nurses." *Journal of Health Economics*, Vol. 14, no. 4 (October), pp. 443-76.

Hoopes, Terence J., and Kevin Maroney. 1992. "Summary of Federal Legislation Affecting Private Employee Pension Benefits." In John A. Turner and Daniel J. Beller, eds., *Trends in Pensions 1992*. Washington, DC: GPO, pp. 635-49.

Hutchens, Robert. 1981. "Distributional Equity in the Unemployment Insurance System." *Industrial and Labor Relations Review*, Vol. 34, no. 2 (January), pp. 377-85.

Ippolito, Richard A. 1985. "The Economic Function of Underfunded Pension Plans." *Journal of Law and Economics*, Vol. 28, no. 3 (October), pp. 611-51.

_____. 1987. "The Implicit Pension Contract: Developments and New Directions." *Journal of Human Resources*, Vol. 22, no. 3 (Summer), pp. 441-67.

Johnson, William G., Marjorie L. Baldwin, and John F. Burton, Jr. 1996. "Why Is the Treatment of Work-Related Injuries So Costly? New Evidence from California." *Inquiry*, Vol. 33, no. 1 (Spring), pp. 53-65.

Johnson, Terry R., and Daniel H. Klepinger. 1994. "Experimental Evidence on Unemployment Insurance Work Policies." *Journal of Human Resources*, Vol. 29, no. 3 (Summer), pp. 695-717.

Katz, Lawrence F., and Alan B. Krueger. 1992. "The Effect of the Minimum Wage on the Fast-Food Industry." *Industrial and Labor Relations Review*, Vol. 46, no. 1 (October), pp. 6-21.

Katz, Lawrence F., and Bruce D. Meyer. 1990. "Unemployment Insurance, Recall Expectations, and Unemployment Outcomes." *Quarterly Journal of Economics*, Vol. 105, no. 4 (November), pp. 973-1002.

Kaufman, Bruce E. 1989. "Labor's Inequality of Bargaining Power: Changes over Time and Implications for Public Policy." *Journal of Labor Research*, Vol. 10, no. 3 (Summer), pp. 285-98.

_____. 1991. "Labor's Inequality of Bargaining Power: Myth or Reality?" *Journal of Labor Research*, Vol. 12, no. 2 (Spring), pp. 151-66.

_____. 1996. "Why the Wagner Act? Reestablishing Contact with Its Origins." In David Lewin, Bruce E. Kaufman, and Donna Sockell, eds., *Advances in Industrial and Labor Relations*, Vol 7. Greenwich, CT: JAI Press.

_____. 1997. "Labor Markets and Employment Regulation: The View of the 'Old' Institutionalists." In Bruce Kaufman, ed., *Government Regulation of the Employment Relationship*. Madison, WI: Industrial Relations Research Association.

Kochan, Thomas A., and Paul Osterman. 1994. *The Mutual Gains Enterprise: Forging a Winning Partnership among Labor, Management, and Government.* Boston: Harvard Business School Press.

Kuhn, Peter. 1992. "Mandatory Notice." *Journal of Labor Economics,* Vol. 10, no. 2 (April), pp. 117-37.

Krueger, Alan B. 1990. "Incentive Effects of Workers' Compensation Insurance." *Journal of Public Economics,* Vol. 41, no. 1 (February), pp. 73-99.

_____. 1991. "The Evolution of Unjust-Dismissal Legislation in the United States." *Industrial and Labor Relations Review,* Vol. 44, no. 4 (July), pp. 644-60.

_____. 1992. "Reply [to Stieber and Block]." *Industrial and Labor Relations Review,* Vol. 45, no. 4 (July), pp. 796-99.

_____. 1994. "Observations on Employment-based Government Mandates, with Particular Reference to Health Insurance." In Lewis C. Solmon and Alec R. Stevenson, eds., *Labor Markets, Employment Policy, and Job Creation.* Boulder, San Francisco, and Oxford: Westview Press, pp. 297-326.

Lazear, Edward P. 1990. "Job Security Provisions and Employment." *Quarterly Journal of Economics,* Vol. 105, no. 3 (August), pp. 699-726.

_____. 1995. *Personnel Economics.* Cambridge, MA: MIT Press.

Levine, David I. 1991. "Just-Cause Employment Policies in the Presence of Worker Adverse Selection." *Journal of Labor Economics,* Vol. 9, no. 3 (July), pp. 294-305.

_____. 1997. "They Should Solve Their Own Problems: Reinventing Workplace Regulation." In Bruce Kaufman, ed., *Government Regulation of the Employment Relationship.* Madison, WI: Industrial Relations Research Association.

Levine, David I., and Laura D'Andrea Tyson. 1990. "Participation, Productivity, and the Firm's Environment." In Alan S. Blinder, ed., *Paying for Productivity: A Look at the Evidence.* Washington, DC: The Brookings Institution, pp. 183-237.

Linneman, Peter D., Michael L. Wachter, and William H. Carter. 1990. "Evaluating the Evidence on Union Employment and Wages." *Industrial and Labor Relations Review,* Vol. 44, no. 1 (October), pp. 34-53.

McDonald, Ian M., and Robert M. Solow. 1981. "Wage Bargaining and Employment." *American Economic Review,* Vol. 71, no. 5 (December), pp. 896-908.

Meyer, Bruce D. 1990. "Unemployment Insurance and Unemployment Spells." *Econometrica,* Vol. 58, no. 4 (July), pp. 757-82.

_____. 1994. "Natural and Quasi-Experiments in Economics." National Bureau of Economic Research Technical Working Paper No. 170.

_____. 1995. "Lessons from the U.S. Unemployment Insurance Experiments." *Journal of Economic Literature,* Vol. 33, no. 1 (March), pp. 91-131.

Meyer, Bruce D., W. Kip Viscusi, and David L. Durbin. 1995. "Workers' Compensation and Injury Duration: Evidence from a Natural Experiment." *American Economic Review,* Vol. 85, no. 3 (June), pp. 322-40.

Moffitt, Robert, and Walter Nicholson. 1982. "The Effect of Unemployment Insurance on Unemployment: The Case of Supplemental Benefits." *Review of Economics and Statistics,* Vol. 64, no. 1 (February), pp. 1-11.

Mortensen, Dale T. 1970. "Job Search, the Duration of Unemployment, and the Phillips Curve." *American Economic Review,* Vol. 60, no. 5 (December), pp. 847-62.

Moss, David A. 1996. *Socializing Security Progressive-Era Economists and the Origins of American Social Policy.* Cambridge, MA: Harvard University Press.

Neumann, George R., and Melvin W. Reder. 1984. "Output and Strike Activity in U.S. Manufacturing: How Large Are the Losses?" *Industrial and Labor Relations Review*, Vol. 37, no. 2 (January), pp. 197-211.

Neumark, David, and William Wascher. 1995. "The Effect of New Jersey's Minimum Wage Increase on Fast-Food Employment: A Re-evaluation Using Payroll Records." National Bureau of Economic Research Working Paper No. 5224.

Paxson, Christina H., and Nachum Sicherman. 1996. "The Dynamics of Dual Job Holding and Job Mobility." *Journal of Labor Economics*, Vol. 14, no. 3 (July), pp. 357-93.

Pigou, A. C. 1920. *The Economics of Welfare*. London: Macmillan.

Polivka, Anne E. 1996. "Are Temporary Help Agency Workers Substitutes for Direct Hire Temps? Searching for an Alternative Explanation of Growth in the Temporary Help Industry." Unpublished paper, Bureau of Labor Statistics.

Reder, Melvin W., and George R. Neumann. 1980. "Conflict and Contract: The Case of Strikes." *Journal of Political Economy*, Vol. 88, no. 5 (October), pp. 867-86.

Rees, Albert. 1963. "The Effects of Trade Unions on Resource Allocation." *Journal of Law and Economics*, Vol. 6, no. 2 (October), pp. 69-78.

Reynolds, Morgan O. 1991. "The Myth of Labor's Inequality of Bargaining Power." *Journal of Labor Research*, Vol. 12, no. 2 (Spring), pp. 167-83.

Ruhm, Christopher J. 1992. "Advance Notice and Postdisplacement Joblessness." *Journal of Labor Economics*, Vol. 10, no. 1 (January), pp. 1-32.

_____. 1994. "Advance Notice, Job Search, and Postdisplacement Earnings." *Journal of Labor Economics*, Vol. 12, no. 1 (January), pp. 1-28.

_____. 1996. "The Economic Consequences of Parental Leave Mandates: Lessons from Europe." National Bureau of Economic Research Working Paper No. 5688 (July).

_____. Forthcoming. "Policy Watch: The Family and Medical Leave Act." *Journal of Economic Perspectives*.

Rundle, James R. 1994. "The Debate over the Ban on Employer-Dominated Labor Organizations: What Is the Evidence?" In Sheldon Friedman, Richard W. Hurd, Rudolph A. Oswald, and Ronald L. Seeber, eds., *Restoring the Promise of American Labor Law*. Ithaca, NY: ILR Press, pp. 161-76.

Shepard, Ira, Paul Heylman, and Robert Duston. 1989. *Without Just Cause: An Employer's Practical and Legal Guide on Wrongful Dismissals*. Washington, DC: Bureau of National Affairs.

Siwolop, Sana. 1996. "Overtime vs. Time Off: Debating the Choice." *New York Times*, August 18, Internet edition.

Sockell, Donna, and John Thomas Delaney. 1987. "Union Organizing and the Reagan NLRB." *Contemporary Policy Issues*, Vol. 5, no. 4 (October), pp. 28-45.

Stieber, Jack, and Richard N. Block. 1992. "Comment on Alan Krueger, 'The Evolution of Unjust Dismissal Legislation in the United States.'" *Industrial and Labor Relations Review*, Vol. 45, no. 4 (July), pp. 792-96.

*St. Louis Post-Dispatch*. 1996. "Clinton Vetoes Republican Labor Measure." July 31, p. 5A.

Stout, Hilary. 1996. "Clinton to Seek Wider Family-Leave Law." *Wall Street Journal*, June 25, p. A2.

Sullivan, Daniel. 1989. "Monopsony Power in the Market for Nurses." *Journal of Law and Economics*, Vol. 32, pt. 2 (October), pp. S135-78.

Summers, Lawrence H. 1989. "Some Simple Economics of Mandated Benefits." *American Economic Review Papers and Proceedings*, Vol. 79, no. 2 (May), pp. 177-83.

Thaler, Richard H. 1992. *The Winner's Curse: Paradoxes and Anomalies of Economic Life*. Princeton, NJ: Princeton University Press.

Topel, Robert H. 1983. "On Layoffs and Unemployment Insurance." *American Economic Review*, Vol. 73, no. 4 (September), pp. 541-59.

_____. 1984. "Experience Rating of Unemployment Insurance and the Incidence of Unemployment." *Journal of Law and Economics*, Vol. 27, no. 1 (April), pp. 61-90.

Trejo, Stephen J. 1991. "The Effects of Overtime Pay Regulation on Worker Compensation." *American Economic Review*, Vol. 81, no. 4 (September), pp. 719-40.

U.S. Bureau of the Census. 1995. *Statistical Abstract of the United States: 1995*, 114th edition. Washington, DC: GPO.

U.S. Chamber of Commerce. 1994. *Analysis of Workers' Compensation Laws*. Washington, DC: U.S. Chamber of Commerce.

U.S. General Accounting Office. 1993. *Dislocated Workers: Worker Adjustment and Retraining Notification Act Not Meeting Its Goals*. Report GAO/HRD-93-18. Washington, DC (February 23).

Weil, David. 1996. "Regulating the Workplace: The Vexing Problem of Implementation." In David Lewin, Bruce E. Kaufman, and Donna Sockell, eds., *Advances in Industrial and Labor Relations*, Vol. 7. Greenwich, CT: JAI Press, pp. 247-86.

_____. 1997. "Analyzing Regulatory Performance: Insights on the Implementation of Federal Workplace Policy." In Bruce Kaufman, ed., *Government Regulation of the Employment Relationship*. Madison, WI: Industrial Relations Research Association.

Weiler, Paul. 1990. *Governing the Workplace: The Future of Labor and Employment Law*. Cambridge, MA: Harvard University Press.

Wellington, Alison J. 1991. "Effects of the Minimum Wage on the Employment Status of Youths: An Update." *Journal of Human Resources*, Vol. 26, no. 1 (Winter), pp. 27-46.

Zachary, G. Pascal. 1996. "Many Firms Refuse To Pay for Overtime, Employees Complain." *Wall Street Journal*, June 24, pp. A1, A10.

# Chapter 5

# The Regulation of Labor Markets: Balancing the Benefits and Costs of Competition

Dale Belman
*University of Wisconsin–Milwaukee*

Michael H. Belzer
*University of Michigan*

The labor markets of the United States have become increasingly competitive over the last two decades. Some of this has been the result of factors beyond the domain of government. The evolution of markets, the introduction of new technologies, the improvement of transportation and communications, and the rapid economic development of many nations have each contributed to increased competition in labor markets. But shifts in the direction of government policy have also increased competition.

For the first seventy years of this century, labor market policies increasingly limited and directed competition through public regulation of wages, hours, and conditions of work. The policies of the last twenty years have been far more mixed. Certain types of regulation, notably those intended to ameliorate the social consequences of markets, have been extended. Legislation, such as the Americans with Disabilities Act, the Civil Rights Act of 1991, and the Family Medical Leave Act, has increased employee rights, extended government's role in labor markets, and further enmeshed market processes within an institutional framework. In contrast, government direction of the economic functions of labor markets has been sharply curtailed as price mechanisms have won increasing acceptance as the primary regulator. Since the 1970s federal and state policy makers have loosened, repealed, and reinterpreted laws directly governing the employment relation, such as area wage standards, work at home, minimum wages, eligibility requirements for unemployment insurance, disability standards under workers' compensation, and employer tactics in labor relations. Inaction in adapting regulation to changes in the employment relationship—changes such as widespread use of subcontractors and temporary workers in place of conventional employees—has likewise exposed an increasing portion of the labor force to the forces of the unconstrained market. The role of the price mechanism in labor markets has also been magnified by the economic deregulation of core transportation industries—airlines, trucking, and railroads, along with telecommunication and banking. Movement toward more openness in trade has had parallel effects in manufacturing. Such policies have placed wages and conditions of work in competition to an extent not seen for nearly a century. Current state and federal legislation portends continuing movement toward market regulation in the near term.

Has this reduction in government's economic role in labor markets and concomitant increase in competition been, on balance, good for employees and society? There are strong arguments and many advocates for the view that increased competition is almost always beneficial. But there are also reasons to believe that there are sizable parts of the economy where unrestrained competition may not improve the efficiency of markets or the bundle of goods and services available to society; where it may undercut other essential dimensions of labor market performance; where the gains from increased competition do not accrue to the employees immediately affected; or in general, where the social consequences of unfettered competition may outweigh the economic gains. The issue is not whether the economic functions of society should be organized around markets but how markets are best organized: whether economic processes are better left unrestrained, or whether the well-being of individuals and society are better served by harnessing some of these processes through regulation and institutionalization.

This chapter is an initial effort to clarify the issues involved in government's economic role in markets. The first section outlines the forms of government intervention affecting labor markets and argues that contrary to popular perception, there has been no singular movement toward increased regulation of the employment relationship. The second develops the traditional economic arguments against government intervention in markets. The third parallels the second in providing theoretic arguments for the benefits of regulation. The final section illustrates the consequences of the reduction of governments' role in markets from the experience of the last twenty years. Here we review current research on the effects of deregulation in the trucking and construction industries on wages and working conditions. The conclusion draws together the various issues addressed in this essay and suggests policy changes which would help restore the position of employees in the economy.

## Has Government Become Increasingly Interventionist?

Is government becoming more involved in the employment relationship? Certainly there are specific laws and administrative acts which have increased this role, but government has de facto and de jure pulled back from involvement in labor markets. We turn first to an overview of the ways in which government intervenes: the legal framework, economic and social regulation, and macroeconomic and competitiveness policy, and then to a discussion of how this has changed over the last two decades.

In the United States the employment relationship is fundamentally a private agreement between the employer and employee. One of government's roles in the labor market is to establish and enforce the legal structure within which the private agreement is struck. This *legal framework*—a mixture of common law, legislation, court rulings, and administration—establishes the rules of the employment relationship.[1] These rules cover issues as diverse as determining what constitutes legal tender for payment of wages, the order of payment of creditors in a bankruptcy, the conditions under which an employee can quit or be dismissed, and the forums in which parties can seek redress. They define what the parties agree to and what they can expect from their contract as well as the limits within which economic activity occurs and the range of acceptable practices.

This framework is prerequisite to complex market transactions. The rules are too comprehensive to be negotiated anew for each employment situation. Necessity does not render the framework neutral. The structure of rules—what topics are subject to determination by the parties, who is permitted to make such determinations, and who is compelled to sue for their rights—affects the balance of power between employers and employees and the range of employment practices which are subject to the pressures of the market. Changes in the framework, brought about by legislation, court decisions, or administrative rule making, can change both the process and rewards of the employment relationship. It may also affect employment practices by taking certain aspects of the employment relationship "out of competition" or restoring them to competitive determination.[2]

Government is not simply a passive umpire of equity disputes. Federal, state, and local governments play an immediate role in markets when they engage in *economic regulation*—the direct regulation of economic processes including prices and quantity—or *social regulation*—regulation intended to ensure the market attains socially desirable ends.[3] These forms of regulation affect conditions of employment directly when they are applied to labor markets. Product market regulation may have equally great, albeit less direct, effects on employees as changes in product markets act on labor markets through derived demand.

The number of statutes that directly regulate economic conditions in labor markets, setting wages or affecting labor supply, is small (see Weil, this volume). The most prominent are the Fair Labor Standards Act (FLSA), with its stipulation of minimum wages and overtime rates; prevailing wage laws such as the Davis-Bacon, Walsh-Healy, and Service Contracts Acts, which require that federally funded contracts pay labor rates equivalent to those earned in similar occupations in the private sector; and the federal and state unemployment insurance system, which provides temporary income to the involuntarily unemployed. Employees outside the scope of the FLSA are typically covered by state minimum wage laws; thirty-two states have little Davis-Bacon acts, i.e., prevailing wage laws for construction employees working on state-funded projects.[4,5] Although the number of statutes regulating economic process in labor markets is small, their scope is broad. Minimum wage laws covered 87.1% of the labor force in 1990, while the overtime provisions of the FLSA covered two-thirds of all employees (Ehrenburg and Smith 1994). The scope of prevailing wage laws is more difficult to estimate as there are no direct measures of the number of employees who benefit from these laws. Twenty to twenty-five percent of all construction is funded by the public sector, and prevailing wage statutes govern the expenditure of most of these funds.[6] Unemployment insurance covered 94% of the labor force in 1994 (McMurrer and Chasanov 1995).

Regulation of product markets has typically been found where industries were both monopolized and produced goods or services believed essential to the health or economic well-being of society or in sectors where unlimited competition was believed to cause instability or unreliability sufficient to endanger wider economic processes or retard the development of other parts of the economy. The industries most consistently subject to product market regulation have been interstate transportation industries such as trucking; railroads and airlines; public utilities such as telephone, gas and electric services; financial services; and agriculture. Regulation of railroads, trucks, and water carriers, overseen by the Interstate Commerce Commission (ICC), limited entry, established routes, and regulated the prices charged by firms. The Civilian Aviation Board (CAB) subjected airlines to similar regulatory policies. Power, gas, and telephone were subject to both price and service regulation by state utility boards, the Federal Power Commission, and the Federal Communications Commission. As it has been limited to specific sectors of the economy, product market regulation has affected a smaller portion of the labor force than labor market regulation. In 1976, immediately prior to deregulation,

6.7% of the labor force was employed in economically regulated industries: 4.2% in transportation, 1.5% in telecommunications, and 1.1% in other utilities.[7]

Social regulation of labor and product markets has the purpose of assuring socially desirable outcomes which would not be achieved were market processes left to themselves. These regulations have been extensive and varied and have included limiting hours of work, mandating conditions of work, regulating safety and health in the workplace, restricting the type of work performed by certain classes of employees, and requiring certain capacities and conduct from employees. For example, in the years between 1890 and 1914, many states acted to limit the total hours of work, the hours at which work was permissible, and the occupations of children and young workers and also imposed educational responsibilities on their employers. This was done to protect the health, safety, physical development, and morals of employees who were not fully able to make decisions for themselves.[8] Laws establishing safety conditions in factories, another early form of social regulation, were intended to improve the conditions of work and life for employees and protect communities from the expense of supporting injured employees. Social regulation of product markets, as this has affected employees, has protected the public from employment practices which endangered the public's safety or health. Hours of service requirements for railway employees and truck drivers were implemented to reduce accidents caused by overtired employees. Similarly, current requirements for health and vision certification for transportation employees are intended to safeguard the public from the hazards which might otherwise result.[9]

Although the government's role in labor markets is most obvious in policies which structure the employment relationship or regulate specific practices and markets, macroeconomic and competitiveness policies are increasingly important determinants of conditions in labor markets. Macroeconomic policymakers' decisions on money supply and interest rates can have large effects on employment and wages throughout the economy. Competitiveness policies, policies which establish the scope and rules of competition, are also increasingly important to the performance of labor markets. Legislation on the extent of and access to markets—such as laws governing imports, exports, and immigration—and laws governing market conduct—such as those concerning dumping and anti-trust, establish the competitive position of firms and of their employees.

How have these various forms of regulation changed between 1975 and 1995? There have been notable extensions of the social regulation with passage of the Americans with Disabilities Act of 1990 (ADA), the Family Medical

Leave Act of 1993 (FMLA), and the Workers Adjustment and Retraining Notification Act of 1988 (WARN). The purpose of earlier legislation such as Title VII of the Civil Rights Act, the Age Discrimination in Employment Act, and the Occupational Safety and Health Act have been advanced over the last two decades, though somewhat uncertainly under some administrations, by their respective agencies—the Equal Opportunity Employment Commission (EEOC), the Office of Federal Contract Compliance (OFCCP), and the Occupational Safety and Health Administration (OSHA). Courts have also afforded employees some additional rights in the workplace through the broadening of public policy, implied contract, and implied covenant of good faith and fair dealing exceptions to the employment-at-will doctrine (see Edwards, this volume). The Employee Retirement and Security Act of 1974 (ERISA) and Comprehensive Omnibus Budget Reconciliation Act of 1986 (COBRA) directly regulated the terms of employment by imposing uniformity in provisions and reporting on employee retirement systems and providing continuation of employee health benefits for some classes of separated workers.

Such gains have been offset by reductions in regulation and reversion to the employment-at-will doctrine. Most notable has been the reduction in effective economic regulation of labor and product markets. The federal minimum wage declined in purchasing power and relative to the U.S. median wages between 1973 and 1995. Similarly, changes in the formula for determining the federal prevailing wage in construction and the repeal and revision of the state prevailing wage laws steadily reduced the wage floor on public projects. Federal and state unemployment insurance laws were restructured in the 1980s by changes in requirements for repayment of federal loans and revisions of the extended benefits program, adoption of more stringent monetary eligibility standards and stricter disqualification provisions by states, and by taxation of benefit payments. This has reduced the effectiveness of the program both as a source of income for the unemployed and as a macroeconomic stabilizer.[10]

Deregulation of product markets has been both more extensive and visible. Starting in the late 1970s the transportation and telecommunications industries were subject to administrative, legislative, and judicial deregulation. This trend continues with current federal and state legislation deregulating the electric power industry. Such changes have increased employees' exposure to competitive conditions and have caused the deterioration of the terms of employment for many employees.[11,12]

Retrenchment has not been limited to reductions in economic regulation. Court decisions on retiree medical insurance benefits have transformed such insurance into a gratuity subject to termination except where the employer has explicitly committed to its maintenance. The substitution of annuities for conventional pension plans and the advent of deferred compensation plans for managerial employees have also deregulated the employment relationship by freeing firms from the rules governing pensions. A long series of decisions by the NLRB and the courts has broadened employers' range of action in their relations with unions.[13] Even areas such as civil rights and affirmative action, in which regulation has been extended in the recent past, may be subject to rollbacks by the courts or referenda in the next several years.

Macroeconomic and competitiveness policies have also evolved in ways which increase competition in labor markets. The Federal Reserve's policy of holding unemployment to the Non-Accelerating Inflationary Rate of Unemployment (NAIRU) and above the level of unemployment accounted for by frictional and structural factors keeps unemployment at historically high levels and places downward pressures on wages in many labor markets. The severity of the recessions in the early 1980s may have been caused, in part, by monetary policies intended to reduce national "wage leadership" by unions in heavy manufacturing and construction (Brand 1985). Competitiveness in manufacturing industries and their associated labor markets has been intensified by the globalization of production and by treaties such as NAFTA, GATT, and bilateral agreements. The consequences of these agreements, increased trade with countries with lower wages and poorer working conditions, have been particularly severe for employees with limited formal education (Sachs and Shatz 1994).[14,15] The open immigration policies of the United States have also played a role in the decline in the real wage of the less skilled workers in the U.S. since the 1970s (Borjas, Freeman, and Katz 1991).

Some of the advances in social legislation of the last two decades are attributable to the consequences of economic deregulation. Requirements for drug and alcohol testing of transportation employees, particularly of truck drivers, was a response to the significant decline in the quality of the trucking labor force following deregulation. Similar problems with the capability and training of the personnel of low-cost, start-up airlines has recently caused revision of the FAA inspection system and regulations on carriage of hazardous materials. Economic deregulation may have brought with it an increased need for social regulation and active intervention.

In sum, the record on government involvement in markets has been mixed and somewhat contradictory over the last twenty years. There have been some notable advances, but these have been balanced and possibly over balanced by the diminution of government's economic role in labor markets. In combination with other changes in economic structures, this reduction in economic regulation has increased competitive pressures in labor markets.

## Arguments against Regulation

Prevailing economic theories of firm and consumer behavior provide an integrated set of arguments against government involvement in the economic functions of markets.[16] In the world defined by these theories, government cannot improve on and may well impair market outcomes, except under limited circumstances. Although possibly disadvantageous to specific groups, deregulation results in efficiencies beneficial to society as a whole.

The theories are structured around a stylized model of markets in which firms maximize profits and employees (consumers) select their best possible bundle of commodities (and leisure) given their endowments (such as employees' skills and abilities and firms' capital stock) and the prices offered in the market. Given a competitive market in which consumers choose "rationally" and freely, in which consumer satisfaction is non-decreasing with consumption of goods and leisure, in which firms' production technologies are not characterized by economies of scale or scope and are well known, and in which consumers and firms are mobile and have complete information about commodities and work, price competition is efficient and provides the goods, services, and leisure most valued by society.

Government regulation of markets can have no constructive role in such an economy. Suppose that government desires to increase employees' earnings and intervenes by establishing a "minimum wage" above the competitive wage. Some employees realize an improvement in their incomes and labor income may rise. From the perspective of society as a whole, such gain is illusory. It is partly a redistribution of income from owners of other factor inputs. There are, however, real economic losses. A higher wage will result in higher prices for goods produced with labor and a shift in production technique away from labor toward other relatively less expensive inputs. This reduces demand for labor's services and results in reduced employment of labor through layoffs or reduced hours. Production is inefficient because producers use too little labor but too much capital, energy, and other inputs and so do not take advantage of society's endowment of inputs. Costs rise, output is reduced, and the total of available consumption goods are smaller and less desirable than that which was available prior to imposition of the minimum wage. Based on this model, society would be better off with an unregulated regime, in this case a regime without a minimum wage. Removal of the minimum wage would reduce the income of some employees but would increase production and the total consumption of society.[17]

In accordance with prevailing theories, regulation may also be objectionable because it prevents employees from arranging their leisure, consumption, and conditions of work to best fit their desires. Presumably, employees in a competitive market can choose suitable work and hours to fit their needs and wants. Those who desire shorter hours, safer conditions, or greater security from dismissal are at liberty to find employers who offer such employment packages. Others less desirous of these conditions can also freely seek employment contracts which address their particular wants. Laws which regulate the conditions of labor preclude at least some employees from establishing their most desired balance of consumption but do not improve the consumption of other employees (who have previously attained the now regulated conditions through individual bargaining). For example, a law which limits hours of work forces at least some employees, those who are prepared to work long hours, to be able to consume more commodities away from their best consumption bundle. The condition of those who value leisure more highly (and so already chose fewer hours) is not improved.[18]

Extensions of this approach suggest that government intervention is often a consequence of interest groups manipulating public policy to their economic advantage. In this view, interest groups use regulation as a means of redistributing income. The decline in their fortunes precipitated by deregulation is not an unfortunate byproduct of attaining greater social welfare but the reapportionment of rents by society. In this view, compensatory payments would defeat the purpose of deregulation.

Government intervention can improve on market outcomes under some circumstances. Where there are externalities, public goods, incomplete information, resource immobility or monopsony power, or economies of scale or scope markets will not achieve efficient outcomes, and some form of intervention may be required. Whether such conditions are common, sufficiently severe to warrant intervention, and whether government's efforts are more costly than the conditions themselves are matters of dispute. For example, some argue that government is a more common source of problems such as monopoly power than the private market. If true, the withdrawal of government from economic regulation would leave pockets of inefficiency, but it would, on net, benefit society.

The case for deregulation of markets does not derive solely from theory. Deregulation has produced tangible benefits, particularly for consumers. Consumer gains include reductions in the cost of air travel as a result of deregulation in the transportation industry, improvements in a variety of telecommunications' services and reductions in the cost of long distance telephone service as a result of deregulation of telecommunications, and reductions in the cost of clothing and electronics from lowering of barriers to trade. The gains of deregulation do not accrue solely to consumers, nor are they solely monetary. Heywood and Peoples (1994) and Hirsch and Macpherson

(1997), for example, find that deregulation of trucking led to increased minority employment in for-hire truck driving.

## Arguments for Regulation

Although the analysis of regulation has been dominated by arguments against market regulation for at least two decades, some attention has been given to why it may be beneficial to use regulation to limit competition. The price system can be corrosive of efficiency where production utilizes public goods or involves externalities, where information about the terms of employment is asymmetric between employers and employees, where "cream skimming" by some employers will prevent others from offering more efficient employment packages, where ease of entry depresses prices and prevents prior entrants from recovering their costs, or where long periods of slackness in labor markets drives down wages and working conditions.

Efficiency also does not ensure that market outcomes will be acceptable to society, and regulation may be required to achieve goals such as ending child labor or protecting the public from unsafe or unethical practices. Unconstrained markets may also produce undesirable distributions of power and economic resources. As suggested by Polanyi (1944), regulation may also be required to slow the disruption of social structure brought on by dynamic market systems.[19]

### Arguments Related to Economic Efficiency

*Public goods.* Where efficiency requires shared investments and cooperation among producers, the price system creates strong incentives for firms to utilize the resulting industry benefits without paying for them—to free ride. Absent barriers to such conduct, free-riding firms will be able to provide goods and services at reduced prices. Over time, other producers are compelled either to forgo shared investment activities or leave the market. Although the consequences of free riding can be foreseen by the participants in the market, the economic logic is difficult to resist without extra-market rules and enforcement.

The decline of the apprenticeship system and the present shortage of skilled construction labor is an example of such a "public goods problem." The growth of the nonunion sector has been fueled by the ability of nonparticipating employers to draw on a pool of employees trained in union apprenticeship programs without participating in such programs. The consequent decline of the organized sector and its training programs, a reflection of the success of the nonunion sector, has resulted in a shortage of skilled labor throughout the industry. Although the need for greater investment in training is obvious to everyone in the market, there are no enforcement mechanisms to support the scale of training currently required. Similar issues are faced by other industries such as interstate trucking where problems with poaching have caused major carriers to discontinue training programs.

*Economies of scope.* Economies of scope exist where the costs of the joint production of a set of commodities is less than the total cost of producing each of the commodities individually. Joint production is socially beneficial because it lowers overall costs, but economies of scope do not of themselves ensure the commercial success of joint production. Production of one or several of the joint commodities may be more profitable than joint production of all of the commodities. Under such conditions, unregulated producers will "cream skim," produce only the individually profitable commodities. The cost of producing a full range of goods is increased, production is inefficient, and some commodities may not be produced at all. Efficiency requires either regulation of entry or the requirement that entrants to the market provide a full range of products. The grant of partial monopoly to the postal service and the service requirements imposed on utilities are examples of regulation intended to protect economies of scope.[20]

Joint production and the consequent problems with unrestrained competition are not only relevant to industry product markets, they may also involve associated labor markets. Teaching hospitals provide a complex joint product. One dimension is conventional hospital services. Another is the development and testing of new health care services. A third, and one which is central to the medical system's ability to sustain itself, is training for doctors and other personnel. A fourth, related to those preceding, is provision of low-cost or free medical services to low-income populations. In the past, teaching hospitals have been permitted higher fees on conventional services in order to subsidize training and advanced medical care. This is changing as financial restraint and increased competition in the industry has made insurers and government administrators reluctant to pay more than the actual costs of such services. Teaching and research functions become financially burdensome, and there is movement toward the reduction or elimination of such services. In the short term, competitive pressures result in a loss of medical services and, in the longer term, may pose a challenge to the system of medical education in the United States.

Progressive employment structures offer many advantages to firms, employees, and society: high quality products, superior efficiency, above-average wages and benefits, shared decision making, and improved job security. Firms' ability to implement such strategies may be limited by competition with firms using more traditional employment strategies (Levine and Tyson 1990). High-performance work systems typically incorporate compressed pay scales and due process in discipline as a strategy to increase employee commitment to the firm. The wage structure of progressive employers renders them vulnerable to losing their best employees to more traditional firms. Similarly, due process may attract an excess number of employees who expect to be subject to discipline. Both disadvantage progressive firms and may restrict progressive practices to narrow sectors of the economy—thereby denying the benefits of such practices to many employees and firms as well as to society at large.

*Imperfect competition.* Free mobility of labor between firms, industries, and markets is necessary for employees to earn the full value of their skills and abilities. Where mobility is sufficiently limited, employees become subject to various forms of imperfect competition and may suffer substandard wages and working conditions.[21] There are two distinct forms of imperfect competition (Kaufman, this volume). The first, the classic case of monopsony or oligopsony, is where employees are restricted to a particular market by geography and skills and the number of employers is limited. Such employees are subject to exploitation, as they earn less than their marginal revenue product. The second occurs when employees are constrained to particular sets of markets despite skills which qualify them for a broader set of opportunities. This type of constraint, often the result of occupational segregation by race, ethnicity, or gender, causes an oversupply of labor to some markets. Individual employers lack power over wages and employees are paid their marginal revenue product, but their compensation and working conditions are below those which would be achieved were mobility unconstrained.

The typical example of the first form of imperfect competition, one which seems dated in the current economy, is the single-employer town in which finding alternative employment requires moving considerable distances and having the economic resources for the move. But imperfect competition has never been solely a phenomenon of company towns and is not just a historic oddity. It can occur when employees with specific skills are limited to a small number of employers. Occupational immobility is not unusual because where skills are specific to an occupation, opportunity cost of leaving an occupation and moving into the general labor market is high. In combination with some geographic immobility, employees face limited employment opportunities, and employers may be vested with power over terms of employment. Similar problems may confront employees where employer associations establish common employment policies in an industry or region. Such associations have been effective in the past (Kaufman, this volume). For example, before collective bargaining, the baseball owners' association was able to cap players' earnings, and players had no alternative but to accept the owner's offer.

Long-term employees may also be subject to imperfect competition if there are large costs to leaving an employer prior to retirement. Back-loaded compensation systems, particularly pension plans in which retirement income is determined by earnings in the last years of employment, make it very costly for long-service employees to leave their position (Ippolito 1987). The health care system of the United States also discourages job mobility because of the expense of keeping up payments when not employed and the risk of going uninsured. Such factors decrease interfirm mobility and provide employers with power over career employees.

The second form of imperfect competition is associated with discrimination and labor market segmentation, the existence of restrictions on intermarket mobility unrelated to employee productivity. Segregation of labor markets by race and gender is a primary source of immobility both in the past and at present (see Becker 1971; Gordon, Edwards, and Reich 1982; and Bulow and Summers 1986). There are additional sources of immobility. Recent immigrants may find employment opportunities limited to specific occupations and industries. This may cause overcrowding and accompanying problems with low wages, work intensification, and poor working conditions in periods of large scale domestic and international migration. The return to equilibrium is often slow and may, as the history of the needle trades indicates, wait on the movement of immigrants' children to other occupations and industries. Individual background may also be a source of immobility. Before deregulation the long-haul agricultural products sector of the trucking industry employed many workers with felony records or prior employment problems. These employees had few alternatives and formed a captive, low-wage labor force for the industry. Immobility and consequent oversupply of labor may also occur in markets which are easy to enter but difficult to leave. Credit for the purchase of a truck tractor and the accompanying job is readily obtained; this encourages entry into the over-the-road trucking industry. But it may be difficult to dispose of the debt and exit the industry without large losses or bankruptcy. Such asymmetries cause large inflows of employees into a market when times are good, inadequate and slow exit when times are poor, and excessively low wages and poor working conditions.

*Externalities.* In labor markets the issue of externalities rests on whether employers pay the full social cost of the labor they employ or whether they transfer part of the cost to other parties: the employee, other employers, or the community. There are large externalities in health care costs. Employers who do not provide health care may be subsidized by other employers through spousal and dependent coverage and by public agencies. A study by the Institute of Industrial Relations at the University of California found that the State of California paid $1 million in health care costs for 408 employees and their dependents in a single large demolition project (Davidson 1989).

Low-wage employment can also impose a variety of costs on communities. Craypo (1993) reports that a middle-sized midwestern town suffered substantial increases in public costs following construction of a new meat-packing plant by Iowa Beef Processing. Although the jobs offered by IBP were sufficiently attractive to bring many new employees into the community, the combination of low wages and high turnover swelled the low-wage, tenuously employed population. This population required additional educational, medical, and social services; and the costs of such services exceeded the tax revenues generated by the plant.

*Asymmetric information.* A strength of competition is that it motivates producers to search for means of lowering product costs and so increases efficiency and social well-being. The same incentives may cause firms to debase product quality and alter the terms of employment in ways not readily apparent to the other parties. For example, following Hurricane Andrew's devastation, investigators found that severe structural damage was often attributable to the failure of builders to adhere to hurricane resistance codes. Similarly, an important producer of baby foods was recently found to have adulterated fruit juices with sugar water and citric acid.

Employees face similar problems with asymmetric information. Retirement packages are complex and meaningful information may be difficult to obtain from employers. Even with access, understanding, verifying, and holding employers to agreements may be difficult. Working conditions, particularly where they involve exposure to substances that are hazardous over the long term, involve similar problems of access and evaluation of information. Where such conditions exist, there is ample opportunity for some employers to gain a competitive advantage by misleading employees about their terms of employment.

Competitive practices based on manipulation of information harm consumers and employees because they do not receive the product/conditions to which they agreed. They suffer economic losses and may suffer personal consequences from such practices. These practices are equally harmful to firms and to industries. Where consumers/employees have difficulty knowing when they have received quality goods/employment for their money, some producers will improve their performance by reducing quality. Other producers will be compelled to follow suit and reduce their quality or withdraw from the industry. Over time, the quality of the industry's products/employment terms will drift toward the lowest level acceptable to consumers and employees. On the consumer side, regulation in the form of labeling requirements and enforcement of minimum product standards through inspection aids in preventing such behavior and ensures an economically efficient and diverse market. On the employee side, requirements for the provision of information, promulgation of minimum standards, and supervision of employer actions may all be required to ensure protection of employee interests.

*Destructive competition.* Some industries may be too competitive—destructively competitive—in the sense that competition reduces both static and dynamic efficiency and produces socially unsatisfactory terms of employment. Problems with destructive competition, the inability to realize normal returns for extended periods, are typically associated with industries which are characterized by high fixed costs, substantial excess capacity, and costly factor mobility. But labor may be subject to problems with destructive competition in industries which are labor intensive, have low costs of entry, and can draw on a large pool of labor. Labor shares many of the characteristics of capital intensive industries: the fixed cost of maintaining a worker and family is high, but the marginal cost of providing an added hour or day of work is low. Labor, particularly low-wage labor, is also comparatively immobile since the need to earn a living requires workers remain employed except for brief periods. In combination with an excess supply of labor, these characteristics may place labor in a position in which it has to accept a wage below that required to maintain its condition.[22]

Commercial success in labor-intensive industries such as apparel and trucking depends, to a great degree, on reducing the cost of labor. Under conditions in which the supply and demand for labor are in balance, firms reduce labor costs through improving labor productivity and other efficiencies. However, where there is a surplus of labor available—excess capacity—firms can reduce costs by reducing the price of labor toward its marginal cost. This will produce low wages and substandard working conditions and, as a consequence, will make recruiting, training, and retaining an adequate labor force difficult.

Large numbers of small firms magnify these tendencies. The combination of high labor costs and low capital costs encourages entry by small proprietors. The success of such business often depends on proprietors working long hours under inferior conditions. Such actions not only fail to provide proprietors adequate returns on investments, they further undercut wages and working conditions and spoil prices for other firms. These problems are ongoing as ease of entry and the lack of business experience of many market participants encourages a constant flow of entrants. This impedes the adjustments required to restore wages and returns to capital.[23] The ongoing problems with prices and wages and work force quality may result in increased costs, reduced product quality, and a lack of innovation in the industry.

The truckload segment of the trucking services industry fits many of the characteristics of a destructively competitive industry.[24] Research suggests that long-haul drivers earn a modest annual income despite working more than sixty hours a week. Long hours of driving combined with additional uncompensated hours for waiting and other tasks have driven compensation down toward the legal minimum wage. Owner-operators, a group which provides a substantial portion of industry capacity, frequently work in excess of eighty hours per week while losing their initial investment (in industry parlance, "eat their trucks"). Low pay and poor working conditions and consequent problems with retaining a skilled labor force have reduced the reliability of service of the motor transportation system (Schulz 1996).

*Appropriation and economic inertia.* The economic theory of the firm suggests that markets compel firms both to operate at their production frontier, at peak economic efficiency, and provide strong incentives for firms to implement new technologies and techniques. Although this may characterize some dimensions of firm behavior, the private sector has often lagged in implementation of efficient labor practices. Government has been essential to the propagation of efficient labor practices beyond the group of innovative firms.

The federal government played a central role in the implementation of the eight-hour day.[25] Before World War I, scientific managers and industrial psychologists established that fatigue increased and work declined sharply after eight hours. Practical experiments found that conversion to an eight-hour day was inexpensive because the increase in sustained work effort balanced the decline in working time. Despite such evidence, few employers shifted to eight-hour schedules voluntarily. It required the action of the War Labor Board during the war to make the standard workday eight hours. The steel strike of 1919 and the efforts of Secretary of Commerce Herbert Hoover were required to induce the steel industry to move from the twelve-hour turn to the eight-hour day in 1923 (Hunnicutt 1988).

The source of this reluctance is difficult to pinpoint. It may be due to issues of appropriation and the locus of decision making in firms. If improvements in working conditions accrue mostly to employees, then managers, whose decisions are oriented toward how the firm gains from various policies, may ignore such innovations. This logic is reflected in the documented bias of employers toward implementing employee suggestions that improve firm efficiency and against those which improve working conditions. Gouldner (1954) suggests that management prefers to invest in machinery and technology rather than in employment structures because the former are more concrete and appear more reliable. Although it is possible to argue deductively from economic theory that firms will implement any innovation which directly or indirectly increases their profitability, the record indicates that markets have not been sufficient to spread efficient and innovative labor policies without government support.

*Consequences of competition under conditions of less than full employment.* An implication of the neoclassical model of markets is that all resources, including labor, will be fully employed. Full employment ensures that resources are allocated efficiently. Holders of resources such as labor are protected against the consequences of shifts in economic conditions and policies (such as deregulation) by the rapid reallocation of resources implicit in full employment. Under such conditions the consequences of movement toward increasingly competitive markets and of policies which promote such change are transitional and limited.

Under conditions of less than full employment, however, increased competition in product and labor markets will depress wages and working conditions for extended periods. Increased competition in product markets reduces the price of goods and services and this shifts the demand curve for labor inward. In a system with full employment, the labor supply curve of the firm is highly elastic. The response to the decline in demand for labor will not be a reduction in the wage but the movement of employees to other industries at the national wage standard. This process is impeded in the absence of full employment. Where there is less than full employment in the national labor markets, employees are likely to have trouble finding equivalent positions elsewhere and face the possibility of extended unemployment if they leave or are separated from their current employer. The adjustment process is slowed and the industry labor supply curve labor becomes kinked. The firm's labor supply is inelastic below the prevailing wage because employees cannot leave the firm or industry easily but is highly elastic above that wage as workers are drawn from other industries (Reynolds 1948). With this structure of labor supply, an inward shift in demand will depress wages and working conditions.

The pressures from chronic slackness in labor markets are particularly acute as the terms and conditions offered for work are vulnerable to degradation. First, unlike many other markets, the supply side of the labor market is inherently atomistic. Employees are perpetually competing with one another for jobs, for wages, and for the other rewards of employment. This is heightened by their limited capacity to manage without employment for extended periods. The aggregate supply curve of labor is relatively inelastic, and the terms and conditions of work decline significantly in response to increased competitive pressures.[26] Second, standards of work are determined more by social constraint than physical limitation. For example, although forty hours is the current standard work week, people can, and in the past regularly did, work fifty to sixty hours per week. Social limitations are more subject to erosion than physical limitations. Marginal workers requiring employment will tend to offer more hours and effort and will accept greater risk and inconvenience for a given wage than will established employees. This places downward pressure on wages and working conditions. Under conditions of less than full employment, such pressures will be magnified by the increased number of marginal workers. The bird of passage, rather than those committed to an occupation and locale, will establish conditions for the majority.

At issue is whether labor markets are typically characterized by full employment. Full employment certainly occurs in particular labor markets and sometimes characterizes national labor markets. However, labor markets have been relatively slack, and unemployment has not recently approached the 3% to 4% rate which was considered full employment for more than twenty years. The failure to achieve full employment reflects, in part, the policy of the Federal Reserve of keeping inflation low by keeping labor markets slack. The unemployment rate preferred by the Federal Reserve, the "NAIRU" rate of between 5% and 6.5% unemployment, is above the level of unemployment associated with frictional and structural factors. Under such conditions, policies which increase competition in markets are likely to substantially worsen the conditions of labor in particular markets and limit the improvement of wages, compensation and working conditions for most employees.

### Arguments Not Related to Economic Efficiency

*Social values.* Although price-driven systems provide high levels of efficiency in the short term, they do not ensure outcomes society considers desirable in the longer term. The employment of young children may be economically efficient for the firms employing them, but social concerns about the long-term health, education, adult productivity, and civic responsibility of those children nonetheless leads to restrictions on the age at which children can be hired for various types of work. Similarly, regulation of the hours of work, vision, and drug use of transportation employees reflects the public's belief that it is at risk without such regulation.

In some instances, social regulations are implemented because of economic externalities. Child labor is restricted, in part, because parents may fail to consider the consequences to society of having a large class of adults with inadequate education. We regulate employment conditions for transportation employees because firms fail to incorporate the total costs to society of accidents caused by tired or impaired employees. Safety regulation of work may reflect the need to internalize medical and social costs which would otherwise have been thrust onto the community. Much of social regulation is, however, undertaken to achieve noneconomic ends and may impede economic efficiency. For instance, the once widespread blue laws reflected a religious desire to promote church attendance and a more secular desire for regular leisure and family time.

*Distributional consequences of markets.* Differing regulatory "regimes" may affect the distribution of income, working conditions, and the "life chances" of various social groups.[27] Issues of distribution have not been prominent in the discussion of deregulation. This reflects a tendency of economists to treat distribution as either outside the purview of their profession or irrelevant because greater efficiency both improves the general well-being of society and permits compensation to the losers.

In contrast, institutional economists emphasized the distributional consequences of the rules governing markets. Economic actors are organized into bargaining groups and these compete with one another for social and economic resources.[28] Intergroup bargaining, part of the day-to-day interaction between employers and employees, takes place within a framework of rules. It is not possible in even a modestly complex society to have an employment relationship without rules, and these rules (legal regimes) influence the relative bargaining power of employers and employee and the distribution of resources in society. The situation of the injured employee and of all employees is very different where a workers' compensation system exists against a system in which employees are dependent on their employer or the courts. Compared to a system which gives the employer the power to dismiss an injured worker without recompense, a system in which a government body systematically extracts funds from employers and provides clear rules and due process to injured employees produces both greater income for the injured and income security for all employees.[29] In addition, shifting the economic costs of accidents from employees to employers provides a powerful incentive to improve workplace safety.

What then are the distributional consequences of a deregulated regime relative to the current structure? This cannot be answered in the abstract because a deregulated regime still has rules. In the United States it would be the historic regime of property rights, liberty of contract, and formal equality of legal and economic power. Under this regime the employer makes the rules and the employee either accepts them or seeks a more satisfactory contract with another employer. With this underlying structure, movement toward deregulation reduces employee rights and places fewer restrictions on employer prerogatives. For example, redefinition of the period during which overtime is measured from a week to a month provides the employer an advantage because employers can more readily meet immediate needs for labor without paying a penalty for overtime. With time off in lieu of pay, employees become subject to more variable schedules. Broadening the scope of the market without extending the rules affecting labor, as is done by many trade agreements, may also free employers from the accretion of rules restricting their liberty of action.[30]

Distribution may be an issue even within the more narrow scope of economic deregulation. Economic theory provides no assurance that the gains from reduced product prices and improved services are evenly distributed throughout the population or that the advantage of the gains accruing to employees balances their loss of wages and employment. Lee and Scott (1996) find that the balance of the gains from increased apparel imports accrued to importers rather than producers or consumers. Borjas and Ramey (1994) find that increased wage inequality is associated with increases in the trade deficit and suggest that this reflects increased exposure of durable goods industries to import competition. DeNardo, Fortin, and Lemieux (1996) find that the decline in the real minimum wage and in union membership accounts for about one-fifth of the increase in wage inequality of the last twenty years.

Whatever the efficiency effects of deregulation, movement toward a regime of increased property rights will shift power and its perquisites toward the owners and managers of property. Movement toward a less regulated employment relationship will likely increase wage and income inequality. As shifts in social distribution have far-reaching consequences for society, the evaluation of regulatory change should account for equity as well as efficiency considerations.

*Regulation as a means of providing social stability in periods of dynamic change.* In *The Great Transformation* (1994), Polanyi argued that underlying the regulation of labor markets was the need to protect social structures from the disruptive consequences of rapidly changing economic markets. Regulation does not stop economic transition but moderates the pace to allow social relations to adapt to emerging economic institutions.

Such was the case for the system of poor relief developed in England in the 1820s which, through the Speedhamland agreement, addressed unemployment in rural areas by subsidizing agricultural employment. This system, which evolved because poor houses could not provide for the large number of unemployed, had deleterious consequences for agricultural labor markets. Nevertheless, in a period of social instability and uncertainty, it served to prevent starvation, moderated rural poverty, and helped to prevent economic disruption from evolving into political disaffection.

Current government interventions can play a similar role. Trade adjustment assistance is intended to reduce the cost to individuals of policies which make the U.S. economy more open. The five-year transition period provided in legislation deregulating electric power in California is likewise intended to allow incumbents and consumers to adapt to the emerging structures and to reduce the potential for entry by precarious providers. The long transition period for the North American Free Trade Agreement serves to allow change without sudden shifts in markets.

## Deregulation and Labor Market Performance: Two Case Histories

We now turn to two studies of deregulation and deinstitutionalization in labor markets: the consequences of the economic deregulation in trucking and the effects of the repeal of state prevailing wage laws and the weakening of the legal status of unions for the construction industry. These cases flesh out the concepts developed above and suggest that the arguments against unrestrained competition involve more than theoretic concerns.

*Intercity Trucking*

The deregulation of the trucking industry provides an example of the effects for labor of ending economic regulation of product markets. The consequences have included a considerable decline in wages, rapid deterioration in working conditions, and increasing income inequality between owners and managers and employees in the industry. Despite industry recognition of substandard wages and labor shortage, market forces have proven inadequate to bring drivers earnings to the standard expected by similarly skilled workers in other industries.

Trucking is an inherently competitive industry with strong tendencies toward underpricing and destructive competition. Although firms may service a metropolitan area, a region, or the entire nation, their customer bases frequently center on the city in which the firm is located. Carriers whose customers regularly ship to a particular location may establish regular service and a customer base in additional cities, but it is common that the carrier's trucks will unload in a city in which it has little or no presence. If the firm moves an empty truck to the next place it has a load—"deadheads" the truck—it pays for the movement but earns no revenue. This provides an incentive to secure a load by charging a price below the fully allocated costs of the truck. In the extreme, the firm may accept a payment which only covers fuel and wages or fuel alone.

One carrier's front haul, the trip out of the home city on which it needs to recoup its costs and earn a profit, is another's backhaul, on which it is willing to charge a reduced price. The home city firm can offer schedules and reliability which allow it to charge more than backhaulers, but the availability of backhauls caps the price charged on front hauls. The pressure on prices can be powerful because backhauls are offered not only by substantial firms but also by minimum scale operations and owner-operators who may be willing to charge only the cost of fuel, gambling that the load will take them to another region which offers better loads. Such competition compels firms to charge less than their fully allocated costs on some front hauls.

This cost/price structure causes problems for firms, shippers, employees, and the public and limits the industry's role in the national transportation system. Before regulation in 1935, the industry suffered from unsatisfactory rates of return and high levels of turnover among firms. The extremity of price competition required that labor costs remain low. Drivers were paid low mileage rates and typically were not paid for non-driving labor. Drivers maintained their earnings through extended hours, high speeds, and minimizing time spent on unpaid duties such as maintenance. The result was a flexible, inexpensive, but unreliable system which posed a threat to public safety and undermined the health and well-being of the labor force (Childs 1985). Low wages and poor working conditions prevented the industry from recruiting the labor force required for a more reliable system.

The system of regulation established under the Motor Carrier Act of 1935 created inefficiencies, but it addressed the problems of the industry, of shippers, and of the public and provided a basis for the resolution of labor's issues. The ICC limited competition by regulating entry, establishing fixed routes, and restricting backhauls. The commission addressed the dual issue of ensuring that rates were compensatory and preventing firms from taking undue advantage of the limits on competition by setting rates through rate bureaus and tariff filings. This regulatory structure increased firms' profitability, stabilized the industry, and greatly improved the reliability of service. Public concerns about safety were addressed through hours of service rules which limited drivers to no more than ten hours of driving without a break of eight hours and restricted total driving time to sixty hours in seven days.

Although the hours of service rules helped drivers, they did not resolve the problem of low earnings or the accompanying incentives to break the rules. Regulation did provide the foundation for improving the conditions of work. Limitation of entry and the creation of fixed routes rendered organizing simpler and more secure for the International Brotherhood of Teamsters (IBT). Over a period of thirty years the Teamsters organized most general freight carriers and brought them within a single framework—the National Master Freight Agreement (NMFA). Wages rose to become comparable with those of steel and auto workers. Jointly administered pension and health funds provided workers with substantial improvements in their economic situation. Truck driving evolved into a good job attractive to stable employees with high school diplomas. Employees could expect to work until retirement. The continued exemption of the industry from the overtime provisions of the Fair Labor Standards Act reflected the success of regulation and unionization in ensuring the quality of jobs.[31] The improved profitability of the industry also reduced the need for strict oversight as major carriers voluntarily adhered to the standards.

Deregulation, begun by the I.C.C. in 1977 and institutionalized in the Motor Carrier Act of 1980, opened entry onto routes and into the industry, eliminated rate making, permitted unlimited backhauling, and allowed carriers to engage in price discrimination.[32,33] The abolition of rules limiting entry unleashed an avalanche of new motor carriers, while elimination of collective rate making allowed these carriers to offer service at very low prices. The intensity of the competition changed the structure of the industry. The previously unified general freight industry divided into truckload (TL) and less-than-truckload (LTL) segments.[34] New (and therefore nonunion) TL carriers entered the market and took existing general freight carriers' TL freight away by offering faster service at very low prices. Part of the low price came from greater efficiencies; TL carriers didn't need the expensive terminal structure used by existing common carriers, but part came from substantially lower wages. Firm turnover increased as new entry was balanced by the bankruptcy of more than 150 major carriers. Operating margins declined, and return on equity slipped after 1980 and remain low (Belzer 1994:36-40).

The intensity of competition altered the employment structure of the industry. The Teamsters' place in the industry declined as rapid turnover replaced organized carriers with nonunion firms. Union membership in the trucking services industry dropped by more than half, from 56.6% to 24.1%, between 1978 and 1990 (Hirsch 1993). The effect was largest in the TL sector where the union lost all bargaining power. Although unionization dropped by 27 percentage points in intercity general freight, a majority of LTL employees have remained union members and the union has retained bargaining power.[35]

Wages and working conditions have declined dramatically. Average annual earnings fell at least 27% between 1978 and 1990; the decline in hourly wages and the deterioration of working conditions have been more marked. Long haul TL drivers spend many hours waiting for loads, loading and unloading, and maintaining their trucks. Before deregulation, union members were paid for this time and it was counted against total hours of service. With the decline of union coverage, the proportion of drivers receiving pay for these duties has fallen. As a result, drivers extend their hours of work and driving to compensate for unpaid time, even when this places them outside the hours of service limits. Eighty hours of work per week is not unusual, particularly in the nonunion TL sector (Belzer 1995b).[36] With average annual earnings of TL drivers running about $23,000, hourly wages are not much above the legal minimum (Belzer 1995a).[37]

Owner-operators, independent contractors who provide a tractor and drive it, have faced equally serious problems. They may earn more than nonunion employees; a survey by *Owner-Operator* magazine found that the owner-operators average net earnings after direct expenses but before taxes varied between $21,000 and $44,700 in 1995 (Witconis 1995). The higher earnings of owner-operators are misleading because they do not participate in mandatory benefits, such as unemployment insurance or workers' compensation, or voluntary benefits, such as health insurance or pension and profit sharing plans, and are liable for the employer share of the FICA tax. Adjusting for these additional expenses suggests that many owner-operators are worse off than employees and may engage in a form of self-exploitation.[38] Owner-operators are also subject to additional problems with unpaid work beyond those suffered by employees as only one-third receive compensation for deadheading. The earnings of owner-operators have fallen at least as much as those of employees; the real earnings of owner-operators in the household moving industry declined by 31.8% between 1980 and 1992.

Pension coverage has also declined. At the beginning of deregulation in 1979, 59.3% of blue-collar employees in the industry were covered by pensions. By 1993 this had declined to 43.3%. Much of the decline is attributable to the decline in the IBT and its associated institutions. Employees in trucking are transient among employers and may work for several firms during their career. The multi-employer pension system established between the industry and the IBT permitted employees to vest and continue accumulating service as they moved among participating employers. Although pension coverage of union members has fallen since 1979, 81.3% of blue-collar union members remain participants in 1993. The nonunion sector has extremely high employee turnover and lacks the institutions needed for a portable pension system. As a result, only 28.5% of nonunion employees report participating in a pension system.

Deregulation has also been associated with increased income inequality in the industry. Burks' (1996) analysis of ICC data on Class I carriers—carriers who receive most of their revenue from intercity operations—suggests the average real annual salary of officers of trucking firms rose by 2.1% annually between 1980 and 1992, from $70,511 in 1980 to $88,959 in 1992 in 1982-1984 base-year dollars. In contrast, drivers' real earnings fell by 2.9% annually, from $30,401 to $23,880 over the same period.

The low wages and poor working conditions have had serious consequences for the industry, for employees, and for the public. It has converted middle-class jobs with reasonable benefits and retirement possibilities into low-wage jobs which are unlikely to provide career employment. Low earnings and limited benefits are obviously disadvantageous to employees and create public costs through increased demand for medical and other social services. Such costs will probably increase over time as employees with inadequate pensions retire and poor working conditions force an increasing number to leave the industry at an age when it is difficult to find a job which will maintain their earnings.

The industry has faced increasing problems in recruiting and maintaining a work force needed to provide adequate quality service, particularly in TL. Before deregulation the typical worker of the industry was reasonably educated, had graduated from high school, and had considerable experience in the industry. Following deregulation and a multitude of bankruptcies, TL firms could draw on experienced workers who had become dislocated by the failure of other carriers. As this work force has aged, new recruitment became necessary, but poor compensation and bad working conditions have made the industry unattractive to any but less educated and inexperienced workers. Such employees have been inexpensive but have been less stable and responsible than the previous labor force. Truckload firms have experienced high levels of turnover, frequently 100%, and consequent problems with the reliability and quality of service.[39] Problems with obtaining an adequate supply of skilled employees have been exacerbated by requirements for drug and alcohol testing of employees. The requirement for Commercial Driver Licenses has also reduced the supply of labor because it is more difficult for drivers to conceal suspended and revoked licenses with licenses from other states.

The industry's response to this shortage of labor has varied. Several major firms have initiated expensive recruitment and training programs and several have actively recruited employees from Ireland and Australia. Others have poached employees from the firms which provide training. This has, to some degree, made training uneconomical. Firms have also invested in technologies, such as automatic transmissions, which reduce the skills required of the drivers.[40] What has not been observed are the wage adjustments predicted by economic theory. The experience of firms has been that efforts to improve recruitment and retention by raising wages has substantially reduced profit margins and placed firms at a competitive disadvantage.[41] Although a major firm is planning to raise some wages in 1997, the industry appears to have become trapped in a low wage/low productivity equilibrium.[42]

Economic deregulation and the externalities associated with intensively competitive markets have compelled extensive and intrusive social regulation. Following evidence that drivers were hiding their bad driving records by holding licenses from multiple states, Congress required that states establish a uniform licensing standard for a single Commercial Drivers License in 1986. The threat to public safety posed by poor working conditions and a poorly trained labor force resulted in passage of the Motor Carrier Act of 1991 and the imposition of mandatory and expensive drug and alcohol tests for drivers. Other regulations established stricter standards for truck maintenance. Such regulations have created a complex regulatory structure which places substantial burdens on firms and enforcement agencies (see Belzer 1994:16-20).

To summarize, the intensity of competition which followed economic deregulation of trucking has reduced employee compensation and caused a sharp deterioration in working conditions. By its own admission, these conditions are now a constraint on the continued development of the industry. Although the public has gained from inexpensive transportation, it has taken on the burden of decreased safety, an increased need for detailed and intrusive regulation of the industry, and the increased social costs associated with low-wage employment.

*Construction Industry*

Deinstitutionalization has taken a different form in construction than trucking. The key event in trucking was the end of economic regulation of the market by the Interstate Commerce Commission. In construction it has been the result of policy shifts which affected labor directly: the weakening or repeal of federal and state prevailing wage laws and shifts in the interpretation of the National Labor Relations Act (NLRA) on issues of double breasting.[43] More generally, it results from a policy regime that made organizing new workers more difficult and a macroeconomic regime that undercut labor's ability to strike (Allen 1994).

Unlike most industries, construction workers are attached primarily to their occupation rather than their employer. Employment is project based and, since employers are typically too small to retain large staffs between projects, employees must be highly mobile between employers. In contrast with most other jobs with similarly high mobility, most trades in construction require considerable skill and experience. Employees need to be sufficiently skilled in their trade to complete assigned work without direct supervision. This employment structure poses challenges to employers, the industry, and employees. Employers need access to a pool of labor on short notice and need to know that the employees will have the requisite skills.[44] The industry needs training programs which produce adequate numbers of new journey workers. Employees face problems with obtaining benefits, such as pensions and health care, which in other industries are typically provided by employers. They also need an orderly means of locating their next job when a project ends and of allocating work among their fellow tradesmen.

Unions earned a central role in the employment relationship in construction by resolving these challenges. Hiring halls provided employers a means of recruiting skilled workers from local, regional, and national labor markets. Unions resolved free-rider problems with apprenticeship training by compelling organized firms to participate in both the financing and training of employees and oversaw programs to ensure that trainees learned the full range of job skills and participated in the classroom portion of the program. Apprenticeship standards also provided criteria by which to judge prospective employees. The hiring hall system provided employees with information about available work and served to allocate that work to those currently without jobs. Jointly managed insurance programs allowed employees to move between employers while retaining benefits needed to make the work attractive as career employment.

The central role of unions in the construction industry led to a high level of organization. Allen (1994) found that 42% of employees in the industry were union members in 1966, with substantially higher levels of organization in the more highly skilled trades categories such as electricians and plumbers. Although this structure was both cost efficient and self-sustaining overall, it could lead to large increases in compensation when labor markets were tight (Allen 1984, 1986a, 1986b, 1988b).

Prevailing wage laws for public works also act to regulate employment conditions in construction. These laws, the federal Davis-Bacon Act and parallel state laws, require that workers on publicly funded construction projects earn wages similar to those paid most employees in privately funded projects. They are intended to guard against the adverse consequences of public construction work being awarded to the lowest bidder.

The need to submit the lowest bid pressures contractors to search for means of lowering their costs, including continued efforts to reduce wages and benefits. Contractors search out low-cost labor locally and look to import low-cost labor from other regions. As government accounts for 25% to 30% of construction expenditures (Pagnucco 1996), low-bid requirements place downward pressures on wages throughout the local construction labor market. The consequent decline in wages disadvantages the construction workers and their families and may place substantial burdens on communities which are faced with increasing demands for services from a low-income population (Craypo 1993 and this volume). In addition, the low-bid process encourages contractors to underbid their true costs. This can cause both additional charges (overruns) to meet the desired standards and increased maintenance costs associated with substandard construction. Prevailing wage laws help avoid these problems by preventing contractors from lowering their bids by cutting wages and benefits. Improved efficiency and lower profits, rather than wages, become the means of winning public contracts.

Deregulation in construction has taken two forms. First, a series of decisions by the NLRB undermined organization in the industry by making it easier for contractors to operate without the construction unions (*R. J. Smith Construction Company* [1971], *Peter Kiewit and Sons, Inc.* [1973], and *Peter Kiewit and Sons, Inc.* [1977]). *Smith* allowed contractors to withdraw from union recognition agreements unless the union could show that it had a majority of employees on a project.[45] The *Kiewit* decisions weakened limitations on double breasting by allowing contractors to establish nonunion subsidiaries more freely. This permitted experienced firms to shift work from union to nonunion subsidiaries more readily. Contractors were quick to take advantage of these decisions. Allen (1994) found that by 1983, 22 of the 43 largest union contractors had nonunion subsidiaries. The sharp decline in unionization in the 1970s and 1980s, from 41.9% in 1970 to 22% in 1992, was in his estimation largely attributable to the legal sanction of double-breasted operations by the *Kiewit* decision.

The other aspect of deregulation has been the weakening and repeal of prevailing wage laws over the last fifteen years. The formula for determining area wages under the Davis-Bacon Act was weakened in 1985 by an administrative shift from a 30% to a 50% rule. Both rules take the modal wage for a particular trade in a specific labor market as the prevailing wage. Under the 30% rule, the prevailing wage was set at the wage paid to at least 30% of the employees. Under the new rule, the prevailing wage is set at the modal wage only when 50% or more of the labor force receives that wage. In the absence of a modal wage cluster which met the rule to the penny, the prevailing wage was set at the average wage—which was generally lower. State prevailing wage laws also have been weakened. They have been repealed or declared unconstitutional in ten states.[46] Other states have altered their formulas and reduced the coverage of their laws. The net effect has been to either eliminate coverage by prevailing wage statutes or lower the wage required to comply with the statute.

What are the consequences of deregulation of employment relations in construction? One already mentioned has been the erosion of the union as the central institution in the industry. Union density in the industry has fallen to about half its 1970 level, from 41.9% to 22% in 1992. Construction union membership had also declined, from 3.2 million in 1979 to 2.9 million in 1989 (Allen 1994). The decline in union density was accompanied by a decline in both absolute and relative earnings. In 1960 the average hourly wage in construction was 126% of the manufacturing wage. Having improved their position in the tight labor markets of the 1960s, construction employees were earning 147% of the manufacturing wage by 1970.[47] The changes in unionization and recessions of the 1970s reduced construction earnings to 127% of the manufacturing wage by 1980. Wages continued to fall after that to 119% in 1990 and then to 114% of the manufacturing hourly wage by 1995. Weekly earnings followed a similar pattern, rising from 135% of weekly earnings in manufacturing in 1960 to 156% in 1970, and then returning to 136% in 1980. Weekly wages then fell steadily to 127% in 1990 and to 121% in 1995. Real earnings also declined over this period. Taking 1970 as a base and using the Personal Consumption Expenditure (PCE) deflator from the GDP accounts, average real wages were $3.91 per hour in 1960, $5.24 in 1970, $5.01 in 1980, $4.37 in 1990, and $4.10 in 1995.[48] In all, purchasing power fell by 21.8% over the last twenty-five years. This is a larger decline than has been suffered by either the manufacturing sector or the balance of the labor force. Benefits have fallen equally sharply. Pension coverage fell from 41% to 33% of the construction labor force from 1979 to 1993. The proportion of employees reporting that their firm offered medical insurance to any employees fell from 59% to 53%.[49]

Is the decline in earnings and benefits related to deinstitutionalization? Current research does not report the effect of declining unionization on wages, but Philips et al. have estimated the effect of repealing the little Davis-Bacon Acts. The gross decline in wages following repeal was 7.5% for the union and nonunion sector. Using a more sophisticated model which controls for the effects of other factors, the authors find repeal causes wages to decline by between 5.1% and 11.0%.[50]

The training system for the industry is also threatened by deregulation. On the union side, this system has been financed by a combination of employee and employer contributions. Apprentices contribute by earning a lower wage before becoming a journey worker. Employers contribute a fixed amount per work hour for each employee. Organized firms cannot free ride by hiring trained journey workers without participating in the apprenticeship system. The same is not true in the nonunion sector. Here, lacking a means of ensuring participation in the apprenticeship system, there is a significant free-rider problem and the apprenticeship system is quite weak. Bilginsoy (1997) finds that depending on the trade, union apprenticeship programs enrolled between 58% and 97% of registered apprentices in 1989. The union programs are also more successful than the nonunion programs, with lower cancellation rates (between 18% and 66% on the union side against 42% to 84% for nonunion programs) and higher completion rates (between 30% and 69% on the union side against 7% to 48% for nonunion programs). The lower graduation rate among nonunion apprentices is related to the lack of oversight to assure that apprentices receive comprehensive on-the-job and classroom training (Philips, Mangum, Waitzman, and Yeagle 1995). The result is that although the union represents a minority of employees in the construction industry, joint labor-management programs account for both a majority of entering apprentices and an even larger proportion of those graduating to journeyman status.

In essence, the nonunion sector has depended on union apprenticeship programs for trained employees and engaged in large scale free riding (Allen 1986a). Predictably, the decline of the union and its apprenticeship system has resulted in a declining supply of trained employees. This problem is more acute in the absence of prevailing wage laws. Prevailing wage laws encourage apprenticeship training by allowing contractors to pay less than the prevailing wage to registered apprentices. Philips, Mangum, Waitzman, and Yeagle (1995) find that the repeal of Utah's prevailing wage law caused both a rapid decline in unionization among plumbers and consequently in the number of enrollees in the apprenticeship programs. Although some large nonunion firms have developed nontrade-based proprietary training, the industry over-all has been unable to evolve an effective training system without participation of the union (Allen 1994). The result has been a growing shortage of skilled labor, a problem reported by the trade press and acknowledged by the president of the Associated Builders and Contractors, the trade organization for the nonunion sector (Tomsho 1994).

The deinstitutionalization of employment relations in construction may also affect safety and construction quality. Waitzman (1996) finds that accident rates are lower in states with prevailing wage laws and decline with the strength of the law. Using annual data on states by three digit SIC construction industries and incorporating controls for average worker's age, establishment size, unemployment rate, income, rainfall, and union density, Waitzman finds that relative to states with strong prevailing wage laws, those without prevailing wage laws have a 16.3% higher injury rate. Those with weak laws have a 14.3% higher injury rate. Lastly, those with "average" laws have an 8.2% higher rate. Repeal of state prevailing wage laws is also associated with an increased number of cost overruns. Philips et al. find that the occurrence of cost overruns on state road contracts increased from 2.0% to 7.3% after repeal. Similarly, although the bid prices fell relative to state engineers' estimated costs from 91% to 89% following repeal, the actual cost rose from 93% to 95%. In a study of violations of prevailing wage laws on public housing projects, the inspector general of HUD found that the use of low-wage/low-skill labor was associated with substandard work and increased maintenance costs (HUD Audit Report 1985).

A final consequence of deinstitutionalization has been the casualization of employment in construction. Under the employment structure that prevailed before deinstitutionalization, individuals could spend most of their working life in the industry. The benefits system provided health and retirement security needed by older employees, and the hiring hall ensured employment to older workers even when age reduced their productivity. The emerging structure is quite different. Health and pension benefits are becoming less common while the lack of an orderly means of allocating work reduces the employment prospects of older employees. Allen reports that counter to the trend in the broader labor force, the average age of construction employees fell from 37 to 35.7 between 1977-78 and 1989. The proportion of the labor force over age 45 fell from 31.1% to 23.7%. These data fit with the work of Philips, Mangum, Waitzman, and Yeagle which find that the response to declining wages in construction in Utah has been both an outward migration of skilled workers and increased movement in and out of construction employment as wages fluctuated relative to those of other industries. Deinstitutionalization appears to be converting career jobs capable of supporting families into jobs which are only attractive to younger single workers with limited commitment to the industry.

The experience of deregulation in construction suggests that a healthy and self-sustaining labor market has dimensions other than compensation. Providing an adequate level of training and obtaining worker commitment to the industry is important not only to employees but also for the industry's capacity to operate efficiently and provide a quality product. The erosion of the institutions which formerly provided these outcomes, the construction unions and prevailing wage laws, continues to reduce the performance of construction labor markets and the industry. Any analysis of the effect of altering labor market policies which does not account for such broader institutional consequences is necessarily incomplete.

An element common to both cases is that deregulation and deinstitutional-ization have, to a great degree, benefited consumers at the expense of worsening the terms of employment. Both industries are labor intensive, and in the absence of legal and institutional limits, reductions in the price of labor are central to a successful competitive strategy. These markets apparently lack an effective mechanism for balancing the competing demands of these groups; a role of regulation was to establish such balance. The trade-off between consumer and worker welfare also complicates measurement of the effects of deregulation. Assessments of competitive policies have focused on the gains accruing to consumers. Where policies influence the quality of employment, these effects should be incorporated in the appraisal (Kreuger and Summers 1988). These cases suggest that an assessment of deregulation which was cognizant of the consequences for both consumers and employees would be less favorable than one that focused solely on consumer welfare.[51]

## Conclusion

Perhaps the most popular public policy slogan since the 1970s has been that deregulation will cure what ails us. Deregulation appeals to quintessential American values since it favors liberty over control and individualism over collectivism. This chapter has argued that our economy, like our society, has always been and always will be regulated. To a significant extent we merely have exchanged market for institutional regulation. While this exchange is by no means complete and direct and indirect economic regulation remain core governing structures in our economy, public policy over the past two decades has decidedly favored market over institutional regulation. Social regulation, the institutional framework governing our noneconomic behavior, has expanded dramatically over the past two decades and remains a growing influence, but deregulation has deinstitutionalized many of our economic relationships.

Workers in the United States have faced increasingly competitive conditions over the last two decades. Some of this has been the result of factors beyond the domain of government: the natural evolution of markets, the introduction of new technologies, and the continuing economic progress of developing countries. Much has been the result of changes in government policy. The deregulation of transportation and communications; the ongoing opening of trade (particularly trade with developing countries); the contraction of social insurance programs such as unemployment insurance and workers compensation; the decline in the minimum wage; the reduction of the protection of concerted activity; and other shifts in policy brought on by legislation, by administrative decisions, and by courts have increased the role of the price mechanism and of competition in labor markets.

Although increased competition has produced benefits, particularly for consumers, theory and experience indicate that such benefits often entail costs for other groups. There are market structures and economic conditions under which increased competition is detrimental to employees, to consumers, to firms, or to society at large. The costs to employees and to society of many recent policy changes have been substantial. As we have reviewed, deregulation of trucking has converted well-paid middle-class jobs with good benefits into low-wage jobs with few benefits and has imposed safety risks and regulatory burdens on society. Similarly, the devitalization of the NLRA and weakening of prevailing wage laws has reduced compensation and safety in the construction industry, has initiated an exodus of skilled workers, and threatens the system of training in the construction industry. Expanded trade with developing countries, trade which is often founded on differences in compensation and working conditions, reduced employment in the manufacturing sector by 1.2 million net jobs between 1978 and 1990. Continued expansion of this trade threatens greater losses (Sachs and Shatz 1994). The decline in union membership and the value of the minimum wage has had ill effects on employees, not the least in increasing wage inequality (DeNardo, Fortin, and Lemieux 1996). Such examples argue that public concern with pro-competitive policies is not a groundless fear of change but a legitimate response to serious issues.

What changes in policy are suggested by this review? First, deregulation and shifts in employment practices have opened gaps in the laws protecting labor. These need to be closed. Extension of the minimum wage and overtime protections of the FLSA to employees in the interstate trucking industry would be an important step in improving the conditions of work in that industry. Similarly, more careful review of claims of independent contractor status in trucking, in construction, and other industries would do much to bring "employees" back under the protection of employment law. Second, it would be sensible to reinvigorate and extend the current structure of employment legislation to mitigate the consequences of increased competition and distribute its gains more equitably. If the new competitive economy will reduce job tenure and require employees to shift jobs more often, we need to ease such transitions by strengthening the unemployment insurance system and altering it to better cover those in nontraditional employment. Similarly, if the new economy is creating a variety of new forms of employment relations—increased use of independent contractors and temporary employees—we need to rewrite the labor laws to extend protections and requirements for equitable treatment for benefits to these new classes of employees. Finally, policies which encourage competition on the basis of the price and condition of labor need to be rethought. Part of the improvement in the economic performance of the

United States has been achieved by worsening the conditions of our labor force. This has advanced the competitiveness of the U.S. relative to other nations, but it has also pushed countries such as Japan, Korea, and Germany toward equivalent policies. Retaining competitiveness by this path will almost certainly require additional and ongoing sacrifices from our labor force. Recent trade agreements also increasingly expose the labor force to competition from countries with much lower labor standards. This will further magnify the pressures on the labor force in exposed industries and throughout the economy. It is past time for both a public debate of the policies which advance economic performance at labor's expense and a serious attempt to establish an international economic system that does not reward the exploitation of labor.

Recognizing the costs of unfettered competition is not synonymous with abandoning market organization or policies which support competition. It suggests a need to change our views from one which under various arguments takes competition as a goal of government policy, to one which views competition as a force to be harnessed to economic and social purposes. This requires a more informed and nuanced appraisal of current policies and proposed changes. We need to ask whether a policy lowers prices, improves services, and so benefits consumers. But we also need to ask how policies affect the wages, hours, and conditions of work; whether they promote or undermine institutions which provide training and maintain standards; and whether they require additional regulation and additional costs to maintain the public good. We also need to be more knowledgeable and clever in developing policies so that they serve multiple ends, improving the welfare of consumers and advancing the condition of employees. Similarly, research on the effects of competition on employees and society needs to be more global in its scope. Rather than limiting research to wages and benefits, the inquiry should be broadened to encompass issues such as employment conditions, training, employee demographics and careers, the structure of work, and the cost of additional regulation and social services. Only such breadth of inquiry can provide an accurate picture of current policies and policy changes.

### Acknowledgment

The authors wish to thank Amy Wells, Paula Voos, Kristen Monaco, Michelle Brown, and Clare Belman for their insightful comments

### Endnotes

[1] Common's term was "legal foundations" (Commons 1932).

[2] In the U.S. the employment-at-will doctrine has given employers a broad right of unilateral action and this, in turn, subjected virtually all aspects of the employment relationship

to market forces. For example, prior to workers compensation legislation, the handling of work-related injuries was part of the private employment relationship and subject to competitive determination in the manner of wages and hours. Employees seeking restitution might sue employers but use of the courts was expensive, time consuming, and uncertain and was not an option for most employees. Workers' compensation legislation altered this by holding employers financially responsible for such injuries and ensuring employees both compensation and due process where payment was challenged. By subjecting employers to common requirements, taking policy on injuries "out of competition," both employees and progressive employers were safeguarded from the practices of those seeking minimum short-term labor costs.

[3] The restaurant industry provides an example of the distinction between these forms of regulation. Federal and state wage-and-hours laws affect fundamental economic aspects of the employment relationship by establishing the minimum wage employees can be paid, the definition of a normal work week, and the rate to be paid employees for "excessive" hours of work. In contrast, local and state sanitation codes establish social requirements for employers and employees, such as testing employees for tuberculosis and the wearing of hair nets to ensure that patrons receive clean and sanitary food, as well as nonlabor conditions such as the temperature at which food must be stored and the hours for the sale of liquor.

[4] A major exception is interstate truck drivers who are neither covered by the FLSA nor, as they are in interstate commerce, state law.

[5] Some municipalities, notably Baltimore, have passed "living wage" legislation which requires city contractors to pay more than the federal minimum. Baltimore established its living wage at $6.10 per hour in 1966 and will increase it to $7.70 in 1998. Maryland has recently passed a similar law for state contractors (*Washington Post*, November 11, 1996, p. A1).

[6] Estimate provided by A. Pagnucco, Building Trade Department, AFL-CIO (by letter of December 28, 1995).

[7] *Employment, Hours and Earnings*, U.S. DOL (1976).

[8] Between 1904 and 1913, 17 states prohibited workers under age 18 from working as night messengers to protect them from exposure to the evening activities of hotels and houses of ill repute (Brandeis 1935:432).

[9] Occupational licensing is a ubiquitous form of labor market regulation which is difficult to fit into a simple typology. It has the function of assuring the public that practitioners possess the minimum level of skill necessary and meet current standards of practice. Licensing may also provide incumbents with economic power by allowing them to limit entry and establish training practices at variance with actual requirements of the profession. Recognizing such trade-offs, courts have acted to limit professions anticompetitive practices, such as advertising bans by bar associations or limitations on the nature of practices by medical associations, while allowing for continued oversight over standards of practice and training.

[10] Although UI coverage has risen since the 1960s, from 71% in 1963 to 94% in 1994, fewer workers are qualifying for payments. Of the unemployed, 48% qualified for payments in 1963; this had fallen to 36% in 1994. In 1963 the overall unemployment rate was 5.7%, while the covered unemployment rate (those who were unemployed and receiving UI benefits) was 4.3%. In 1994 the unemployment rate was 6.1%, but the covered rate was 2.5%.

Only 42% of those who were employed full time for one year prior to the start of their unemployment received benefits (Congressional Research Service as cited in McMurrer and Chasanov 1995).

[11] Deregulation has reduced wages and employment in trucking, airlines, and railroads. In trucking, deregulation has reduced both wages and narrowed the union wage differential, with average wages declining a nominal 26.8% between 1978 and 1990 (Belzer 1995b). In airlines, the primary effect of deregulation has been to reduce job security; wage decline has paced the fall in real wages in the broader economy (Johnson 1995). Recent research on railroads also finds wage decline following deregulation, albeit after considerable delay. Wages increased modestly for several years following deregulation, partially as a tradeoff for substantial reductions in employment. More recently, wages have begun to decline and are estimated to have fallen about 10% in real dollars between 1986 and 1990 because of deregulation. Employment in Class I railroads fell from 548,000 in 1975, the year prior to passage of the Railroad Revitalization Regulatory Reform Act of 1976, to 271,000 in 1993 (MacDonald and Cavazullo 1996).

[12] These same forces may have worked to the advantage of other employees, notably managers and professionals. Berks (1996) finds that in the late 1980s, the compensation of officers of trucking firms increased while driver compensation declined. National earnings distributions also became more unequal over the last two decades as the real earnings of those in the top 10% of the earnings distribution increased and those of the majority of employees fell (Bernstein, Mishel, and Schmitt 1996).

[13] Examples may be found in the greater permissiveness in the use of the lockout and of replacement workers, in the increased scope for employer speech in certification campaigns, and in the limitation of protections for concerted activity.

[14] The importance of competition based on labor conditions is reflected in the debates over enforceable labor standards in the NAFTA and GATT agreements.

[15] See Belman and Lee (1995) for a summary of the literature on the effects of trade on wages. Murphy and Welch (1991) and Borjas, Freeman, and Katz (1991) find that increased trade reduced the wages of those with less than a college degree and raised the earnings of those with a college degree.

[16] Although literature focuses on government intervention in product markets, similar reasoning is used to argue for repealing the NLRA (Reynolds 1987, 1984) and privatizing social security (Pinera 1996).

[17] It would be possible to implement a redistributional scheme which would leave no one worse off and make at least some better off. Although such a scheme might be implemented by government, Coase (1960) suggests that private bargaining may produce a more efficient outcome.

[18] The redistributional effects of regulation may render an entire group such as labor better off. If the demand for labor is overall inelastic, an increase in the minimum wage will result in an increase in labor income despite the decline in hours. The redistribution from the owners of other factors renders an equivalent part of society worse off.

[19] An alternative view is provided in this volume by Addison and Hirsch.

[20] See Bailey and Friedlander (1982) for a detailed discussion of these issues.

[21] Free mobility does not require that all employees be willing to change employers. Job shifting by a sufficient number of "marginal" employees will keep employees' wages at the market rate. When job movement declines to the point at which employers have only a few vacancies, employers may be in a position to put off filling the opening or finding sufficient applicants with reservation wage below the mean of the occupational wage distribution. Under such conditions, market restraints on wages will be weak and mobility may be said to be impeded.

[22] See Kaufman 1996 and this volume.

[23] Although these conditions are deleterious for the employees and small firms participating, it may work to the advantage of users of industry services, larger employers, those brokering industry services, and lending institutions.

[24] Others suggest that trucking is a conventionally competitive industry (Hirsch and Macpherson 1997).

[25] The eight-hour day is distinct from the forty-hour week. The former provided substantial efficiency gains to firms, while the effects of the latter were less favorable.

[26] Unemployment insurance and the trend toward two-earner families have increased labor's ability to withdraw from the market. Recent employment trends, declining UI recipiency rates, increased consumer debt, and dependence on the second income may again be making labor market withdrawal more difficult.

[27] Income distribution is valued not only for itself but for all that comes with it: the opportunity to live a more pleasant life, to obtain adequate health care, send one's children to good schools.

[28] Neoclassical economics models competition as occurring within bargaining groups: employees compete with employees, employers compete with other employers.

[29] Solow (1990) makes a similar argument about the distributional consequences of different institutional frameworks. Using a game theoretic model, he finds that unemployment insurance provides important disincentive for the unemployed to chisel against the standard wage. This increases employees' ability as a group to improve the standard wage and appropriate a greater share of the available economic surplus.

[30] Such problems are less important when trade is opened between countries with similar levels of economic development because labor standards will be similar. The same is not true when trade is opened between countries of very different levels of economic development.

[31] *Report of the Minimum Wage Study Commission* 1981:Chp. 6.

[32] Pressure for deregulation came from many sources, notably shippers, but economists provided the intellectual support for deregulation in the late 1970s. In their analysis, regulation of an inherently competitive industry introduced significant allocative inefficiencies. Restrictions on backhauls wasted fuel and capacity; fixed routes and the need for obtaining certification to haul new products or change route structure impeded the response of the transportation system to changing conditions. Most important, however, were restrictions on entry and collective rate making which combined to keep shipping rates high and provided little incentive for the improvements or innovation in the quality of service. In this view, the wages and working conditions earned in the regulated segment of the industry were rents resulting from a shared monopoly on road transportation.

[33] Previously carriers had been required to handle particular products over which they had authority regardless of quantity and as common carriers were not allowed to charge smaller shippers higher prices. After deregulation, carriers could segment the market, specialize in particular types of freight, and price discriminate, all of which became essential to survival.

[34] TL carried shipments which could be picked up from a shipper and delivered to a customer in a single movement. LTL took smaller shipments which were consolidated at a terminal before being shipped to another terminal, deconsolidated, and delivered to the customer.

[35] The IBT is currently threatened by the spread of nonunion regional carriers in LTL. These carriers were founded by Consolidated Freightways and Roadway, the largest organized national LTL carriers, as double-breasted operations but now operate as unaffiliated competitors.

[36] Drivers often do not log non-driving hours since they are paid by the mile driven and non-driving time is not compensated but is counted against their maximum hours of service.

[37] Data on the hours of over-the-road drivers is difficult to obtain. As noted, although drivers are required to log both driving and on-duty hours, underreporting is routine. CPS data is not particularly useful both because it does not distinguish between over-the-road, local delivery and other drivers in the trucking services industry and because of ambiguity of noncompensated time. Belzer estimates hours by extrapolation from driver mileage data provided in reports to the ICC and the DOT.

[38] Witconis finds a three-cent difference in cost per mile between a small firm and an owner-operator. Two cents of this difference is accounted for by the exemption of owner-operators from workers compensation insurance.

[39] J.B. Hunt, the second largest carrier in the industry, reports 100% turnover in drivers annually with consequent problems with the reliability and quality of service (Schulz 1996).

[40] *Traffic World*, December 9, 1996, pp. 26-27.

[41] MS Carriers reported that 75% of the cost of a wage increase granted in 1992 came out of the firm profits (*Wall Street Journal*, September 23, 1996).

[42] For example, J.B. Hunt, a major TL carrier, increased the wages of their random route drivers by 32% in February of 1997 (Schultz 1996).

[43] The rules under which firms can maintain union and nonunion subsidiaries.

[44] Because periods of employment are very short, screening costs would represent a very high proportion of total labor costs if all applicants had to be screened on every project.

[45] Prehire agreements committed employers to union recognition on all projects for a specified period of time. It resolved the problem of determining union status in an industry in which attachment to employers was often shorter than the period required to conduct a recognition election.

[46] Florida (1979), Alabama (1980), Utah (1981), Arizona (1984), Colorado (1985), Idaho (1985), New Hampshire (1985), Kansas (1987,) and Louisiana (1988) repealed their prevailing wage laws. Oklahoma's law was declared unconstitutional in 1995.

[47] BLS *Employment and Earnings* establishment data (1997).

[48] The CPE deflator is used to avoid problems with the change in the measurement of housing costs in the CPI as well as the current controversy over biases in that index.

[49] This is due almost entirely to falling collective bargaining coverage, which declined from 42.6% in 1979 to 25.4% in 1993. The nonunion sector has increased its pension coverage over this period, from 10% to 18%, while pension coverage in the union sector has fallen from 83% to 75%. The decline in medical insurance is also driven by deunionization.

[50] For a dissenting view of the work of Philips et al., see Thieblot (1996).

[51] Addison and Hirsch (this volume) adopt this latter standard.

## References

Allen, S. G. 1984. "Unionized Construction Workers Are More Productive." *Quarterly Journal of Economics* (May), pp. 251-74.

_____. 1986a. "Unionization and Productivity in Office Building and School Construction." *Industrial and Labor Relations Review* (January), pp. 187-201.

_____. 1986b. "The Effect of Unionism on Productivity in Privately and Publicly Owned Hospitals and Nursing Homes." *Journal of Labor Research* (Winter), pp. 59-68.

_____. 1988a. "Declining Union Efficiency in Construction." *Industrial and Labor Relations Review* (April), pp. 212-42.

_____. 1988b. "Further Evidence on Union Efficiency in Construction: The Facts and the Reasons." *Industrial Relations* (Spring), pp. 232-40.

_____. 1994. "Developments in Collective Bargaining in Construction in the 1980s and 1990s." In Paula Voos, ed., *Contemporary Collective Bargaining in the Private Sector.* Madison, WI: Industrial Relations Research Assn., pp. 411-46.

Becker, Gary S. 1971. *The Economics of Discrimination.* 2nd ed. Chicago: University of Chicago Press, p. 168.

Belman, Dale, and Thea Lee. 1996. "International Trade and the Performance of U.S. Labor Markets." In R. Blecker, ed., *U.S. Trade Policy and Global Growth.* New York: M. E. Sharpe, pp. 61-108.

Belzer, Michael H. 1993. "Collective Bargaining in the Trucking Industry: The Effects of Institutional and Economic Restructuring." Diss., Cornell University.

_____. 1994. *Paying the Toll: Economic Deregulation of the Trucking Industry.* Washington, DC: Economic Policy Institute.

_____. 1995a. "Labor Law Reform: Some Lessons from the Trucking Industry." *Proceedings of 47th Annual Meeting* (Washington, DC). Madison, WI: Industrial Relations Research Association, pp. 403-13.

_____. 1995b. "Collective Bargaining after Deregulation: Do the Teamsters Still Count?" *Industrial and Labor Relations Review*, Vol. 48, no. 4 (July), pp. 636-55.

Bernstein, J., L. Mishel, and J. Schmitt. 1996. *State of Working America: 1996-1997.* Washington, DC: Economic Policy Institute.

Bailey, E., and A. F. Friedlander. 1982. "Market Structure and Multi-product Industries." *Journal of Economic Literature.* Vol. 20 (September), pp. 1024-48.

Bilginsoy, C. 1997. "Apprenticeship Training in the U.S. Construction Industry." *Report to the Construction Alliance.* New York State School of Industrial and Labor Relations, Cornell University.

Borjas, G. J., R. B. Freeman, and L. Katz. 1991. "On the Labor Market Effects of Trade and Immigration." NBER Working Paper 3761, Cambridge, MA: National Bureau of Economic Research.

Borjas, G. J., and V. Ramey. 1994. "Rising Wage Inequality in the United States: Causes and Consequences." *American Economic Review* (May), pp. 10-16.

Brand, H. 1985. "The Decline of Workers' Incomes, the Weakening of Labor's Position." *Dissent* (Summer), pp. 286-98.

Brandeis, E. 1935. "Labor Legislation." In J. Commons et al., eds., *History of Labor in the United States, 1896-1932*, Vol. 3. New York: MacMillan Company.

Bulow, Jeremy I., and Lawrence H. Summers. 1986. "A Theory of Dual Labor Markets with Application to Industrial Policy, Discrimination and Keynesian Unemployment." *Journal of Labor Economics*, Vol. 4, no. 3, part 1, pp. 376-414.

Burks, Stephen V. 1996. "Wage Segmentation in the General Freight Trucking Industry." Paper presented at the 1996 Annual Meeting of the Transportation Research Forum, San Antonio, Texas. October 17-19, 1996.

_____. 1997. "Labor Market Segmentation in the For-Hire Motor Freight Industry." Ph.D. Dissertation Prospectus, Economics Department, University of Massachusetts–Amherst.

Childs, William R. 1985. *Trucking and the Public Interest: The Emergence of Federal Regulation, 1914-1940*. Knoxville, TN: University of Tennessee Press.

Coase, R. 1960. "The Problem of Social Cost." *The Journal of Law and Economics*, Vol. 3, pp. 1-44.

Commons, J. R. 1932. *Legal Foundations of Capitalism*. New York: Macmillan.

Craypo, C. 1993. "Strike and Relocation in Meatpacking." In C. Craypo and B. Nissen, eds., *Grand Designs: The Impact of Corporate Strategies on Workers, Unions and Communities*. Ithaca, NY: ILR Press, pp. 185-208.

Davidson, C. 1989. "Impact of Out-of-Area Workers in Non-Residential Construction on Contra Costa County: A Case Study of the USS-POSCO Modernization." Center for Labor Research and Education, Institute of Industrial Relations, University of California–Berkeley.

DeNardo, John, Nicole M. Fortin, and Thomas Lemieux. 1996. "Labor Market Institutions and the Distribution of Wages, 1973-1992: A Semiparametric Approach." *Econometrica*, Vol. 65 (September), pp. 1001-46.

Ehrenberg, R. G., and R. S. Smith. 1994. *Modern Labor Economics: Theory and Public Policy*, 5th ed. New York: Harper Collins.

Gordon, David M., Richard Edwards, and Michael Reich. 1982. *Segmented Work, Divided Workers*. Cambridge, UK: Cambridge University.

Gouldner A. W. 1954. *Patterns of Industrial Bureaucracy*. Toronto: Free Press.

Heywood, J. S., and J. H. Peoples. 1994. "Deregulation and the Prevalence of Black Truck Drivers." *Journal of Law and Economics*, Vol. 37 (April), pp. 133-55.

Hirsch, Barry T. 1993. "Trucking Deregulation and Labor Earnings: Is the Union Premium a Compensating Differential?" *Journal of Labor Economics*, Vol. 11, no. 2, pp. 279-301.

Hirsch, B. T., and D. A. Macpherson. 1997. "Earnings and Employment in Trucking: Deregulating a Naturally Competitive Industry." In James Peoples, ed., *Regulatory Reform and Labor Markets*. Norwell, MA: Kluwer Academic Publishers (forthcoming).

HUD Office of the Inspector General. 1985. *HUD Audit Report on Monitoring and Enforcing Labor Standards*.

Hunnicutt, B. W. 1988. *Work Without End: Abandoning Shorter Hours for the Right to Work*. Philadelphia, PA: Temple University Press.

Ippolito, R. 1987. "Why Federal Workers Don't Quit." *Journal of Human Resources*, Vol. 22, pp. 281-99.

Johnson, N. B. 1995. "Pay Levels in Airlines since Deregulation." In Peter Capelli, ed., *Airline Labor Relations in the Global Era*. Ithaca, NY: ILR Press, pp. 101-15.

Kaufman, B. Forthcoming. "Why the Wagner Act? Reestablishing Contact with Its Original Purpose." In David Lewin, Bruce Kaufman, and Donna Sockell, eds., *Advances in Industrial and Labor Relations*, Greenwich, CT: JAI Press.

Kelly, Ken. 1996. "Trucks Reinvented." *Traffic World* (December 9), pp. 26-27.

Krueger, A., and L. H. Summers. 1988. "Efficiency Wages and the Inter-industry Wage Structure." *Econometrica*, Vol. 56, no. 2 (March), pp. 259-93.

Lee, T., and R. Scott. 1996. "The Cost of Trade Protection Reconsidered: The Case of U.S. Steel, Textile and Apparel." In R. Blecker, ed., *U.S. Trade and Global Growth*. Armonk, NY: M. E. Sharpe.

Levine, D. I., and L. Tyson. 1990. "Participation, Productivity and the Firm's Environment." In A. S. Blinder, ed., *Paying for Productivity: A Look at the Evidence*. Washington, DC: Brookings.

MacDonald, J. M., and L. C. Cavazullo. 1996. "Railroad Deregulation: Pricing Reforms, Shipper Response and the Effect on Labor." *Industrial and Labor Relations Review*, Vol. 50, no. 1 (October), pp. 80-91.

McMurrer D. P., and A. B. Chasanov. 1995. "Trends in Unemployment Insurance Benefits." *Monthly Labor Review* (September), pp. 30-39.

Minimum Wage Study Commission. 1981. "Exemptions from the Fair Labor Standards Act." *Report of the Minimum Wage Study Commission*, Vol. 4. Washington, DC: U.S. Government Printing Office.

Murphy, K., and F. Welch. 1991. "The Role of International Trade in Wage Differentials." In M. Kosters, ed., *Workers and Their Wages*. Washington, DC: American Enterprise Institute.

National Commission for Employment Policy. 1995. *Unemployment Insurance: Barriers to Access for Women and Part-time Workers*. Washington, DC: U.S. Department of Labor.

Philips, P., G. Mangum, N. Waitzman, and A. Yeagle. 1995. "Losing Ground: Lessons from the Repeal of Nine "Little Davis-Bacon Acts." Working Paper, Economics Department, University of Utah.

Polyani, K. 1944. *The Great Transformation*. New York: Reinhold.

Reynolds, Lloyd. 1948. "Toward a Short Run Theory of Wages." *American Economic Review*, Vol. 38, no. 2 (June), pp. 289-308.

Reynolds, Morgan. 1978. *Making America Poorer: The Cost of Labor Law*. Washington, DC: Cato Institute.

_____. 1984. *Power and Privilege: Labor Unions in America*. New York: Universe Books.

Sachs, J. D., and H. J. Shatz. 1994. "Trade and Jobs in U.S. Manufacturing." Brookings Papers on Economic Activity, 1.

Schulz, John D. 1996. "A 32 Percent Pay Raise: J. B. Hunt Gambles on Pay Increase to Alleviate its Chronic Driver Shortage." *Traffic World* (September 16), pp. 43-44.

Schultz, Richard J. 1995. "Chronic Shortage of Truckload Drivers Spurs Innovative, Long-range Solutions." *Traffic World* (March 27), pp. 30, 32.

Solow, R. 1990. *Labor Markets as a Social Institution*. Cambridge: Basil Blackwell.

Thieblot, A. J. 1996. "A New Evaluation of Impacts of Prevailing Wage Law Repeal." *Journal of Labor Research*, Vol. 17, no. 2 (Spring), pp. 297-322.

Tomsho, R. 1994. "Labor Squeeze." *Wall Street Journal* (February 27), p. A1.

Waitzman, N. 1996. "Worker Beware: The Relationship between the Strength of State Prevailing Wage Laws and Injuries in Construction, 1976-1991." Mimeo.

Witconis, Leon. 1994. "1995 Cost Per Mile/Economic Report." *Owner-Operator* (September), pp. 29-36.

CHAPTER 6

# Alternative Perspectives on the Purpose and Effects of Labor Standards Legislation

CHARLES CRAYPO
*University of Notre Dame*

Some 180 federal statutes currently regulate labor markets (Commission on the Future of Worker-Management Relations 1994:45; Weil, in this volume). Although the core legislation was enacted in the 1930s, subsequent laws and amendments, administrative decisions, and judicial interpretations constantly change the body of such regulation. In 1940 just 7 major federal laws were in force, more than twice that number in 1970, 19 in 1980, and 26 in 1994 (GAO 1994). Two that directly regulate wages and hours are the Davis-Bacon Act of 1931 and the Fair Labor Standards Act of 1938 (FLSA).

Davis-Bacon and "Little Davis-Bacon" Acts at the state level require contractors working on government-funded construction projects to pay their employees no less than the "prevailing" wage for each occupation in that area. The Wage and Hours Division of the U.S. Labor Department surveys contractors and other interested parties and, using predetermined formulas, calculates prevailing wages for crafts employed in commercial, residential, heavy, and highway construction. Individual state agencies do the same under their guidelines.

In 1979 the Labor Department reported that government-determined prevailing rates and union-negotiated wages were the same in "slightly less than half" of all construction work during the 1970s (Hearings 1979:111). In the decade after 1979, nine states repealed their Little Davis-Bacon Acts, reducing the number covered to 30 from a high of 42 in 1979. Another dozen or so states debated doing so and, in several instances, weakened existing laws. Thus by the mid-1980s the estimated ratio of coverage of state and federal acts together had fallen to about one-third of the work and somewhere between one-fifth and one-quarter under the federal law alone (Thieblot 1986:38-40). The ratio doubtless is smaller today due to construction union decline. Even

221

so, leadership in the 1994-96 Congress tried unsuccessfully to repeal the federal law (Bill to Repeal the Davis-Bacon Act, S. 141 and H.R. 500).

The FLSA, also administered by the Wage and Hour Division, establishes minimum wage rates and maximum hours of work per week for most workers and industries and regulates the use of child labor. In 1938 the minimum hourly rate was $0.25. In October 1996 it was raised to $4.75 from $4.25, increasing to $5.15 in 1997. The law mandated time-and-a-half pay for hours of work beyond 44 at passage and 40 soon after. Bills before Congress in 1997 would permit employers to give employees one and a half hours of unpaid time off for each hour of overtime worked within a two-week period.

Until the 1960s the minimum rate remained close to the accepted definition of a "living wage"—enough for a full-time worker to support a family of three or four. But the act covered only about half the eligible work force and specifically exempted many of the lowest wage industries. During the next three decades FLSA coverage was expanded to include most workers, but the mandated rate fell much below the living wage. This will be true even after the $0.90 increase approved in 1996. The gap between the federal minimum wage and the living wage has given rise to political movements in several states and cities to adopt "living wage" rates above the federal level.

This analysis examines Davis-Bacon and the FLSA from orthodox neoclassical and institutional perspectives. These models ask different questions; interpret the origins, purposes, and performance of regulatory labor laws differently; and make or imply opposite policy recommendations. This chapter begins with the legislative histories of both statutes to determine the economic thinking and policy objectives behind them. It then examines the neoclassical approach to legislated standards in general and to Davis-Bacon and the FLSA in particular and does the same for institutional approaches. The chapter concludes with an assessment of the relative contributions of the contrasting models to our understanding of labor standards legislation in modern industrial society.

## Legislative History of Federal Minimum and Prevailing Wage Laws

Legislative histories provide a basis for comparing the perceptions, methods, and conclusions of individuals and groups responsible for these laws with those of the alternative perspectives. What were their concerns and why did the supporters of these laws think they would solve the problems?

### The Davis-Bacon Act

The purpose of Davis-Bacon was never in doubt. Throughout the congressional committee hearings and floor discussion accompanying its passage—no real debate ever occurred—the object clearly was to prevent local or outside contractors from importing cheap labor as a way of lowering costs and, on that basis, of submitting low bids on federal construction projects.[1] The effect of such low bidding, all agreed, was to put the government in the politically embarrassing position of seeming to undermine jobs and wages at a time when it was trying to revive industry and earnings through public projects.

Moreover, by 1931 it was evident that no amount of "preventive incantation" by President Hoover or anyone else was going to convince Americans that the economy was fundamentally sound (Galbraith 1954:94). Something had to be done, especially in the construction industry, where the temporary and transient nature of projects encouraged destructive wage cutting. The national mood was getting angry and a prevailing wage law would, according to Congressman Robert Bacon (D-NY), do much "to quiet the discontent which increases to serious proportions especially during times of economic depression, times such as we are having today" (Hearings 1931:21).

Davis-Bacon thus became law when it did because of the Depression, but its rationale was the vulnerability of the construction industry and not the business cycle as such. Indeed, Bacon had been introducing such legislation since 1927 in response to wage cutting in construction following passage the year before of a nationwide federal building program. He became involved in the issue, he said, when an out-of-state company was the low bidder on a veterans' hospital project in his district. The company brought in low-wage migrant labor to do the work at substandard wages. Individual states had been enacting wage-and-hour laws since before the turn of the century, but this and similar experiences elsewhere showed that they could not address the problem when federal funds were involved.[2]

The way he and other reformers saw it, construction was unstable even in the best of times and chronically so in the worst. Twice before his bills had won unanimous committee approval but advanced no further. Now it was a law whose time had come. A new ten-year federal building program was underway at a cost of a half-billion dollars, perhaps the largest such investment to date. Congress wanted to distribute these funds broadly and equitably, Bacon said, but low-wage competition was defeating the purpose. The House Labor Committee voted out the bill unanimously and by the time it got to the floor the Senate had so approved it without debate. President Hoover signed it into law without delay.

Everyone seemed to support prevailing wages in 1931. Second to none in this was Hoover, even though he had recently opposed an unsuccessful collective bargaining bill. In the 1930 election Democrats had gained control of the House and nine additional seats in the Senate. Finally, wage cutting on government projects contradicted presidential efforts to persuade employers not to slash wages in the wake of the 1929 market crash. Hoover wanted them to maintain wages and also make capital investments to sustain purchasing power, create jobs, and inspire confidence.[3]

Several cabinet members and agency heads testified in favor of Davis-Bacon. Even the president's newly appointed Committee on Unemployment endorsed it, suggesting that any job losses that might result were not a primary concern. Labor Secretary Doak revealed that the administration had planned to write prevailing wage requirements into federal construction contracts the preceding year but had been advised that it could not do so without legislation to that effect (Hearings 1931:4).

Both the unions and the industry's only national trade association supported legally standardized wages but disagreed on their administration. The question was what should be the prevailing rate? The AFL wanted union wages to be designated as such but endorsed the bill anyway "as the best thing we can get" (Hearings 1931:18). The General Contractors' Association supported prevailing rates in principle: "It is contrary to the best interests of the construction industry and society at large for contractors and other employers to utilize the present surplus of workmen as a means of depressing wages or establishing excessive hours of labor." But it withheld final support because the bill left rate determination to government contracting officials and local industry. GCA wanted Washington to decide. That was objectionable to the bill's drafters, however, who wanted to avoid the impression that government was fixing wages rather than observing those determined in local markets or collective bargaining (*Congressional Record* 1931:6511).

Labor and the Democratic leadership preferred that the prevailing rate be the union wage; established contractors and the GOP wanted something between that and the low-bid wage but were prepared to accept the union wage if necessary to avoid the lowest. Hoover's assistant war secretary, for example, testified that even without the law he had persuaded a local contractor to pay bricklayers a "fair" $1.25 an hour rather than the low $0.75 or the union $1.50" (Hearings 1931:18). The final bill left the matter to local determination.

Everyone—industry, unions, communities, and government—understood and wished to avoid casualization of construction labor markets. Casual labor had become the norm in agriculture and longshoring and, with the worsening economy, was now appearing in manufacturing, construction, and elsewhere. A condition of chronic labor surplus, irregular work, and low pay was spreading nationally. Unemployed men and women were appearing outside factory gates and other workplaces in search of jobs that lasted only a day or so. Those selected worked under the terms offered. Those not went away to return the following day. Employers began retaining core workers and hiring others as needed from the growing contingent labor force. In longshoring, for example, "in addition to the relatively small cadre of workers who regularly offer their services, there [were] also many newcomers competing with them for jobs" (Larrowe 1955:49).

Congressman Blanton of Texas raised the lone voice in opposition to Davis-Bacon in the House on constitutional and states' rights. He used the same arguments the Supreme Court had used in striking down federal minimum wage laws during the 1920s: workers cannot be deprived of their right to work for less than the minimum without due process of law, and states cannot be preempted in matters involving local labor markets (e.g., *Adkins v. Children's Hospital*, 261 U.S. 525 [1923]). "We are thus proposing by this pernicious bill to interfere with a sacred, inalienable right that has given initiative and independence to men for ages past," he warned (*Congressional Record* 1931:6507). His alarm had nothing to do with the state of the construction industry but everything with the politics of federal intervention. As Moss (1996:77-96) shows, when regulatory responsibility was left to the states, "degenerative competition" followed when they began competing with one another to see which could best avoid such statutes and attract business fleeing regulation elsewhere.

Other speakers, however, expressed apprehension over industrial trends generally and in labor markets specifically. They kept coming back to the threat of low-wage competition. "At the present time employees are competing with each other for employment," Bacon said, "and the natural result is that they in their anxiety to secure work underbid each other" (*Congressional Record* 1931:6517). If casualization could occur in construction, with its relatively high wages and strong unions, then which workers and industries were secure against destructive market forces? As one congressman put it:

> In these days of improved methods and modern machinery we find the employer class generally resisting wage increases and work-period reductions. . . . With consumption falling far behind production and resulting in economic stagnation, it is our chief concern to maintain the wages of our workers and to increase them wherever possible. (Congressional Record 1931:6513)[4]

## The Fair Labor Standards Act

To socially privileged New Deal reformers there was much worth saving in American capitalism. But they had long been convinced that capitalism had to be saved from capitalists. This required, among other things, a legal floor on wages. Frances Perkins, daughter of a successful industrialist and wife of a finance analyst (Bernstein 1970:111-14), had written in a 1933 Labor Non-Partisan League pamphlet:

> As a nation, we are recognizing that programs long thought of as merely labor welfare, such as shorter hours, higher wages, and a voice in the terms and conditions of work, are really essential economic factors for recovery and for the technique of industrial management in a mass production age. (Fraser 1991:330)

The wage-and-hour aspect of their agenda therefore aimed at the most vulnerable workers. During the 1936 presidential campaign, Roosevelt promised such legislation to help restore economic growth with full employment, rising wages, and industry profits (Brandeis 1957:217). Davis-Bacon thus preserved local wage standards in construction, and the Wagner Act protected worker rights to unionize and union rights to represent and bargain for them. Now the administration was coming to the aid of unorganized, low-wage workers with a bill to ensure them a "living wage." New Deal economists were aware of the possible unemployment effects of minimum wage laws, but that contingency did not override their primary objective of driving the low-wage worker and employer out of the market.

The legislative history of the FLSA is unmistakable on this count. Individuals and organizations supported it because experience and analysis convinced them that labor markets play hostage to the machinations of employers that either set out to use low wages as a competitive weapon or have no choice but to do so as a result. Their reasoning was that if a job does not afford a customary living standard, then it should not exist; it causes or is caused by negative market externalities and unequal bargaining power and is both socially and economically destructive. Individuals, families, and communities are made to subsidize low-wage employers and therefore to pay the price of such dysfunctional competition. A firm that cannot pay the same wage that its competitors have to pay and still survive should not be in business, because it must be either an inefficient producer in other ways or an outright "wage chiseler."

Secretary Perkins, Sidney Hillman, and economists and lawyers from the Roosevelt "brain trust" drafted what became the Connery-Black Bill (Fraser 1991:391-94). Congressional hearings were held in June 1937, a time when the economy appeared to be recovering from nearly eight years of depression. Industrial production, income, and employment were up but still below their 1929 levels, and unemployment was estimated at 14% (Hession and Sardy 1969:704-11; Hearings 1937, Part 1:156). Moreover, although none of the witnesses and legislators could know it at the time, the current boom would end later that year and the economy sink back into depression.

Economists, government officials, union leaders, and businessmen who testified generally supported the bill, but for different reasons and with varying degrees of enthusiasm. Economists showed that industry had cut wages and increased work hours following the Supreme Court's 1935 nullification of labor standards under the National Recovery Act (NRA) of 1933. They and administration officials claimed that a federal minimum wage would (1) establish a floor on wages to discourage wage cutting within industries and among geographic regions, (2) put a ceiling on hours of work to discourage employers from working low-wage labor long hours instead of hiring more employees at shorter hours, (3) encourage firms to invest in capital and technology in order to make workers productive enough to justify the higher wages, and (4) prohibit employers from using child labor to lower costs (cf. Hearings 1937).

William Green and John L. Lewis, speaking for organized labor, gave qualified support provided the minimum rate was not high enough to jeopardize negotiated wages. As it turned out, they had nothing to fear. BLS testimony (Hearings 1937, Part 2:338) revealed that average wages in fewer than a dozen industries were low enough to be affected by the proposed $0.40 an hour minimum, and three of them had been specifically exempted. This is especially revealing in view of the fact the final bill called for a $0.25 rate and even narrower coverage.

Northern manufacturers in mobile industries such as cotton textiles supported the measure enthusiastically; major business and trade associations, including the Chamber of Commerce and the National Association of Manufacturers, did so in principle but with considerably less enthusiasm, agreeing that mandated minimums were in the national interest but insisting they be modest in nature and hopefully anticipating restoration of the defunct NRA *industry* codes. Representatives of multiplant operations in the North and the South testified against the bill as an unwarranted wage equalizer.

A leading Senate supporter confirmed that the bill was intended to complement Davis-Bacon and Wagner Act provisions. It provides "collective bargaining through a government agency, for the men and women who are not organized, who are working in small industries, who are subject to the tyranny and oppression of sweatshops and chiselers." Where no union existed or was likely to exist, he said, the government would play that role by establishing "for the lowest wage groups a decent, reasonable minimum wage and maximum hours" (*Congressional Record* 1938:7650). His characterization thus closed the circle of regulatory legislation to include all or most working Americans, union members via Davis-Bacon and the Wagner Act, and nonunion workers via the FLSA.

## Alternative Interpretations of Labor Standards Legislation

*The Neoclassical Case against Labor Market Regulation*

The neoclassical market approach analyzes and evaluates labor standards laws using a scarcity-choice-equilibrium model. The logic is impeccable given the necessary assumptions. The competitive firm's labor demand curve slopes downward because the physical product of each additional worker declines while the product price remains constant. The rational employer thus hires additional workers to the point where the marginal value product of the last one hired equals the wage paid to that and all the workers. Under these conditions, an arbitrary wage increase above the equilibrium causes some workers to cost more than their productive worth and hence to become unemployed. Mandated wages and wage increases therefore harm some of the employees they are intended to help.

Such laws also raise the cost of doing business and cause marginal firms to earn less than competitive profit rates and eventually go out of business, creating an inefficient allocation of both capital and labor. Consumers in turn are harmed by the high prices and less than optimal production of goods and services. Finally, the larger economy is constrained because mandated wage increases do nothing to improve the labor productivity needed to pay for them.

Regulation, from this perspective, is unnecessary—even counterproductive—and by implication unfair.[5] Each worker freely and rationally chooses what his or her worth will be, within the boundaries of their financial resources and natural abilities, because each chooses how much time, effort, and money to invest or not invest in acquiring formal education and training. This bundle of "human capital" determines the individual's productive value. Large bundles produce high output and get rewarded accordingly; small bundles produce low output and low rewards.

*The Neoclassical Case against Davis-Bacon*

Neoclassical studies of prevailing wages ask three basic questions consistent with the logic of the model. Does the act favor union workers and contractors over nonunion individuals and firms? Are protected (union) project bids higher than unprotected (nonunion) bids and, if so, by how much? Finally, do prevailing wage laws make the industry inefficient, more expensive, and unfair?

These issues are difficult to investigate using large data bases. A unionized project cannot be rebid and performed under nonunion conditions. The critical research therefore depends on case study data. (See, Goldfarb and Morrall 1978; Gould and Bittlingmayer 1980; Thieblot 1986.) Excess costs are estimated by assuming that without Davis-Bacon contractors would substitute low-paid for high-paid labor, either nonunion for union workers or union workers at below union wages. The total number of hours worked on a particular project is then multiplied by the average wage difference between union and non-union labor to obtain the precise amount of cost inefficiency.

On the basis of these findings and the logical expectations of the model, neoclassical analyses criticize prevailing wage laws on numerous counts. Davis-Bacon may have been justified during the 1930s, they conclude, but has been made obsolete by economic expansion and improved employment relations; it is difficult, if not impossible, to administer fairly and efficiently; it inflates the cost of public construction, as demonstrated by cost comparisons of specific projects and in government sample surveys; it discourages small businesses from expanding employment and output; it destroys work incentives, which in turn delays completion schedules and encourages poor product quality; and it imposes unfunded mandates on local governments by requiring them to pay premium prices for roads and other projects. Finally, and importantly, it unfairly excludes nonunion workers, particularly women and minority youths, by preventing them from acquiring job skills and work experiences.

In view of these flaws and the difficulty in trying to remedy them satisfactorily, most neoclassical commentary favors outright repeal. Prevailing wages are deemed blatant price-fixing, offensive to conservative and liberal economists alike. The liberal Walter Heller, for example, observed that "a government that is dead serious about fighting inflation ought to put an end to the laws that make government an accomplice in cost and price-propping actions . . . such as the Davis-Bacon Act" (cited in Bourdon and Levitt 1980:93). No other piece of labor legislation is treated as disdainfully in the professional literature. The following excerpt is illustrative:

> A reasonably thorough search of the literature reveals that no professional economist has testified in favor of the Davis-Bacon Act, nor do labor economics textbooks offer a brief in favor of the Act. In fact, the professional literature overwhelmingly recognizes the Act as a device to uphold the pay standards and employment of the building trades unions, protecting them from the cold winds of competition that are so intolerant of monopoly pricing and inefficient methods. (Reynolds 1982:297)

This opposition extends beyond the majority of economists to include conservative think tanks, the corporate affiliates of the Business Roundtable (major users of commercial construction services), nonunion contractors represented by the Associated Builders and Contractors (ABC), and some labor

law specialists and state and federal agencies (e.g., Gujarati 1967; Business
Roundtable 1978; Goldfarb and Morrall 1978, 1981; GAO 1979; Gould and
Bittlingmayer 1980; Reynolds 1982; Congressional Budget Office 1983;
Thieblot 1986).

## The Neoclassical Case against the Fair Labor Standards Act

Market analyses of wage-and-hour legislation focus mainly on wages and,
within that, on the employment effects of increases in minimum rates. A survey
of the literature in the early 1980s found that "the employment/unemployment
effect of the minimum wage continues to be a pivotal issue around which present-day debate centers" (Brown et al. 1982:487). Neoclassical theory suggests
that unskilled, inexperienced workers would be most susceptible to the adverse
employment effects of increases in either the rate or the coverage. FLSA coverage is now quite complete, therefore research has focused on the demand for
teenage workers following rate increases (Filer, Hamermesh, and Rees 1996:
171). As expected, studies estimate that for every 10% increase in the minimum
rate or in the effective coverage, some 1% to 2% fewer teenagers will be
employed (Kennan 1995; Filer, Hamermesh, and Rees 1996:168-76; Ehrenberg
and Smith 1996:117-27; Brown et al. 1982). Thus a majority of U.S. economists
has consistently opposed recent efforts to increase the minimum.[6]

Neoclassical research also finds adverse effects beyond employment. Minimum wages do little to cure poverty or redistribute income equitably because
so many recipients are teenagers or secondary wage earners from middle-class
families. Moreover, they deprive recipients of fringe benefits because affected
employers have to pay higher wages rather than provide security; they prevent
unskilled workers from exchanging present low pay for on-the-job training to
improve future earnings; and they encourage promising youngsters to drop
out of school to take jobs previously held by school dropouts.

The neoclassical literature does consider situations that might mitigate
these harmful effects. An increase in the minimum could "shock" firms into
using productive factors more efficiently and improve productivity, lower
product price and increase output, and increase labor demand, thus offsetting
the negative employment effects. Existing wages could be inefficient (i.e., too
low) because of monopsony in labor markets. Or higher minimum wages
could discourage low-paid, low-productivity workers from shirking on the job
by raising the cost to them of losing their jobs and trying to find others in the
face of increased unemployment caused by the mandated wages. While such
scenarios are possible in theory, they are seldom pursued in practice, on
grounds they presume unrealistically high levels of industrial mismanage-
ment, non-competition among employers, and efficiency wage effects. In the

absence of such likelihood, neoclassical critics often show more than a hint of scientific exasperation at the inability of the public to see the logical defect in regulatory laws that destroy jobs and businesses and of disdain for groups and organizations that promote them.

No increases in federal minimum rates or coverage were advocated and none enacted throughout the 1980s. One researcher even wondered whether the issue was that important. If the minimum wage affects mainly secondary workers, many from middle-class families, and the overall share of teenagers in the labor force is shrinking; and if most workers, young and old, earn more than the legal minimum; and if it does not cure poverty or reduce inequality, then why the concern? He concluded the minimum wage is indeed "over-rated" by both critics and advocates (Brown 1988). In any event, neoclassical literature had effectively discredited the minimum wage as a useful analytical concept and dismissed it as a viable policy option. Mandated wages had acquired the stigma of special interest legislation. The intellectual debate would be rekindled in the 1990s, however, with the controversial research and findings of a group of academic revisionists whose work is discussed below.

## Perspectives Favoring Labor Standards Legislation

Institutional labor economics in America appeared before the turn of the century in response to neoclassical failure to study labor markets rather than labor theories and therefore to address chronic unemployment and low wages among hourly workers and consider government interventionist remedies (Kaufman 1993:30-35). Based on empirical evidence from the field and historical and comparative studies, they argued that real labor markets seldom conform to the competitive ideal but instead are full of imperfections and externalities that nullify the theory and of structural and social interactions that are unaccounted for in the theory but which produce outcomes the opposite of those predicted. If left unattended, these conditions lead to widespread labor devaluation, productive inefficiency, and declining competitiveness and living standards.

At the heart of the institutional perception, then, is the conviction that society gets the labor market outcomes it wants, not those determined by some economic law, and that society therefore must assume a responsibly interventionist role.[7] Three alternative groups of labor economists who reject key concepts and conclusions of neoclassical equilibrium models are discussed here: John R. Commons and the old institutionalists of the Wisconsin School, the post-WWII neoclassical revisionists, and a contemporary group of applied labor economists at the University of Cambridge. Excluded are the "new institutionalists" (see Dow in this volume) who use alternative equilibrium models such as efficiency wage theory and either do not directly address labor regulation issues or do so from much the same choice-theoretic perspective as traditional neoclassical analysis.

## The Old Institutionalists

The old institutionalists described by Kaufman in this volume were the principal architects of the policy response to neoclassical rejection of labor standards legislation during the Progressive Era and the Great Depression. Their empirical study and observation led them to support regulatory laws on grounds widespread unemployment and poverty wages resulted from market imperfections and externalities originating in social institutions rather than as the inevitable price of overall progress. Such socially determined conditions included too little or too much competition in labor markets, either of which could be devastating in the absence of institutional protections. Market imperfections generated market externalities absorbed by individual workers, working-class households and industrial communities in the form of low wages, bad working conditions, and social welfare expenditures (Moss 1996:60-65).

Commons analyzed the process by which this occurs in studies of American shoemaking (1909), meatpacking (1904) and other industries, and in his and Andrews' analysis of labor policy (1936). What Commons called the "menace of competition" occurs when sustained market expansion alters traditional relationships and pits workers against employers, prompting some of the latter to compete by driving down labor standards, that is, by putting labor into competition. In meatpacking, for example, he found that competitive wage cutting begins as a strategic choice by one or more firms but once underway and shown to be successful, it soon becomes the norm for all firms and a race ensues to see which firm can pay the least and which labor group will work for the least. Vulnerable labor, in most instances unorganized, had no choice but to accept these terms if it wished to work, and capital had no choice if it wished to compete.

Commons and Andrews (1936) justified protective legislation on grounds labor markets do not work the way neoclassicals say they do because the theory assumes things that are not so and omits things that are. Individual workers, for example, have little bargaining leverage unless they cannot be replaced. They also lack the knowledge of the market the model presumes, and family obligations make them immobile. They are not atomistic, independent sellers of labor but interdependent members of ethnic, racial, and gender groups that are easily divided.

At the time, most production workers suffered from an "abundant supply of cheap [immigrant] labor" in nearly every industry they tried to find jobs. Cutthroat competition ruled: "[T]he wage that the cheapest laborer—such as the partially supported woman, the immigrant with low standards of living, or the workman oppressed by extreme need—is willing to take, very largely fixes the wage level for the whole group." Such destructive competition leveled efficient and inefficient firms. "When an employer can hire workers for practically his own price," they observed, "he can be slack and inefficient in his methods, and yet, by reducing wages, reduce his cost of production to the level of his more able competitor" (p. 48). The purpose of legislated standards was to compensate for this lack of bargaining power by ensuring a wage sufficient to afford workers the accepted social standard of living.

Their empirical studies of state minimum wage laws convinced Commons and Andrews that legislated standards alleviate the degenerative effects of low wages and enhance productivity by increasing worker desire and ability to produce. The data revealed that the earnings of targeted workers increased following passage of state minimum rates; that only those "parasitic" firms "whose existence depended on the bounty of others" were adversely affected; that not many workers were displaced and the wages of skilled workers brought down, as AFL leaders had feared; and that worker "incentive and output" were not diminished, probably "just the opposite" (pp. 48-64).

*Postwar Neoclassical Revisionists*

An influential group of post-war labor economists not only defended regulation but challenged the traditional competitive labor market model, particularly its theory of marginal productivity. But they were trying to improve the neoclassical model, not displace it, by identifying where it did not conform with real-world structures and outcomes. Prominent among this group were Richard Lester, John Dunlop, Clark Kerr, and Lloyd Reynolds. Together they advanced the method of inquiry into how labor markets work and for a time influenced labor economic analysis and teaching in the U.S. (Kaufman 1988).

Unlike the Wisconsin scholars, most of whom either had been trained in the German historical tradition, which resisted the classical emphasis on natural law and deductive reasoning, or had learned it from Richard Ely and Commons at Wisconsin, the revisionists were the products of traditional neoclassical teaching exemplified by John R. Hicks' *Theory of Wages*. What they shared with Commons and the others, however, was a preference for interdisciplinary work and empirical, inductive field study—and a mistrust of ideal models and deductive methods. Often their experiences as applied labor market economists during World War II put them at odds with traditional theory, and they became frequent critics, sometimes reluctantly, of the conventional wisdom.

Their case studies of specific postwar labor markets produced much the same empirical evidence and led to many of the same conclusions as that of the old institutionalists. The postwar group confirmed that labor was not nearly as mobile as thought, especially in the upper reaches of skill and earnings where it made the greatest difference; that firms followed a variety of labor policies, not just the market model; and that wage dispersion among workers having similar jobs and skills was the result, instead of the standard competitive wage in Hicks' text. They also could see that labor markets are not auctions, as orthodox neoclassical economists held, but instead are institutional structures exhibiting power imbalances, social stratification, irrationality, lack of information, and other distinguishing human characteristics; also that unions, internal labor markets, and demographic differences among workers give rise to noncompeting labor groups and subsequent wage rigidities (Kaufman 1988:45-74).

Richard Lester in particular challenged the reliability and usefulness of neoclassical theory in explaining wage dispersions in actual markets. His wartime experience measuring area wage and benefit patterns and gathering postwar data and talking with company officials persuaded him there was no single competitive wage. Instead, in the absence of unions, firms set wage levels to position themselves strategically within markets and maintained such positions over time without losing workers or having to attract them from other employers. When unionized, they tended to conform to negotiated patterns and content themselves with narrower wage dispersions. He also found that the quality of workers differed little among firms despite such differentials, except at the extremes (Lester 1988:92-96).

These were telling empirical criticisms of neoclassical accuracy and usefulness. Nevertheless, except for the Lester-Stigler-Machlup debate discussed below, these criticisms were more ignored than confronted. In any event, the influence of the postwar revisionists fell into decline, and today their work is seldom referenced in academic labor journals, undergraduate texts, and graduate reading lists. Orthodox analysis today is centered in equilibrium models and for that reason bears little resemblance to that of the postwar empiricists.

*Cambridge U.K.*

Like the old institutionalists, the Cambridge U.K.-applied economists eschew equilibrium models in favor of empirical studies of a historical, structural, and analytical nature. Frank Wilkinson, Jill Rubery, Roger Tarling, and Simon Deakin presently are the core of this group.

Their model explains how households, firms, industries, nations—any discernible productive units—create and distribute wealth (Wilkinson 1983; Tarling 1987; Tarling and Wilkinson 1987). They use a productive systems analysis with emphasis on labor market stratification.[8] Key is the high-wage economy, that is, the need to maintain and reproduce a skilled, secure labor force in competitive economic environments, an observation at least as old as Adam Smith,[9] based on the argument that a high-paid, continuously educated, trained, and experienced work force is essential to achieving and maintaining a highly productive, prosperous, and competitive productive system.

The defining concept is that production processes are both technically and socially determined. Technical and social relationships are interactive and together determine how firms respond to their external environments and how these responses in turn affect the external environment in a constantly evolving process of virtuous or vicious productive cycles. Owners, managers, and workers—the principal components of the firm as a productive system— have mutual interests in maximizing technical efficiency because each stands to gain from the resultant value added. Cooperation rather than hostility is therefore both natural and beneficial. But they have competing interests in the distributional process where one party gains at the expense of the other.

If, for example, managers and shareholders use their hierarchical social relationship with labor to distribute the net income (the difference between production costs and product revenues) disproportionately in their favor, workers resent the outcome and lose interest in maximizing future technical efficiency because they do not see themselves sharing in the results. They withhold cooperation either in formal job actions or informal acts of sabotage. But if the surplus is distributed in a more egalitarian manner or reinvested in the productive process, including enhancement of worker skill and security, both the technical and the social relations of production improve and with it the firm's potential competitiveness and operating surplus.

Thus the cooperative system is more functional (constructive) than the adversarial, which in this context is dysfunctional (destructive). This resembles the old institutional concept of destructive competition based on low-wage labor. Local labor markets can offer too little competition as a result of concentrated industrial structures or collusive employer associations or too much as a result of product market pressures to cut labor costs in order to gain a cost advantage or to protect existing market shares and returns on investment. Unrestrained competition as a result of excess production capacity, industry deregulation, or large pools of substitute low-wage labor leads to employer preoccupation with short-term profit performance.

This in turn encourages low-wage employer strategies: union avoidance, work intensification, production relocation, and similar adversarial initiatives. These give the adversarial employer short-term advantages over those that prefer to focus on long-term innovation and cooperation but are not able to do so and survive under short-term labor cost pressures. Dysfunctional systems thus drive out functional (Biricree and Konzelmann 1997), and Levitan and Belous (1979:17-18), among others, have observed that in the U.S. hourly pay tends to be lowest in those industries and occupations that most closely resemble textbook competition.

Cambridge U.K. analysis of stratified labor markets also distinguishes between advantaged and disadvantaged labor. Where dual labor market theory sees a two-tiered segmentation of primary and secondary workers, they see a seamless gradation of segmented work groups distributed hierarchically among occupationally "good" and "bad" jobs. Movement of individual workers up and down the hierarchy is frequent but uneven and sporadic, depending on the extent and effectiveness of institutional barriers that impede or enhance mobility and on the state of the economy, expansion facilitating overall upward movement and stagnation overall downward movement.

Disadvantaged workers lack the necessary resources to compete successfully in markets where applicants for good jobs are routinely screened on the basis of their formal credentials and social networking is at a premium. Unable to pass the screening, they are consigned to the bad jobs, those that pay badly and offer poor working conditions and little chance for advancement, because they have been socially downgraded and therefore occupied by workers who also have been socially devalued, often because they and the work they do are associated with "women's" work: cleaning, caring, cooking, clerical, catering. Advantaged workers, by contrast, have access to the necessary credentials and networks and, as a result, qualify for and get the good jobs (Wilkinson 1983).

Undesirable labor market outcomes can be traced to social structuring in response to changing productive environments. Decline in goods-producing jobs as a result of deindustrialization, for example, removed workers from the institutional protections associated with "good" hourly jobs in modern industrial democracies (i.e., unions and labor standards laws). Simultaneous increases in service and retail employment channels workers into jobs having social value but few protective institutions and as a result are downgraded and devalued regardless of their social and economic contribution.

Both the Cambridge U.K. group and the old institutionalists integrate product and labor markets in the analyses of jobs and earnings because the two are interactive rather than independent in this regard. The effects of such interaction can be positive or negative. Union bargaining power in key transportation and telecommunications industries, for example, was strengthened by government regulation during the postwar decades, only to be weakened by subsequent deregulation. This has been the experience in trucking (Belzer 1994; Belman and Belzer, in this volume), telecommunications (Keefe and

Boroff 1994), and airlines (Cremieux 1996). The attack on Davis-Bacon and a series of unfavorable court rulings contributed to similar union decline in construction (Allen 1994:432-35).

## Institutional Defense of Davis-Bacon

Bourden and Levitt (1980) concluded in their review of Davis-Bacon literature in the late 1970s that the data used in impact studies were incomplete and inconclusive and the underlying nonmarket purpose of prevailing wage legislation therefore neglected:

> [A]ttention has to be paid to the original intent of [Davis-Bacon], subsequently reaffirmed by Congress, which was in part to establish the principle that wages should not be an element in the competition for government contracts. While antithetical to economists' and others' belief in the value of competitive markets, this principle is central to the philosophy of trade unionism and, indeed, to most of the existing legislation on labor standards. Thus, debates over the cost impact of the act quickly become entangled in more philosophical arguments over the proper role of government in regulating markets. (Bourden and Levitt 1980:93)

This observation sums up the institutional critique that while neoclassical economists find Davis-Bacon inefficient and inequitable on the basis of downward-sloping demand curves, its purpose is to turn contractors from wage-based competition to that based on innovation, quality, capitalization, and marketing, objectives that ultimately benefit all the stakeholders, including the community, through higher productivity and greater marketability. As evidence, institutionalists cite historical and empirical examples such as the early experiences of the San Francisco building trades.

From the turn of the century until the 1920s, the Bay Area Building Trades Council participated in wage, employment, and training decisions through its bilateral relationship with major contractors. Following WWI, however, the employers launched a citywide open shop movement to eliminate union representation and establish unilateral control through their industrial association:

> From 1921 to the mid-1930s, the San Francisco construction industry was a case study in the managerial domination of a labor market. The Industrial Association assumed the centralized reins it had wrested from the BTC, but on the board of *this* barony sat representatives of Levi Strauss, Westinghouse, Southern Pacific, and other pillars of corporate San Francisco. Under their aegis, everything from apprentice training to job specifications to wage rates were regulated

so as to maximize productivity and minimize the possibility of workers exerting collective will. The employers and personnel experts who designed and operated the new system tried to convince craftsmen that acquiescence would yield them benefits far beyond what their devastated unions could offer. (Kazin 1987:270-71)

But area wages and conditions instead deteriorated relative to those in other cities. Contractors soon complained of skilled labor shortages and proceeded to wrest control of local apprentice programs from the unions. But they trained too many applicants and created pools of low-paid or unemployed craftsmen, which effectively discouraged additional entry into the trades (Kazin 1987:250, 271-72). Any short-term productivity gains from overtraining presumably were lost with the next generation of young, inadequately trained workers. These and similar experiences elsewhere explain why the AFL began lobbying a decade *before* the Great Depression for national legislation to protect prevailing wages against low-wage contractors.

A number of studies, not all of them institutional, show prevailing wage laws do not increase final and long-term construction costs in specific instances despite imposing higher direct costs (e.g., Mandelstamm 1965; Bourden and Leavitt 1980:91-103; Allen 1983). The most recent work in this regard comes from institutional labor economists at the University of Utah (Azari-Rad et al. 1994; Philips et al. 1995). In the tradition of Lester and other postwar empiricists, they go beyond the immediate bid price to assess the long-term effects of prevailing wage legislation, in this instance beyond the immediate cost-benefit estimates of particular building projects.

They examined experiences in Utah and eight other states that repealed Davis-Bacon laws between 1979 and 1988. Few of the benefits predicted in the neoclassical model actually occurred. Instead, when efficiency is measured by actual project costs at completion rather than by accepted bids, savings to taxpayers and the state are either minimal or nonexistent. Second, real wages in construction fell in Utah both absolutely and relative to those in other industries and states. Repeal accelerated union decline in the share of construction work, as theory and observation would predict, but wages fell for both union and nonunion workers, as would not have been predicted. Nor did lower direct labor costs lower per-unit costs. Less new capital equipment was introduced than before and lower labor productivity resulted. Total construction employment increased slightly, but total construction wages fell disproportionately, thus reducing tax revenues.

Third, repeal was followed by construction labor shortages and a less-skilled labor force. In the absence of a coordinated effort by nonunion contractors, as in the San Francisco case, individual employers were reluctant to invest in worker skill and training, and these also went into decline following repeal. Earnings reductions discouraged young workers from entering and completing apprenticeships and individual nonunion contractors from making human capital investments in workers who were less likely to stay with them or even make careers in the industry. The same thing happened overall in construction; the open shop segment had 60% of the market nationwide in the early 1980s but accounted for only 10% of total training expenditures (Allen 1994:423). Moreover, the number of minority workers recruited into the Utah construction industry actually declined. Finally, job injury rates rose an average 15% in the repeal states, which is much above the national average and confirms earlier findings that construction industry accidents decline with greater length of worker service.

The most frequent scenario found following repeal is that nonunion contractors bid even below their operating costs in order to take the work away from union contractors. Union firms are then forced either to leave the industry or to create nonunion subsidiaries to compete against open shop operators. For their part, union craftsmen resign themselves to the nonunion trend, put their union cards in their shoes, so to speak, and go to work for low-wage companies.

According to field interviews in the Utah study, when unions made wage, benefit, and work rule concessions to help contractors stay competitive, the nonunion contractors required their workers to accept comparable reductions in order to maintain pay differentials and get costs low enough to make good on their low project bids. Movement of skilled labor from union to nonunion jobs temporarily equalized the skill factor, which until then had been the comparative advantage of the higher wage union contractors. These findings illustrate the institutional claim that unregulated labor markets can create conditions in which price (the nonunion bid) determines cost (union and nonunion wages) rather than costs determining product price.

Finally, even the anticipated immediate cost savings did not always occur. Low-wage, low-bid contractors had lower on-time and within-cost completion rates than did the rest of the industry and frequently had to request upward readjustments of their original bid prices in order to complete projects. Separate studies by government agencies also reveal higher long-term maintenance and repair costs on nonunion, low-bid projects than on union work (Belman and Voos 1995). Thus when long-run total costs and benefits are taken into account, the gains from repeal become problematic. Savings from lower direct labor costs may be more than offset by the inefficiencies of low bidders and the reduced tax revenues.

## Institutional Defense of Minimum Wage Legislation

Institutional defense of minimum wages includes empirical case studies and theoretical analyses of their impact on employment (in response to neoclassical allegations), living standards, worker productivity, and economic competitiveness. The case studies began after the turn of the century when states started passing minimum wage laws affecting women workers because the courts prohibited similar legislation for males (Moss 1996:99-113). Government researchers examined changes in the wages paid in affected jobs before and after passage of these laws, which seemed the logical way to proceed. They found that low-wage jobs generally paid more after the law and relatively few if any of the higher paying jobs were eliminated (e.g., Obenauer and von der Nienburg 1915).

Richard Lester and other postwar neoclassical revisionists duplicated these findings. Lester (1946) obtained survey data on wage-employment practices in 58 southern firms (out of 430 surveyed) and from the results concluded that marginal analysis was a theoretically logical but practicably limited concept in explaining employer response to wage increases. Managers do not know their marginal costs at particular levels of output but behave as if such costs decline with increasing production up to capacity utilization, meaning that the firm responds by trying to expand its product market rather than by laying off workers and cutting production.

Neoclassicals felt compelled to defend orthodoxy. Fritz Machlup (1946) and George Stigler (1946) protested that employers know equilibrium points of production intuitively, that Lester's survey was scientifically flawed, and that he did not really understand marginal productivity theory. They were well advised to protest, for if Lester was right, then who was to know the employment effect of a minimum wage raise. Indeed, in a subsequent article Lester (1947) argued precisely that. The empirical evidence is overwhelming, he reiterated, that divergent wage rates persist within labor markets and among comparable workers: "Such matters are elementary and commonplace to a student of labor, but they seem to be largely overlooked by theorists of the marginalist faith" (p. 148).

In the 1990s another group of revisionists using much the same investigative method but with more sophisticated equipment and techniques at hand produced similar findings and interpretations. In a number of empirical studies, David Card, Alan Krueger, and Lawrence Katz concluded that modest increases in minimum wage rates have little if any negative impact on teenage employment and, in fact, may even increase it. Instead of using large data bases to test the theory, this new generation of labor researchers also went into the field. They surveyed employment changes generally and in fast-food restaurants in particular, both before and after increases in federal and state minimum wages. Among other things, they found that fast-food employment increased overall in New Jersey following that state's increase above the federal minimum and rose fastest in those restaurants that had paid the lowest wages. More surprising, perhaps, in those adjacent Pennsylvania areas where no increases had occurred, fast-food employment actually fell slightly. They found similar outcomes in Texas fast-food restaurants following the 1990-91 federal increase. Separate studies of earnings among California teenagers in *all* industries following that state's sizable rate increase showed subsequent wage increases averaging 10% but with no reduction in overall teenage employment (Card and Krueger 1995:Chps. 2 and 3).

These findings clearly were at odds with the neoclassical literature and prompted one reviewer to conclude, just as the debate over the 1996 minimum wage increase was heating up, that "we just don't know how many jobs would be lost if the minimum wage were increased to $5.15" (Kennan 1995:1964). The result, at least for the moment, was to erode orthodox certainty. The issue now was "whether the problem [of contradictory findings] lies with the use of a theory of labor demand that is too simple or with the research methods used to test that theory" (Ehrenberg and Smith 1996:124). The debate was opened but confined to issues *within* the neoclassical paradigm rather than between it and alternative models.

Moreover, some neoclassicals held to the view that jobs *will* be lost regardless. Authors of a standard labor text referred to the fast-food industry studies, noted the mounting criticism in the literature regarding their method and reliability, and concluded that "while the impact of the minimum wage on employment, especially that of young workers will undoubtedly continue to receive a great deal of research and public policy discussion, the best evidence remains that the overall impact of the law is to lower employment of unskilled workers while increasing the earnings of those who are able to get jobs" (Filer, Hamermesh, and Rees 1996:175).

By contrast, old institutionalists and productive systems economists argue the case for minimum wages on the basis of historical and systemic studies. The empirical case for productive systems analysis in the U.S. is that large, monopsonistic firms dominated communities and wage decisions during earlier stages of industrial development, resulting in the serious market imperfections and externalities identified and described by Commons and others. Once organized by industrial unions, however, the previous hegemony of these employers now became a source of productive dependency and the basis for these unions to negotiate better wages and benefits and of the community to collect revenues and payrolls. It was only after their power in product markets was compromised by deregulation, globalization, entry of new domestic producers—often aggressive wage cutters—that these employers were less able and prepared to pay high wages and revenues through higher product prices and productivity gains. The massive industrial restructuring of the 1970s and 1980s put effective downward pressure on labor and community living standards and created the need for mandated wage floors (Craypo and Nissen 1995).

The Cambridge U.K. group challenges the application of human capital theory to labor standards legislation. The model is logically flawed, they say, because "we are presented with an argument of impregnable circularity in which the outcome—low pay—is used as evidence for the alleged cause: low skill and personal inefficiency" (Wilkinson 1992:7). In other words, low-wage workers must be unskilled and inferior because if they were skilled and superior they would be high-paid workers. If a job pays well, it must require human capital to perform; if it does not, then it must not. Thus to the Cambridge critics, "the outcome, low pay, is used as the only evidence for the alleged cause" (Brosnan and Wilkinson 1988:9).

All reference to job content and responsibility is lost in the conventional analysis, they claim. To say that human capital theory explains widening earnings disparities is to measure the worth of a job by what it pays and without regard to what is required of the worker to perform it satisfactorily and reliably. Devalued workers get devalued jobs on grounds they have little or no recognizable skills. The measurement of productive value is thus shifted from the job to the worker. When, for example, the college degree becomes a proxy for labor market skill (i.e., for productivity), the effect is to make human capital in the form of college degrees the cause of high earnings, when in fact the earnings may simply reflect the role of formal education in screening applicants for high-paying jobs. Neoclassical theory thus explains high pay as the result of college-acquired skills, but college skills may be acquired largely because people know that the best jobs go to the best educated, but that advantaged households are best able to give their members the best education.[10]

As with the postwar revisionists, the Cambridge economists try to explain how labor markets work through empirical investigation rather than deductive theorizing. Their studies show that actual income returns on education and training differ considerably along demographic lines (Wilkinson 1981). Women's part-time jobs in England, for example, typically pay less than higher paying jobs for which they are qualified but customarily do not get (Horrell, Rubery, and Burchell 1989). Detailed studies of job content and requirements other than formal credentials show that the lowest paying jobs, particularly those held by women, often demand greater skill, experience, and responsibility than higher paying jobs held by men (Craig et al. 1982). Thus, because they are devalued workers, the social value of the services they provide may be greater than the rewards. Galbraith (1992) points out that low-wage labor presently subsidizes whole industries and occupations that exist largely to make life more comfortable and less expensive for high-income households: "The economically fortunate, not excluding those who speak with greatest regret of the existence of this class, are heavily dependent on its presence" (p. 31).

Cambridge U.K. policy recommendations also parallel those of the old institutionalists. Commons and associates believed that government intervention has to directly affect labor market practices and outcomes if it is to correct market imperfections and avoid negative externalities—such as mandated workers' compensation rather than employers' liability laws when the latter were shown to have encouraged expenditures on litigation rather than on accident prevention (Moss 1996:68-74).[11] The Cambridge group therefore advocates high minimum wages and protected trade unionism as important remedies to low-wage earnings as part of the high-wage economy, which in its view spurs producers to innovate in order to raise worker productivity high enough to pay for itself. On the labor supply side, high wages assure a healthy, reliable, and trainable labor force and thus eliminate the need for social welfare expenditures traceable to negative externalities. High labor productivity supports high wages, and high wages generate high productivity.

The policy goal of the Cambridge group is to generate a sufficient number of good jobs to ensure sustained industrial growth, regular productivity gains, and high and equitable living standards (i.e., jobs affording good pay and security in return for lifetime work and training commitments by labor). When good jobs are available, people do what is necessary to get them, whether it be formal education or vocational training, informal (on-the-job) training or job networking. Neoclassical concern about the harmful effects of market intervention on worker incentives to acquire human capital are unnecessary. Labor supply takes care of itself. Demand for labor creates its own supply when the rewards are ample and attainable. But labor supply does *not* create its own demand (except when it is low paid), therefore high growth rates and labor standards should be policy priorities, not income supplements to workers and wage subsidies to employers, which subsidize imperfections and externalities and devalue the work by driving wages down to their subsidized levels. As Commons noted (1893:176) more than a century ago, "The experience of England demonstrates that poor relief tends to lower wages by the amount of the relief."

## Conclusion

Neoclassical and institutional perspectives differ completely on minimum and prevailing wage laws because they differ fundamentally on the structure, behavior, and performance of the modern industrial economy. Neoclassicals ask how many and which workers will lose jobs as a result of such laws; institutionalists ask what prompted their passage in the first place. The former respond to issues raised in the logic of the competitive model, the latter to the labor problems of productive systems. The first uses deductive and the latter inductive methods. They are like ships passing in the night.

The institutional perspective prevailed under the New Deal and into the post-WWII years because of the enormity of the economic crisis of the 1930s and the collective memory of the experiences then with unregulated labor markets. But since that time the neoclassical perspective has prevailed. Academic and policy interests shifted from unions and collective bargaining and by implication from income distribution and purchasing power, to technology and training, industrial competitiveness, structural unemployment, and welfare dependency, and by implication to minimizing direct and indirect labor costs.

Human capital theory did not replace or defend marginal productivity theory when the latter came under attack from postwar neoclassical revisionists, but it did change the analytical focus from the demand for labor (jobs) to the supply of labor (workers). The effect was to shift responsibility for good and bad jobs and earnings from the policies and actions of employers and governments to those of individual workers and households. As a result, current debates over labor standards legislation are not so much contemplated as pre-ordained. Not only are individuals paid their worth, according to the neoclassical model, but by implication also what they deserve for having made the choices they did, given their capabilities. After they make their choices and the outcomes are apparent, market losers should not expect government to step in and reverse things.

In the 1960s orthodox marginal productivity and human capital theory effectively replaced institutional case studies and social analyses of jobs and workers. Old institutionalists and postwar revisionists therefore did not influence neoclassical economics as much as demonstrate that almost no amount of empirical evidence can shake the orthodox faith in competitive market models. Far from taking alternative perspectives seriously, traditional neoclassical eyes glaze over at the mention of social wage formation.

For their part, institutional minimum wage advocates—as opposed to neoclassical revisionists—dismiss neoclassical research into labor standards as being more irrelevant than wrong. To them, as with proponents of the original FLSA, the relevant question is not how many secondary wage earners are made unemployed but how many bad jobs are eliminated. Linder (1989:155), for example, argues that "by downplaying the number of jobs destroyed by a statutory minimum wage, proponents unwittingly undermine the most cogent grounds for supporting it—namely, that the jobs it destroys are low wage and unproductive."

Nevertheless, the effect of neoclassical dominance is that minimum and prevailing wage laws are judged mainly on the basis of policy objectives and market outcomes for which they were never intended. Review of the legislative histories of Davis-Bacon and the FLSA shows they were part of a larger effort to avoid or remedy deteriorating labor standards. Market forces and failures put wages in situations in which firms in wage competition can destroy trust and motivation among stakeholders and make the productive system dysfunctional. These concerns and this analysis have an unfamiliar ring today, with our perception of wages as costs of production rather than sources of purchasing power, but in 1931 and 1938 mandated labor standards were seen as necessary to complement unions and collective bargaining in shoring up a faltering productive system. The remaining option, which no one in power wanted, was *direct* government control of labor standards and labor-management relations.

Failure of neoclassical and institutional perspectives to agree involves more than competing paradigms and methodologies. Competing interests in distributional outcomes also come into focus. Opponents of regulation are correct, for example, when they say that proponents often stand to benefit financially because they are vulnerable to competition; but institutionalists are equally correct when they say that opponents often gain from deregulation because they hold power in unregulated markets. Therefore, to insist that we intervene in labor markets only to undo previous intervention is to defend the status quo, which means to preserve the existing social structure of jobs and workers, that is, the current distribution of social advantages and disadvantages.

But what is the status quo? Neoclassicals look at relatively low levels of unemployment and labor-management conflict and conclude that existing labor laws should be curtailed or repealed and no new ones enacted. Institutionalists look at the same economy and see large numbers of low-paying jobs, increasing underemployment, and widening income disparities. On that basis they advocate strengthening these laws. Mishel et al. (1997), for example, report on the proliferation of low-wage jobs and low-income households (especially among young households and displaced workers); stagnant wages and longer hours; growing worker insecurity; increasing polarization of wealth, income, and taxation; persistent U.S. trade deficits; and comparative wage and productivity declines. The cost of nonintervention, they insist, is more of the same.

## Endnotes

[1] See, e.g., Congressman Welch's (D-CA) remarks in introducing the bill. *Congressional Record* 1931:6505.

[2] Kansas passed the first prevailing wage law in 1881 as part of an eight-hour statute. New York approved similar legislation a few years later, and within a decade several other mainly western states followed. Bacon modeled his federal bills after New York's progressive provisions.

[3] Manufacturers did maintain wages for a year but then nullified the effort by laying off workers. They also declined to invest. It was not good business to create additional capacity when they were not selling what they already were producing (McElvaine 1984:73-75).

A month after Hoover signed Davis-Bacon, a National Industrial Conference Board survey of the nation's largest manufacturers showed that wage cutting was more widespread than commonly thought. Average earnings had been cut 20% in the past six months. Employers agreed with Hoover's wage policy, the article concluded, but could no longer comply in the face of increasing competition based on wages (*New York Times*, April 11, 1931:2).

[4] This perception and the consequent belief that the purpose of the law was to promote the highest wage possible were so pervasive in 1931 that the *New York Times* reported final passage of the "Davis-Bacon maximum wage bill" because, in the paper's words, the law ensured "the highest wage scale prevalent in any community where public works are undertaken under Federal contract" (*Maximum Wage Bill Is Passed by House*, March 1, 1931:6).

[5] J.B. Clark, the principal American progenitor of marginal productivity theory, made it a point to show that all workers get the value of their productive worth, partly in response to Henry George's widely publicized claims to the contrary (Seligman 1971:314-15). Those employed in a given workplace, he explained, are homogeneous (interchangeable) factors of production and therefore each is, so to speak, the marginal worker and as such is paid the equilibrium wage commensurate with his or her worth: the "share of income that attaches to any productive function is gauged by the actual product of it," he concluded (Clark 1899:3).

[6] A 1966 survey revealed that 61% of university economists and 79% of business economists opposed increasing the minimum or broadening its coverage (Levitan and Belous 1979:5-6). The ratio remained high in the 1970s (Reynolds 1982) and thereafter; a 1993 survey found 77% of economists believed that increases lead to job losses, compared to a 1996 poll that found 84% of Americans in favor of an increase (Rosenbaum 1996:A-12).

[7] John Stuart Mill observed that regulatory labor laws involve conflicting interests and for that reason are enacted only when the "ruling portion" of society, as he put it, agrees to a more equitable distribution. Production of goods and services is entirely a matter of natural resources and human ingenuity, he continued, but their distribution among the social classes is "a matter of human institutions solely." Wealth and income therefore depend "on the laws and customs of society . . . and are very different in different ages and countries; and might be still more different, if mankind so chose" (Cited in Heilbroner 1996:133-34).

[8] Their rejection of neoclassical equilibrium is in the tradition of Cambridge theorist Joan Robinson. Her 1930s analyses forced the profession to concede that actual firms seldom are either perfect competitors or pure monopolists but mostly monopolistic competitors or oligopolists in between. She eventually abandoned equilibrium models altogether, however, on grounds they are inherently contradictory and therefore of little practical use in either understanding or coming to grips with industrial society's economic problems (e.g., Robinson 1971, 1978).

Static market models, she explained, logically require movement from one equilibrium point to another, as in the conventional supply/demand diagram, but this in turn requires movement across *both* time and space. Time refuses to stand still, however, while spatial movement brings the variables being watched into natural equilibrium. Hypothetical buyers and sellers therefore have time to respond to changing conditions. When they do so the points of intersection along the supply and demand functions move farther from rather than closer toward some natural equilibrium. The neoclassicist, she said, is "using a metaphor based on space to explain a process that takes place in time" (Robinson 1978:138). The result is analytical indeterminacy, in which the model cannot reliably predict labor market effects, including those of minimum or prevailing wages.

[9] Smith observed that national policy should be to institutionalize high wages in order to maximize national wealth. Such levels require the employer "to supply [workers] with the best machinery which either he or they can think of," so that goods are "produced by so much less labor than before that the increase of [labor's] price is more than compensated by the diminution of its quantity." Besides, he said, high wages are "but equity" for those "who feed, clothe and lodge the whole body of the people" (Smith 1976:Book I, Chp. 8, pp. 96-97). This is an accepted and frequent argument. Advocates of the Wagner Act, for example, defended it on grounds it was essential if the U.S. hoped to get out of the Depression and establish a high-wage economy (Kaufman 1997).

[10] Thurow's "job competition" model is useful in locating the Cambridge U.K. analysis within the Cambridge U.S. context. In his analysis "the marginal product resides in the job and not in the man" and "earnings depend upon the job he acquires and not directly upon his own personal characteristics" (1975:77). Competition among workers for the job produces a market-clearing wage equal to its marginal product. The Cambridge U.K. group accepts that the job determines the value of the work but not that the market necessarily clears at that value; low-wage labor is more likely to be devalued and therefore the true value of the job disguised.

[11] Compare Wilkinson (1992) and Moss' (1996) detailed analysis of Commons' work in this regard.

## References

Allen, Steve. 1983. "Much Ado about Davis-Bacon: A Critical Review and New Evidence." *Journal of Law and Economics*, Vol. 26 (October), pp. 707-36.
_____. 1994. "Developments in Collective Bargaining in Construction in the 1980s and 1990s." In Paula B. Voos, ed., *Contemporary Collective Bargaining in the Private Sector*. Madison, WI: Industrial Relations Research Association, pp. 411-45.
Azari-Rad, Hamid, Anne Yeagle, and Peter Philips. 1994. "The Effects of the Repeal of Utah's Prevailing Wage Law on the Labor Market in Construction." In Sheldon Friedman, et al., eds., *Restoring the Promise of American Labor Law*. Ithaca, NY: Cornell ILR Press, pp. 207-22.

Belman, Dale, and Paula B. Voos, eds. 1995. *Prevailing Wage Law in Construction: The Costs of Repeal to Wisconsin*. Milwaukee, WI: Institute for Wisconsin's Future.

Belzer, Michael H. 1994. "The Motor Carrier Industry: Truckers and Teamsters under Siege." In Paula B. Voos, ed., *Contemporary Collective Bargaining in the Private Sector*. Madison, WI: Industrial Relations Research Association, pp. 259-302.

Bernstein, Irving. 1970. *Turbulent Years: A History of the American Worker, 1933-1941*. Boston: Houghton Mifflin.

Birecree, Adrienne M., and Suzanne J. Konzelmann. Forthcoming. "Productive Systems, Competitive Pressures, Strategic Choices and Work Organization: An Analytical Framework." *International Contributions to Labor Studies*.

Bourden, Clinton C., and Raymond E. Levitt. 1980. *Union and Open Shop Construction: Compensation, Work Practices, and Labor Markets*. Lexington, MA: Lexington Books.

Brandeis, Elizabeth. 1957. "Organized Labor and Protective Legislation." In Milton Derber and Edwin Young, eds., *Labor and the New Deal*. Madison, WI: The University of Wisconsin Press, pp. 193-237.

Brosnan, Peter, and Frank Wilkinson. 1988. "A National Statutory Minimum Wage and Economic Efficiency." *Contributions to Political Economy*, Vol. 7, pp. 1-48.

Brown, Charles. 1988. "Minimum Wage Laws: Are They Overrated?" *Journal of Economic Perspectives*, Vol. 2 (Summer), pp. 133-45.

Brown, Charles, Curtis Gilroy, and Andrew Kohen. 1982. "The Effect of the Minimum Wage on Employment and Unemployment." *Journal of Economic Literature*, Vol. 20 (June), pp. 487-528.

_____. 1983. "Time-Series Evidence of the Effects of the Minimum Wage on Youth Employment and Unemployment." *The Journal of Human Resources*, Vol. 18 (Winter), pp. 3-31.

Business Roundtable. 1978. *Coming to Grips with Some Major Problems in the Construction Industry*. Report No. 2, New York.

Card, David Edward, and Alan B. Krueger. 1995. *Myth and Measurement: The New Economics of the Minimum Wage*. Princeton, NJ: Princeton University Press.

Clark, John Bates. 1899. *The Distribution of Wealth* (1956 reprint). New York: Kelley & Millman.

Commission on the Future of Worker-Management Relations. 1994. U.S. Department of Labor/U.S. Department of Commerce. Washington, DC:GPO.

Commons, John R. 1893. *The Distribution of Wealth*. New York: Macmillan.

_____. 1904. "Labor Conditions in Meat Packing and the Recent Strike." *Quarterly Journal of Economics*, Vol. 19 (November), pp. 1-32.

_____. 1909. "American Shoemakers, 1648-1895: A Sketch of Industrial Evolution." *Quarterly Journal of Economics*, Vol. 24 (November), pp. 39-98.

Commons, John R., and John Andrews. 1936. *Principles of Labor Legislation*. 4th ed., 1967 reprint. New York: Harper.

Congressional Budget Office. 1983. *Modifying the Davis-Bacon Act: Implications for the Labor Market and the Federal Budget*. Washington, DC: CBO.

Congressional Record. 1931. House, 71st Congress, 3d Session, Vol. 74, Pt. 7, February 28.

_____. 1938. Senate, Bill 2475 "To Provide for the Establishment of Fair Labor Standards," Vol. 81, no. 7, pp. 7648-655.

Craig, Christine, Jill Rubery, Roger Tarling, and Frank Wilkinson. 1982. *Labor Market Structure, Industrial Organization and Low Pay*. Cambridge: Cambridge University Press.

Craypo, Charles, and Bruce Nissen, eds. 1993. *Grand Designs: The Impact of Corporate Strategies on Workers, Unions, and Communities.* Ithaca, NY: ILR Press.

Cremieux, Pierre-Yves. 1996. "The Effect of Deregulation on Earnings: Pilots, Flight Attendants, and Mechanics, 1959-1992." *Industrial and Labor Relations Review,* Vol. 49 (January), pp. 223-42.

Ehrenberg, Ronald G., and Robert S. Smith. 1996. *Modern Labor Economics: Theory and Public Policy.* 6th ed. Reading, MA: Addison-Wesley.

Filer, Randall K., Daniel S. Hamermesh, and Albert Rees. 1996. *The Economics of Work and Pay.* 6th ed. New York: Harper Collins.

Fraser, Steven. 1991. *Labor Will Rule: Sidney Hillman and the Rise of American Labor.* New York: The Free Press.

Galbraith, John Kenneth. 1954. *The Great Crash: 1929.* Boston: Houghton Mifflin.

_____. 1992. *The Culture of Contentment.* Boston: Houghton Mifflin.

General Accounting Office (GAO). 1979. *The Davis-Bacon Act Should Be Repealed.* Washington, DC: GPO.

Goldfarb, R.S., and J.F. Morrall. 1978. "Cost Implications of Changing Davis-Bacon Administration." *Policy Analysis,* Vol. 4 (Fall), pp. 439-53.

Gould, John P., and George Bittlingmayer. 1980. *The Economics of the Davis-Bacon Act: An Analysis of Prevailing-Wage Laws.* Studies in Economic Policy. Washington, DC: The American Enterprise Institute.

Gujarati, D.N. 1967. "The Economics of the Davis-Bacon Act." *Journal of Business,* Vol. 40 (July), pp. 303-16.

Hearings. 1931. *Regulation of Wages Paid to Employees by Contractors Awarded Government Building Contracts,* 71st Congress, 3rd Session, on H.R. 16619, January 31.

Hearings. 1937. *Bills to Provide for the Establishment of Fair Labor Standards in Employment in and Affecting Interstate Commerce and for Other Purposes,* Joint Hearings, 75th Congress, 1st Session, June 2-5.

Hearings. 1979. *Oversight to Examine the Administration of the Davis-Bacon Act,* Senate Subcommittee on Housing and Urban Affairs, 66th Congress, 1st Session, May 2.

Heilbroner, Robert. 1996. *Teachings from the Worldly Economists.* New York: Norton.

Hession, Charles H., and Hyman Sardy. 1969. *Ascent to Affluence: A History of American Economic Development.* Boston: Allyn and Bacon.

Horrell, S., J. Rubery, and B. Burchell. 1989. "Unequal Jobs and Unequal Pay." *Industrial Relations Journal,* Vol. 20 (Autumn), pp. 176-91.

Kaufman, Bruce E. 1988. "The Postwar View of Labor Markets and Wage Determination." In Bruce E. Kaufman, ed., *How Labor Markets Work: Reflections on Theory and Practice by John Dunlop, Clark Kerr, Richard Lester, and Lloyd Reynolds.* Lexington, MA: D.C. Heath and Company, Lexington Books, pp. 145-203.

_____. 1993. *The Origins and Evolution of the Field of Industrial Relations in the United States.* Ithaca, NY: ILR Press.

_____. 1997. "Why the Wagner Act? Reestablishing Contact with Its Original Purpose." In David Lewin, Bruce Kaufman, and Donna Sockell, eds., *Advances in Industrial and Labor Relations.* Greenwich, CT: JAI Press.

Kazin, Michael. 1987. *Barons of Labor: The San Francisco Building Trades and Union Power in the Progressive Era.* Urbana, IL: University of Illinois Press.

Keefe, Jeffrey, and Karen Boroff. 1994. "Telecommunications Labor-Management Relations after Divestiture." In Paula B. Voos, ed., *Contemporary Collective Bargaining in the Private Sector.* Madison, WI: Industrial Relations Research Association, pp. 303-71.

Kennan, John. 1995. "The Elusive Effects of Minimum Wages." *Journal of Economic Literature*, Vol. 33 (December), pp. 1949-65.

Larrowe, Charles P. 1955. *Shape-Up and Hiring Hall: A Comparison of Hiring Methods and Labor Relations on the New York and Seattle Waterfronts*. Berkeley: University of California Press.

Lester, Richard A. 1946. "Shortcomings of Marginal Analysis for Wage-Employment Problems." *American Economic Review*, Vol. 36 (March), pp. 63-82.

_____. 1947. "Marginalism, Minimum Wages, and Labor Markets." *American Economic Review*, Vol. 37 (March), pp. 135-48.

_____. 1988. "Wages, Benefits, and Company Employment Systems." In Bruce E. Kaufman, ed., *How Labor Markets Work: Reflections on Theory and Practice by John Dunlop, Clark Kerr, Richard Lester, and Lloyd Reynolds*. Lexington, MA: D.C. Heath and Company, Lexington Books, pp. 89-115.

Levitan, Sar A., and Richard S. Belous. 1979. *More Than Subsistence: Minimum Wages for the Working Poor*. Baltimore, MD: The Johns Hopkins Press.

Linder, Marc. 1989. "The Minimum Wage as Industrial Policy: A Forgotten Role." *Journal of Legislation*, Vol. 16, no. 1, pp. 151-71.

Machlup, Fritz. 1946. "Marginal Analysis and Empirical Research." *American Economic Review*, Vol. 36 (September), pp. 519-54.

Mandelstamm, A.B. 1965. "The Effect of Unions on Efficiency in the Residential Construction Industry: A Case Study." *Industrial and Labor Relations Review*, Vol. 18 (July), pp. 503-21.

McElvaine, Robert S. 1984. *The Great Depression: America, 1929-1941*. New York: Times Books.

Mishel, Lawrence, Jared Bernstein, and John Schmitt. 1997. *The State of Working America, 1996-97*. Armonk, NY: M.E. Sharpe.

Moss, David A. 1996. *Socializing Security: Progressive-Era Economists and the Origins of American Social Policy*. Cambridge: Harvard University Press.

Obenauer, Marie L., and Bertha von der Nienburg. 1915. *Effect of Minimum Wage Determinations in Oregon*. Bureau of Labor Statistics, Bulletin No. 176. Washington, DC: GPO.

Philips, Peter, Garth Mangum, Norm Waitzman, and Anne Yeagle. 1995. *Losing Ground: Lessons from the Repeal of Nine "Little Davis-Bacon" Acts*. Working Paper, Economics Department, University of Utah.

Reynolds, Morgan O. 1982. "Understanding Political Pricing of Labor Services: The Davis-Bacon Act." *Journal of Labor Research*, Vol. 3 (Summer), pp. 293-309.

Robinson, Joan. 1971. *Economic Heresies: Some Old-fashioned Questions in Economic Theory*. New York: Basic Books.

_____. 1978. *Contributions to Modern Economics*. New York: Academic Press.

Rosenbaum, David E. 1996. "The Minimum Wage: A Portrait." *New York Times*, April 19, pp. A-1, A-12.

Seligman, Ben B. 1971. *Main Currents in Modern Economics: Volume Two, The Reaffirmation of Tradition*. New York: Free Press.

Smith, Adam. 1976. *An Inquiry into the Nature and Causes of the Wealth of Nations* (1776). Chicago: University of Chicago Press.

Stigler, George. 1946. "The Economics of Minimum Wage Legislation." *American Economic Review*, Vol. 36 (June), pp. 358-65.

Tarling, Roger, ed. 1987. *Flexibility in Labor Markets*. London: Academic Press.

Tarling, Roger, and Frank S. Wilkinson, eds. 1987. *The Level, Structure and Flexibility of Costs*. London: Academic Press.

Thieblot, Armand J. 1986. *Prevailing Wage Legislation: The Davis-Bacon Act, State Little Davis-Bacon Acts, the Walsh-Healy Act, and the Service Contract Act*. Philadelphia, PA: Industrial Research Unit, The Wharton School, University of Pennsylvania.

Thurow, Lester R. 1975. *Generating Inequality: Mechanisms of Distribution in the U.S. Economy*. New York: Basic Books.

Wilkinson, Frank, ed. 1981. *The Dynamics of Labor Market Segmentation*. London: Academic Press.

_____. 1983. "Productive Systems." *Cambridge Journal of Economics*, Vol. 7, pp. 413-29.

_____. 1992. *Why Britain Needs a Minimum Wage*. London: Institute for Public Policy Research.

CHAPTER 7

# Workplace Safety and Health Regulations: Rationale and Results

JOHN F. BURTON, JR. AND JAMES R. CHELIUS
*Rutgers University*

The scope of this chapter is the regulation of workplace safety and health in the U.S. This topic provides a particularly good vehicle for examining the usefulness of the theories considered in this volume. Dating back to the 19th century, occupational safety and health regulation is the oldest form of government intervention in the labor market. Since several types of regulatory intervention have been tried over this period and because major elements of the regulation have been conducted at the state level (with substantial differences among jurisdictions), there is a long and diverse record to consider.

We begin with a brief review of what has happened to workplace safety and health in the last one hundred years. We then succinctly discuss the various approaches to prevention of injuries and diseases that have been used during this time period, such as safety standards issued and enforced by governments. Most of the chapter examines several of the theories that have been offered about the preferable ways to achieve workplace safety and health and about the optimal level of safety and health. Some of the prevention approaches are associated with particular theories, and to a limited degree, we examine the empirical evidence concerning the effectiveness of the various prevention approaches in order to provide a rough test of the validity of the various theories.

The theories we focus on vary in terms of their attitude toward government regulation. In "pure" neoclassical economics, government intervention will either be ineffective or deleterious. In "modified" neoclassical economics, such factors as limits of knowledge or mobility by workers may justify some limited forms of intervention in the economy. In the "old" institutional economics perspective, even more intervention would be supported, including government assistance to workers to deal collectively with employers. The greatest degree of intervention is associated with the "government mandate theory," which is more likely to be propounded by lawyers than economists.

We also examine the transactions cost economics strand of the "new" institutional economics, which is agnostic about the value of government intervention, and the "law and economics" approach, which is generally opposed to any government role except, perhaps, the minimal intervention supported by modified neoclassical economics.

We make no pretense that this list of theories used to assess government regulation of health and safety is exhaustive.[1] Nor are the boundaries between the various theories precisely defined: there is, for example, a substantial overlap between the views of the modified neoclassical economists and the old institutional economists.[2] We nonetheless believe our taxonomic scheme is useful because it spans a broad array of attitudes about the desirability of various types of government regulation.

A distinction between safety and health is used in this chapter. Workplace safety is concerned with injuries and fatalities that result from traumatic episodes. Workplace health is concerned with occupational diseases and fatalities resulting from diseases. The distinction is relevant for the data on the extent of the health and safety problem, for the types of prevention approaches that may be effective, and for the usefulness of the various theories.

## What Has Happened to Workplace Safety and Health?

The rapid industrialization of the U.S. economy in the 19th and early 20th centuries was associated with a surge of workplace injuries, diseases, and deaths. The number and frequency of fatalities resulting from accidents are generally viewed as the most reliable overall indicators of trends in safety since fatalities are less subject to reporting errors than injuries or diseases, which are more likely to be affected by variations in record-keeping requirements under various regulatory arrangements.[3]

The peak in the number of workplace fatalities was reached in 1907 when more than 7,000 workers were killed in just two industries: railroading and bituminous mines (Somers and Somers 1954:9). The fatality rate resulting from accidents significantly declined during the 20th century. The rate dropped by about half between 1912 (when the rate was in the range of 49 to 57 fatalities per 100,000 workers) and 1950 (Somers and Somers 1954:207). Then, from 27 deaths per 100,000 workers in 1950, the workplace fatality rate per 100,000 workers dropped to 21 in 1960, 18 in 1970, 13 in 1980, 9 in 1990, 4 in 1992, and 4 in 1994 (National Safety Council 1995:12). The corresponding numbers of death were 15,500 in 1950, 13,800 in 1960, 13,800 in 1970, 13,200 in 1980, 10,100 in 1990, 4,965 in 1992, and 5,000 in 1994.[4] While much of the decline reflects improvements in medical treatment and a shift in employment away from dangerous industries and occupations, much is also undoubtedly due to improvements in workplace safety.[5]

The workplace injury rate, unlike the fatality rate, has not continued to decline continuously throughout the 20th century. A substantial decline in the injury frequency rate did occur between 1926 and 1932, but this was followed by an "over-all plateau" from 1932 to 1946 (Somers and Somers 1954:208). The injury frequency rate then dropped significantly from 1948 to 1958, when the rate began to increase in a process that lasted until 1970 (Chelius 1977:13). Since 1972, when the Bureau of Labor Statistics (BLS) introduced new measures of workplace safety, changes in incidence rates have provided a mixed picture. The total cases injury frequency rate (including relatively minor injuries) declined from 10.6 cases per 100 workers per year in 1973 to 7.5 in 1983, then climbed to 8.3 in 1992, and dropped to 7.5 cases per 100 workers in 1995. The total lost workday cases frequency rate was 3.3 per 100 workers in 1973, increased to 4.2 in 1979, and then declined in an irregular pattern to reach 3.4 cases per 100 workers in 1995. Meanwhile, the number of lost workdays per 100 workers, a measure of severity of the injuries (plus occupational illnesses), increased from 53.3 per 100 workers per year in 1973 to 93.8 days per 100 workers in 1992, when the BLS discontinued the series (Burton and Schmidle 1995:III-25; Bureau of Labor Statistics 1997).

There are several reasons why the accuracy of the data on the frequency of workplace injuries can be challenged (Smith 1992:559-65). For example, from 1981 to 1988, the Occupational Health and Safety Administration (OSHA) used an inspection procedure that provided incentives for employers to underreport their injuries. Then, starting in 1986, OSHA began to levy substantial fines for underreporting. These changes in OSHA policies may help explain part of the apparent decline in the total case frequency rate from the 1970s to the 1980s and the subsequent increase in the rate until 1992.

The data on workplace diseases and deaths resulting from the diseases are even more problematical. The estimates of the current number of occupational diseases and deaths differ widely. The BLS reported about 495,000 workplace illnesses in 1995, which is equivalent to 0.6 illnesses per 100 workers per year (Bureau of Labor Statistics 1997). However, Barth (1997:12-16) provides several reasons why the BLS numbers may be low and reports an estimate for 1992 of 1.3 million cases of occupational diseases and almost 60,000 fatalities resulting from occupational diseases. One reason for underreporting is the latency period associated with many work-related diseases, which makes identification of the cause of many diseases difficult. While most factors suggest that the current data undercount the number of diseases, there also may be overinclusion of some conditions, such as back disorders, which currently meet the legal tests for workers' compensation benefits and thus are likely to be counted as work-related in the BLS data, even though the primary cause may be the aging process (Burton 1992). Given the difficulties with measuring the current number of occupational diseases and deaths resulting from diseases, the assessment of trends in these measures is infeasible.

The essence of this review is that workplace fatalities from accidents have declined throughout the 20th century, but trends for workplace injuries show no such continuing improvement. Periods of substantial declines in injury frequency rates (such as the 1920s and 1940s) are mixed with periods of relative stability in frequency rates (the 1930s) and with periods when injury frequencies increase (the 1950s and arguably the period from 1983 to 1992). The evidence on trends in occupational diseases is inconclusive, which complicates an overall assessment. The conclusion by Dorman (1996:18) that "on balance, the statistical evidence points toward worsening conditions in U.S. workplaces" may be overly pessimistic, but at best there is no apparent overall improvement in workplace safety and health in the last twenty-five years.

## Prevention Approaches

Employers voluntarily devote significant resources to improving workplace safety and health in order to reduce costs resulting from injuries and diseases (such as training replacements) or simply because they are persuaded an active prevention program is the right thing to do. Likewise, employees have strong incentives to avoid injuries and diseases because of the economic and noneconomic consequences, including pain.

Despite these strong incentives for employers and employees to avoid workplace injuries and diseases, all industrialized countries also rely on government regulation to encourage prevention. Over the last 150 years, several approaches to the prevention of workplace injuries and diseases have been adopted as government policy in the U.S., either by the states or the federal government. Some of the approaches, such as safety standards, have prevention as their sole or dominant goal, while other approaches, such as workers' compensation, have compensation of disabled workers as an additional goal. They are presented here in an order that roughly corresponds to their historical origin, although their use has overlapped in time so the chronology is not orderly.[6] The descriptions of the approaches are brief and are augmented in later sections in connection with the various theories about how improved workplace safety and health should be achieved.

*Laissez-faire economics.* The essence of this theory is that government should establish the legal framework for the operation of the economy (such as defining property rights and enforcing contracts). The government should not, however, directly intervene in the operation of the economy because the interests of individuals (in their roles as consumers and workers) and employers will lead to the proper allocation of resources, including the use of resources to prevent workplace injuries.

*Negligence suits.* Workers sue their employers for workplace injuries caused by the employers' negligence in this approach.[7] The damages provided compensation for the worker, and the threat of damages provided incentives to employers to prevent workplace accidents. This legal remedy was available to workers throughout the 19th century, but was largely eliminated by workers' compensation programs when they were established.

*Government standards.* The promulgation and enforcement of safety standards represents the earliest form of protective labor legislation in the U.S. Most states enacted safety laws between 1877 and 1910 (Somers and Somers 1954:200), although they were generally ineffective (Chelius 1974:700-29). The perception that injury rates were increasing in the 1960s and that state efforts were inadequate help explain the adoption of the Occupational Safety and Health Act (OSHAct) of 1970, which established a regulatory scheme largely controlled by the federal government.

*Workers' compensation.* The first workers' compensation statutes to survive constitutional challenges were enacted in 1911, and by 1920 all but six states had passed such statutes. The statutes provide compensation to workers disabled by work-related injuries and diseases or to the survivors of workers killed at work. Prevention has also been an important goal of workers' compensation since the initial laws, primarily through the use of experience rating that relates the employer's insurance premiums to the previous benefits payments by the industry and (for larger employers) by the firm.

*Government promulgation of information about risks and remedies.* Prior to the enactment of the OSHAct in 1970, the federal government's role in the field of industrial safety was limited to promotion, education, and technical assistance (Somers and Somers 1954:212). These activities have continued in recent decades, such as the publication of data on injuries and illnesses by the BLS.

*Collective bargaining and other policies that empower workers at a local level.* Collective bargaining agreements can outlaw unsafe activities or explicitly require employers to pay a wage premium for unsafe work. If workers are injured, unions can help them obtain workers' compensation benefits. Safety committees containing management and union representatives are found in many collective bargaining contracts. In recent years, a few jurisdictions in the U.S. and Canada have mandated safety committees with management and employee representation for all employers, including nonunionized firms.

## Promoting Safety and Health Using Pure Neoclassical Economics Theory

The neoclassical theory of work injuries and related empirical evidence are examined in Thomason and Burton (1993) and Ehrenberg (1988). The prevention approach consistent with the neoclassical economics theory is laissez-faire economics, i.e., minimal government intervention.[8] We assume for this initial presentation a "pure" version of neoclassical economics, such as that presented and criticized by Dorman (1996:35-41).

*The Pure Neoclassical Economics Theory*

Pure neoclassical economics theory assumes a competitive world, where workers at the margin are mobile and possess accurate information concerning both the risks of employments and the costs of accidents. Workers are assumed to maximize their utility, not just their pecuniary income. Because workers are free to choose between hazardous and nonhazardous employment, hazardous employers must pay a wage greater than that paid by nonhazardous employers. On the assumption that insurance arrangements for employers or workers, such as workers' compensation or private disability insurance, are unavailable,[9] the equilibrium wage will include a risk premium equal to the expected costs of injuries borne by workers employed in the hazardous firm.[10] As a result of the employer paying a risk premium, employment and wages net of the risk premium will be less than if the employer were nonhazardous and did not pay the premium, while in the product market, the firm's price will be higher and output will be lower than if the risk premium were not paid.[11]

The employer has an incentive to invest in safety (such as guards for machinery and training of workers) in order to improve the firm's accident rate and thus reduce the risk premium paid by the employer. The firm will make safety investments until the marginal expenditure on safety is equal to the marginal reduction in the risk premium. Since there is a rising marginal cost to investments in safety, equilibrium will occur with a positive value for the risk premium, which means that in equilibrium, there will be some workplace injuries. In the neoclassical approach, eliminating these remaining accidents would cost more than the benefits resulting from their elimination. The resources that would be needed to further reduce injuries have alternative uses that are more beneficial for employers, workers, and society. In the parlance of economists, there are opportunity costs for the resources used to reduce the level of workplace accidents because there are alternative opportunities for the resources. Use of the resources to improve workplace safety beyond the point where the marginal costs of safety equal the marginal reductions in the risk premium reduces the overall efficiency of the economy since these re-sources are not being allocated to their best possible use.[12]

This version of neoclassical economics provides incentives to workers to avoid workplace accidents. The risk premium fully compensates the worker for the expected costs of work injuries in a hazardous firm. This is described as ex ante compensation since the worker receives the premium prior to the accident. However, the worker who is actually injured does not receive any additional ex post compensation (i.e., compensation after the injury), which provides the worker a strong incentive to avoid the injury and to return to work if the workplace injury does occur.

Variants on neoclassical economics theory can be generated by changing some of the assumptions involved in the previous discussion. For example, sup-pose all workers purchase actuarially fair insurance covering the full costs of work injuries in order to reduce the uncertainty associated with the possibility of work injuries. This means that the worker will be indifferent about whether he is injured, and furthermore, if injured, has no incentive to return to work since the ex post compensation provided by the insurance benefits fully replaces the wages lost due to the work injury. This is an example of the moral hazard problem, in which the availability of insurance increases the quantity of the events that are being insured against (i.e., the occurrence of injuries and the duration of the resulting disabilities). While the additional assumption of actu-arially fair insurance available to workers may reduce the incentives to workers to avoid injuries and to return to work, the result is added incentives to employ-ers to reduce the frequency and severity of workplace injuries since the costs are higher due to the disability insurance.[13] One strategy pursued by employers is insurance schemes that shift part of the costs of injuries to workers (through the use of deductibles and coinsurance) in order to provide incentives to work-ers to avoid workplace injuries and to return to work if such injuries occur.

## Arguments Why the Pure Neoclassical Economics Theory is Faulty

The criticisms of the pure neoclassical economics theory by the propo-nents of the "old" institutional economics (OIE) theory are examined at length in Kaufman (1997) and will only be restated here as they particularly apply to workplace safety and health. A particularly sharp criticism of the neoclassical economics theory is provided by Dorman (1996), who contrasts the neoclassi-cal economics view to a common sense position on occupational safety and health that includes many elements of the OIE theory. We are unaware of any economist who considers the pure version of neoclassical economics adequate for the purposes of analyzing safety and health regulation, although this may reflect our lack of discernment of the dismal science.[14] In any case, some of the criticisms of the pure neoclassical approach will be accepted at least in part by the "modified" neoclassical economists.

One of the attacks on pure neoclassical economics relates to imperfections in the labor market. Critics assert that workers lack sufficient information about the working conditions associated with particular jobs and thus can easily underestimate the risks of workplace injuries and demand inadequate risk premiums. The lack of information is likely to be a special problem for diseases, where the uncertain etiology and the long latency periods of many occupational diseases seem likely to result in the underestimation of risks associated with disease-prone jobs.

Another attack on neoclassical economics pertains to worker mobility. Critics allege that even if workers can perceive the risks associated with hazardous employment, they have a limited ability to move to less hazardous jobs. Lack of mobility can result from several problems with the labor market, not the least of which is widespread involuntary unemployment. Moreover, even if workers have the ability to move, the critics argue that employers do not have to pay compensating differentials to attract workers because of the inequality of bargaining power between labor and management (due in part to excessive supply in the labor market resulting from involuntary unemployment).

Rose-Ackerman (1988:355-57) also argues that the labor market does not generate proper risk premiums because certain costs are not borne by workers but are externalized. Because of programs such as welfare and Medicaid, which are financed from general revenues, individuals do not bear all the costs of their illnesses and injuries. Furthermore, individuals may not properly account for the pain and suffering of their friends and families that result from work injuries. Thus, she argues, "individuals may fail to take into account all the social cost of their risky employment decisions."

Finally, the neoclassical economics approach can be critiqued because it assumes that employers (1) are aware they are paying risk premiums because of the firm's accidents, (2) are aware that investments in safety can reduce the frequency or severity of those accidents, and (3) are motivated to take advantage of the opportunities to improve workplace safety.

### Evidence on the Labor Market

There is evidence on the operation of the labor market that can be used to assess the validity of the criticisms of the pure neoclassical economics approach.

*Worker knowledge.* On the assumption of worker knowledge of workplace risks, for example, Ehrenberg and Smith (1996:252-53) report that the proportions of employees in various industries who consider their work dangerous is closely related to the actual injury rates published by the government for those industries. The authors conclude that "while workers probably cannot state the precise probability of being injured, they do form accurate judgments about the relative risks of several jobs." In contrast, Viscusi (1993:1918) refers to a sizable literature in psychology and economics documenting that individuals tend to overestimate low probability events, such as workplace injuries. As a result of this misperception of risks, the level of the risk premium demanded by workers for low-risk jobs will be too large. However, because workers will underestimate the additional risks associated with higher hazard jobs, they will demand smaller marginal increases in the risk premiums for the jobs with higher actual risks than they would if they accurately estimated those higher risks. This means, for example, that the extra risk premium demanded by workers to move from very safe to moderately safe jobs will be less than the additional risk premium that the workers would demand if they accurately perceived the hazards associated with the two jobs.

*Worker mobility.* Ehrenberg and Smith (1996:253) conclude that job mobility among American workers is relatively high, as evidenced by the large fraction of the labor force that is "in the market" at any given time. For example, over 25% of men and women in the 25 to 34 year age group have been with the current employer for less than a year. Moreover, Viscusi (1993:1920) reports that workers are more likely to quit once they learn about adverse properties of jobs, such as higher than expected injury rates. The magnitude of this adaptive behavior is substantial: the manufacturing industry quit rate would drop by one-third if all industries eliminated their job risks. The result of the turnover in response to job risks, according to Viscusi, "is that more experienced workers on hazardous jobs receive higher compensating differentials."

*Compensating differentials.* There is a burgeoning literature on compensating wage differentials for the risks of workplace death and injury. Ehrenberg and Smith (1996:255) report that studies have generally found that industries having the average risk of job fatalities (about 1 per 10,000 workers per year) pay wages that are .5% to 2% higher than the wages for comparable workers in industries with half that level of risk. Viscusi (1993:1931) also reports on 17 studies that have estimated statistically significant wage premiums for the risks of job injuries.[15] The total amount of risk premiums implied by these various estimates is substantial; probably the upper bound is the Kniesner and Leeth (1995:55) figure of $200 billion in risk premiums in 1993.[16]

The wage premiums received by workers to accept higher risk can be used to calculate the implicit value that workers place on their lives. The survey by Viscusi (1993) of 24 labor market studies found that a majority of estimates for the implicit value of life are in the $3 million to $7 million range in 1990 dollars.

These estimates reinforce the impression that the labor market is operating as the neoclassical economists argued.

That impression must be qualified, however. There are a number of methodological hurdles that studies of risk premiums must surmount. For example, the jobs that have a higher risk of workplace death generally have other undesirable features, such as night shifts or noisy environments, and unless the studies are done carefully, the compensating differentials for these features may be attributed to the risks of death, thereby increasing the magnitudes of the statistical estimates of the risk premiums for workplace fatalities. While researchers are aware of this problem, the limitations of the available data sets mean that the empirical results showing risk premiums must be used with caution. There are, moreover, some studies of the labor market that do not find any evidence of compensating wage differentials (such as Leigh 1991).

The most telling attack on the compensating wage differentials evidence is by Dorman (1996), who argues that most studies have been improperly specified. Dorman finds (pp. 98-100) that after controlling for industry-level factors, the only evidence for compensating wage differentials pertains to unionized workers. For nonunion workers, the inclusion of industry-level data in regressions eliminates the risk premium for fatalities and produces a *negative* risk premiums for injuries. Since Dorman attacks the validity of the previous compensating wage differential results, he also denies the validity of the estimates of the implicit value of life that are based on these risk premiums.

Even prior to the publication of Dorman (1996), some of the economists who surveyed the literature on compensating wage differentials and the implicit value of life reached qualified conclusions about the validity of the neoclassical economics theory. Ehrenberg and Smith (1996:255), for example, conclude that the studies of compensating wage differentials for the risks of injury or death on the job "are generally, but not completely, supportive of the theory."[17] And even if every empirical study found a risk premium for workplace fatalities and injuries, the evidence would not conclusively validate the pure neoclassical economics approach. Viscusi (1993) provides the ultimate qualification:

> Furthermore, all of these results are premised on an assumption of individual rationality. If individuals do not fully understand the risk and respond to risks in a rational manner, then the risk tradeoff that people are actually making may not be those that researchers believe they are making based on objective measures of the risk. (p. 1938)

*Assessment of the pure neoclassical economics theory concerning the labor market.* The studies of worker knowledge of risks, worker mobility, and compensating wage differentials do not provide support for the pure version of neoclassical economics. On the other hand, the evidence from the studies also contradicts an extreme version of the criticism of neoclassical economics that views the assumptions of neoclassical economics so unrealistic that the existence of compensating differentials is considered implausible. In our view, the evidence indicates there are enough knowledge, mobility, and compensating wage differentials to provide considerable stimulus to workplace safety, even though the economic incentives are less than those postulated by the pure version of neoclassical economic theory.[18] Thus efforts to augment the incentives to safety provided by the pure version of neoclassical economics are warranted.

### Appropriate Regulations for Safety and Health in Both the Modified Neoclassical Economics Theory and the Old Institutional Economics

*General strategy for regulation.* Many economists endorse a "modified" version of neoclassical economics theory that recognizes that limited types of government regulation of safety and health are appropriate in order to overcome some of the attributes of the labor market that do not correspond to the assumptions of pure neoclassical economics. The attributes include the lack of sufficient knowledge by employees about the risks of various jobs and the possible lack of sufficient knowledge or motivation of employers about the relationship between expenditures on safety and the reduction in risk premiums. In general, the adherents of the old institutional economics theory would accept the rationale for and types of government regulations supported by the proponents of modified neoclassical economics (as well as other regulations discussed in the next section).

*Government promulgation of information about risks and remedies.* Efforts to overcome the imperfections in the labor market caused by inadequate knowledge by workers and employers of the hazardous nature of jobs and the opportunities to reduce risks would be endorsed by the OIE and the modified neoclassical economists (although the latter would want to compare the costs with the benefits of such efforts).

Examples of such efforts include the Oregon safety initiative that provides consultative visits to employers and safety education for workers. A study of Oregon employers that received the voluntary consultations and were later subjected to regular safety inspections showed an 88.7% decrease in the number of serious hazards (Chelius and Moscovitch 1996:88-89). At the federal level, an example is the 1983 OSHA Hazard Communication standard, which requires labeling of hazardous substances and notification to workers and customers and which is estimated to save 200 lives per year (Viscusi 1996:124).

OSHA also requires employers to maintain a log of workplace injuries and illnesses that is available for inspection by employees and to post an annual summary of the information. The BLS publishes information on injuries indicating differences among occupations and industries in terms of frequency and severity of workplace injuries, as well as extensive information on the factors causing these injuries.

There is additional direct evidence of the importance of knowledge in facilitating the operation of the labor market. Viscusi (1993:192) found that when workplace injuries occur, one result is increased turnover. The evidence discussed in the next section indicating that unionized workers receive greater risk premiums and are more likely to file workers' compensation claims than nonunion workers indirectly confirms the importance of information and assistance to workers.

*Workers' compensation and experience rating.* The workers' compensation program in each state relies on two levels of experience rating to promote safety. Industry-level experience rating establishes an insurance rate for each industry that is largely based on prior benefit payments by the industry. Firm-level experience rating determines the workers' compensation premium for each firm above a minimum size by comparing its prior benefit payments to those of other firms in the industry.

In the pure neoclassical economics model, the introduction of workers' compensation with experience rating should make no difference in the safety incentives for employers (compared to the incentives provided by the labor market without workers' compensation). Consider a variant of neoclassical economics with these assumptions: workers cannot purchase insurance covering the costs of work injuries; there is perfect experience rating (a firm's premiums depend solely on its own record of benefit payments); and the workers' compensation premium is actuarially fair (the premium is equal to expected benefit payments and does not include a loading factor for administrative expenses). Under these assumptions, the risk premium portion of the wage paid by the employer will be reduced by an amount exactly equal to the amount of the workers' compensation premium.[19] Also, under these assumptions, the employer has the same economic incentives to invest in safety after the workers' compensation program is established that the employer had prior to the introduction of the program.[20]

If the workers' compensation policy covers the full expected losses of the worker, the result is the same as the previously discussed variant in which workers can purchase disability insurance policies covering their full expected losses. Workers will be indifferent about whether they are injured and if injured have no incentive to return to work since the ex post benefits provided by workers' compensation fully replace the wages lost to the injury. This set of assumptions also provides incentives for employers to develop workers' compensation plans to deal with the moral hazard problem that shift part of the costs of injuries to workers (through the use of deductibles and coinsurance) in order to provide incentives to workers to avoid workplace injuries and to return to work should such injuries occur.

Once the assumptions such as perfect experience rating and actuarial fair premiums are relaxed, the effect of establishing a workers' compensation program on the safety incentives provided solely by the labor market is unclear. An example from Thomason and Burton (1993:S7) illustrates one possible outcome. If a firm is not perfectly experience rated because premiums are determined by the experience of all firms in the industry, the firm's incentive to invest in safety will be reduced (compared to the incentives postulated in the pure neoclassical model) since improvements in the firm's accident rate will have little impact on the firm's workers' compensation premium because the savings from the reduced benefit payments to this firm's workers will be shared with all other firms in the industry. This is another example of the moral hazard problem, where the creation of insurance leads to a greater incidence of the event being insured against.

The essence of the pure neoclassical economics approach is that the introduction of workers' compensation (1) will lead to reduced incentives for workers to avoid injuries, assuming that they did not purchase private disability insurance plans prior to the introduction of workers' compensation; and (2) will lead to reduced incentives for employers to prevent accidents, if assumptions such as perfect experience rating are dropped.

In contrast, the OIE approach argues that the introduction of workers' compensation with experience rating should improve safety because the limitations of knowledge and mobility and the unequal bargaining power for employees mean that the risk premiums generated in the labor market are inadequate to provide employers the safety incentives postulated by the pure neoclassical economics approach.[21] Commons (1934:804-05), a leading figure in the OIE approach, claimed that unemployment is the leading cause of labor problems, including injuries and fatalities, because slack labor markets undercut the mechanism that generates compensating wage differentials. Commons asserted that experience rating provides employers economic incentives to get the "safety spirit" that would otherwise be lacking. The modified neoclassical economics approach would also accept the idea that experience rating should help improve safety by providing stronger incentives to employers to avoid accidents, although they probably would place less emphasis on the role of unemployment in undercutting compensating wage differentials and more emphasis on the failure of employers to recognize the costs savings possible from improved safety without the clear signals provided by experience-rated premiums. Where the OIE theorists would probably disassociate themselves from the modified neoclassical economics theorists would be the latter contingent's emphasis on the moral hazard problem aspect of workers' compensation, which could result in more injuries.

A number of recent studies of the workers' compensation program provide evidence that should help us evaluate the virtues of the pure neoclassical economics, the modified neoclassical economics, and the OIE approaches.[22] However, the evidence is inconclusive. One survey of the literature by Boden (1995:285) concluded that "research on the safety impacts has not provided a clear answer to whether workers' compensation improves workplace safety." In contrast, a recent survey by Butler (1994:I-87) found that with the exception of the study by Chelius and Smith (1983), most recent studies provide statistically significant evidence that experience rating "has had at least some role in improving workplace safety for large firms." Based on our knowledge of the literature, we believe the Butler conclusion is more reasonable, although additional research is clearly warranted in order to support this finding. Some estimates of the magnitude of the safety effect are substantial: Durbin and Butler (1997) suggest that a 10% increase in workers' compensation costs may reduce fatality rates by 4.1% to 15.4%. This evidence on experience rating is consistent with the positive impact on safety postulated by the OIE approach and the modified neoclassical economists and inconsistent with the pure neoclassical view that the use of experience rating should be irrelevant or may even lead to reduced incentives for employers to improve workplace safety.[23]

There is also evidence that the presence of workers' compensation benefits leads to changes in worker behavior. Thomason and Burton (1993:S8) summarize a number of studies that found the reported frequency and severity of workers' compensation claims increase in response to higher benefits, which suggests that a moral hazard problem exists. Caution is needed in interpreting these studies, however, since the increased frequency or severity reported in the claims can result from a "true injury effect" (workers take more risks as a result of higher benefits and as a result actually experience more injuries) or from the "reporting effect" (workers report claims that would not have been reported as a result of the higher benefits and/or extend their period of reported disability because of the higher benefits). Most studies of the relationship between workers' compensation benefits and the frequency and severity of claims have not distinguished between the true injury and reporting effects. Durbin and Butler (1997) conclude that the latter effect dominates, which implies that the concerns of modified neoclassical economists that the use of workers' compensation benefits to provide ex post compensation for injured workers will lead to more injuries may be exaggerated.

*The incidence of workers' compensation costs.* The OIE considered the workers' compensation program to have a feature that promotes safety in addition to experience rating, namely, the distribution of the costs of workplace injuries to consumers and/or employers. The modified neoclassical economists accept much of the rationale for this approach, but differ about the degree to which workers also bear the costs of the workers' compensation program.

There were several theories offered by the old institutional economists about who should bear the costs of the workers' compensation program.[24] According to the trade-risk theorists, such as Dawson (1915:278), because industrial injuries arise out of the production of goods and services, the prices for these items should include the costs of workers' compensation insurance. This view is best captured by the slogan attributed to Lloyd George, the English statesman: "The cost of the product should bear the blood of the working man."

Downey (1924) introduced the least social cost theory as a justification for workers' compensation in which he argued that injured workers "are precisely those least able to bear the burden of economic loss themselves" (pp. 14-15). If employers are held legally responsible for workplace injuries or fatalities, the employer will purchase insurance and will incorporate this cost in the price of goods and services. "This method secures the widest, the least burdensome, and perhaps on the whole the most equitable distribution of the cost of industrial accidents and disease." A common aspect of both the Dawson and Downey theories is that all of the costs of workplace injuries will be shifted forward to consumers in the form of higher prices.

The least social cost theory was reformulated by Witte (1930:411-18). He noted that workers' compensation benefits did not replace all of the income losses experienced by injured workers and therefore workers will also bear part of the costs of industrial accidents. Witte also denied that employers could transfer all of the remaining compensation costs to consumers by charging higher prices. Rather, employers would be required to absorb part of the cost of accidents in the form of lower profits. Thus Witte argued that the costs of work injuries would be shared by customers in the form of higher prices, by employers in the form of lower profits, and by workers in the form of the portion of lost wages that were not replaced by benefits.

The essence of these various OIE theories concerning the incidence of the costs of the workers' compensation program is that they either assumed workers did not bear any of the costs (because, for example, the costs of the program were incorporated into higher prices and thus were borne by consumers) or that workers shared in the costs only to the extent that they suffered the loss of that portion of wages not replaced by workers' compensation benefits. The OIE did not consider the possibility that workers might also help pay for the workers' compensation program by having their pre-injury wages or employment reduced, which is the position of the modified neoclassical economists.

There was, to be sure, a contemporaneous statement of the notion that wages might be reduced as a result of the introduction of workers' compensation:

> And just as the employee's assumption of ordinary risks at common law presumably was taken into account in fixing the rate of wages, so the fixed responsibility of the employer, and the modified assumption of risk by the employee under the new system, presumably will be reflected in the wage scale.

Who was the author of this trenchant analysis, written in the spirit of neoclassical economics? Why, none other than U.S. Supreme Court Justice Pitney in the 1917 decision upholding the constitutionality of the New York workers' compensation statute, *New York Central Railroad Co. v. White* (243 U.S. 188 at 201-02)!

A recent survey of the empirical literature on the incidence of the costs of the workers' compensation program reached this conclusion (Chelius and Burton 1994:I-158): "a substantial portion of workers' compensation costs (and even, according to some estimates, all of the costs) are shifted onto workers" in the form of lower wages. We also concluded that not only do workers pay for workers' compensation, but that to a large extent this financing of workers' compensation through the reduction in wages "is a fair deal for workers, since more expensive benefits lead to a roughly equivalent drop in wages." But even if this is a fair deal and represents the conventional wisdom of modified neoclassical economists, it is not the deal envisaged by the old institutional economists, who assumed that the workers' compensation statutes designed to help workers would shift most or all of the cost of the program to consumers in the form of higher prices or employers in the form of lower profits.

## Appropriate Regulations for Safety and Health in the OIE Approach

While the modified neoclassical economists and the OIE would largely agree on the desirability of several prevention approaches, such as the use of experience rating in workers' compensation, the OIE endorsed another approach to promoting health and safety that many modified neoclassical economists would not support.

*Collective bargaining and other policies that empower workers at a local level.* Unions can help overcome workers' lack of knowledge about unsafe conditions and their unequal bargaining power by several methods. Collective bargaining agreements can outlaw unsafe activities or at least explicitly require employers to pay a wage premium for unsafe work. If workers are injured, unions can help them obtain workers' compensation benefits, thereby increasing the financial incentives for employers to improve workplace health and safety. In addition, there are joint labor-management efforts to improve workplace safety that take two primary forms. First, there are safety committees established by many collective bargaining contracts that assume responsibility for certain activities, such as formulation of health and safety rules, participation in inspections conducted by OSHA, and inspection and enforcement of rules established by the collective bargaining process. Second, there are several jurisdictions in the U.S. and Canada with laws that mandate joint labor-management committees in all firms above a certain size, whether or not they are unionized.[25] These committees have been assigned roles such as conducting inspections.

The beneficial effects predicted by the OIE approach for these efforts appear to be achieved. Several studies, including Smith (1986), Weil (1991), and Adler, Goldoftas, and Levine (1997), concluded that the Occupational Safety and Health Act enforcement activity was greater in unionized firms than in nonunionized firms. The latter authors (p. 436) suggested this was because "the union safety representative has less fear of reprisal for calling in an outside regulator than a nonunion worker might have."

Moore and Viscusi (1990:118) find that unionized workers receive larger compensating wage differentials for job risks than unorganized workers, and Dorman (1996:97-100) found that unionized workers were the only workers who received a positive differential for risk. Hirsch, Macpherson, and Dumond (1997:213) concluded that "union members were substantially more likely to receive workers' compensation benefits than were similar nonunion workers." The authors suggest that unionized workers fare better "because workers are provided with information from their union representatives, supervisors are more likely to inform injured workers about workers' compensation filing procedures . . . and management has less discretion and ability to monitor workers and penalize them for questionable claims." Thus unionized workers appear to do better than nonunionized workers in terms of enforcement of safety laws and in receipt of ex ante compensation (risk premiums in the wage) as well as ex post compensation (workers' compensation benefits).

There is little evidence on the impact of legally mandated safety committee on workplace safety and health. Chelius and Moscovitch (1996:87-88) describe the recent Oregon law that requires every company with 10 or more employees to establish a labor-management safety committee, which must meet monthly. Weil (1995:279) concluded that the mandated safety committees increased the extent of employee involvement and the union impact on enforcement activities. Subsequent to the adoption of the law, fatalities in Oregon dropped by almost 40%, but other aspects of the Oregon safety environment were also changed, such as a substantial increase in safety inspections by the state, and thus it is hard to know how much credit should be given to the safety committees.[26]

Disentangling the effect of mandatory safety committees is also complicated in Canada, because all the provinces have established a system known as the Internal Responsibility System with three elements: (1) joint health and safety committees (JHSCs), (2) the right for individuals to refuse unsafe work, and (3) the right of employees to be informed of unsafe hazards in the workplace. Lewchuk, Robb, and Walters (1996:234-36) studied Ontario workplaces and found that where JHSCs existed prior to the establishment of the Internal Responsibility System, their effectiveness in improving workplace injury and illness rates was increased by the establishment but that JHSCs formed reluctantly by the parties as a result of the establishment of the IRS had no clear effect.

While the beneficial effects on workplace safety and health of mandatory safety committees for all firms (unionized or not) has limited empirical support, the evidence clearly indicates that unions do facilitate prevention of workplace injuries and compensation of those workers who are injured. This evidence provides support for the OIE justification of institutional intervention into the economy to improve workplace safety.

### Promoting Safety and Health Using the New Institutional Economics Theory

A number of strains of the "new" institutional economics (NIE) theory are surveyed by Dow (1997). NIE authors generally argue that market forces encourage efficient forms of economic organization without government assistance and that opportunities for efficiency-improving public intervention are rare. We consider only the Coase theory/transaction costs economics strain of NIE in this section.

*The Coase theory and transaction costs economics.* In the absence of costs involved in carrying out market transactions, changing the legal rules about who is liable for damages will not affect decisions involving expenditures of resources that are expended to increase the combined wealth of the parties. The classic example offered by Coase (1988:97-104) involves the case of straying cattle that can destroy crops growing on neighboring land. The parties will negotiate the best solution to the size of the herd, the construction of a fence, and the amount of crop loss due to the cattle whether or not the cattle-rancher is assigned liability for the crop damages.

Coase recognized that the assumption that there were no costs involved in carrying out transactions was "very unrealistic." According to Coase (1988):

> In order to carry out a market transaction, it is necessary to discover who it is that one wishes to deal with . . . and on what terms, to conduct negotiations . . . , to draw up the contract, to undertake the inspection needed to make sure that the terms of the contract are being observed, and so on. These operations are often . . . sufficiently costly . . . to prevent many transactions that would be carried out in a world in which the pricing system worked without cost. (p. 114)

The goal of transactions costs economics is to examine these costs and to determine their effect on the operation of the economy. As Coase and other scholars of transactions costs, including Williamson (1985), have demonstrated, one conclusion is that when transactions costs are significant, changing the legal rules about initial liability can affect the allocation of resources.

*Evidence concerning changes in liability rules.* Workplace safety regulation provides a good example of a change in liability rules, since in a relatively short period (1910-1920), most states replaced tort suits (the employer is only responsible for damages if negligent) with workers' compensation (the employer is required to provide benefits under a no-fault rule) as the basic remedy for employees injured at work. Evidence from Chelius (1977:44-45) "clearly indicated that the death rate declined after workers' compensation was instituted as the remedy for accident costs." This result suggests the high transactions costs associated with the determination of fault in negligence suits were an obstacle to achieving the proper incentives to workplace safety and that the institutional features of workers' compensation, including the no-fault principle and experience rating, were a relatively more efficient approach to the prevention and compensation of work injuries.[27]

An interesting study that also suggests that institutional features can play a major role in determining the effects of changing liability rules is Fishback (1987). He found that fatality rates in coal mining were higher after states replace negligence law with workers' compensation in those states that had state-run workers' compensation funds (exclusive or competitive), but there was no statistically significant effect on fatalities of establishing workers' compensation if the state solely relied on private carriers to provide the workers' compensation insurance. Fishback (pp. 322-23) suggested that the difference between his general results (that the introduction of workers' compensation was associated with higher fatality rates) and those of Chelius may be due to the high supervision costs that existed in coal mining in the early 1900s.

The focus on transactions costs provided by this component of the NIE theory thus appears to provide a useful supplement to the neoclassical economics theory, since it appears that such institutional features can have a major effect on the change in the economic incentives resulting from revision in liability rules.[28] Moreover, the Coase theorem provides a useful lesson that just because there is a market failure, there is no prima facie case for government regulation. Rather, each situation has to be examined to see if the benefits of regulation outweigh the costs.

## Promoting Safety and Health Using the Law and Economics Theory

Law and economics (L&E) theory draws on neoclassical economics and transaction cost economics but is distinctive in the extent to which it examines legal institutions and legal procedures. Two branches of law and economics theory will be analyzed: tort law and employment law.

*Theoretical stimulus of tort law to safety.* When negligence is the legal standard used for tort suits, an injured employee may sue his employer for damages when the employer is at fault. If the employer has not taken proper measures to prevent accidents and thus is at fault, the employer will be liable for all of the consequences of the injury.[29] The standard for the proper prevention measure was developed by Judge Learned Hand and restated by Posner (1972) as

> the judge (or jury) should attempt to measure three things in ascertaining negligence: the magnitude of the loss if an accident occurs; the probability of the accident's occurring; and the burden [cost] of taking precautions to prevent it. If the product of the first two terms, the expected benefit, exceeds the burden of precautions, the failure to take those precautions is negligence. (p. 32)

Posner argued that proper application of this standard will result in economically efficient incentives to avoid accidents.[30] As Chelius (1977:34-35) notes, the added costs of determining liability in a court may appear to be inconsistent with achieving an efficient use of resources, since legal fees are usually a significant percentage of the total award. The benefits of legal proceedings, however, *may* outweigh their costs if the incentives created by such a system are more accurate than those present under alternative systems.[31]

*Evidence on the tort law stimulus to safety.* The generally accepted view is that tort suits were largely ineffective as remedy for workplace injuries in the late 1880s and early 1900s. Not only were workplace injuries and fatalities increasing, but employees were generally unsuccessful in suits, in large part because of legal defenses available to employers, such as the contributory negligence defense that eliminated any recovery if the worker was negligent, even if the employer was negligent to a greater degree. The leading legal treatise on workers' compensation (Larson and Larson 1997:Sec. 4.50) concludes that "the precompensation loss-adjustment system for industrial accidents was a complete failure. . . ." However, Berkowitz and Berkowitz (1985:160) indicate that workers were beginning to enjoy considerable success with tort suits at the beginning of the workers' compensation era. Perhaps the tort system if left in place for workplace injuries would have evolved and produced a major stimulus to workplace safety.

There are two types of empirical evidence that indicate skepticism is nonetheless warranted about the stimulus to workplace safety from tort suits. First, as previously discussed, Chelius (1977) found that the replacement of the negligence remedy with workers' compensation led to a reduction in workplace fatalities. (The Fishback [1987] results provide a qualification to this general result.) Second, in other areas of tort law, there is a major controversy among legal scholars about whether the theoretical incentives for safety resulting from tort suits actually work. One school of thought is exemplified by Landes and Posner (1987:10), who state that "although there has been little systematic study of the deterrent effect of tort law, what empirical evidence there is indicates that tort law . . . deters, even where, notably in the area of automobile accidents, liability insurance is widespread . . . and personal safety might be expected to be of greater concern than the potential financial consequences of an accident."[32]

An opposing view on the deterrent effects of tort law is provided by Priest (1991), who finds almost no relationship between liability payouts and the accident rate for general aviation and states that "this relationship between liability payouts and accidents appears typical of other areas of modern tort law as well, such as medical malpractice and products liability."

A recent survey of the deterrent effects of tort laws by Schwartz (1994: 378-79) distinguished between a strong form of deterrence (as postulated by Landes and Posner) and a moderate form of deterrence, in which "tort law provides a significant amount of deterrence, yet considerably less than the economists' formulae tend to predict." Schwartz surveys a variety of areas where tort law is used, including motorist liability, medical malpractice, and product liability, and concludes that sector by sector the evidence undermines the strong form of deterrence but provides adequate support for the deterrence argument in its moderate form (pp. 422-23). As to workers' injuries, Schwartz (1994:391-93) cites the Chelius and Fishback studies and concludes "it is unclear whether a tort system or workers' compensation provides better incentives for workplace safety; in an odd way . . . neither study is out of line with the general idea that a properly designed set of liability rules can produce beneficial results."

Based on both the ambiguous historical experience of the impact of workers' compensation on workplace safety and the current controversy over the deterrence effect in other areas of tort law, the law and economics theory concerning tort law does not provide much assistance in designing an optimal policy for workplace safety and health.[33] We will be even more assertive in our assessment of the virtues of tort law as a strategy for improving workplace safety and health: we are sufficiently persuaded of the favorable effects of workers' compensation experience on safety and sufficiently skeptical of the deterrent effects of tort suits that we would resist the use of tort suits to deal with work injuries unless much more compelling evidence of the deterrent effect is produced.

### Promoting Safety and Health: The Conflict between the Government Mandate Theory and the Law and Economics Theory

*The government mandate theory.* The government mandate theory argues that the promulgation and enforcement of government standards will improve workplace safety and health. A good example of this approach is McGarity and Shapiro (1996). Part of their strategy is to attempt to refute three critical claims of the abolitionists: that is, those who would abolish OSHA. These claims are that (1) workplace risks have decreased dramatically in recent decades, (2) OSHA regulations are costly but ineffective, and (3) economic incentives from risk premiums and workers' compensation have generated those reductions in risk that have occurred. The first two claims are discussed below; the third claim is challenged on the basis of the objections to the evidence on compensating wage differentials and the deterrent effect of experience rating, plus an argument that workers' compensation experience rating in any case would provide an insufficient incentive for safety because workers' compensation benefits only replace a portion of the economic losses caused by work-related injuries and diseases.

In addition to refuting the three claims of the abolitionists, plus critically examining a variety of other topics, such as risk analysis, cost-benefit analysis, and congressional mistreatment of OSHA, McGarity and Shapiro (1996) provide a positive case why OSHA is necessary.

OSHA can help plug the considerable gap left by the failure of economic incentives by insisting that employers take additional

safety and health precautions pursuant to their general duty to provide employees with a safe and healthful employment. Exercising its
standard-setting authority to protect employees from significant
risks, OSHA can insure that employers invest in protective technologies.

OSHA has comparative institutional advantages over uncritical
reliance on economic incentives to generate safety and health precautions. . . . OSHA's capacity to write safety and health regulations
is not bounded by any individual worker's limited financial resources. Likewise, OSHA's capacity to stimulate an employer to
action does not depend upon the employees' knowledge of occupational risks or bargaining power. In other words, the "workers in a
particular firm may be unskilled, nonunion, and speak Spanish
rather than English, but OSHA can still force their employer to
improve conditions." (p. 697)

The government mandate theory is basically a legal theory, although much
of the supporting evidence involves reinterpretation of studies conducted by
economists. The government mandate theory would not be endorsed by many
economists, including the OIE. Commons and Andrews (1936), for example,
criticized at length the punitive approaches that used factory inspectors in the
form of policemen, since this turned employers into adversaries with the law.
The OIE theory rather favored regulatory methods that enlisted the profit
motive to reduce injuries, such as experience rating. The minimum standards
supported by the OIE were those developed by a tripartite commission, involving employers, employees, and the public, rather than standards promulgated by the government. While the OIE theory is thus unsympathetic to the
government mandate theory, the sharpest attack is derived from the law and
economics (L&E) theory, which tends to be dominated by anti-regulation
economic analysis.

*The L&E theory concerning consequences of government regulation.* As
indicated by Schwab (1997), L&E scholars make a distinction between
mandatory, minimum terms (standards) and those terms that are merely
default provisions (or guidelines) that employers and employees can agree to
override. Most employment laws, including workplace safety laws, create standards and are thus objectionable to the L&E scholars.

Willborn (1988) has articulated the standard economic objections to
mandatory terms.[34] Employers will treat newly imposed standards like exogenous wage increases and in the short run will respond by laying off workers.
In the long run, employers will try to respond to mandates by lowering the
wage. The final wage-benefits-standards employment package will make

workers worse off than they were before the imposition of the standards—
otherwise the employers and workers would have bargained for the package
without legal compulsion.

There are possible responses to the L&E objections to standards. The
proponents of the government mandate theory argue that standards may solve
workers' information or mobility problems. The approach also asserts that
workers have inadequate bargaining power resulting from factors such as
involuntary employment and that standards help produce outcomes that
would result from bargaining among equals. There also may be external costs
that bargains between workers and employers do not consider, such as the
medical care that society is required to provide indigent injured workers.
Another possible argument in favor of standards is that the result may redistribute income to workers, which is desirable from a normative standpoint
even if inefficient.[35] The essence of these arguments by the government mandate theorists and others supportive of standards is that the impact of regulations, such as those promulgated under the OSHAct, should be an improvement in workplace safety. The expected result would be even more beneficial
for regulation of health, since the information deficiencies are greater for
health than for safety.

*Evidence on the economic justification of OSHA standards.* The evidence
suggests that the OSHAct has done little to improve workplace safety. The
workplace fatality rate declined by 57% between 1970 (the year the OSHAct
was enacted) and 1993. However, Kniesner and Leeth (1995:49) point out
that the drop in the frequency of workplace fatalities from 1947 to 1970 (the
13 years prior to OSHA) was 70% larger than the drop in the 13 years after
OSHA and assert that "OSHA might actually have slowed the downward
trend in fatal injuries." Kniesner and Leeth (p. 49) also found "no downward
trend in either the total frequency of workplace injuries or the frequency of
injuries resulting in at least one lost workday." Smith (1992:558) found that
between 1971 and 1990, the percentage of manufacturing workers experienc-
ing lost workday injuries "exhibits considerable yearly variation but no hint
whatsoever of a downward trend . . . [while] the number of lost workdays per
hundred manufacturing workers . . . has a pronounced upward trend, rising
from 73 days in 1975 to 104 days by 1990!"

Despite the assertion by McGarity and Shapiro (1996:591-92) that the
OSHA abolitionists claim workplace risks have decreased dramatically over
the last several decades, that is not the general thrust of the arguments of the
economists quoted above. In an interesting twist, while Kniesner and Leeth
argue that the drop in workplace fatalities had actually slowed after OSHA,
McGarity and Shapiro (1996:594-95) argue that the number of fatalities have

declined at a greater rate since Congress created OSHA. As for nonfatal accidents, McGarity and Shapiro (p. 595) provide data indicating that the total number of accidents has been declining in the post-OSHA period, but the number of serious injuries has been rising. This is basically consistent with the finding of the economists quoted above.

Several possible reasons have been offered for the apparent failure of the OSHAct to improve workplace safety. Kniesner and Leeth (1995:49) note that the self-employed account for about 9% of the work force but about 20% of all workplace fatalities; these workers are not covered by the OSHAct. In addition, BLS found that 40% of recent workplace fatalities were from transportation accidents and about 20% from assaults and other violent acts, and Kniesner and Leeth (1995:49) argue these leading causes of workplace deaths "are unlikely to be reduced much by OSHA inspections."

OSHA's ineffectiveness in part may be due to the lack of inspection activity, since the average establishment is only inspected once every 84 years.[36] According to Kniesner and Leeth (1995:48), "the federal government has six times more fish and game inspectors than workplace health and safety inspectors." But the evidence also suggests that transferring resources from walleye inspection to wall-to-wall plant inspections may be imprudent. Kniesner and Leeth (p. 50) reviewed the empirical studies of OSHA inspections and concluded "that OSHA has reduced injuries by no more than 4.6%. OSHA's impact, however, may be considerably smaller than 4% to 5%, considering that the majority of studies have found neither an abatement nor a deterrence effect from OSHA inspections." Smith (1992:566-71) provided a more exhaustive review of the studies of OSHA inspections and reached a similar conclusion: the studies "suggest that inspections reduce injuries by 2% to 15%" although the estimates often are not statistically significant (and thus cannot be confidently distinguished from zero effect).

Several recent studies have provided a more favorable assessment of the OSHA inspection process. Weil (1996) examined the custom woodworking industry and found that OSHA inspections resulted in improved compliance with a set of OSHA standards particularly relevant for that industry. However, Weil was unable to determine if the improved compliance with OSHA standards resulted in lower injury rates. Even more promising results were provided by Gray and Scholz (1991), who examined firms that had been inspected more than once for exceeding OSHA exposure limits for dangerous substances and found that the effect of an inspection leading to a penalty was to reduce the firm's injury rate by 20% over the following three years. However, even Dorman (1996:196), who supports an aggressive public policy to reduce workplace injuries, provided a qualified interpretation of such evidence: "These new results portray an OSHA with unfulfilled potential for improving working conditions . . . however, even the most optimistic reading indicates that . . . more vigorous enforcement alone cannot close the gap between U.S. safety conditions and those in other OECD countries."

Supporters of the government mandate theory, as represented by McGarity and Shapiro (1996), are more optimistic about the potential impact of OSHA inspections:

> Analysts who have attempted to isolate OSHA's impact using econometric models have produced inconsistent results. To the abolitionists these equivocal results suggest that OSHA is ineffective. However, a more plausible interpretation is that they demonstrate OSHA's unrealized potential. (p. 596)

OSHA inspections might be more effective if the size of the monetary penalties were increased or if criminal sanctions were utilized more frequently.[37] But some critics of OSHA are skeptical this would help; Kniesner and Leeth (1995:55) argue that "the economic incentives to improve safety by reducing compensating wage differentials and workers' compensation expenses far surpass the safety-enhancing incentives from the relatively small fines currently imposed by OSHA."[38] Even if OSHA fines were doubled, the amounts would be far surpassed by these other sources of economic incentives.

While the inspection and fines approach to improving safety relied on by OSHA is thus of questionable effectiveness based on the evidence concerning trends in workplace fatalities and injuries and the studies of the impact of inspections, some critics of OSHA have identified other problems. Kniesner and Leeth (1996:50-51) argue that the annual compliance costs with OSHA health and safety standards are $11 billion (considering the effect on productivity and the cost of OSHA-mandated capital equipment), while the upper range of the benefits of OSHA in terms of reducing injuries is $3.6 billion a year. This unimpressive cost-benefit ratio is in part a result of the excessive stringency of some of the various safety and health standards that have been promulgated by OSHA. Viscusi (1996:124-25) examined OSHA standards using an implicit value of life of $5 million as the standard for efficient regulation. Four of the five OSHA safety regulations adopted as final rules had costs per life saved of less than $5 million; only the 1987 grain dust standard with $5.3 million per life saved failed the efficiency test proposed by Viscusi. In contrast, only one of the five OSHA health regulations adopted as final rules had costs per life saved of less than $5 million, namely, the 1983 Hazard Communication standard that cost $1.8 million per life saved. The four health standards that failed the efficiency tests had costs that ranged from $17.1 million per life saved (the 1987 benzene standard) to $72,000 million per life saved (the 1987 formaldehyde standard).

The Viscusi analysis has been challenged by Stone (1997:187-88), who specifically focuses on the formaldehyde standard.[39] Viscusi confined his analysis of the benefits of the standard to the number of lives saved without considering the other beneficial effects of OSHA standards, such as reductions in the number of injuries and illnesses. Stone indicates that the OSHA regulations typically prevent roughly 5 to 25 injuries for every life saved. However, the formaldehyde standard has an extraordinarily high ratio of reduced illnesses to reduced fatalities. According to OSHA's estimates, the standard prevents approximately 17,000 illnesses per year and 0.6 deaths per year, for a ratio of 30,000 avoided illnesses for every life saved. Stone, using an implicit value of a typical avoided illness or injury of $20,000 to $50,000 (which he attributes to Viscusi) calculates that the illness-reduction benefits of the OSHA formaldehyde standard are between $340 million and $850 million annually, with a midpoint of about $600 million. Since OSHA estimates that the annualized cost of the standard is only $64 million, Stone argues that the cost-benefit test of efficiency is clearly met.

The proponents of the government mandate approach have concerns about the use of cost-benefit analysis that transcend the misapplication in a particular instance. For example, McGarity and Shapiro (1996:622-30) provide eight objections to cost benefit analysis, ranging from paralysis by analysis to the elitist perspective of the experts who prepare cost-benefit analysis. Two objections against cost-benefit analysis worth further elaboration are the bias against protective legislation. McGarity and Shapiro (1996:630) argue that most health and environmental regulation was enacted to protect some members of the public from the harmful aspects of conduct engaged in by other members of the public. Subjecting these regulations to cost-benefit analysis "reflects a bias against the protective approach that Congress adopted in the protective legislation." The final objection is that cost-benefit analysis is inconsistent with technology-based standard setting, which is basically the approach that OSHA currently uses to decide the appropriate stringency of OSHA standards. This approach does not consider the costs and benefits of a proposed standard, but rather the technological and economic feasibility of the standard. McGarity and Shapiro (1996) defend this approach with this rationale:

> OSHA's technology-based approach may appear awkward, but it is usually effective, and it is not irrational. The mandate is a pragmatic way to balance efficient and other important social values in

the context of workplace risks, and it permits OSHA to implement its mandate more effectively than if it had to defend its cost and benefit calculations. (p. 632)

To be sure, cost-benefit analysis of health standards issued under the OSHAct is not legal, and so those standards that fail the cost-benefit test (considering both lives saved plus injuries and illnesses avoided) do not violate the letter and presumably the purpose of the law. But to the extent that the rationale offered by the government mandate theorists for regulation of health is that workers lack enough information to make correct decisions and therefore the government is in a better position to make decisions about how to improve workplace health, the evidence on the variability and magnitude of the cost/benefit ratios for OSHA health standards is disquieting. Rather than OSHA standards reflecting interventions in the marketplace that overcome deficiencies of the marketplace, the explanation of why the stringency of regulation varies so much among industries would appear at best to be a result of technology-based decisions that could well aggravate the alleged misallocation of resources resulting from operation of the market and at worst could reflect relative political power of the workers and employers in various industries.[40]

## Conclusions and Observations

We examined several variants of economic theory—ranging from pure neoclassical economics to law and economics theory—that are potentially useful in designing government regulations that will provide an optimal policy for workplace safety and health. For each theory we identified prevention approaches that appear particularly suitable (or unsuitable) for that theory. For example, laissez-faire economics is a prevention approach that is particularly compatible with neoclassical economics, while collective bargaining and other policies that empower workers are prevention approaches consistent with old institutional economics.

We also reviewed the empirical evidence concerning the various prevention approaches. The evidence was used not only to evaluate the usefulness of the particular approaches but also to provide an indirect test of the value of the economic theory associated with that approach. In a survey as brief as this chapter, we were required to be selective in the economic theories, the prevention approaches, and the empirical evidence we considered, but we believe the material we examined warrants several conclusions.

The pure version of neoclassical economics theory clearly suggests that appropriate levels of workplace safety can be achieved by the government adopting a laissez-faire approach to prevention. The theory postulates that workers and employers will interact in the labor market by taking into account the differential risks of various jobs and the result will be compensating wage differentials that both compensate workers for the possibility of workplace injuries and provide incentives to employers to improve workplace safety. Because there are costs associated with improving safety, the equilibrium in the labor market will include a residual level of risk. The empirical evidence indicates that the labor market does produce substantial levels of risk premiums and to that extent the pure neoclassical economics theory is supported. However, there is also evidence that strongly suggests that the incentives to safety produced by the laissez-faire approach are incomplete, and thus the pure neoclassical theory provides a necessary but insufficient basis for designing a safety policy.

The old institutional economics theory as well as a modified version of neoclassical economics suggest that safety can be enhanced by intervention in the labor market such as experience rating for workers' compensation. The empirical studies we examined generally support the postulate that experience rating improves workplace safety, thus both providing evidence that the neoclassical theory is an insufficient basis for a safety policy and providing validation for the modified version of neoclassical theory and portions of the old institutional economics theory. There is also evidence that empowerment of workers through collective bargaining and the use of safety committees— which are prevention approaches advocated by the old institutionalist economists—promote workplace safety. One area where the OIE theory has deficiencies is the notion that the costs of the workers' compensation program can be largely shifted to consumers and employers.

We have examined only one strain of the new institutional economics, namely transactions costs economics. In a world without transactions costs, changing the liability rules would make no difference in resource allocation. Transactions costs theory does not imply that in the presence of transactions costs a particular liability scheme (such as a negligence standard) is necessarily a better approach to safety. Rather, the theory indicates that in the presence of high transactions costs, different liability schemes may produce different outcomes, and therefore the actual effect of these schemes must be investigated. The evidence that shifting from a negligence standard for workplace injuries to the no-fault approach of workers' compensation produced a drop in workplace fatalities validates this central tenet of transactions costs economics.

One of the two strains of the law and economics theory we examined was that the use of the negligence suits provides optimal incentives to accident prevention. Although the evidence on the deterrent effects of tort law is subject to various interpretations, we found the approach and thus the theory wanting because of the historical experience with workplace injuries (where the replacement of negligence suits with workers' compensation led to a reduction of workplace fatalities) and the current evidence suggesting that tort suits do not promote safety to the degree postulated by Posner and Landes.

We also considered the employment law strain of the law and economics theory, which recognizes that government intervention is occasionally warranted (for example, in the presence of externalities that mean market prices do not reflect all costs associated with a particular activity) but which has a strong aversion to government standards, since in general they are assumed to denigrate the solutions the parties would otherwise reach voluntarily. In sharp contrast to the L&E theory is government mandate theory, which suggests that government intervention in the form of the promulgation and enforcement of safety standards would improve workplace safety and health.

The evidence indicates that the OSHAct has been largely ineffective in reducing workplace fatalities and injuries. Moreover, the evidence suggests that the OSHA standards are of varying stringency and often unjustified in terms of costs and benefits, and thus supports the anti-standards approach to safety suggested by law and economics theory. Caveat emptor is a useful adage.

The overall conclusion of this review of the theories, prevention approaches, and empirical evidence is that what appears to work best to improve workplace safety and health is a rather eclectic mix of approaches and theories. We are least impressed by the arguments and evidence pertaining to pure neoclassical economics and the government mandate theory, which reflect the extremes in terms of the extent of government regulation that is desirable. But among the remaining theories, there surely is no single theory that would suffice as an underpinning for designing government regulations that would optimize the amount of workplace safety. Nor is there a single prevention approach (such as laissez-faire economics or workers' compensation) that is sufficient to produce that optimal level of safety. We hope that our survey of the prevention approaches and the evidence concerning their effectiveness will be of value to researchers and policymakers in designing a multifaceted prevention policy.

We found writing this chapter to be a challenge, which upon reflection seem to warrant several observations. First, the theories are overlapping and within each theory there are proponents who make different assumptions and use different models. Thus it is not easy to frame predictions that uniquely distinguish among theories in order to provide tests of those theories.

Second, the evidence on the effectiveness of many of the prevention approaches is ambiguous. Depending on the data base, the model specification, and the statistical technique used, the results differ on a number of topics, such as the existence and magnitude of compensating wage differentials, the effect of experience rating, and the effectiveness of OSHA inspections. The good news is that during the last thirty years, the quantity and quality of empirical research on the topics in this chapter have markedly increased. The hope is that our zone of disagreement will narrow with continuing research.

Third, there is a marked tendency for advocates of various theories and prevention approaches to interpret the empirical evidence in a manner most sympathetic to the viewpoint they espouse. The conflicting studies about the effect of experience rating on safety, the existence of compensating wage differentials for risk of injury, and a myriad of other topics are subject to various interpretations, and in too many cases the interpretations are predictable from the background and theoretical orientation of the author. We salute scholars such as Ehrenberg and Smith (1996), who mixed their endorsement of the evidence supporting compensating wage differentials with a mega-grain of salt.

Fourth, a consequence of the tendency of researchers and reformers to divide into "camps" supporting one prevention approach (e.g., OSHA or workers' compensation) is that not enough consideration is given to the relative strengths and weaknesses of each approach and to the possible synergistic interrelationships among the programs that can possibly enhance the overall effectiveness of our efforts to promote workplace safety and health. For example, most modified neoclassical economists would recognize that a major limitation to the effective operation of the labor market is the lack of worker knowledge of the risks of occupational diseases and the long latency period between exposure to toxic substances and the resulting disease. These factors suggest that compensating wage differentials and experience rating under workers' compensation will not provide adequate incentives to prevent occupational diseases and that OSHA potentially can make a major contribution in promoting workplace health. On the other hand, given the evidence suggesting the relative ineffectiveness and infrequency of OSHA inspections that are largely devoted to finding violations of safety standards and the hostility of employers to these inspections, the promotion of safety can perhaps best be left to the economic incentives from workers' compensation and compensating wage differentials.

This does not mean that separate prevention approaches for safety and for health are always desirable; indeed, one challenge is to identify unexploited synergistic relations among the prevent approaches. Examples of potential interprogram strategies not currently utilized in most states include the use of workers' compensation claims data to help target OSHA inspections and the use of OSHA data on occupational illnesses to help decide which diseases should be compensable in workers' compensation statutes.

Finally, we have relied on the existing empirical evidence to assess the various prevention approaches and economic theories because we think it is impossible to choose among the theories in terms of their logic or intellectual appeal. One consequence of this reliance on empirical evidence is that the assessment of the various approaches and theories is likely to evolve over time as the weight of evidence about what works changes. An example is the use of experience rating in workers' compensation. From 1911 (when experience rating was incorporated into the initial workers' compensation program in Wisconsin) until about 1970, experience rating was assumed to work based on theory. Then, when some of the first empirical studies of experience rating done in the 1970s did not find evidence of a beneficial effect of experience rating on safety, the approach and the underlying theory were generally out of favor. In the last decade or so, however, the studies of experience rating generally find that the approach does matter for safety (due, perhaps, to improved methodology of the studies and the higher costs of workers' compensation in recent decades, which may have made the economic incentives more obvious and compelling to employers), and so we have provided a more favorable review of the approach and the supporting theory than we would have a decade ago.

We anticipate that as evidence accumulates concerning the effectiveness of other approaches to workplace safety, our views of the various theories and prevention approaches will also evolve. Thus the limited information currently available suggests that joint labor-management safety committees are an effective stimulus to safety, but additional and more refined studies of that topic may change our views about the value of the approach. Moreover, studies of other countries may force us to refine our views about the best theories and approaches to achieve workplace safety. For example, the limited evidence suggests that compensating wage differentials are not found in the German labor market, and so what appears to be generally safe workplaces in that country must be due to a different mix of prevention approaches and theories. Thus our survey of what theories and prevention approaches best promote workplace safety and health must be recognized as bounded by time and geography. Having stated that qualification, we nonetheless hope that our study will help academics and policymakers improve the health and safety of workers.

### Dedication and Acknowledgments

This chapter is dedicated to the memory of James R. Chelius, who died in June 1997. Bruce Kaufman had recruited Jim to write about workplace safety and health because of his distinguished record of research in this area. When Jim became ill, I was honored to be asked to help prepare the chapter. Jim was able to actively participate in the preparation of several drafts of the paper, and so he truly is a coauthor even though the final version does not reflect the additional insights and corrections he would have provided.

I acknowledge the useful comments made on earlier drafts of the chapter by Peter Barth, Lee Benham, Bruce Kaufman, Stewart Schwab, Robert Smith, Emily Spieler, Terry Thomason, and Steven Willborn. I accept responsibility for remaining errors of fact or interpretation.

John F. Burton, Jr.

## Endnotes

[1] We do not, for example, consider the "critical legal studies" theory nor many of the strains of the "new" institutional economics theory discussed by Dow (1997).

[2] Several of the economists who commented on drafts of this paper made clear they recognized that the assumptions of pure neoclassical economics were not satisfied in the real world and thus some types of intervention (such as experience rating of workers' compensation premiums) were warranted if properly designed. These economists do not consider themselves "institutional" economists, however, and so we have established the "modified" neoclassical economics category for their domain.

[3] Although fatalities are more likely to be accurately reported than injuries and diseases, there nonetheless are substantial variations among the estimates of the number of deaths resulting from workplace accidents, as discussed by Smith (1993:562).

[4] In 1992, when the National Safety Council (1995:4) reported 4,965 workplace deaths and a rate of 4 deaths per 100,000 workers, the Census of Fatal Occupational Injuries prepared by the U.S. Bureau of Labor Statistics reported 6,083 fatal work injuries and a rate of 5 fatalities per 100,000 employed (Toscano and Windau 1993).

[5] According to Toscano and Windau (1993:Table 5) the two major industry groups with the highest fatality rates in 1992 were agriculture, forestry, and fishing (24 fatalities per 100,000 workers) and mining (27 fatalities per 100,000 workers), while the two major industry groups with the lowest fatality rates were finance, insurance, and real estate (2 fatalities per 100,000 workers) and services (2.2 fatalities per 100,000 workers). The shifting employment from the former to the latter industry groups since 1912 helps explain the decline in the overall workplace fatality rate. Dorman (1996:16-18) constructed fatality rates for the period from 1980 to 1990 in which he held industry mix constant, and still found a substantial drop in the fatality rate (from about 8.5 to 5.5 fatalities per 100,000 workers).

[6] The historical chronology is not followed in later sections, where each prevention approach is discussed in connection with the theory of safety and health with which the approach is most closely related.

[7] Negligence is one type of tort (or civil wrong) that requires fault by the tortfeasor. Another type of tort that is not examined in this chapter but that could be used for workplace injuries is strict liability, which holds the tortfeasor liable without fault. In general, a tortfeasor is responsible for full damages resulting from the tort.

[8] The minimal government intervention includes enforcement of contracts that parties have freely negotiated.

[9] We will discuss the consequences of dropping the assumption that disability insurance is not available to workers later in this section, and we will discuss the consequences of dropping the assumption that workers' compensation is not available for employers in the next section.

[10] The expected costs include lost wages, medical care, and the disutility caused by the injury.

[11] This discussion of the consequences of the employer paying a risk premium assumes that the firm is earning a normal rate of return; if the firm is earning excess profits, the payment of the risk premium will reduce profits. The relative importance of price and output adjustments in the produce market and the employment and wage adjustments in the labor market depend on the relative elasticities of supply and demand in the two markets.

[12] Some critics of the neoclassical approach argue that in an economy with idle resources, there are no opportunity costs associated with the use of resources to improve safety. This implies that resources should be devoted to improving safety so long as there is any positive increment to safety resulting from the use of resources.

[13] If workers are assumed to be risk averse prior to the availability of actuarially fair insurance, employees will demand a risk premium that in part compensates them for the uncertainty about whether they will be the particular workers who will be injured. The availability of insurance that provides ex post compensation means that workers do not need to worry in advance about whether they will be the injured workers. This will lead to a reduction in the risk premium portion of the wage that is greater than the increase in the insurance premium paid by the worker. The result will be that the total wage paid by the employer (including the risk premium) will be less when the workers can buy insurance than if they cannot, and the reduction in the total wages reduces the incentive for the employer to invest in safety.

[14] In comments on an earlier draft of this paper, a referee provided a different assessment of the number of adherents to pure neoclassical economics. He states "my perspective is that a great many economists believe this model in its *as if* form . . . in the sense that they believe real world labor markets function pretty much as if the assumptions of the pure model were indeed true, at least for the aggregate, market-type outcomes economists generally look at."

Perhaps the difference between the referee and us has to do with the level of analysis, since there may be many economists who feel that the pure neoclassical economics theory is adequate for "aggregate, market-type outcomes." However, in the specific area of safety and health regulation, we believe almost all labor economists would endorse the use of experience rating for employers, even though (as discussed in the text) in the pure neoclassical economics model, the introduction of workers' compensation with experience rating should make no difference in the safety incentives for employers.

[15] According to Viscusi (1993:1929), the chief recent methodological addition to the studies of risk premiums has been the inclusion of a workers' compensation variable, in recognition that the availability of workers' compensation benefits will reduce the risk premiums needed by the worker. Inclusion of this variable has raised the estimates of the wage-risk tradeoff and the implicit value of life.

[16] Ehrenberg and Smith (1996:note 17 at p. 267) state that "the compensating wage differential for a complete elimination of risk can be extrapolated to 4%." Clinton (1997:Table B-26 at p. 328) reports that the total of wages and salaries in the U.S. in 1993 was $3,095.3 billion. Four percent of this total of wages and salaries suggests that compensating wage differentials were about $125 billion in 1993, which is considerably less than the Kniesner and Leeth figure of $200 billion.

[17] Another example of an economist who provided a muted endorsement of the validity of the evidence is Viscusi (1993:1931), who concludes, "Perhaps the best way to interpret these studies is that there is a value-of-life range that is potentially pertinent. The wage-risk relationship is not as robust as is, for example, the effect of education on wages."

[18] We do not accept the strict standard for judging the theory of compensating wage differentials offered by Dorman (1996:26): "Once we accept the postulates of free choice in the labor market and worker rationality in making that choice, it appears to be an inescapable conclusion that offsetting wage differentials must *fully* compensate workers for taking on greater risks."

While this test might be appropriate for evaluating the pure version of neoclassical economics, we think it is logically consistent to conclude that, given the limitations of knowledge and mobility in the labor market, wages which contain premiums that only partially compensate for risk are plausible.

[19] For example, suppose the employer had been paying 30 cents per hour as a risk premium portion of the wage prior to the establishment of the workers' compensation program. Then a workers' compensation program is established that provides benefits with an expected value of 10 cents per hour. Given the assumption of actuarial fair premiums, the employer will pay a workers' compensation premium of 10 cents an hour, and the risk premium portion of the wage will be reduced to 20 cents per hour. (This example assumes workers are risk neutral.)

[20] Extending the example from the previous note, if prior to the workers' compensation program, the employer could reduce the risk premium portion of the wage by 15 cents per hour by investing 15 cents per hour in safety equipment, then subsequent to the establishment of the workers' compensation program, the 15 cents per hour investment in safety equipment will lead to a 10 cents per hour reduction in the risk premium portion of wages and a 5 cents per hour reduction in the workers' compensation premium.

[21] Moss (1996:59-76) presents an excellent recent synopsis of the OIE view on experience rating as a stimulus to prevention of industrial accidents and unemployment.

[22] Robert Smith properly noted that most of the studies of the safety incentives resulting from experience rating contrast (1) workers' compensation with experience rating with (2) workers' compensation without experience rating, and thus do not compare (1) workers' compensation with experience rating with (3) the labor market without any benefits for workplace injuries. If there is no difference between (1) and (2), however, it is unlikely that there will be any difference between (1) and (3). Moreover, Chelius (1974) did compare (1) and (3) and found that the workplace fatality rate dropped after states adopted workers' compensation programs. The Chelius study is further examined in connection with our discussion of tort suits.

[23] The evidence that experience rating "works" does not prove that compensating differentials fail to provide any economic incentives to employers to improve workplace safety, only that the incentives can be augmented by use of experience rating.

[24] The discussion of the institutional economists in this subsection is largely based on Williams and Barth (1973:21-23).

[25] Rhinehart (1994:I-77) indicated that "at least 13 states currently require employers to establish safety and health programs and 13 states require joint safety and health committees for at least some employers."

[26] Eaton and Nocerino (1996) examined the effectiveness of health and safety committees in the public sector in New Jersey. They found no significant correlation between two measures: (1) the perceptions of effectiveness by participants in the committees, and (2) reported levels of illnesses and injuries. They also found that the mere existence of a committee did not significantly affect reports of injuries and illnesses but that certain aspects of committee performance (such as worker involvement) were associated with fewer reported illnesses and injuries.

[27] Lee Benham has pointed out that this analysis assumes that the level of fatalities were too high under the tort system. High transactions costs can result in fatality rates that are too high as well as too low, compared to the number of fatalities that would occur in an economy without transactions costs. Thus the reduction in fatalities associated with the substitution of workers' compensation for tort suits does not necessarily prove that workers' compensation is the more efficient approach to the prevention of work injuries.

We accept this indictment of our logic. While we agree that not all reductions in injuries and fatalities are economically justified (in the sense that after some point the costs of further reductions are greater than the additional benefits), in the context of the magnitude of the fatality rates that existed in the economy in the early 20th century, we assume that any reductions that resulted from the introduction of workers' compensation reflect the greater efficiency of this program compared to tort suits.

[28] The transactions costs analysis strain of the NIE theory is related to the OIE theory. Indeed, Williamson (1985) acknowledged the concept of "transaction" came from John R. Commons, and much of Commons (1934) is about the influence of property rights as they influence economic activity and the allocation of resources.

[29] This formulation of the negligence standard assumes that the employee is not also negligent.

[30] The negligence standard must be formulated in terms of the marginal expected accident costs and prevention costs in order to achieve proper allocation decisions, as discussed by Posner (1992:163-67).

[31] Epstein (1982:801-03) argues that negligence is an inefficient system and that the theoretical arguments offered in its support are flawed.

[32] Just in case tort law does not have a deterrent effect, Landes and Posner (1987:13-14) add this rationale for their economic structure of tort law: "Even if tort law does not have a significant effect on behavior, the theory advanced in this book is not refuted. Ours is a theory of the rules of tort law rather than of the consequences of those rules for behavior. It might seem that if the rules had no effect on behavior, an efficient set of rules would be one that minimized the costs of using the legal system and would thus consist solely in a rule of no liability applied in all cases. But this conclusion does not necessarily follow. . . . The doctrinal structure would still be economic even if the social function of tort law was to assuage feelings of indignation and avert breaches of the peace rather than to promote an efficient allocation of resources to safety."

[33] The limitations of negligence law as a stimulus to safety may be due to the substantial transactions costs associated with establishing liability, as discussed in the previous section.

[34] The guidelines (or waivable terms) are not subject to these economic objections because (following the Coase theorem) parties can write around inefficient legal terms assuming that transactions costs are low.

[35] The distributive impact of inefficient rules is complex. For a general treatment, see Craswell (1991). Stewart Schwab, in comments on our paper in which he applied Craswell's analysis to labor markets, concluded that if all workers value safety identically, they will benefit from a standard if and only if it is efficient. However, when different workers value safety differently, both efficient and inefficient safety standards have different distributional effects on different subgroups of workers.

[36] This estimate was provided by former AFL-CIO Secretary-Treasurer Thomas R. Donahue, who is quoted in O'Neill (1992:1).

[37] The experience with the federal Coal Mine Health and Safety Act (CMHSA) of 1969, which is administered by the Mine Safety and Health Administration (MSHA), arguably indicates that an inspection program can improve workplace safety. Weeks (1989:193-94) reported that the fatality rate in coal mining showed no trend from 1933 until 1970, and then declined to half the pre-CMHSA rate by 1980. However, there was no statistically significant decline in the fatality rate from 1980 to 1987, which weakens the argument. Also, as Weeks discusses (p. 197), other factors than MSHA regulation can affect the fatality rate. One factor is the payment of black lung benefits to disabled workers and their survivors, a program that was also established by the CMHSA and that was paying about $1.6 billion a year to beneficiaries when Weeks wrote his article. Weeks stated that "the federal black lung program may be a rare instance in which compensation is an incentive to control hazards." In light of the differences in the time trends for fatalities during the 1970s and the 1980s, and the possibility that the source of the decline in fatality rates after the enactment of the CMSHA may have been due to economic incentives, we are reluctant to view the MHSA regulatory approach as providing persuasive evidence that a more aggressive OSHA inspection policy would be more effective in reducing workplace injuries and fatalities.

[38] Kniesner and Leeth (1995:55) estimate that in 1993, firms paid more than $55 billion for workers' compensation and $200 billion for compensating wage differentials, while OSHA and state safety programs assessed fines of $160 million, which makes the total of the first two approaches greater than OSHA fines by a ratio of 1,594 to one.

[39] The Viscusi analysis has also been criticized by Dorman (1997:188-89), who challenges the use of $5.3 million as the value of life, both because the econometric evidence leading to any valuation of human life is suspect and because Viscusi has elsewhere advocated that the value of life should vary among groups of workers depending on factors such as their level of income. In this context, Dorman argues that since the risk premium for unionized workers is higher than the premium for nonunionized workers, Viscusi's logic would suggest that the value of life for union workers should be greater than the value of life for nonunion workers. Dorman argues that we should reject this implausible interpretation of the econometric evidence.

[40] The role of politics in determining the stringency of OSHA regulations in various industries could be based on further examination of the OIE and the NIE, which is a task beyond the scope of this chapter. Those interested in examining the NIE analysis of institutions such as OSHA should consider the complex models of the state that combine both the public good-providing and redistributive view of the state, as discussed by Rutherford (1996:119-23). A leading modern proponent of this view is Douglas North, whose views are summarized in North (1997). Rutherford (1996:120) examines the differences and similarities between the old and new institutional economics and, in this particular area, notes the similarities between Commons and North, who are respectively leading figures among the old and the new institutional economists.

# References

Adler, Paul S., Barbara Goldoftas, and David I. Levine. 1997. "Ergonomics, Employee Involvement, and the Toyota Production System: A Case Study of NUMMI's 1993 Model Introduction." *Industrial and Labor Relations Review*, Vol. 50, no. 3 (April), pp. 416-37.

Barth, Peter S. 1997. "Workers' Compensation and Work-Related Illnesses and Diseases in 1997." Unpublished paper presented to the Third International Congress on Medical-Legal Aspects of Work Injuries.

Berkowitz, Edward D., and Monroe Berkowitz. 1985. "Challenges to Workers' Compensation: An Historical Analysis." In John D. Worrall and David Appel, eds., *Workers' Compensation Benefits: Adequacy, Equity, and Efficiency*. Ithaca, NY: ILR Press, pp. 158-79.

Boden, Leslie I. 1995. "Creating Economic Incentives: Lessons from Workers' Compensation Systems." *Proceedings of the Forty-Seventh Annual Meeting* (Washington, DC). Madison, WI: Industrial Relations Research Association, pp. 282-92.

Bureau of Labor Statistics. 1997. "Workplace Injuries and Illnesses in 1995." News Release USDL 97-76 of the U.S. Department of Labor.

Burton, John F., Jr. 1992. "Compensation for Back Disorders." In John F. Burton, Jr. and Timothy P. Schmidle, eds., *Workers' Compensation Desk Book*. Horsham, PA: LRP Publications, pp. I-123-I-128.

Burton, John F., Jr., and Timothy P. Schmidle, eds. 1995. *1996 Workers' Compensation Year Book*. Horsham, PA: LRP Publications.

Butler, Richard J. 1994. "Safety Incentives in Workers' Compensation." In John F. Burton, Jr. and Timothy P. Schmidle, eds., *1995 Workers' Compensation Year Book*. Horsham, PA: LRP Publications, pp. I-82-I-91.

Chelius, James R. 1974. "The Control of Industrial Accidents: Economic Theory and Empirical Evidence." *Law and Contemporary Problems* (Summer-Autumn), pp. 700-29.

_____. 1977. *Workplace Safety and Health*. Washington, DC: American Enterprise Institute.

Chelius, James R., and John F. Burton, Jr. 1994. "Who Actually Pays for Workers' Compensation? The Empirical Evidence." In John F. Burton, Jr. and Timothy P. Schmidle, eds., *1995 Workers' Compensation Year Book*. Horsham, PA: LRP Publications, pp. I-153-I-159.

Chelius, James R., and Edward Moscovitch. 1996. *Toward a Safer Workplace: Reform and Deregulation of Workers' Compensation*. Boston, MA: Pioneer Institute for Public Policy Research.

Chelius, James R., and Robert S. Smith. 1983. "Experience-Rating and Injury Prevention." In John D. Worral, ed., *Safety and the Workforce*. Ithaca, NY: ILR Press, pp. 128-37.

Clinton, William J. 1997. *Economic Report of the President*. Washington, DC: U.S. Government Printing Office.

Coase, R.H. 1988. *The Firm, the Market, and the Law*. Chicago, IL: The University of Chicago Press.

Commons, John R. 1934. *Institutional Economics: Its Place in Political Economy*. New York, NY: MacMillan.

Commons, John R., and John Andrews. 1936. *Principles of Labor Legislation*. 4th ed. New York: Harper & Bros.

Craswell, Richard. 1991. "Passing on the Costs of Legal Rules: Efficiency and Distribution in Buyer-Seller Relationships." *Stanford Law Review*, Vol. 43, no. 2 (January), pp. 361-98.

Dawson, Miles M. 1915. "The Constitutionality of Workmen's Compensation and Compulsory Insurance Laws." *Case and Comment*, Vol. 22 (September).

Dorman, Peter. 1996. *Markets and Mortality: Economics, Dangerous Work, and the Value of Human Life*. Cambridge, UK: Cambridge University Press.

_____. 1997. "Correspondence on Benefit-Cost Analysis." *Journal of Economic Perspectives*, Vol. 11, no. 2 (Spring), pp. 188-90.

Dow, Gregory K. 1997. "The New Institutional Economics and Employment Regulation." In Bruce E. Kaufman, ed., *Government Regulation of the Employment Relationship*. Madison, WI: Industrial Relations Research Association.

Downey, H.E. 1924. *Workmen's Compensation*. New York: Macmillan Company.

Durbin, David, and Richard Butler. 1997. "Prevention of Disability from Work Related Sources." Preliminary draft of chapter to be included in Terry Thomason, Douglas Hyatt, and John F. Burton, Jr., eds., *Disability in the Workplace: Prevention, Compensation, and Cure*. Madison, WI: Industrial Relations Research Association. Scheduled for publication in 1998.

Eaton, Adrienne E., and Thomas Nocerino. 1996. "The Effectiveness of Health and Safety Committees: Results of a Survey of Public Sector Worksites." Unpublished paper, School of Management and Labor Relations, Rutgers University.

Ehrenberg, Ronald G. 1988. "Workers' Compensation, Wages, and the Risk of Injury." In John F. Burton, Jr., ed., *New Perspectives on Workers' Compensation*. Ithaca, NY: ILR Press, pp. 71-96.

Ehrenberg, Ronald G., and Robert S. Smith. 1996. *Modern Labor Economics: Theory and Public Policy*. 6th ed. Reading, MA: Addison-Wesley.

Epstein, Richard A. 1982. "The Historical Origins and Economic Structure of Workers' Compensation Law." *Georgia Law Review*, Vol. 16, pp. 775-819.

Fishback, Price V. 1987. "Liability Rules and Accident Prevention in the Workplace: Empirical Evidence from the Early Twentieth Century." *Journal of Legal Studies*, Vol. 16, pp. 305-28.

Gray, Wayne B., and John T. Scholz. 1991. "Do OSHA Inspections Reduce Injuries? A Panel Analysis." National Bureau of Economic Research (NBER) Working Paper No. 3774.

Hirsch, Barry T., David A. Macpherson, and J. Michael Dumond. 1997. "Workers' Compensation Recipiency in Union and Nonunion Workplaces." *Industrial and Labor Relations Review*, Vol. 50, no. 2 (January), pp. 213-36.

Kaufman, Bruce E. 1997. "Labor Markets and Employment Regulation: The View of the 'Old' Institutionalists." In Bruce E. Kaufman, ed., *Government Regulation of the Employment Relationship*. Madison, WI: Industrial Relations Research Association.

Kniesner, Thomas J., and John D. Leeth. 1995. "Abolishing OSHA." *Regulation*, No. 4, pp. 46-56.

Landes, William M., and Richard A. Posner. 1987. *The Economic Structure of Tort Law*. Cambridge, MA: Harvard University Press.

Lanoie, Paul. 1992. "The Impact of Occupational Safety and Health Regulation on the Risk of Workplace Accidents: Quebec, 1983-87." *Journal of Human Resources*, Vol. 30, pp. 643-60.

Larson, Arthur, and Lex K. Larson. 1997. *Larson's Workers' Compensation: Desk Edition*. New York: Matthew Bender.

Leigh, J. Paul. 1991. "No Evidence of Compensating Wages for Occupational Fatalities." *Industrial Relations*, Vol. 30, no. 3 (Fall), pp. 382-95.

Lewchuk, Wayne, A. Leslie Robb, and Vivienne Walters. 1996. "The Effectiveness of Bill 70 and Joint Health and Safety Committees in Reducing Injuries in the Workplace: The Case of Ontario." *Canadian Public Policy*, Vol. 33, no. 3, pp. 225-43.

McGarity, Thomas O., and Sidney A. Shapiro. 1996. "OSHA's Critics and Regulatory Reform." *Wake Forest Law Review*, Vol. 31, no. 3 (Fall), pp. 587-646.

Moore, Michael J., and W. Kip Viscusi. 1990. *Compensation Mechanisms for Job Risks: Wages, Workers' Compensation, and Product Liability*. Princeton, NJ: Princeton University Press.

Moss, David A. 1996. *Socializing Security: Progressive-Era Economists and the Origins of American Social Policy*. Cambridge, MA: Harvard University Press.

National Safety Council. 1995. *Accident Facts*. Itasca, IL: National Safety Council.

North, Douglas C. 1997. "Prologue." In John N. Drobak and John V. C. Nye, eds., *The Frontiers of the New Institutional Economics*. San Diego, CA: Academic Press, pp. 3-12.

O'Neill, Colleen M. 1992. "OSHA Inspection Once-in-Lifetime Experience." *AFL-CIO News*, May 11.

Posner, Richard A. 1972. "A Theory of Negligence." *The Journal of Legal Studies*, Vol. 1, no. 1, pp. 29-66.

_____. 1992. *Economic Analysis of Law*. 4th ed. Boston, MA: Little, Brown and Company.

Priest, George L. 1991. "The Modern Expansion of Tort Liability: Its Sources, Its Effects, and Its Reform." *Journal of Economic Perspectives*, Vol. 5, no. 1, pp. 31-50.

Rhinehart, Lynn. 1994. "State Initiatives on Injury and Illness Prevention: Comprehensive OSHA Reform Needed." In John F. Burton, Jr. and Timothy P. Schmidle, eds., *1995 Workers' Compensation Year Book*. Horsham, PA: LRP Publications, pp. I-76 to I-81.

Rose-Ackerman, Susan. 1988. "Progressive Law and Economics—And the New Administrative Law." *Yale Law Journal*, Vol. 98, pp. 341-68.

Rutherford, Malcolm. *Institutions in Economics: The Old and the New Institutionalism*. Paperback ed. Cambridge, Eng.: Cambridge University Press.

Schwab, Stewart J. 1997. "The Law and Economics Approach to Workplace Regulation." In Bruce E. Kaufman, ed., *Government Regulation of the Employment Relationship*. Madison, WI: Industrial Relations Research Association.

Schwartz, Gary T. 1994. "Reality in the Economic Analysis of Tort Law: Does Tort Law Really Deter?" *UCLA Law Review*, Vol. 42, no. 2 (December), pp. 377-444.

Smith, Robert S. 1986. "Greasing the Squeaky Wheel: The Relative Productivity of OSHA Complaint Inspections." *Industrial and Labor Relations Review*, Vol. 40, no. 1 (October), pp. 35-47.

_____. 1992. "Have OSHA and Workers' Compensation Made the Workplace Safer?" In David Lewin, Olivia S. Mitchell, and Peter D. Sherer, eds., *Research Frontiers in Industrial Relations and Human Resources*. Madison, WI: Industrial Relations Research Association, pp. 557-86.

Somers, Herman M., and Anne R. Somers. 1954. *Workmen's Compensation*. New York: John Wiley & Sons.

Stone, Robert F. 1997. "Correspondence on Benefit-Cost Analysis." *Journal of Economic Perspectives*, Vol. 11, no. 2 (Spring), pp. 187-88.

Thomason, Terry, and John F. Burton, Jr. 1993. "Economic Effects of Workers' Compensation in the United States: Private Insurance and the Administration of Compensation Claims." *Journal of Labor Economics*, Vol. 11, no. 1, Part 2 (January), pp. S1-S37.

Toscano, Guy, and Janice Windau. 1993. "Fatal Work Injuries: Results from the 1992 Census." *Monthly Labor Review*, Vol. 116, no. 10 (October), pp. 39-48.

Viscusi, W. Kip. 1993. "The Value of Risks to Life and Health." *Journal of Economic Literature*, Vol. 31 (December), pp. 1912-46.

_____. 1996. "Economic Foundations of the Current Regulatory Reform Efforts." *Journal of Economic Perspectives*, Vol. 10, no. 3 (Summer), pp. 119-34.

Weeks, James L. 1989. "Is Regulation Effective? A Case Study of Underground Coal Mining." *Annals of the New York Academy of Sciences*, Vol. 572, pp. 189-199.

Weil, David. 1991. "Enforcing OSHA: The Role of Labor Unions." *Industrial Relations*, Vol. 30, no. 1 (Winter), pp. 20-36.

_____. 1995. "Mandating Safety and Health Committees: Lessons from the States." *Proceedings of the Forty-Seventh Annual Meeting* (Washington, DC). Madison, WI: Industrial Relations Research Association, pp. 273-81.

_____. 1996. "If OSHA Is So Bad, Why Is Compliance So Good?" *Rand Journal of Economics*, Vol. 27, no. 3 (Autumn), pp. 618-40.

Willborn, Steven L. 1988. "Individual Employment Rights and the Standard Economic Objections: Theory and Empiricism." *Nebraska Law Review*, Vol. 67, no. 1 & 2, pp. 101-39.

Williams, C. Arthur, Jr., and Peter S. Barth. 1973. *Compendium on Workmen's Compensation*. Washington, DC: National Commission on State Workmen's Compensation Laws/Government Printing Office.

Williamson, Oliver E. 1985. *The Economic Institutions of Capitalism*. New York: The Free Press.

Witte, Edwin E. 1930. "The Theory of Workmen's Compensation." *American Labor Legislation Review*, Vol. 20, no. 4 (December), pp. 411-18.

# CHAPTER 8

# Collective Bargaining Regulation in Canada and the United States: Divergent Cultures, Divergent Outcomes

DAPHNE GOTTLIEB TARAS
*University of Calgary*

A recurrent theme in comparative industrial relations scholarship is that industrial relations (IR) systems develop from the complex interplay of managers, workers and their representatives, and governments, all linked to a social, political, and economic environment. Because each system exists within this broad societal context, the prognosis for a successful transplant of the features of one system into another is therefore relatively poor (Kahn-Freund 1974; Bok 1971). This is a proposition that ought to be kept in mind as scholars examine whether the attractive features of one country's system can be imported to fix the apparent ailments of another country's system. For example, in the last dozen years the American labor law regime governing collective bargaining has been subject to growing criticism for a variety of flaws and has been identified as a principal cause of the sharp decline in U.S. union density (Weiler 1986; Commission on the Future of Worker-Management Relations 1994). At the same time, Canada's relative strength and stability in IR have attracted attention. Despite various predictions that Canadian union density would follow the American pattern of decline, Canadian unionization has remained stable in aggregate for the past two decades.[1] Among the many explanations is the effectiveness of the administrative and regulatory mechanisms which govern the collective bargaining regime.[2] The Canadian system is seen by some as suggesting avenues for the reform of American law (Weiler 1983; Gould 1993).

This prescription is based, in part, on the tantalizing notion that Canada and the U.S. form a distinct "North American" IR model, and thus parts of one IR system are relatively interchangeable with those of another. On closer inspection, however, this idea appears problematic, a theme developed in much greater detail in this chapter. In particular, this chapter describes the Canadian collective bargaining regime and demonstrates a significant rupture within the "North American" model. Hence U.S. labor law reform initiatives based on cherry picking from a foreign Canadian setting may prove to have little effect because of the lack of home-grown "fit" between the law and the underlying societal values.

A substantial body of IR literature exists on comparative Canadian-American trends and outcomes (e.g., Chaison and Rose 1991; Meltz 1985; Meltz and Verma 1996; Troy 1991a, 1991b; Riddell 1993). Perhaps the broadest and most empirically grounded treatment of comparative public policy directions and outcomes is contained in an anthology compiled by Card and Freeman (1993). After reviewing the evidence, the editors concluded that small differences in public policy approaches do matter in outcome measures. But two perplexing questions remain: What are the determinants of these small differences? and, Do multiple small differences cumulate into two significant, identifiable national patterns? If so, American policy analysts who use Canada as a "natural experiment" must develop greater sensitivity to the confounding effects of a host of independent and intervening variables.

Discussion is limited to the labor law regime, although the general approach could be extended to the broader corpus of employment law. The chapter is divided into three parts. The first part provides an overview of Canada's distinctive statutory and administrative treatment of labor unions and collective bargaining. The second part searches for the *origins* of Canada-U.S. differences. The differences, while quite real, are often tangible manifestations of the underlying constructs which determine the trajectory of Canadian public policy.

The next section reviews six explanatory variables that account for Canada's divergence. They are tightly interwoven and difficult to treat as mutually exclusive. For the sake of greater clarity, however, each ingredient is introduced into the analysis separately: (1) decentralization of labor jurisdictions; (2) Canadian national values; (3) a third-party voice for labor unions; (4) the role of William Lyon Mackenzie King; (5) historic contingencies and societal pressures at critical junctures during which labor statutes were conceived, a point examined through Canada's statutory treatment of company unions; and (6) Canadian pragmatism in brokering competing interests (French/English, U.S./British, federal/provincial), the practice of which spills over onto labor relations.

The theme of the chapter, that Canadian-American labor law regimes rest on different social and historical experiences, is further illustrated with three significant contemporary issues in which Canada had the potential to converge with U.S. approaches but chose instead to strengthen the environment for collective bargaining. First, the 1982 Canadian Charter of Rights and Freedoms offered substantial protection for individual rights, but Canada continued to facilitate a collective rights regime. Second, even when Canadian and American statutes are similarly worded, Canadians are more restrictive of employer activities, particularly during organizing campaigns. Third, Canada has unequivocally rejected the American right-to-work approach.

## The Broad Strokes: Similarities and Differences in Labor Law Regimes

Commenting on the period from the 1940s to the early 1970s (the years before there was any noteworthy divergence in Canadian-American union density rates), the eminent labor policy scholar H.D. Woods concluded an examination of Canadian labor policy with the statement that "contrary to much popular opinion, the Canadian and American systems differ to a marked degree" (1973:336). Canada amalgamated its own distinctive approach to labor regulation with a version of the American Wagner Act, and in "the interplay of these combined elements" is found the uniqueness of the Canadian system.

In both Canada and the U.S., 19th century labor unions were treated as criminal conspiracies in restraint of trade, and both countries subsequently enacted laws to loosen the legal obstacles to freedom of association and offer the right to take collective action. Though Canada was almost a decade later than the U.S. in forcing employers to recognize unions (1944 versus 1935), in other respects the Canadian state acted earlier and more aggressively in regulating labor relations.[3]

The first key legislative development was the Conciliation Act of 1900 which both founded the federal Department of Labor and established a scheme of voluntary government-assisted conciliation. The Railway Labor Disputes Act of 1903 was passed in the wake of the Canadian Pacific Railway strike. The 1903 act compelled the cessation of conflict until a three-person board of conciliation issued its report. The need to move away from the voluntary approach in a broader range of industries became apparent during a series of strikes in the coal mines, brought about by intolerable working conditions and employers' refusal to recognize the legitimacy of unions and of collective bargaining.

The government intervened dramatically and forcefully in extending its reach and powers when the Industrial Disputes Investigation Act was enacted in 1907 (the IDIA, also known as An Act to Aid in the Prevention and Settlement of Strikes and Lockouts in Mines and Industries Connected with Public Utilities), which codified the basic pillars of the distinctive Canadian aversion to industrial unrest. The three elements of the IDIA were (1) compulsory investigation of labor disputes by government-appointed neutrals, (2) the use of investigatory reports to inform public opinion and bring pressure on the parties to compromise, and (3) the absolute prohibition of work stoppages pending investigation.

What vision of labor relations drove early Canadian policymakers? While there are many subcomponents to the institutional perspective on "labor problems" which was gaining saliency in the U.S. at this time (outlined in Kaufman's chapter earlier), by contrast Canadian policymakers tended to see labor relations predominantly as a source of strife and a destabilizing influence on society. Because of the central importance of industries that produced fuel for residential and industrial consumption and the railways that kept the supply lines of the country running, industrial unrest was particularly intolerable because it posed a clear danger to citizens. The image of starving Saskatchewan farmers freezing to death in their heroic efforts to settle the inhospitable prairies was used to advance early labor legislation.

There is ample evidence that labor unrest was viewed as pathological and malevolent (King 1918; Ferns and Ostrey 1955:65). Little credence was given to the alternative explanations that conflict was a normal expression of the inherent defects of a capitalist system or of human behavior in superior/subordinate employment relations or of destructive competition in either product or labor markets (described in the Kaufman chapter). Canada's explicit regulation of the collective bargaining milieu was due to a fervent belief by the key policymaker of the day, William Lyon Mackenzie King, that government conciliation efforts would improve communication, strip away accumulated hostility, and cleanse the parties of their resentments to usher in a partnership of labor and capital, with labor on the job and capital advancing industry.

For eighteen years, the IDIA was amended and extended to other industries. When the IDIA Act was declared unconstitutional in 1925 because the federal government had exceeded its jurisdiction in that the IDIA legislation usurped provincial powers, the majority of provinces passed enabling legislation that moved the IDIA approach from the federal to provincial sphere. Subsequent provincial experimentation with the passage of labor laws, which began in the late 1930s, was halted as World War II allowed the federal government to assume greater powers in labor relations under the War Measures Act. After a flurry of ineffective Orders-in-Council aimed at stabilizing wartime labor unrest, the federal government finally yielded to political pressure in 1944 and merged the key elements of the American National Labor Relations (Wagner) Act (1935) model with the IDIA, to form PC 1003, the first comprehensive modern labor statute that guaranteed both statutory rights and their enforcement through an administrative apparatus.

The broad outlines of the American Wagner Act were adopted in PC 1003. Workers were given the right to choose the form of representation they desired, free of employer interference. Employers were made to understand their legal duty to recognize and negotiate with their employees' selected unions. The vote of the majority for union certification overrode the individual freedom to contract. There could be only one bargaining agent for a group of employees.

PC 1003 gave meaningful powers to Canadian labor boards—investigative, adjudicative, and conciliatory authority—which were critical in ensuring speedy resolution of complaints. In the U.S., the Wagner Act had specified a similar arrangement, but the 1947 Taft-Hartley amendments bifurcated the duties necessary to enforce labor statutes. This has created a major impediment to effective administration of statutes (Gould 1993; Weiler 1983), notwithstanding recent attempts to expedite the process (NLRB 1997).[4]

Sims, a former provincial labor board chair, draws attention to the effects of the different approaches to enforcement:

> The original National Labor Relations Board had full administrative and adjudicative control over the NLRA. Happily, in contrast, PC 1003 left Canadian boards with control of both aspects of board business. Both countries have administrative tribunals, but these tribunals are very different in structure and processes. As a result, Canadian boards, particularly those with strong bipartite representation, have been able to offer quicker and more "user friendly" processes than their U.S. federal counterpart. (Sims 1994:4)

PC 1003 was not the precise equivalent of the Wagner Act, either in its content or its underpinnings. In contrast to the sweeping vision underlying the Wagner Act (Keyserling 1960; Gross 1985; Kaufman 1996), Canada's legislation presents "a picture of a strategic but temporary compromise, authored by an uncertain political regime" (Russell 1994:148). (Some of the marked differences are laid out by Russell [1994:144-48], who argues that PC 1003 was less liberal and more parsimonious than the Wagner Act.) PC 1003 arose in the wake of a flurry of CIO-affiliated industrial organizing, which was seen by those in power as inimical to industrial peace and politically destabilizing (Abella 1973). As a result, unfair labor practices for both parties were specified. Great attention was paid to the precise mechanisms for certification of bona fide trade unions, those that could demonstrate concretely that they existed for the purpose of collective bargaining rather than to foment revolution. World War II saw a great wave of strikes, and Canadian unions made it clear that the price of greater harmony in Canada was protective legislation.

Canada's longstanding preoccupation with industrial peace became espe-cially salient during World War II. PC 1003 incorporated the IDIA's rules and procedures. Strikes were prevented until the expiry of collective agreements, and cooling-off periods and a sequence of steps before strikes could legally occur were specified. A prohibition was put on strikes and lockouts during the term of a collective agreement, with a related duty to include in collective agreements a means of resolving mid-contract disputes (generally the use of third-party arbitration) without any recourse to work stoppage.[5]

In contrast to the Wagner Act, which was situated within the Great Depression and efforts at national economic recovery (Kaufman 1996), mac-roeconomic stabilization was never a stated objective of the public policy drafters of PC 1003 (Thompson 1994:63; Woods 1983). PC 1003 was driven by political expediency and brokerage politics during World War II, although some of its antecedents are philosophical.

Though both countries have adopted certain common principles, signifi-cant differences were present at the outset or emerged over time. The 1947 Taft-Hartley amendments caused some of the rupture in common approaches (e.g., enabling right to work, altering the structure and duties of the labor board), and provincial legislation subsequent to PC 1003 further advanced the discrepancies (e.g., offering greater union security protections, guaranteeing rights to striking workers). A selection of noteworthy statutory differences is found in Table 1.[6] A number of other differences that arise from the broader powers of labor boards in Canada will be discussed later in this chapter. These differences include the rapidity with which unions are certified, the ability of boards to impose certifications, and the philosophy underlying the determina-tion of employer unfair labor practices during union organizing drives.

The Taft-Hartley route has never received support from Canadians, who instead concentrated on strengthening collective bargaining. Some in Canada lament that the Wagner Act was not ambitious enough and argue that more comprehensive labor legislation is required. As Adell puts it, "Sadly, Wagnerism has thus become a contributor to . . . the polarization of the workforce" and has denied legally enforceable forms of workplace representation to workers who do not fit the Fordist conception of the workplace. It has delimited the scope of issues and left a host of contemporary crises to be handled by the prolifera-tion of new statutes and regulatory bodies (e.g., human rights, employment, and pay equity). There is little doubt that the model has "added to the frag-mentation, polarization, and adversarial bent of employer-employee relations" (Adell 1994:124-25). Adams (1994) makes the argument that the enforcement mechanisms, the "administrative approach" inherent in the Wagner Act model, have had perverse consequences; in making nonunion industrial autocracy the

## TABLE 1
### Selection of Noteworthy Canadian-American Differences

| Differences | Canadian Approach | American Approach |
|---|---|---|
| Jurisdiction | Fragmented constitutional responsibility. Federal government responsible only for industries and activities specified in the British North America (BNA) Act of 1867. Provincial governments have complete authority to design labor codes. | Federal laws passed by Congress preempt state laws if the two conflict. Broad definition of interstate commerce tends to expand the scope of federal powers in labor relations. |
| Bargaining Issues | Since collective bargaining is the preferred instrument of labor market regulation for distributive issues, there is greater scope of appropriate issues for bargaining. (Adams 1995:8). Bargaining subjects are not classified using the American mandatory/permissive schema. | Bargaining subjects are classified as mandatory (wages, hours, and other crucial conditions of employment), permissive (bargained over only if union and employer mutually consent), and illegal (e.g., closed shop provisions). |
| Striking Workers | Canadian codes have significant protections for striking workers. Quebec and British Columbia prohibit replacement workers. All jurisdictions protect job rights of workers engaged in lawful strike activities. Striking workers are entitled to resume employment in preference to replacement workers. | If strike is due to employer unfair labor practices, striking workers are entitled to return to their jobs, even if replacement workers must be dismissed. Workers striking over economic issues can be re-placed, and employers need not reinstate strikers where they have been replaced. *Mackay* doctrine gives employers the right to pursue legitimate business interests. |
| Ban on Company Unions | Management domination and interference is prohibited, but nonunion forms of employee representation are not an unfair labor practice per se. Most labor statutes consider only trade unions as appropriate for bargaining and will not certify nonunion forms (Taras 1997a). | NLRA Section 2(5) defines labor organization broadly. Section 8(a)(2) prohibits management domination and interference in a labor organization. Together, these two sections ban most nonunion forms of employee representation. |
| Strikes and Lockouts | Canadian statutes prohibit strikes and lockouts while a collective agreement is in force. Either or both parties may request labor minister to appoint a mediator. Cooling-off period is required if mediation fails. Strike votes and notice periods are required. | Most collective agreements contain a mutual renunciation of work stoppages during the life of the agreement. The NLRA limits the use of economic sanctions by requiring notice periods. Strike votes are not required by law, (except in Taft-Hartley emergency disputes) but are left to union constitutions. |
| Union Security Provisions | No jurisdiction has outlawed union security provisions. Seven jurisdictions compel universal dues collection. | NLRA Section 14(b) enables states to pass right-to-work laws. Taft-Hartley made the closed shop illegal. |
| Board Appointments and Powers | Board members' appointments confirmed by lieutenant governor or other figurehead. Appointments process tends to be depoliticized. Board composition is bipartite or tripartite, with a government appointed chair and an equal number of labor and management representatives. Boards have full administrative and adjudicative responsibilities. Board powers over matters within statutes are broad. Privative clauses in statutes tend to limit court intervention. (Quebec has an Office of the Labor Commissioner-General and a Labor Court.) | NLRA Section 3(a) specifies five members appointed by the President with advice and consent of Senate. The general counsel of the board also appointed by President with advice and consent of Senate. Taft-Hartley created the office of the general counsel and gave it control of board's administration, field examiners, and all decisions to seek court enforcement. NLRB has an almost entirely adjudicative role. Appointment process is highly political (Aaron 1985; Cooke and Gautschi 1982), and Board budget is politicized (NLRB Report, 1977). |

legitimate default mode of industrial relations and forcing workers to be proactive in demanding collective representation, the complex rules and procedures act to discourage unionization. Nevertheless, even critics of the Wagner model acknowledge that "when assessed against the ideal, Canada falls far short, but from an American perspective where collective bargaining has diminished by an even greater degree, the Canadian version of Wagnerism is a relative success" (Adams 1994:3). As Thompson (1994) puts it, Canada's legislation has "achieved most of its objectives in those environments [blue collar] for which it was originally designed" (p. 64). There are many ideas in Canada for incrementally improving or even overhauling the Wagner model (Adams 1994; Adell 1994; Forrest 1994; Russell 1994; Sims 1994; Thompson 1994), but there is little momentum for dramatic change in the face of high union density figures.

Though Canada currently has 2.3 times the union density of the U.S., this was not always the case. A cursory examination of divergent trends in union density in Table 2 reveals that from 1920 until Canadian public servants were given the right to unionize in the mid-1960s, union density trend lines were quite similar. The average absolute difference in density percentages from 1920 to 1965 was only 2.5% (derived from subtracting Canadian from American density percentages and dividing the sum by the number of years). Though the passage of the Wagner Act gave union density figures a considerable boost in the U.S. (by 1939, 28.6% of U.S. workers were unionized, compared to only 17.3% of Canadians), Canadian density figures caught up to American density figures shortly after the passage of PC 1003. The U.S. Taft-Hartley (1947) and Landrum-Griffin (1959) amendments are not correlated to any appreciable divergence between the two countries, and by the early 1960s, the two union density figures were virtually identical. Canadian figures rose a few percentage points after the unionization of public servants and stabilized. The precipitous drop in American rates began in the mid-1970s and continued over the next decades. Although the latest revision of Canadian density figures in the far right column of Table 2 shows a drop from 1990 to 1996, the absolute number of workers who belong to unions has not changed appreciably. The decline in the recent trend line is due to structural changes in the economy and labor market (growth of the less unionized service sector and downsizing of the heavily unionized public service).

Beginning with Weiler (1983), scholars have examined explanations of American union decline and tested them against the Canadian experience in a "natural experiment" (Riddell 1993:116). The general consensus is that laws do matter, particularly when management is "on the offensive" (Lawler and West 1985; Lawler 1990). Weiler attributed declining American density to the lack of a labor law regime supportive of unionization and strongly urged that

TABLE 2

Union Membership as a Percentage of Nonagricultural Paid Workers
in the United States and Canada, 1920-96.

| Year | United States | Canada (1) | Canada (2) |
|------|---------------|------------|------------|
| 1920 | 17.6 | 16.0 | — |
| 1925 | 12.8 | 14.4 | — |
| 1930 | 12.7 | 13.9 | — |
| 1935 | 13.5 | 14.5 | — |
| 1940 | 22.5 | 16.3 | — |
| 1945 | 30.4 | 24.2 | — |
| 1950 | 31.7 | 28.4 | — |
| 1955 | 31.8 | 33.7 | — |
| 1960 | 28.6 | 32.3 | — |
| 1965 | 30.1 | 29.7 | — |
| 1970 | 29.6 | 33.6 | — |
| 1975 | 28.9 | 35.6 | — |
| 1980 | 23.2 | 37.1 | 35.7 |
| 1985 | 18.0 | 38.1 | 36.4 |
| 1990 | 16.1 | 36.2 | 34.5 |
| 1991 | 16.1 | 36.3 | 34.7 |
| 1992 | 15.8 | 37.4 | 35.7 |
| 1993 | 15.8 | 37.6 | 35.8 |
| 1994 | 15.5 | 37.5 | 35.6 |
| 1995 | 14.9 | — | 34.3 |
| 1996 | 14.5 | — | 33.9 |

Source: U.S.: pre-1985 from L. Troy and N. Sheflin, *Union Source Book: Membership, Finances, Structure, Directory* (West Orange, NJ: Industrial Relations Data and Information Services, 1985), and quoted in Riddell (1993:110); the years 1985 to 1995 from *Statistical Abstract of the United States 1996*, 116th ed., Table No. 681. 1996 from U.S. Bureau of Labor Statistics. Canada (1) from *Directory of Labor Organizations in Canada* (multiple years including 1994/95). 1950 number is unavailable and 1951 number is substituted in table above. Canada (2) from *Directory of Labor Organizations in Canada 1996*.

American law adopt some of the features of the Canadian approach. Meltz (1986:143) found little impact on density of variations in the distribution of employment by industry and argued that differences in legislation and in the presence of labor-oriented political parties in Canada both have more discernable effects. Adams (1989) reviewed the importance of statutory differences and attributed their emergence to the influence of the New Democratic Party. Riddell's (1993) analysis explored a variety of alterative explanations for the unionization differential, including structural changes in the economy and labor force, public versus private sector coverage, public opinion, and the costs of unionization to employers. After eliminating these explanations, he concluded that "on the whole these findings support the hypothesis that much of the Canada-U.S. unionization gap can be attributed to intercountry differences in the legal regime pertaining to unions and collective bargaining and to differences in overt management opposition to unions (itself possibly a consequence of differences in collective bargaining laws and their administration)" (p. 143). Riddell's article was part of the *Small Differences That Matter* anthology comparing labor market and income maintenance policies in Canada and the U.S. The editors Card and Freeman concluded that even seemingly small differences "in safety-net systems, labor market regulation, and labor market conditions" led to appreciable differences in outcome measures.

My concern with explanations that rest on public policy frameworks is that they tend to treat public policy as an exogenous force. As Riddell (1993) properly asks, "Do the laws in each country not simply reflect the underlying values held by the citizens of the respective societies? Canada-U.S. differences in the legal framework governing collective bargaining and in the extent of union organization may thus be jointly endogenous outcomes of fundamental value differences between the two societies" (p. 138). The next section of this chapter attempts to situate Canada's regulatory regime within its philosophical, social, and political environment. By identifying six forces that interact to produce public policy, I will demonstrate that the differences in legal regimes arise from the pressures that caused them to come into being and from the spirit with which they are enforced and adjudicated.

## Six Explanatory Variables

*How a 19th Century Constitution Inadvertently Set the Stage for Decentralization, Experimentation, and Diffusion*

Canada's inadvertent decentralization of labor law is a fact on the ground which has greatly affected the subsequent development of Canadian experimentation and regulation. To put the Canadian case in a nutshell, originally Canada was supposed to have a strong, central federal government and weaker provincial governments. The allocation of jurisdictional powers between the federal and provincial governments in the British North American Act (BNA Act) of 1867 gave the central government exclusive jurisdiction over the important matters of that century, including military, banking, communications, and interprovincial transport systems. Provinces were dealt the lesser matters of the health and education of their citizenry and control over natural resources. As Canada's economy developed, the scope of the provinces evolved into the significant wielding of power over labor matters. A series of important decisions by the Judicial Committee of the British Privy Council (which until 1949 had ultimate authority in determining the direction of the then-colonial Canada), of which the most critical was the 1925 *Toronto Electric Power Commissioners v. Snider et al.*, caused a rapid and unanticipated devolution of federal power.[7]

Today there exist eleven separate jurisdictions in Canada: the federal government and ten provinces. Each has complete authority over all aspects of labor codes and employment standards, minimum wage legislation, human rights laws, and so on.[8] The federal jurisdiction does not override provincial legislation in any aspect of employment relations which is under the exclusive jurisdiction of the provinces. Thus, except in exceptional circumstances, national standards cannot take precedence over provincial policies (Hogg, 1985:461-66).

As a result, only 10% of the work force (employed in industries specifically mentioned in the BNA Act as falling within federal jurisdiction) is covered by federal labor laws, while the remainder of working Canadians are protected by the regulatory regime of the province in which they are employed. On the negative side, there is an increased burden on larger employers and unions to manage the complexity entailed by 11 jurisdictions. As Andrew Sims has put it, "Provincialization has led to too much law and too much inconsequential diversity. This adds to the cost of doing business . . . and has tended to disenfranchise labor relations practitioners in favor of lawyers" (Sims 1994:6). On the positive side, this decentralization has led to a rich tradition of experimentation and the cross-fertilization of ideas.

Provincial legislation has tended to move labor regulation in the direction of guaranteeing greater influence to employees. For example, in 1964 Quebec was the first government in North America to grant the right to strike to all public employees except police and firefighters. In 1977 Quebec was first in the world to amend its labor code to provide a comprehensive ban on the use of replacement workers during a work stoppage (Boivin and Déom 1995). Quebec is also unique in North America in having a decree system which since 1934 has allowed the minister of labor the power to extend collective agreements to nonunionized segments of an industry (Berniar 1993).

One of the more interesting contemporary examples of the diffusion of innovation is the Artists and Producers Professional Relations Tribunal. This experiment, which originated in Quebec, has moved to the federal sphere. It offers statutory protection for an emerging employment model involving a flexible, contract, and mobile work force with specialized skills. The notion that employment is long term, which is a view entrenched in current labor laws and their emphasis on settling a binding collective agreement, gives way in this experiment to a different form of employment relationship. In this context, Saskatchewan has provided for greater protection of part-time workers and British Columbia has examined similar legislation. The future dissemination of these initiatives throughout the jurisdictions is worth watching.

It is very difficult to muster national support in a country as large, diverse, and fragmented as Canada, with defined blocks of the country traditionally voting for different parties. Not only was the French/English situation problematic politically, but regionalism in general plagued the country and limited the capacity of any particular governing federal party to build nationwide alliances. Had the federal government controlled most employment relations matters, as is the case in the U.S., likely the Canadian regulatory movement might have stalled in ways comparable to that of our neighbors. Regional contentiousness is evident in the 1995 Federal Task Force to review changes in the Canada Labor Code (Sims 1995), in which the most difficult issue to broker was Quebec's unions' demands for the same "anti-scab" legislation that they are accustomed to in that province. The Clinton administration's recent impasse in facilitating change to national health care drives this point home. In Canada the idea of universal health care protection was originally implemented in Saskatchewan, and once it was judged as successful, it quickly spread.

The capacity to implement a provincial "pilot project" which covers the majority of workers in that province has made a strong impact on the advancement of labor innovation. Indeed, there is evidence of innovation and subsequent diffusion in such areas as protections for striking workers (which have spread broadly), legislation banning the use of replacement workers during strikes and lockouts (in Quebec, British Columbia, and until 1995, Ontario), first contract arbitration (in British Columbia and now being considered in the federal jurisdiction), labor board-directed certifications after employer unfair labor practices (in British Columbia and Ontario), union security clause protections (in seven jurisdictions), and statute-driven expedited certifications (Nova Scotia, Newfoundland, and Ontario). There are also pockets of practices which did not spread, including Ontario's pay equity legislation, introduced by the NDP government and defanged by the Conservatives and Quebec's decree system.

### Canadians Are Not Merely "Decaffeinated" Americans: The Canadian Weltanschauung

In the previous section the importance of decentralization was described. The question remains, though, Why did Canadian jurisdictions innovate in the direction of entrenching collective bargaining? (By contrast, decentralization in the U.S. has enabled close to half the states to pass right-to-work laws.) The general argument here is not that Canadians have watered down American values or as some have argued are "decaffeinated" Americans but rather that Canadian values derive from a different wellspring altogether. The homogenization of North American culture (with the exception of Quebec) through exposure to popular media makes it increasingly difficult to put one's finger on the differences precisely. A number of important works have been written on Canadian-American differences, including works by Lipset (e.g., 1986a, 1986b, 1989) and earlier by Horowitz (1968:Ch. 1).

One of the more prominent propositions explaining the development of national values is Hartz's (1964) fragmentation thesis, which traces the effects of immigrant groups striving to embody and entrench the values they carried with them at their point of emigration from the old country. At vital points in Canadian evolution, influential groups of citizens operated as a "feudal fragment" trying to preserve a remnant of their British deference to hierarchy, to authority, together with an overlay of respect for "red Toryism" (that is, economic conservatism with simultaneously held principles of collective rights and state intervention in providing comprehensive social welfare policies). There was no revolutionary overthrow of British influences. Over time, Canadians were encouraged to consider themselves part of a "mosaic" of diverse ethnic groupings, and the notion of hyphenated Canadianism was accepted—French-Canadian, Italian-Canadian, Jewish-Canadian, and so on. By contrast, in the U.S., the guiding principle of the "melting pot" required that new citizens drop their old allegiances and assimilate quickly into the American mainstream. As well, the settlement of the Canadian hinterland proceeded in a more orderly, state-directed fashion than was the case in the American west, and major institutions like the railways, banks, and national police (RCMP, formerly the NWMP) directed Canadian settlement (Innis 1930). It is commonly believed that Canadians are more deferential to authority, more accepting of collective rights, and more willing to forego individual freedoms where they clash with social norms (e.g., the Canadian acceptance of gun control, of enforced seat belt laws, of higher income tax rates than the U.S., and of universal access to medical care). Lipset labels Canada as "leftist collectivist," which is probably an overstatement, but it does capture the historic Canadian tendency toward corporatism, which can be juxtaposed to the American national values of egalitarianism and individualism.[9]

Another critical element in the Canadian blend of environmental factors setting the stage for labor-management interaction is the behavior of employers. There is considerable evidence of antiunion activity within the U.S. and a growing concern that more and more American employers are willing to mount a scorched earth campaign rather than accept a unionized work force

(Weiler 1990a:302). A burgeoning antiunion consultancy industry (Kaufman and Stephan 1995) is becoming brazen enough to openly tout union-defeating success rates in home pages on the World Wide Web. Opposition to unions is widespread and increasingly is accepted behavior (Kochan, Katz, and McKersie 1986; Lawler 1990). There are a variety of often cited reasons for this phenomenon (detailed in Strauss 1995).

Though there exist a few noteworthy cases of Canadian firms committing unfair labor practices rather than acquiesce to union certifications, by and large Canadian employers accept the basic premises of collective bargaining, including the legitimacy of unions as agents of the common aspirations of employees (Thompson 1995). The balance of power, however, clearly has shifted toward management in Canada, just as it has in many other nations.[10]

This is evident even in the Canadian public sector as governments are increasingly willing and likely to unilaterally impose cutbacks on their employees and bypass the collective bargaining procedure altogether, spurred on by deficit-reduction political mandates (Panitch and Swartz 1993). In both public and private sector union-management relations, there is a considerable increase in hard bargaining as annual average wage increases are approaching zero and a growing experimentation with mutual gains techniques. Despite similar changes in economic environments throughout the 1980s, Canadian private sector manufacturing unions fared significantly better in their wage outcomes than did their American counterparts (e.g., Widenor 1995), a finding variously interpreted as due to the greater militancy of Canadian unions, their larger density (perhaps a proxy measure for bargaining power), as well as the cost advantages to multinational corporations of a low Canadian dollar translated into more generous wage settlements. What we do not see, however, is much evidence of American-style union avoidance, nor is there a strong consulting industry to aid management in achieving its desires. The widely held view is that the Canadian regulatory system imposes constraints on the exercise of managerial choice which mitigate the more virulent antiunion tactics found in the U.S. (Weiler 1983; Chaison and Rose 1991a; Adams 1989).

Employers, on the whole, are simply more constrained in Canada because of both the social milieu and the regulatory regime. Interestingly, employers are as likely to express antiunion sentiments in Canada as in the U.S. Three quantitative studies support this claim. The first study by Saporta and Lincoln (1995) used the "class consciousness and class formation" data set of U.S. attitudes in 1980 and Canadian attitudes in 1982. The authors created a subset of managerial employees and found no statistically significant differences between Canadian and American managers for any of the industrial relations survey questions analyzed (p. 558). The second is a 1992 survey of 64 managers in 38 Canadian and American-owned firms operating in the Canadian petroleum industry, in which Taras (1994) asked, "To what extent is the maintenance of a union-free environment in all or some of your operations a priority in your company?" Sixty percent of respondents scored their company as either a 4 or 5, on a five-point scale with 5 representing "top priority." There were no significant differences based on company ownership, and many prominent Canadian firms held vigorously union-free preferences. American-owned firms, however, were significantly more likely to have lower levels of union penetration than were Canadian or European-owned firms and were much more likely to practice union substitution strategies (such as formal nonunion employee representation plans), pay wage premiums to nonunion employees over the union rate, and employ hard bargaining with unions in certified locations (Taras 1994:299, Table 8-1, p. 351). In the third study of a cross-section of 106 Canadian firms from 1990-94, Thompson concluded that "the hard-line approach of American employers toward their unions and employees has little acceptance in Canada, although most Canadian employers would prefer not to have a union" (1995:126). The similarities in attitude among firms was strong, as evinced by his Tables 5.3 and 5.4 (1995:113-14). Canadian firms are resigned to the reality of working within unionized structures and they reluctantly accept the legitimacy of collective bargaining.

The three studies in tandem suggest that it is not increased U.S. managerial animus toward unions per se which is driving American union decline, since Canadian unions are relatively healthy despite virtually identical Canadian antiunion managerial sentiments. Canadian managers' preferences are less likely to be enacted into practice than are American. With both a strong political watchdog in the NDP since pre-WWII days and a labor law regime which has certain weapons to deter pathological employers (including rapid reinstatements of wrongly terminated employees and in some jurisdictions board-directed certifications and first contract arbitrations), there is little maneuverability for the Canadian employer who might prefer in other circumstances to remain nonunion. While the desire to avoid unions might continue to exist in Canada, what is missing is the *tradition* of union avoidance. Having failed to sink a strong tap root, an antiunion stance lacks a sustaining structure.

What of Canadian workers? Again, the surface similarities between Canadian and American workers are more noteworthy than are the differences. There is little disagreement that Canadian and American workers currently hold similar views when asked identical questions (Troy 1991a:18-19; Freeman and Rogers 1995; Gallup Reports, various years; Riddell 1993).[11]

Saporta and Lincoln (1995) demonstrate that Canadian and American workers hold similar attitudes toward specific industrial relations issues, albeit with Canadian workers appearing "marginally more in the middle than their U.S. counterparts" (Saporta and Lincoln 1995:563).[12] Regional differences in subsamples appear more sizable than binational differences.

After comparing Gallup polls from 1949 to 1985, Riddell (1993:139-41) concluded that "Canadians and Americans evidently have very similar attitudes toward unions . . . thus there is no empirical support for the view that the Canada-U.S. unionization differential can be attributed to fundamental differences in social attitudes toward unions and collective bargaining" (pp. 140-41).

If there are few Canadian-American differences in measurable surface attitudes, to what do we attribute the different industrial relations outcomes? There are two possibilities here. First is that attitudes genuinely converge but that IR outcomes diverge as a result of different environmental factors (e.g, the degree of competitive pressures on businesses, differences in labor regulations, etc.). Alternatively, these attitude surveys do not present a valid portrait of the two nations. Survey questions of managers and of workers do not probe deeply into the psyches of the respective citizenries and are not likely to capture the underlying clusters of values which lead to action or inaction, aggressiveness or passivity, and political support or opposition to public policy initiatives. At best, these survey questions tap only the most superficial sentiments about unions. The extant literature does not permit resolution of these competing explanations. Moreover, I am not proposing that there is one simple explanation for intercountry divergence. National cultures are but one of six explanatory variables. I offer evidence in three illustrative cases at the end of this chapter of the actual *behavior* of the Canadian system when faced with challenges.

## The Importance of a Multiparty Democracy

The collectivist aspirations of a sizeable segment of Canadians found its expression in a viable political party, the New Democratic Party (formerly called the Cooperative Commonwealth Federation, or CCF). In Quebec, where the NDP did not make inroads, unions aligned themselves with other parties. The movement of labor into the political arena had enormous ramifications for the regulation of employment relations. Until the founding of the CCF, mainstream Canadian unions tended to adopt American "business unionism." In the early 1940s, however, an alliance was formed between the new CCF party and the union movement. Significant electoral support for the CCF, and later the NDP, caused governments of the day to pay homage to the third party's strongly articulated and disciplined call for labor law reform and the guarantee of a statutory regime to entrench collective bargaining.

It can be argued that though unions had been strenuously lobbying over some years for a Wagner-like legal document, PC 1003 was enacted in the 1940s only when Prime Minister Mackenzie King perceived a serious election campaign threat to his Liberal party. Public opinion poll results showed a sharp rise in CCF support (Pickersgill 1960:571). Early in 1944 Gallup asked both Americans and Canadians: "Most people believe the government should not be controlled by any one group. However, if you had to choose, which would you prefer to have control of the government—big business or labor unions?" The response was,

|  | United States | Canada |
| --- | --- | --- |
| Big Business | 63% | 35% |
| Labor Unions | 37% | 65% |

At the time this poll was taken, the CCF party was campaigning strenuously for labor reform and obviously managed to persuade substantial numbers of voters that labor unions were ill-served by the prevailing regime. There is evidence from Mackenzie King's diaries that this poll in particular, and fear of electoral defeat generally, were instrumental in driving the federal government to draft comprehensive legislation. Although Mackenzie King had been lobbied unrelentingly for a Wagner Act type of labor legislation by the organized labor movement over the World War II years, and despite his concerns that a strike wave was endangering wartime production, he was unprepared to act in the absence of a genuine threat to his tenure in office. This tendency toward delay and obfuscation was a marked characteristic of his decision making as prime minister. After four decades of political seasoning, he was far too pragmatic a politician to take any concrete steps without the convergence of considerable pressure from a variety of sources.

The composition of electoral sentiments such as those in the 1944 Gallup poll described earlier underscore the realistic fear held by both provincial and federal governments across Canada that failure to offer basic protections for labor organizing and bargaining to appease labor supporters would drive voters into the arms of the rival CCF/NDP. Peter Bruce (1989) traces the adoption of strong legislative measures to promote collective rights in employment directly to the influence of the NDP, either as the provincial governing party spearheading labor law reform in a number of provinces (including British Columbia, Saskatchewan, Manitoba, and Ontario) or as a strong and vociferous opposition and a serious electoral threat. Although the NDP has never formed a government at the federal level, it is a significant player at the provincial level, and the latter covers 90% of Canadian employment.

312     EMPLOYMENT REGULATION

*William Lyon Mackenzie King: Architect of Labor Regulation*

While labor law in the U.S. was swayed at a critical decade by the distinctive agenda and forceful personality of Senator Robert Wagner, the linkage between a single person and the statutory regime in Canada is even tighter. For over four decades, William Lyon Mackenzie King's imprimatur can be found in virtually all collective bargaining laws from their infancy at the turn of the century to their entrenchment in the mid-1940s.

A brief biography is in order. Mackenzie King's education in industrial relations was both broad and deep. As a university student attending Universities of Toronto, Chicago, and then Harvard, he was exposed to a superb assembly of scholars, and he read prodigiously. In Chicago he worked at Hull House, the famous settlement center and was greatly influenced by his professor, Thorstein Veblen. For a brief period, Mackenzie King flirted with socialism and believed himself an ardent socialist (an enthusiasm that waned rapidly when he traveled to England in 1899 and attended Fabian socialist gatherings). In 1897 he left Chicago to begin a doctorate at Harvard in economics and focused his research on trade unions. In the brief interregnum between universities, Mackenzie King wrote a series of newspaper articles based on his eyewitness empirical investigations exposing the appalling conditions in the needle trade sweat shops. These articles, in tandem with his educational qualifications, launched his brilliant parliamentary career.

Mackenzie King entered the newly formed Ministry of Labor as its resident expert in 1900 and was called upon to investigate and mediate some of Canada's most difficult labor disputes. He was the principal architect of early federal government legislation, including the 1907 IDIA. In 1914 he was called upon by the Rockefeller interests to solve a vicious labor dispute in the coal mines of Colorado, which resulted in King's invention of the joint industrial council plan (Gitelman 1987). This plan bypassed the need for union recognition while establishing a formal mechanism for employee representation. He returned to Canada as leader of the Liberal Party and eventually enjoyed remarkable longevity, 22 years, in office as prime minister.

There is little doubt that he was a peerlessly shrewd politician and that his pursuit of electoral success led him to moderate (even to the point of sacrificing) his early zeal for social reform:

> Once in office, King discovered that society was indeed dominated by carnivorous beasts who would not bow to the simple application of reason and that, aside from the political realities, the attempt to reform society had to be carried out against the intense and unwavering opposition of established interests and their agents. This was

not the type of activity that he had any stomach for because it produced, in the short run, more apparent social discord and national division than the lack of reform might manifest in the long. (Bercuson in King 1918: xxiii)

Despite his early enthusiasm for government intervention in labor relations, by the time he became prime minister, only the application of sustained political pressure was likely to activate his support for legislation.

Mackenzie King's watchword was conciliation, whether voluntary or by government fiat. Through the magic of the conciliation process, he believed that the veils of self-interest would fall and that the parties would come to appreciate the "public interest." As his biographers put it,

> he appreciated both the actual power of the rich and the potential power of the poor. The power of the rich he believed to be an agency of beneficence; the potential power of the poor to be an agency of chaos. He believed, however, that an equilibrium between the two might be maintained; and he worked to create faith in the powers of "conciliation." (Ferns and Ostrey 1955:328)

What he knew of economic history from his academic training, confirmed by what he observed directly as he ventured into the heart of labor disputes, was that "the early stages of industrialization have been characterized by acute social tension" (Ferns and Ostrey 1955:65). While his legacy is muddied by his self-aggrandizing propaganda and impenetrably dense and moralistic recounting of his position (e.g., King 1918; Craven 1980), his interventions consistently compelled state intervention to restore industrial peace. This motive was well understood. The prime minister of the day, Sir Wilfrid Laurier, recounted that the IDIA "was not passed with the object of conciliating the labor vote. It was passed with the sole object of preventing the untold misery and mischief wrought by strikes" (quoted in Ferns and Ostrey 1955:72).

Mackenzie King is a perplexing figure in labor relations. On the one hand, he sought to impose order from chaos and fervently yearned for a humane society in which "Reason" and "Truth" would prevail (King 1918). To create greater discipline, King drafted laws which emphasized third-party expertise (the role of government as "impartial umpire" [Craven 1980]) and prohibited work stoppage. The failure of employers to ameliorate abusive treatment of their workers would be a victory for "Evil," just as self-serving and narrow union demands would divert humanity toward disorder. If "Reason" won the day, he envisioned benevolent paternalism. He was an ardent proponent of employee representation systems, whether union or nonunion, and believed that union supporters should be protected from unjust dismissal simply for expressing their prounion stance. He did not characterize unions as monopolist, as rent-extractors, or even as purveyors of collective goods. Rather, unions were one of many parties in an ongoing relationship with each other, the purpose of which was to advance civilization. On the other hand, he was suspicious of unions and greatly disagreed with union recognition strikes. He utterly failed to appreciate the intensity of employers' distaste for employees' legitimate selection of a union as bargaining agent, and thus for forty years he refused to legislate compulsory recognition. Despite Mackenzie King's rhetoric,

> there is no evidence that Mackenzie King ever worked to strengthen the legal and political foundations of union recognition or to limit the effects of the open shop system on the power to bargain. He consistently advocated legislation directed to strengthening the state's power to investigate labor disputes, to compel arbitration and conciliation, and by this device to blunt the ultimate weapon possessed by the wage-earners, i.e., their power to withhold their labor. (Ferns and Ostrey 1955:65)

A stream of sentiment has run through the development of Canadian labor laws that has consistently stressed reason over passion and humanism rather than macroeconomic planning. There was a strong moral tone in King's energies:

> For Industry and Nationality alike, the last word lies in the supremacy of Humanity. . . . The national or industrial economy based on a lesser vision, in the final analysis, is anti-social, and lacks the essentials of indefinite expansion and durability. The failure to look beyond the State, and beyond Industry as a revenue-producing process, has brought chaos instead of order. . . . The sacredness of human personality is more important than all other considerations. (King 1918:28)

More than sixty years later, the same sentiments were less floridly expressed by Paul Weiler in his book on Canadian labor policy: "The economic function is the beginning, not the end, of the case for collective bargaining. . . . The true function of economic bargaining consists in its *civilizing* impact upon the working life and environment of employees" (Weiler 1980:29).

A final contrast involving the role of individuals in contributing to government regulation of labor relations must be made here. Previously, I began this section by comparing Mackenzie King to Robert Wagner in terms of influencing particular pieces of legislation. However, Mackenzie King was the driving intellectual architect of the underlying approach to labor regulation as well as to the regulation itself. For the former role, the more appropriate foil is the American John R. Commons, whose vision made a pivotal contribution to U.S. labor regulation (described in the Kaufman chapter in this volume). Commons and the Wisconsin school generally stressed that labor and management must fashion their own accords in order to have a commitment to honoring them and that third-party intervention in labor disputes was to be avoided (Commons and Andrews 1920). At the heart of the American regulatory approach was voluntarism. Mackenzie King favored government intervention, because he saw it was both feasible and felt it to be the morally correct position. He believed first that the state realistically could find and employ appropriate third-party expertise (and here he viewed his own early career as the exemplar) and take on the role he described as "impartial umpire" (Craven 1980), and second, that the state was duty-bound to protect the interests of citizens against the discord created by irrationality between labor and management.

### Historical Contingencies and Societal Pressures: The "Company Union" Issue

There are many instances in the histories of the two countries where significant differences emerged that were to have an impact on labor relations. While the Wagner Act was strongly influenced by the Depression, PC 1003 bore the mark of World War II. Canada's traditional allegiance to Great Britain led to Canada entering the war more than two years before the December 7, 1941, Pearl Harbor attack forced an American declaration of war. When Canada's Parliament opened its session in January 1939, Prime Minister Mackenzie King quoted with approval former Prime Minister Sir Wilfrid Laurier's statement that "when Britain is at war, Canada is at war and liable to attack" (Pickersgill 1960:12). Britain declared war on September 3, 1939, and Canada made its commitment official exactly one week later with the united support of the Canadian Parliament. The war effort was the consuming preoccupation of Canadians in the five years leading up to the passage of PC 1003, and a focus on all-out production in critical industries made the creation of mechanisms for labor-management cooperation an urgent matter.

In this section, I discuss the impact of historical contingencies in the context of the little-known topic of Canada's treatment of nonunion representation because it is most salient in the wake of the Dunlop Commission investigation and the TEAM Act proponents' recent attempt to amend Section 8(a)(2) of the NLRA. The reasons Canada and the U.S. diverged on the company union issue are illustrative of the different political and economic contexts during the passage of labor acts. In both countries, restrictions against management domination have outlawed true company "sham" unions. The

Wagner Act Section 8(a)(2) in tandem with Section 2(5) has this effect (Jenero and Lyons 1992; Finkin 1994). In Canada every jurisdiction has enacted legislation similar to Section 8(a)(2), but formal nonunion forms of employee representation continue to be lawful provided they are not deliberately designed to thwart union organizing. (For a fuller discussion of this issue, see Taras 1997a, 1997b.) They continue to exist today, alongside a viable union presence, and without being imperiled by collective bargaining statutes. The company union movement was at least as significant in Canada as it was in the U.S. in the years prior to the passage of the Wagner Act (estimates quoted in Taras 1997b). Deliberate but subtle adjustments to the Wagner model allowed nonunion employee representation to persist in Canada.

There are two major explanations for this intercountry difference: first is the influence of Mackenzie King (which has been described broadly in the previous section), and second is the institutional setting for the passage of labor laws. The decade that intervened between the Wagner Act and Canada's federal attempt at comparable legislation involved a basic realignment of economic and political forces. These years were characterized by the emergence of union organizing along industrial (CIO-affiliated) lines, which threatened business and political interests. Preoccupation with Canadian participation in World War II meant a fierce emphasis on uninterrupted productivity (MacDowell 1978). The constellation of forces which had an impact on the drafting of Canadian laws were different than the pressure points which underpinned the Wagner Act (Keyserling 1960; Kaufman 1996, 1997) and the Taft-Hartley amendments (Gross 1985).

Despite its sensitivity to local concerns and positive record of accomplishment in improving personal relations, Senator Wagner identified as its major flaw the company union movement's inability to take wages out of competition: "The company union . . . has failed dismally to standardize or improve wage levels, for the wage question is a general one whose sweep embraces whole industries, or States, or even the Nation. Without wider areas of cooperation among employees there can be no protection against the nibbling tactics of the unfair employer who is willing to degrade standards by serving for a pittance (NLRB 1985:22-26, quoted in Kaufman 1996). Wagner was a passionate enemy of company unions.

In contrast to the American disavowal of company unions, Canada was inclined to favor state intervention which tended to sideline the union movement (MacDowell 1978; Rudin 1972). When called upon to intervene in a series of contentious labor struggles during the course of World War II, the federal government consistently recommended substituting formal nonunion forums in place of trade unions to end recognition strikes. The prime minister was not merely a figurehead in this debate but had a strong vested stake in perpetuating his 1914 invention of the joint industrial council for the Rockefeller interests (Gitelman 1987). There was no comparable figure to Senator Wagner to sound the call against company unions in Canada; quite the reverse was true. Not only did Mackenzie King advocate nonunion forums to break recognition strikes in the private sector, but in his own role as employer of the civil service, he built the nonunion National Joint Council plan rather than allow government employees to unionize.

During World War II, the need for all-out production actually made elements of company unionism quite attractive. Cooperation between workers and managers was much desired and was particularly attractive by contrast to the contentious disputes occurring in unionizing industries. Proponents of company unions touted their virtues to policy makers, and in the end the employer arguments proved persuasive. The National War Labor Board inquiry of 1943 criticized the "new type of labor leader" who irresponsibly preferred to stoke his ambition by attempting "to organize quickly by stirring up labor unrest." Even the mainstream Canadian union movement (the TLC) was more preoccupied by the issue of how to achieve statutory protection for "responsible" unions rather than a comprehensive ban against company unions. Instead of obliterating company unions' existence, the TLC argued that "only bona fide trade unions or genuine employees' organizations should be accorded benefits under any proposed collective bargaining legislation. We are firm in our view that the counterfeit species of so-called employee-organization, usually known as the 'company union' . . . should be denied any standing under a collective bargaining act" (NWLB 1943:69). The concept of union responsibility guided the future statutory provisions that required unions to demonstrate their financial accountability, their legal status, and their purpose of bargaining with employers to effect agreement rather than foment revolution. It was clear that the emphasis in Canada's legislation was to be on certification procedures of narrowly defined trade unions. The Wagner Act prohibition on company unions was diluted, although certification of trade unions (narrowly defined) which were influenced or dominated by management was forbidden.

Over the years, the NLRA Section 8(a)(2) prohibition has risen to prominence in policy-making circles. There is a great debate over its continued relevance, and the lack of employee voice mechanisms in the growing nonunion sector has prompted a group of prominent American companies to join forces in lobbying for legislative change through the TEAM Act proposal. There is no such debate in Canada, as there are no legislated barriers to nonunion representation. Thus Canadians by and large view nonunion employee representation as a nonissue.

*Brokering Competing Interests: Seeking a Balance*

Canadians have a long history of searching for that elusive middle ground that would hold together the disparate elements of Canadian society in a loose, decentralized alliance within a fragile federal system (Taylor 1993). In fact, brokerage theory has dominated Canadian political science. Its premise is that "national political parties must encompass all the essential interests in the country if both a majority is to be secured and minority rights guaranteed. . . . Parties, it is believed, are supposed to act as agents of consensus and as aggregators of interests rather than as instruments of choice" (Smith 1984: 355). Within its borders, Canada's struggle to reconcile English and French elements—"two nations warring within the bosom of a single state"—is well known. Internationally, Canada spent a good deal of its history on an uncomfortable perch, attempting to be the "honest broker" between Great Britain and the U.S. Great pride was taken in United Nations peacekeeping, in which Canadians would insert themselves between two warring factions in order to suspend conflict.

In the labor relations setting, Roy Adams (1989) concludes, "Pragmatism, rather than deeply held conviction, was the wellspring of Canadian policy" (p. 57), but that pragmatism was ideologically driven by the desire to find a compromise position for all combatants. *Seeking a Balance* is the title of the 1995 Sims Task Force to investigate reform to Canada's federal Labor Code sections pertaining to collective bargaining. It is an apt title, for it captures Canada's attempts throughout the drafting of all labor codes and regulations to equalize the power of unions and employers and avoid tipping the balance too far in any single direction.

## Three Contemporary Examples

This section of the chapter is meant to illustrate how the six explanatory variables interact to produce tangible intercountry differences in the labor regulation arena. Not all six variables are salient in any single illustrative case. The three cases were chosen because they are contemporary, concrete, and demonstrate how two or more of the six variables interact to produce noteworthy Canadian-American differences in labor regulation.

*Individualism and Collectivism: How the Charter of Rights and Freedoms Is Applied*

Illustrative of Canadian acceptance for the need to achieve a workable political compromise is the manner in which the modern Canadian constitution was crafted. After more than 100 years with a constitutional document which did much to affect jurisdictional divisions but was silent on individual rights, Canada created a rights-based constitution in 1982 called the Canadian Charter of Rights and Freedoms. The charter guaranteed certain fundamental freedoms including freedom of association, freedom of thought, belief, opinion, and expression, and equality before and under the law. Advocates of the Charter praised its recognition of the multifaceted complexion of Canadian society, while detractors feared "Americanization," whereby a powerful judiciary would challenge parliamentary enactments (Smiley 1983).

To operationalize the American Bill of Rights, the American judiciary was left to interpret the scope of its unqualified individual rights. By contrast, the Charter offered the courts a specific test to help in its deliberations. Section 1 of the Charter states that the fundamental rights are subject to "such reasonable limits prescribed by law as can be demonstrably justified in a free and democratic society." This is a tacit presumption that a fettering of individual rights is necessary for society and that in a democracy there must be an obligation to subordinate some rights for the good of the majority. The onus rests with those who seek to limit fundamental rights to prove demonstrable justification.

The willingness of Canada's Supreme Court to hear Charter cases challenging the existing statutory collective bargaining framework caused consternation that union activities were unprotected from Court incursions. (A review of cases is in Swinton 1995.) The question which struck real fear within the union movement was whether the Supreme Court might apply the Charter so as to erode existing union rights (Carter 1987; Carter and McIntosh 1991).[13]

The landmark Charter case came in 1991 and it involved the constitutionality of a union security arrangement found in a collective agreement. Under this arrangement and in accordance with the labor laws of the majority of Canadian jurisdictions, all members of the bargaining unit would pay union dues regardless of whether they personally chose to be members of the union. In *Lavigne v. Ontario Public Service Employees Union* (1991), 81 D.L.R. (4th) 545 (S.C.C.), the central issue was whether the use of union dues for the union's political activities was inconsistent with the Charter's guarantees of freedom of association and freedom of expression. If the union dues arrangement was found to be inconsistent with Charter rights, the onus was on the union to demonstrate that the arrangement could be a "reasonable limit" that could be "demonstrably justified" as beneficial to Canadian society.

In the U.S., the comparable case might be *Abood v. Detroit Board of Education* (1977), 431 U.S. 209 (U.S.S.C.), in which the agency shop permitted by Michigan legislation was held by the Supreme Court to violate Abood's First

Amendment rights to freedom of speech and freedom of belief. The Supreme Court reasoned that unions are by their nature political organizations and, therefore compulsory financial support of them violates an individual's rights. Had the Canadian Supreme Court taken the American approach, it would have paved the way toward a right-to-work movement in Canada.

Canada took a sharp departure from the American decision. In a close decision, four of the seven judges held that the union security arrangement was not inconsistent with the Charter's guarantees of freedom of association. However, on the second important question of whether the compulsory and universal collection of union dues could be justified even if it encroaches on Canadians' fundamental freedoms, the judges were unanimous. All seven held that this clause could be considered a reasonable limit on the Charter's guarantees. Political activity by unions was viewed as a legitimate extension of collective bargaining. This was evident particularly in the interactions between organized labor and the NDP, which resulted in significant statutory amendments to labor acts. Thus the Supreme Court issued a strong signal that an important element in collective bargaining regime was not inconsistent with Charter rights (by a narrow margin) and was demonstrably justifiable (by a unanimous decision).

The importance of the Supreme Court's stance in *Lavigne* is in what it did not do, given the potential offered by Charter rights, and the *Lavigne* case should be viewed in this light. It is one of judicial restraint, and it would seem that after a strong flurry of charter challenges (115 cases touching on collective bargaining between 1982 and 1990 listed by Ryan [1990]), the Supreme Court is becoming more reluctant to strike down legislation or interpret the Charter so as to expand its meaning (Russell and Morton 1990; Swinton 1995). Rather, the diffusion of Charter principles into the employment relationship is being accomplished by the involved parties themselves, through the careful drafting of collective agreements to contain clauses prohibiting discrimination and through the seepage of Charter-based reasoning into labor board decisions and into arbitration awards. The poor likelihood of winning the two-fold test in the Charter probably discourages disgruntled parties from pursuing their cases beyond the normal administrative and dispute resolution mechanisms.

The Charter strategy of limiting individual rights underscores the Canadian protection of collectivism, described earlier as characteristic of Canadian national values. The Charter was created to meet historical contingencies that had little to do with labor relations but nevertheless made its mark in labor regulation. Finally, the Charter provides Canadians with a mechanism for applying brokerage politics to disputes and is markedly different from the American interpretation of the Bill of Rights.

*Union Organizing and Management Unfair Labor Practices: The "Squeaky Clean" Canadian Standard*

The contrasting approaches taken by Canadian and American labor law regimes to employer campaigning during union organizing drives was described by Weiler (1983). He recommended substantial alterations of the American union election system, based on his experiences with Canadian "instant elections." In this section of the chapter, I trace the Canadian approach through three related issues, all dealing with the common theme of facilitating entry of worksites into the collective bargaining milieu: restrictions against employer campaigning, expedited union certification procedures, and directed certifications.

The issue is more subtle than simply enforcing an expedited certification procedure. Even without expedited union certifications, the Canadian approach is substantially divergent from the American. The heart of the difference is philosophical. Canadian labor boards have adopted a *relativistic* interpretation based on an analysis of differential powers of employees and employers, while the American approach is a more absolute and literal application of freedom of expression. To arrive at this conclusion, I contrast Canadian and American approaches through both the statutory provisions for free speech and the important jurisprudential holdings which advance or inhibit campaigning.

The current American situation fosters an unquestionable right to campaign, a right which was codified in the 1947 Taft-Hartley Act through an amendment of the NLRA to include section 8(c). The section specified that "the expressing of any views, argument, or opinion, or the dissemination thereof . . . shall not constitute . . . an unfair labor practice . . . if such expression contains no threat of reprisal or force or promise of benefit." Judicial interpretations of 8(c) have led to vigorous management campaigning during union organizing drives and the overt expression of strong antiunion opinion by employers to their employees. For example, in *General Shoe Corporation and Boot and Shoe Workers Union, AFL*, 77 NLRB 124 (1948), the employer campaigned unrelentingly, making strongly disparaging comments about the union. Despite this employer activity, the NLRB concluded that "these statements contained no threat of reprisal or promise of benefit and appear to be only such expressions of opinion as are excluded from our consideration in an unfair labor practice case by reason of Section 8(c) of the amended act." Another noteworthy American example is *Livingston Shirt Corporation and Amalgamated Clothing Workers of America, CIO*, 107 NLRB 400 (1953). In this case, supervisors made statements to employees predicting that the plant would close if the union was victorious. The company president then gave a speech that reassured employees of their rights to self-organization without fear of reprisal. The day before the first election, the company president made an "antiunion, noncoercive speech to the assembled employees." By Canadian standards, it is hard to imagine that such an antiunion speech would be found to be *noncoercive*, as the standard is much different.

In Canada, the simple reference to a fundamental freedom of speech right cannot prop up management's intrusion into a union organizing campaign. Though employer free speech is explicitly recognized in the statutes of at least four Canadian jurisdictions (British Columbia, Alberta, Ontario, and Manitoba), with language virtually identical to NLRA 8(c),[14] labor board interpretations of free speech provisions have created significant restrictions.

Canadian labor board decisions have been exquisitely sensitive to vulnerability of employees within an employment relationship (an approach that was shared with Americans until the Taft-Hartley amendments). This sensitivity is reflected in a number of decisions, including the Ontario decision *Pigott Motors (1961) Ltd.* (1962), 63 C.L.L.C. at para. 16, 264, and British Columbia case *Consumer Pallet Limited* (1974), 74 C.L.L.C. at 16, 129. The leading Canadian decision on captive audience speeches is *American Airlines Inc. v. Brotherhood of Railway, Airline and Steamship Clerks, Freight Handlers, Express and Station Employees*, [1981] 3 C.L.R.B.R. 90 at 91-109. It stands in stark contrast to the post-Taft-Hartley American approach.[15]

In *American Airlines*, the vice chair of the Canada Labor Relations Board, Claude Foisy, argued that:

> we cannot stress enough the unique relationship that exists between an employer and his employees and the privileged position that puts the employer in to influence those employees. From this unique relationship, the employee perceives the awesome power of the employer to fire him/her at any time, in other words, the power over life and death. . . . Under such circumstances, what must an employee feel? Let us, for a moment, ask ourselves some of the questions that must go through an employee's mind.

> "What if the employer finds out [that I have been involved in union organizing]? Has the employer already found out? Why is he looking at me in that peculiar manner? How will this affect my future? Will the union be certified? If not, . . . ?"

> Any involvement by the employer in the exercise by the employee of his/her basic right to join a union puts unfair pressure on the employee. An employee joining a union must not be put in a situation of second class citizen who is adhering to a secret society and being ashamed of it. Either the right is recognized or it is not; if it is, it must be exercised in full light and without fear.

Two earlier cases set an extremely high hurdle for employers to leap without falling afoul of unfair labor practice provisions. In *General Aviation Services Ltd.* (1979), 2 Can. L.R.B.R. 98, the board said that "in judging the actions of an employer during a union organizing campaign among its employees, the test is to what extent, if any, the employer departs from a *stance of strict neutrality.*" The standard articulated by the British Columbia Board in *Fleetline Parts and Equipment Ltd.* (decision number 29/80) is that "in the context of an attempt by a union to organize a group of employees, the employer retains the right to communicate with its employees, however, *the employer's exercise of the right must be squeaky clean.*"

Thus employer actions in Canada are viewed through the eyes of employees. Employer free speech is an extremely risky exercise and one which cannot be taken lightly by employers. To avoid violating the law, employers are advised to observe union organizing from the sidelines, regardless of the natural temptation to enter the fray and express their views.

To what extent does the squeaky clean Canadian standard affect organizing outcomes? Greater union organizing vitality in Canada is due to a host of factors, including the relative ease of obtaining certification without a drawn-out, emotional, and expensive battle. In a 1996 study Meltz and Verma demonstrate the vitality of new union certifications in Canada, arguing that unions in the five provinces they examined (British Columbia, Ontario, Quebec, Saskatchewan, and Newfoundland) were out-organizing American unions in the U.S. "not only in proportion to the size of the labor force but in absolute numbers" (Metz and Verma 1996:4). Unions in Canada were more than ten times as active in filing for certifications as were their American counterparts over a fifteen-year period from 1980 to 1995. In that same period, the certification rates were 69.2% in Canada and 47.17% in the United States (p. 6).

Table 3 illustrates the statutory requirements for certification across the Canadian jurisdictions. Table 3 indicates that many Canadian jurisdictions allow that a sufficient show of support for the union (via petition or signing union membership cards) can be the basis for automatic certification without a secret ballot vote. Where certification is automatic, the success rate for unions appears to be considerably higher. Even in jurisdictions which require votes, however, the Canadian union win rate is higher than the American: 75.25% in Nova Scotia, 51.2% in Alberta, and 58.3% in British Columbia (considering only the average of the years in which compulsory votes were in effect).

In jurisdictions which require votes, efforts are made by labor boards to expedite procedures. One study of Ontario from 1982 to 1990 found that accelerated certification procedures "significantly reduce the effect of illegal managerial practices designed to influence worker choice with respect to the

## TABLE 3
### Statutory Provisions Regarding Certifications

| Jurisdiction | Procedure: How to demonstrate adequate support for certification | Time between Application and Certification | Board Directed Certification | Directed First Collective Agreement |
|---|---|---|---|---|
| Federal | 35% support to apply for vote; 50% support to automatically certify | No statutory directive. Average of 119 days in cases without public hearing; 1995 Sims Task Force recommendation is for 30-45 days, and that a "fast-track" certification be developed. | No. 1995 Sims Task Force recommendation is for directed certification where egregious unfair labor practices have occurred. | Unclear in Sections 99(1) and (2). Sims Task Force recommends that Board direct the inclusion or withdrawal of specific collective agreement terms in order to rectify failure to bargain in good faith. |
| Newfoundland | 40% support, followed by compulsory vote. | 5 days between application and vote (S. 47). | No. | No. |
| Prince Edward Island | 50% to show support; board may order vote. | No statutory directive. | No. | No. |
| Nova Scotia | 40% support, followed by compulsory vote. | 5 days in total. 3 working days after employer notified (S. 25). | Board may use directed certification if unfair labor practices. | No. |
| New Brunswick | 50% support for board consideration of automatic certification; 40-60% support to apply for a vote. | No statutory directive. | Board may use directed certification if unfair labor practices. | No. |
| Quebec | 50% support for automatic certification; 35% support to apply for a vote. | No statutory directive. | No. | No. |
| Ontario | Until 1995: 55% support for automatic certification; 40% support to apply for vote. Since 1995, compulsory vote after showing 40% support. | 5 working days after certification filed with board [S 8(5)] | Board may use directed certification if unfair labor practices. | Board can impose first agreement if parties apply, and if any of four conditions are present, including bad faith bargaining. |
| Manitoba | 65% support for automatic certification; over 45% support for Board supervised vote. | No statutory directive. | May allow interim certification while dispute ongoing. May certify if unfair labor practices. | No. |
| Saskatchewan | 25% support, followed by compulsory vote. | No statutory directive. | No. | No. |
| Alberta | 40% support, followed by compulsory vote. | No statutory directive; board tries for under one month. | No. | No. |
| British Columbia | 55% support for automatic certification; over 45% to apply for a vote. | No statutory directive. | Board may use directed certification if unfair labor practices. | Board may order compulsory interest arbitration. |

*Source:* Review of the federal and provincial labor codes. Some details provided in *Industrial Relations Legislation in Canada*, 1995-96 ed., compiled by Human Resources Development Canada.

representation decision . . . specifically, accelerated certification procedures limit the employer's ability to erode favorable union sentiment during an organizing campaign. . . . [T]he extent of illegal managerial resistance and its impact on union support are much smaller in union representation elections in Ontario than in the United States" (Thomason 1994:224). Indeed, Ontario, which is one of the largest and most active jurisdictions in Canada, requires its labor board to determine the outcome of certification applications by vote within five working days.

Where there is a card procedure only rather than a vote (in the federal jurisdiction), delays are somewhat more tolerated, as employees have had the ability to document their support for a union over the course of a union organizing drive. Nonetheless, the delays in some situations are noteworthy. In the federal sphere, time delays in certification processes became unacceptable and were attributed to administrative inefficiencies rather than to employer conduct. Over a five-year period (1990-95), in cases where no representation vote or public hearing was held, it took on average 119 days to deal with a certification application. Public hearings are held in about 12% of certification applications. Cases involving public hearings took close to one year to resolve. The Sims Task Force felt that a more realistic time line should be between 30 and 45 days and recommended that dramatically expedited procedures be put in place for uncontested situations (Sims Task Force:58-61).

How is it possible for a board to handle the administration required for these expeditious procedures? In Alberta the average time from application to certification for the 205 applications received was 20 days. This average time included a number of mail-in representation votes, which require about 14 days longer to complete that in-person votes (ALRB 1993/94). When an application is received, the board schedules a hearing for within 8 to 10 working days and has suggestions for vote arrangements prepared prior to the release of a report of the hearing. If there are no objections, the hearing gets cancelled. The board schedules a vote for within 3 to 4 working days of the hearing. Alberta is a large, relatively sparsely populated province. To facilitate vote arrangements, since 1988 the board has appointed a network of deputy returning officers (DROs), each serving a defined geographic area of the province. These DROs were assembled by selecting from the list of returning officers available from the electoral office, as they had experience administering political elections. The Alberta board issued them union election kits and portable polling stations, so they are prepared well in advance of a phone call advising them that an election must be scrutinized. There are other provinces which employ similar tactics to speed up the period between application and certification. In British Columbia, for example, employment standards officers also conduct votes and field investigations for the labor board.

The philosophy underlying these comparatively rapid certifications is that employers have had many years to demonstrate the degree of their concern for employee well-being. The union has only a narrow window of opportunity to canvass employees. Allowing employers to run campaigns, as is done in the U.S., might tip the balance of power to the employer side. As employees are considered uniquely vulnerable to employer pressures, the sooner the organizing campaign is over, the better.

In addition to the expeditious processing of certification applications, particularly in jurisdictions which require votes, there are a number of other powers held by boards in various jurisdictions. One of the most contentious is the capacity of a board to issue a directed certification in cases where unfair labor practices have made it impossible to be assured of what the outcome of the election might have been in the absence of management interference. The British Columbia Board has the ability to impose a first collective agreement. Both powers are rarely exercised and are reserved for only the most egregious situations. The latest data (from the BCLRB Annual Report, 1994) is that as *remedies*, these are completely ineffective. Of the dozen times the board directed the certification, the parties failed to conclude a first collective agreement on their own. Where boards imposed a collective agreement, the parties generally fail to conclude a subsequent collective agreement. Why then did the 1995 Sims Task Force recommend directed certification for the federal Canada Labor Board? Apparently, these powers are exceedingly important as *deterrents*. In the words of a board chair: "Without these powers, when managers go to their labor lawyers and say, 'What can happen to me if I fire some of the union activists?' the lawyers basically advise against this but shrug. With these powers, lawyers have to say, 'You will likely be certified *because* of your actions,' and management has to think twice" (Interview 1996). The Ontario Board chose to exercise its powers in February 1997 by directing the certification of a unit of employees at Wal-Mart, even though the union lost the certification vote by a considerable margin. The decision, a very contentious one, was due to a subtle adverse inference employees might draw from Wal-Mart's refusal to answer direct questions about the future of the store during the organizing drive, in contrast to its normally open and participatory culture.[16]

The Canadian approach to resolving unfair labor practice disputes demonstrates the Canadian tolerance for state intervention into disputes, a role Mackenzie King strenuously argued was appropriate in labor relations. The enhanced powers of Canadian labor boards are consistent with this responsibility. In many jurisdictions, these powers came into being when the NDP was the governing provincial party. Canadian labor boards were given a broad range of powers that allow them to play the role of "impartial umpire" and craft rapid and meaningful judgments when brokering competing interests in union-management disputes.

*Canada's Union Security Clauses: The Antithesis of the American RTW Approach*

Differences between Canadian and American approaches to labor are most starkly apparent in the evolution of union security clauses. In the United States, 21 states have exercised their limited labor jurisdictional powers to enact right-to-work (RTW) legislation which prohibits unions and management from negotiating and concluding collective agreements that enforce universal union membership or dues deductions. The argument tendered by RTW supporters is that such clauses override individual political freedoms of members of the bargaining unit who do not wish to join or support the union.

Canada never adopted the American treatment of union security issues. While union security clauses always were within the scope of bargaining issues between the parties, the most important development in Canadian regulatory intervention came as a result of a landmark 1946 decision by Justice Rand in his investigation of the turbulent Ford Motor Company dispute. To settle a bargaining impasse, Justice Rand devised a system of universal dues deductions for members of the certified bargaining unit, regardless of whether or not they chose to join the union. He framed his decision in the context of making operational the underlying premises of collective bargaining:

> Certain declarations of policy of both Dominion and Provincial legislatures furnish me with the premises from which I must proceed. . . . [T]he social desirability of the organization of workers and of collective bargaining where employees seek them has been written into laws. . . . The corollary from it is that the labor unions should become strong in order to carry on the functions for which they are intended. This is machinery devised to adjust, toward an increasing harmony, the interests of capital, labor and public in the production of goods and services which our philosophy accepts as part of the good life; it is to secure industrial civilization within a framework of labor-employer constitutional law based on a rational economic and social doctrine. . . . [T]he power of organized labor, the necessary co-partner of capital, must be available to redress the balance of what is called social justice; the just protection of all interests in an activity which the social order approves and encourages. (Rand 1958: 1251-53)

In tackling the issue of dues check-off provisions, Justice Rand also addressed the free-rider problem inherent in RTW legislation:

> Employees as a whole become the beneficiaries of union action, and I doubt if any circumstance provokes more resentment in a plant

than this sharing of the fruit of unionist work and courage by the non-member. It is irrelevant to try to measure the benefits in a particular case; the protection of organized labor is premised as a necessary security to the body of employees. (Quoted in *Canadian Labor Law Reports* 1989, section 2007)

The Rand formula was a classic Canadian compromise that protected the rights of workers to refuse union membership and protected unions against free riders in their bargaining units. Shortly thereafter, Canadian legislators across multiple jurisdictions began to expressly incorporate union security arrangements into labor statutes.

Today, 7 out of the 11 Canadian jurisdictions (federal, British Columbia, Manitoba, Newfoundland, Quebec, Ontario,[17] and Saskatchewan) make the Rand formula mandatory. Saskatchewan has a mandatory union shop directive. Of these seven, most have provisions built into the statutes which specify that bargaining unit members who for religious reasons cannot contribute dues to a union must donate an equivalent amount to a registered charity. The *Lavigne* decision, described in an earlier section of the chapter, was the decisive victory for the entrenchment of the Canadian approach to union security even in the face of a Charter which made room for constitutional challenges. Over 90% of Canadian collective agreements contain mandatory dues deductions, and as Table 4 illustrates, at a minimum the Rand formula or even stronger union protection is the norm.

TABLE 4
Union Security Clause Provisions in Canadian Collective Agreements

| Union Security Provision | Canada-wide 1994 (%) | Alberta - 1995 (%) |
|---|---|---|
| Closed Shop | 9.0 | 22.4 |
| Union/Modified Shop | 42.3 | 45.9 |
| Rand Formula | 39.2 | 29.3 |
| Maintenance of Membership | 3.0 | 2.1 |
| Open Shop | 6.5 | 0.3 |

*Source:* Canadian figures from Giles and Starkman (1995:Figure 13.2); Alberta figures from Alberta Labor.

The only Canadian jurisdiction to have investigated the RTW option is Alberta, and therefore the breakdown of current union security provisions in that province is also provided in Table 4. A concerted attempt was made to introduce RTW in Alberta in 1994. It is worth examining the ensuing debate and the forces which ultimately defeated RTW. Alberta arguably is the most "Americanized" of the Canadian provinces. It has a union density of 26%, well below the national average. A lobby effort initiated by the Citizen's Coalition Against Forced Unionism garnered sufficient support in the Alberta legislature to pass a motion calling for a study of the impact of a movement toward RTW in Alberta. The Alberta Economic Development Authority was assigned responsibility for overseeing the study, and it was headed by Elaine McCoy, the former Alberta minister of labor, with a bipartisan committee. The McCoy committee publicized its mandate and invited submissions.

Although 225 submissions were received, it is significant that only a dozen were from major employers. While various unions wrote detailed defenses against RTW, the few employer-side reports were split. Unexpectedly, the majority of Alberta employers who responded to the call for submissions were *opposed* to RTW. One of the most startling submissions was written on behalf of the employer coalition group, Construction Labor Relations (CLR), whose members are directly affected by closed shop provisions. In the early 1980s, CLR orchestrated a provincewide lockout of its unionized employees, which resulted in the shift of the industry from unionized to virtually union-free over a one-year period. Unions have been retrieving their lost membership since then, and as the parties have restored relations after this traumatic event, efforts have been made to transform the relationship between the unions and construction industry. According to the RTW submission of CLR President R. Neil Tidsbury, the CLR "invested in the nurturing of more effective working relationships and more rational and responsive negotiation and problem-solving processes . . . Much has been gained as we have dragged ourselves from the antagonism and hostility of the 1980s." He urged Alberta to resist RTW because of its deleterious effects on union confidence, a vital component in a bargaining relationship:

> The levels of stability and market sensitivity that have been achieved in the unionized construction industry have been built in the face of waves of restructuring, economic turbulence, ever intensifying competition, and new approaches to fiscal management. The attitudinal shift, the pragmatism, among bargaining parties and the resulting stability and market sensitivity are significant though fragile. . . . We are fearful at the prospect [that RTW will bring] of confrontational lobbying and ideological warfare deflecting their [union] agendas and marring the relationships which . . . are vitally necessary.

> [Having carefully examined the fortunes of U.S. RTW states, the lack of demand among workers for RTW in Alberta, the decisions of the Alberta Labor Relations Board, and so on.] We have concluded that there is no substantive problem to be corrected nor any identifiable potential return to offset the risk we have identified from the

intensely emotional and ideological consideration of "right to work" legislation. We have concluded that the suggestion of "right to work" legislation for this province at this time is driven solely by ideology, at a time when all parties in the province need to be pragmatically addressing their attention and creativity and energies toward productivity, quality, competitiveness, and growth.

After reviewing the submissions, the McCoy committee unanimously rejected the RTW option for Alberta, arguing that it could produce none of the benefits espoused by its advocates. Though the RTW movement suffered a considerable defeat, it persists in its lobbying efforts and the issue is likely to resurface in Alberta. There are no signs that any other jurisdictions in Canada are interested in giving RTW a sympathetic hearing.

Union security clauses have a critical impact in maintaining the financial health of Canadian unions and keeping union coffers high. Perhaps as a result, Canadian unions have taken a more militant stance in the face of hard bargaining, have retained resiliency against employer and government attacks, and have demonstrated greater vitality in new union organizing (Meltz and Verma 1996). The relationship between compulsory Rand agreements, union financial viability, and union organizing efforts is a topic worthy of further investigation by scholars who seek to explain Canada-U.S. divergences in union density.

## Implications

Was there ever a "North American model"? While the broad strokes of Canadian and American approaches are similar, particularly in that a majority of worker support leads to a union having exclusive bargaining rights for the unit as a whole, nevertheless a more nuanced examination of intercountry features reveals significant disjunctures. I would argue that in this century, the two systems were closest during the period from 1944 to 1947—from the grudging acceptance of forced recognition of unions in PC 1003 for reasons of political expediency only, to the passage of the Taft-Hartley Act in 1947, which led the way to employer campaigning, reduced union security, and bifurcated the powers of the labor board. The two countries converged briefly only because strong pressures were brought to bear on Canada's governing party to accept Wagner Act principles. Further, because Canadian concerns with radical unionism propelled lawmakers to incorporate union unfair labor practice sections into PC 1003, there was little momentum for a major recrafting of federal law subsequent to the adoption of PC 1003. The home-grown preoccupation of Canadians with industrial peace and with achieving a balance continued to flourish. While provincial labor laws exhibit diversity, there is not a single province that has departed from a basic commitment to uphold the principles of free collective bargaining. The PC 1003 approach had enduring appeal because it achieved a strong fit with Canadian values and managed to find a compromise position among competing interests.

By contrast, I would speculate the Wagner Act was more firmly situated in the concerns of a particular era, and as time progressed, it became increasingly decoupled from American values and behaviors. Kaufman (1996) argues that the Wagner Act was "first and foremost a macroeconomic recovery measure." The law was born in the Depression and thus issues of economic recovery and stabilization were central concerns—concerns that probably have diminished greatly since then. Others have written that the act was motivated by the desire to foster industrial self-government, achieve dignity in the workplace, and enhance social justice (Keyserling 1960; Gross 1965). Despite controversies over the precise determinants of the Wagner Act, there is consensus, however, that collective bargaining under the Wagner Act "was intended to be more than a system of checks and balances based on countervailing power" (Gross 1985:10) but rather was designed to encourage unionization. In failing to provide a union unfair labor practice section, however, and lacking a better balance between union and management interests, it gave credibility to managements' sustained lobbying for legislative change, ultimately manifest in the Taft-Hartley Act. Gross (1985) argues that the NLRA, since incorporating the Taft-Hartley amendments, is a deeply conflicted document.

Alternatively, I would argue that the Taft-Hartley/Wagner Act merger might be deeply internally conflicted but might also provide a better external match with American society and values. After all, broader employment law reform has not stalled in the U.S.: it has moved in the direction of protecting individual employee rights (Weiler 1990). Unless there are extraordinary social, economic, and political pressures, as there were in the years leading up to the passage of the Wagner Act, individual rights are favored over collective rights. RTW states enacted labor legislation. The recent attempt (thwarted by President Clinton's veto) to incorporate TEAM Act amendments into the NLRA would have loosened the company union prohibition and allowed greater forms of worker participation for nonunion employees. In contrast, even relatively mild reform efforts to restore the promises of the Wagner Act have been defeated (e.g., the Carter administration's 1977 proposals to return the labor board to its pre-Taft-Hartley administrative powers). Despite the steep downward trend line in union density, the Dunlop Commission has been unable to mobilize sufficient support for installing the types of legislative adjustments that might arrest union decline. Could it be that the movement toward a union-free America simply provides a better fit with American values, political alliances, and economic pressures?

## Summary and Conclusions

In this overview of the Canadian approach, six driving factors were identified: decentralization, national values, political party advocacy, leadership, historical contingencies, and how competing interests are brokered. The convergence of some or all of these six driving factors resulted in three main recurring themes in Canada's regulation of collective bargaining: (1) the collectivist Canadian tendency and the greater acceptance of corporatism (as evinced in the electoral strength of the NDP, in various health care policies, and in the acceptance of the Rand formula); (2) the willingness of Canadians to explore trade-offs between collective and individual rights (as evinced in the Charter's "justifiable limits" clause and the rejection of RTW in Canada); and (3) a high degree of pragmatism in the administration of the law in a direction (as evinced in expeditious certification processes) which has enhanced rather than diminished effectiveness. The institutional features of the Canadian environment, including the multiple jurisdictions, have facilitated incremental statutory change to labor codes, and successful experimentation has spread. As well, the various labor boards' interpretations of their powers to adjudicate competing claims and to create efficient administrative procedures has smoothed various potential roadblocks, including eliminating the capacity of the parties to delay labor board action. Thus the ability to administer justice efficiently in Canada sits in stark contrast to the procedural delays, multiple levels of decision making, and legislative paralysis which have created fragility in the U.S. collective bargaining regime.

The regulation of labor relations is deeply embedded in the national context. It consists of two equally important components: first is the statutory regime, which in some important aspects differs markedly in Canada from that of the U.S. The second component is the implementation of the laws. Many of the prominent features of the Canadian system have to do with the various labor boards' interpretation of their powers to act expeditiously and effectively, rather than with the precise statutory directives (which in the case of employer free speech were virtually identical in both countries). It is the interaction of the statutes with effective guardianship of their intent that leads to the power of the Canadian model. Clearly, the will to enforce the law, which is a reflection of differences in national values and culture, is at least as great a spur to collective bargaining as is the law itself.

Given the fate of the U.S. Dunlop Commission report, the Canadian experience is instructive. The success of reform to the regulatory regime is dubious when the enactment of laws is used as a mechanism to drive societal transformation. Rather, statutory regimes are deeply embedded within the ethos of a nation, and unless there is convergence of law and values, the law becomes a hollow instrument. There is little evidence of a constellation of pressures emerging in the U.S. to mobilize support for labor reform in the direction of strengthening any of the precepts of the Wagner Act model. In Canada, it is not simply the statutes that drive the regulation of labor relations but also the attitudes of the parties, the interpretation of judicial holdings, and the power of labor boards to determine their own administrative procedures free of interference from government. It is improbable that these features could be transported into the U.S. without significant political trade-offs that might differ markedly in the U.S. from those that were struck in Canada. Successful transfer of the features of the Canadian approach might well require a "reengineering" of the national soul.

## Acknowledgments

I am grateful for the helpful input at an early stage in this chapter from Andrew Sims. Bruce Kaufman, Allen Ponak, and Chris Albertyn made many constructive suggestions for improvement. Funding from the Alberta Energy Company's Strategic Research Fellowship Program is gratefully acknowledged. An earlier version of this chapter was presented at the Conference on Collective Bargaining and Public Policy, University of Minnesota, October 1996.

## Endnotes

[1] The strength and fortunes of the Canadian union movement are the subject of vigorous debate. Those who argue that Canadian and American scenes are sharply divergent include Chaison and Rose (1991), Lipset (1986), Meltz and Verma (1996), Kumar (1993), and Weiler (1993). On the other side, Leo Troy has mounted a series of essays (e.g., 1991a and 1991b) accusing the "Canadian crowd" of misrepresenting union density rates so as to allow public sector vitality to obscure declines in private sector union density which he argues simply lag behind those experienced in the U.S. My intent is to avoid becoming embroiled in this dispute. It is important to note, however, that despite differences in national context and law, the notion of *divergence* took hold only after public sector employees were given the right to unionize in the mid-1960s. Until that time, union density figures were broadly comparable. A second matter which complicates this debate is that the 1996 *Directory of Labor Organizations in Canada* (produced by the Bureau of Labor Information) has revised its union density figures in accordance with changes to the Statistics Canada Labor Force Survey. The old method of calculation would show 1996 Canadian density as 38% and holding stable, while the new calculations report 1996 density as 33.9% and declining slightly over the previous four years. See Table 2 of this chapter, which reports both old and new annual union density figures.

[2] The role of the Wagner model is contentious. As Roy Adams (1994:2) put it, "By most objective standards the Wagner Act model must be judged a long term failure" (see also Weiler 1986). Beatty (1987) provides provocative critiques of both law-makers' and organized

labor's failure to protect the rights of the weakest members of society, domestic workers and agricultural workers. Forrest (1994) argues that women and female-dominated occupations have been badly served by the Wagner Act influence in Canada.

[3] The comparable American labor legislation was the 1898 Erdman Act, which Congress adopted after a highly publicized strike in the railways. The law required an Interstate Commerce Commission to mediate railway labor disputes, provided for arbitration, and enforced arbitration awards. The Erdman Act applied only to railways, and it was declared unconstitutional in 1908. The next attempt was the Railway Labor Act of 1926, which in 1936 was amended to include the airline industry. The 1932 Norris-LaGuardia Act announced a national policy to secure a place for collective bargaining, protect unions and bargaining relationships from antitrust laws, to limit the availability of injunctive relief in labor disputes, and to ban "yellow dog" contracts. The National Industrial Recovery Act was passed shortly after Norris-LaGuardia, and it was declared unconstitutional. The NLRA was proposed by Senator Robert F. Wagner, passed by Congress, and its constitutional validity was tested and upheld by a divided Supreme Court in 1937. The Taft-Hartley Act significantly revised the NLRA in 1947 and, some argue, tipped the balance too far toward management (Gross 1995:11-16). The final major revision of the NLRA came in 1959 with the Landrum-Griffin Act, which was aimed at union electoral reporting and disclosure of union financial affairs.

[4] See, for example, NLRB Chairman William Gould's speech to the Canadian Industrial Relations Association conference, Brock University, June 1996. In an attempt to seek injunctive relief against employer misconduct, the labor board increasingly has used NLRA Section 10(j). Invoking 10(j) requires applying to the courts, and this fact alone can take in excess of 65 days (Rose and Chaison 1996:6). In Canada, by contrast, labor boards can issue injunctive relief directly and have broader powers generally.

[5] In reality Canada has an abysmal record of days lost due to strikes in relation to other countries. The statutory freeze might inadvertently contribute to positional rigidities and give the parties greater time to prepare for prolonged work stoppages. For a recent review of the Canadian record, see Gunderson, Hyatt, and Ponak (1995). There are many competing explanations for Canada's volatility, including unemployment rates, inflation, real wages and industrial composition.

[6] A useful source for further description of Canadian-American-Mexican differences in industrial relations laws was recently produced by the Secretariat, Commission for Labor Cooperation, North American Agreement on Labor Cooperation. The Preliminary Report to the Ministerial Council is entitled, "Labor and Industrial Relations Law in Canada, the United States, and Mexico" (1996:31-34). A three-volume series on comparative labor principles among the three countries is planned.

[7] The *Snider* case caused the Industrial Disputes Investigation Act to be declared unconstitutional, as the IDIA's federal conciliation board procedure infringed on property and civil rights. The Privy Council held these rights to be exclusively within provincial jurisdiction. Earlier, ten of twelve members of the Supreme Court of Ontario upheld the IDIA because labor relations were vital to "peace, order and good government," the assurance of which was a federal responsibility.

[8] Within each jurisdiction are statutory and administrative subdivisions based on whether employees work in the public sector or the private sector. For example, in the federal jurisdiction, public employees are covered by the Public Service Staff Relations Act of 1967 (PSSRA), while private employees are covered by the Canada Labor Code. A comprehensive

description of the jurisdictions is found in Adams' *Canadian Labor Law* (1985), albeit with the warning that some of the specific details are now out-dated.

[9] More recent work on the Canadian identity argues that these conventional labels no longer are accurate. Canadians currently are in the throes of a transition away from deference, the brokerage of competing interests, and accommodation of diversity, moving instead toward populism, regional competition, and rights-driven demands over the apportionment of benefits. Three recent Canadian essayists give U.S. pause. Simpson (1993) believes that "Canada's traditional political culture in the 1980s cracked like river ice in spring. No single current produced the crack-up; it arose from the confluence of powerful new economic, demographic and political factors, and the resurgence of older currents" (p. 1). Newman (1995) argues that the conventional picture of Canadians as more deferential to political authority has changed fundamentally from 1985 to 1995, as Canadians have moved from "deference to defiance." In his commentary on the state of the nation, Gwyn (1995) laments challenges to the "Canadian values of tolerance, civility, and decency" (p. 289) arguing that we have arrived at "some kind of historical discontinuity" (p. 253). Nevertheless, most would agree that the early collectivist and corporatist values were operative at the time when regulatory approaches to labor were entrenched.

[10] Perhaps only the weak Canadian dollar relative to U.S. currency is propping up employment in unionized sectors and preserving union viability. There remains a heated debate as to whether Canadian union density is on the precipice of a cliff (Troy 1991a, 1991b on one side; and Meltz 1985, 1986; Meltz and Verma 1996; Chaison and Rose on the other). In a speech to the Canadian Industrial Relations Association, Thomas Kochan warned in 1984 that Canadians seemed over fixated with the status quo and that the parallels between the two countries should serve as a wake-up call to Canadians.

[11] In a controversial article, Lipset (1986a) stated the view that the Canadian-American differential in union density rates could be due to disparate social values. He used American public opinion polls to demonstrate that American union decline is correlated with an upsurge in antiunion attitudes. This thesis was quickly discredited when scholars demonstrated that Canadian public opinion poll findings were "remarkably similar" to those conducted in the U.S. (e.g., Riddell 1993).

[12] From Saporta and Lincoln's Table 1 (p. 557), it is evident that whatever statistically significant differences exist between Canadian and American workers, they are relatively small and readily explained by differences in statutory treatments of strikes and the hiring of replacement workers. The overwhelming impression is of similarities rather than differences.

[13] Canada's courts also have been significantly less intrusive in the collective bargaining realm. It is rare that the courts overturn labor board decisions, adopting instead a policy of curial restraint. Where there is a privative dispute resolution clause in a collective agreement or a statute, the courts tend to review cases only for "excess of jurisdiction" or "patent unreasonableness." A series of holdings (with some exceptions) confirm the refusal of Canadian courts, over many years, to intrude upon matters resolvable between union and management, by grievance or interest arbitration, or by labor boards (*Labor Law Casebook* 1991:798-807). This is a dramatic difference from the situation in the United States, in which Block and Roomkin (1996) assert that the jurisdictional demarkation is relatively blurred, with the result that it is quite likely that a higher court will agree to hear an NLRB decision. From 1990 to 1996, on average the courts overturned or only partially enforced 17% of NLRB decisions (NLRB 1997).

[14] For example, Ontario's Labor Relations Act (1995), Section 70, specifies that "No employer . . . shall participate in or interfere with the formation, selection or administration of a trade union or the representation of employees by a trade union or contribute financial or other support to a trade union, but *nothing in this section shall be deemed to deprive an employer of the employer's freedom to express views so long as the employer does not use coercion, intimidation, threats, promises or undue influence*" (emphasis added). In some Canadian jurisdictions, employer statements are proscribed: both Newfoundland and Saskatchewan prohibit employers from threatening plant closure during a labor dispute.

[15] The pre-Taft-Hartley leading American case *N.L.R.B. v. The Fedderbush Co. Inc.*, 121 F. 2nd 954 (1941) at 957, is quoted with great favor in Canadian cases. In *Fedderbush*, Judge Learned Hand eloquently sets employer free speech within the context of employment:

> The privilege of "free speech," like other privileges, is not absolute; it has its seasons; a democratic society has an acute interest in its protection and cannot indeed be without it; but it is an interest measured by its purpose. The purpose is to enable others to make an informed judgement as to what concerns them, and ends so far as the utterances do not contribute to the result. Language may serve to enlighten a hearer, though it also betrays the speaker's feelings and desires; but the light it sheds will be in some degree clouded, if the hearer is in his power. Arguments by an employer directed to his employees have such an ambivalent character . . . the relations between the speaker and the hearer is perhaps the most important. What to an outsider will be no more than the vigorous presentation of a conviction, to an employee may be the manifestation of a determination which it is not safe to thwart.

[16] Ontario Labor Relations Board, *United Steelworkers of America v. Wal-Mart Canada*, decision issued February 10, 1997. The vote was 151 to 43 against the Steelworkers Union. The Board decision was not unanimous. See "Why Wal-Mart lost the case," and "What the labor relations board said," *Globe and Mail*, February 14, 1997, B10; and "Wal-Mart's cheer fades as union certified," *Globe and Mail*, February 15, 1997, B4. The outcome of this case is uncertain: employees are asking for the board to reconsider, and the company is preparing an appeal.

[17] Ontario's Labor Relations Act (1995) has a slightly different formulation. Section 47 makes a Rand formula compulsory only at the request of a trade union. It would be an unfair labor practice for management to refuse the union's request during bargaining.

## References

Aaron, Benjamin. 1985. "The NLRB, Labor Courts, and Industrial Tribunals: A Selective Comparison," *Industrial and Labor Relations Review*, Vol. 39, no. 1, pp. 35-45.

Abella, Irving. 1973. *Nationalism, Communism, and Canadian Labor*. Toronto: University of Toronto Press.

Adams, George. 1985. *Canadian Labor Law: A Comprehensive Text*. Aurora, Ontario: Canadian Law Book Inc.

Adams, Roy J. 1989. "North American Industrial Relations: Divergent Trends in Canada and the United States." *International Labor Review*, Vol. 128, no. 1, 1989, pp. 47-64.

_____. 1994. "The 'Administrative Approach' and Union Growth in Canada and the United States, 1929-1955." *Proceedings of the 31st Conference* (Calgary). Quebec: Canadian Industrial Relations Association, pp. 29-40.

_____. 1995. "A Pernicious Euphoria." *Canadian Labor and Employment Law Journal*, Vol. 3, no. 3/4, pp. 321-56.

Adell, Bernard. 1994. "Jurisification under Wagnerism: The Need for a Change in Direction." *Proceedings of the 31st Conference* (Calgary). Quebec: Canadian Industrial Relations Association, pp. 123-42.

Alberta Economic Development Authority. 1995. *Report on Right to Work*. (McCoy Committee). Alberta.

Beatty, David M. 1987. *Putting the Charter to Work: Designing a Constitutional Labor Code*. Kingston, Ontario: McGill-Queen's University Press.

Bemmels, Brian, E.G. Fisher, and Barbara Nyland. 1986. "Canadian-American Jurisprudence on 'Good Faith' Bargaining." *Industrial Relations*, Vol. 41, no. 3, pp. 596-620.

Berniar, J. 1993. "Juridical Extension in Quebec: A New Challenge Unique in North America." *Relations industrielles/Industrial Relations*, Vol. 48, pp. 745-61.

Block, Richard N., and Myron Roomkin. 1996. "The Role of the Courts of Appeals in Interpreting the National Labor Relations Act: A Preliminary Analysis." Paper presented to the Conference on Collective Bargaining and Public Policy, University of Minnesota (October).

Boivin, Jean, and Esther Déom. 1995. "Labor-Management Relations in Quebec." In Morley Gunderson and Allen Ponak, eds., *Union-Management Relations in Canada*. 3d ed. Toronto: Addison-Wesley, pp. 455-93.

Bok, Derek. 1971. "Reflections on the Distinctive Character of American Labor Law." *Harvard Law Review*, Vol. 84, pp. 1394-463.

Bruce, Peter G. 1989. "Political Parties and Labor Legislation in Canada and the U.S." *Industrial Relations*, Vol. 28, pp. 115-41.

_____. 1990. "The Processing of Unfair Labor Practice Cases in the United States and Ontario." *Relations industrielles/Industrial Relations*, Vol 45, no. 3, pp. 481-511.

Card, David, and Richard Freeman. 1993. *Small Differences That Matter*. Chicago: University of Chicago Press.

Carter, Donald D. 1987. "The Comparative Effects of U.S. and Canadian Labor Laws and Labor Environment in the North American Competitive Context: The Canadian View." *Canadian-United States Law Journal*, Vol. 12, pp. 241-47.

Carter, Donald D., and Thomas McIntosh. 1991. "Collective Bargaining and the Charter: Assessing the Impact of American Judicial Doctrines." *Relations industrielles/Industrial Relations*, Vol. 46, no. 4, pp. 722-50.

Chaison, Gary, and Joseph Rose. 1991. "Continental Divide: The Direction and Fate of North American Unions." In D. Sockell, D. Lewin, and D. B. Lipsky, eds., *Advances in Industrial and Labor Relations*. Greenwich, CT: JAI Press, pp. 169-205.

Commission on the Future of Worker-Management Relations. 1994. *Report and Recommendations*. Washington, DC: U.S. Department of Labor and Department of Commerce.

Commons, John R., and John B. Andrews. 1920. *Principles of Labor Legislation*. 2d ed. New York: Harper and Bros.

Cooke, William N., and Frederick A. Gautschi III. 1892. "Political Bias in NLRB Unfair Labor Practice Decisions." *Industrial and Labor Relations Review*, Vol. 35, no. 4, pp. 539-49.

Craven, Paul. 1980. *'An Impartial Umpire': Industrial Relations and the Canadian State 1900-1911*. Toronto: University of Toronto Press.

Ferns, H.S., and B. Ostry. 1955. *The Age of Mackenzie King*. London: William Heinemann Ltd.

Finkin, Matthew W., ed. 1994. *The Legal Future of Employee Representation.* Ithaca, NY: ILR Press.

Forrest, Anne. 1994. "Women and Unions: What's P.C. 1003 Got to Do with It?" *Proceedings of the 31st Conference* (Calgary). Quebec: Canadian Industrial Relations Association, pp. 87-100.

Freeman, Richard B., and Joel Rogers. 1995. "The Worker Representation and Participation Survey: Preliminary Findings." *Proceedings of the 47th Annual Meeting* (Washington, DC). Madison, WI: Industrial Relations Research Association.

Giles, Anthony, and Akiva Starkman. 1995. "The Collective Agreement." In Morley Gunderson and Allen Ponak, eds., *Union-Management Relations in Canada.* 3d ed. Don Mills, Ontario: Addison-Wesley, pp. 339-71.

Gitelman, Harold M. 1987. *Legacy of the Ludlow Massacre: A Chapter in American Industrial Relations.* Philadelphia: University of Pennsylvania Press.

Gould, William B. 1993. *Agenda for Reform.* Cambridge, MA: MIT Press.

Gross, James A. 1985. "Conflicting Statutory Purposes: Another Look at Fifty Years of NLRB Law Making." *Industrial and Labor Relations Review,* Vol. 39, no. 1, pp. 7-18.

Gunderson, Morley, Douglas Hyatt, and Allen Ponak. 1995. "Strikes and Dispute Resolution." In Morley Gunderson and Allen Ponak, eds., *Union-Management Relations in Canada.* 3d ed. Don Mills, Ontario: Addison-Wesley, pp. 373-411.

Gwyn, Richard. 1995. *Nationalism without Walls: The Unbearable Lightness of Being Canadian.* Toronto: McClelland and Stewart.

Hartz, Louis. 1964. *The Founding of New Societies.* New York: Harcourt Brace and World.

Hogg, P. 1985. *Constitutional Law of Canada.* 2d ed. Toronto: Carswell.

Horowitz, Gad. 1968. *Canadian Labor in Politics.* Toronto: University of Toronto Press.

Innis, Harold. 1930. *The Fur Trade in Canada.* Toronto: University of Toronto Press.

Jenero, K. A., and C. P. Lyons. 1992. "Employee Participation Programs: Prudent or Prohibited?" *Employee Relations Law Journal,* Vol. 17, no. 4, pp. 535-66.

Kahn-Freund, Otto. 1974. "Uses and Misuses of Comparative Law." *Modern Law Review,* Vol. 35.

Kaufman, Bruce E. 1996. "Why the Wagner Act? Reestablishing Contact with Its Original Purpose." In David Lewin, Bruce Kaufman, and Donna Sockell, eds., *Advances in Industrial and Labor Relations,* Vol 7. Greenwich, CT: JAI Press, pp. 15-68.

_____. 1997. "Company Unions: Sham Organizations or Victims of the New Deal?" *Proceedings of the 49th Annual Meeting* (New Orleans). Madison, WI: Industrial Relations Research Association.

Kaufman, Bruce E., and Paula E. Stephan. 1995. "The Role of Management Attorneys in Union Organizing Campaigns." *Journal of Labor Research,* Vol. 16, no. 4, pp. 439-54.

Keyserling, Leon H. 1960. "The Wagner Act: Its Origin and Current Significance." *George Washington Law Review,* Vol. 29.

King, William Lyon Mackenzie. 1918 and 1973. *Industry and Humanity.* Toronto: University of Toronto Press.

Kochan, Thomas A., Harry C. Katz, and Robert McKersie. 1986. *The Transformation of American Industrial Relations.* New York: Basic Books.

Kumar, Pradeep. 1993. *From Uniformity to Divergence: Industrial Relations in Canada and the United States.* Kingston, Ontario: Queen's University IRC Press.

Labor Law Casebook Group. 1991. *Labor Law.* 5th ed. Kingston, Ontario: Industrial Relations Center, Queen's University.

Labor Relations Board. 1994. *Annual Report: April 1, 1993-March 31, 1994.*

Lawler, J. J. 1984. "The Influence of Management Consultants on the Outcome of Union Certification Elections." *Industrial and Labor Relations Review*, Vol. 38, pp. 38-51.
_____. 1990. *Unionization and Deunionization: Strategy, Tactics, and Outcomes*. Columbia, SC: University of South Carolina Press.
Lawler, J. J., and R. West. 1985. "Impact of Union-Avoidance Strategy in Representation Elections." *Industrial Relations*. Vol. 24, pp. 406-20.
Lipset, Seymour Martin. 1986a. "North American Labor Movements: A Comparative Perspective." In S. M. Lipset, ed., *Unions in Transition: Entering the Second Century*. San Francisco: Institute for Contemporary Studies, pp. 431-51.
_____. 1986b. "Historical Traditions and National Characteristics: A Comparative Analysis of Canada and the United States." *Canadian Journal of Sociology*, Vol. 11, pp. 113-55.
_____. 1989. *Continental Divide: The Values and Institutions of the United States and Canada*. Toronto and Washington: Howe Institute and National Planning Association.
MacDowell, Laurel Sefton. 1978. "The Formation of the Canadian Industrial Relations System during World War Two." *Labor/Le Travailleur*, Vol. 3, pp. 175-96.
Meltz, Noah. 1985. "Labor Movements in Canada and the United States." In Thomas A. Kochan, ed., *Challenges and Choices Facing American Labor*. Cambridge, MA: MIT Press, pp. 315-34.
_____. 1986. "Interstate vs. Interprovincial Differences in Union Density." *Industrial Relations*, Vol. 28, pp. 142-58.
Meltz, Noah, and Anil Verma. 1996. "Beyond Union Density: Union Organizing and Certification as Indicators of Union Strength in Canada and the United States." *Proceedings of 33rd Conference* (St. Catherines, Ontario). Quebec: Canadian Industrial Relations Association.
National Labor Relations Board. 1985. *Legislative History of the National Labor Relations Act 1935*. Volumes 1 and 2. Washington, DC: GPO.
_____. "In Three-Year Report, NLRB Chairman Gould Assesses Agency Decisions, Initiatives; Sees Progress in Labor Relations Environment." Released by NLRB March 7, 1997, R-2202.
Newman, Peter C. 1995. *The Canadian Revolution 1985-1995: From Deference to Defiance*. Toronto: Viking.
Panitch, Leo, and Donald Swartz. 1993. *The Assault on Trade Union Freedoms: From Wage Controls to Social Contract*. Toronto: Garamond Press.
Pickersgill, J.W. 1960. *The Mackenzie King Record, Volume 1: 1939-1944*. University of Chicago Press and University of Toronto Press.
Rand, Justice I.C. 1958. "Rand Formula." *Canadian Law Reports* 2150.
Riddell, W. Craig. 1993. "Unionization in Canada and the United States: A Tale of Two Countries." In David Card and Richard Freeman, eds., *Small Differences That Matter*. Chicago: University of Chicago Press, pp. 109-47.
Rose, Joseph B., and Gary N. Chaison. 1996. "Immediacy and Saliency in Remedying Employer Opposition to Union Organizing Campaigns." McMaster University School of Business Working Paper #416.
Rudin, B. 1972. "Mackenzie King and the Writing of Canada's *Anti* Labor Laws." *Canadian Dimension*, Vol. 8, pp. 42-48.
Russell, Bob. 1994. "Wagnerism in a Post-Fordist Era." *Proceedings of the 31st Conference* (Calgary). Quebec: Canadian Industrial Relations Association, pp. 143-54.
Russell, Peter, and F. L. Morton. 1990. "Judging the Judges: The Supreme Court of Canada's First One Hundred Charter Decisions." Paper presented at the Canadian Political Science Association Meetings (University of Victoria).

Ryan, Cynthia. 1990. "Collective Bargaining Laws under the Charter: A Digest of Case Law." *Research and Current Issues*, no. 61. Kingston, Ontario: Queen's University Industrial Relations Center.

Saporta, Ishak, and Bryan Lincoln. 1995. "Managers' and Workers' Attitudes toward Unions in the U.S. and Canada." *Relations industrielles/Industrial Relations*, Vol. 50, no. 3, pp. 550-66.

Simpson, Jeffrey. 1993. *Faultlines: Struggling for a Canadian Vision*. Toronto: Harper-Collins.

Sims, Andrew C.L. 1995. *Seeking a Balance: Canada Labor Code, Part 1, Review*. Ottawa, Ontario: Government of Canada.

_____. 1994. "Wagnerism in Canada: A Fifty-Year Check-Up." H.D. Woods Memorial Lecture. *Proceedings of the 31st Conference* (Calgary). Quebec: Canadian Industrial Relations Association.

Smiley, Donald V. 1983. "The Constitution Act, 1982: A Dangerous Deed." In K. Banting and R. Simeon, eds., *And No-One Cheered*. Toronto: Methuen.

Smith, David E. 1984. "The Federal Cabinet in Canadian Politics." In Michael S. Whittington and Glen Williams, eds., *Canadian Politics in the 1980s*. 2d ed. Toronto: Methuen.

Strauss, George. 1995. "Is the New Deal System Collapsing: With What Might It Be Replaced?" *Industrial Relations*, Vol. 34, no. 3, pp. 329-49.

Swinton, Katherine. 1995. "The Charter of Rights and Public Sector Labor Relations." In Gene Swimmer and Mark Thompson, eds., *Public Sector Collective Bargaining*. Kingston, Ontario: Queen's University IRC Press.

Taras, Daphne Gottlieb. 1994. *The Impact of Industrial Relations Strategies on Selected Human Resource Practices*. Ph.D. diss., University of Calgary.

_____. 1997a. "Company Unionism in Canada: Legal Status and Legislative History." *Proceedings of the 49th Annual Meeting* (New Orleans). Madison, WI: Industrial Relations Research Association.

_____. 1997b. "Why Nonunion Representation is Legal in Canada." Unpublished manuscript. Faculty of Management, University of Calgary.

Taylor, Charles. 1993. "Shared and Divergent Values." In *Reconciling the Solitudes: Essays on Canadian Federalism and Nationalism*. Montreal: McGill-Queen's University Press, pp. 155-86.

Thomason, Terry. "The Effect of Accelerated Certification Procedures on Union Organizing Success in Ontario." *Industrial and Labor Relations Review*, Vol. 47, no. 2, pp. 207-26.

Thompson, Mark. 1994. "Wagnerism in Canada: Compared to What?" *Proceedings of the 31st Conference* (Calgary). Quebec: Canadian Industrial Relations Association, pp. 59-72.

_____. 1995. "The Management of Industrial Relations." In Morley Gunderson and Allen Ponak, eds., *Union-Management Relations in Canada*. 3d ed. Don Mills, Ontario: Addison-Wesley, pp. 105-29.

Troy, Leo. 1991a. "Canada's Labor Policies: A Paradigm for the United States?" *Government Union Review*, Vol. 12, no. 4, pp. 1-31.

_____. 1991b. "Convergence in International Unionism Etc.: The Case of Canada and the U.S." *British Journal of Industrial Relations* (December).

Weiler, Paul. 1980. *Reconcilable Differences*. Toronto: Carswell.

_____. 1983. "Promises to Keep: Securing Workers' Rights to Self-Organization under the NLRA." *Harvard Law Review*, Vol. 96, no. 8, pp. 1769-827.

_____. 1986. "Milestone or Tombstone: The Wagner Act at Fifty." *Harvard Journal on Legislation*, Vol. 1, no. 3, pp. 1-31.

_____. 1990. *Governing the Workplace*. Cambridge, MA: Harvard University Press.

Woods, H.D. 1983. *Labor Policy in Canada*. 2d ed. Toronto: Macmillan.

Widenor, Marcus R. 1995. "Diverging Patterns: Labor in the Pacific Northwest Wood Products Industry." *Industrial Relations*, Vol. 34, no. 3, pp. 441-63.

# CHAPTER 9

# The Affirmative Action Debate

MARY F. RADFORD
*Georgia State University*

Government regulation of the employment relationship takes a variety of forms. Since the beginning of the 20th century, government has played a dominant role in policing worker safety and in directly controlling employees' wages and hours. In the areas of hiring and firing, however, the principle that prevailed until the middle of the century mandated against government involvement. This principle is known as the "employment-at-will" doctrine.

The employment-at-will doctrine allows an employer or employee to commence or terminate the employment relationship at any time and for any reason whatsoever. From the standpoint of business owners, this meant that employers were free to hire whomever they chose and to fire whenever they felt like it, free from any government regulation or oversight. Prior to the 1960s, the employment-at-will doctrine thus allowed employers to make employment decisions that reflected markedly discriminatory treatment of members of minority groups and women. The result of this treatment is illustrated by 1964 unemployment rates, which were twice as high among blacks as among whites, and by the fact that those black men and women who were employed were clustered almost exclusively in lower level blue-collar positions. Unemployment rates for women were also higher than those for men. Furthermore, employers were allowed to segregate jobs and to require, for example, that certain management-level positions be occupied only by men. In an attempt to remedy injustices of this type, Congress began in the early 1960s to enact a series of civil rights laws that severely restricted the employment-at-will doctrine. With the emergence of these laws, government's previous stance of non-involvement in the hiring and firing processes changed dramatically.

As originally designed, the antidiscrimination laws did not dictate whom an employer must hire or whom an employer could not fire. Rather, the laws prohibited an employer from imposing different hiring or firing standards on

343

an individual because of the individual's race, color, sex, religion, national origin, age, or disability. However, either out of respect for the social origins of the law or fear of being sued under it, many employers went a step further and began affirmatively to hire members of certain historically disadvantaged groups (e.g., blacks and women). Many of these actions withstood judicial challenge. Additionally, in attempts to remedy past discrimination by employers, courts themselves imposed affirmative action requirements on defendants in employment discrimination suits. At the same time, federal and state governments intervened directly in the employment relationship by adopting affirmative action plans whose sole purpose was to ensure that the governments and those who contracted with them would hire and retain members of the historically disadvantaged groups.

The term "affirmative action" became both a buzzword and a battle cry. Proponents of affirmative action speak glowingly of its potential to wipe out the effects of prior discrimination and to raise minority groups to their deserved status in our society. Opponents speak disparagingly of how "the quota system" not only penalizes individuals who played no part in perpetrating the prior discrimination but also stigmatizes those who are theoretically benefiting from it. The tension that characterizes the affirmative action debate is centered on the question of whether affirmative action is in fact an appropriate mechanism for achieving equality for women and minorities in the workplace or merely a subtle but definite form of the type of discrimination that the Constitution and the civil rights acts were designed to prohibit.

The dualistic nature of affirmative action affords ample opportunity for government participation on either side of the issue. On the one hand, the legislative and executive branches of states and the federal government regulate the hiring of millions of workers through grants, contracts, and other incentive programs that require employers to engage in affirmative action. Also, Title VII of the Civil Rights Act of 1964 allows courts and the Equal Employment Opportunity Commission (EEOC) to order affirmative action as a resolution for discrimination suits filed against employers. On the other hand, the federal courts and the EEOC are empowered to handle (and, in the case of the EEOC, to initiate) a variety of employment discrimination cases, including those cases of "reverse discrimination" which arise when a member of a majority group complains that preferential treatment of a minority group or individual has denied him his right to be treated equally regardless of his race or gender.

The affirmative action debate is played out in many arenas. Sociologists and psychologists dispute whether affirmative action will break down racial and gender barriers or in fact make them more apparent. Politicians argue as to whether the government should have any role in promoting social change or at best should just ensure that the nondiscrimination laws are enforced. Legal scholars argue on the one hand that affirmative action is against the law and on the other hand that it is the law.

Implicit in most debates is that the two sides are arguing about the same concept. Yet there is a basic incongruity in the affirmative action debate in that, although many people have an opinion about affirmative action, few can accurately or adequately describe what the term means. The purpose of this chapter is, first, to explore the various meanings of affirmative action by examining its sources in the law, its manifestations in the employment context, and its treatment by the courts. The fundamental contours of the affirmative action debate will then be fleshed out through a review of the major jurisprudential theories on affirmative action. Next, the chapter examines whether affirmative action truly results in effecting a change in the social and economic status of women and minorities. At the conclusion, some predictions will be offered as to what direction the debate will take over the next five years.

## Legal Definitions of Affirmative Action

The inability of most people to define the term "affirmative action" is understandable in light of the fact that there exist in the current statutes, executive orders, and government regulations only a very few clearly delineated or comprehensive definitions of the concept. The Constitution of the United States contains no reference to affirmative action. Of relevance in the affirmative action debate is the Equal Protection Clause of the Fourteenth Amendment which provides that no state shall "deny to any person within its jurisdiction the equal protection of the laws." The following is a brief historical sketch of the development of the affirmative action concept in the executive and congressional arenas:

- Kennedy Executive Order 10925. The term "affirmative action" first appeared in Executive Order 10925, which was signed by President John F. Kennedy on March 6, 1961. The Kennedy executive order followed a series of orders issued by every president since Franklin D. Roosevelt that required government contractors to agree not to discriminate against employees or job applicants because of race, creed, color, or national origin. The Kennedy executive order additionally mandated that these contractors agree to "take affirmative action to ensure that applicants are employed and employees are treated during employment without regard to their race, creed, color, or national origin."

346 EMPLOYMENT REGULATION

- The Civil Rights Act of 1964. This antidiscrimination act did not contain any mandate that an employer engage in "affirmative action." Title VII of the act makes it an "unlawful employment practice" for an employer to make employment decisions about an individual "because of such individual's race, color, religion, sex, or national origin." (One 1994 study indicates that about 80% of private sector employees work for employers that are subject to the mandates of Title VII [Bloch 1994:100].)

- Johnson Executive Order 11246. This 1965 order reiterated almost verbatim the words of the Kennedy executive order. The regulations promulgated under Executive Order 11246 now apply to an estimated 16,000 companies in the United States, covering some 25 million workers (Berkman 1995:A30).

- Nixon Executive Order 11478. At the beginning of the Nixon administration, the Office of Federal Contract Compliance established a number of area-wide compliance programs designed to implement the Johnson executive order. Of these programs, the "Philadelphia Plan" is the best known. The comptroller general refused to honor the Philadelphia Plan on the ground that it imposed quotas in violation of Title VII. The comptroller general took his disagreement to Congress, where he convinced the Senate to attach a rider onto its supplemental appropriations bill that would essentially defeat any application of the Philadelphia Plan or similarly designed plans. The Senate passed the rider but President Nixon convinced the House to defeat it and promised to veto any appropriations bill that contained the rider.

- Congressional attempts to prohibit affirmative action. Congressional ratification of affirmative action became more explicit in 1971-72, when Senator Sam Ervin introduced a series of proposed amendments to Title VII that would explicitly prohibit all affirmative action programs promulgated under the Johnson executive order. The sound defeat of these amendments was seen as formal congressional sanction of the system of affirmative action goals and timetables that constituted the revised Philadelphia Plan.

- Civil Rights Act of 1991. The main purpose of the new Civil Rights Act was to "strengthen and improve federal civil rights laws," particularly in light of a 1989 Supreme Court decision that had "weakened the scope and effectiveness of federal civil rights protections" (CRA 1991, preamble, Sec. 1). Although both houses of Congress had carried on extensive discussions of affirmative action during the debates, the only reference to it in the new Act appears in Sec. 116: "Nothing in the amendments made by this title shall be construed to affect court-ordered remedies, affirmative action, or conciliation agreements that are in accordance with the law."

- Equal Employment Act of 1995. Congress again addressed affirmative action in 1995, when it considered but did not pass the "Equal Employment Act of 1995." This act, whose principal senatorial sponsor was Robert Dole, would have clearly prohibited any agency of the federal government from intentionally discriminating against or granting "a preference" to any individual or group based on race, color, national origin, or sex.

- Clinton Executive Order 13005. President Bill Clinton added his contribution to the series of executive orders on affirmative action in government contracting with Executive Order 13005 (5/16/96). For the first time, however, the presidential focus of affirmative action shifted from members of the traditional minority groups (classified by race, national origin, and gender) to individuals who lived in areas of "general economic distress." "General economic distress" is defined in this order with reference to the poverty and unemployment rate rather than to any racial or ethnic group.

A quick glance at the dates of the executive and congressional actions described above shows a gap between the mid-1970s and 1990. During this period the affirmative action debate shifted from the executive and congressional arenas to the courtroom.

## Judicial Pronouncements: From *Bakke* to *Adarand*

The Supreme Court of the United States has on several occasions examined whether affirmative action plans are valid both under Title VII of the Civil Rights Act and under the United States Constitution. While the theories behind the antidiscrimination mandate of Title VII and the equal protection mandate of the Constitution are substantially similar, the Court obviously has a longer history of decision making under the Constitution. One challenge to observers of developments in the affirmative action arena has been that the Court has at times applied different logic in the constitutional cases (which deal primarily with government employers) than in the Title VII cases (which deal primarily, although not exclusively, with private employers). The Court's decisions have not been confined to affirmative action in employment but cover also affirmative action as it relates to education, minority set-asides for government contracts, and minority set-asides in the transportation and communications industries. No overview of the Court's employment law cases would be complete without at least a summary of their holdings in these related cases.

- *Bakke.* The first and perhaps best known Supreme Court decision on affirmative action is *Regents of the University of California v. Bakke*, 438 U.S. 265 (1978). Bakke sued the university system when he was denied a place in the entering class of the medical school of the University of California at

Davis. The medical school had a special admissions program whereby it reserved 16 of the 100 places in its entering class for minorities. Bakke claimed that this program violated Title VII of the Civil Rights Act as well as the Fourteenth Amendment of the Constitution. The Court agreed. However, the Court refused to close completely the question of affirmative action plans in that it would not go so far as to prohibit the university from any consideration of race in the course of its admissions process.

- *Weber.* One year after *Bakke*, the Court decided the seminal employment discrimination case of *United Steelworkers of America v. Weber*, 443 U.S. 193 (1979). The case involved a challenge to an affirmative action plan that constituted part of the United Steelworkers and Kaiser Aluminum master collective bargaining agreement. The agreement established an in-house training program in which 50% of the spaces were reserved for blacks. Writing for the majority, Justice Brennan stated the Court's position quite clearly: "We hold that Title VII does not prohibit such race-conscious affirmative action plans." Justice Brennan also explained that a "permissible" affirmative action plan must (1) mirror the purposes of Title VII ("to break down old patterns of racial segregation and hierarchy"), (2) "not unnecessarily trammel the interests of the white employees," (3) not "create an absolute bar to the advancement of white employees," and (4) be a "temporary measure" that "is not intended to maintain racial balance but simply to eliminate a manifest racial imbalance" (*Weber*, 443 U.S. at 208-09).

- *Stotts.* Five years later, in *Firefighters Local Union No. 1784 v. Stotts*, 467 U.S. 561 (1984), the Supreme Court again visited the issue of affirmative action plans in the employment context and held that Title VII prohibited affirmative action plans that interfered with bona fide seniority systems. In this case, Justice Byron White made the sweeping statement that the policy behind the section of Title VII that authorizes court-ordered affirmative action was "to provide 'make-whole' relief only to those who have been actual victims of illegal discrimination" (*Stotts*, 467 U.S. at 580). This statement raised two related questions which the Court was forced to address in later cases. The first question was whether a court could order or approve affirmative action relief only if there had been a finding of actual discrimination by the employer. If so, the second question was whether the relief ordered had to be limited to those individuals who had actually suffered from the discrimination.

- Post-*Stotts* decisions. Decisions in the subsequent three years more clearly delineated the contours of the affirmative action debate among the then-sitting members of the Court while attempting to answer the two questions raised in *Stotts*. In *Wygant v. Jackson Board of Education*, 476 U.S. 267 (1986), a public school system's collective bargaining agreement geared the hiring of minority teachers to the percentage of minority students and limited layoffs of these teachers at the expense of more senior white teachers. Because the plan involved a state employer, the Court's analysis was based on its previous constitutional jurisprudence. The Court rejected the layoff plan as a violation of the Equal Protection Clause of the Constitution because it unnecessarily burdened the senior white employees who had lost their jobs. The Court also did not find the purpose of providing role models for minority teachers to be "compelling" enough to justify the blatant race-based preference.

In *Local 28, Sheet Metal Workers Intern. Ass'n. v. EEOC*, 478 U.S. 421 (1986), the Court upheld fines for contempt that were levied on a union that had violated judicially mandated goals for hiring minorities. The plan in question in this case was a hiring goal rather than a plan that resulted in the layoff of majority-group workers. Also, the defendant was a union rather than a public employer. Four members of the Court stated that court-ordered, race-conscious affirmative action relief need not be limited to those individuals who were the actual victims of prior discrimination. The deciding fifth vote, cast by Justice Lewis Powell, seemed limited to the egregious nature of the union's noncompliance as well as the fact that no innocent third parties were injured by the plan.

One year later, in *U.S. v. Paradise*, 480 U.S. 149 (1980), the majority of the Court echoed Justice Powell's opinion when it stated that race-based affirmative action by the government is appropriate when there has been a finding of past government action that was "long-term, open, and pervasive" discriminatory conduct.

- Voluntary plans. In *Local 93, Firefighters v. Cleveland*, 478 U.S. 501 (1986), the Court distinguished a plan that was adopted under a consent decree as a "voluntary" plan that was thus subject to fewer restrictions than the court-ordered plan involved in the *Weber* case. In this case, a strong majority (six justices) agreed that a voluntary affirmative action plan could be adopted even if it benefited persons other than those who had actually suffered from the employer's past discrimination.

In 1987, in *Johnson v. Santa Clara Transportation Agency*, 480 U.S. 616 (1987), the Court faced a more individualized form of voluntary affirmative action than that of its previous cases. The transportation agency, a public employer, had concluded that women were significantly underrepresented in certain job categories. The agency thus promoted a woman who had scored slightly lower on a prepromotion test than her male counterparts because it considered her gender as a "plus" factor in the decision. The Court upheld this approach.

- Minority set-aside cases. In *City of Richmond v. J.A. Croson Co.*, 488 U.S. 469 (1989), the Court struck down the city's minority set-aside plan because Richmond had not made a preliminary finding of past discriminatory action by anyone in the Richmond construction industry. The Court refused to accept the effects of past societal discrimination as a compelling enough reason to justify race-conscious action by the municipal government.

  The Court did not reach the same conclusion one year later in *Metro Broadcasting, Inc. v. FCC*, 110 S. Ct. 2997 (1990), a case that involved an FCC program to increase the licensure of minority radio and television broadcasters. In his final year on the Court, Justice Brennan wrote for the majority in *Metro Broadcasting* that "benign," race-conscious affirmative action mandated by Congress need not be limited to remedial measures designed to compensate past victims of government discrimination.

- *Adarand*. The holding in *Metro Broadcasting* that accepted "benign" affirmative action was effectively reversed in 1995 after Justice Brennan and Justice Thurgood Marshall had retired from the Court. *Adarand Constructors, Inc. v. Pena*, 515 U.S. 2097 (1995), involved another congressional affirmative action program that provided a financial incentive to government contractors who hired minority subcontractors. The Court applied strict scrutiny to this race-based program and found that it violated the Fifth Amendment to the Constitution. The Court confirmed that a finding of systemic and egregious discrimination by the government would justify a race-based remedial program so long as the program was a narrowly tailored remedy.

The series of Supreme Court cases that culminated with the *Adarand* case cast some doubt on the continued viability of a variety of affirmative action programs. First, *Adarand* confirms that any race-based program sponsored by a public employer, whether federal or local, must meet the demands of strict scrutiny. The *Adarand* holding would seem to indicate that such a program would be upheld only if an initial finding of past governmental discrimination was made, combined with an assurance that the program itself was not too broad to survive strict scrutiny. The cases preceding *Adarand* that dealt with court-ordered affirmative action dictate that a court must find some "egregious" prior discrimination in order to justify any order requiring affirmative action. Additionally, such an order is more likely to be upheld if it does not result in unnecessary intrusion on the rights of majority-group workers. Private employers' discretion to engage in voluntary affirmative action under

Title VII is much broader than the discretion of the courts to order such action. One question that remains open after *Adarand* is whether affirmative action plans adopted pursuant to Executive Order 11246 will continue to be treated as "voluntary" plans or will instead be construed to constitute the type of government action that entails a stricter scrutiny.

## Forms of Affirmative Action in the Workplace

As noted above, while many people have opinions about affirmative action, few can articulate a precise definition of the term. Instead, taking the "I know it when I see it approach," employers and employees alike generally define affirmative action by offering examples. Most of the examples revolve around classifications made on the basis of race (usually favoring the black race), sex (usually favoring women), or national origin (often favoring those of Hispanic origin). For the purpose of efficiency and with full realization that women constitute a majority rather than a minority in many countries, these classifications will be referred to as classifications made on the basis of minority status.

Some employers and employees equate the term affirmative action with quotas. Quotas involve statistical comparisons of the proportion of minorities in the employer's work force with the proportion of minorities in a designated pool. Affirmative action in this context is defined as the hiring or promoting of members of minority groups for the sole purpose of achieving a specified proportion of those groups in the work force or in certain ranks within the work force. The employer's action in these circumstances may or may not be tied to merit. For example, an employer may strive to employ a proportion of the minority group that mirrors the proportion of qualified minority applicants in the applicant pool. Presumably, then, no individual who is not qualified will be hired, but some qualified members of the majority group may be passed up in favor of similarly qualified minorities. On the other end of the spectrum, an employer may wish to employ a proportion of minorities that represents the proportion of that minority group in the general population. Particularly in the more highly skilled positions, such an approach may well result in the hiring of minimally or even unqualified minorities instead of qualified members of the majority group. Quotas are generally frowned upon by the courts.

In a more individually oriented context, some describe affirmative action as the choice by an employer to hire a member of a minority group over a member of the majority group for a specified position. Once again, the employment decision may or may not also be tied to merit. If the goal of hiring a minority is the sole determining factor in the employment decision, the employer may hire a minority who is not qualified while passing up a qualified member of the majority group or may simply refuse to consider the applications of individuals who are not members of the targeted minority group. On the other hand, the minority status of the applicant may be simply a tie-breaker—that is, the employer who is faced with two similarly qualified applicants may choose to hire the minority group member. Between these two extremes, minority status may be a motivating or "plus" factor in that the employer may hire a minority group member who is somewhat less qualified (lower test score, fewer years of experience) than the majority applicant under the theory that the goal of hiring a minority overrides the relative inequality of the applicants' credentials.

Affirmative action need not always take the form of a determinant in a hiring or promotion decision. An employer who wishes to hire more members of a minority group may choose instead to recruit aggressively at historically black colleges or to instigate a new training program that targets women who have exhibited management potential. This type of affirmative action is generally more palatable in that majority group applicants do not see themselves as blatantly denied a job or promotion which is granted to a minority group applicant. One commentator refers to this approach as "good affirmative action," as opposed to "bad affirmative action," which is the use of preferences as job determinants (Eastland 1996). On the other hand, it is arguable that an extensive investment of resources into the hiring or promoting of members of minority groups must eventually result in a denial of benefits or positions to members of the majority group.

## Why Employers Engage in Affirmative Action

Basically, an employer engages in affirmative action for one (or any combination) of four reasons: (1) the employer is required to do so by law or otherwise ordered by a court to do so, (2) the employer has no independent desire to engage in an affirmative action program but perceives that the program will be instrumental in accomplishing another goal of the employer, (3) the employer perceives that an affirmative action program will have a direct beneficial effect on the employer's business, or (4) the employer desires to engage in affirmative action to remedy perceived injustices in society. Commentators and some courts refer to plans that are established for the first reason as "involuntary" affirmative action and all other plans as "voluntary" affirmative action (Zimmer 1994:1115; Player 1988:313).

### Involuntary Affirmative Action

Executive Order 11246 requires the government as an employer to engage in affirmative action. Involuntary court-ordered affirmative action is also authorized by Title VII of the Civil Rights Act. Section 706(g)(1) allows a court that has found that an employer has intentionally engaged in prohibited discrimination to "order such affirmative action as may be appropriate," including reinstatement or hiring or "any other equitable relief as the court deems appropriate." This section would seem to give the court broad powers to force an employer to engage in a program that is designed to achieve and maintain a higher proportion of minorities in its work force. However, this section takes on a much more narrow cast when read in light of other relevant sections of Title VII. For example, section 703(j) cannot be ignored when considering the validity of court-ordered affirmative action. This section states clearly that Title VII shall not be interpreted to require an employer to grant preferential treatment to any individual for the sole purpose of remedying an imbalance in the employer's work force. Another section of Title VII that is relevant to court-ordered affirmative action is subsection (2) of section 706(g). This subsection provides that a court may not order the reinstatement or hiring of an individual who was fired or not hired for any reason other than the minority classification (e.g., poor credentials, poor job performance, dishonesty).

*Voluntary Affirmative Action*

Many employers have "voluntarily" initiated affirmative action plans for the three other reasons described above. Some employers institute such plans even when they prefer not to because they have discovered that an affirmative action program is a prerequisite for another goal the employer wishes to achieve. The goal may be a simple one, such as the avoidance or settlement of a lawsuit. For example, the EEOC, which is authorized to negotiate with employers to settle pending discrimination claims, may include an affirmative action program as part of the conciliation agreement (29 C.F.R. Chp. 14, Sec. 1608.6). Alternatively, the employer may choose to implement an affirmative action program in order to be eligible for federal funding (Civil Rights Act, T. VI) or for work under a government contract (Exec. Order 11246).

It is arguable that the type of "voluntary" affirmative action described above is more coerced than voluntary. However, the second and third reasons for establishing "voluntary" plans truly reflect an uncoerced decision by an employer. An employer might engage in an affirmative action program if the employer perceives that the affirmative action program will have a direct beneficial effect on the employer's business. In this case, the employer views affirmative action as a strategy for ameliorating its productivity or the marketability of its products rather than as an indirect means of acquiring government funding or immunity from a lawsuit. For example, a bank that operates offices in a major metropolitan area may determine that an increased visibility of black branch managers will boost its business prospects. A television station may choose to hire a female rather than a male anchorperson in order to attract a wider array of viewers. A law firm that represents management in employment discrimination cases might choose to hire a black woman litigator whose presence in the courtroom will help dissipate a jury's suspicion of its clients. In the *Weber* case, Justice Brennan noted how ironic it would be if Title VII were to be interpreted to prohibit private voluntary affirmative action plans. After pointing out that Section 703(j) (which provides that employers would not be forced to grant racial preferences in order to achieve a balanced work force) was designed to "avoid undue regulation of private business," Justice Brennan observed that a statutory prohibition against private affirmative action plans would "augment the power of the federal government and diminish traditional management perspectives" (*Weber*, 443 U.S. at 206-07). However, as noted above, the Supreme Court of the United States would seem to frown on even private plans unless their purpose is to ameliorate the effects of prior discrimination.

The final reason why an employer might choose to engage in affirmative action is simply that the employer wishes to play a role that it perceives will better our traditionally discriminatory society. For example, an architectural firm that has never intentionally discriminated in the past may decide that it would like to sponsor a promising young black architect. The firm then turns down other "better qualified" architects in order to achieve its socially oriented goal. Some would argue that such an altruistic employer would be a rare find in that business owners rarely make decisions that are not motivated at some level by their own economic interests. Such an approach, however, is not unusual with public employers. In 1989, the township of Piscataway, New Jersey, made such a decision. The school system in the township had not discriminated in hiring faculty; in fact, the percentage of black teachers in the system exceeded the percentage of available black employees in the work force. The township faced the prospect of extensive cutbacks and found itself forced to lay off teachers in order of seniority. Two teachers of equal qualifications, a black teacher and a white teacher, had begun working for the school system on exactly the same day. The system decided to lay off the white teacher because the black teacher was the only black teacher in the business education department and the system was committed to maintaining a culturally diverse faculty. The Court of Appeals for the Third Circuit examined the school board's motivation in light of the earlier *Weber* and *Johnson* cases and determined that the affirmative action plan did not pass muster under Title VII. (*Taxman v. Board of Education of Piscataway*, 91 F.3d 1547 [3d Cir. 1996]). The court pointed out that the purpose articulated by the school board—that is, the achievement of diversity in the school system's faculty—

was not one of the purposes of Title VII. In fact, the court went so far as to say that the *only* time a voluntary affirmative action plan would be valid would be when its purpose was to remedy the effect of past discrimination by the employer school system. While the *Weber* and *Johnson* plans had focused on eliminating the effects of past discrimination, the school board's plan seemed motivated more by the social goal of maintaining a diverse environment. The Court of Appeals found that that type of goal did not outweigh Title VII's basic prohibition against considering an individual's race when making an employment decision.

## Jurisprudential Theories of Affirmative Action

Jurisprudential discussions of affirmative action are beset with a series of dichotomies: neutrality vs. reverse discrimination, victims vs. sinners (or, more precisely, nonvictims vs. nonsinners), compensatory justice vs. distributive justice, benign discrimination vs. invidious discrimination, and individual rights vs. group rights. An interesting irony of these discussions is that theorists on either side envision the same goal: a society in which an individual's race or sex or national origin or other status is not viewed as a negative factor. The arguments for the most part revolve around the ways and means of reaching that goal.

For some theorists, affirmative action is simply the reverse of the type of discrimination that is prohibited by the laws of the United States. These purists (referred to also as "neutralists" [Tribe 1986:202] or "fair shakers" [Abram 1986:1313]) label as invalid any circumstance in which an employer considers an individual's race, color, religion, national origin, sex, age, or disability in the course of making an employment decision. Proponents of this theory argue as follows: The Constitution of the United States mandates that states and the federal government shall not deny equal protection of the laws to individuals (U.S. Constitution, Amends. V, XIV). As stated by William Bradford Reynolds, former Assistant U.S. Attorney General, "[I]t is clear beyond doubt that the intent of the [Fourteenth] Amendment was to command that all government decisions be made on a race-neutral basis; that the amendment was meant to guarantee equal opportunity, not equal results; and that it would not permit preferences by reason of race" (Daly 1985:2-3). Additionally, the federal antidiscrimination laws prohibit public and private employers from making employment decisions that are based on an individual's minority status. Title VII of the Civil Rights Act specifically states that the act is not designed to require an employer to grant preferential treatment to employees of any minority group merely because there is an imbalance of members of that group in the employer's work force (Civil Rights Act, T. VII, §703(j)). Recent revisions to the Civil Rights Act indicate that the antidiscrimination laws are violated whenever an individual's race, color, religion, national origin, or sex was a "motivating factor" in an employment decision (Civil Rights Act, T. VII, §703). Therefore, prohibited discrimination occurs in any circumstance in which the individual's race or other characteristic plays a role, regardless of whether the employer is hiring a black individual or a white individual, a man or a woman, a Baptist or a Jew, and regardless of why the employer chose to consider the characteristic.

The purist stance was perhaps best articulated in Justice John Marshall Harlan's famous dissenting statement in the 1986 case of *Plessy v. Ferguson*: "Our constitution is color-blind." From this viewpoint, there is virtually no difference between discrimination and affirmative action—and both are definitely and in all circumstances illegal.

Opponents of this theory counter the purists' reliance on the Constitution by arguing that the Fourteenth Amendment in its historical context was passed primarily to protect blacks from hostile state action (Fiss 1976:85-86). Drew S. Days III, former Solicitor General of the United States, points out that "[t]he Congress that ratified the Civil War amendments itself engaged in affirmative action. The Freedman's Bureaus were explicitly designed to benefit blacks, and they used racial classification" (Daly 1986:4). Legal philosopher Ronald Dworkin criticizes the purist stance even more strongly: "There is no language in the Constitution whose plain meaning prohibits affirmative action. Only the most naive theories of statutory construction could argue that such a result is required by the language of . . . the Civil Rights Act of 1964 or any other congressional enactment" (Dworkin 1985:298). These proponents of affirmative action argue that a society that has historically discriminated against certain classes of individuals owes that group some remedial action. (For this reason, these theorists are sometimes referred to as "social engineers" [Abram 1986:1313].)

Opponents and proponents of affirmative action often clash on the notions of victimization and "sin." As noted above, early affirmative action cases questioned whether affirmative action should be available only to those who actually had been victimized by the prior discrimination of the employer, rather than to more recent job applicants who had not suffered from the employer's actions. Stephen Carter (1988) describes this concept of victimhood as "bilateral individualism, because it invents a reality in which the only victims are those who have suffered at the hands of transgressors" (p. 421). Dr. Benjamin Hooks, former Executive Director of the NAACP, responds to the "victims-only" argument by stating that "all black folks are victims of discrimination. Therefore, we were all intended to be helped by these laws" (Daly 1985:10). On the other hand, Ronald Fiscus (1992) views this notion "that all blacks are the equivalent of members of a single family" as "in a word, racist." He explains that this notion "equates, legally and morally, individual black men and women with their racial identity" (p. 10).

The label of victim is not restricted to those who have suffered from or continue to suffer from past discrimination. Purists point out that innocent members of the majority group (nonsinners) may easily be victimized by an affirmative action program that denies them benefits while favoring members of the minority group. Such an approach is manifestly unjust, observes Judge Richard Posner (1974), because "the nonminority people excluded because of the preference are unlikely to have perpetrated, or to have in any demonstrable sense, benefited from, the discrimination" (p. 16). On the other hand, Derrick Bell is very suspicious of this claim: "I wonder whether the claim that whites are victimized by affirmative action is sincere, or whether it is nothing more than a self-aware appropriation of victim status for self-gain. . . . The myth that racial remediation programs are responsible for whites' economic woes persists despite the fact that whites continue to be employed at rates vastly outpacing African-Americans" (Bell and Singer 1993:276).

Kathleen Sullivan (1986) characterizes the overall themes of victims/nonvictims and sinners/nonsinners as unduly focused on the past rather than "justifying affirmative action as the architecture of a racially integrated future" (p. 80). Fiscus criticizes the approach because it is based on a model of compensatory rather than distributive justice. He explains that compensatory justice is the "claim to compensation for discrete and 'finished' harm done to minority group members or their actions," while distributive justice is "the claim an individual or group has to the positions or advantages or benefits that would have been awarded under fair conditions" (Fiscus 1992:8). Fiscus justifies affirmative action in the form of proportional quotas under the distributive justice model but is quick to point out that under this model "individuals or groups may *not* claim positions, advantages, or benefits that they would *not* have been awarded under fair conditions" (p. 13). Kent Greenawalt, on the other hand, feels that the distinction between the Aristotelian models of compensatory and distributive justice "largely collapses" in the affirmative action context because both rest "on assertions of past injustice" (Greenawalt 1975:579).

The affirmative action debate at times revolves around a perceived distinction between "benign" as opposed to "malign" or invidious discrimination. Some theorists argue that affirmative action is not illegal because illegal discrimination occurs only when an employer intentionally makes a negative employment decision based on an individual's minority status. For example, a white man who refuses to hire blacks or women is engaging in the type of action that the antidiscrimination laws were designed to prevent. On the other

hand, an employer who engages in affirmative action is not performing an illegal act because the discrimination involved is "benign" discrimination in favor
of individuals who traditionally have suffered due to their minority status.
These theorists contend that true equality in society will not be achieved
unless individuals in these groups are placed on an equal footing with those
who have always enjoyed this society's benefits. Proponents of benign discrimination are not opposed to preferential treatment of individuals in certain
groups because they see the preference as a way of society paying its debt to
these groups and of eventually achieving an environment in which race, sex,
and all the other characteristics will no longer play a role.

Opponents of affirmative action argue that even "benign" discrimination
may have malign effects. These theorists attack the notion that all blacks or
members of other minority groups are in fact benefited by affirmative action.
Led by such visible spokespersons as Justice Clarence Thomas, these theorists
argue that many minority group members are opposed to affirmative action
because it stigmatizes them and confirms stereotyped notions about their
inferiority (Smith 1996:9). In *Confessions of an Affirmative Action Baby*
(1991), Stephen Carter describes his feeling upon realizing that he had been
accepted to Harvard Law School because of his race: "The insult I felt came
from the pain of being reminded so forcefully that in the judgment of those
with the power to dispose, I was good enough for a top law school only
because I happened to be black" (p. 16).

Proponents of affirmative action as "benign" action are comfortable with
an analysis of rights that focuses on groups rather than on individuals. Owen
Fiss justifies affirmative action if its purpose is to advantage groups that have
been historically disadvantaged. He refers to his theory as "an ethical view
against caste, one that would make it undesirable for any social group to
occupy a position of subordination for an extended period of time" (Fiss
1976:128). He rationalizes a "special judicial solicitude on their behalf" without which certain segments of our society would continue as a "perpetual
underclass" (p. 133). Former U.N. Ambassador Morris B. Abram, on the
other hand, highlights the danger of this group-oriented action:

> The social engineers' approach also fails to confront the problem of
> *who decides* what groups are sufficiently disadvantaged to deserve
> special treatment. They offer no mechanism for neutral decision
> making on this issue. . . . In the absence of any neutral decision-
> making mechanisms, the attempt to end discrimination through
> color-conscious remedies must inevitably degenerate into a crude
> political struggle between groups seeking favored status. (Abram
> 1986:1321)

The focus on individual as opposed to group rights was emphasized by the Supreme Court in the *Adarand* case. In that case, Justice Sandra Day O'Connor harkened back to Justice Powell's statement in *Bakke* that "it is the individual who is entitled to judicial protection against classifications based upon his racial or ethnic background because such distinctions impinge upon personal rights, rather than the individual only because of his membership in a particular group" (115 S.Ct. at 2111, citing 438 U.S. at 299).

## Affirmative Action: Do We Need It? Does It Work?

The debate of politicians, judges, and scholars revolves around whether affirmative action is constitutional and fair. Perhaps the more pragmatic questions are these: Do we need affirmative action at all? If we do, does it work to accomplish our goal? Proponents of affirmative action explain that it is designed to address the inferior economic position held by women and minorities in the American workplace. Because this inferior position results from past discrimination, affirmative action is a necessary component of an equal opportunity system (Clayton 1992:4). The proponents remind us that before the Civil Rights Act of 1964 became effective, blatant and overt discrimination by employers against women and minorities was not only legal but also well-accepted. One probable effect of this discrimination was that female and minority workers were underrepresented in the workplace, particularly in positions of high compensation and power. For example:

- In 1964 unemployment rates for black men and black women were roughly double those for whites, and unemployment rates for women of both races were higher than the rates for males of the same races (3.4% for white males age 20 or over, 7.7% for black males, 4.6% for white women, and 9.0% for black women) (Bloch 1994:42).

- In 1966, 85% of black men who worked for private employers and 69% of black women held blue-collar positions, as compared to 39% of white men and 37% of white women (Feagin and Feagin 1988:44).

- In 1966 the average white male who had graduated from high school earned 40% more than his nonwhite male counterpart. This gap became progressively wider as the education level of each group increased (Bell 1992:809).

- In 1965 women earned $.60 for every dollar earned by men (Feagin and Feagin 1986:45).

- A study of federal employees in 1962 indicated that blacks comprised 18.1% of employees in the lower grades (GS 1-4) and only .8% of employees in the highest grades (GS 12-18). Women also were grossly underrepresented in the higher grades, comprising only .10% of employees grade 13-18 in 1971 (Kellough 1989:31-37).

Have the relative economic positions of women and minorities improved since the dawn of affirmative action programs? Statistics are available that support both affirmative and negative responses to that answer. These are examples of the evidence that is cited to show that the plight of women and minorities has improved:

- Unemployment rates for both white women and black women are now lower than those for white and black men (Bloch 1994:42; U.S. Dept. of Labor 1996).

- In 1994, for every dollar earned by white men, black men earned $.75, white women earned $.72, and black women earned $.63 (National Council for Research on Women 1995:4).

- In the two decades following enactment of the first civil rights laws, blacks and women increased their proportional representation in the highest grades of federal government employment (blacks to 6.4% in GS 12-18 by 1984 and women to .27% in GS 13-18 by 1984) (Kellough 1989:31-37).

- The proportion of managers who are women grew substantially between 1980 and 1990 (from 27% to 35% for white women and from 3% to 7% for women of color) (National Council for Research on Women 1995:6), and the proportion of women and blacks who hold managerial or professional positions increased between 1983 and 1994 (40.9% of women workers in 1983 up to 48.1% in 1994, 5.6% of black workers in 1983 up to 7.1% in 1994) (U.S. Dept. of Commerce 1995).

On the other hand, equally compelling evidence indicates that women and minorities not only have a long way to go but, in some cases, may be worse off now than they were thirty years ago. For example:

- In 1990 only 6.3% of women managers and 3.6% of minority managers earned incomes in the top 20% (National Council for Research on Women 1995:4).

- College-educated women earn 29% less than college-educated men and their average pay is only $1,950 higher than the average high-school-educated white man (National Council for Research on Women 1995:4).

- The average income of black families in the late 1980s was lower than the average income for black families in the 1970s (Bell 1992:808). The median income for black families (in constant 1993 dollars) was $21,969 in 1970 and $21,542 in 1993 (U.S. Dept. of Commerce 1995).

- In 1970 median black income was 61.3% of median white income; by 1989 median black income had decreased to only 56.2% of median white income (Bell 1992:812)

- In 1993, 12.2% of whites lived at or below the poverty level, while 33.1% of blacks lived at or below the poverty level (U.S. Dept. of Commerce 1995).

- By 1992 the gap between the unemployment rates for blacks and whites had increased from that of 1964: 13.4% for black males as opposed to 6.3% of white males and 11.7% for black females as opposed to 5.4% for white females (Bloch 1994:42). While national unemployment rates had decreased by 1995, the substantial gap still remained: 10.7% for black men as opposed to 4.8% for white men and 8.2% for black women as opposed to 4.4% for white women (U.S. Dept. of Labor 1996).

- The pace at which Fortune 500 companies are adding women to their boards of directors has slowed steadily since 1994, with a 9% increase between 1993 and 1994, slowing to only a 3% increase between 1995 and 1996 (Catalyst 1996).

- As of 1995 white men comprised only 33% of the American population but still comprised 85% of partners in law firms, 85% of tenured professors, 80% of the House of Representatives, 90% of the U.S. Senate, and 95% of Fortune 500 CEOs (National Council for Research on Women 1995:6).

It is obvious that a variety of factors have contributed to the statistical situation outlined above. Educational opportunities for women and minorities have increased, but relative rates of achievement in many public schools have gone down. The drug culture has dominated the lives of certain segments of our society, particularly low-income black families. The number of single mothers raising children has increased substantially. The number of women who enter the work force on career-oriented paths has also increased. Thus it is difficult to use these statistics to make any definitive evaluation of whether affirmative action has worked.

Perhaps more telling are those studies that concentrate particularly on the implementation of Executive Order 11246, which requires the federal government and all federal contractors to engage in affirmative action. Unfortunately, these studies are also inconclusive.

In 1984-85 Jonathon S. Leonard conducted studies of the enforcement mechanisms employed under the executive order and of the impact of the executive order on the employment of women and blacks. He concluded that the enforcement mechanisms were targeted more at large white-collar-intensive establishments than at those establishments that had a relatively small proportion of women and minorities (Leonard 1984:383). Despite this poorly targeted enforcement, he found several positive effects of affirmative action. He concluded as follows:

> In the contract sector affirmative action has increased the demand relative to white males for black males by 6.5%, for nonblack minority males by 11.9%, and for white females by 3.5%. For a program lacking public consensus and vigorous enforcement, this is a strong showing. (Leonard 1984:459)

A 1989 study examined the effect of the goals and timetables instituted by the federal government in 1971 as part of its equal employment opportunity program. The study found no significant gains by blacks in the higher grades of government employment, where blacks had been traditionally underrepresented. There were slight increases in the proportion of women employed in these higher grades, but women still remained substantially underrepresented in these grades. On the other hand, examination of the rates of employment in particular government agencies indicated that the agencies that experienced the most substantial increase in employment of women and blacks in the higher grades were those that had had the lowest proportion of women and blacks in these grades prior to the instigation of the affirmative action program. The author of this study made three general observations. First, he concluded that the problem at hand (the underrepresentation of women and blacks in high-level government positions) was complicated dramatically by broader social inequities. Second, he found that the goals and timetables had not altered substantially the trends for hiring women and blacks. Third, he concluded that the goals and timetables had had some impact and definitely had a symbolic value that would be important for minorities and women who were considering jobs in the public sector (Kellough 1989:108-15).

A 1994 study took a somewhat different approach to determining whether government regulation of the employment process justified the problems inherent in giving preferred treatment to certain members of the society. This study focused in part on the differences in hiring practices between those firms that contract with the federal government (and thus are covered by the Executive Order 11246 affirmative action requirement) and those firms that are noncontractors. The results confirmed an earlier 1990 study that showed that "contractors have fostered significantly higher growth in the employment rates of protected class members [women and minorities] than noncontractors" (Bloch 1994:96). However, when attempting to reconcile this conclusion with the increasing gap in the unemployment rate among blacks and white, the author of the study observed that "the contractor-noncontractor differences primarily represent demographic shifts across these two employer categories rather than net economywide gains for minorities" (p. 103).

As noted above, opponents of affirmative action argue that affirmative action constitutes nothing more than reverse discrimination against white males. What is more, argues Richard Epstein (1995), government-mandated affirmative action is unnecessary because "the same political forces arrayed on behalf of affirmative action could still find their voice inside private organizations" (p. 180). However, Epstein's claim that "the forces for diversity and affirmative action are simply too powerful to be denied" (p. 180) begs the question that the above-described statistics cannot seem to answer. That question is simply this: Even if we assume that women and minorities have made economic strides in the past thirty years, were those strides made because of or in spite of affirmative action? As the affirmative action debate rages into the 21st century, a variety of issues remain to be resolved.

## Future Direction of the Affirmative Action Debate

After the *Adarand* case, described above, it is clear that government-sponsored affirmative action plans, to the degree they retain the race or gender categories, will be subject to the same level of scrutiny that is applied to any governmental action that takes race or gender into account. Within the next two to three years, the Supreme Court will probably be called upon often to decide which programs meet that standard of scrutiny. *Adarand* made it clear that an affirmative action plan based on race will be subjected to strict scrutiny. Consequently, the government will need to show both a compelling governmental purpose for the plan and that the plan is narrowly tailored to fit that purpose. The Court's decision in *Adarand* indicated that actual past discrimination by the employer that was of a "pervasive, systematic, and obstinate" nature will justify race-based affirmative action by a government. In the recent future, the Court will very likely be called upon to decide whether other justifications are significantly compelling so as to justify race-conscious treatment.

Congress, the President, the Supreme Court, and the states will most likely keep their focus on the extent to which government-sponsored affirmative action plans will be allowed. In the November, 1996 election, the state of California passed an anti-affirmative action initiative that prohibits preferential treatment in government actions, including government employment. Other states caught up in the rhetoric of the political debates will attempt and probably pass such initiatives too. President Clinton's recent executive order illustrates what will most likely be the approach of the executive branch during his second term. Affirmative action for federal employers and government contractors will not be abolished completely but instead will be focused less on the race and gender categories and more on the hiring and implementation of members of economically disadvantaged groups. While this change may have only a marginal effect on the hiring of minorities and minority contractors, it remains to be seen whether women will be deemed to have been traditionally economically disadvantaged.

The long-term focus will more likely shift to affirmative action plans that are put in place voluntarily by private employers for any of the reasons described above. The fate of these plans is in some ways dependent upon the fate of government-sponsored plans but private plans have traditionally been given greater leeway by the courts.

The post-*Adarand* years will see a proliferation in the number of "reverse discrimination" lawsuits brought by whites or males who feel disadvantaged by an employer's affirmative action plan. The threat of such suits will surely result in a decrease in the number of "quota"-type affirmative action plans.

On the other hand, if Epstein is correct in his prediction that "the forces for diversity and affirmative action are simply too powerful to be denied," private employers will become more and more inclined to make employment decisions based on race or gender for compelling business reasons. What is ironic is that in all of the cases in which the Supreme Court examined private plans, it was made clear that the purpose behind the plan should mirror the spirit of Title VII—that is, the correction of the lingering effects of past discrimination. If the Court holds private employers to this rule, then employers would not be authorized to take race-conscious or gender-conscious affirmative action simply because it makes good business sense. Consider, for example, a company that builds hardware and software for "virtual reality" communications. Such a company and industry have no history of past discrimination if for no other reason than that neither existed even a few years ago. If this company decides to hire a black saleswoman to market its product to black-owned businesses, Title VII would seem to offer the company no protection from a lawsuit.

If a court or Congress takes this approach, the various camps involved today in the affirmative action debate will splinter and new alliances will be formed. For example, some current opponents of affirmative action argue that the government should not be in the habit of "social engineering" and thus should be involved only minimally, if at all, in business decisions. These opponents would probably favor an approach that allows business-oriented decision making, even if it is race conscious or gender conscious. However, other current opponents of affirmative action take the purist stance that any type of discrimination for whatever reason is wrong. These opponents, who would not accept the notion of "benign" discrimination in government-oriented affirmative action programs, could not logically accept an approval of such action even on a private scale. In fact, this group may be the most vocal harbingers of the danger for abuse with such an approach. Some current proponents of affirmative action favor affirmative action because it raises certain societal groups to an equal level in our society. These proponents also would focus quickly on the danger that a "business decision" may easily result in a majority group members getting a job selling products in majority-group communities. These proponents of affirmative action would then find themselves arguing that race or gender should not be allowed to be a consideration in hiring or promotion decisions. The current proponents of affirmative action who justify such action as remedial would have difficulty arguing that race or gender can be considered as a corrective feature if the business or industry has no history of past discrimination.

Race-based affirmative action in government-sponsored programs may well have met its demise with *Adarand* and the variety of state and federal initiatives that are designed to invalidate it. However, the affirmative action debate will not die as quickly or as fast, particularly since more and more employers are making hiring or promotion decisions that consciously take race or gender into account. The debate will continue to involve not only private employers but also all three branches of federal and local governments. Perhaps the only prediction that can be made safely is that the shifting contours of the debate will have the kaleidoscopic effect of separating and regrouping politicians, judges, theorists, and voters whose current stance seems—to them, at least—so solidly rooted as to be both unquestionable and timeless.

## Acknowledgment

The author expresses her thanks to J. Parker Gilbert for his invaluable assistance in the preparation of this work.

## References

Abram, Morris B. 1986. "Affirmative Action: Fair Shakers and Social Engineers." *Harvard Law Review*, Vol. 99, no. 6 (April), pp. 1312-26.

Bell, Derrick. 1992. *Race, Racism, and the Law*. 3d ed. Boston: Little, Brown & Co.

Bell, Derrick, and Linda Singer. 1993. "Making a Record." *Connecticut Law Review*, Vol. 26, no. 1 (Fall), pp. 265-84.

Berkman, Harvey. 1995. "Many 'Tentacles' to Race-Based Federal Policies." *The National Law Journal*, April 24, p. A1.

Bloch, Farrell. 1994. *Antidiscrimination Law and Minority Employment*. Chicago: University of Chicago Press.

Carter, Stephen L. 1988. "When Victims Happen to be Black." *Yale Law Journal*, Vol. 97, no. 3 (February), pp. 420-47.

_____. 1991. *Confessions of an Affirmative Action Baby*. New York: Basic Books.

Catalyst. 1996. "Boards Add Women at Slower Pace." *The Atlanta Journal-Constitution*, December 6, 1996, p. F-1.

Clayton, Susan D., and Faye J. Crosby. 1992. *Justice, Gender, and Affirmative Action*. Ann Arbor: University of Michigan Press.

Daly, John Charles. 1985. "Affirmative Action and the Constitution." *Proceedings of Public Policy Forum 64* (Washington, DC, May 21, 1985) Washington, DC: American Enterprise Institute for Public Policy Research, pp. 1-29.

Dworkin, Ronald. 1985. *A Matter of Principle*. Cambridge: Harvard University Press.

Eastland, Terry. 1996. "Special to *Insight*: Should Washington Halt Race-based Policies for Hiring and Contracting? Yes: Restore the Standard of the Civil Rights Act of 1964." *Insight Magazine*, May 6.

Epstein, Richard A. 1995. *Simple Rules for a Complex World*. Cambridge: Harvard University Press.

Feagin, Joe R., and Clairece Booher Feagin. 1986. *Discrimination American Style: Institutional Racism and Sexism*. Malabar: Robert E. Krieger Publishing Co.

Fiscus, Ronald J. 1992. *The Constitutional Logic of Affirmative Action*. Durham: Duke University Press.

Fiss, Owen M. 1976. "Groups and the Equal Protection Clause." *Equality and Preferential Treatment: A Philosophy and Public Affairs Reader*, pp. 87-154.

Greenawalt, Kent. 1975. "Judicial Scrutiny of 'Benign' Racial Preference in Law School Admissions." *Columbia Law Review*, Vol. 75, no. 3 (April), pp. 559-602.

Kellough, J. Edward. 1989. *Federal Equal Employment Opportunity Policy and Numerical Goals and Timetables*. New York: Praeger.

Leonard, Jonathon S. 1984. "The Impact of Affirmative Action on Employment." *Journal of Labor Economics*, Vol 2, no. 4, pp. 439-63.

_____. 1985. "Affirmative Action as Earnings Distribution: The Targeting of Compliance Reviews." *Journal of Labor Economics*, Vol. 3, no. 3, pp. 363-84.

National Council for Research on Women. 1995. "Affirmative Action: Beyond the Glass Ceiling and the Sticky Floor." *Issues Quarterly*, Vol. 1, no. 4.

Posner, Richard A. 1974. "The *DeFunis* Case and the Constitutionality of Preferential Treatment of Racial Minorities." *Supreme Court Review*, Vol. 1974, pp. 1-25.

Player, Mack A. 1988. *Employment Discrimination Law*. St. Paul, MN: West Publishing Co.

Smith, Steven. 1996. "Justice Thomas: The Record Speaks." *The Defender*, Vol. 11, no. 6 (May/June), pp. 1, 8-9.

Sullivan, Kathleen M. 1986. "Sins of Discrimination: Last Term's Affirmative Action Cases." *Harvard Law Review*, Vol. 100, no. 1 (Nov.), pp. 78-98.

Tribe, Laurence H. 1986. "In What Vision of the Constitution Must the Law Be Color-Blind?" *John Marshall Law Review*, Vol. 20, no. 2 (Winter), pp. 201-207.

U.S. Department of Commerce. 1995. *Statistical Abstract of the United States*. 115th ed. Washington, DC: GPO.

U.S. Department of Labor. 1996. *Employment and Earnings*. January-April. Washington, DC: GPO.

Zimmer, Michael J., Charles A. Sullivan, and Richard F. Richards. 1994. *Cases and Materials on Employment Discrimination Law*. Boston: Little, Brown and Company.

## Cases

*Adarand Constructors, Inc. v. Pena*, 515 U.S. 2097 (1995)
*City of Richmond v. J.A. Croson Co.*, 488 U.S. 469 (1989)
*Firefighters Local Union No. 1784 v. Stotts*, 467 U.S. 561 (1984)
*Griggs v. Duke Power Company*, 401 U.S. 424 (1971)
*Johnson v. Santa Clara Transportation Agency*, 480 U.S. 616 (1987)
*Local 28 of Sheet Metal Workers Intern. Ass'n. v. EEOC*, 478 U.S. 421 (1986)
*Local 93, Firefighters v. Cleveland*, 478 U.S. 501 (1986)
*Metro Broadcasting, Inc. v. FCC*, 110 S. Ct. 2997 (1990)
*Plessy v. Ferguson*, 163 U.S. 537 (1896)
*Regents of the University of California v. Bakke*, 438 U.S. 265 (1978)
*Taxman v. Board of Education of Piscataway*, 91 F3d 1547 (3d Cir. 1996)
*U.S. v. Paradise*, 480 U.S. 149 (1980)
*U.S. v. Virginia*, 116 S.Ct. 2264 (1996)
*United Steelworkers of America v. Weber*, 443 U.S. 193 (1979)
*Wygant v. Jackson Board of Education*, 476 U.S. 267 (1986)

# Chapter 10

# Government Regulation of Workplace Disputes and Alternative Dispute Resolution

Lamont E. Stallworth
*Loyola University Chicago*

As this country prepares to set sail to improve government efficiency and effectiveness in resolving workplace disputes and to use alternative dispute resolution processes as an integral tool to effectuate our important and hard fought for workplace civil rights, we should remain ever mindful of the importance of these workplace civil rights statutes. Indeed, the courts have spoken of workplace civil rights statutes such as Title VII as involving rights of the highest order.[1]

A historical perspective and knowledge from where we have come as an industrial and civilized society in the workplace civil rights area will provide us with a better appreciation of "where we are today, and how and why we got here, and where we want to be tomorrow." As this country approaches the year 2000 and the 21st century, the workplace dispute resolution systems which are put in place today shall undoubtedly be institutionalized and shall provide the "model" for the next century. History may also provide us with a greater understanding and sensitivity as to why claimant employees often perceive that they have been treated if not unlawfully, at least unfairly. It is the opinion of the author that the perception of unfair treatment is the primary genesis for the ever-increasing number of what I term "diversity-statutory-based workplace disputes."[2]

In the previous chapters, the authors addressed the topic of "government regulation of the employment relationship" from a theoretical perspective. This chapter, however, will address and examine the government regulation of workplace disputes from more of a historical and legal perspective. Specifically, the chapter will examine the manner with which workplace disputes or grievances were historically resolved. Second, this chapter will explore the current state of the law and practice related to workplace dispute resolution. A particular focus will be placed on the government's promotion and use of alternative dispute resolution and conflict management in handling statutory-based workplace disputes.[3]

Third, the chapter will also touch upon the six primary catalysts or factors prompting such government efficiency and promotion of workplace dispute resolution ADR initiatives. These catalysts are (1) public and business community criticism,[4] (2) external statutory case law,[5] (3) increased civil litigation jury damage awards, (4) workplace civil rights and protective workplace legislation,[6] (5) mandated government enforcement agency efficiency and ADR initiatives,[7] and (6) employer-sponsored workplace dispute resolution systems and ADR programs.[8]

The chapter will address these areas within the context or backdrop of the relevant statutory case law, the dramatically changing demographic diversity in the workplace, and the changing psyche of the American worker.[9]

Lastly, the chapter will suggest some pragmatic solutions to several critical public policy and practical issues related to the governmental and private resolution of workplace disputes including the proposing of a National Workplace Dispute Resolution Act (NWDRA).

## Workplace Dispute Resolution Systems and the Law: Then and Now

From a historical perspective, our industrial society adopted, as a matter of public policy and practice, that there would be limited government intervention in the workplace and endorsed the right of the employee and employer to form employment relationships. This philosophy was premised, in large part, on the theory of permitting employers and employees a significant degree of self-regulation and adhering to the principle of employment at will.[10] Under the former, for example, government generally would not intervene in the employment relationship, and later with the enactment of the Wagner Act, the government in most instances preferred to have management and labor unions utilize collective bargaining as means of self-regulation of their relationship.[11] Under this latter labor-management relationship scheme, unionized workers were generally protected from the arbitrary treatment of foremen and supervisors. With the advent and adoption of seniority provisions and grievance and arbitration procedures, unionized workers and their employers had both an objective criteria upon which such employment decisions as holiday pay, vacation time, promotions, and layoffs were determined. A worker's seniority most often was the criteria for employment benefit decisions and layoff decisions. Furthermore, where a dispute arose over the manner by which a worker was treated, that worker generally had access to a grievance procedure which often culminated in final and binding arbitration using a disinterested outside third party as the private judge.[12]

The same contractual protections and formal grievance procedures, which are now also called "employee voice systems,"[13] did not generally exist for the nonunion worker. It was not unusual for the nonunion worker to be subject to the vagaries and arbitrary treatment of supervisors in the assignment of work, compensation, promotion and even layoff and termination. In many instances, these types of treatment served as the catalyst for workers to form and join labor unions.[14] However, the nonunion worker as an employee at will, in the absence of any other relevant statutory protection, could be terminated for any reason—good or bad—and have no real recourse. Furthermore, even in those instances where the employee may have had some kind of "open-door policy" to handle worker complaints,[15] workers more often than not were reluctant to resort to such "open-door" voice mechanisms.[16]

In addition to the inadequacy of legitimate internal workplace dispute resolution systems, workers generally did not fare any better when they resorted to the courts to address disputes involving work-related injuries and accidents.

*Early Employer-sponsored Open-Door Policies*

Informal and formal open-door policies designed to serve as employee voice or employer-promulgated grievance procedures (EPGPs) have come in various forms. Some workplace dispute resolution systems were relatively informal open-door policies; others were more lengthy and formalized fair treatment systems involving ombudspersons, neutral corporate officials, involving formal three- or four-step grievance procedures, culminating in the dispute being resolved by either corporate officials or outside arbitrators.

Such informal or formal open-door policies (or EPGPs) were utilized as early as the 1940s, according to a study completed by the National Industrial Conference Board.[17] Eli Lilly & Company was one of the early employers which implemented the practice and policy of resolving workplace disputes on the basis of informal discussion and investigation. Eli Lilly & Company later instituted a six-step grievance procedure to supplement its initial dispute resolution system.[18]

Other early corporate pioneers in the use of formal workplace dispute resolution systems included Northrop Corporation (1946), IBM (1950), and Trans World Airlines (1950s).[19] Northrop Corporation was one of the first employers to adopt final and binding arbitration for its nonunion work force. The primary catalyst for Northrop's decision to implement a final and binding arbitration system using an outside neutral was in reaction to two unsuccessful unionizing attempts. Northrop had previously employed only an open-door policy program.[20] According to one observer, Northrop's dispute resolution system "was avant-garde then and is still avant-garde" and is considered to be the "cadillac" of employer-promulgated grievance procedures.[21] Northrop's system covered not only hourly nonexempt employees who were subject to unionization but also its salaried nonsupervisory exempt employees in clerical, administrative, technical, and engineering positions.[22] A number of other employers have adopted the Northrop model which provides for an outside arbitrator as the terminal stage.[23]

### Brown & Root: Contemporary Advanced Employer-initiated Dispute Resolution Systems

Another employer which recently has received considerable attention because of its workplace dispute resolution system is Brown & Root.[24] Brown & Root is a large, international, nonunion construction and engineering firm. Brown & Root's "dispute resolution program" (DRP) began in June 1993 and covers only its domestic operations. The DRP was created with input from employees and managers of the company with assistance from an experienced consulting firm. The program is founded upon two principles: fairness and freedom from retaliation. It is overseen by senior management and provides for internal and external dispute resolution options. Internal options include listening, referral, discussion of options, informal fact-finding, shuttle diplomacy and mediation inside the company for any type of workplace problem. The four levels of options are set forth in a written employee booklet. At level one, an employee may use an open-door policy. An employee may also meet with the personnel office of their business unit or with corporate employee relations or other specialized offices as appropriate. An employee may also call off the record, either anonymously or with all the identifying details of a problem, to an employee hotline staffed by advisors.

At level two, any unresolved problem may be brought to the DRP administrator who can arrange dispute resolution conferences. The options at this level may include informal mediation by trained internal neutrals, arbitration, and in-house mediation. The lead DRP professional is an experienced mediator who reports to a human resources manager. The DRP professional serves in a role similar to that of an ombudsperson.

At levels three and four of the DRP, statutory-based workplace disputes may be submitted to external mediation or arbitration at the request of the employee.

A unique aspect of the DRP is the provision for the company to provide legal reimbursement of legal consultation for employees up to $2,500. Mandatory arbitration is a condition of employment for disputes that might otherwise go to court. Any employee, however, is free to consult with or appeal to any relevant government regulatory body. Where the arbitration option is exercised, the arbitrator is assigned through a private dispute resolution provider such as the American Arbitration Association, JAMS/EnDispute, and U.S.

Arbitration and Mediation, for example. The arbitrator is also vested with the same remedial authority of a federal court judge.

There are approximately 500 cases annually handled through the DRP at levels two through four; 1% to 2% of the cases actually go to arbitration. Of the cases which are submitted to DRP, 70% are resolved within one month.[25]

The workplace dispute resolution systems of Northrop Corporation and Brown & Root may not be perfect. Indeed, it is fair to say that there is no ideal design for a workplace dispute resolution system. However, the dispute resolution systems promulgated by these two employers certainly can serve as models for other employers who are committed to creating fair systems which are free from retaliation.[26]

## Internal Tribunals and Peer Review Systems

A number of employers have not been satisfied with the underutilization of open-door programs and employer-sponsored grievance procedures. One response to this dissatisfaction has been the establishment and implementation of internal tribunals and peer review panels. The internal tribunals and peer review panels are designed to resolve conflicts over promotion, disciplinary actions, and discharges. The peer review panels may consist of three peers of the aggrieved worker and two management representatives. The decisions of peer review panels are final and binding on the worker and the employer.[27] Included among those employers who have implemented internal peer review panels and tribunals are Federal Express Corporation, General Electric, and Citicorp. According to one observer, this trend represents an effort by companies to broaden employees' rights in disciplinary matters. Companies also say the peer boards build an open, trusting atmosphere; deter union organizing; and perhaps most importantly, stem the rising number of costly lawsuits claiming wrongful discharge and discrimination.[28]

## Criticisms of Employer-sponsored Systems

There is no consensus as to the reasons and motives for employers instituting internal workplace dispute resolution systems. In 1980 Berenbeim asserted that the most important factor for an employer implementing a dispute resolution system is to avoid unionization.[29] Other observers and scholars have cited a host of other factors and motives for employer-sponsored workplace dispute systems. Based on his 1986-88 survey of several hundred companies, David Ewing found some 16 factors or influential developments prompting employers to institute workplace dispute systems. The most important of these factors include the following: (1) "crumbling of the pillars" (managers and executives today are not revered in the way their predecessors were); (2) "the influence of education" (that one out of every four workers who enters the work force has a college degree, the willingness to joust with supervisors has increased); (3) "everybody here has an accent" (as mobility, diversity, and homogeneity have increased in the work force, so have conflicts in expectations and values among well-meaning employees); (4) "the view from the top" (management initiative); (5) employees' desire to participate in decisions affecting them; (6) participative management; (7) erosion in the employment-at-will doctrine; and (8) state protective antidismissal legislation. With the decline in union organization, Ewing notes, "companies are feeling more pressure, not less, to do what union leaders might be doing in the area of employee rights."[30]

Gentile, however, has summarized the influential developments or factors as follows: (1) employer concern over the continued erosion, though minimal during the 1970s, of the employment-at-will doctrine; (2) an employer change in the personnel philosophy that viewed employees as "human resources" to be preserved and protected in the workplace environment; (3) employer concern over the proliferation of protective legislation in the employment field—this "produced an atmosphere in which it is considered desirable, whenever possible, to settle complaints within the company because the alternative is costly resolution by a third party"; (4) a change in employee concerns, such as "privacy, due process, and participation"; and (5) some concern in certain industries of "the constant specter of unionization."[31]

R. Theodore Clark, Jr., has also suggested a number of factors and motives influencing employers' decision to institute workplace dispute resolution systems. These factors include (1) the litigation explosion,[32] (2) excessive damages and litigation expenses,[33] (3) the decline in union-represented employees,[34] (4) statutory encouragement of arbitration,[35] and (5) judicial encouragement of arbitration as evidenced by the *Gilmer* decision.[36]

Interestingly, Clark does not suggest that union avoidance was the primary motive behind many employers' decision to institute internal workplace dispute resolution systems. According to Clark, this point is most easily demonstrated by the fact that many employer-initiated arbitration procedures being adopted today frequently cover managerial and supervisory personnel who are exempt from collective bargaining under the National Labor Relations Act (NLRA). Clark points out that supervisory personnel are not targets for union organizing campaigns.[37]

## External Statutory Case Law and ADR: *Gardner-Denver* and *Gilmer*

As suggested by Clark and other observers, the impacts of external law and court decisions have also served as important catalysts prompting the promulgation of employer-sponsored workplace dispute resolution systems and the use of alternative dispute resolution processes. Two of the more significant catalysts were the Supreme Court's decisions in two landmark decisions, *Alexander v. Gardner-Denver Co.*[38] and *Gilmer v. Interstate/Johnson Lane Corp.*[39]

### The Gardner-Denver Decision

The Supreme Court in *Alexander v. Gardner-Denver Co.*[40] addressed the potential preclusive effect of labor arbitration on a Title VII cause of action. The Gardner-Denver Company discharged Alexander, a black drill press trainee, allegedly for producing an excessive amount of scrap. Alexander claimed that his discharge violated the just cause provision of the applicable collective bargaining agreement. He filed a racial discrimination complaint with the Colorado Civil Rights Commission, which referred it to the Equal Employment Opportunity Commission (EEOC). The arbitrator upheld Alexander's discharge, finding that the Gardner-Denver Company had just cause. Alexander subsequently sued under Title VII. The lower courts, relying on the arbitration award, granted the Gardner-Denver Company summary judgment.

The Supreme Court unanimously reversed and held that neither the doctrines of election of remedies or waiver nor the federal policy favoring arbitration of employment disputes precluded a trial de novo on the Title VII claim. The Court also refused to adopt the NLRB's policy of deferral to arbitration awards in Title VII litigation.

The Supreme Court provided several compelling reasons to support its decision. The Supreme Court observed that Congress intended to vest final responsibility for the enforcement of private Title VII rights in the federal courts. According to the Court, it was the intention of Congress that Title VII supplement rather than supplant other discrimination remedies. In the Court's words:

> Title VII's purpose and procedures strongly suggest that an individual does not forfeit his private cause of action if he first pursues his grievance to final arbitration under the non-discrimination clause of a collective bargaining agreement. . . . In submitting his grievance to arbitration, an employee seeks to vindicate his contractual right under [the] collective bargaining agreement. By contrast, in filing a lawsuit under Title VII, an employee asserts independent statutory rights accorded by Congress. The distinctly separate nature of these . . . rights is not vitiated merely because both were violated as result of the same factual occurrence.[41]

The Court also rejected the argument that by proceeding to arbitration Alexander had elected his remedies. The Court observed that Congress had set forth precise jurisdictional prerequisites for civil rights actions without mentioning arbitration. Therefore, the Court concluded that Title VII clearly provided for relief in several nonexclusive fora and that it was not inconsistent to allow arbitration to resolve contractual rights while allowing the federal judiciary to resolve statutory rights.[42]

The *Gardner-Denver* Court also dismissed the related argument that by proceeding to arbitration, Alexander waived his Title VII rights. The Court reasoned that unlike the union (whose responsibility it was to protect the collective rights of the bargaining unit members), Title VII protected the rights of the individual employee. The Court intimated its distrust of the institutional nature of the collective bargaining process:

> A further concern is the union's exclusive control over the manner and extent to which an individual grievance is presented. In arbitration, as in the collective-bargaining process, the interests of the individual employee may be subordinated to the collective interests of all employees in the bargaining unit. Moreover, harmony of interest between the union and the individual employee cannot always be presumed, especially where a claim of racial discrimination is made, and a breach of the union's duty of fair representation may prove difficult to establish. In this respect, it is noteworthy that Congress thought it necessary to afford the protections of Title VII against unions as well as employers.[43]

Because waiving these rights would defeat the paramount congressional purpose behind Title VII, the Court determined that the individual statutory rights conferred by Title VII could form no part of the collective bargaining process.[44]

While acknowledging that arbitration was well suited for resolving contractual disputes, the Court concluded that arbitration was inappropriate for resolving Title VII disputes. The Court based its distinction on the arbitrator's desire to effectuate the parties' intent rather than the requirements of the legislation.[45] Nevertheless, the Court gave lower courts a means by which to accommodate arbitration in Title VII litigation. In the Court's opinion, the arbitration award may be admitted as evidence in the litigation, and its evidentiary weight would be determined by the lower courts. The *Gardner-Denver* Court commented:

> *We adopt no standards as to the weight to be accorded an arbitral decision, since this must be determined in the court's discretion with regard to the facts and circumstances of each case.* Relevant factors include the existence of provisions in the collective-bargaining agreement that conform substantially with Title VII, the degree of procedural fairness in the arbitral forum, adequacy of the record

with respect to the issue of discrimination, and the special competence of particular arbitrators. Where an arbitral determination gives full consideration to an employee's Title VII rights, a court may properly accord it great weight. This is especially true where the issue is solely one of fact, specifically addressed by the parties and decided by the arbitrator on the basis of an adequate record. But courts should ever be mindful that Congress, in enacting Title VII, thought it necessary to provide a judicial forum for the ultimate resolution of discriminatory employment claims. It is the duty of courts to assure the full availability of this forum.[46]

## Significance of Gardner-Denver

The Supreme Court's holding in *Gardner-Denver* was quite narrow. *Gardner-Denver* did not preclude either the lower federal courts from accommodating arbitration awards in subsequent Title VII litigation or the arbitrators from accommodating an employer's equal employment legal responsibilities in interpreting and applying labor contracts. Indeed, *Gardner-Denver* suggests ways of accomplishing both types of accommodation. The Court's decision, however, begged the question of when such accommodations are appropriate. The delineation of an appropriate role for grievance arbitration in equal employment opportunity law may also provide insight into its use in resolving employment discrimination or workplace disputes outside the collectively bargained grievance procedure.[47]

Judge Harry Edwards suggests that arbitration is an appropriate vehicle for resolving employment discrimination disputes that are factual in nature and require only the application of established law. Employment discrimination cases raising unsettled issues of public law, however, should be left to the courts and administrative agencies. Judge Edwards cautions that the use of arbitration and other forms of alternative dispute resolution should not be allowed to sanction the replacement of public fora, protecting basic legal values, with private fora, resolving disputes on the basis of nonlegal social mores. Further, many issues of public law require a choice between conflicting public values. Such conflicts should be resolved by judges and other officials charged with lawmaking in the public interest rather than private dispute resolvers.[48] Judge Edwards also notes that a collectively bargained grievance and arbitration procedure may be ill suited as a forum for resolving complex employment discrimination issues. If arbitrators stray far outside the boundaries of traditional contract interpretation, their awards may not command the high level of deference that they currently receive from the courts. He suggests that arbitration procedures are best used and perhaps should be confined to claims that an employer's conduct violated both the contract and the law.[49]

*Gilmer: Alternative Dispute Resolution and Enforceability of Private Agreements to Arbitrate*

Since the Supreme Court's decisions in *Gardner-Denver*, one question that has been raised is whether private agreements to arbitrate "all employment disputes," specifically age discrimination claims, are enforceable in court. This issue was resolved in *Gilmer v. Interstate/Johnson Lane Corporation*,[50] a dispute arising in a nonunion setting and in the securities industry.[51]

In *Gilmer*[52] the Court held that the Federal Arbitration Act (FAA)[53] compelled arbitration of a claim under the Age Discrimination in Employment Act,[54] where the claimant had signed an agreement in a securities registration application to arbitrate all employment disputes.[55] *Gilmer* sharply limited the reach of a line of labor cases that had protected access to the courts for the vindication of statutory employment rights.[56]

Robert Gilmer, age 62, was terminated from his position as manager of financial services at Interstate/Johnson Lane Corporation (Interstate). He had worked for Interstate, a member of the New York Stock Exchange, for six years and was earning about $145,000 at the time of his termination. Gilmer believed he had been discharged because of his age and, therefore, filed a charge of age discrimination with the Equal Employment Opportunity Commission. When Gilmer sued in federal district court, Interstate moved to stay the proceedings and to compel arbitration under the Federal Arbitration Act. Interstate pointed to the arbitration agreement contained in Gilmer's securities registration application with the NYSE, whereby Gilmer agreed "to arbitrate any dispute, claim or controversy" arising between Gilmer and Interstate that "is required to be arbitrated under the rules, constitutions or by-laws of the organizations with which I register."[57] Among the disputes which NYSE rules require to be arbitrated are those "arising out of the employment or termination of employment of such registered representative."[58] The NYSE rules made the duty to arbitrate a mutual one, an obligation of both the employer and the employee.[59] The employer was bound as a member of the NYSE, and the employee was bound by the registration application.

Gilmer resisted arbitration on the basis of the *Gardner-Denver*[60] line of cases, which held that the arbitration of an employment dispute under a collective bargaining agreement did not preclude subsequent resort to a judicial forum in order to enforce statutory employment rights. Gilmer argued that nondiscrimination statutes, being central to national policy, could not be adequately resolved in arbitration because the rights invoked by such statutes deserve the protection and publicity of a judicial forum.

Interstate insisted on arbitration on the basis of a line of FAA cases decided after *Gardner-Denver*. These cases held that the Federal Arbitration

Act demands enforcement of private agreements to arbitrate statutory claims arising under antitrust,[61] securities,[62] and racketeering laws. These cases are often called the *Mitsubishi* trilogy, named after the first case to hold statutory claims arbitrable.

In an opinion by Justice White, the Court ruled 7-2 against Gilmer.[63] The Court held that the FAA applies to agreements to arbitrate statutory employment claims of age discrimination, since *Gardner-Denver* and its progeny apply only in the collective bargaining context.[64] By an agreement to arbitrate a statutory claim, the claimant is not foregoing a substantive right but is submitting that right to an arbitral rather than a judicial forum.[65] While the Court understood that Mr. Gilmer's agreement to arbitrate was a condition of employment, one exacted of all securities dealers in the industry, it found that mere inequality of bargaining power was not reason to deny enforcement of an agreement absent coercion or fraud.[66]

Although there is debate and concern over the propriety and implications of *Gilmer*,[67] the law as it stands today supports the enforceability of private employment contracts to arbitrate age discrimination claims. However, the *Gilmer* Court also held that notwithstanding any outcome in arbitration, the EEOC could independently pursue the EEO matter in court. The *Gilmer* rationale has also been applied to sexual harassment and other age discrimination claims.[68]

## The Effect of *Gardner-Denver* and *Gilmer* on Workplace Dispute Resolution and ADR

As will be discussed later, the Supreme Court decisions in *Gardner-Denver* and *Gilmer* and their progenies have prompted many employers, labor organizations, and government policymakers to reexamine the potential utility of public and private methods to resolve more efficiently and effectively the literally 100,000 and more statutory-based workplace disputes made annually.[69] Many of these statutory-based claims are without merit and are essentially claims of alleged unfair treatment, cloaked in terms of unlawful treatment. Many of these claims, however, are also based on good faith "perceptions" of unfair treatment.[70] Notwithstanding, these many "perception-based disputes" must be accorded an appropriate degree of procedural as well as substantive due process treatment by the government, as are those workplace claims which are subsequently proven to have merit. A number of agencies, particularly the EEOC, have attempted to institute more effective and efficient methods to resolve the many workplace disputes which arise within their respective jurisdictions by adopting case priority systems.[71]

## The Effect of Workplace EEO Legislation and ADR Public Policy

In addition to the Supreme Court's decisions in *Gardner-Denver* and *Gilmer*, the enactment of legislation expressly incorporating and encouraging the use of alternative dispute resolution has also prompted employer and worker disputants to consider and/or use alternative dispute resolution as an alternative to the administrative agency procedures and court litigation.[72]

As it relates to the resolution of workplace disputes, there are two primary pieces of legislation which expressly encourage the use of alternative dispute resolution, the Americans with Disabilities Act and the Civil Rights Act of 1991. These statutes both contain similar provisions which read as follows:

> Where appropriate and to the extent authorized by law, the use of alternative means of dispute resolution, including settlement negotiations, conciliation, facilitation, mediation, fact finding, mini trials, and *arbitration*, is encouraged to resolve disputes arising under the Acts.

Although other federal agencies have recently announced programs to use alternative dispute resolution,[73] the Equal Employment Opportunity Commission has most recently received considerable public attention which has prompted the agency to adopt an ADR Public Policy Statement encouraging and implementing the use of voluntary mediation.[74] The EEOC's ADR Public Policy Statement was based, in large part, on the results of a one-year pilot mediation study.[75] The results of the study affirmed that voluntary mediation can be an effective means to assist the agency in managing its usual case inventory of some 80,000 to 100,000 cases per year.[76]

### Current Status of EEOC Voluntary Mediation Program

At the current time, the EEOC is attempting to implement mediation programs in its 25 district and area offices located throughout the country. The EEOC expects to complete its national implementation of mediation by September, 1997.[77] The EEOC plans to use law school interns as mediators as well as professional mediators.[78] In a number of district offices, the EEOC also plans to use trained EEOC staff members as mediators. This is an interesting reversal of policy. In the ADR Task Force's earlier words, it was believed that "by facilitating resolution where agreement is possible, ADR (could) free up commission resources to place greater emphasis on identifying discrimination in the workplace and perform more expeditious and thorough investigations in those cases that are not resolved through alternative processes.[79] It remains to be seen whether the commission's use of staff as mediators is the most effective use of agency resources and staff, particularly where there is an increasing corps of private professional EEO mediators available to serve as mediators. A number of these private mediators are willing to serve on a for-fee, reduced fee, or even pro bono basis.[80] A more effective alternative would be for the commission to actively develop a public/private partnership using government contract mediators or affording the disputants the free choice to select a private for-fee mediator. This is the model in which the Chicago, St. Louis, and Kansas City EEOC district offices and the Illinois Human Rights Commission have recently agreed to participate.[81]

It is further suggested that a more effective and sorely needed use of agency staff would be for the commission to use staff as technical assistants for unrepresented disputants, most of whom are claimants. Among other things, this would directly address the commission's obligation to address the imbalance of power which often exists where unsophisticated and inexperienced claimants are permitted to participate in mediation. The use of staff members in this capacity and that as actual representatives (where probable cause has been found) has been adopted by other state government agencies.[82] Furthermore, the use of staff members in this capacity would to some degree assure that the public policy prohibiting discrimination in the workplace is being upheld. This is the undisputed mission of the commission.[83]

In addition to adopting a policy of using a combination of EEOC staff members, law student intern mediators, and private professional mediators, a number of the EEOC district offices have or will be attempting to identify which cases are most eligible or appropriate for mediation. This selection process is directly related to the commission's new case categorization process discussed earlier.[84] Under this program, it has been decided that "B" category cases are most appropriate for mediation, particularly those cases where there is a continued employment relationship.[85] The issue related to the unrepresented disputant, most often claimants, and the underfunding of EEOC's mediation strategy are critical issues which must be addressed. Otherwise, it is doubtful that the EEOC's goal of eventually resolving approximately 10% of all eligible cases through mediation can be achieved. Currently, each district office has been provided $8,000 for ADR and mediation training of staff.[86] This underfunding and need to actively include external professional mediators must be immediately addressed; otherwise, as one EEOC official stated, mediation will continue to be implemented in "baby steps."[87]

With successful pilot mediation programs, the support of EEOC Chairman Casellas and an ADR Task Force directing its implementation, the future use of voluntary mediation in resolving EEO workplace disputes has considerable promise. Much of EEOC's efforts at this point have been more procedural than substantive.

## Federal and State EEO Enforcement Agency ADR Initiatives: Early Empirical Findings

In addition to the EEOC, there have been a number of state EEO enforcement agencies which have experimented with the use of mediation and final and binding arbitration to resolve employment disputes. First among these agencies is the Illinois Human Rights Commission (IHRC), the Illinois Department of Human Rights (IDHR), and the Massachusetts Commission against Discrimination (MCAD).[88]

The EEOC has not fully implemented mediation programs in each of its district and area offices; however, it is contemplated that by September 1997 nationwide mediation programs will be in place. Consequently, there is little if any available empirical evidence as to how well any EEOC-sponsored mediation programs are currently operating. However, there is some empirical statistical evidence available related to ADR programs sponsored by the Illinois Human Rights Commission, the Illinois Department of Human Rights, and the Massachusetts Commission against Discrimination. These statistics again support the utility of voluntary mediation in this area.[89]

The empirical data from these undertakings provide valuable insights into both the impediments and facilitative factors which will affect the future use of alternative dispute resolution systems, particularly the mediation of statutory-based workplace disputes.

## Employer-sponsored Conflict Management Systems and ADR Programs and Due Process

In addition to government-initiated efficiency efforts (via policies, procedures, and supporting ADR processes) to resolve workplace disputes, many private employers have taken steps to design and implement conflict management or employee voice systems.[90] As discussed earlier, these "employee voice systems," or what have been called Employer Promulgated Grievance Procedures (EPGPs), have taken many forms, including but not limited to employer open-door policies, the use of ombudspersons, peer review, peer mediation, mandatory or "imposed" final and binding arbitration, and voluntary final and binding arbitration.[91] In some instances, employers such as Brown & Root have subsidized the use of mediation and final and binding arbitration.[92] However, there is considerable controversy related to the propriety or fairness of employer-mandated or "imposed" final and binding arbitration programs, particularly as a precondition to employment or in some instances as a condition of continued employment. Indeed, the Dunlop Commission[93] and the Brock Commission (also called the Commission on Excellence in State and Local

Government) have opposed the implementation of such mandated or "imposed" predispute arbitration programs notwithstanding the Supreme Court's decision in *Gilmer*. Senator Russ Feingold (D-Wisconsin) and Representative Patricia Schroeder (D-Colorado) have proposed legislation to reverse the Supreme Court's decision in *Gilmer*.[94]

## Voluntary Mediation

There has been, however, a broader acceptance of voluntary mediation as opposed to final and binding arbitration by workplace disputants. Generally, voluntary mediation has been viewed as offering a number of unique benefits and advantages.[95] It has been suggested that for a number of reasons, mediation is well suited to resolve workplace disputes arising within an internal grievance procedure or in conjunction with an agency or court-connected dispute resolution system.[96]

There are a host of reasons why mediation is well suited for the resolution of workplace disputes. Among these is the recognition that many workplace disputes involve highly emotional issues. It is said that the loss of employment is the third most stressful life event. Similarly, disputes related to sexual harassment or professional relationships which have gone awry occur in a charged atmosphere. A mediator can assist the disputants in venting their anger and frustrations in a conducive setting that allows disputants to feel that their positions have been heard and then advance to "problem solving" the dispute. The assurance and existence of privacy and confidentiality is also another reason which makes mediation suitable for resolving workplace disputes, particularly employment discrimination disputes involving claims of harassment. In such disputes, the employee wishes the behavior stopped quickly and permanently. The employee also wishes to convey to the offender the effect of the harassment. The respondent-employer, on the other hand, also wishes to stop the complained-of behavior but also wishes to maintain their public image and reputation. Employers are also concerned that a public resolution of a dispute may have a "narcotic" or "me too" effect on other employees. Specifically, the nonconfidential resolution of a dispute will prompt other employees to file claims in order to obtain some otherwise unwarranted monetary settlement. The confidentiality which mediation provides affords both disputants to arrive at a mutually acceptable resolution of their dispute in a more private fashion.

Creativity of settlement outcomes is another benefit derived through mediation which usually does not exist in arbitral or other adjudicatory processes. In mediation, a problem-solving process, the disputants can deal with a host of nonlegal and nonmonetary issues. In dealing with these issues, a wide variety of mediated or interest-based solutions may be agreed upon; for example, retaining an otherwise terminated employee on a consultant basis until they secure regular employment, maintaining one's health insurance benefits until retirement or eligibility for Medicare, corporatewide sexual harassment training or even providing guaranteed loans to terminated managers in order to invest in a new business. One of the major reasons for many disputants electing to use mediation is cost savings. For the respondent-employer, the possibility of avoiding the vagaries or unpredictability of a jury trial is quite attractive.[97] Also, the significant cost incurred related to discovery costs, witness fees, attorney fees, and the consumption of management witness time makes mediation even more attractive to respondent-employers. It has been estimated that the cost for an employer to defend a single discrimination claim is $81,000, and in sexual harassment cases, the cost for one Fortune 500 company approximated $6.7 million annually.[98] From the claimant's perspective, the cost to litigate a claim approximates $25,000, as compared to a $1,000 to $3,000 cost of mediation.[99]

Speed and the success rate of mediation is also a benefit derived from mediation. It has been estimated that an employment discrimination charge is typically mediated within 67 days after agreement to mediate versus 294 days to have a charge investigated by an EEO enforcement agency.[100] In addition to speed, the success rate of resolving employment disputes is another significant advantage derived from mediation. Settlement rates range to 56%. However, it is more likely that settlement rates in agency-connected mediation programs are in the 50% range.[101] There are a host of reasons why disputants elect to use mediation and ultimately settle;[102] however, suffice it to say that even a settlement rate of 52% generally assists the agency in managing their case inventory. But equally important, it effectuates the cornerstone of such antidiscrimination statutes as Title VII and the Civil Rights Act of 1991 that these disputes should be "conciliated" and not litigated. This is a public policy objective which has been overlooked for some time.[103] There are, of course, a number of potential disadvantages to mediation, particularly where the disputants abuse the process and do not bargain in good faith or where there is an undue imbalance of power and resources between the disputants, often where claimants are unrepresented.[104] However, generally many of these disadvantages can be addressed prior to disputants exercising the alternative mediation option, thus permitting the disputants to voluntarily make "informed decisions" to resolve their disputes.[105]

## Model Employment Termination Act

There have been a number of other initiatives to attempt to bring procedural and substantive due process to the worker, particularly in discharge and dismissal cases. The most significant of these initiatives is the Model Employment Termination Act.[106] META is a product of the National Conference of Commissioners on Uniform Laws. Among other things, central to META is the use of arbitration to resolve discharge and dismissal complaints. META specifically provides for the following:

- Covers employees who have worked more than part time for the same employer for at least one year.
- Includes workers to be fired for reasons such as theft, assault, substance abuse, insubordination, inadequate performance, and improper off-duty conduct (job-related).
- Provides for good-cause protection, while extinguishing tort actions for wrongful discharge.
- Employer and employees to set the standard of what makes up "good cause."
- Enforcement by state-appointed, publicly funded professional arbitrators who can award up to three years' front pay (instead of reinstatement and back pay).

Some 45 states have modified the employment-at-will doctrine, and Montana enacted its Wrongful Discharge from Employment Act (WDFEA) in 1987. However, the Model Employment Termination Act (META) has not met with universal acceptance. Indeed, the AFL-CIO has concluded that META offers very little real benefit.[107]

## ABA's Due Process Protocol for the Arbitration and Mediation of Statutory Workplace Disputes

In the wake of the Supreme Court's decision in *Gilmer* and in reaction to a number of unfair employer-sponsored arbitration programs, a number of labor and employment attorneys who represent labor, management, civil rights and liberties organizations, and labor-management neutrals drafted a document called the Due Process Protocol in May of 1995. The purpose of the Due Process Protocol was to provide some basic elements or guidelines for arbitration and mediation programs to be used in the resolution of statutory-based employment disputes. The Due Process Protocol was subsequently recommended by the Section of Labor and Employment Law of the American Bar Association.[108] The delegates approved the following standards for ADR in the workplace:

- Employees should have the right to be represented by a person of their choice.

- The fee for that representation should be determined by agreement between the employee and the representative, but the arbitrator should have authority to provide for fee reimbursement by the employer as part of the remedy.[109]
- Employees should have access to all information reasonably relevant to mediation or arbitration of their claims.
- A roster of available arbitrators and mediators with experience in employment matters should be established, and training should be provided by government agencies, bar associations, and academic institutions acting under the auspices of a designating agency, such as the American Arbitration Association.
- Mediators and arbitrators should be selected using a list procedure, with a certain number of strikes available to the parties.
- The arbitrator's award should be final and binding, and the scope of review should be limited.
- The section members did not achieve consensus on one important issue: whether an agreement to mediate or arbitrate statutory employment disputes should be made a condition of employment, or whether the decision to mediate or arbitrate individual cases should be made only after the dispute arises.[110]

## SPIDR's ADR in the Workplace Committee

The use of mediation, arbitration, and other workplace dispute resolution processes are not devoid of a number of significant public policy and practical issues which must be addressed to ensure fair and "legitimate" workplace dispute resolution systems. Included among these issues to be addressed are the accessibility to quality dispute resolution processes by members of all socioeconomic groups, imbalance of power and the unrepresented claimant, assurance of diversity of neutrals, and the propriety of mandating or imposing dispute resolution processes such as arbitration and mediation.

These issues are presently being examined by the Law and Public Policy Committee of the Society of Professionals in Dispute Resolution. Under SPIDR's ADR in the Workplace Initiative, for the first time since 1912, a systematic examination is being conducted to determine and recommend guiding principles as to the elements and safeguards which should be incorporated into employer-sponsored and agency and court-connected workplace dispute resolution programs. As reported in the *Daily Labor Report*:

> The initiative has three tracks: an employment track, an organized work force track, and an international track. The employment track

is intended to develop guiding principles for the use of ADR in resolving statutory claims in employment discrimination claims. The track will work in three different areas: (1) mediation of claims brought to federal and state agencies; (2) propriety of participating in systems that mandate arbitration as a condition of employment; and (3) design and use of ADR processes under employer-sponsored internal dispute resolution programs.[111]

It is anticipated that the committee will issue its initial report and recommendations related to the employment track in 1998.

## National Workplace Dispute Resolution Act: A Proposal

It has been said that "alternative dispute resolution continues to be a solution in search of a problem."[112] This assertion is, of course, subject to debate. However, it may be more accurate to assert that there is a need to have a systematic and institutional marriage between the undisputed problem related to this country's statutory-based promise of workplace civil rights and establishing efficient methods for resolving workplace civil and protective rights, using alternative dispute resolution, particularly mediation. In the author's opinion, there is a need to have a statutory or presidential executive order to promote effectively the use of "structured negotiations" or mediation of workplace disputes. This is particularly the case under Title VII, where the initial objective of "conciliating" these disputes was the cornerstone of that statute. This public policy objective of conciliation, or presumably mediation, is the rationale for the proposed National Workplace Dispute Resolution Act (NWDRA). As it stands today, there is underutilization of voluntary mediation which only serves to perpetuate the overburdened dockets of our public justice system and cause the expenditure of scarce public resources.[113]

As suggested by the EEOC's ADR Public Policy Statement, the forthcoming mediation guiding principles of the ADR in the Workplace Committee of the Society of Professionals in Dispute Resolution and ABA's ADR Due Process Protocol, a number of elements and safeguards should exist in what the author terms a "fair and legitimate" mediation program. Among other things, this includes the qualifications of the mediator and the effective addressing of imbalance of power issues. It is under these conditions that the preliminary elements of the proposed National Workplace Dispute Resolution Act are being offered. These elements are as follows:

1. Any federal contractor receiving federal funds in the amount of $50,000 or more would be required to establish internal dispute resolution programs, providing as a voluntary option access to external third-party neutrals or mediators.

2. Affected federal contractors would be mandated to participate in mediation where the claimant has filed a charge and the claimant expressly seeks mediation. Similarly, claimants of affected federal contractors should be mandated to participate in mediation where the "respondent federal contractor" has expressed a desire to mediate. The mediation outcome would be voluntary, however. The relevant government regulatory agency would provide technical assistance to the unrepresented disputant, where a formal charge has been filed. This may also be carried out by providing support to and services from the Legal Services Corporation, area law schools and civil rights organizations, and members of the state and local bar associations.

3. All agencies, including Section 706 or worksharing agencies and federal courts, would be required to participate and cooperate in "certified" mediation programs administered by private mediation centers.[114] At a minimum, this means that government regulatory workplace entities and the courts would cooperate with the "certified" mediation center in informing disputants of the mediation alternative (e.g., distribute informational packets) and cooperate with external entities (mediation centers) which would provide a conduit to trained mediators.

4. In pre-formal charge disputes, there should also be a tolling of statutory time limits where the disputants voluntarily enter into an agreement to attempt to resolve a workplace dispute internally without filing a formal charge and where the internal dispute resolution system is "fair and legitimate" and regular. The disputants would have ninety days within which to resolve the dispute. Where the dispute process does not resolve the matter, the employer must formally advise the claimant that the ADR process has been concluded. Such voluntary private tolling agreements shall also be enforceable in court.

5. The filing of an internal grievance by an employee with the affected federal contractor and subsequently the mediation center constitutes a "nominal filing" with the appropriate agency and thus tolls the applicable statutory time limits. As stated above, the tolling period shall be for a reasonable time period and not to exceed ninety days unless otherwise mutually and formally agreed by the disputants.

6. Wherever possible, the federal government and/or the federal contractor shall assist in subsidizing the cost of the mediation.

7. Prospective federal contractors which have such internal dispute resolution programs and agree to abide by the National Workplace Dispute Resolution Act shall be afforded preferred consideration in the awarding of federal contracts in the amount of $50,000 or more.

8. All Section 706 or worksharing EEO enforcement agencies must comply with any mediation guidelines of the National Workplace Dispute Resolution Act and the EEOC's ADR Public Policy Statement, including any guidelines related to the representation and technical assistance for unrepresented disputants.
9. The matters discussed in mediation are confidential and shall not be used in any subsequent administrative or court proceedings.
10. Although participation in the mediation may be mandated, any settlement outcome is strictly voluntary and may not be mandated or imposed.
11. The destruction of any relevant evidence or documents shall subject that offending party to any civil and appropriate criminal sanctions.[115]
12. The disputants agree not to engage in any retaliation against any participants, fellow workers, or associates of participants of the internal grievance system or mediation program. Such retaliation shall subject the offending party to any appropriate civil sanctions.
13. Affected government contractors who violate or fail to comply with the NWDRA shall be subject to disbarment from future federal contracts.

The elements detailed above are not intended to be exhaustive but rather serve to accomplish the goal of "actually" getting workplace disputants to attempt to resolve their disputes voluntarily. This is an undisputed public policy objective. NWDRA breathes life and purpose into those statutes that merely "encourage" the use of ADR but do not effectuate actual participation of workplace disputants in mediation. NWDRA also creates an efficient and effective public/private partnership between government regulatory agencies and private mediators. NWDRA will also enhance the probability of settlement outcomes which do not erode the underlying applicable statutes and public policies and enforcement mission of government workplace regulatory agencies. The proposed act would also serve to enhance the effectuation of government efficiency and effectiveness of the resolution of workplace disputes.

## Future Prospects for Workplace Dispute Resolution and ADR

It is beyond debate that as a matter of public policy and as evidenced by statute and court decisions, internal workplace dispute resolution systems, conflict management, and alternative dispute resolution will become the most effective means to resolve statutory and nonstatutory-based workplace disputes during the next century. These processes will also become more formalized, and in many instances they will be set forth in employee handbooks which are enforceable in court. Furthermore, more disputants, particularly workers, will eagerly resort to such alternative processes. This will particularly be the case as a result of the decreased state and federal government funding of various enforcement agencies such as the EEOC. Because of this, more workplace disputants, particularly workers, will be faced with one of two options: (1) wait for extended periods to have their workplace disputes resolved through either administrative agency processes or the court, or (2) opt into a variety of either employer-sponsored workplace dispute resolutions systems or agency/court-connected ADR programs.

Based on empirical research in this area, it is fair to conclude that many, if not most, employees will readily opt to use a "perceived or believed to be fair" workplace dispute resolution system prior to filing an external formal charge or lawsuit.[116] Where the worker has decided to file a legal action externally, research also indicates that these workers are more interested in resolving their dispute using an ADR process.[117] Empirical research further indicates, however, that employers are more reluctant to agree to resolve statutory-based disputes once a formal legal action is taken.[118] This reality raises a critical public policy question as to whether disputants should be mandated to participate in ADR processes as a precondition to the expenditure of agency or court public resources to resolve the matter.[119] Evidence further suggests, at least at the judicial level, that more courts are mandating the participation of disputants in nonbinding and nonadjudicative dispute resolution processes such as mediation or nonbinding arbitration as a precondition to a trial.[120] Whether administrative enforcement agencies should adopt similar rules or policies is debatable and remains to be seen. However, it is reasonable to conclude that the greater the opportunities whereby disputants can communicate and/or negotiate using a third-party neutral, the greater the probability of settlement. This would be in harmony with the public policy supporting workplace disputes resolution processes and ADR.

Before traveling down this path of mandated participation (not mandated outcomes), however, certain safeguards must be in place to ensure that the underlying purposes and policies of the related public policies are not eroded. Among other things, this includes the addressing of the issue of imbalance of economic and informational power which often exists between a worker and the employer in such disputes.

The apparent desire and trend by employers to "impose" or mandate final and binding arbitration as a condition of employment will most likely continue, absent the enactment of legislation prohibiting such programs.[121] It should be noted, however, that a number of commissions, including the Dunlop and Brock Commissions, have opposed the use of Gilmer-type mandated arbitration programs. In addition, the EEOC has also taken a position opposing such mandated dispute resolution processes. Consequently, it is fair to conclude that the jury is still out on this score. However, the type of workplace dispute systems promulgated by Northrop Corporation, Brown & Root, and Federal Express will most likely serve as models for the future. Each of these systems provide nonadjudicatory, interest-based means to resolve disputes as an option. In those cases in which these interest-based dispute resolution alternatives either do not resolve the matter or the worker wishes to opt for an adjudicatory dispute resolution process (or external administrative agency or court process), that latter option should still be made available.

As we approach the 21st century, the critical challenges for the industrial relations and human resources professional and union representatives will be to (1) obtain a thorough knowledge about workplace dispute resolution systems, (2) be able to support and implement appropriate and fair workplace dispute resolution systems for their particular organizations, and (3) recognize the need and benefit of obtaining dispute resolution skills themselves. The use of formalized workplace dispute resolution systems and alternative dispute resolution may serve as the basis for a new calling and role for the industrial relations and human resources professional and union representative. The 21st century will also require a formalized and cooperative partnership between our public justice system and private and public professional dispute resolvers.

## Acknowledgments

The author would like to express appreciation to Vida E. Stanius, Associate Director, and Ruth Hollemans of the Center for Employment Dispute Resolution and to Kelly Salita, graduate assistant at the Institute of Human Resources and Industrial Relations, Loyola University Chicago, for their assistance in preparing this chapter. The comments and conclusions are, however, solely those of the author.

## Endnotes

[1] See, e.g., *Fogerty v. Fantasy, Inc.*, 114 S. Ct. 1023 (1994) (Title VII is a policy "Congress considered of the highest priority."); *Independent Federation of Flight Attendants v. Zipes*, 491 U.S. 754, 759 (1989); *United States v. Paradise*, 480 U.S. 149, 167 (1987); *Guardians Association v. Civil Service Commission of New York*, 463 U.S. 582, 600 (1983); *Consolidated Foods Corp. v. Unger*, 456 U.S. 1002, 1003 (1982) (Blackmun, J., concurring); *New York Gaslight Club, Inc., et al. v. Carey*, 447 U.S. 54, 63 (1980); *Christianburg Garment Co. v. EEOC*, 434 U.S. 412, 418 & 419 (1977); *Franks v. Bowman Transportation Co.*, 424 U.S. 747, 763 (1976); *Emporium Capwell Co. v. Western Addition Community Org.*, 420 U.S. 50, 66 (1975); *Bradley v. School Board of Richmond*, 416 U.S. 696, 719 (1974); *Alexander v. Gardner-Denver Co.*, 415 U.S. 36, 47 (1974).

[2] See Martin H. Malin and Lamont E. Stallworth, "Grievance Arbitration: Accommodating an Increasingly Diversified Work Force," *Labor Law Journal* (Aug. 1991) at 551; Lamont E. Stallworth and Martin H. Malin, "Conflict Arising Out of Work Force Diversity" in

*Arbitration 1993: Arbitration and the Changing World of Work, Proceedings of the Forty-Sixth Annual Meeting*, National Academy of Arbitrators 104 (1993).

[3] The term alternative dispute resolution is used here to describe the use of such processes as negotiations, mediation and arbitration or adjudication, and other hybrid processes. These processes are used to resolve conflicts instead of submitting the matter for resolution to an administrative agency or the courts. The term workplace dispute resolution systems or processes is used to describe primarily internal or administrative agency/court-connected conflict management programs such as open-door policies, EEO mediation and arbitration, employee peer review systems, etc.

[4] For examples of research critical of government enforcement agencies see, Alfred W. Blumrosen, *Modern Law: The Law Transmission System and Equal Employment Opportunity* (Univ. Wisc. Press, 1993); James A. Gross, *Broken Promise: The Subversion of U.S. Labor Relations Policy, 1947-1994* (Temple Univ. Press, 1995); Michael Arndt, "Overworked, Ineffective: EEOC Can't Keep Up," *Chicago Tribune* (February 12, 1995); and Derek Bell, *Faces at the Bottom of the Well: The Permanence of Racism* (Basic Books, 1992).

[5] *Lincoln Mills v. Textile Workers Union*, 353 U.S. 448 (1957); *Steel Workers v. Louisville-Nashville Railroad*, 325 U.S. 483 (1944); *Gateway Coal Co. v. UMW*, 414 U.S. 368 (1974); *Glover v. Mumford*, 503 F.2d. 878 (5th Cir. 1974); *Alexander v. Gardner-Denver Co.*, 415 U.S. 36 (1974) [hereinafter referred to as *Gardner-Denver*]; *Gilmer v. Interstate/Johnson Lane Corporation*, 520 U.S. 20, 111 S. Ct. 1647 (1991) [hereinafter referred to as *Gilmer*].

[6] The Americans with Disabilities Act and the Civil Right Act of 1991 contain provisions which expressly encourage the use of such alternative dispute resolution processes as negotiations, mediation, early case evaluation, etc. to resolve EEO disputes. In addition, the Judicial Improvement Act (Dec. 1, 1990) authorizes experimentation with ADR in the federal district courts. And the Administrative Dispute Resolution Act requires each federal agency to adopt a policy that recognizes ADR as a means of dispute resolution and case management in adjudications, rulemaking, litigation, etc.

[7] OSHA Reinventing; NLRB-ALJ Mediation and EEOC-ADR Public Policy Statement and Case Processing Program. Pub. L. No. 102-166, 105 Stat. 1081 (1991). National Labor Relations Board (1994). *Fifty-Ninth Annual Report of the National Labor Relations Board for the Fiscal Year*, Washington, DC: GPO (1994). NLRB, National Labor Relations Board (doc.), New Release, "Statement by William Gould, Chairman National Labor Relations Board on FY 1997 Authorization," Washington, DC, 20570 (June 13, 1996). U.S. Department of Labor, Occupational Safety and Health Administration, OSHA (doc) "Reinventing OSHA: A Progress Report," *Job Safety and Health Quarterly*, Vol. 7, no. 1 (Fall/Winter 1995).

[8] Alan F. Westin and Alfred G. Feliu, *Resolving Employment Disputes without Litigation* (Bureau of National Affairs, 1988) [hereinafter cited as *Resolving Employment Disputes without Litigation*]; and see, Cathy A. Costantino and Christina Sickles Merchant, *Designing Conflict Management Systems: A Guide to Creating Productive and Healthy Organizations* (Jossey-Bass, 1995) [hereinafter cited as *Designing Conflict Management Systems*] and William L. Ury, Jeanne M. Brett and Stephen B. Goldberg, *Getting Disputes Resolved: Designing Systems to Cut the Cost of Conflict* (Jossey-Bass, 1988) [hereinafter cited as *Getting Disputes Resolved*].

[9] The federal government's earlier intervention into what now might be called a "statutory-based" diversity dispute includes *Muller v. Oregon*, 208 U.S. 412 (1908) (sex-based discrimination); *Steele v. Louisville-Nashville Railroad*, 323 U.S. 192 (1944) (racial based discrimination by a labor organization). For an article discussing the litigious nature or psyche of contemporary workers, see, e.g., Michele Hoyman and Lamont E. Stallworth, "Who Files Lawsuits and Why: An Empirical Portrait of the Litigious Worker," *Illinois Law Review*, Vol. 1981, no. 1.

[10] The concept of employment at will is that an employee who did not have an employment contract for a fixed term could be discharged or terminated at any time for good cause, bad cause, or no cause at all. See, Horace G. Wood, *A Treatise on the Law of Master and Servant* (1877). The American courts adopted this concept and applied it to all workers who were not guaranteed continued employment in individual employment contracts.

[11] One fundamental purpose of the Wagner Act or the National Labor Relations Act was to encourage the use of collective bargaining as a means of self-regulating the economic relationship between employers and labor organizations.

[12] Robben W. Fleming, *The Labor Arbitration Process* (Illini Books, 1967).

[13] "Grievance Procedures in Nonunionized Companies," *Studies in Personnel Policy No. 109*, (National Industrial Conference Board, Inc., 1950); Bureau of National Affairs, "Policies for Unorganized Employees," *PPF Survey No. 125* (April, 1979); Ronald Berenbeim, "Nonunion Complaint Systems: A Corporate Appraisal," *The Conference Board Report No. 770* (1980); David W. Ewing, *Justice on the Job* (Harvard Business School Press, 1989); Alan F. Westin and Alfred G. Feliu, *Resolving Disputes without Litigation* (BNA, 1988).

[14] Richard B. Freeman and James L. Medoff, *What Do Unions Do?* (Basic Books, Inc., 1984).

[15] Douglas M. McCabe, *Corporate Nonunion Complaint Procedures and Systems: A Strategic Human Resources Management Analysis* (Praeger, 1988).

[16] Joseph Gentile, "The Structure and Workings of Employer-Promulgated Grievance Procedures and Arbitration Agreements," in James L. Stern and Joyce M. Najita, eds., *Labor Arbitration under Fire* (Cornell University Press, 1997) at 137 [hereinafter cited as *Labor Arbitration under Fire*].

[17] Id., note 11.

[18] Id. at 143.

[19] David Ewing, *Justice on the Job* (Harvard Business School Press, 1989); *Resolving Employment Disputes without Litigation* at pp. 45-46. And, see *Labor Arbitration under Fire* at pp. 144-146.

[20] *Labor Arbitration under Fire* at pp. 146-147.

[21] Id. at p. 147.

[22] Id. at p. 146.

[23] Id. at p. 148.

[24] Mary P. Rowe, "Dispute Resolution in the Nonunion Environment: An Evolution toward Integrated Systems for Conflict Management?" in Sandra Gleason, ed., *Frontiers in*

*Dispute Resolution in Labor Relations and Human Resources* (1997). "Case Study: Brown & Root's Options," *Workforce Strategies* (BNA), Vol. 4, No. 10 (October 25, 1993).

[25] Id.

[26] Mary P. Rowe, "Specifications for an Effective Integrated Complaint System" in Robert Shoop, et al., eds., *Sexual Harassment on Campus* (Simon and Schuster, Forthcoming, 1997).

[27] Douglas McCabe, *Corporate Nonunion Complaint Procedures and Systems* (Praeger, 1988) at pp. 22-23. Also see, Larry Reibstein, "More Firms Use Peer Review Panel to Resolve Employees' Grievances," *The Wall Street Journal* (Dec. 3, 1986) at p. 29.

[28] Id. Also see, John D. Coomke, "Peer Review: The Emerging Successful Application," *Employee Relations Law Journal*, Vol. 9 (Spring, 1984) at p. 659, and Fred C. Olson, "How Peer Review Works at Control Data," *Harvard Business Review*, Vol. 62 (Nov.-Dec., 1984) at p. 58.

[29] Supra note 16 at p. 139.

[30] Supra note 16 at p. 140.

[31] Ronald Berenbeim, "Nonunion Complaint Systems: A Corporate Appraisal," *The Conference Board Report No. 770* (1980).

[32] John J. Donohue, III, and Peter Siegelman, "The Changing Nature of Employment Discrimination Litigation," *Stanford Law Review*, Vol. 43 (1991). And see, *Labor Arbitration under Fire* at p. 162 where Theodore Clark reports that:
- The number of employment discrimination cases filed in the last two decades has increased an unbelievable 2,166%.
- In 1986-87, 118,444 unlawful employment discrimination charges were filed: 66,305 with the EEOC and 52,139 with state and local human rights agencies.
- The Educational Fund for Individual Rights estimates that there was a total of less than 200 state court wrongful discharge cases filed annually in the 1970s but that the number pending as of 1987 was estimated at more than 20,000.
- A California study of 120 wrongful discharge cases that went to a jury verdict revealed that plaintiffs won in 68% of the cases, with an average verdict of $650,000 and a median verdict of $177,000.
- Several studies show that the *average* cost for attorneys' fees to defend a wrongful discharge case ranges from $80,000 to $90,000. In many cases, the cost of defending a wrongful discharge case is many times the average.

[33] *Labor Arbitration under Fire* at 163.

[34] Id. at 164.

[35] Id.

[36] Id. at 165.

[37] Id. at 166-167.

[38] *Gardner-Denver.*

[39] *Gilmer.*

[40] *Gardner-Denver*, 415 U.S. 36 (1974).

[41] See Harry T. Edwards, "Labor Arbitration at the Crossroads: The Common Law of the Shop v. External Law," *Arbitration Journal* (June, 1977).

[42] *Gardner-Denver* at 59-60.

[43] Id. at 58 n. 19.

[44] Id. at 59-60.

[45] Id.

[46] Id. at 60 n. 21 (emphasis added). See also, Dennis R. Nolan and Roger I. Abrams, "American Labor Arbitration: The Maturing Years," 35 Univ. Fla. L. Rev. 557, 619 (1983) (characterizing *Gardner-Denver* as inviting parties to construct arbitration procedures to allow courts to give awards substantial weight). See, Michele Hoyman and Lamont E. Stallworth, "The Arbitration of Discrimination Grievances in the Aftermath of Gardner-Denver," *Arbitration Journal* (September, 1984) at p. 49. Martin H. Malin and Lamont E. Stallworth, "Grievance Arbitration: Accommodating an Increasingly Diversified Work Force," *Labor Law Journal* (August, 1991) at 551. Also see, W. R. Grace & Co. v. *Local Union 759, International Union of the United Rubber, Cork, Linoleum & Plastic Workers*, 461 U.S. 757 (1983).

[47] There is ongoing debate over whether the collectively bargained grievance and arbitration procedure can serve as a model for employment dispute resolution in the nonunion setting. See, Alfred W. Blumrosen, "Exploring Voluntary Arbitration of Individual Employment Disputes," 16 Univ. Mich. J.L. 249 (1983); Jack Stieber and Michael Murray, "Protection against Unjust Discharge: The Need for a Federal Statute," 16 Univ. Mich. J.L. 319 (1983); Julius G. Getman, "Labor Arbitration and Dispute Resolution," 88 Yale L.J. 916 (1979).

[48] Harry T. Edwards, "Alternative Dispute Resolution: Panacea or Anathema?" 99 Harv. L. Rev. 668, 671-72 (1986).

[49] Harry T. Edwards, "Arbitration of Employment Discrimination Cases: A Proposal for Employer and Union Representatives," 27 Lab. L.J. 265, 273 (1976).

[50] *Gilmer*.

[51] See, e.g., Martin H. Malin, "Arbitrating Statutory Employment Claims in the Aftermath of Gilmer," *Saint Louis University Law Journal*, Vol. 77 (1995).

[52] For a law review article that predicted most of *Gilmer*, see note, "Agreement to Arbitrate Claims under the Age Discrimination in Employment Act" 104 Harv. L. Rev. 568 (1990). See also, note, "Arbitrating Claims under the Age Discrimination in Employment Act of 1967: Gilmer v. Interstate/Johnson Lane Corp." 59 Univ. Cin. L. Rev. 1415 (1991); Case Comment, "Overcoming the Presumption of Arbitrability of ADEA Claims: The Triumph of Substantive over Procedural Values," 138 Univ. Pa. L. Rev. 1817 (1990).

[53] 9 U.S.C. sec. 1 et seq. (1925) (hereinafter cited as FAA).

[54] 29 U.S.C. sec. 621 et seq. (1990) (hereinafter cited as ADEA).

[55] More specifically, the Court held that "Gilmer has not met his burden of showing that Congress, in enacting the ADEA, intended to preclude arbitration of claims under that Act." *Gilmer*, at 35.

[56] Id. at 33-34.

[57] Id. at 23.

[58] Id.

[59] See Legg, Masib & Co. v. MacKall & Coe, Inc., 351 F. Supp. 1367 (D.D.C. 1972).

[60] Gardner-Denver (an employee's statutory right to trial de novo under Title VII of the Civil Rights Act of 1964 is not foreclosed by prior submission of his claim to final arbitration under the nondiscrimination clause of a collective bargaining agreement; the labor arbitrator's decision that employee was discharged for just cause does not preclude employee from resort to federal court suit under Title VII to vindicate claim of racial discrimination arising from the same factual setting addressed in arbitration); Barrentine v. Arkansas-Best Freight System, Inc., 450 U.S. 728 (1981) (employees' wage claims under the Fair Labor Standards Act are not barred by the prior submission of their grievances to the contractual dispute resolution procedures); McDonald v. City of West Branch, Michigan, 466 U.S. 284 (1984) (in a Sec. 1983 action, a federal court should not afford res judicata or collateral estoppel effect to an award in an arbitration proceeding brought pursuant to the terms of a collective bargaining agreement, and hence employee's Sec. 1983 action was not barred by the arbitration award). A similar principle is elucidated in Atchison, Topeka & Santa Fe Railway Co. v. Buell, 480 U.S. 557 (1987) (railway employee retains right to bring FELA [Federal Employers' Liability Act] action for damages even though the alleged injury was caused by conduct which may have been subject to arbitration under the RLA, because FELA provides substantive protection against conduct that is independent of the employer's obligations under the collective bargaining agreement, and it afforded fuller remedy to employee).

[61] Mitsubishi Motors Corp. v. Soler Chrysler-Plymouth, Inc., 473 U.S. 614 (1985) (FAA compels enforcement of private contract to arbitrate Sherman Act claims).

[62] Shearson/American Express Inc. v. McMahon, 482 U.S. 220 (1987); Rodriguez de Quijas v. Shearson/American Express, Inc., 490 U.S. 477 (1989).

[63] Gilmer. The dissent would have held that "arbitration clauses contained in employment agreements are specifically exempt from the coverage of the FAA," so that Gilmer could not be required to submit his claim to arbitration. Id. at 36 (Stevens, J., dissenting). The dissent concluded that "the exclusion in sec. 1 should be interpreted to cover any agreements by the employee to arbitrate disputes with the employer arising out of the employment relationship, particularly where such agreements to arbitrate are conditions of employment." Id. Moreover, the dissent believed that "compulsory arbitration conflicts with the congressional purposes animating the ADEA," which was to eradicate employment discrimination through an independent judiciary. Id. at 41.

[64] Id. at 34-35.

[65] Id. at 26

[66] Id. at 33.

[67] Christine G. Cooper, "Where Are We Going with Gilmer?—Some Ruminations on the Arbitration of Discrimination Claims," 11 St. Louis Univ. Pub. L. Rev. 203 (1992).

[68] Alford v. Dean Witter Reynolds, Inc., 905 F.2d 104 (5th Cir. 1990). And see, Willis v. Dean Witter Reynolds, 948 F.2d 305 (6th Cir. 1991). Mago v. Shearson Lehman Hutton, Inc., 956 F.2d 932 (9th Cir. 1992) (where reversing a federal district court decision against Shearson Lehman Hutton Inc., the Ninth Circuit held that plaintiff Dano Mago failed to carry her burden of proving that Congress, in enacting Title VII, intended to preclude arbitration of employment discrimination claims). Relying on the Supreme Court's decision in

*Gilmer*, the court said that an arbitration clause contained in an individual contract may require arbitration of bias charges filed under Title VII as well as age discrimination charges such as those involved in *Gilmer*.

The court added, however, that on remand, Mago may pursue her alternative argument that the arbitration clause is an unenforceable "adhesion" contract under state law because she was compelled to sign in order to obtain a job with Shearson Lehman.

Writing for the Ninth Circuit, Judge J. Clifford Wallace observed that *Gilmer* instructed that "courts should remain attuned to well-supported claims that the agreement to arbitrate resulted from the sort of fraud or overwhelming economic power that would provide grounds for the revocation of any contract." Id. at 934. In Mago's case, Wallace said the district court should decide in the first instance whether the arbitration clause is enforceable as a matter of contract law because Mago lacked any power to negotiate over or change its terms. Id. See, *Dancu v. Coopers & Lybrand*, 778 F. Supp. 832 (E.D.Pa. 1991) (the court held in an age and wrongful discharge case that the arbitration clause in the partnership between claimant Dancu and C&L is within the scope of the Federal Arbitration Act). The federal court rejected a broad interpretation of an FAA provision that excludes arbitration clauses in contracts of workers engaged in foreign or interstate commerce.

[69] Donald B. Reder, "Mediation as a Settlement Tool for Employment Disputes," *Labor Law Journal* (September, 1992) at 602, 605-606. Kilborn, "Backlog of Cases is Overwhelming Job-Bias Agency: Some Workers Giving Up," *New York Times* (Nov. 6, 1994). Matthew Davis, "Mediating ADA Claims," *The National Law Journal* (Nov. 18, 1996): 1, 14-15.

[70] Lamont E. Stallworth and Martin H. Malin, "Conflict Arising out of Work Force Diversity," *Arbitration 1993: Arbitration and the Changing World of Work, Proceedings of the Forty-Sixth Annual Meeting*, National Academy of Arbitrators 104 (1993). Lamont E. Stallworth and Leslie Christovich, "The Equal Employment Opportunity Act and Its Administration: The Claimant's Perspective," *Thirty-Eighth Proceedings of the Industrial Relations Research Association* (1985).

[71] "Charges of Disability Discrimination Boost EEOC Intake by 22% in Fiscal 1993," *Daily Labor Report* (Jan. 13, 1994) AA1-Z. EEO Policy Statement on Alternative Dispute Resolution, EEOC Notice No. 915.002 (July 17, 1995) in *Daily Labor Report* at E-13 (July 18, 1995). "EEOC Takes First Step toward Offering ADR Option," *Daily Labor Report* (April 26, 1995): DLR No. 80: AA-1, E-1 to E-2. "Alternative Dispute Resolution," *The United States Law Week*, 65 LW 2519 (Feb. 11, 1997). "Illinois Human Rights Commission and CEDR Offer ADR for Job Bias Cases," *World Arbitration & Mediation Report*, Vol. 5, No. 4 (April, 1994) at 76.

[72] Note 6, supra. And see, Stallworth and Malin note 70, supra. And see, U.S. Equal Employment Opportunity Commission, *Annual Report of the Equal Employment Opportunity Commission for the Fiscal Year* (Washington, DC: GPO, 1994). EEOC, U.S. Equal Employment Opportunity Commission (doc.), News Release, "Commission Votes to Incorporate Alternative Dispute Resolution into its Case Charge Processing System: Defers Decision on State and Local Agencies" (April 28, 1995). Chairman Gilbert F. Casellas, U.S. Equal Employment Opportunity Commission: Priority Charge Handling Procedures (June, 1995) (unpublished government document).

[73] Deborah Billings, "Labor Department to Seek Comment on Expanded Dispute Resolution Program," *Daily Labor Report* (Feb. 2, 1997), A-4 to A-5.

[74] EEOC's ADR Public Policy Statement (July, 1995). And see, Craig A. McEwen, "Mediation in Equal Employment Cases," *ABA Dispute Resolution Journal* (1993). And see, Craig A. McEwen, *An Evaluation of the Equal Employment Opportunity Commission's Pilot Mediation Program: Center for Dispute Settlement*. Washington, DC (Contract No. 2/0011/0168; and Elizabeth Rolph and Erik Moller, *Evaluating Agency ADR Programs: User's Guide to Data Collection and Use*, Rand Institute for Civil Justice (DRU-843-ACUS/IC) (September, 1994).

[75] Craig A. McEwen, *An Evaluation of the Equal Employment Opportunity Commission's Pilot Mediation Program: Center for Dispute Settlement*. Washington, DC (Contract no. 2/0011/0168). Under the EEOC Pilot Mediation approximately 58% of cases submitted to mediation were successfully resolved.

[76] It should be noted that, as discussed later, a number of state EEO enforcement agencies implemented formal mediation programs prior to the EEOC's pursuit of its mediation programs. See note 88.

[77] Rinat Fried, "EEOC Mediation Program Nears Launch Despite Snags," in *The Recorder* No. 230 (November 25, 1996).

[78] Id.

[79] Id. at p. 1 and 6.

[80] Recently, the EEOC district and area offices in Chicago, St. Louis and Kansas City, Kansas entered into a cooperative mediation program with the Center for Employment Dispute Resolution (CEDR) in Chicago. Under the ADR Consortium mediation program, EEO disputants are afforded the opportunity to select voluntarily for fee, reduced fee and pro bono. CEDR is the program administrator of the ADR Consortium. The William and Flora Hewlett Foundation provided support to initiate this program.

[81] Id.

[82] See, e.g., Iowa Code section 654A.7 (financial analyst and legal assistance), Minn. Stat. section 583.26 (financial analyst and farm advocates); Colo. Rev. Stat. section 6-9-106(3) (mediator assists). See, e.g., Cal. Fam. Code Stats. 1993, Ch. 219 at 154 (support person).

[83] Supra note 74.

[84] Chairman Gilbert F. Casellas, U.S. Equal Employment Opportunity Commission: Priority Charge Handling Procedures (June, 1995) (unpublished government document).

[85] See, McEwen note 74, supra.

[86] *The Recorder*.

[87] *The Recorder*. And, see Nadya Aswad, "Chairman Frustrated by Commission Enforcement Efforts under New Plan," *Daily Labor Report* (Dec. 23, 1996), C-1.

[88] The Illinois Human Rights Commission commenced its voluntary mediation and final and binding arbitration program in 1993. "Illinois Human Rights Commission and CEDR Offer ADR for Job Bias Cases," *World Arbitration and Mediation Report*, Vol. 5, no. 4 (April, 1994), pp. 76-77.

[89] Note 88, supra.

[90] See generally, e.g., "Employment ADR Issues and Procedures," *Dispute Resolution Journal* (January, 1997).

[91] Westin, *Resolving Employment Disputes without Litigation* and Constantino and Merchant, *Designing Conflict Management Systems*. Lamont E. Stallworth and Carolyn Hernandez, "Labor Arbitration and Alternative Methods of Resolving Employment Discrimination Disputes," *Workplace Topics* (July, 1992). William Ury, Jeanne M. Brett, and Stephen Goldberg (1988), *Getting Disputes Resolved: Designing Systems to Cut the Cost of Conflict* (Jossey-Bass Publishers, 1988). Douglas McCabe, *Corporate NonUnion Procedures and Systems* (New York, Connecticut, and London: Praeger Publishers) (1988). Mary P. Rowe, "Specifications for an Effective Integrated Complaint System" (Simon and Schuster, forthcoming 1997).

[92] Brown & Root, *Dispute Resolution Journal*. Supra note 26.

[93] *Report and Recommendations*, Commission on the Future of Worker-Management Relations (December, 1994). Chaired by John D. Dunlop, former Secretary of Labor and Professor Emeritus, Harvard University, one of the areas of the commission's focus was employment regulation, litigation, and dispute resolution.

[94] See, e.g., S.B. 2012 introduced by Senator Russ Feingold (D-Wis), which would amend Title VII of the Civil Rights Act and other antidiscrimination statutes to prohibit employers from requiring employees to submit discrimination claims to employment arbitration. Senator Feingold asserts that the immediate problem with the growing practice of securities firm, and now other employers in information technology, legal services, and insurance fields, of requiring their employees to submit claims of discrimination, including sexual harassment, to mandatory and binding arbitration. *Daily Labor Report* (April 15, 1994), pp. A3-A4. And see H.R. 4981, introduced by Representative Patricia Schroeder (D-Colo.), which would forbid agreements to arbitrate prospective claims but would allow parties to agree to arbitrate statutory issues only after a specific claim has arisen. H.R. 4981, called the Civil Rights Procedures Protection Act, would overturn *Gilmer* by amending seven federal laws, including Title VII of the Civil Rights Act, the Age Discrimination in Employment Act, the American with Disabilities Act, the Family and Medical Leave Act, and the Rehabilitation Act of 1973, to provide that the protections and procedures of those laws cannot be overridden by contract, other federal statutes of general applicability, or by any other means. It would not, however, preclude employees from voluntarily agreeing to submit discrimination claims to arbitration or other alternative dispute resolution procedures once a claim arises. *Daily Labor Report* (August 18, 1994), pp. A1-A2.

[95] Donald B. Reder, "Mediation as a Settlement Tool for Employment Disputes," *Labor Law Journal* (September, 1992).

[96] Carol A. Wittenberg, Susan T. MacKenzie and Margaret Shaw, Chapter 15, "Employment Disputes" in Dwight Golann, ed., *Mediating Legal Disputes: Effective Strategies for Lawyers and Mediators* (Little Brown, 1996) [hereinafter cited as *Mediating Legal Disputes*].

[97] Cheryl Niro, "The Decision Tree: A Systematic Approach to Settlement Decisions," *Illinois Bar Journal* 82 (March, 1994).

[98] Supra note 96 at p. 445.

[99] Supra note 96 at p. 445.

[100] Supra note 96.

[101] Supra note 75 and see, Lamont E. Stallworth and Linda K. Stroh, "Who IS Seeking to Use ADR? Why Do They Choose to Do So?" *Dispute Resolution Journal* (January-March, 1996).

[102] Supra note 101.

[103] When Title VII was enacted, it was envisioned that the charges filed under the act would be primarily "conciliated" and litigated.

[104] Lamont E. Stallworth, "Ruminations about Professional Responsibilities and Ethics for the EEO Neutral and ADR Providers: The Unrepresented Claimant, Power Imbalance and Designing ADR Programs." Speech hosted by the American Arbitration Association. September 22-23, 1995, Washington, D.C. And see, *Mediating Legal Disputes* at pp. 449-455 for other disadvantages.

[105] J. Richard, "The Law of Requisite Variety," in *The Magic of Rapport* (Meta Publications, 1987), 15-17.

[106] See, e.g., Randall Samborn, "At Will Doctrine under Fire," *National Law Journal* (October 14, 1991). John L. Zalusky, "A Union View of Nonrepresented Employees Grievance Systems," in *Labor Arbitration under Fire*.

[107] *Labor Arbitration under Fire* at 195-198.

[108] *U.S. Law Week*, 65 LW 2519 (February 11, 1997).

[109] For a comprehensive court decision reviewing major court decisions and the literature related employment ADR, see *Cole v. Burns International Security Services, et al.* (Judge Harry T. Edwards), Case No. 96-7042 (February 11, 1997), *Daily Labor Report* No. 29 (February 12, 1997: E-1 to E-23.

[110] Supra note 108.

[111] "Dispute Resolution Group Announces Initiative to Examine ADR in Workplace," *Daily Labor Report* No. 209 (October 29, 1996), at p. A2.

[112] Denenberg, Tia Schneider, and R.V. Denenberg. "The Future of the Workplace Dispute Resolver," *Dispute Resolution Journal* (June, 1994), pp. 48-58.

[113] See Stallworth and Stroh note 101, where the researchers found almost a 50-50 split in employers and claimants expressing an interest in mediation. However, also see McEwen note 75 supra where he finds that claimants are overwhelmingly more interested in mediation than respondent employers. One of the major barriers to the rise of mediation has been getting both disputants to agree to mediation. A number of courts have adopted a policy of mandated mediation as a condition precedent to a trial.

[114] The term "certified mediation program" is used here to describe any mediation program, which conforms to the EEOC's ADR Public Policy Statement, the ABA's ADR Protocol, AAA's National Rules for the Resolution of Employment Disputes and SPIDR's ADR in Employment Public Policy Report and Recommendations (forthcoming, 1998), for example.

[115] See, e.g., Daniel Wise, "Texaco Taps Armstrong, Higginbotham: Pillars of New York Bar Seen Salvaging Oil Company in Public Relations Mess," *New York Law Journal* (November 14, 1996).

[116] See Donohue, III and Siegelman note 32, supra.

[117] Supra note 101.

[118] Supra note 101, and McEwen note 32 supra.

[119] Former Senator John Danforth proposed S.B. 2327 the "Employment Dispute Resolution Act of 1994" in the 103rd Congress. S.B. 2327 provided for mandated participation in EEO mediation where at least one of the disputants has expressed an interest in mediation.

[120] See, e.g., Nancy Rogers and Craig McEwen, Chapter 7, "Mandatory Mediation and Settlement Pressures" in *Mediation: Law, Policy & Practices*. Clark, Boardman and Callaghan (1994) (2nd edition).

[121] Supra note 94.

# CHAPTER 11

# Alternative Regulatory Approaches to Protecting Employees' Workplace Rights

RICHARD EDWARDS
*University of Nebraska*

Contemporary contention over the rights that employees exercise in the workplace reflects, as do struggles over other aspects of the employment relationship, the growing inadequacy of traditional arrangements in the face of drastically changing employment circumstances. Yet the basic issue remains: In private, nonunionized companies, what workplace rights should employees possess? Indeed, what rights do they possess already, given rapidly changing legal interpretations?

These questions are increasingly being asked by American managers, workers, public policymakers, and organization theorists. Employers explore these questions because, as they seek new ways to recruit and retain high-producing employees (the key ingredient in high performance workplaces), they find that issues of "decent treatment"—mainly workplace rights—are at least as important as high wages. Less positively, employers are interested in workplace rights because increasingly they are being litigated, and companies seek to minimize their legal exposure.

Workplace rights are also of vital interest to employees for perhaps obvious reasons: workplace rights are crucial to defining the quality of the workers' daily employment experience. As Gordon (1996:34) noted in his last book, when interviewing rank-and-file workers and local union officials, he expected workers to want to talk about such matters as job security; instead, they "inveighed against speed-up, hostility, petty aggravations, capricious threats and punishments, and—perhaps most bitterly—crude, arrogant and often gratuitous exercises of power." The continuing importance of these matters to workers was confirmed in the recent and extensive survey of employees by Freeman and Rogers (1995); the survey's most powerful finding is a widespread and strongly felt worker desire for more "voice" at the workplace.

Voice is a way to achieve and enforce workplace rights, and rights directly limit the employer's power.

Changes now occurring, however, offer a significant challenge to workers' traditional advocates. Some of the most important innovations and potentials for advancing workers' status are now appearing outside the pale of traditional worker protections, requiring new ways of conceptualizing workers' interests and how to further them. Unfortunately, many workers' advocates, no less than laggard managements, are susceptible to overly long adherence to cherished old forms of struggle and too tardy recognition of the new possibilities, especially those associated with the market. Yet the new circumstances offer an important opportunity to rethink our approach to employee workplace rights.

In the debate about the proper role of government in regulating the American labor market, only three possible *regimes* are usually recognized: an unrestricted market in which labor commodities are traded freely and competitively[1]; a regulated market in which workers bargain collectively, through state-certified unions under government-set bargaining rules; and a regulated market in which government directly enforces certain minimal conditions of employment (e.g., workplace safety, overtime pay). Each of these three regimes has associated with it a by now well-known vector of economic and social benefits and costs.

These three traditional regimes treat workplace rights quite differently. In the free-market model, workplace rights appear as one among many possible desiderata for which the job-seeker or seller of labor may bargain; depending upon the weighting of workplace rights relative to other elements in the worker's utility function, the job-seeker may bargain strongly or weakly for workplace rights as part of his or her employment contract. To the extent that workplace rights are costly to the employer (e.g., by inhibiting managerial flexibility in ways that reduce profitability), employers will try to avoid having to provide workplace rights. Thus individual bargaining between sellers and buyers of labor are the means in this regime by which the inevitable tradeoffs are determined, and while little scholarly attention has been devoted to this topic, it is usually assumed that workplace rights constitute as appropriate a target for such bargaining as any other elements (e.g., wages) of the employment relationship.

By contrast, the other two regimes—collective bargaining and government direct regulation—assume that ordinary market competition (individual bargaining) is not an appropriate or adequate mechanism for determining workplace rights. Why workplace rights should be treated differently is not so clear. In the real world, of course, collective bargaining and direct regulation appeared because widespread segments of society, workers in particular, were dissatisfied with the actual results—the paucity of workplace rights—that emerged from market determination; child labor protections, hours regulation, workplace safety laws, and others derive directly from a refusal to accept the market's results. But this historical evolution does not explain why workplace rights should not be left to the market.

Of course these three traditional regimes for regulating the employment relationship are not the only possibilities.[2] One alternative model, now termed "binary economics," was offered by Louis O. Kelso. Kelso and co-author Patricia Kelso (1991:12, 22) note that "capital instruments must be recognized equally with labor as an input factor," and so they conclude that a fully democratic capitalism can only be achieved through mass (but not nationalized) ownership of capital, or what they term "every citizen's right to become a capital worker as well as a labor worker." The method for achieving this outcome is employee stock ownership plans (ESOPs), in which the employees of a firm use the firm's own revenue stream to create a broadening of the ownership base of industry.[3] ESOPs change the employment relationship and the treatment of workplace rights in particular by, in effect, making employees their own employers.

Weitzman (1984:85, 110, 111, 120-21) developed a second approach with his ingenious "share-economy" model in which "under a share contract, worker compensation is tied to a formula that makes it vary inversely with the firm's level of employment." The purpose of this far-reaching schema is to abolish "the illusion that the welfare of a firm's employees is independent of the economic condition of the employer" by making "explicit what is already inherently true in a capitalist market economy—namely that the worker gets but a part of the product and, for better or worse, ultimately depends on the capitalist for employment and income, just as the capitalist depends on the worker for profits." The model results in several unusual outcomes, at both the macro and micro level, but perhaps most relevantly for our discussion, it creates a permanent "excess demand for labor without inflation" and thereby generates much greater competition among employers for workers; "[w]hen it is in the economic interest of an employer to please his workers, he will very quickly discover what makes them happy and endeavor to bring it about." The enhanced competition for labor is expected to produce greater dignity for workers, improved working conditions, even the end of "nonfunctional discrimination," although no specifically different method of securing workplace rights is foreseen.

Freeman (1994:236) has proposed, not without substantial cautions, a more modest plan for building both greater employee "voice" and greater productivity-enhancing cooperation through introduction of European-style works councils at the enterprise level. He notes that "[p]roviding collective representation and venues for participation for American workers will require new labor institutions and changes in labor law." Drawing upon comparisons of European and Canadian labor experiences, he concludes that "legal protection for the establishment of modes of worker representation is necessary to ensure that employees have a collective voice in firms, and that once in place, such institutions can create cooperative and productive labor relations" and that "[s]uch councils or committees would need real power in some areas, say for regulating occupational health and safety, dealing with grievances, obtaining information about company plans, or for joint consultation in decision-making on training." In this plan, they would not have the right to bargain over wages or strike, but rather they would secure workplace rights via a greatly enhanced worker voice.[4]

We have also seen the real growth—without benefit of a theoretical model or academic recognition, so to speak—of a variety of incipient regulatory mechanisms rooted in the marketplace itself. Rent-a-judge, based on the contending parties' private contractual agreement to abide by the "judge's" ruling, has become a favored way of resolving some workplace disputes without the expense or delay of invoking the official judicial process. Private sector mediation and arbitration provide other do-it-yourself dispute resolution processes. In the garment industry, management and unions have experimented with jointly employing their own inspectors to supplement governmental policing of compliance with regulations on workplace labor standards. In other settings, we see similar innovative private arrangements springing up to address particular problems.

Thus alternate regulatory mechanisms have appeared in both theoretical and real forms; unfortunately, the theoretical ones typically lack real-world manifestations, and the new real-world possibilities, as responses to specific situations, are typically not suited for wider application. What particularly characterizes the emerging real-world alternatives is their dependence on the market—that is, they tend to be arrangements that re-channel and utilize market forces so that the power of markets is harnessed for the realization of the desired employment regulation.

The recent evolution of workplace rights in the U.S. offers an opportunity for remaking employment relations in ways that could benefit both employers and workers. It might be possible, for example, for employees to obtain more effective protection than they now receive at the workplace while their employers gain relief from regulatory burdens, reduce their litigation liability, and profit from more committed and productive employees. But this outcome is hardly inevitable, perhaps not even likely, and other outcomes adverse to *both* employers and their workers may ensue.

## Defining Workplace Rights

*Rights* may be thought of as a category of goods, although with some very special characteristics. Most broadly, rights are legitimate and enforceable claims or privileges that individuals obtain through membership in a group; rights entitle or protect those individuals in some specific way from the prevailing system of governance. The legal scholar Neil MacCormick (1982:143) argues that "rights always and necessarily concern human goods, that is, concern what it is, at least in normal circumstances, good for a person to have. When positive laws establish rights, for example expressly by legislation, what they do is secure individuals (or members of a particular defined set of individuals) in the enjoyment of some good or other." Thus rights may be thought of as one way that societies distribute "goods" (broadly construed), other methods being market exchanges, elections, gifts, and government programs providing services or subsidies. To be legitimate, rights as claims must derive from recognized or accepted authority.

Individuals possess rights because they are members of a group or category for whom such rights are defined; nothing further—no performance nor promise of performance on the part of the individuals within the group—is required. Consider, for example, the right to vote. Individuals possess this right by virtue of their being citizens in good standing (nonfelons of majority age); they do not need to do anything further to "earn" the right to vote. Predefined status— membership in the relevant group or category—determines access to a right.

Rights entitle individuals in some specific way within the established system of governance, or protect them in some specific way from that system, so rights are exercised in opposition to or as a limitation on the ordinary exercise of legitimate power. Dworkin (1977:11) said it best when he noted that "individual rights are political trumps held by individuals. Individuals have rights when, for some reason, a collective goal is not a sufficient justification for denying them what they wish, as individuals, to have or to do, or not a sufficient justification for imposing some loss or injury upon them."

*Workplace rights* are rights that employees exercise in the workplace, that is, in the context of work, and they can be defined following the more general definitions of rights just given. Workplace rights are legitimated claims or privileges—a form of "goods"—that an employee may exercise as a result of being an employee and that he or she may use as protection from the established workplace governance. Both membership (being an employee) and limitation of legitimate power are inherent in the meaning of workplace rights, just as with other rights. One unusual but important feature of workplace rights is that the employer may fire the worker (that is, exclude him or her from the rights-defining group) and thereby deprive the employee of the opportunity to exercise his or her workplace rights.

Workplace rights (like all rights) can be distinguished from *quid pro quo* or *contractual benefits*, which are benefits earned in return for some performance or promise of performance by the individual. Examples include wages and other employee emoluments that a worker may negotiate in the employment contract; as quid pro quo benefits, they typically depend on individual performance and are available differentially to different workers depending upon performance.

In contrast to these sharp distinctions in theory, the line between workplace rights and quid pro quo benefits in the real world of work is often blurred. A claim may appear in some guises or in some circumstances or in some enterprises as a right, in others as a quid pro quo benefit; employers and workers frequently dispute whether a particular claim is a right or not, and such arguments not infrequently spill over into the nation's courts. But these practical difficulties in marking the boundaries (and the fact that the boundaries change over time) do not vitiate the usefulness of the conceptual distinction between rights and other claims; indeed, they demonstrate the opposite, because both employers and workers know the great practical importance attached to whether a claim falls on one side or the other of this boundary— that is after all what the argument is all about.

Within this framework, we can identify several types of workplace rights, according to the sources from which they derive. One set of workplace rights derives from the law; I will call these rights *statutory rights*, although I mean to include more broadly in this category rights that come from constitutional protections and common law as well as statutes per se.[5] These are the rights most immediately identified with the direct government-regulation regime of the labor market. A second set of rights, which I term *collective contract rights*, grows out of collective bargaining and is expressed in the bargained contract. Note that for individual workers, collective contract rights (e.g., the right to a grievance procedure) function similarly to statutory rights, in that for an individual, they are non-negotiable, mostly unrelated to individual performance, and usually alienable only if the employee is fired. Collective contract rights assume primary importance in a labor market regime of generalized collective bargaining.

A third set of workplace rights, what I call *enterprise rights*, consists of those claims or privileges that employers unilaterally grant or promise to their workers. Such rights may be established by the highest echelons of the firm's management, for example, as protections against counter-productive petty tyranny of foremen and middle-level managers—a historically important development, as it turned out, in the evolution of the modern corporation.[6] Similarly, such rights may be instituted by management as part of a competitive labor market strategy to attract and retain the most talented and productive employees—a significant and highly visible factor today, especially in those industries dependent upon highly educated work forces.[7]

Examples of enterprise rights include the right to petition beyond one's immediate supervisor, the right to a grievance or complaint system, the right to relief from nepotism or arbitrary foreman's actions, the right to (limited) due process in discipline procedures, the right to have one's job clearly defined, the right to a "just cause" standard in dismissal, and the right to have one's "say" in various promotion, disciplinary, and other proceedings. Enterprise rights are idiosyncratic for each firm and typically expressed in the firm's employee handbook, which usually lists the various workplace duties, rules, practices, legal obligations, and other matters of concern to the employee and also specifies the worker's rights. Employers may use other methods besides handbooks in promulgating enterprise rights.

Enterprise rights differ in one important respect from statutory rights. For the latter, for instance the right to organize a union or serve on a jury, being dismissed for exercising one's rights is illegal (though not, as we know, uncommon). Enterprise rights, by contrast, create a legal conundrum: Is an enterprise right really a "right"? Or is it just an employer's gift or "gratuity," since any time the worker exercises the right, the employer may fire the worker, thereby extinguishing the relationship upon which the right is founded. It is on this question that the courts have recently and dramatically changed their answer. First, however, let us consider why markets, at least unaided markets, may not be an appropriate mechanism for determining workplace rights.

## The Inadequacy of the Market

Most job-seekers and jobholders, in evaluating their potential or current employment, apparently consider many dimensions of any job; employees desire employment that is stable and secure, doing meaningful work, in safe conditions, at adequate wages, with appropriate benefits, in which they receive decent treatment and some opportunity for occupational or professional advancement. A contract establishing an employment relationship necessarily covers, explicitly or implicitly, all of these dimensions, for example by establishing a presumption of job security or not, by defining decent treatment through enterprise rights or not. Some of these dimensions (e.g., benefits) may be seen as close substitutes for higher wages, whereas others (e.g., decent treatment) are more perceived as complements. Given that the employment relationship inevitably involves, by commission or omission, these multiple dimensions, it would be surprising if one method of arriving at a contract would turn out to be most efficient for all dimensions. In particular, individual bargaining in the market falls short vis-à-vis workplace rights.

For some and perhaps most elements of the employment relationship, it is widely acknowledged that workers can bargain their interests efficiently through ordinary market exchange. For example, wages are quid pro quo benefits, and both the quid and the quo can usually be well defined for the individual worker.[8] Of course employees would always like higher wages, and unions by exercising monopoly power can help them obtain higher wages; but here the issue is not the efficiency of bargaining but rather the relative power (initial endowments) within efficient bargaining. Likewise, there is little support even among employees for government wage setting, other than for the minimum wage and overtime. Little intervention is needed to correct the market process for wage determination. For other elements of the employment relationship, those elements that are rights-like, however, market determination is either inefficient or not available at all.

Consider the situation where individuals must bargain for their workplace rights; in the absence of statutory rights and collective contract rights, this process reduces to bargaining over enterprise rights. Several features peculiar to the labor market make ordinary market competition less than optimal for determining enterprise rights.[9]

First, job-seekers (and employees) typically lack critical information, especially about the actual content and efficacy of enterprise rights, and they cannot obtain such information except at great cost; these conditions create a significant and chronic information asymmetry between job-seekers and potential employers, a serious source of market failure (Laffont 1990). Enterprise rights are almost always different for each firm. Moreover, information about them is often closely guarded: Nonunion private sector employers typically regard their own packages of enterprise rights as "proprietary," partly to reduce litigation and partly as a competitive labor market strategy. Indeed, most firms will disclose information about enterprise rights only to current employees, even requiring them for example to sign for employee handbooks and threatening disciplinary action against employees who make unauthorized disclosure of the information to persons outside the firm. When enterprise rights are firm specific and proprietary, obtaining information about them is very costly for job-seekers. High information costs to labor—or employers' possession of what is sometimes called "private information"—produces a systemic condition of information asymmetry in bargaining.

Second, enterprise rights are of ambiguous legal enforceability, a de jure situation that results in part from the structural inequality in the labor market between employers and employees.[10] One employer typically bargains with many employees, and the rights-like portions of the proposed employment relationship are usually not individually bargained but offered as a similar package to all employees (or large groups of them). But unless an element of the employment contract has been individually bargained, it has not, until recently, been legally enforceable—judges have instead termed it an "employer gratuity." Even with some dramatic changes in judicial interpretations (reviewed below), enterprise rights remain of problematic legal enforceability. When key elements of a contract being bargained are not enforceable, markets cannot work efficiently, without appeal to further mechanisms such as reputational effects; but these mechanisms are themselves highly implausible.[11]

Third, a worker typically has a great problem of ensuring de facto compliance (as distinct from its legal standing) for the rights portion of an individually bargained contract; this problem results from the very nature of enterprise rights. Any right negotiated by an individual job-seeker is essentially a promise by the employer to honor the right at some unspecified time in the future, when the employee needs to exercise the right. Of course, various formal methods of ensuring compliance are hypothetically available (e.g., bonding or litigation), but they are highly costly and mostly unrealistic except in the most egregious cases. Nor does it appear that informal mechanisms such as implicit contracts or reputational effects offer a plausible short cut around this difficulty for individual workers, since such information is costly to disseminate. With poor assurance of actual contract compliance, individual bargaining works poorly.

Fourth, enterprise rights like other workplace rights have significant aspects of (firm-wide or local) public goods, so individual bargaining results in a less than optimal level of enterprise rights being achieved. An employer bargaining with one worker (who, say, has an especially favorable bargaining position) cannot easily provide that worker with seniority-based job protections or a workplace free of ambient contaminants without offering similar benefits to nearby or similar workers. In some cases the public-good aspect may be inherent or derive from technical considerations: if the employer provides seniority rights for one worker, others will necessarily be affected; removing air contaminants for one worker will mean that others nearby will benefit as well. In other cases, the public-good aspect may derive from social considerations: providing grievance rights for only some workers will be seen as unjust by excluded workers or even all workers. It is well known that ordinary market competition will not produce the optimal level of a public good, because individual demanders have an incentive not to reveal their true preferences, and this finding is fully applicable to enterprise rights.

There are several other unusual features of labor markets and enterprise rights—the limited effectiveness of recontracting due to the reduced efficacy of "exit," certain economies of scale in the provision of enterprise rights, and other externalities—that further diminish the efficiency of individual bargaining for enterprise rights. All of these features increase the complexity and reduce the effectiveness of individual contracting for enterprise rights.

Given all of these considerations, it is little wonder then that workers seek to appeal to means other than individual bargaining to gain workplace rights. Their choice should be seen not (only) as a strategy to improve their chances of a favorable outcome but as potentially in fact a socially rational choice reflecting the character of the rights-like elements of the employment contract. It may be presumed that it is on this latter basis that the public so frequently supports them—how else to explain why calls for governmental intervention in wage bargaining have never gained much public support (except for setting a minimum wage and overtime pay), whereas there is usually substantial support for intervention vis-à-vis the rights-like elements?

These various features force us to conclude that the unaided free market is not an appropriate mechanism for determining workplace rights, and so for a half century workers have depended upon other mechanisms. But, as I review very briefly, the two principal alternative mechanisms relied upon, collective bargaining and government direct regulation, have become highly ineffective or enfeebled.

## The Limited Reach of Collective Bargaining

Collective bargaining, whatever its other merits and problems, provides a direct and highly effective alternative to the market for the determination of workplace rights; in particular, collective bargaining provides a method for overcoming those specific weaknesses of the market enumerated above. First, unions are long-lived and have professional staffs, making them far superior to individual job-seekers in collecting information about specific workplaces; the problem of asymmetric information is greatly reduced, because unions can typically enter bargaining with information much more similar to employers. Second, when a union acts as the workers' bargaining agent and enters an agreement with the employer, the legal status of the contract is unambiguous and its enforcement entails no difficulties beyond ordinary contract jurisprudence. Third, because the union maintains a continuing relationship with the employer and likely processes the rights claims of many employees, the employer's compliance (or failure to comply) is regularly demonstrated to the union through repeated cases where workers seek to exercise their rights; this information can be shared, and so every worker benefits by learning from other workers' experiences the extent to which the employer will likely respect the rights promised. And finally, the union, like the firm itself, provides an entity wherein the local public-goods aspects of workplace rights can be internalized. Indeed, the unions' superior ability to handle workplace rights is surely one of the most important reasons that workers have supported unions.

Assessing the overall strengths and weaknesses of collective bargaining goes far beyond the scope of this paper, but suffice it say that unions today cannot serve as general agents in bargaining for workers' rights for one simple but powerful fact: they represent far too few workers to be able to protect the labor interest at large. Although where they exist unions continue to be effective in achieving and administering workplace rights, their coverage is just too limited for them to serve as the central mechanism in a future labor market regime. It is sometimes difficult to grasp just how thoroughly the U.S. private sector has been deunionized: American unions today organize fewer than one out of every eight private sector workers, with virtually no presence in the most technologically advanced sectors. Nor are unions likely to increase their share any time soon, given their severe problems—employer hostility, adverse legal circumstances, foreign competition, changing labor force demographics, and internal union weaknesses.

To see why the unions have so little chance to win a significantly larger share (or even halt their decline), look at the arithmetic. Simply to maintain their current private sector share, each year unions must recruit enough new members to keep up with growth in the employed labor force (around 2%), to compensate for normal attrition in the union sector (perhaps 3%), and to replace those members lost though employers' decertification efforts (less than 1%). As is now well known, recent union organizing has fallen far short of even this modest goal. For example, in 1992 the union share was 12.7%; to maintain that share in 1993, unions would have had to attract approximately 410,000 new members. But in 1993, all unions combined won 82,262 new employees through the NLRA election process. Unfortunately, decertification elections initiated by employers during 1993 deprived unions of 12,027 members. So the "net" addition was just 70,235—about 17% of the number needed to maintain their prior year's share, resulting in a decline in the share to 12.3%. And 1993 was actually better than the preceding years: during the prior four years, unions won only about 16% of their "replacement" needs.[12]

The real problem is that the recent horrendous recruiting results are only the latest part of a very long slide for American unions. The private sector union share has been declining continuously since 1955. And the last time unions won enough NLRB elections to add 400,000 new private sector members was 1953. Freeman (1988:65) has rightly called this process "the effective de-unionization of most of the U.S. labor force." Of course, the past may not predict the future well, but to construct a scenario in which unions are able again to represent a significant share of the work force requires extremely implausible assumptions.

The success of the collective bargaining framework, during its heyday from, say, the mid-1940s through the mid-1970s, was based on a kind of "win-win" situation. Neither unions nor employers were totally satisfied with the results, but it is clear that the NLRA system produced benefits for both parties. As Freeman and Medoff (1984) have shown, unions increased productivity while obtaining higher wages, creating conditions in which profits could also increase. Indeed, the collective bargaining system began seriously to fall apart when employers perceived that a win-win situation no longer existed and that collective bargaining no longer served their interests. This is a powerful lesson: It probably is not possible to maintain a system based on the cooperation of the social partners when either partner thinks the system is not producing benefits for it. And it is unclear that such a system can be successfully reimposed.

There are many good reasons to support unions and labor law reform. Reforming labor law makes sense as a matter of justice. Reform would reduce the cynicism created by a labor law that promises workers the right to unionize but as a practical matter makes unionization extremely difficult. Reform might save existing unions, sustain a labor-based middle class, and reduce racial disparities, thereby contributing to political stability. But among the good reasons to support labor law reform, a realistic hope that it could restore a situation in which unions would represent more than a tiny fraction of private sector workers is probably not one.

## The Limited Effectiveness of Statutory Regulation

Like collective bargaining, direct statutory regulation of the workplace constitutes an obvious mechanism for overcoming the weaknesses of the market's determination of workplace rights, a mechanism that has been frequently resorted to. First, by establishing rights through statute (or judges' rulings), the rights immediately become public knowledge rather than being proprietary, and information about them is limited only by the costs of dissemination; "private information" or asymmetric access to information is rendered relatively trivial. Second, statute-based rights are legally unambiguous (once the case law is settled) and present no novel juridical issues. Third, enforcement costs are shifted from the individual worker to the regulating public agency, and so, if the agency commits sufficient enforcement resources, workers can be assured of the employer's de facto compliance. And fourth, statutes address the local public-goods aspects of workplace rights by setting the socially optimal level of rights directly. This straightforward approach to handling workplace rights undoubtedly accounts for the public's support for the enormous expansion in recent decades of statutory rights.

Despite its straightforwardness, direct workplace regulation turns out to have very definite limits to its effective application. Direct regulation has the opposite problem from unions: although coverage is extremely broad, much regulation is not very effective. Or rather, American workplace regulation works tolerably well when directed at workplace phenomena that are simple, transparent, available for ex post reconstruction (e.g., from records), and easily monitored; otherwise, it is typically too clumsy, remote, and inefficient to be very useful.

I do not want to overstate the case, because some regulation is clearly effective and beneficial. For example, despite some problems, the minimum wage and overtime provisions of the Fair Labor Standards Act are important labor safeguards. Antidiscrimination legislation has opened up new jobs to excluded groups. So, too, the Occupational Safety and Health Act has clearly been helpful in disseminating information and raising consciousness about job safety.

Most workplace phenomena needing adjudication are highly complex, however, and direct regulation, when aimed at these issues, is likely to be a highly faulty protection device. For example, if we look to the real regulatory (not just information dissemination) benefits of OSHA—benefits that make a difference on the shop floor—the evidence suggests that they are very, very slight; OSHA might reduce the risk of workplace injuries by something on the order of 1% to 3% at most, and perhaps nothing at all (Viscusi 1986). Similarly, the Employee Retirement Income Security Act clearly brought some benefits, early vesting of pensions, for example; but if we look at the regulatory operations of ERISA, it is very hard to find substantial benefits for *workers*—as contrasted with accountants, lawyers, and corporate profiteers (U.S. Congress 1986). A third example is the 1988 Worker Adjustment and Retraining Notification Act; Addison and Blackburn (1994:187) found that the implementation of this law has resulted in almost no increase in notification of workers, and indeed, "the major change in notice apparently took the form of shifting workers from informal notice to no notice at all."

Workplace regulation is intrinsically a difficult task: The U.S. has somewhat more than five million job sites, and they are all different, with different technologies, work forces, management philosophies, physical layouts, and workplace cultures. When regulators write rules in Washington (or Sacramento or Springfield) to cover this myriad of workplaces, they confront a difficult choice. Either the rules must be made very complicated to fit the differences among many workplaces, in which case the rules become extremely complex to administer, impose a large regulatory burden, and are susceptible to lengthy challenges, or the regulations are made simple enough to be easily administered but then are frustratingly inappropriate (and costly) when applied to such differentiated workplaces. Neither approach serves well.

Some would argue that regulation has not really been tried in the United States and that if we just gave it a chance—hired enough OSHA inspectors to really do the job, for example—it would work. But this view ignores the political context of regulation: the politics of this country, at least since the 1960s, has been hostile to effective regulation. Indeed, the Republicans have lived for a generation on berating regulation, and in every election for the past 20 years, if a presidential candidate wanted to be successful, he had to swear off further regulation. President Clinton was elected primarily because he claimed to be a "New Democrat," not one of the old "tax-and-spend-and-regulate"-type Democrats, and again in the 1996 election, neither major candidate wanted to be identified with increased regulation.

So as I read the record of workplace regulation, there exists this disconnect: While it is sometimes possible at both the national and state levels to get new regulation passed, the actual impact at the shop floor or job-site level of the new regulation is to bring remarkably few benefits to employees. Those regulations that were imposed first tended to address the simplest and most urgent problems, like wages, hours, obvious safety measures, or overt discrimination, for which direct regulation works most effectively. Now, however, further regulation would necessarily mean going beyond those relatively simple aspects of workplaces, and so additional regulation is likely to be correspondingly less and less effective. Workers' advocates have much more power in Washington and the nation's statehouses to get new statutory protections passed than they do in the factories and offices to get old or new protections enforced. This creates the peculiar situation in which democratic forces can sometimes impose new regulation that is irritating and/or truly burdensome to employers but not very helpful to workers.

If the traditional protective mechanisms have become as enfeebled as the preceding sections suggest, yet ordinary market bargaining remains as inefficient for determining workplace rights as ever, we might well ask: Is there not some other way to deal with the rights-like aspects of the employment relationship? In particular, is it possible to build upon developments already emerging within the private sector—those arrangements that draw upon and re-channel market forces so that the power of markets is harnessed for the realization of the desired employment regulation? Is it possible to make individual bargaining work more effectively for employees?

## The Growing Importance of Enterprise Rights

In contrast to the slow demise of the two traditional protection mechanisms, enterprise rights are becoming much more important in practice. Enterprise rights have traditionally been limited by the "at-will" doctrine, originally enunciated in the 1884 landmark case of *Payne v. Western & Atlantic Railroad*, which gives the employer an unfettered right to terminate an employment contract.[13] The at-will doctrine in practice became the basis for denying legal recognition to virtually all workplace rights as follows: courts reasoned that since an employer could fire a worker at any time for any cause without committing an illegal act, whenever an employee claimed any right, the employer could legally fire the worker, rendering the employee's "right" a nullity. Therefore, the "right" existed only because the employer *chose* to permit it; instead of being a legally enforceable claim, the employee's "right" was in fact an employer gratuity, not an enforceable claim.

Before 1980, the at-will doctrine was accepted in all fifty states as the basic rule of employment law, except for those explicit intrusions created by specific statutory and collective contract rights. Starting about 1980, however, the legal landscape for employees' rights changed dramatically in favor of workers. State courts provided the leadership for this change because they have final jurisdiction over all labor contracts, except for cases involving constitutional questions, aspects specifically preempted by federal statutes (such as the NLRA), or by diversity of citizenship. During much of this period conservative Republicans dominated the national executive, but state supreme court justices proved to be much more sympathetic to workers' interests, not surprising perhaps since many of them were appointed by Democratic governors.

The first non-statute, noncollective-contract-based intrusion on at-will was what came to be known as the public policy exception. Courts in most states have refused to sanction the dismissal of employees for actions required for important public policies. For example, they protected employees who refused to commit an illegal act or who reported a workplace illegality to authorities or who miss work due to jury duty or military service. Although in practical terms quite minor, this exception created the opening for larger changes to come (McWilliams 1986; Winters 1985).

The judges' second intervention, known as the implied contract exception, dramatically reversed direction and became the true basis for the sea change in workers' enterprise rights. During the 1980s, courts in 41 states accepted the doctrine that employee handbooks, personnel manuals, and employers' oral promises can be interpreted as elements of an *implied* contract between employer and employee, and this implied contract can alter at-will status. For example, if a handbook lists employee misbehaviors that will trigger dismissal, courts have sometimes interpreted the employer's issuing of the handbook as implying a promise not to dismiss employees for other than one of the listed "good causes" (Edwards 1993:Ch. 7; McWilliams 1986; Parks and Schmedemann 1994).

Courts in nine states have opened a third exception to at will, termed the implied covenant of good faith and fair dealing. This exception has perhaps even greater potential for creating change, although its impact so far is limited because so few states have yet adopted it. Courts in these states have vested employment contracts with a requirement that the employer exercise good faith and fair dealing toward the employee. For example, a Massachusetts court (in *Fortune v. National Cash Register*) nullified National Cash Register's firing of a long-time at-will employee when the employee showed that the company's main purpose in firing him was to avoid paying a bonus.

These various exceptions to at will opened the courts to aggrieved workers and increasingly involved them in administering workplace relations. Although the data here are notoriously poor, various estimates (see Shepard et al. 1989; Dertouzos and Karoly 1992) suggest that in any given year there are 20,000 to 25,000 cases before the courts involving unjust dismissal alone. And as one legal reporter (Wald and Wolf 1985:545) rather delicately put it, as a result of the substantial awards won by employees, "plaintiff's bar has become receptive to handling wrongful discharge cases on a contingency fee basis." Lawyers in pursuit of settlement fees have become agents of change.

Little wonder. Several studies suggest that workers frequently win their cases and that they are obtaining substantial awards. One nationwide study found that plaintiffs (employees) recovered damages in 78.9% of defamation cases, 70.0% in sex discrimination and harassment cases, 58.4% in wrongful discharge cases; the average jury award for the plaintiff was $602,302 (reported in Shepard et al. 1989). Dertouzos and colleagues (1988) studied 120 wrongful discharge jury trials in California between 1980 and 1986 and concluded that the plaintiffs won 67.5% of those cases; the average jury award was $646,855 and the median was $177,000. Another study in California found that in 1987 plaintiffs won 61% of the time and the average award was $596,340 (Bureau of National Affairs 1988). Moreover, the Dertouzos et al. (1988) study found that employers paid an average of about $81,000 in legal fees to defend themselves, *whether they won or lost*.

Employers of course respond to the possibility of litigation, and so there are *indirect* costs arising from the threat of litigation (Connolly et al. 1983); these costs turn out to be far more significant economically than the direct costs. In an important second study, Dertouzos and Karoly (1992:13) found that the indirect costs on employers are "100 times more costly than the direct legal costs of jury award settlements and attorneys fees." They note (p. 63) that "the threat of wrongful termination suits changes firms' human resource practices in a manner that increases the cost of doing business . . . in effect, firms have responded to increased wrongful termination liability by treating labor as more expensive." Dertouzos and Karoly estimate that the decline in employment resulting from these indirect costs is roughly equivalent to the effect of a *10%* wage increase.

Despite the courts' new thinking and the subsequent growing litigation, enterprise rights remain of ambiguous legal enforceability. For one thing, employers have responded to the courts' interventions by rewriting their handbooks, featuring in particular prominent disclaimers that seek to preclude their interpretation as contracts; however, courts have sometimes refused to recognize disclaimers (Edwards 1993:177-81). One study (Schmedemann and Parks 1994:687) makes the distinction between handbooks as legal contracts and handbooks as moral obligation (especially in the eyes of employees) and notes that "[a]lthough these two spheres overlap considerably, they are not identical."[14]

Moreover, the courts' entry is a mixed blessing at best for both employers and workers, because they are an extremely poor mechanism for administering industrial relations. Courts are costly, have long delays, require lawyers and other expensive legal personnel, are overly formal, produce capricious awards, and perhaps most unfortunately, they create winners and losers rather than mediating disputes in a way that allows the parties to go back to working together.

Thus American industrial relations have come to a crossroads. Although the union-centered, NLRA-based system of the early postwar period has greatly declined and is unlikely to be revived, and the direct regulation regime of the later postwar period may have reached and even exceeded the limits of its effectiveness, a new system has not yet emerged. Unless some new common ground is discovered, it is likely that future industrial relations in the United States will be characterized by some market elements, significant and growing intervention by statutory regulation and by the courts, increasing costs on employers, and decreasingly effective protection for workers. This is an exact description of a dead-weight loss; fortunately, it also creates the classic conditions within which to construct a "win-win" solution.

## Toward a New Approach

It may be possible to fashion a new approach to protecting workers' rights, one that creates a "win-win" arrangement for employers and workers, by drawing upon elements from each of the regimes described above. Both employers and employees have demonstrated their interest in ensuring fair treatment on the job. Employees' concerns are evident in the thousands of lawsuits they file to obtain fair treatment but also in their clear expressions of interest in both having more "voice" and in seeking cooperative work relations with their employers.[15] And many employers evidently want to provide fair treatment (doing so is likely to promote high productivity), and in fact *many employers already promise fair treatment in the employee handbooks that they give to their workers.*[16] These promises—enterprise rights—are unilaterally granted to workers by their employers, and they cover some of the most important due process issues. Unfortunately, as noted, enterprise rights are inappropriate elements for bargaining by individual workers under present market rules. Unions once provided a means to internalize plant-level or enterprise-specific externalities within the bargaining (unions also brought other consequences as well), but they represent too few workers to provide this social good today.

The first element in finding a common ground must be the recognition that employees need and deserve some special workplace protections. In the competitive market, under the present rules, an individual worker typically cannot bargain efficiently for the rights-like elements of the employment contract. Since workers cannot bargain efficiently for workplace rights, there is a very large demand for achieving such protections in other ways—that is, through collective bargaining, direct regulation, or the courts. This is the reason, I believe, why there is such a pervasive, continuing, and apparently successful appeal to legislatures, Congress, and the courts for workplace protections. (In a revealing contrast, the same petitioners are quite unsuccessful when asking for intervention on wage bargaining, where workers *can* bargain effectively.)

The second element in finding common ground is the understanding that while workers need and deserve certain job rights, the conservative impulse to rely on markets to deliver them is often correct. As Coase (1960) and others have argued, showing that the market fails is logically insufficient to justify regulation; it is also necessary to demonstrate that government intervention would be superior. And much workplace regulation manifestly fails this test. The advantage of the market is that, in contrast to the clumsiness of direct regulation of the workplace, it promotes flexible and highly differentiated arrangements, accommodating workplace protections to the manifest differences in individual workplaces.

A superior approach would be to incorporate new elements from the three traditional labor market regimes to change how markets work, so job-seekers could more effectively use market competition to achieve their rights.

Employers promise enterprise rights to recruit and retain high-quality workers. This competition among employers is, from a social welfare perspective, now used inefficiently for worker protections. A market-based system that permitted workers to bargain efficiently for workplace protections would offer the prospect of reconciling to the greatest extent possible the conflicting needs of employers and workers.

A more effective market-driven system could be implemented by introducing some pro-competition rules, similar in nature to what we do in other situations to promote competition. For example, the Truth in Savings Act requires banks to state consumer interest rates clearly, using the annual percentage yield (APY) method, thereby facilitating comparison shopping by borrowers. Limited liability facilitates entrepreneurial activity. Other laws require food processors to list their ingredients, brokers to refrain from insider trading, and auto insurers to write their policies in understandable English. All are designed to promote more effective competition, and similar interventions are needed for workplace rights.

How then would a new market-based system address the market weaknesses vis-à-vis workplace rights described earlier?

*To overcome "private information" or asymmetric access to information, employee handbooks should be mandatory and public.* Effective competition would be enhanced if job-seekers had fuller information about job rights in prospective places of employment. Firms' failure to disclose this information serves no compelling private or public interest and inhibits market functioning. The government should supply a prototype handbook, modeled on existing private sector handbooks, so that employers currently without handbooks could, if they so chose, avoid any costs of development. All employers, or at least those with more than, say, twenty workers, should be required to provide an employee handbook to each job-seeker, and such handbooks should be public documents.

*To ensure unambiguous legal enforceability, employee handbooks should be made legally enforceable by statute.* Efficient market operation is hindered by having unresolved or ambiguous law on the enforceability of key elements of employment contracts. The very real cost of this ambiguity is apparent in the growing expenses associated with litigation to resolve workplace disputes. When job-seekers are recruited by a company, perhaps in part on the basis of the enterprise rights promised, both employee and employer should have a clear assurance that the contract they are making is enforceable. This also would make competition work more effectively for the worker.

*To reduce the costs of actual contract compliance enforcement, an independent dispute resolution service should be established.* The government now provides a very high-cost service (the courts) for resolving disputes; all parties—workers, employers, and the public—bear some of the costs involved. Costs for all could be reduced if the government would expand its mediation and dispute resolution service, so that employee grievances or disputes—I am talking here about *nonunion* cases—could be resolved in a mediation and arbitration setting that emphasizes quick, simple, inexpensive, and legitimate resolutions. (A different model, used in a number of European countries, employs labor courts that specialize industrial disputes.) Such a system could encourage and give deference to *private* mechanisms of dispute resolution, such as private arbitration, rent-a-judge, mediation, and so on. Our increasing reliance on the civil courts clogs court dockets, puts substantial and unnecessary burdens on employers, denies most workers effective redress for unfair treatment, and creates a competitive disadvantage for domestic employers in world markets.[17]

*To address the public-goods aspects of workplace rights, a system to guarantee employee "voice" should be mandated in all but the smallest workplaces.* In the collective bargaining sector, this mechanism would be the union itself. In some nonunion workplaces, voice might be achieved via works councils of the kind that Freeman and others have suggested. But in general a quite different system would be needed, along the lines of a plan called "Choosing Rights" that I have proposed elsewhere (Edwards 1993:Ch. 9).

"Choosing Rights" utilizes employee handbooks to guarantee rights to employees while preserving maximum flexibility for employers. The basic idea is simple: Every firm over a threshold size, say twenty employees, would be required by statute to have an employee handbook (or handbooks). The handbook would be distributed to employees and job-seekers and be on record as a public document. The handbook would be recognized in law as a binding and enforceable employment contract.

An employer could adopt a handbook in one of two ways. First, the employer could simply choose and implement a "standard handbook." For this purpose, a special public-private commission would be chartered to develop a set—ten or more—of standard or prototype handbooks. The principal considerations in drawing up such handbooks would be that each must provide basic workplace protections and rights while offering a distinctive and diverse array of specific rights. The point is to ensure that while each handbook offers a comparable overall *level* of protections, it does by means of a different specific *mix* of rights.

For example, there are several alternative ways of assuring job security. One handbook might offer substantial severance pay, another permit dismissal for just cause only, a third might establish employees' rights to consultation and "say" in decisions involving possible job losses, and a fourth guarantee continued employment over some period (e.g., three years) with the possibility of reduced hours or pay if the company makes a loss. The employer could simply choose whichever standard handbook was most compatible with the enterprise's circumstances or philosophy and implement it.

Second, the employer could write its own specially tailored handbook, which it could put into effect upon the firm's employees ratifying it. This option would allow the employer to include in its handbook exactly those conditions, rules, terms, procedures, and rights that it believes would be most helpful to its business. No restrictions would be placed on what the employer included or omitted from the handbook, except that the employer would know that the handbook could only be put into effect when its employees approved it.

The process for approval would be a simple, NLRB-supervised election asking workers to choose between the employer's specially tailored handbook and one of the standard handbooks (selected by the employer). In effect, while free to write any specific provisions, the employer must make its total package more attractive to its employees than at least one of the standard handbooks. On the other hand, the most adverse outcome for the employer would only be the imposition of the standard handbook which it would otherwise have chosen anyway.

"Choosing Rights" would thus move the locus of rules and rights formulation away from regulatory bureaucracies and into the decentralized private sector. It would permit a virtually infinite variation in workplace protections, consistent with the extraordinarily diverse nature of American workplaces; such variation could accommodate the diverse demands of all the differences in management philosophies, gender and ethnic compositions of labor forces, regional customs, production technologies, workplace cultures, and market conditions. Yet it would also ensure basic workplace protections for nonunion, private sector workers. And it would give firms and individuals a direct and daily self-interest in doing so.

Undoubtedly, the system would need to be fleshed out with further operational requirements (see Edwards 1993:208-30). For example, one standard handbook could be designated as the "default" option; it would prevail in workplaces where the employer, after a reasonable period, had failed to promulgate a handbook by either of the methods outlined above. Similarly, there would need to be rules about how frequently, and by what methods, an employer could change or switch handbooks. The enhanced arbitration service described above would be necessary for resolving workplace disputes.

The introduction of these rules would open up new ways to shape employment relations. Public policy, rather than being driven to further protective legislation by default, could be based on market-based or statute-based methods, depending on the specific purpose and circumstances of the intervention. Market forces—competition among employers in offering diverse workplace regimes, competition among workers in seeking out those workplace regimes they most desire—would retain a leading role in this system, thereby facilitating private, decentralized, and efficient arrangements. Unions would gain a new and significant opportunity to serve and lead unorganized workers in achieving and enforcing workplace rights. And most importantly, the system would create a win-win situation in which workers would gain more effective assurances of fair dealing at the workplace and employers would realize reduced litigation costs, relief from regulation, and a more committed and productive work force.

## Endnotes

[1] Below I refer to market competition based on this model as "individual bargaining" to distinguish it from market processes associated with collective bargaining.

[2] I do not consider other possibilities such as European co-determination, cooperatives, command-economy direction of labor, guild systems, etc., which have not played any role in American debate.

[3] Kelso and Hetter (1967) first popularized ESOPs.

[4] See also Freeman (1990); Freeman and Rogers (1993); and Rogers and Streek (1995).

[5] For some purposes it may be important to distinguish among these categories of law-based rights.

[6] See, for example, Nelson (1975) and Edwards (1979).

[7] Although everyday workplace life and customs may often develop in such a way as to permit workers various perquisites in practice, I reserve the term "enterprise rights" to refer to those claims or privileges explicitly and unilaterally granted, usually in written form, by employers to their employees.

[8] I am considering here the exchange of the wage for labor time; as much literature has shown (e.g., Edwards 1979; Gordon 1996), an exchange of the wage for productive work is much more problematical.

[9] The several arguments made in this section are explained more fully in Richard Edwards, *Rights at Work: Employment Relations in the Post-Union Era* (Washington, DC: Brookings, 1993), Chapter 3.

[10] One could apply a Tiebout-type model to argue that structural inequality is irrelevant to efficient market outcomes; for reasons why this argument is not plausible for labor markets, see Edwards (1993:Ch. 3).

[11] Black and Loewenstein (1991:64), for example, note that, "analysis of implicit contracts typically appeal to adverse reputational effects as providing employers with an incentive to honor their agreements, although this argument is almost never spelled out in much detail. Upon reflection, there are several reasons for doubting the effectiveness of reputation as an

enforcement mechanism." The Boston *Globe*'s story (p. 51) of January 10, 1991, "Digital Breaks Its No-Layoff Tradition," reported on how one employer ended its 33-year implicit promise to its employees; similar stories have been written since about Texas Instruments, IBM, Xerox, Polaroid, ATT, and many other corporations.

[12] Calculated from Bureau of National Affairs (1994); National Labor Relations Board (various years), and U.S. Department of Labor (various years).

[13] The court in *Payne* (at 507) declared that "men [sic] must be left, without interference, to buy and sell where they please, and to discharge or retain employees at will for good cause or for no cause, or even for bad cause without thereby being guilty of an unlawful act *per se*."

[14] "[E]mployers should consider the effect of language which combines promise-making statements with a disclaimer. Our results suggest that employees may deem such language to bind the employer morally, but not legally. As a result, the employee may perceive that the employer also is unwilling to stand behind its promises. While these perceptions may reduce the chances of a lawsuit should termination occur, they may also reduce the employee's commitment to the employer" (Schmedemann and Parks 1994:687).

[15] These results are strongly evident in the findings of a recent major and in-depth survey of worker attitudes (Freeman and Rogers 1995:18); their conclusions: "Most American employees want more involvement and greater say in their jobs. Many—sometimes a majority, sometimes a large minority—also want some form of workplace organization or policy that provides them with *group* as well as individual voice. . . . At the same time, virtually all employees—including union members and those interested in joining unions—strongly prefer *cooperative* relations with management to conflictual ones . . ." (emphasis in original).

[16] Of course companies may have extended these promises never intending to honor them; however, as the New Jersey Supreme Court declared in the precedent-setting Woolley case (at 1266): "It will not do now for the company to say it did not mean the things it said in its [employee] manual to be binding. Our courts will not allow an employer to offer attractive inducements and benefits to the work force and then withdraw them when it chooses."

[17] There is strong support among workers for arbitration and other "alternative dispute resolution" methods, especially if such systems were jointly run by management and employees and independent of government (Freeman and Rogers 1995:15).

## References

Addison, John T., and McKinley L. Blackburn. 1994. "Policy Watch: The Worker Adjustment and Retraining Notification Act." *The Journal of Economic Perspectives*, Vol. 8, no. 1 (Winter), pp. 181-90.

Black, Dan A., and Mark Loewenstein. 1991. "Self-Enforcing Labor Contracts with Costly Mobility." In R. Ehrenberg, ed., *Research in Labor Economics* (Vol. 12). Greenwich, CT: JAI Press, pp. 63-83.

Bureau of National Affairs (BNA). 1994. "NLRB Representation and Decertification Elections Statistics." Mimeo (May).

_____. 1988. *Daily Labor Report*, no. 25 (Feb. 8).

Coase, Ronald. 1960. "The Problem of Social Cost." *Journal of Law and Economics*, Vol. 3, no. 1, pp. 1-44.

Connolly, Walter B., Gary Murg, and Clifford Scharman. 1983. "Abrogating the Employ-
    ment-at-Will Doctrine: Implications for Personnel Policies and Handbooks." *Preven-
    tive Law Reporter*, Vol. 2 (December), pp. 53-60.
Dertouzos, James, Elaine Holland, and Patricia Ebener. 1988. *The Legal and Economic
    Consequences of Wrongful Termination*. Santa Monica, CA: The Rand Corporation.
Dertouzos, James, and Lynn A. Karoly. 1992. *Labor Market Responses to Employer Liabil-
    ity*. Santa Monica, CA: The Rand Corporation.
Dworkin, Ronald. 1977. *Taking Rights Seriously*. Cambridge, MA: Harvard University Press.
Edwards, Richard. 1979. *Contested Terrain: The Transformation of Work in the Twentieth
    Century*. New York: Basic Books.
_____. 1993. *Rights at Work: Employment Relations in the Post-Union Era*. Washing-
    ton, DC: The Brookings Institution.
*Fortune v. National Cash Register Co.*, 373 Mass. 96, 3364 N.E.2d 1251.
Freeman, Richard. 1990. "Employee Councils, Worker Participation, and Other Squishy
    Stuff." *Proceedings of the Forty-Third Annual Meeting*. Madison, WI: Industrial Rela-
    tions Research Association, pp. 328-37.
_____. 1988. "Contraction and Expansion: The Divergence of Private Sector and Pub-
    lic Sector Unionism in the U.S." *The Journal of Economic Perspectives*, Vol. 2, pp. 63-
    88.
Freeman, Richard (ed.). 1994. *Working under Different Rules*. New York, Russell Sage
    Foundation.
Freeman, Richard, and James Medoff. 1984. *What Do Unions Do?* New York: Basic Books.
Freeman, Richard, and Joel Rogers. 1995. "Worker Representation and Participation Sur-
    vey: Second Report of Findings." Mimeo. Princeton, NJ: Princeton Survey Research
    (June 1).
_____. 1993. "Who Speaks for Us? Employee Representation in a Nonunion Labor
    Market." In B.E. Kaufman and M.M. Kleiner, eds., *Employee Representation: Alterna-
    tives and Future Directions*. Madison, WI: Industrial Relations Research Association.
Gordon, David M. 1996. *Fat and Mean: The Corporate Squeeze of Working Americans and
    the Myth of Managerial "Downsizing."* New York: The Free Press.
Gould, William F., IV. 1992. "The Employment Relationship under Siege: A Look at Recent
    Developments and Suggestions for Change." *Stetson Law Review*, Vol. 22, no. 1 (Fall),
    pp. 15-25.
Kelso, Louis O., and Patricia Hetter Kelso. 1967. *Two-Factor Theory: The Economics of
    Reality*. New York: Random House.
_____. 1991. *Democracy and Economic Power: Extending the ESOP Revolution
    through Binary Economics*. Lanham, MD: University Press of America.
Laffont, Jean-Jacques. 1990. *The Economics of Uncertainty and Information*. Cambridge,
    MA: MIT Press.
MacCormick, Neil. 1982. *Legal Right and Social Democracy*. New York: Oxford University
    Press.
McWilliams, Kelley. 1986. "The Employment Handbook as a Contractual Limitation on the
    Employment At-Will Doctrine." *Villanova Law Review*, Vol. 31, pp. 335-75.
Nelson, Daniel. 1975. *Managers and Workers: Origins of the New Factory System in the
    U.S., 1880-1920*. Madison, WI: University of Wisconsin Press.
Parks, Judi McLean, and Deborah A. Schmedemann. 1994. "When Promises Become Con-
    tracts: Implied Contracts and Handbook Provisions on Job Security." *Human Resource
    Management*, Vol. 33, no. 3 (Fall), pp. 403-23.

*Payne v. Western & Atlantic Railroad*, 81 Tenn. 507 (Tenn. 1884).

Rogers, Joel, and Wolfgang Streek. 1995. *Works Councils: Consultation, Representation, and Cooperation in Industrial Relations.* Chicago: University of Chicago Press.

Schmedemann, Deborah A., and Judi McLean Parks. 1994. "Contract Formation and Employee Handbooks: Legal, Psychological, and Empirical Analyses." *Wake Forest Law Review*, Vol. 29, no. 3, pp. 647-718.

Shepard, Ira Michael, Paul Heylman, and Robert L. Duston. 1989. *Without Just Cause: An Employer's Practical and Legal Guide on Wrongful Discharge.* Washington, DC: BNA Books.

U.S. Congress, Committee on Education and Labor. 1986. *Oversight Hearings on Employee Benefit Plans.* Washington, DC: GPO.

U.S. Department of Labor. Various years. *Employment and Earnings* (January issue). Washington, DC: GPO.

U.S. Departments of Labor and Commerce, Commission on the Future of Worker-Management Relations. 1994. "Fact Finding Report." Washington, DC: GPO.

U.S. National Labor Relations Board. Various years. *Annual Report.* Washington, DC: GPO.

Viscusi, Kip. 1986. "The Impact of Occupational Safety and Health Regulation, 1973-1983." *Rand Journal of Economics*, Volume 17 (Winter), pp. 567-80.

Wald, Martin, and David W. Wolf. 1985. "Recent Developments in the Law of Employment at Will." *Labor Lawyer*, Vol. 1 (Summer), pp. 533-54.

Weitzman, Martin. 1984. *The Share Economy: Conquering Stagflation.* Cambridge, MA: Harvard University Press.

Winters, Richard Harrison. 1985. "Employee Handbooks and Employment-at-Will Contracts." *Duke Law Journal*, Vol. 1985, pp. 196-220.

*Woolley v. Hoffman-LaRoche, Inc.* 491 A.2d 1257 (1985) at 1266.

# CHAPTER 12

# Implementing Employment Regulation: Insights on the Determinants of Regulatory Performance

## DAVID WEIL
### Boston University

> Notwithstanding all that has been said regarding the progress of legislation for the protection of the workers, it is scarcely worth consideration if the laws are not enforced. More important than the hasty enactment of additional laws is the adoption of methods of administration that will enforce them. It is easy for politicians, or reformers, or trade union officials to boast of the laws which they have secured for labor, and it is just as easy to overlook the details, or appropriations, or competent officials that are needed to make them enforceable. (Commons and Andrews 1936:448)

Analysts are often implored to "cut to the chase" when examining the performance of legislation or regulatory interventions and address the question, Did it work? While the importance of this question is self-evident, it often obfuscates the related question of, *Why* did the legislation work? Or, more commonly, Why did it fail? Though policymakers periodically face the question whether to keep or dispose of an entire area of regulation, the far more common decision concerns how to make an existing agency or regulatory program operate more effectively. Thus as Commons and Andrews imply above, the factors affecting the administration of regulation are as critical an area of enquiry as is the desirability of regulatory intervention itself.

Other chapters in this volume discuss the rationale for various pieces of federal workplace regulatory policy and assess their general performance. In contrast, this essay focuses on how the structure of the regulatory system itself affects the performance of employment regulation. It provides a framework for examining this question and presents evidence from a variety of studies relating to the underlying determinants of regulatory performance.

The chapter begins by charting the growth of federal workplace regulations and describing the increasing diversity of regulatory targets, objectives, and methods employed to enforce and administer them. The next three sections discuss the sequence of relationships that connect de jure to de facto employment regulation via (1) the structure of regulatory enforcement, (2) the impact of enforcement on firm compliance behavior, and (3) the relation of compliance with labor market and public policy outcomes. The chapter concludes with a discussion of how implementation and administration might be reformed to improve regulatory performance in the future.

## The Growth and Diversity of Federal Workplace Regulation

Since the passage of the Railway Labor Act in 1926, federal government regulation of the workplace via statute and executive order has grown significantly. In 1940 the U.S. Department of Labor administered 18 regulatory programs; by 1960 it administered 40; in 1975, 134; and by 1994, the number had reached 180 (Dunlop 1976; Commission on the Future of Worker-Management Relations 1994a).

The 26 most important federal workplace regulations are listed in Table 1, broken into six major categories of activity: labor standards, benefits, civil rights, occupational health and safety, labor relations, and hiring and separation decisions. Federal workplace regulation has experienced three major periods of growth: the first in the mid-1930s, the second in the early 1970s, and most recently between 1986 to 1993. In the most recent period, Congress passed employment policy statutes addressing employment discrimination for disabled workers, notification of layoff resulting from reductions in business operations, and a number of statutes regarding specific hiring and firing procedures.

Almost all federal labor regulations[1] place the employer as the target of regulation, with the intent to alter the behavior of the employer by making him or her conform to a set of baseline policies regarding the employment relationship. It can therefore be argued that the "purpose" of federal labor laws (de jure although perhaps not de facto) is to create a floor for employer behavior in the labor market.[2]

The efficiency justification for establishing these floors is that they redress externalities arising in the labor market. Private employers do not face the full costs of their policy choices. For example, in the area of safety and health, if injury and illness levels arising from the profit-maximizing choices by firms exceed the injury level desirable from a social perspective, there is justification for government intervention in this labor market. Similarly, recent legislation to require advanced notice of plant closings can be justified on efficiency grounds if employers' incentives to provide advanced notice to employees before a major plant closing are too close to the time of the actual closure, because employers do not factor in the adjustment costs for individual workers and their communities.

Other labor policies fit less well under the externality model.[3] Minimum wages are justified usually along equity criteria: employers should not be allowed to pay below the minimum wage, because no person should work on a full-time basis and not achieve a basic standard of living. Overtime standards were originally passed along similar grounds at the turn of the century because of the excessive hours worked in many industries.[4] These laws were later justified on the grounds of employment promotion: restrictions on overtime would force employers to hire more workers.

Efficiency explanations of labor laws suggest that regulations result from rational choices on the part of policymakers or, in more sophisticated law and economics frameworks, the equivalent outcomes arising from Pareto optimizing trades between political coalitions (see Schwab in this volume). Equity explanations more readily reflect the intense political struggles that underlay many pieces of federal labor market policy. Both types of explanations can provide insight into the origins of employment regulation. Thus one can interpret the passage of the National Labor Relations Act in 1935 as a social welfare enhancing solution to a full employment problem (Kaufman, this volume) or as a political response to the growing militancy of unskilled workers in the rapidly expanding mass production industries and consequent concerns about the havoc uncontrolled strikes and shutdowns would have on the economy.[5] The passage of OSHA thirty-five years later arose from concerted efforts by manufacturing and building trades labor unions to enhance their ability to bargain over issues of safety and health as much as from explicit or de facto efforts to deal with externalities arising from occupational injuries (Bokat and Thompson 1988).

Whether efficiency concerns ultimately dominate social equity aims, or whether both objectives are trumped by other objectives, a study of regulatory performance must recognize that federal regulations arise from multiple, sometimes contradictory, roots and cannot therefore be regarded as a seamless web of logically interconnected interventions. This heterogeneity in regulatory objectives has led to equal (or greater) heterogeneity in (1) the regulatory tools and apparatus used by the government, (2) the definition of regulatory targets, and (3) the workplace outcomes regulations seek to affect.

The 180 statutes administered by the Department of Labor draw upon a variety of enforcement and penalty systems, relying on an equally varied assortment of regulatory agents (see below). In order to internally administer this smorgasbord of programs, the Department of Labor relies on no less than twenty different types of major adjudication procedures and many more minor procedures (Commission on the Future of Worker-Management Relations 1994b). While certain regulatory programs administered by the DOL have coordinated enforcement (e.g., enforcement of overtime, minimum wage, and child labor within the Wage and Hours Division), coordination across major programs has often been (and remains) a difficult problem.

Heterogeneity in the structure of federal regulations also leads to heterogeneity in the intended target(s) of labor regulation. The term "employer" masks a myriad of parties whose behavior the legislation is ultimately directed toward. The "employer" in question can vary widely, from the manager of a plant, to the CEO of a company, to the owners of the firm as a whole. For example, a CEO may ultimately be criminally responsible for an egregious violation of OSHA standards. However, many OSHA standards ultimately require changes in operating practices made by managers many layers lower in the corporate structure. Similarly, plant supervisors or line foremen may be responsible for systematic violation of overtime standards or the use of contract labor in violation of child labor restrictions. Thus principle-agent problems abound in defining the "employer" whose behavior must be monitored and in some cases changed.

Finally, the labor regulations listed in Table 1 seek to affect a diversity of labor market outcomes. Most of the regulatory programs attempt to directly affect employment outcomes in the areas of labor standards, benefits, safety and health, and hiring and separation. These range from general requirements (payment of the minimum wage) to highly specific ones (the voluminous safety and health standards promulgated under OSHA). A second set of programs address issues regarding the treatment of the work force particularly in relation to civil rights objectives, ranging from specific prohibitions against pay discrimination (Equal Pay Act) to the more general set of activities dealt with under Title VII, ADA, and EO 11246. Finally, a third set of programs in the area of labor relations are directed toward the *process* of setting conditions at the workplace. The NLRA in particular sought to create a system of private industrial jurisprudence where conditions of work and disputes arising within the employment relation could be worked out by the parties themselves.

Analyzing regulatory performance must take into account this heterogeneity in tools, targets, and outcomes. The following section provides a framework for doing so.

## Determinants of Regulatory Performance

Regulatory policies are implemented via the actions of government, employers, employees, and/or other agents (e.g., other levels of government,

TABLE 1

Major Federal Workplace Regulations

| Labor Statute or Executive Order | Acronym | Date of Passage | Description |
|---|---|---|---|
| *Labor Standards* | | | |
| Fair Labor Standards Act | FLSA | 1938 | Establishes minimum wage, overtime pay and child labor standards |
| Davis-Bacon Act | — | 1931 | Provides for payment of prevailing local wages and fringe benefits to workers employed by contractors and subcontractors on federal contracts for construction, alteration, repair, painting or decorating of public buildings or public works |
| Service Contract Act | SCA | 1963 | Provides for payment of prevailing local wages and fringe benefits and safety & health standards for employees of contractors and subcontractors providing services under federal contracts |
| Walsh-Healy Act | — | 1936 | Provides for labor standards, including wage and hour, for employees working on federal contracts for the manufacturing or furnishing of materials, supplies, articles, or equipment |
| Contract Workhours and Safety Standards Act | CWHSSA | 1962 | Establishes standards for hours, overtime compensation, and safety for employees working on federal and federally funded contracts and subcontracts |
| Migrant and Seasonal Agricultural Workers Protection Act | MSPA | 1983 | Protects migrant and seasonal agricultural workers in their dealings with farm labor contractors, agricultural employers, associations, and providers of migrant housing |
| *Benefits* | | | |
| Employee Retirement and Income Security Act | ERISA | 1974 | Establishes uniform standards for employee pension and welfare benefit plans, including minimum participation, accrual and vesting requirements, fiduciary responsibilities, reporting and disclosure |
| Consolidated Omnibus Budget Reconciliation Act | COBRA | 1986 | Provides for continued health care coverage under group health plans for qualified separated workers for up to 18 months |
| Unemployment Compensation provision of the Social Security Act | — | 1935 | Authorizes funding for state unemployment compensation administrations and provides the general framework for the operation of state unemployment insurance programs |
| Family Medical Leave Act | FMLA | 1993 | Entitles employees to take up to 12 weeks of unpaid, job-protected leave each for specified family and medical reasons such as the birth or adoption of a child or an illness in the family |

TABLE 1 (Continued)

Major Federal Workplace Regulations

| Labor Statute or Executive Order | Acronym | Date of Passage | Description |
|---|---|---|---|
| *Civil Rights* | | | |
| Title VII of the Civil Rights Act | — | 1964 | Prohibits employment or membership discrimination by employers, employment agencies, and unions on the basis of race, color, religion, sex, or national origin; prohibits discrimination in employment against women affected by pregnancy, childbirth, or related medical condition |
| Equal Pay Act | — | 1963 | Prohibits discrimination on the basis of sex in the payment of wages |
| Executive Order 11246 | EO 11246 | 1962 | Prohibits discrimination against an employee or applicant for employment on the basis of race, color, religion, sex, or national origin by federal contractors and subcontractors and requires federal contractors and subcontractors to take affirmative action to ensure that employees and applicants for employment are treated without regard to race, color, religion, sex, or national origin |
| Age Discrimination Employment Act | ADEA | 1967 | Prohibits employment discrimination on the basis of age against persons 40 years and older |
| Americans with Disabilities Act | ADA | 1990 | Prohibits employment discrimination against individuals with disabilities; requires employer to make "reasonable accommodations" for disabilities unless doing so would cause undue hardship to the employer |
| Rehabilitation Act (Section 503) | — | 1973 | Prohibits federal contractors and subcontractors from discriminating in employment on the basis of disability and requires them to take affirmative action to employ, and advance in employment, individuals with disabilities |
| Anti-retaliatory provision-Surface Transportation Assistance Act | STAA | 1978 | Prohibits the discharge or other discriminatory action against an employee for filing a complaint relating to a violation of a commercial motor vehicle safety rule or regulation or for refusing to operate a vehicle that is in violation of a federal rule, or because of a fear of serious injury due to an unsafe condition |
| *Occupational Health & Safety* | | | |
| Occupational Safety & Health Act | OSHA | 1970 | Requires employers to furnish each employee with work and a workplace free from recognized hazards that can cause death or serious physical harm |

TABLE 1 (*Continued*)

Major Federal Workplace Regulations

| Labor Statute or Executive Order | Acronym | Date of Passage | Description |
|---|---|---|---|
| Federal Mine Safety & Health Act | MSHA | 1969 | Requires mine operators to comply with health and safety standards and requirements established to protect miners |
| Drug Free Workplace Act | DFWA | 1988 | Requires recipients of federal grants and contracts to take certain steps to maintain a drug free workplace |
| *Labor Relations* | | | |
| National Labor Relations Act | NLRA | 1935 | Protects certain rights of workers including the right to organize and bargain collectively through representation of their own choice |
| Labor-Management Reporting & Disclosure Act | LMRDA | 1959 | Requires the reporting and disclosure of certain financial and administrative practices of labor organizations and employers; establishes certain rights for members of labor organizations and imposes other requirements on labor organizations |
| Railway Labor Act | RLA | 1926 | Sets out the rights and responsibilities of management and workers in the rail and airline industries and provides for negotiation and mediation procedures to settle labor-management disputes |
| *Hiring & Separation Decisions* | | | |
| Employee Polygraph Protection Act | PPA | 1988 | Prohibits the use of lie detectors for pre-employment screening or use during the course of employment |
| Veterans' Reemployment Rights Act | VRR | 1940 | Provides reemployment rights for persons returning from active duty, reserve training, or National Guard duty |
| Immigration Reform & Control Act (Employment provisions) | IRCA | 1986 | Prohibits the hiring of illegal aliens and imposes certain duties on employers; protects employment rights of legal aliens; authorizes but limits the use of imported temporary agricultural workers |
| Workers Adjustment & Retraining Act | WARN | 1988 | Requires employers to provide 60 days advance written notice of a layoff to individual affected employees, local governments, and other parties |

*Source*: Adapted from GAO (1994), Table 2.1; Figure 2.1.

labor unions, employer associations). For each of the 26 major regulations, Table 2 indicates which agency (or in some cases agencies) play this role. In most cases,[6] a division of the U.S. Department of Labor (e.g., the Wage and Hour Division, Occupational Safety and Health Administration) acts as the enforcement agent. The Department of Labor (DOL) exercises its authority either because of a legislative mandate providing it jurisdiction over all private sector workplaces or authority granted it arising from government's role as a major purchaser of services and products.

The task of the DOL is to ascertain whether or not a firm is conducting its human resource policies in a manner consistent with the six categories of regulatory programs and then to change the behavior of those firms that are not. As Table 2 indicates, the majority of workplace regulations provide the DOL or other enforcement agents with a variety of civil and in some cases criminal sanction to provide incentives to change behavior.

Enforcement of OSHA and MSHA are indicative of the administrative process underlying many workplace regulations. The process is depicted in Figure 1. Based on a set of health and safety standards promulgated through a separate administrative procedure, OSHA and MSHA enforcement personnel are authorized to inspect selected workplaces to monitor compliance with those standards (Mintz 1985).[7] In the course of those inspections, enforcement officers may cite the employer for one or more violations of standards. Citations may result in both an abatement order (stating how the problem should be corrected and within what time period) and may result in a penalty, depending on the severity, number of workers exposed, and previous history of the employer. Both features of the citation may be modified in post-inspection meetings between the employer, the inspection officer, and—where present—a representative of the work force. The citation(s) may also be appealed through formal administrative review processes established under both acts.

Despite the variations in enforcement features, an implicit model of regulatory performance underlies workplace regulation. Assessing the performance of a regulatory intervention rests in part on the sequence of activities embodied (or assumed) in the original legislation and elaborated upon through administrative code to lead ultimately to the desired labor market outcomes.

Evaluation of labor policies often proceeds by assuming a direct connection between labor statutes and labor market outcomes. The labor statute is evaluated based on whether it has led to the desired change in the labor market outcome. While this approach provides insight into the overall question of efficacy, it can mask underlying reasons that firms are moving toward or away from desired outcomes for reasons unrelated (but perhaps correlated) with

TABLE 2

Enforcement Features of Federal Workplace Regulations

| Labor Statute or Executive Order | Principal Enforcement Agency | Fed. Contract Necessary for Coverage | Penalty/Sanctions | | |
|---|---|---|---|---|---|
| | | | Civil Monetary Penalties | Other Major Civil Sanctions | Criminal Sanctions |
| *Labor Standards* | | | | | |
| FLSA | DOL-WHD | | ✓ | Unpaid wages; Liquidated/punitive damages | |
| Davis-Bacon Act | DOL-WHD | ✓ | | Unpaid wages; Debarment | |
| Service Contract Act | DOL-WHD | ✓ | | Unpaid wages; Debarment | |
| Walsh-Healy Act | DOL-WHD | ✓ | | Unpaid wages; Liquidated/punitive damages; Debarment | |
| CWHSSA | DOL-WHD | ✓ | ✓ | Unpaid wages; Liquidated/punitive damages; Debarment | ✓ |
| MSPA | DOL-WHD | | ✓ | Unpaid wages | ✓ |
| *Benefits* | | | | | |
| ERISA | DOL-PWBA; PBGC; IRS | | ✓ | | ✓ |
| COBRA | DOL-PWBA Treasury-IRS | | | | |
| Unemployment Compensation | DOL-ETA | | | | |
| FMLA | DOL-WHD | | ✓ | Unpaid wages; Liquidated/punitive damages | |
| *Civil Rights* | | | | | |
| Title VII | EEOC | | ✓ | Unpaid wages; Liquidated/punitive damages | (state or local) |
| Equal Pay Act | EEOC | | ✓ | Unpaid wages; Liquidated/punitive damages; Debarment | ✓ |

TABLE 2 (Continued)
Enforcement Features of Federal Workplace Regulations

| Labor Statute or Executive Order | Principal Enforcement Agency | Fed. Contract Necessary for Coverage | Penalty/Sanctions | | |
|---|---|---|---|---|---|
| | | | Civil Monetary Penalties | Other Major Civil Sanctions | Criminal Sanctions |
| EO 11246 | DOL-OFCCP | ✓ | | Unpaid wages; Debarment | |
| ADEA | EEOC | | | Unpaid wages; Liquidated/punitive damages | ✓ |
| ADA | EEOC | | | Unpaid wages; Liquidated/punitive damages | ✓ (state or local) |
| Rehabilitation Act (Section 503) | DOL-OFCCP | ✓ | | Unpaid wages; Debarment | |
| Anti-retaliatory provision-STAA | DOL-OSHA | | | Unpaid wages | |
| *Occupational Health & Safety* | | | | | |
| OSHA | DOL-OSHA | | ✓ | | ✓ |
| MSHA | DOL-MSHA | | ✓ | | ✓ |
| DFWA | DOL-OFCCP | ✓ | | Debarment | |
| *Labor Relations* | | | | | |
| NLRA | NLRB | | | | |
| LMRDA | DOL-OAW | | ✓ | | ✓ |
| RLA | NMB | | | | ✓ |
| *Hiring & Separation Decisions* | | | | | |
| PPA | DOL-WHD | | ✓ | Unpaid wages | |
| VRA | DOL-VETS | | | Unpaid wages | |
| IRCA (Employment provisions) | DOL-WHD | | ✓ | | ✓ |
| WARN | None | | ✓ | Unpaid wages | |

*Source:* Adapted from GAO (1994), Table 2.1; Figures 2.3, 2.5.

FIGURE 1
Schematic Structure of MSHA and OSHA

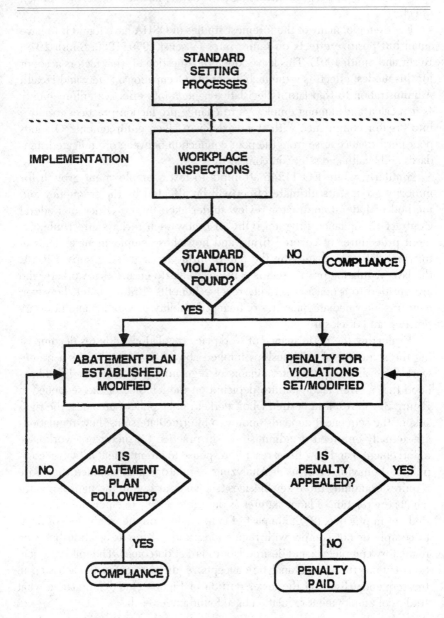

the labor statute. More importantly, the approach provides little guidance in the question of *why* a given labor statute is having its intended or unintended effect.

For example, many of the foremost studies of OSHA have found it to have small but positive effects on injury rates (Viscusi 1979, 1986; Smith 1979; Ruser and Smith 1991). This leaves open the question of what factors account for this modest effect: Is it the inability of the Occupational Safety and Health Administration to translate its legislative agenda into effective enforcement? Is it recalcitrance among employers to change production practices to move into greater compliance with standards even given enforcement? Or does poor performance arise from the poor connection between promulgated standards and health and safety outcomes?

Similarly, while EO 11246 attempts to foster employment growth for minority groups, its ultimate effect will be affected by the frequency and method of federal contractor review undertaken by the Office of Federal Contract Compliance Program (OFCCP), how such reviews affect employment procedures of covered firms, and how those employment policies in turn translate into changes in the rate of hiring for targeted groups. ERISA, the laws regulating private sector pensions, seeks to ensure that workers who are entitled to a pension actually receive benefits. Enforcement, however, concerns intermediate measures of financial viability, accounting and fiduciary practice, and disclosure.

Evaluating the performance of workplace regulations requires decomposing the sequence of relationships implied above. Figure 2 depicts a framework for evaluating the determinants of regulatory performance. The likelihood that a given labor statute (depicted on the left side of the sequence in Figure 2) will result in desired labor market/public policy outcomes (the right side of the sequence) depends upon two intermediate steps: how regulations are actually enforced or administered in practice ("structure of workplace enforcement") and how firms react in response to enforcement activity ("compliance behavior of firms"). Analyzing regulatory performance therefore requires examining three key linkages (shown as arrows in the figure) regarding (1) the relation of labor statutes as described in law to enforcement as carried out in practice, (2) the impact of enforcement on the willingness of firms to comply or not comply with regulations, and (3) the association between regulatory compliance and desired labor market outcomes. The following sections lay out the central analytic concepts required to examine each step in the sequence (listed in the lower portion of Figure 2) and summarize what studies of employment regulation have found under each.

FIGURE 2

Implementation Determinants of Regulatory Performance

| ASPECT OF REGULATION | Labor Statute | Structure of Workplace Enforcement | Compliance Behavior of Firms | Labor Market/Public Policy Outcomes |
|---|---|---|---|---|
| ANALYTIC CONCEPTS | Regulatory objectives | Role of enforcement agency | Deterrence incentives via regulatory system | Direct labor market outcomes |
| | Regulatory targets | Penalty/sanction policy | Internal costs of compliance | Larger public policy objectives |
| | Formal regulatory structure | Employee rights/reporting requirements | Human resource policies | Unintended consequences |
| | | Workplace agents | Market structure/other external factors | |

## From Statute → Enforcement: Resource Limitations and the Role of Employee Rights

The intentions of labor legislation and executive orders are translated into practice via enforcement. There are three ways that enforcement can be undertaken under labor regulation: (1) the responsible government agency can initiate enforcement; (2) employees can initiate enforcement (via rights of private action); or (3) a mix of the above, where employees trigger enforcement, bring government action, and/or use private rights through the courts. The first step in assessing regulatory performance requires analyzing how well these methods translate the intentions of government policies as stated in legislation into effective enforcement activity.

### Government Enforcement and the Problem of Resource Limitation

Most of the workplace policies depicted in Table 1 require some enforcement action on the part of the U.S. government. Part of this enforcement action is triggered by complaints and other rights granted to employees under those laws (see next section). The laws, however, also create independent authority in portions of the DOL for undertaking these actions.

There is considerable divergence between the enforcement implied in statutes to actual enforcement as carried out by federal departments. The Department of Labor relies upon 800 inspectors in its Wage and Hour Division to enforce overtime, minimum wage, child labor, and other labor standards covered by the FLSA. OSHA's inspection force has never exceeded 1,500 and currently hovers around 1,200 (Siskind 1993).

Staffing limitations give rise to large regulatory backlogs. In 1993 the EEOC had 87,942 complaints filed with it (versus the 56,228 complaints it received in 1981). In that year the commission pursued a mere 481 lawsuits. In a similar vein, in 1993 the DOL pursued only 2,295 wage and hour cases, while 46,121 such complaints were filed with the Wage and Hour Division (Commission on the Future of Worker-Management Relations 1994a:135).

Resource limitations substantially lower the probability that a workplace will be inspected in a given year by the government. The annual probability of receiving an inspection for one of the six million establishments covered by OSHA is well below .001. The ability of government agencies to fulfill their legislative mandates therefore relies upon an agency's ability to deploy very constrained resources in an effective manner. One response to the severe resource constraints faced by all regulators has been the use of enforcement/inspection targeting. The difficulties of targeting can be seen in the case of OSHA. Historically, OSHA has focused on specific industrial segments: construction, manufacturing, and in the early 1970s maritime industries.[8]

OSHA's programmed inspection programs (which constituted about 53% of inspections in 1993)[9] attempt to further refine targeting by conducting randomized inspections of eligible establishments in specific SIC industries selected according to industry-level injury rates (U.S. Department of Labor 1994). Different industry or standard-based targeting priorities have existed under OSHA's different administrators (Wokutch 1990). However, while industry targeting is possible, establishment-level targeting cannot be pursued because of the absence of injury data at the workplace level for OSHA enforcement staff.[10]

As a result, targeting has been imperfect at best, and OSHA resources have been skewed toward certain industries as a result of both explicit program policies and implicit targeting arising from factors discussed below. While most industries continue to face nominal levels of inspection threat, others have received more intense scrutiny over time: the annual probability of receiving an inspection in an establishment in 1993 was less than .01 for the service sector, .03 for manufacturing, and .09 for construction. However, for certain segments within these industries the probability was far higher: for the largest 2,000 construction contractors in the U.S. the annual probability of receiving an inspection at one of its construction sites was about .50, while within manufacturing, annual inspection probabilities for establishments in blast furnace and basic steel products industries (SIC 331) equaled about .42.[11]

Other programs with equally constrained budgets have done less targeting than OSHA. Studies of compliance reviews conducted by the OFCCP to enforce affirmative action goals under EO 11246 found that the probability of receiving a compliance review was unrelated to establishment size, minority employment, or change in minority employment in the early 1970s (Heckman and Wolpin 1976). This targeting policy still seemed to characterize OFCCP reviews by the end of that decade (Leonard 1990).

*Government Enforcement and Penalty Policy*

The other method for enforcement agents to increase the incentives to comply with workplace regulations is via penalty policies. As the final three columns of Table 2 indicate, there is considerable variation across federal workplace regulations concerning the use of civil penalties and sanctions and, in some cases, criminal sanctions. Civil sanctions for many regulations require the payment of unpaid wages and less frequently punitive damages. For workplace regulations directed toward federal contractors (e.g., Davis Bacon, Walsh-Healy, EO 11246), debarment from future work represents a severe penalty available to the government. Many regulations also carry civil monetary penalties ranging from $10 per each day of violation of CWHSSA up to $70,000 for each repeat violation committed under OSHA. Finally, most workplace regulations provide for criminal sanctions for cases of willful and/or repeat violations of statutes (which include in several cases the possibility of imprisonment).

In practice, the principal enforcement agents of federal workplace policies levy penalties far below permissible maximums on average. Average OSHA penalties in 1993 were $275 per violation and $366 per serious violation (the category of violations with a potential penalty of $70,000). Administrative policies under other labor regulations make the potential incentive effects of penalties small. Under FLSA, when a minimum or overtime violation is found, the typical procedure is to negotiate a settlement with the employer to pay affected employees the differences between what they should have been paid and what they were actually paid (Ehrenberg and Schumann 1982; Ashenfelter and Smith 1979; Card and Krueger 1995).[12] The more severe penalties for FLSA in Table 2 are invoked for a relatively small subset of cases where an employer falsifies records, refuses to comply, or exhibits a pattern of repeat violations. Awards for backpay under EO 11246 are even less frequent than those sought under FLSA: backpay awards have been granted to a fraction of potentially eligible recipients, and such awards were phased out entirely after 1980 by the Reagan and Bush administrations (Leonard 1990).

Loss of revenue arising from debarment for violating regulations enforced via the federal government's role as contractors (e.g., Davis-Bacon, SCA) can have potentially high impact on contractors. But debarment is infrequently used as a tool of enforcement. The case of EO 11246 is instructive. Less than one contractor per year was debarred for violation of EO 11246 in the early 1970s (Goldstein and Smith 1976). Despite more stringent enforcement efforts in the mid to late 1970s, debarment was still seldom carried out. By 1990 fewer than 30 firms had been debarred in the OFCCP's entire history of enforcement (Leonard 1990). Thus the practice of penalty policy often falls short of what is allowed by legislation.

*Individual Rights, Collective Agents and Enforcement*[13]

Virtually all major federal workplace regulations provide employees with an important role in the process of implementation. Table 3 depicts a subset of these roles for the surveyed legislation: the right to initiate an agency action and the right to pursue private action in courts either as the first step in seeking to change employer behavior or after administrative remedies have been exhausted. In addition, most legislation establishes reporting/disclosure requirements that seek to inform employees of their rights, employer duties,

TABLE 3

Employee Rights and Reporting Requirements under Federal Workplace Regulations

| Labor Statute or Executive Order | Designated Employee Rights | | | Reporting/Disclosure Requirements | | | |
|---|---|---|---|---|---|---|---|
| | Employee right to initiate agency action | Private right of action available to employee | Private right of action, after exhaustion of administrative remedies | Forms completed or filed w/ agency | Payroll/other business data must be collected | Notices must be posted in workplace | Data on injuries and complaints reported |
| *Labor Standards* | | | | | | | |
| FLSA | ✓ | ✓ | | | ✓ | ✓ | |
| Davis–Bacon Act | ✓ | ✓ | | | ✓ | ✓ | |
| SCA | | | | ✓ | ✓ | ✓ | |
| Walsh–Healy Act | | ✓ | | | ✓ | ✓ | |
| CWHSSA | | ✓ | | ✓ | ✓ | ✓ | |
| MSPA | | | ✓ | ✓ | ✓ | | |
| *Benefits* | | | | | | | |
| ERISA | | ✓ | ✓ | ✓ | | | |
| COBRA | | ✓ | ✓ | ✓ | | | |
| Unemployment compensation | | | | | ✓ | | |
| FMLA | ✓ | ✓ | | | ✓ | ✓ | |
| *Civil Rights* | | | | | | | |
| Title VII | ✓ | ✓ | ✓ | ✓ | ✓ | ✓ | |
| Equal Pay Act | ✓ | ✓ | | ✓ | ✓ | ✓ | ✓ |
| EO 11246 | | | | | ✓ | ✓ | ✓ |
| ADEA | ✓ | ✓ | | | ✓ | ✓ | |
| ADA | ✓ | ✓ | ✓ | | ✓ | ✓ | ✓ |
| Rehabilitation Act | | | | | | ✓ | ✓ |
| STAA | | | | | | ✓ | ✓ |

TABLE 3 (*Continued*)

Employee Rights and Reporting Requirements under Federal Workplace Regulations

| Labor Statute or Executive Order | Designated Employee Rights | | | Reporting/Disclosure Requirements | | | |
|---|---|---|---|---|---|---|---|
| | Employee right to initiate agency action | Private right of action available to employee | Private right of action, after exhaustion of administrative remedies | Forms completed or filed w/ agency | Payroll/other business data must be collected | Notices must be posted in workplace | Data on injuries and complaints reported |
| *Occupational Health & Safety* | | | | | | | |
| OSHA | ✓ | | | ✓ | | ✓ | ✓ |
| MSHA | | | | ✓ | | ✓ | ✓ |
| DFWA | | | | ✓ | | ✓ | ✓ |
| *Labor Relations* | | | | | | | |
| NLRA | | ✓ | | ✓ | | ✓ | |
| LMRDA | | ✓ | | | | ✓ | |
| RLA | | | | | | | |
| *Hiring & Separation Decisions* | | | | | | | |
| PPA | | ✓ | | ✓ | | ✓ | |
| Veterans Reemployment Act | | ✓ | | | ✓ | | |
| IRCA | | ✓ | | ✓ | | ✓ | |
| WARN | | ✓ | | | | ✓ | |

*Source:* Adapted from GAO (1994), Figures 2.6, 2.7.

or employer performance under the statute (these are depicted in the final two columns of Table 3).

Regulations promulgated during the two most recent surges of workplace legislation/executive orders (in 1969-74 and 1988-93) have increased the number of regulations providing workers with a right to initiate civil actions under such laws as Title VII, ADA, PPA, and WARN. This has resulted in an enormous increase in the number of cases filed under employment law relative to other categories of litigation. This can be seen in Figure 3 which depicts relative growth in five categories of lawsuits (total civil, business litigation, personal injury, labor law, and employment law) filed in federal district courts between 1971 and 1991. The fastest growing category in relative terms over the period has been litigation on employment law, which went in absolute terms from 4,331 cases filed in 1971 to 22,968 cases in 1991. As a result, employment law went from comprising about 6% of the 69,465 civil cases filed in federal district courts in 1971 to about 16% of the 146,790 civil cases filed in 1991.[14]

Given the enforcement limitations discussed above, the conditions under which employees exercise their rights either to initiate suits or agency action therefore fundamentally affects achievement of policy goals in the workplace. There is little reason to believe that workers uniformly exercise rights granted them under various labor policies. A number of empirical studies have shown different propensities for individuals to litigate civil claims (see, for example, Hoyman and Stallworth 1981; Shavell 1991). Other studies have documented factors affecting workers' use of grievance procedures in union and nonunion workplaces (see Peterson [1992] for a review of the union literature and Feuille and Delaney [1992] and Chachere and Feuille [1993] on use of grievance procedures in nonunion workplaces). This literature suggests that factors related to the individual (sex, education, background), the workplace environment (size, degree of conflict, management and union policies), and the specific grievance or civil problem involved affect under what circumstances individuals use their rights.

Worker use of the rights granted them under labor laws can depend on the perceived benefits versus costs of exercising those rights from the perspective of an individual worker. The benefits of exercising a right are a function of the impact of a given piece of labor legislation on the outcome of concern to the worker.[15] For example, initiating an OSHA inspection potentially improves working conditions for the worker by diminishing or removing the risk of an injury or illness. More generally, the benefits received for a worker increase as a function of either the severity of the problem subject to regulation and faced by the worker and of the potential relief offered by the labor

FIGURE 3

Litigation in the Federal District Courts, 1971-1991

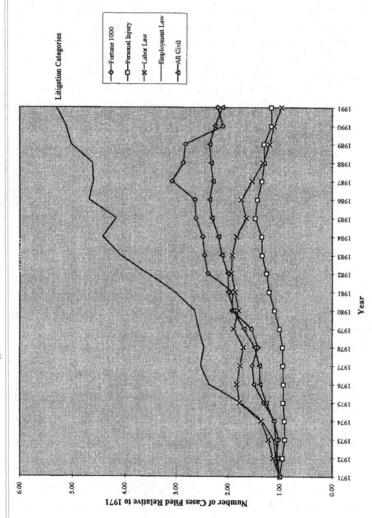

*Source:* Commission on the Future of Worker-Management Relations (1994a).

legislation. Thus the perceived benefit of exercising a right are increased by the degree that current conditions differ from those proscribed by labor statutes.

In order to ascertain the magnitude of these benefits, workers must acquire information on the *current* and *legally permissible* level of a regulated outcome. The cost of exercising rights are primarily a function of the costs of gathering information regarding (a) the existence of basic rights under applicable workplace regulations as well as the standards to which employers are held accountable,[16] (b) the particular labor market problem giving rise to the labor policy,[17] and (c) specific details of how the law is administered (e.g., the procedures to initiate a complaint inspection under OSHA or FLSA or how to apply for unemployment benefits). In addition to information-related costs, workers face costs arising from potential employer retaliation. These costs may arise from the psychic costs associated with fear of retribution at the job site or, in the extreme, being fired.[18]

Different attributes of the workplace will influence the costs of gathering information or the probability of retaliation. For example, employees in large workplaces would seem to face lower costs than those in small workplaces all else equal, because "whistleblowers" are less likely to be detected in a large workplace. Further, large firms are more likely to provide information on employee rights as part of formalized human resource policies (Foulkes 1980; Dunlop 1988).

Workers will systematically underutilize their rights if decisions are made on an individual basis as a result of the divergence between receiving benefits and bearing costs on an individual versus group basis. Employee exercise of workplace rights displays positive externalities on the benefit side. If an individual only perceives the benefits accruing directly to them from filing such a claim, they will "underinvest" in exercise of rights because the collective (workplace) benefits arising from their action are not factored into the individual decision. For example, single violations of labor standards like overtime provisions of FLSA are usually associated with a larger pattern of violation across a group of employees. An individual claim for backpay may cause an investigation into the employer's overtime pay practice which in turn may lead to workplacewide compliance with FLSA from that point forward.

The divergence between costs on an individual versus collective level may also lead to underutilization of rights. The information requirements of pursuing a case have significant fixed cost elements arising from the requisite time to learn the law and procedures on the one hand and to gather evidence and make a case on the other. While workers can (and do) use outside counsel as a means of making these assessments, the use of lawyers also entails significant costs. As a result of the existence of positive externalities in regard to benefits and the structure of information costs, relying on individual exercise of worker rights results in usage of those rights below what is optimal for the workplace as a whole.[19]

A collective workplace agent can potentially solve the problem described above. It can do so first by internalizing the positive externality to workers arising from a claim as a representative of all workers in the unit. A workplace agent can also gather and disseminate information thereby lowering the cost of information acquisition faced by individuals. The specific elements required of such an agent are straightforward: (1) interests allied with those of the individual worker—specifically an interest in the implementation of labor regulations consistent with those of covered workers (implying institutional independence from the employer); (2) a means of efficiently gathering and disseminating information on rights, administrative procedures, and the nature of workplace risks; and (3) a method of providing some type of protection against employer discrimination against individual workers for their exercise of rights.

### Unions and the Enforcement of Federal Labor Regulations

While a number of different arrangements can potentially satisfy these conditions, labor unions potentially fulfill many of them through their basic agency functions.[20] Specifically, unions act as purveyors of workplace-based public goods regarding labor policies both by internalizing the benefits relating to worker exercise of rights across workers in the unit and by lowering the costs of information acquisition.

As the elected representative of workers, a union has an incentive to act on behalf of the collective interests of members in the bargaining unit. This means that a union will not base perceptions of the benefit of pursuing a claim under laws based on the preferences of an individual worker at the margin but based on inframarginal evaluations of those benefits. In facing this allocation problem, a union can vertically aggregate preferences for the "public goods" represented by workplace regulations, following the model of public goods described in Samuelson (1955).[21]

Unions can efficiently gather and disseminate information on the existence of workplace laws and rights created by those laws. Unions provide this information formally through educational programs, in apprenticeship training, or through supplying educational materials. Informally, union leaders or staff alert members of their rights where a problem or issue arises. Unions also provide information on the existence of specific underlying problems, particularly in the area of safety and health (see Viscusi 1983). As above, this information may be collected and disseminated through formal programs or channels or informally via the union structure or fellow workers.

Unions also offer individual workers assistance in the actual exercise of their rights. This may result from the operation of committees established under collective bargaining, as is common in safety and health or via the help of union staff who can trigger inspections, oversee pension fund investments, or assist members in filing unemployment claims. Most importantly, unions can substantially reduce the costs associated with potential employer discrimination by helping affected employees to use antidiscrimination provisions of the labor policies and providing this protection via collective bargaining agreements regulating dismissals. The formal protection offered by a collective agreement provides security unavailable in the vast majority of nonunion workplaces, even where a grievance procedure exists (Feuille and Delaney 1992).

Thus if unions act on behalf of the collective preferences of the workers in the bargaining unit, they can be expected to induce greater usage of rights. In this sense, exercise of *individually based* rights still requires an agent operating in the *collective interest*. Government labor market policies should be more strenuously enforced, and employers should operate in a higher state of regulatory compliance in unionized workplaces than in otherwise comparable nonunion workplaces. A survey of research on workplace regulations solidly supports these predicted differences between union versus nonunion enforcement and compliance outcomes for many of the federal labor regulations discussed in this chapter. The results of these studies are summarized in Table 4.

Table 4 portrays positive union enforcement effects on a variety of labor regulations. Unions affect enforcement of FLSA overtime provisions by wholly incorporating those provisions into collective bargaining language and ensuring their enforcement via contract administration. Unions also raise the probability that workers will file suits under the WARN Act. Unions improve employees' ability to appeal employers' pension eligibility, vesting, disclosure, funding, fiduciary responsibility, and termination decisions in federal court as one means of enforcing the provisions of ERISA. In particular, unions seem to increase employee access to federal courts via class action suits in the case of single employer plans, although their impact on ERISA enforcement among multi-employer pension plans is less clear (Langbert 1995).

The cases of OSHA and MSHA are particularly illustrative of the agency role played by unions. Unions have large impacts on an array of enforcement outcomes under both OSHA and MSHA. Unionized workplaces are far more likely to be inspected than nonunion workplaces with comparable characteristics. This union effect is remarkably consistent across industry sectors (Weil 1990, 1991, 1992) and stable over time.[22] In addition, once an inspection has

TABLE 4

Impact of Labor Unions on Enforcement and Compliance with Federal Workplace Regulations

| Labor Statute or Executive Order | Union Impact on Enforcement | Union Impact on Employer Compliance | Study |
|---|---|---|---|
| Fair Labor Standards Act—Overtime Provisions | Inclusion of premium pay standard in collective agreements | Increase in the probability of compliance for unionized workers | *Enforcement:* BNA (1992) *Compliance:* Ehrenberg and Schumann (1982); Trejo (1991) |
| ERISA | Improve access to courts in single employer pension cases, primarily via class action and collective suits | Require more strict adherence to eligibility and financial management standards by employers | *Enforcement:* Langbert (1995) *Compliance:* Freeman (1985) |
| OSHA | Higher inspection probabilities; longer inspections; shorter abatement durations; and higher penalties | Higher rates of compliance with specific OSHA standards | *Enforcement:* Weil (1991, 1992, 1994) *Compliance:* Weil (1996a) |
| MSHA | Higher inspection probabilities; longer and more intense inspections; shorter abatement durations; higher penalties; lower penalty reductions via administrative procedures | N/A | Weil (1990) |
| EO 11246 | No impact on probability of receiving a federal contract compliance review | N/A | Leonard (1985) |
| ADA | N/A | Raise the probability that firms comply with four core practices required by ADA | Stern and Balser (1996) |
| Unemployment Compensation | N/A | Increase in the percentage of use of unemployment insurance for eligible workers | Blank and Card (1989) Budd and McCall (1994) |
| WARN | Increase the probability of filing suit under WARN | No impact on the probability of providing advance notice to affected workers | *Enforcement:* GAO (1993); Ehrenberg and Jakubson (1990) *Compliance:* Addison and Blackburn (1994a) |

been initiated, unionized establishments receive longer and more intense inspections, which result in detection of a higher number of violations and lead to higher penalties than *comparable* nonunion workplaces. Once again, these effects are robust across industries and over time.

Thus, with the exception of unions' neutral impact on contract compliance reviews under EO 11246, available empirical studies of enforcement indicate that unions act as agents that assist employee exercise of rights. Given this agency role, unions also increase the degree of employer compliance with regulations, as will be discussed in detail in the following section.

## From Enforcement → Compliance: Determinants of Compliance Behavior

The second stage of analyzing regulatory performance regards the impact of de facto enforcement (as described in the previous section) on employer compliance with the specific provisions of workplace regulations. The definition of compliance differs across labor regulations. In some cases, compliance can be measured by the object of the labor market regulation: Compliance with minimum wage laws is measured by the presence of wage scales below that provided in the law for those workplaces and workers covered by those standards. Compliance with overtime provision of FLSA can be defined as providing covered workers with premium pay for hours worked in excess of 40 hours. Compliance with other labor laws must be measured by more complex measures: OSHA and MSHA are built around enforcement of pages and pages of Code of Federal Regulations subparagraphs describing specific technology, work practice, information, screening, and other practices. Monitoring ERISA compliance requires highly technical background in the administration of pension plans.

### Determinants of Workplace Compliance

The behavioral model embodied in most federal labor policies is gaining employer adherence to standards primarily via the threat of inspection, compulsion, and fines. Thus compliance with standards is secured either through the direct pressure arising from inspection activities (triggered either by the agency or covered workers) or through deterrence effects and the consequent voluntary decision to comply with labor policies. Thus firms are assumed to act in accordance with the model of crime initially set out by Becker (1968) and Stigler (1970), where crime (or here regulatory noncompliance) is a decreasing function of the return to crime or the avoidance of costs arising from regulatory compliance. Holding constant compliance costs, employers will choose not to comply with a labor regulation if it is easy to escape detection and/or because assessed penalties in the event of being detected are small. Compliance can therefore be increased through more aggressive enforcement policies, either by increasing the probability of inspections or the penalties received for violations (Polinsky and Shavell 1984, 1996; Shavell 1991).

Holding constant government enforcement policies, an employer's willingness to comply will also be affected by the costs associated with bringing human resource practices chosen on the basis of firm-level optimization decisions into line with practices required by law. For a regulation like minimum wage, willingness to comply will be a function of the difference between the current wage and the minimum wage and the employer elasticity of demand for labor (which in turn derives from market demand and the degree of product market competition). For OSHA, it will be the cost of changing production or work organization practices to comply with applicable OSHA standards. Once again, the intensity of product market competition will affect firms' willingness to bear these compliance costs.

In this latter sense, the probability of compliance is a function of employer choices regarding human resource/industrial relations (HR/IR) policies (that is, the set of policies governing a firm's labor market policies). Human resource policies, in turn, arise from the choices taken by firms in addressing (1) competitive conditions in their industry, (2) the nature of the technology and capital available to and used by the firm, (3) the labor supply available to the employer, (4) the longevity of the employment relationship (e.g., the level of turnover), and (5) specific characteristics of the product or service being produced. The degree to which employers resist compliance with a statute arises from how far statutes force them away from private choices arising from the above external and internal conditions.[23]

Other internal features of firms not directly related to the benefits and costs of noncompliance affect a firm's compliance choices, including plant and company size, the nature of ownership and degree of control exerted by owners, labor/management relationships, and characteristics of the firm's organizational structure (e.g., its degree of centralization). This includes the "corporate culture" of a firm and its sensitivity to public perceptions of fair play and decency. These factors condition the way that a firm perceives that nature of external factors, how it reacts and sets policies, and how it implements policies once chosen. Indicative is the recent sensitivity of firms in the retail and apparel industries to highly publicized reports regarding the use of child labor and prison labor.[24]

Compliance must therefore be analyzed both as a direct consequence of regulatory incentives as well as the indirect result of other choices correlated but not causally linked to compliance behavior. The above discussion suggests a ranking of compliance factors: Compliance with a labor policy or more sensibly with a set of policies will be a function of the larger HR/IR choices made by regulated employers. These in turn will reflect pressures exerted by external forces to the firm and decision processes, culture, and relationships internal to that firm. Overlaid on this will be the weighing of benefits and costs of compliance suggested by deterrence theory. As a result, compliance will vary on the basis of product market characteristics, technology and work organization, and firm structure, as well as from enforcement practices.

*Evidence on Compliance*

Compliance with labor market policies has not received a great deal of attention in the academic literature. A number of studies, however, provide informative evidence.

A 1960s study of minimum wage regulation (DOL 1965) reported virtually complete compliance with the standard. However, since compliance was measured as the percent of all private sector establishments paying at least the minimum wage level at that time, the true state of compliance was entirely masked by the vast majority of establishments that pay more than the minimum (and in many cases not even covered by FLSA). A far more careful study of minimum wage compliance by Ashenfelter and Smith (1979) draws on data from the Current Population Survey (CPS) for workers paid on an hourly basis and in industries completely covered by FLSA in 1973. Based on this sample, the authors found compliance rates of 69% for the country as a whole. Compliance was found to vary positively with age (the older the worker, the more likely their pay was in compliance with minimum wage). Compliance was also found to be higher for those groups "whose wage rates would be lowest in the absence of a minimum wage" (p. 343). Thus those firms with the highest incentive *not* to comply in fact were more likely to comply with the law, particularly surprising given the low enforcement and penalty outcomes described above. Passage of an increase in the minimum wage in 1975 lowered the overall rate of compliance to 60% for the sample of covered workers, although patterns of higher compliance for those groups with the lowest potential wage rates persist.

In a more recent study of the impact of minimum wages in California, Card and Krueger (1995) find compliance rates of about 69% among a sample of covered workers in 1987. Compliance fell to about 54% following passage of an increase in the minimum wage from $3.35 to $4.25 in 1988 (p. 84), although the authors find far higher compliance rates for teenagers following the increase.[25]

Ehrenberg and Schumann (1981, 1982) provide estimates of compliance with overtime standards of FLSA. Also using CPS data for workers in industries entirely covered by FLSA overtime standards, the authors find far higher levels of compliance than in the minimum wage studies, ranging from about 77% to 90% depending on how compliance is defined. For workers in industries with only partial coverage of overtime restrictions, the authors estimate compliance at the lower end of the above range, in the vicinity between 75% and 80%. A similar range of compliance estimates also using CPS data is found in Trejo (1991), for 1974, 1976, and 1978.

In addition to overall compliance, Ehrenberg and Schumann also provide estimates of compliance determinants related to individual, firm, and industry characteristics, as well as to government enforcement effort. Most significantly in terms of this essay, they find that government enforcement has small positive but statistically insignificant effects on compliance status.[26]

Compliance with OSHA has been the subject of a number of studies. Most of these studies measure compliance as the absolute number of violations cited by OSHA for noncompliance with health or safety standard. Bartel and Thomas (1985) find that second OSHA inspections discover about one-half the number of violations than detected in initial inspections (for those establishments receiving multiple inspections). Relying on longitudinal data in manufacturing, Gray and Jones (1991a, 1991b) and Scholz and Gray (1990) document similar declines in the number of total violations arising from repeat enforcement. While these studies indicate firm responsiveness to enforcement, the enormous number of standards potentially applicable to a given establishment makes such a broad definition of compliance problematic.

An alternative approach by Weil (1996a) uses an industry and standard-specific approach to improve the measurement of compliance. The study examines compliance with a particular subset of standards (those regarding machine guarding) in one industry (custom woodworking) over a 20-year period. Its findings are consistent with the responsiveness to regulatory pressure displayed in the other OSHA studies. Despite extremely low enforcement probabilities (less than 5% per year), low fines (about $300 per inspection), and the high cost of compliance ($5,000-$15,000 for a typical plant), Weil estimates baseline levels of compliance of about 60%. The study also finds large increases in the probability of compliance given one additional OSHA inspection, other factors held constant. Since the study carefully controls for other, nonenforcement determinants of compliance, this suggests surprising levels of sensitivity to weak regulatory incentives.

Defining compliance with the affirmative action provisions of EO 11246 can be tricky since the executive order requires a multi-step process for compliance. A firm must draft and have approved (if reviewed) a hiring plan specifying goals and timetables on paper (as opposed to their adoption in practice). The drafting, review, and approval of such plans represents the first step of compliance, while assuring subsequent adherence to the plan represents the subsequent step toward compliance. Despite extremely low probabilities of review and the even lower probabilities of debarment, Leonard (1990) presents evidence of high rates of compliance with the first step requirements by covered contractors. The connection between drafting the plan and adherence to affirmative action goals will be discussed in the next section.

Compliance with WARN can be measured by the formal provision of advance notice of closure to workers by their employers in the event of a plant shutdown or "mass layoff." Studies of WARN indicate that it has had little impact on compliance so measured. Addison and Blackburn (1994a) show relatively unchanged rates of advanced notice provision pre- and post-WARN. Using data from Displaced Worker Surveys, they find little difference between voluntary notice provided by firms before passage of the act and notice given under WARN's mandatory requirements. They also show little change in the length of notice (Addison and Blackburn 1994b). This is in part reflective of the wide exemptions under that law. It also may indicate significant firm-level incentives to provide notice even absent requirements, as shown by the pre-1988 prevalence of voluntary advance notification of workers.[27]

## Unions and Compliance Behavior

Given the relative disparity in enforcement in union and nonunion workplaces described in the previous section, one would expect to find differentials in compliance along union/nonunion lines. These differentials exist under a variety of workplace regulations, as shown in the third column of Table 4. The "internalization" of overtime enforcement via collective bargaining leads to systematically higher rates of compliance with FLSA in unionized workplaces (Ehrenberg and Schumann 1981, 1982; Trejo 1991). Ehrenberg and Schumann estimate noncompliance with overtime standards of 25% among nonunion workplace versus 18% for comparable union workplaces.

The presence of a labor union raises the probability of compliance with OSHA standards appreciably among the sample of plants studied by Weil (1996a). The probability of complying with standards, holding other factors constant, increases from .44 for nonunion plants to .63 for a comparable workplace where a union is present. Unions also seem to raise the level of compliance with the eligibility and vesting requirements under ERISA.[28] Freeman (1985) finds that unions lower the likelihood that pensions will incorporate vesting requirements more liberal than required by ERISA (resulting, for example, in unionized employees working on average 70 hours longer to qualify for full pension benefits than nonunion workers). This suggests that unions lead employers to adhere more closely to the letter of ERISA.

Unionization is also associated with higher levels of compliance with core activities mandated by the Americans with Disabilities Act (ADA). Specifically, Stern and Balser (1996) show that employers in unionized firms are far more likely to comply with a set of four ADA compliance requirements—(1) distributing information on ADA rights, (2) assigning a person or department to handle ADA issues, (3) sending employees for ADA-related training, and (4) developing procedures to create reasonable accommodations for people with disabilities—compared to nonunion firms of comparable size.

Despite their impact on increasing the frequency of WARN filings, unions do not seem to raise compliance with WARN, where compliance is measured as receipt of notice by employees of impending plant closings or mass layoffs. In fact, Addison and Blackburn (1994a) find that higher levels of unionization are associated with *lower incidence* of lengthy notice, all else equal.

### The Compliance Puzzle

The de facto structure of enforcement described above would lead one to predict low rates of voluntary compliance with the web of workplace regulations listed in Table 1, except among unionized workplaces. Yet taken as a whole, the empirical evidence indicates remarkably *high*—although by no means complete—compliance across a spectrum of regulations. This poses an intellectual puzzle. Why are a significant number of firms in regulatory compliance given modest enforcement pressure and the low density of unionization in the private sector?

Voluntary compliance with labor regulations may be consistent with overarching human resource or industrial relations policies in the case of certain firms. In particular, larger firms seeking to build greater stability in their relationships with employees and retain those with job-specific human capital may pursue policies in many ways consistent with regulatory policies. And to the extent that they would not adopt such policies absent standards, their size and public exposure make them more vulnerable (and sensitive) to government enforcement. The fact that most of the enforcement agencies of the DOL have pursued and/or continue to pursue targeting policies tilted toward large workplaces reinforces this sensitivity to potential enforcement action.[29]

At the same time, noncompliance remains a major problem in certain industries and among certain categories of employers within industries. The DOL since the Bush administration has found systematic evidence of noncompliance in the apparel industry, not only with child labor standards but minimum wage, overtime, and OSHA standards. Similar patterns of safety and health violations have been found in the poultry processing industry. These industries represent the flip side of those firms exhibiting high rates of compliance: the high incentives to flaunt labor regulations given intense product market competition and the low levels of inspection probabilities make such behavior rational, à la the crime models of Becker. A firm facing highly competitive conditions in its product market, driven to compete on the basis of minimum cost where labor costs represent a significant percentage of total product cost, works under strong pressures not to comply with labor standards if the expected level of enforcement is low. A similar story may explain the relatively higher rates of noncompliance among small firms in many industries (Brown, Hamilton, and Medoff 1990) exposed to powerful market incentives to ignore regulatory standards.

The central puzzle remains for those establishments in the middle of the compliance distribution, however, where the costs of compliance are presumably nontrivial, yet where firms face relatively low regulatory incentives to comply with labor policies. Why do so many nonunion firms comply with FLSA despite the unlikely event of an employee complaint for nonpayment of overtime wages? Why do the majority of federal contractors comply with the detailed steps required by EO 11246, despite the fact that intensive reviews are rare and the odds of debarment nonexistent? What explains small manufacturers adopting costly machine guarding equipment given tiny odds of meeting an OSHA inspector or incurring significant penalties?

In terms of enforcement, these behaviors may arise from systematic overestimation of the risk of inspection and/or the size of potential penalties (or equivalently high risk aversion to the downside risks posed by noncompliance). This suggests that many firms may be responding to a government bark that is far more fierce (or perceived to be more fierce) than its bite. The historic antagonism of the small business community to workplace regulation (and OSHA in particular) despite its de facto exemption from many workplace regulations is consistent with this explanation.

On the other hand, examining the relationship between enforcement and compliance highlights the behavioral oversimplification inherent in assuming that enforcement is the sole cause of compliance behavior. This point is well summarized by Flanagan (1989) in regard to employer and union compliance with the NLRA:

> The larger lesson of the analysis is that the influence of NLRB policy on compliance is often swamped by factors that are beyond the regulators' sphere of influence. Compliance and enforcement choices that determine the volume of unfair labor practice charges are influenced importantly by incentives that are determined in the market and through collective bargaining. (p. 278)

The framework and empirical evidence described above suggests that the median level of compliance with the suite of labor policies discussed in this chapter varies given characteristics of the industry and the firms within it. While variance in compliance around this median behavior may be determined by the activities of the government, attempting to ascribe the median performance itself to the regulatory regime misses important sources of compliance behaviors.

## From Compliance → Labor Market/Public Policy Outcomes

The final link in assessing the effect of implementation on regulatory performance regards whether compliance with regulatory standards leads to desired labor market and public policy outcomes. Just as many studies assume that legislation on paper translates into effective enforcement and that enforcement translates into compliance, regulatory analyses often presume that compliance with statutes is identical with achieving the underlying purposes of the regulation. The link between compliance and policy outcomes brings this chapter's emphasis on implementation back to the overall question of regulatory performance. The intent of this section is therefore not to replicate what is examined in much greater depth in the rest of this volume (see, for example, Addison and Hirsch), but to indicate how the study of implementation as outlined here can be linked back to the more general question of regulatory performance.

### Compliance and Public Policies: Hidden Complexities

For some regulatory programs, the link between compliance and public policy objective seems simple and transparent. Compliance with FLSA minimum wage or overtime standards or with the prevailing wage standards of Davis-Bacon and Walsh-Healy means that firms are compensating their workers consistent with adopted public policy. Compliance with WARN translates into workers being notified in advance of plant closings.

However, these cases mask hidden complexities. The objective of the minimum wage can be framed as an antipoverty measure and not simply as a means to establish wage floors. Thus firms may comply with current minimum wage levels, but if instability in the jobs paying that wage leads to less than full-time employment, or if the wage itself is insufficient to provide a subsistence income for a typical family supported by the job (even given full-time employment), compliance is not synonymous with policy success. Thus one ultimately cares about characteristics of workers earning the minimum wage according to their labor market participation, hours worked, geographic location, and family structure in order to determine the policy impacts of minimum wage compliance. In this regard, evidence on the impact of minimum wages on poverty is somewhat encouraging (see Gramlich 1976; Card and Krueger 1995:Ch. 9).

Similarly, if the overtime provisions of FLSA are cast as a means to encourage employers to expand employment rather than simply a device to require higher pay for long hours, the true test of regulatory performance is whether those firms who comply with standards expand employment relative to comparable firms facing similar expansion decisions who are not complying with the standards. Empirical studies relating compliance to this particular outcome suggest the size of these employment impacts are small (see Ehrenberg and Schumann 1981, 1982).

The public policy objective of WARN similarly goes beyond formal notification to workers of the impending loss of their job; its original sponsors sought to reduce the amount of dislocation to workers and communities arising from the closure. Does WARN's *formal* advanced warning requirement lead to better post-layoff results for notified workers?[30] A number of studies cast some doubt on this connection. A series of papers by Addison and Portugal (1992) that empirically model the relation of advance notice to job search find general evidence linking extended written notice (as opposed to informal notice) to improvements in job search outcomes. They find "the failure of written notice to be associated with net reductions in jobless duration, with the notable exception of notified white-collar males. In other words, any beneficial impact of notice in permitting workers more easily to transition directly into reemployment is in practice more than counterbalanced by subsequently lower escape rates from unemployment." The authors also find a small but negative association between formal notice and reduction in the probability of a joblessness spell of zero length (a performance measure advocated by Ehrenberg and Jakubson 1989).

The performance of EO 11246 provides a more encouraging model of the potential impact of compliance on regulatory outcomes. The performance of that regulation can be judged either in terms of its impact on employment growth for targeted groups or occupational advance of the same groups. Early analyses of the law revealed significant impacts of coverage (i.e., holding a federal contract in comparison to similar firms not undertaking work for the government and therefore not covered by the executive order) and to a lesser extent of compliance reviews on employment growth of targeted minority groups, particularly black males (Ashenfelter and Heckman 1976; Goldstein and Smith 1976; Heckman and Wolpin 1976).

Studies of the regulatory effect of the agency reveal even larger impacts in the period of the mid-1970s to the end of the Carter administration when enforcement efforts were at their pinnacle (Brown 1982; Leonard 1984a,

1990). Leonard in particular found that while the various enforcement tools used by OFCCP (e.g. progress reports, pre-award reviews, and other forms of monitoring) had negligible impacts on employment growth, the employment *goals* negotiated through the compliance processes result in improvement in employment growth among black men in reviewed workplaces (Leonard 1985). It also proved to be generally successful in the later 1970s in improving occupational advance, increasing minority employment (once again black men in particular) in skilled white-collar occupations (Leonard 1984a).[31]

Other labor regulations present equally complex questions regarding the relationship between compliance and outcomes, but little evidence exists about the nature of this final set of relationships. ERISA was originally designed to ensure that workers who had secured pension benefits at their workplace would actually receive them upon retirement. Yet many of ERISA's complex requirements pertain to the structuring of pension plans (eligibility, reporting requirements, investment, and fiduciary guidelines). These requirements might or might not ultimately lead to improved probability of receipt of pension benefits. In contrast to the studies of FLSA, there has been no systematic investigation of these critical linkages.

OSHA and MSHA require employers to adopt an enormous range of standards regarding everything from permissible technologies to warnings about exposures to certain types of chemicals. Compliance with any one of these standards may actually result in improved safety or health outcomes, but this is once again an open question. While the process of promulgation of new standards turns in part on making this case (and linking it to some statement of relative benefits and costs),[32] the vast majority of OSHA standards were passed without such an explicit test (particularly in regard to safety standards). The body of literature on OSHA performance fails to tease out these final linkages, partially because analyzing the connection between specific standards and safety and health takes one from the analytic world of economics into that of occupational medicine, epidemiology, and related fields.

## Implementation and Performance: Implications for Regulatory Reform

> The history of administration is the story of a series of attempts . . . to make labor laws truly effective. From this point of view the history of American labor legislation may be divided into three stages. . . . First came a "pre-enforcement stage" in which it was assumed that a mere statutory declaration of the rights of workers and the duties of employers was enough. . . . Second came the "enforcement stage" in which a special governmental agency was set up to see that employers

complied with the requirements. . . . Third came the "administrative stage" in which the functions of the special governmental agency in the field of labor legislation was thought of in much larger terms— when its task became the translation of legislative policy into action, by securing the cooperation of both employers and workers in the setting up and enforcing of detailed regulations designed to carry out the general legislative intent. Brandeis (1935)

Employment regulation in the U.S. has been in a state of flux, dating back to the passage of early federal workplace laws in the late 1920s. The result is a large, complex hodge-podge of regulatory systems that no longer conform easily into Brandeis' progressive evolutionary model. There are a variety of proposals and pilot efforts to bring coherence and create a more desirable "fourth stage" of regulation, built upon increased self-regulation by workers and employers, works councils, as well as the use of market forces. The framework depicted in Figure 2 and described throughout this essay points to some of the problems underlying major reform proposals, while also suggesting the outlines of a more modest approach to improving regulatory performance.

## Alternative Regulatory Approaches

Much has been written about alternatives to the "command and control" regulatory system that underlies federal regulation, including several essays in this volume (see in particular the chapters by Levine, Marshall, and Edwards). Critics point out the rigidities of the present system that prevent workers, employers, and regulators from reaching innovative solutions that respond to particular problems at a workplace. These rigidities not only impose excessive costs on society but also prevent the parties from achieving desired outcomes, in part because of the inability of existing regulatory methods to respond to changes in the labor market, technology, work organization, and public expectations.

Rather than relying on regulators as the key enforcement agent, systems drawing on self-regulation would "create incentives for companies and workers to solve their own problems" (see Levine, this volume, for a detailed description of this proposal). This would include the use of works councils or other methods of employee representation that would, among other functions, approve firm-level plans to achieve a given regulatory objective such as safety and health. In its final report, the Dunlop Commission endorsed this direction in principle by "encouraging experimentation with workplace self-regulation procedures in general and with specific reference to workplace safety and health" (Commission on the Future of Worker-Management Relations 1994b:18).

Shifting the focus of regulatory efforts to the parties themselves does not overcome some of the implementation problems described above, however. In particular, the notion of requiring employers to institute employee participation in the formation, approval, and/or administration of internal regulatory systems does not ensure that activity in practice. In the same way, the "choosing rights" system described by Edwards (1993 and in this volume), which requires that firms supply an employee handbook outlining workplace protections and rights, presupposes that firms will comply with that general requirement. More profoundly, it requires that workers act as effective enforcement agents in cases where employment practice diverges from the provisions laid out in the "binding and enforceable" contract represented by the handbook. As in the case of our current regulatory system, both models must still answer the question, Under what circumstances will employees exercise these newly vested rights to the extent necessary to provide for effective systems of self-regulation?[33]

The recent experience of Oregon's OSHA program is instructive. In 1991 the state required all private sector establishments with 11 or more workers to create safety and health committees to oversee workplace safety and health in union and nonunion workplaces. One would expect, among other effects, that mandated committees would improve the performance of nonunion workplaces relative to unionized counterparts in regard to safety and health activities. An analysis of safety and health committee activity in the years following passage of the requirements, however, finds that union/nonunion differentials in a wide range of OSHA enforcement outcomes *grew* between 1989-90 (previous to passage of the committee requirements) and 1992-93 (the first full years of operation). The study results suggest that safety and health committees requirements augment the impact of unions as workplace agents in regard to safety and health while having little effect on nonunion workplaces except among large nonunion employers (Weil 1994, 1997). Comparable results seem to hold for Canadian safety and health committee mandates (Tuohy and Simard 1993).

The absence of effective workplace agents to solve the workplace public-goods problem limits the feasibility of regulatory reforms that are premised on employee participation. In essence, one needs some type of workplace agent before one can vest it with extensive regulatory responsibilities, particularly if those responsibilities often run counter to the interests of the regulated entity. This is not to suggest that such reforms are inherently doomed. However, absent attention to the sequence of implementation questions discussed here—and in particular without bolstering the activities of agents in nonunion contexts—reliance on self-regulation will not provide a simple fix to the problems of workplace regulation.

## A Modest Reform Agenda

The sheer size and complexity of federal regulatory programs, as well as the ingrained methods and expectations of how the government *should* regulate, makes moving away from the present system difficult. Employment regulation could be improved, however, even in its present incarnation. The linkages presented in Figure 2 once again provide guidance.

The review of the compliance literature suggests higher levels of compliance among firms subject to even modest regulatory pressure. Thus well-targeted, deterrence-focused enforcement policies could lead to potentially large improvements in performance, particularly in the sectors where regulatory problems loom large. In order to gain the greatest effect from limited resources, better advantage could be taken of the fact that certain types of firms and certain industries are prone to systematic noncompliance with a number of labor policies (e.g., certain segments of the trucking and construction industries, food processing, apparel). Directing resources toward that subset of covered employers and doing so in a coordinated fashion across regulatory programs may offer the largest payoffs (in terms of improved compliance) for the DOL. Along with improved agency coordination, a deterrence-driven approach requires sophistication in analyzing the determinants of compliance and noncompliance at the industry and firm level as a means to select targets (e.g., using the degree of product market pressure, the cost of compliance, the size of establishments, and other determinants of private compliance incentives) and better access and use of data on the performance of individual workplaces.

Rationalizing the maze of penalty policies listed in Table 2 and bringing de jure and de facto policies in better alignment is also a critical feature of creating credible enforcement to those firms of greatest regulatory concern. The Environmental Protection Agency has far more refined methods of calculating damages associated with noncompliance than employed by the DOL (see U.S. Environmental Protection Agency 1984a, 1984b). EPA converts those damage estimates into penalty policies, thereby reducing variance in initial penalties and in subsequent modifications made in post-inspection discussions and administrative procedures. This has improved the incentives for voluntary compliance among all firms covered by environmental regulations (Smith 1991).

On the other hand, effective targeting also means shifting regulatory resources away from those sectors where employers can be expected (or have exhibited a past willingness) to comply with workplace regulations. Regulatory resources continue to be disproportionately placed on larger companies and establishments because of their higher profile and the agency's ability to affect more workers with fewer resources. However, these firms are often not where the main regulatory problems lie. Similarly, the disproportionate emphasis of enforcement on unionized workplaces, arising from the connection between unionization and utilization of employee rights, reallocate resources away from those workplaces where major problems persist but employees cannot solve the "public goods" problem and trigger enforcement actions. This creates the perverse effect of raising the cost of business for those employers adhering most closely to regulatory standards (unionized firms), thereby undermining their competitive position relative to employers facing lower regulatory costs (nonunionized firms).[34]

Self-regulation, reliance on employee rights, and other methods of decentralized regulatory control may be most applicable to these larger, multiestablishment firms (see Weil 1996b for a detailed discussion of this issue). Workplaces where either union or other solutions to the public-good problem can be realistically drawn upon also are attractive candidates for internal systems to resolve employment disputes effectively within the confines of the workplace, not necessarily requiring the direct involvement of government. One such method is encouraging greater reliance on alternative dispute resolution as a means of resolving problems arising under employment law, via expedited, legally sanctioned, workplace-based processes (Commission on the Future of Worker-Management Relations 1994b; Dunlop and Zack 1997).

The "fourth stage" of regulatory evolution may then be a hybrid system consisting of familiar command and control regulation directed toward those sectors most likely to cause the greatest social burdens with self-regulatory elements better suited to those sectors where the agents of regulatory activity (workers and employers) are able to carry out their respective responsibilities. A mixed system of regulatory implementation may then provide the greatest opportunity for improving the coherence and ultimately the performance of federal workplace regulations.

## Endnotes

[1] In addition to employment relations, provisions of Title VII and ADA are directed toward practices in employment agencies and unions, while the LMRDA addresses the internal practices of labor unions.

[2] Labor relations laws (the National Labor Relations Act and its legislative amendments) are somewhat different. They establish a process of representation and in turn a method for the creation of labor policies by employers and workers through representation by unions. This process-driven piece of legislation therefore sets up a different track of legislative effort. This is discussed further in a later section.

[3] The objectives of labor legislation do not only fit within the standard economic "efficiency vs. equity" dichotomy. The justifications for intervention in employment relations span a broader range of factors, both in terms of political motivation (see footnote 5) and legislative intent. For example, see Linder (1989) for a discussion of the minimum wage as a

form of industrial policy. Kaufman (this volume) provides a more general discussion of the institutionalist conception of labor legislation.

[4] The earliest Supreme Court case dealing with the constitutionality of labor regulations, *Lochner v. New York*, 198 U.S. 45 (1905), concerned state laws limiting hours of work in the baking industry.

[5] In contrast to the straightforward justifications suggested by economic analysis, the origins, growth, and development of labor laws is the subject of wide debate by labor historians, sociologists, and political scientists with interests in the relations of labor and management in capitalist economies. The interpretations, as one would expect, vary according to the conceptual framework of the author. Part of this literature comes from Marxist scholars who often painted U.S. labor laws as the means that the state used to pacify and control class conflict. Economic historians from non-Marxist schools (originating with John R. Commons at the turn of the century) regarded labor legislation as part of a logical historic advancement accompanying the evolution of a pluralist, industrial society. In contrast, economists following the public choice work of James Buchanan explain labor legislation as the result of labor power in legislative process or more generally in terms of the dynamics of legislative voting behavior (see Buchanan and Tullock 1962).

[6] Some labor regulations also draw on other parts of government (particularly the Internal Revenue Service in the cases of COBRA and ERISA) for enforcement—see Table 2.

[7] MSHA specifically requires that all mining operations covered by the act receive at minimum four inspections in the course of the year. OSHA provides for the right of inspection but does not (and cannot for reasons described below) require all covered establishments to actually receive those inspections.

[8] Emphasis has shifted across these segments over time:

% of Inspections by Industry

| Year | Construction | Manufacturing | Maritime | All Other |
|------|-------------|---------------|----------|-----------|
| 1973 | 27.4 | 45.2 | 16.1 | 11.3 |
| 1983 | 49.3 | 42.8 | 1.2 | 6.7 |
| 1993 | 45.7 | 25.0 | 0.1 | 29.2 |

*Source:* Siskind (1993) and author's calculations based on OSHA data.

[9] Average for all state and federal OSHA inspections. Author's calculation based on data from OSHA Integrated Management Information System.

[10] Attempts by several different administrations (including the Clinton administration) to require that firms file required OSHA injury log forms with the agency as a basis for targeting have met stiff opposition from the business community. The ongoing Maine 200 pilot program attempts to use state workers compensation data for firm-level targeting of OSHA enforcement as well as consultation activities (see U.S. Department of Labor 1995).

[11] Based on author's calculations of data from U.S. Department of Commerce (1993), Siskind (1993), and data extracts from the OSHA Integrated Management Information System.

[12] A DOL study (1974) found that backpay settlements provided an average of one-half of the underpayment.

[13] See Weil (1996b) for a more extensive discussion of the issues contained in this section.

[14] See Commission on the Future of Worker-Management Relations (1994a:Exhibit IV-3, p. 134) for a definition of these categories.

[15] For an empirical study of the impact of workplace information provision on worker financial investment behavior, see Bayer, Bernheim, and Scholz (1996).

[16] This is a recurring problem under a number of labor laws. For example, a comprehensive survey of OSHA compliance officers by the General Accounting Office (GAO) concluded that "many OSHA inspectors believe workers' participation [in OSHA] is limited by their lack of knowledge about their rights and lack of protection from employer reprisal" (GAO 1989).

[17] This is particularly true in the case of safety and health laws where occupational risks might not be fully perceived or appreciated (Viscusi 1983; Viscusi and O'Connor 1984).

[18] Fear of such retaliation has been shown to have a dampening effect on use of grievance procedures in both union and especially nonunion environments (Feuille and Delaney 1992).

[19] It is a separate and more difficult question to determine the socially optimal level of workplace exercise of rights. This requires determination of the overall benefits of the labor policy per se and the comparative costs. However, if one believes that government resources must be augmented through the worker exercise of rights, the individual-based solution can be viewed as suboptimal.

[20] Williamson (1985:254) points out, "(u)nions can both serve as a source of information regarding employee needs and preferences." In addition to Williamson, the role of unions in providing basic agency functions is discussed in Freeman and Medoff (1984), particularly in regard to personnel practices and benefits.

[21] There might also be divergences in behavior arising from a number of sources. Median voter models of union behavior would predict that union leadership would tend to pursue policies reflective of more senior members of the unit which might not be synonymous with the public goods solution to benefit valuation. Alternatively, principal/agent divergences in interest may also lead away from optimal behaviors from the perspective of collective worker interests. For example, the union may have incentives to "overuse" certain rights for strategic reasons unrelated to the workplace regulation (e.g., as a source of pressure in collective bargaining or strikes). However, principal/agent divergences in behavior may be moderated both through electoral processes and by worker recourse via duty of fair representation claims which tend to induce unions to pursue activities consonant with the preferences of represented workers.

[22] The union/nonunion differential in annual inspection probabilities among the 2,000 largest construction contractors was virtually constant between 1987 and 1993, with union contractors bearing a .08 higher probability of inspection than nonunion contractors (author's calculation based on OSHA inspection data).

[23] For example, the choice of human resource practices is closely related to the underlying organization of assembly work in the apparel industry, arising from both the highly competitive nature of product market competition in many segments and as a result of the technologies required for sewing (Dunlop and Weil 1996). Automobiles (Pils and MacDuffie

1996) and steel (Ichniowski, Shaw, and Prennushi 1997) practices have greater variance in human resource choices but are still generally constrained by these larger forces.

[24] The disclosure in May 1996 that children were being used to produce clothes in the fashion line promoted by T.V. personality Kathy Lee Gifford led to enormous public pressure on both the retailers and manufacturers providing this clothing line and on the industry as a whole. This pressure led in part to adoption of a number of "codes of conduct" regarding the sourcing of apparel products. See, for example, Bureau of National Affairs, "The Apparel Industry and Codes of Conduct: Executive Summary of Labor Department Report." *Daily Labor Report*, October 22, 1996, pp. E5-E9.

[25] The recent explosion of work on minimum wage pays surprisingly little attention to the issue of compliance.

[26] The study employs a very indirect measure of enforcement effort; however, the number of FLSA compliance actions and compliance budget in the state where the individual worker observation is taken.

[27] Ehrenberg and Jakubson (1990) ascribe higher compliance rates in part to the potentially significant costs of noncompliance, although this seems unlikely given the extremely low rates of suits brought by parties under WARN, the only avenue of enforcement as well as the relatively mild penalties associated with violation.

[28] On the other hand, unions substantially increase the probability of receiving pensions as a benefit policy (Allen and Clark 1987). However, increasing the prevalence pension plans is not the intended purpose of ERISA.

[29] The need to establish common practices across often dispersed, multi-establishment enterprises also leads to higher rates of compliance for the enterprise as a whole. Several of the compliance studies show a positive correlation between multiplant operation and compliance (e.g., Weil 1996a).

[30] The pre-WARN impact of informal notice on job displacement outcomes has been studied extensively (e.g., Addison and Portugal 1992; Swaim and Podgursky 1990; more generally, Addison 1991).

[31] Analyses of the impact of Title VII of the Civil Rights Act of 1964 on the employment and occupational status of blacks shows that it has also had large, positive impacts (e.g., Leonard 1984b). In contrast to EO 11246, its primary effect has been through the impact of private suits brought by individuals under Title VII rather than the direct administrative procedures of the Equal Employment Opportunity Commission. While the EEOC's capabilities to pursue enforcement have been meager, between 1964 and 1981 more than 5000 cases brought (35% of which were class action) were decided by federal district courts alone.

[32] While proving the existence of positive net benefits of regulation is not a statutory requirement (and has been the subject of considerable litigation), OSHA undertakes benefit/cost estimation as part of their standard promulgation procedures.

[33] In the same way, requiring that employee participation systems meet "minimum standards" of practice in regard to operating procedures, compensation, and protection from retribution raises the questions of (1) how minimum standards themselves would be enforced; (2) whether enforcement would lead to compliance with those minimum standards; and (3) whether compliance, in turn, would lead to truly effective systems of representation.

[34] Northrup (in this volume) makes the counter-argument that unions manipulate the regulatory process to advance nonregulatory ends, such as using the threat of OSHA enforcement to bring pressure in collective bargaining forums. Analysis of union versus nonunion OSHA complaint inspections (i.e., those initiated by employees) reveals that these inspections result in comparable detection rates of serious standard violations, thereby providing little evidence of this type of union manipulation in the case of OSHA. These results are available from the author.

## References

Addison, John, ed. 1991. *Job Displacement: Consequences and Implications for Policy*. Detroit, MI: Wayne State University Press.

Addison, John, and Pedro Portugal. 1992. "Advance Notice and Unemployment: New Evidence from the 1988 Displaced Worker Survey." *Industrial and Labor Relations Review*, Vol. 45, no. 4, pp. 645-64.

Addison, John, and McKinley Blackburn. 1994a. "The Worker Adjustment and Retraining Notification Act: Effects on Notice Provision." *Industrial and Labor Relations Review*, Vol. 47, no. 4, pp. 650-62.

_____. 1994b. "Has WARN Warned? The Impact of Advance-Notice Legislation on the Receipt of Advance Notice." *Journal of Labor Research*, Vol. 15, no. 1, pp. 83-90.

Allen, Steven, and Robert Clark. 1987. "Pensions and Firm Performance." In Morris Kleiner, Richard Block, Myron Roomkin, and Sidney Salsburg, eds., *Human Resources and the Performance of the Firm*. Madison, WI: Industrial Relations Research Association, pp. 195-242.

Ashenfelter, Orly, and James Heckman. 1976. "Measuring the Effect of an Antidiscrimination Program." In Ashenfelter, O., and J. Blum, eds., *Evaluating the Labor Market Effect of Social Programs*. Princeton, NJ: Princeton University, Industrial Relations Section.

Ashenfelter, Orly, and Robert Smith. 1979. "Compliance with the Minimum Wage Law." *Journal of Political Economy*, Vol. 87, no. 2, pp. 333-50.

Bartel, Anne, and L. Thomas. 1985. "Direct and Indirect Effects of Regulation: A New Look at OSHA's Impact." *Journal of Law and Economics*, Vol. 28, no. 1, pp.1-25.

Bayer, Patrick, B. Douglas Bernheim, and John K. Scholz. 1996. "The Effects of Financial Education in the Workplace: Evidence from a Survey of Employers." National Bureau of Economic Research Working Paper 5655.

Becker, Gary. 1968. "Crime and Punishment: An Economic Analysis." *Journal of Political Economy*, Vol. 76, pp. 169-217.

Blank, Rebecca, and David Card. 1989. "Recent Trends in Insured and Uninsured Employment: Is There an Explanation?" National Bureau of Economic Research Working Paper No. 2871.

Bokat, Stephen, and Horace Thompson, III. 1988. *Occupational Safety and Health Law*. Washington, DC: Bureau of National Affairs.

Brandeis, Elizabeth. 1935. *Labor Legislation*. Volume IV of *History of Labor in the United States*. John R. Commons, ed. New York: Augustus M. Kelley (Reprints of Economic Classics, 1966), pp. 625-26.

Brown, Charles. 1982. "The Federal Attack on Labor Market Antidiscrimination Law: The Mouse That Roared?" In Ronald Ehrenberg, ed., *Research in Labor Economics*, Vol. 3. New York: JAI Press, pp. 33-68.

Brown, Charles, James Hamilton, and James Medoff. 1990. *Employers Large and Small.* Cambridge, MA: Harvard University Press.

Buchanan, James, and Gordon Tullock. 1962. *The Calculus of Consent.* Ann Arbor, MI: University of Michigan Press.

Budd, John, and Brian McCall. 1997. "The Effect of Unions on the Receipt of Unemployment Insurance Benefits." *Industrial and Labor Relations Review*, Vol. 50, no. 3, pp. 478-92.

Bureau of National Affairs. 1992. *Basic Patterns in Union Contracts.* 13th ed. Washington, DC: Bureau of National Affairs.

Card, David, and Alan Krueger. 1995. *Myth and Measurement: The New Economics of the Minimum Wage.* Princeton, NJ: Princeton University Press.

Chachere, Denise, and Peter Feuille. 1993. "Grievance Procedures and Due Process in Nonunion Workplaces." *Proceedings of the Forty-Fifth Annual Meeting* (Anaheim). Madison, WI: Industrial Relations Research Association, pp. 446-455.

Commission on the Future of Worker-Management Relations. 1994a. *Fact Finding Report.* Washington, DC: U.S. Dept. of Labor and Dept. of Commerce.

Commission on the Future of Worker-Management Relations. 1994b. *Report and Recommendations.* Washington, DC: U.S. Dept. of Labor and Dept. of Commerce.

Commons, John R., and John Andrews. 1936. *Principles of Labor Legislation.* Revised 4th ed. New York: Augustus M. Kelley (Reprints of Economic Classics).

Delaney, John, and Peter Feuille. 1992. "The Determinants of Nonunion Grievance and Arbitration Procedures." *Proceedings of the Forty-Fourth Annual Meeting* (New Orleans). Madison, WI: Industrial Relations Research Association, pp. 529-38.

Dunlop, John T. 1976. "The Limits of Legal Compulsion." *Labor Law Journal*, Vol. 27, no. 1, pp. 67-74.

_____. 1988. "Proceedings of the Twenty-Second Annual Symposium on Labor Law: Should American Labor Law be Applied to Small Business?" *Villanova Law Review*, Vol. 33, no. 6, pp. 1123-39.

Dunlop, John T., and David Weil. 1996. "Diffusion and Performance of Modular Production in the U.S. Apparel Industry." Industrial Relations, Vol. 35, no. 3, pp. 334-55.

Dunlop, John T., and Arnold Zack. 1997. *Mediation and Arbitration of Employment Law Disputes.* San Francisco: Jossey-Bass.

Edwards, Richard. 1993. *Rights at Work: Employment Relations in the Post-Union Era.* Washington, DC: The Brookings Institution.

Ehrenberg, Ronald, and George Jakubson. 1989. *Advance Notice Provisions in Plant Closing Legislation.* Kalamazoo, MI: Upjohn Institute.

_____. 1990. "Why WARN? Plant Closing Legislation." *Cato Review of Business and Government* (Summer), pp. 39-42.

Ehrenberg, Ronald, and Paul Schumann. 1981. "The Overtime Provisions of the Fair Labor Standards Act." In Simon Rottenberg, ed., *The Economics of Legal Minimum Wages.* Washington, DC: American Enterprise Institute.

_____. 1982. *Longer Hours or More Jobs? An Investigation of Amending Hours Legislation to Create Employment.* Ithaca, NY: ILR Press.

Feuille, Peter, and John Delaney. 1992. "The Individual Pursuit of Organizational Justice: Grievance Procedures in Nonunion Workplaces." *Research in Personnel and Human Resources Management*, Vol. 10, pp. 187-232.

Flanagan, Robert J. 1989. "Compliance and Enforcement Decision under the National Labor Relations Act." *Journal of Labor Economics*, Vol. 7, no. 3, pp. 257-80.

Foulkes, Fred. 1980. *Human Resource Policies in Large Nonunion Firms*. Cambridge, MA: Harvard Business School Press.

Freeman, Richard. 1985. "Unions, Pensions, and Union Pension Funds." In David Wise, ed., *Pensions, Labor and Individual Choice*. Chicago: University of Chicago Press.

Freeman, Richard, and James Medoff. 1984. *What Do Unions Do?* New York: Basic Books.

General Accounting Office. 1989. *How Well Does OSHA Protect Workers from Reprisal: Inspector Opinions*. Washington, DC: GAO, T-HRD-90-8.

_____. 1991. *OSHA Action Needed to Improve Compliance with Hazard Communication Standard*. Washington, DC: GAO, HRD-92-8.

_____. 1993. *Dislocated Workers: Worker Adjustment and Retraining Notification Act Not Meeting Its Goals*. Washington, DC: GAO, HRD-93-18.

_____. 1994. *Workplace Regulation: Information on Selected Employer and Union Experiences*. Volume 1. Washington, DC: GAO/HEHS-94-138.

Gleason, Sandra, and Karen Roberts. 1993. "Worker Perceptions of Procedural Justice in Workers' Compensation Claims: Do Unions Make a Difference?" *Journal of Labor Studies*, Vol. 14, no. 1, pp. 45-58.

Goldstein, Morris, and Robert Smith. 1976. "The Estimated Impact of the Antidiscrimination Program Aimed at Federal Contractors." *Industrial and Labor Relations Review*, Vol. 29, no. 4 (July), pp. 523-43.

Gramlich, Edward. 1976. "Impact of Minimum Wages on Other Wages, Employment, and Family Incomes." *Brookings Papers on Economic Activity*, Vol. 7, no. 2, pp. 409-51.

Gray, Wayne, and Carol Jones. 1991a. "Longitudinal Patterns of Compliance with Occupational Safety and Health Administration Health and Safety Regulations in the Manufacturing Sector." *Journal of Human Resources*, Vol. 26, no. 4, pp. 623-53.

_____. 1991b. "Are OSHA Health Inspections Effective? A Longitudinal Study in the Manufacturing Sector." *Review of Economics and Statistics*, Vol. 73, no. 3, pp. 504-8.

Heckman, James, and Kenneth Wolpin. 1976. "Does the Contract Compliance Program Work? An Analysis of Chicago Data." *Industrial and Labor Relations Review*, Vol. 29, no. 4, pp. 544-65.

Hoyman, Michele, and Lamont Stallworth. 1981. "Who Files Suits and Why: An Empirical Portrait of the Litigious Worker." *University of Illinois Law Review*, Vol. 198, no. 1, pp. 115-59.

Ichniowski, Casey, Kathryn Shaw, and Giovanna Prennushi. 1997. "The Effects of Human Resource Management Practices on Productivity: A Study of Steel Finishing Lines." *American Economic Review*, Vol. 87, no. 3, pp. 291-313.

Langbert, Mitchell. 1995. "Voice Asymmetries in ERISA Litigation." *Journal of Labor Research*, Vol. 16, no. 4, pp. 455-65.

Leonard, Jonathon. 1984a. "Employment and Occupational Advance under Affirmative Action." *Review of Economics and Statistics*, Vol. 66, no. 3, pp. 377-85.

_____. 1984b. "Anti-Discrimination or Reverse Discrimination: The Impact of Changing Demographics, Title VII and Affirmative Action on Productivity." *Journal of Human Resources*, Vol. 19, pp. 145-74.

_____. 1985. "The Effect of Unions on the Employment of Blacks, Hispanics, and Women." *Industrial and Labor Relations Review*, Vol. 39, no. 1, pp. 115-32.

_____. 1990. "The Impact of Affirmative Action Regulation and Equal Employment Law on Black Employment." *Journal of Economic Perspectives*, Vol. 4, no. 4, pp. 47-63.

Linder, Marc. 1989. "The Minimum Wage as Industrial Policy: A Forgotten Role." *Journal of Legislation*, Vol. 16, no. 1, pp. 151-71.

Mintz, Benjamin. 1985. *OSHA: History, Law, and Policy*. Washington, DC: Bureau of National Affairs.

Peterson, Richard. 1992. "The Union and Nonunion Grievance System." In David Lewin, Olivia Mitchell, and Peter Sherer, eds., *Research Frontiers in Industrial Relations and Human Resources*. Madison, WI: Industrial Relations Research Association.

Pil, Frits, and John Paul MacDuffie. 1996. "The Adoption of High-Involvement Work Practices." *Industrial Relations*, Vol. 35, no. 3, pp. 423-55.

Polinsky, A. Mitchell, and Steven Shavell. 1984. "The Optimal Use of Fines and Imprisonment." *Journal of Public Economics*, Vol. 24, no. 1, pp. 89-99.

_____. 1996. "On Offense History and the Theory of Deterrence." Olin Program in Law and Economics, Stanford University, Working Paper No. 134.

Ruser, John, and Robert Smith. 1991. "Reestimating OSHA's Effects: Have the Data Changed?" *Journal of Human Resources*, Vol. 26, no. 2, pp. 212-35.

Samuelson, Paul. 1955. "Diagrammatic Exposition of a Theory of Public Expenditure." *Review of Economics and Statistics*, Vol. 37, no. 3, pp. 350-56.

Scholz, John, and Wayne Gray. 1990. "OSHA Enforcement and Workplace Injuries: A Behavioral Approach to Risk Assessment." *Journal of Risk and Uncertainty*, Vol. 3, no. 3, pp. 283-305.

Shavell, Steven. 1991. "Specific versus General Enforcement of Law." *Journal of Political Economy*, Vol. 99, no. 5, pp. 1088-1108.

Siskind, Frederic. 1993. *Twenty Years of OSHA Federal Enforcement Data: A Review and Explanation of the Major Trends*. Washington, DC: U.S. Department of Labor.

Smith, Jeffrey D. 1991. "U.S. EPA Ups the Ante." *EI Digest*. (February), pp. 31-34.

Smith, Robert. 1979. "The Impact of OSHA on Manufacturing Injury Rates." *Journal of Human Resources*, Vol. 14, pp. 145-70.

_____. 1992. "Have OSHA and Workers' Compensation Made the Workplace Safer?" In David Lewin, Olivia Mitchell, and Peter Sherer, eds. *Research Frontiers in Industrial Relations and Human Resources*. Madison, WI: Industrial Relations Research Association, pp. 557-586.

Stern, Robert, and Deborah Balser. 1996. "Regulations, Social Control, and Institutional Perspectives: Implementing the Americans with Disabilities Act." Unpublished manuscript, Cornell University.

Stigler, George. 1970. "The Optimum Enforcement of Laws." *Journal of Political Economy*, Vol. 78, no. 3, pp. 526-36.

Swaim, Paul, and Michael Podgursky. 1990. "Advance Notice and Job Search: The Value of an Early Start." *Journal of Human Resources*, Vol. 25, no. 2, pp. 147-78.

Trejo, Stephen. 1991. "The Effects of Overtime Pay Regulation on Worker Compensation." *American Economic Review*, Vol. 81, no. 4, pp. 719-40.

Tuohy, Carol, and Marcel Simard. 1993. "The Impact of Joint Health and Safety Committees in Ontario and Quebec." Study prepared for the Canadian Association of Administrators of Labor Law.

U.S. Department of Commerce, Bureau of the Census. 1993. *County Business Patterns, 1990*. Washington, DC: Government Printing Office.

U.S. Department of Labor, Wage and Public Contracts Divisions. 1965. *Compliance Survey*. Washington, DC: Government Printing Office.

U.S. Department of Labor, Employment Standards Administration. 1975. *Minimum Wages and Maximum Hours under the Fair Labor Standards Act*. Washington, DC: Government Printing Office.

U.S. Department of Labor, Bureau of Labor Statistics. 1993. *Occupational Injuries and Illnesses in the United States, 1991*. Washington, DC: Government Printing Office.

U.S. Department of Labor. 1994. "The Availability and Use of Data on Occupational Injuries and Illnesses." Report to the House and Senate Appropriations Committees, July. Washington, DC: Author.

U.S. Department of Labor. 1995. *The New OSHA: Reinventing Worker Safety and Health. Report for the National Performance Review*. Washington, DC: Author.

U.S. Department of Labor, Wage and Hour Division. 1996. *Augmented Compliance Program Agreement*. Washington, DC: Author.

U.S. Environmental Protection Agency. 1984a. "Policy on Civil Penalties." EPA General Enforcement Policy #GM-21. Washington, DC: Author.

_____. 1984b. "A Framework for Statute-specific Approaches to Penalty Assessments." EPA General Enforcement Policy #GM-22. Washington, DC: Author.

Viscusi, W. Kip. 1979. "The Impact of Occupational Safety and Health Regulation, 1973-1983." *RAND Journal of Economics*, Vol. 17, no. 3, pp. 567-80.

_____. 1983. *Risk by Choice: Regulating Health and Safety in the Workplace*. Cambridge, MA: Harvard University Press.

Viscusi, W. Kip, and Charles O'Connor. 1984. "Adaptive Responses to Chemical Labeling: Are Workers Bayesian Decision Makers?" *American Economic Review*, Vol. 74, no. 5, pp. 942-56.

Vroman, Wayne. 1990. *Unemployment Insurance Trust Fund Adequacy in the 1990s*. Kalamazoo, MI: W.E. Upjohn Institute for Employment Research.

_____. 1991. "Why the Decline in Unemployment Insurance Claims?" *Challenge*, Vol. 34, no. 5, pp. 55-58.

Weil, David. 1990. "Government and Labor at the Mine Face." Unpublished paper. Boston University.

_____. 1991. "Enforcing OSHA: The Role of Labor Unions." *Industrial Relations*, Vol. 30, no. 1, pp. 20-36.

_____. 1992. "Building Safety: The Role of Construction Unions in the Enforcement of OSHA." *Journal of Labor Research*, Vol. 13, no. 1, pp. 121-32.

_____. 1994. "The Impact of Safety and Health Committees on OSHA Enforcement: Lessons from Oregon." Working Paper No. 112. Washington, DC: Economic Policy Institute.

_____. 1996a. "If OSHA Is So Bad, Why Is Compliance So Good?" *The RAND Journal of Economics*, Vol. 27, no. 3, pp. 618-40.

_____. 1996b. "Regulating the Labor Market: The Vexing Problem of Implementation." In David Lewin, Bruce Kaufman, and Donna Sockell, eds., *Advances in Industrial and Labor Relations*, Vol. 7, Greenwich, CT: JAI Press, Inc., pp. 247-86.

_____. 1997. "Are Workplace Committees Substitutes or Supplements for Labor Unions? New Evidence on an Old Issue." Working paper, Boston University.

Weiler, Paul. 1991. *Governing the Workplace*. Cambridge, MA: Harvard University Press.

Williamson, Oliver. 1985. *The Economic Institutions of Capitalism*. New York: The Free Press.

Wokutch, Richard. 1990. *Cooperation and Conflict in Occupational Safety and Health: A Multination Study of the Automotive Industry*. New York: Praeger.

# Chapter 13

# They Should Solve Their Own Problems: Reinventing Workplace Regulation

David Levine
*University of California*

In the United States, more than one hundred laws regulate everything from safety to discrimination to overtime rules (GAO 1994). Unfortunately, workplace regulations often do not work well for employees, for employers, or for regulators. This chapter outlines a reinvented regulatory system based on giving employers the option of working with employees to solve their mutual problems. That is, employers and employees can create custom plans that achieve the goals of the regulations and meet minimum standards. A key element of this proposal is that the work force (or its representatives) must approve each plan. Furthermore, the work force has the authority to cancel plans that are not protecting them.

The advantages of this system include more interesting work and better jobs for workers, more productive workplaces for owners and managers, and more flexibility for all involved. In addition, this system can increase total compliance, while permitting regulators to focus their efforts on the minority of workplaces with the most serious problems.

## Overview of the Problem

Although typically intended to protect their interests, regulations often do not work well for workers. One problem for workers is that workplaces are not safe. At some point during their career, perhaps one-third of all employees will miss work because of an on-the-job injury or illness. Furthermore, although fatality rates have declined in the last twenty years, rates of workplace injuries (as best we can measure them) have not declined (U.S. Bureau of Labor Statistics 1994:Table 4). In addition, millions of workers are subject to discrimination and sexual harassment each year (Rowe 1990). Unfortunately, most workers who perceive discrimination have no meaningful recourse. The process of appealing to the Equal Employment Opportunity Commission (EEOC) is adversarial and costly, discouraging employees from using it. When an employee *does* pursue an EEOC claim, he or she joins a line almost 100,000 people (eighteen months) long (Duffy 1995).

Finally, the vast majority of employees also would like more involvement in decision making than they find at work. In one recent poll, 90% of respondents with opinions wanted more involvement at work (Commission on Worker-Management Relations 1994a).

Regulations do not work well for managers either. Although the total benefits of workplace regulation probably outweigh the costs, often the tens or perhaps even hundreds of billions of dollars spent on workplace regulations are not cost effective (*Regulatory Systems* 1993). Few regulations provide incentives for managers and workers to discover the most effective means to accomplish the regulations' goals. In addition, many federal rules assume "one size fits all," imposing similar regulations for different industries, regions, and company sizes (Howard 1994). Similarly, laws and regulations often require regulators to use similar enforcement strategies for companies with very different compliance efforts and records. The result is harassment of "good" employers and lack of focus on "bad" ones (*Reinventing OSHA* 1995). Regulatory agencies often create different definitions, inspection schedules, and paperwork requirements with no coherence to the system. Employers also resent laws that discourage employee involvement that might satisfy the goals of both workers and managers.

Finally, regulations do not work well for the regulators. Rules are difficult to modify even decades after the regulators realize they are out of date. For example, one agency used an 18-foot chart with 373 boxes to describe its rulemaking process (*Regulatory Systems* 1993). Inspections are rare, frustrating many regulators' desire to ensure safe, legal, and nondiscriminatory workplaces. For example, the federal government and states together employ about 4,000 safety and health inspectors to cover 6 million workplaces. In addition, rules often require regulators to play "gotcha" and count minor infractions. The resulting system often leads to, as one author put it, "the death of common sense" (Howard 1994). Most regulators would prefer to use common sense in order to assist those companies that want to comply, while focusing enforcement on the worst offenders.

## An Alternative

Fortunately, an alternative exists—one based on creating incentives for companies and workers to solve their own problems. The proposed system is based on *conditional* deregulation, where companies with good records of compliance can choose to work with their employees to improve compliance and face fewer regulations, inspections, and penalties. To ensure the company does not reduce safety, increase discrimination, or otherwise worsen employees' lives, employees or their representatives must approve each alternative plan.

Where the system works, regulations will be more flexible and will achieve their goals more effectively (for example, providing more safety at lower cost). The methods used to meet these goals will be designed to fit the needs of each organization and its work force, reducing the costs of compliance. In addition, more managers and employees will have the authority and the incentive to ensure the company complies. The new system will also provide incentives for companies to be proactive in working with their work force to search out and solve problems. Companies that provide good workplaces will be rewarded with regulatory flexibility. These positive incentives will be in addition to existing negative incentives such as fines, the costs of workers' compensation, or the threat of a union drive. The outcome should be safer, fairer, and less discriminatory workplaces that are both better places to work and more productive.

Importantly, regulators will be able to spend less time and energy at the majority of workplaces that intend to comply with the spirit of the law (even if they do not comply with the letter of each regulation). This change will free up regulatory energy to focus on the "bad actors." (At the same time, some fraction of regulators' resources will need to be redirected to providing training materials and other assistance to workplaces that are moving to the new system.)

The potential disadvantages of the proposed system are equally clear. Companies might merely go through the motions of setting up alternative systems, while reducing safety and ignoring statutory rights of the employees. In this scenario, a system of conditional deregulation will diminish the already weak enforcement powers of the regulators. Self-regulation without oversight is not a recipe for compliance.

*Employees Can Oversee the New System*

Fortunately, one group has an interest both in effective regulation and in a flexible and productive workplace—the work force. A premise of the proposed system is that the employees must collectively approve any plan for achieving a regulation's goal. For example, employees can provide oversight when considering new means to achieve the goals of a safety regulation; they might choose to exchange more flexibility in weekly hours in exchange for ending mandatory overtime; and they can approve an employee involvement group to improve working conditions or safety that might otherwise run afoul of labor law. In all these cases, if the work force agrees, it is often inefficient for the federal government to mandate one-size-fits-all regulations.

There is no single best way to ensure employee involvement in approving the alternative plans. At the same time, the approval process must meet minimum standards concerning adequate information, adequate training, and a fair selection process for employee representatives.

In small workplaces, direct employee vote is often appropriate. (Regulations should contain exemptions or simplified procedures to accommodate the high cost of regulations per employee in very small workplaces.) In unionized settings, the union is a natural representative of the organized work force.

In larger nonunion workplaces, one possibility is to permit companies to voluntarily create employee representation committees (similar to European works councils). Such employee committees would then be able to approve programs to achieve the goals of any or all of a list of regulations. This proposal is consistent with public policy in many European nations, where works councils often have oversight over areas such as workplace safety.

To ensure lack of employer domination, these committees would need to meet minimum standards.[1] Participants would be guaranteed against loss of pay or benefits and against any retribution for their participation (or for choosing not to participate) in any element of the employee oversight system. The selection of members in the representative council would be chosen freely and fairly; they would not be chosen by management. In addition, any mechanism would need to ensure proportional representation of hourly and salaried employees. Mechanisms ranging from random choice among volunteers to elections with secret ballots would be permissible. The initial establishment of such a representative committee would need to be approved by a majority of the work force, as would the dissolution of the committee.

Even with employee-approved waivers, each regulatory arena would remain subject to minimum standards. For example, the employees or their representatives could approve the enterprise's safety program and opt out of many detailed safety regulations. Nevertheless, the safety program would need to meet minimum standards (detailed below), the *goals* of each regulation would still need to be met, and some Occupational Safety and Health Administration (OSHA) regulations would still be in effect. The employees or their representatives could approve the enterprise's alternative dispute resolution program and opt out of some EEOC and other antidiscrimination enforcement, but the dispute resolution procedure would need to meet strict standards. The following sections outline such minimum standards for safety and health, for dispute resolution procedures, for employee involvement programs, and several other areas of regulation.

Each sphere of regulation, from safety to wages and hours, suffers from a common set of problems: rigid, command-and-control regulations, with one set of regulations for all workplaces over a certain size, coupled with an adversarial and legalistic enforcement mechanism. Each sphere of workplace regulation also has similar problems with employer opportunism such as mismeasuring compliance or failing to meet minimum standards. In addition, each sphere has the feature that the work force and the regulators share most objectives. Thus it is not surprising that a unified framework can address such different areas of regulation.

Under the proposal, companies and workers could jointly agree to modify the regulations in any one sphere or in several. This proposal provides the economy of scale of having a single representative body in place for each issue that arises. Because of the common issues that arise in each sphere of workplace regulation, proposals for reform of specific arenas will systematically miss the advantages of a unified framework for employee-monitored self-regulation.

*Relation to Past Literature*

Works councils are mandated in all of the continental European Union members. In most of these nations the councils have rights to information and consultation on a variety of issues. In Germany, Denmark, Luxembourg, and the Netherlands the works council must not only be informed but must also agree to changes in personnel policies such as hiring, firing, and work rules.

This proposal draws on past arguments for mandatory works councils (e.g., Weiler 1990). A key distinction is that it proposes the voluntary creation of employee representation councils specifically to improve the quality and reduce the cost of workplace regulations. This proposal is also related to arguments for decentralized means to achieve the goals of regulations, what John Dunlop has called an "internal responsibility system" (e.g., Bok and Dunlop 1970). A number of authors have noted how employee involvement can advance the goals of regulations and other government programs in specific spheres such as safety (OSHA 1995b) or training (Lynch 1994).

The Commission on the Future of Worker Management Relations (1994b) also endorsed employee involvement to help decentralize regulatory enforcement. Commission member Thomas Kochan noted the commission's approach to improving workplace regulation emphasized separating those "employment relationships with effective workplace institutions that can take on some of the regulatory functions from those without such institutions." While the former can be largely deregulated, the latter still "need to remain subject to the standard approach to regulation and enforcement" (Kochan 1995:357). The commission's proposal (1994b) endorsed separate mechanisms of employee involvement in each sphere, such as safety and dispute resolution, while this proposal emphasizes that the common problem of workplace regulation leads to a common solution.

This proposal is closest to those of Kochan and Osterman (1994:205-06) and Freeman and Rogers (1993:63-4), who also propose voluntarily established employee committees that can further the goals of multiple spheres of workplace regulation while enhancing flexibility and employee involvement. Their proposals emphasize the role of the committees in enhancing employee voice. The system proposed here emphasizes the converse proposal: employee involvement is necessary for improving workplace regulation.

The proposal also draws on the long tradition among economists advocating performance-based regulations. Under this proposal, employers would be able (with their work force) to design alternative means to achieve the goals of any regulation. Furthermore, those with good track records of success would be treated differently from those with poor records of success. For environmental regulations, preliminary evidence indicates that performance-based regulations can achieve results similar to as command-and-control regulations but cost about one-third less. (Moving to performance-based regulations is already a priority of the Clinton administration's proposals for reinventing regulations [Gore 1995].) It is plausible that similar cost savings can be achieved in other spheres of workplace regulation.

Employee involvement is an important complement to performance-based regulations, because measuring performance is so often problematic. For example, rewarding low rates of reported injuries gives managers incentives both to reduce injuries and to penalize employees who report their injuries. Empowering employees to approve the safety plan and to monitor its results reduces the difficulties with managers gaming the performance measurement system.

## Safety and Health

### The Problem

Every year more than 6,000 Americans die of workplace injuries, an estimated 50,000 people die of illnesses caused by workplace chemical exposures, and 6 million people suffer non-fatal workplace injuries. Injuries alone cost the economy more than $110 billion a year (OSHA 1995). These numbers are high in absolute terms and are also high compared with other nations such as Sweden and Japan (even acknowledging difficulties in international comparisons) (Freeman and Rogers 1993).[2]

More regulation does not seem to be the answer: after the IRS, OSHA may be the most hated part of the federal government (see, e.g., Potter and

Youngman 1995:319). The reasons for this hatred are easy to understand. As OSHA describes the problem:

> In the public's view, OSHA has been driven too often by numbers and rules, not by smart enforcement and results. Business complains about overzealous enforcement and burdensome rules. . . . Too often, a "one-size-fits-all" regulatory approach has treated conscientious employers no differently from those who put workers needlessly at risk. (OSHA 1995)

### The Role of Employee Involvement in Improving Safety

Improving safety and health requires that managers and employees actively participate in identifying and eliminating hazards. A number of enterprises have already established mechanisms for such employee involvement. For example, in one survey about 75% of establishments with more than 50 employees and 31% of smaller ones reported having safety and health committees (Commission on Worker-Management Relations 1994b).

*Mandatory programs.* About ten states currently require employers in some or all sectors to sponsor safety committees (Commission on Worker-Management Relations 1994b). A majority of state workers' compensation systems are beginning to require workplaces to establish a safety and health program, at least in hazardous sectors (OSHA 1995). Most of these required programs contain minimum standards similar to those listed below.

Although no careful evaluation exists, preliminary evidence on the effectiveness of such committees is favorable. For example, both state and business officials agree that mandated safety and health committees have contributed to the $1.5 billion decrease in injury costs experienced by Oregon employers between 1990 and 1993 (*Occupational Safety and Health* 1993).

*Voluntary programs.* OSHA's Voluntary Protection Program is a small well-respected program that recognizes companies with excellent safety programs. VPP employers have injury rates about 40% lower than the average of their industries (although it is unclear how much of the decrease is due to the actions measured by the VPP program) (GAO 1992:10). More generally, employers that voluntarily adopt safety and health programs have lower injury and illness rates than do other employers, and their managers often attribute the difference largely to the existence of the program (GAO 1992).

Unfortunately, current federal law discourages rather than encourages such safety and health programs. For example, the definition of "company unions" under the National Labor Relations Act is broad enough to forbid many safety committees. Moreover, OSHA does not systematically provide incentives for proactive safety and health programs. (OSHA does provide a small incentive in that good faith efforts can lower fines slightly.) Even if a safety and health program identifies a better and cheaper way to achieve a safety goal, OSHA does not grant a waiver from its detailed regulations.

*Examples of the New Model*

Fortunately, the situation is changing, and OSHA is moving to encourage proactive safety and health programs. For example, in a pilot program called Maine 200, OSHA targeted 203 companies in Maine with the worst injury records over the preceding years. Each company in this group was allowed to choose either to undergo an immediate and detailed safety inspection or to create a safety and health program meeting certain minimum standards. All but two of the companies opted to create a safety program.

Results thus far have been impressive. Participating companies have identified and eliminated 55,000 hazards in the program's first year—as many hazards as OSHA identified in the entire state during the previous eight years. In addition, the injury rate declined at 59% of these companies, sometimes dramatically (*Reinventing OSHA* 1995:Appendix 1). OSHA is currently expanding this program to any state that will help it identify the companies with the worst safety records.

Similarly, in construction OSHA has begun rewarding worksites with an adequate safety program, defined as having a written safety program and a trained safety person. OSHA rewards such sites by promising that any OSHA inspections will focus only on the four main deadly hazards, not on minor violations such as paperwork violations or poor communication about possible hazards (*Reinventing OSHA* 1995:Appendix 2).

*Ensuring Minimum Standards*

Within the writings of the safety professionals such as industrial hygienists, ergonomists, union safety representatives, and regulators, a consensus is arising about the elements of adequate safety programs. Such programs must ensure both managers and employees have the training to understand safety, incentives to improve safety, and the authority to make safety-enhancing changes. To be more specific, the following elements are common to most proposals for an adequate safety and health program:[3]

- Managers and employees receive training and education about identifying and controlling hazards. They (or outside experts they have chosen) perform periodic joint workplace inspections to identify hazards.

- Managers and employees have incentives to participate fully in the safety and health program. Employees or their representatives have the authority to develop recommendations to the employer with assurance that the employer will respond to recommendations in a timely manner. Employees are protected against retribution due to their contributions to the safety program.
- When accidents occur, an emergency response plan is implemented, and first aid services are available. An investigation to eliminate root causes follows each accident.
- The employer provides appropriate medical surveillance for all health hazards.
- Written records include a description of the safety and health program, records of injuries and illnesses, and plans to abate hazards. These abatement plans have timetables and procedures to track progress.

Good process matters, but so do results. Under this proposal, employers with very high accident and illness rates (compared with their industry) or with fairly high accident rates and no pattern of improvement would lose the presumptions otherwise due to employers with good safety programs. (Employers requesting exemptions would be required to submit their OSHA safety and health logs and workers' compensation records to OSHA so OSHA can compare its safety record with their industry.) For employers with poor safety records, or those in particularly dangerous industries, additional certification of the safety program by a third party such as the workers' compensation insurer may be required. (Workers' compensation insurers are appropriate certifiers because they also save money from reducing injury rates. Several states require these companies to certify safety plans as adequate [OSHA 1995].)

Finally, not all regulations will be automatically waived if the workers approve. In situations with hard to detect hazards that may lead to rare or long to develop harms, even trained employees will have trouble dealing with the scientific complexities involved. In these situations, OSHA should continue to promulgate regulations.

OSHA has already proposed some incentives for excellent safety programs and records: OSHA inspections focused on major hazards, not every hazard; lower fines; and lower priority for random inspections (*Reinventing OSHA* 1995:Appendix 3). Unfortunately, these incentives alone will not be very effective, because fines are almost always trivially small and random inspections are very rare.

OSHA can provide more effective incentives by giving automatic waivers from detailed command-and-control regulations to safety programs that achieve the goals of each rule. In addition, OSHA could agree that for approved safety programs, all complaints except imminent danger would have to satisfy the internal safety procedures before OSHA would inspect the workplace. For example, a worker would have to first submit a suggestion or complaint to the in-house safety committee. Only if this committee then found no need for action (or did not act in a timely fashion) could the worker call in an outside regulator. OSHA does not have time to inspect every complaint and still engage in sufficient random inspections of the most dangerous workplaces; giving deference to excellent in-house systems will permit them to focus their scarce resources on the most dangerous and worst-run workplaces.

*The Role of Employee Oversight in Ensuring the Programs Are Not a Sham*

Permitting companies to exempt themselves from OSHA regulations if they have a safety program runs the risk of companies establishing sham programs that reduce safety. Fortunately, employees have an interest in a safe workplace and are ideally placed to oversee the workplace safety plan. In addition, under this proposal, employees have the threat to revert to detailed regulations coupled with an OSHA inspection if the employer does not follow through on important safety and health improvements. Preliminary case study (Adler, Goldoftas, and Levine 1995) and statistical (Weil 1991) evidence suggest that the combination of employee involvement in health and safety and the ability to call in safety regulators when disputes arise can lead to better outcomes than either one alone.

## Dispute Resolution

The United States is unique among the industrialized nations in permitting companies to fire employees without the need to show cause. Ironically, the U.S. is also unique in having the most expensive and conflict-laden legal system, one that frustrates both employees and managers. Alternative dispute resolution programs such as mediation, arbitration, and ombudsmen have the potential to increase fairness in dismissals, promotions, and other management actions, while reducing costs.[4] The key is to ensure these alternative dispute resolution programs are not mere sham, but actually provide due process under the law.[5]

*The Problem*

Employees have statutory rights to a workplace free of discrimination and sexual harassment. Unfortunately, as noted above, surveys suggest that several million employees each year feel they have been sexually harassed or discriminated against. Evidence of continued discrimination is not just from self-reports. When matched pairs of employees (black and white, Anglo and Hispanic, or male and female) are sent for job interviews, employers are more likely to offer white men employment, especially for better jobs (Bendick et al. 1993; Glaster et al. 1994; Neumark 1995).

Workers also have a statutory right of appealing to the EEOC and eventually the court system for redress. Unfortunately, many workers cannot enforce their statutory rights. As noted above, when employees bring charges before the EEOC, they find themselves at the back of a line almost 100,000 people long (Duffy 1995). When the EEOC does find the employer guilty of malfeasance, most claims do not result in meaningful monetary damages. Lawsuits, although occasionally leading to enormous awards, are largely the preserve of those in high-wage and high-status occupations, almost irrelevant to most of the work force (Donahue and Siegelman 1991).

Even without the backlog, many victims of discrimination do not find EEOC enforcement well suited to their problems. Some find the EEOC process too adversarial. Many do not want to bring formal charges but want low-cost, low-intensity dispute resolution procedures. Sometimes the employee wants nothing more than a formal apology or for the behavior to stop (Rowe 1990). Other employees find the EEOC process too costly, particularly if they need a lawyer at some stage. A third group of employees finds the EEOC process too public. For example, the EEOC process does not permit anonymous complaints as would operate through many companies' in-house ombudsman (Rowe 1990). In short, many employees find themselves with no workable recourse to discrimination: some quit and suffer unemployment or wage declines, while others continue to work after what may have been largely a misunderstanding, with no simple means for clearing up the misunderstanding; and others endure work with bosses who persist in violating their rights (Rowe 1990).

At the same time, nonunion employees in the private sector are employed at will, meaning the firm is allowed to dismiss the employee "for good cause, for bad cause, or even for cause morally wrong" (cited in Steiber 1984:2). Many states have carved out several exemptions to pure employment at will, most importantly based on employers' handbooks or other promises that imply an employment contract (Potter and Youngman 1995:141). Unfortunately, these protections, like those against discrimination, apply in fact primarily to high-wage employees who can afford a lawyer (Commission on Worker-Management Relations 1994b:30).

While many employees feel their rights are not protected, many employers resent the cost of litigation and regulation and what they perceive as EEOC's combative and anti-employer stance (Potter and Youngman 1995:141). Two bad effects can result if employers find it expensive to dismiss people from protected groups. First, fear of lawsuits may stop them from dismissing unsatisfactory employees from these protected groups, reducing efficiency and incentives. In addition, employers may resist hiring the disabled, blacks, or females because they fear future lawsuits. (In fact, almost all EEOC and antidiscrimination cases are about unjust dismissal, not unjust failure to hire [Donahue and Siegelman 1991].) When the courts do find a contract was implied, many employers resent the high costs of lawsuits and the uncertainty and risk relating to the (small) chance of very high damages (Goldstein 1995).

Companies already have some incentives to have good in-house processes for avoiding and resolving cases of discrimination because both discriminating against good workers and becoming involved in the EEOC process are costly. Nevertheless, current employment law does not provide direct incentives for good in-house dispute resolution processes.

### The Role of Employee Oversight in Creating Credible Alternative Dispute Resolution Procedures[6]

While no legal system alone can end all discrimination, this proposal should both reduce discrimination and lower the costs of fighting discrimination. Alternative dispute resolution procedures can reduce costs, increase the speed in which problems are resolved, and increase both employees' and employers' satisfaction. A key element of alternative dispute resolution procedures is that they can be flexible and tailored to the needs of the organization and its members (Commission on Worker-Management Relations 1994b:28). For example, in-house dispute resolution procedures often provide employees with the choice of either confidential or public means of addressing complaints (Rowe 1990; Commission on Worker-Management Relations 1994b:28). In another setting, an employer where many employees are not native English speakers might ensure that any appeals board of workers and managers had at least one native speaker of the accused worker's language. Because so many complaints require primarily better communication, in-house procedures can begin with mediation, not the more legalistic EEOC procedures.

### Ensuring High Standards

A serious problem with alternative dispute resolution procedures is that an employer may establish procedures rigged in its favor. For example, one law firm proposed that employees give up their legal rights in return for the right to use a company-designed dispute resolution program. This program's highest level of appeal was a partner from another large law firm (Commission on Worker-Management Relations 1994b:27). It is not likely that a young woman working in a law firm who accuses her older male boss of sexual harassment will feel that an (older male) partner in a nearby large law firm is a neutral decisionmaker. Other alternative dispute resolution procedures companies have established have had maximum penalties far below those permitted by law, and others have taken years to resolve disputes. Because of these risks, the EEOC has argued that employers cannot require employees to sign away their rights to EEOC hearings just because an employer has an in-house dispute resolution procedure (Bompey and Stempel 1995).

To avoid these problems, any in-house dispute resolution program would need to meet high standards. The first standard is approval by the employees' representation body described above. Employees will be loath to approve a procedure that gives employers the ability to act with no disregard for the facts. At the same time, minority employees cannot have their rights suspended because their colleagues feel a given dispute resolution procedure is adequate. The majority of current employees may themselves discriminate or may just care less about the concerns of the minority than the law does.

Fortunately, a recent high-level commission found that both employers and employees agree on a set of standards alternative dispute resolution procedures must meet if they are to serve as a legitimate form of private enforcement of public employment law. Specifically, these systems must provide (1) a neutral arbitrator who knows the laws in question and understands the concerns of the parties, (2) a fair method by which the employee can secure the necessary information to present his or her claim, (3) a fair method of cost sharing that ensures all employees can afford access, (4) the option for employees to have independent representation, (5) a range of remedies equal to those available through litigation, (6) a written opinion by the arbitrator explaining the rationale for the result, and (7) sufficient judicial review to ensure that the result is consistent with the governing laws.[7] The standards might also require a timely decision. In addition, in cases where due process is in doubt, the worker retains recourse to appeal to the standard court system.[8]

The new system has several possible drawbacks. Unlike court cases, arbitration does not provide clear precedents. In addition, arbitration can lead to different arbitrators imposing different settlements for identical facts without judicial review of the settlement. (Judges would only review whether due process was followed.) These problems will probably not be too serious, because arbitrators try to be consistent with each other both as a measure of professional competence and to ensure repeat employment—employees and employers will not jointly agree on arbitrators with records far from the norm.[9]

While the concern about repeat business reduces the odds of arbitrary and capricious awards, it also implies arbitrators will rarely provide the very large awards that some juries provide. If fear of large (but unpredictable and rare) awards is a major deterrent to employer discrimination, then the new system will not reduce discrimination (Kochan 1995:358). It is likely that reducing the costs of protesting unfair treatment and increasing the probability of sanctions in cases of unfair treatment will protect more workers than the risk of a few large but arbitrary awards.

Problems can also arise when most of the work force would prefer a discriminatory dispute resolution procedure. As noted above, this proposal requires outside neutral arbitration and permits judicial review of due process, precluding the worst abuses. To enhance the rights of minorities further, this proposal expands the right of individuals to bring class-action lawsuits outside the in-house dispute resolution mechanism when employment practices are systematically biased against a group. (This right is broader than the right under current law, because it permits a class-action suit even if only a single employee is in the discriminated against group at this time, if the practice has reduced the number of employees in the group.)

## Employee Involvement

*The Problem*[10]

The National Labor Relations Act makes it illegal for employers to discuss "conditions of employment" with company-sponsored committees of employees. Under Section 8(a)(2) of the National Labor Relations Act, such a committee is an illegal "company union." Thus committees of workers that influence training, work schedules, and promotions are typically not legal. Even a safety committee can easily run afoul of labor law.

The situation is no better at unionized establishments. In high-involvement workplaces such as the Saturn auto factory, workers make many decisions that were once the province of management. Unfortunately, U.S. labor law defines workers performing such "managerial" tasks as managers and does not permit managers all the rights of traditional union members. These legal barriers are important because, as cited above, new forms of work organization with higher levels of employee involvement are desired by most of the work force. In addition, recent research shows that such innovations typically have positive effects on outcomes ranging from product quality to stock market value. (See the evidence reviewed in Levine [1995], which also describes several market imperfections that impede the spread of employee involvement.)

One possible solution is legalizing all forms of employee involvement. For example, Congress is now considering the TEAM Act that permits all employee involvement groups that do not negotiate or enter into collective bargaining agreements with the employer (HR 743 passed the House of Representatives September 27, 1995).

Unfortunately, this approach is not a good solution, because company unions *can* be a threat, even if they do not sign a collective bargaining agreement. As Senator Wagner stated in pushing for the NLRA sixty years ago, company unions posed "one of the great obstacles to genuine freedom of self-organization" (cited in AFL-CIO 1995). Most Americans support the right of employees to form their own organizations free of management domination to bargain with management and to protect employees' rights (Freeman and Rogers 1993:30-2).

If employers can establish company unions of any sort, they can impede workers' right to self-determination. For example, employers who perceive themselves at risk of a union organizing campaign can set up a sham employee representation program that alleviates some employees' perceived need for a union. Employers that already have unions can establish alternative problem-solving mechanisms that bypass the elected representatives of the work force. Moreover, the strong opposition of the American labor movement to the new law makes it likely its passage will do little to increase cooperation and involvement at work (Kochan 1995).

### The Role of Employee Oversight in Ensuring Teamwork Is Not Just a Facade

Under this proposal, employees will need collectively to approve any employee involvement mechanisms that would otherwise run afoul of the NLRA. In organized worksites the union would need to approve the plan. In other workplaces either the democratically chosen employee council or a direct vote would need to approve each exemption. If a high-quality employee representative body approved an employee involvement program, such a program would be exempt from the NLRA ban.

This oversight would make it much less likely that employers would propose sham involvement mechanisms or that they would set up an employee involvement program primarily to weaken a union organizing campaign. If the employees ever felt the group was a sham, they could rescind their approval and the plan would no longer be legal. At the same time, this oversight would increase employees' confidence that the proposed involvement program was in their best interest. Some evidence exists that employee involvement programs are more long-lived in unionized establishments (Drago 1988); presumably, part of the advantage is due to the union's role in discouraging employers from setting up exploitative and short-run programs.

### Ensuring Minimum Standards for the Involvement Groups

Even with employee oversight, several standards would be required of all involvement plans. For example, all participants would be guaranteed against loss of pay or benefits and against any retribution for their participation (or for choosing not to participate) in any employee involvement group. Once an employee involvement group begins, the company could not disband the group without the approval of the employees or their representatives.

## Other Spheres of Regulation

The basic insight that workers have an interest in both effective and efficient workplace regulation implies that the same framework of employee oversight can be applied to other spheres of workplace regulation. This section outlines how employee oversight can improve overtime rules, employee stock ownership plans, and government-subsidized training programs.

### Wage and Hour Regulations

Wage and hour rules also do not always make it easy for a company to implement flexible schedules. Few companies permit someone to choose to work six days one week and four days the next because the company must pay overtime for the sixth day. Also, employers may not offer partial vacation days to salaried employees for fear they will become eligible for overtime (Potter and Youngman 1995:293). Even worse, people who work too few hours or days in a row sometimes run the risk of losing eligibility for unemployment insurance or other benefits. In addition, some employees would prefer time off to higher pay, but companies are not always permitted to offer compensatory time instead of overtime wages (Potter and Youngman 1995:295). At the same time, several million workers work longer shifts than they desire (Kahn and Lang 1992). Any move that simply relaxed overtime rules would worsen this problem.

Employee oversight can help provide flexibility. One possibility is to permit the employees or their representatives to authorize limited forms of flexibility in hours. For example, an employee council might be permitted to approve replacing the 40-hour week with the 160-hour month (or 80 hours in two weeks) to allow for flexible schedules. Employees would have some bargaining power in this process. Thus the council might modify the rules to allow flexible time schedules and compensatory time instead of overtime wages in exchange for the company ending mandatory overtime.

### Employee Stock Ownership Plans

For over a generation, the federal government has given tax subsidies to employee stock ownership plans (ESOPs). When the U.S. Congress created the ESOP program, an important motive was to increase worker commitment and productivity. Over the life of this program, the cost in reduced tax collections due to subsidizing employee stock ownership has been more than $20 billion.[11]

In spite of the continued tax expenditures on this program, "there is no evidence whatsoever that employee ownership itself automatically causes improved productivity or profitability except when combined with employee involvement" (Blasi and Kruse 1991; see also GAO 1987; Quarrey 1986). Nonetheless, under current law ESOP trustees are chosen solely by management. They can be company officers or outsiders such as banks. However, these outsiders often receive large fees and can be replaced at will by management. The potential conflicts of interests are clear, and ESOP trustees often act more for the benefit of managers than for either shareholders or employee-owners. For both reasons, tieing the ESOP subsidy to policies indicative of worker participation is appropriate. Such a change in ESOP legislation can potentially reduce the federal deficit, better meet Congress's original intent, and increase national productivity.

One solution is to restrict the ESOP tax subsidy to employers that permit employees to have oversight over their ESOP shares.[12] For companies with an employee representation council, for example, the council could vote the ESOP shares or could appoint or approve the trustee. Furthermore, employees or their representatives should be able to vote shares held by other retirement plans such as 401(k) defined contribution pensions, stock bonus plans, savings plans, defined benefit pension plans that own company shares, and deferred profit sharing plans. Workers should be able to vote both allocated and unallocated shares of the ESOP. (Unallocated shares are owned by a leveraged ESOP but are not yet purchased by workers.) Following similar logic, the employee representative might also be useful in helping appoint trustees for employees' pension funds.

*Training Programs*

Currently, the federal government and 44 states have created programs to work with employers to provide training (Potter and Youngman 1995:195). A problem with public funding of training is that employers may take public funds and either not provide training, or only provide training they would have even without the government assistance.

Lisa Lynch (1994) notes that in Europe employee oversight via works councils helps ensure training programs are well run. The same logic applies in the United States, implying that public subsidies should be given preferentially to employers whose training programs have been approved by employees or their representatives.

## Critiques

The main critique of in-house systems, even those approved by the work force and meeting high standards, is that some workers will lose compared with the status quo. For example, some safety programs will not listen to valid complaints that an OSHA inspector would have caught, and some in-house dispute resolution procedures will be manipulated by management, endorsed by a discriminatory work force, or poorly run.

These problems are serious because each of these problems will surely arise. At the same time, this critique is unconvincing, because many workers now work in unsafe conditions and are not treated fairly. This proposal must be judged by whether it improves safety, lessens discrimination, and improves the situation for most workers; not whether it reaches perfection. Given the inadequacies of the current system and the likelihood of continuing funding cuts for regulatory agencies, the current system is unlikely to become more effective at protecting workers without dramatic reforms.

Some unions have opposed past proposals for various forms of employee representation committees in the U.S. because they are too close to company unions. At the same time, some managers have resented proposals for works councils as thinly disguised entry points for unions. The evidence supports neither view strongly—for example, no evidence exists that union organizing has increased *or* decreased in states that begin requiring safety committees.

An additional argument against permitting workers to renegotiate regulations in areas such as safety is that they may agree with management (perhaps under the threat of job loss) to reduce safety or other protections below the socially optimal level. (Recall that because of workers' compensation and social security disability insurance, often neither workers nor employers pay the full cost of injuries.) It is likely that workers and managers at some workplaces will agree to reduce safety below the level that OSHA now requires on paper. Unfortunately, given OSHA's resources for enforcement, under the status quo OSHA has almost no ability to enforce safety rules in workplaces where workers and managers do not want to obey them. Thus it is unlikely that many workplaces will reduce their level of safety, although it may remain below the socially optimal level.

One obstacle to the new system is the required change in the priorities of regulators. Currently, as noted above, regulators are often required to inspect after every complaint and to write up all violations, no matter how minor. Under the new regime, many regulations would be waived for workplaces with effective internal systems. Regulators would need to redirect resources from nit-picking inspections to providing training materials and other resources for in-house systems. (Inspections at companies without effective in-house systems would remain an important part of regulators' jobs.) Congress would need to provide sufficient resources for regulators to assist compliance, particularly in the early years when participants in in-house systems will need the most training.

Politically, this proposal has many hurdles. The current system has relatively strong workers' rights on paper but often not in practice. The proposed system weakens some of these formal rights while it intends to enlarge rights in practice. Politically, few proponents of workers' rights are willing to accept this weakening de jure, even if it strengthens rights de facto. After a generation of increased de jure rights for employees, many advocates of employees' rights look to the law, not to employees and employers, to protect workers' rights. These advocates must be willing to trade off some rights on paper to strengthen rights in practice if effective reform is to succeed.

At the same time, many critics of employment protections feel that complete deregulation is the answer. Everyone agrees the current regulatory system has many shortcomings. Unfortunately, continued discrimination coupled with the many imperfections in labor markets makes it unlikely that complete deregulation will enhance the work force's well-being. Similarly, although savings are possible, budget cuts to destroy the limited regulatory capacities of the enforcement agencies are also unlikely to improve things. It is in the long-run interests of both managers and employees to improve regulation, even if not along the lines of this proposal.

## Conclusion

Almost all observers of American workplaces would like regulations to be more flexible and employees to have more involvement on the job. The government has substantial control over the first but must be concerned that any flexibility will be used by employers to defeat the goals of the regulations. In contrast, the government has few mechanisms for encouraging employee participation.[13] Fortunately, the proposed system both promotes flexibility in regulation and, by using employees to monitor management, increases employees' voice in how their workplace runs. The government, thus, moves from discouraging to encouraging employee involvement in decisions at the workplace, at the same time it reduces direct government regulation.

Importantly, the proposed new system is voluntary. Each employer has the option of establishing an alternative system with high standards and employee oversight, or the option to remain subject to the current regulatory scheme. The government provides incentives to those employers with good records of success and good programs to work with their employees to ensure continued progress. Often an important incentive is conditional deregulation from detailed command-and-control regulations.

In short, the status quo provides poor incentives to workers and managers—they have incentives to hit the letter of the regulation but not the goal of the law. The reinvented system provides incentives for workers and managers to achieve and exceed the standards of today. The status quo provides poor incentives for regulators; for example, OSHA inspectors forced to play "gotcha" instead of increasing safety. The reinvented system permits many employees of regulatory agencies to focus on compliance assistance, while others focus on the truly bad apples. Finally, the status quo relies on top-down regulations, while the reinvented process encourages workers and managers to improve compliance with flexibility to meet local conditions.

Under this proposal, an employer can establish an alternative regulatory system in any single area of workplace regulations such as safety, dispute resolution, or wage and hours rules. However, the new system can be fruitfully applied to all these areas of regulation. Moreover, creating a single employee committee to provide oversight for all spheres costs less than creating separate oversight mechanisms. This approach to reinventing regulation, by providing employers incentives to work with their employees, has the potential to both improve workers' lives and improve companies' bottom lines.

## Acknowledgment

Many of these ideas were developed while working at the Council of Economic Advisors in 1994 and 1995. While there I learned from a number of colleagues who were working on reinventing regulation. I remain responsible for all errors and interpretations.

## Endnotes

[1] Kochan and Osterman (1994:207) present a similar list.

[2] Some economists dispute the need for any safety regulation. They assume that workers have good information before taking jobs or that workers learn fairly quickly about hazards and find it easy to move between jobs. In this setting, employers will face market incentives to provide the efficient amount of safety because unsafe employers will need to pay higher wages that compensate workers for hazards.

Unfortunately, the empirical support for this theory is mixed (Brown 1980). In addition, a number of market failures suggest government intervention can have a role. For example, information on safety and (especially) health risks that may take decades to materialize is often far from perfect. Moreover, the presence of social insurance implies that injured workers do not pay the full cost of their injuries; thus the unregulated market will lead to inefficiently little safety. Finally, even if markets work well, we should still favor proposals such as this one that reduce the costs of the politically chosen level of safety regulation.

[3] See, for example, *Reinventing OSHA* (1995:Appendix 3) found at http://www.osha-slc.gov:80/Reinventing/app_3.html.

[4] Levine (1991) explains several market imperfections that may lead employers to have inefficiently or unfairly little protection against unjust dismissal.

[5] The Supreme Court in the *Gilmer* decision ruled that employers can require employees before being hired to agree to use outside arbitration (and to sign away their statutory

rights). Because this decision was based partly on law specific to the securities industry, its applicability to other industries is unclear. The EEOC has argued that such pre-employment contracts should not be binding in other industries (EEOC 1995).

[6] This section draws on the Commission on the Future of Worker-Management Relations (1994b:29).

[7] For more detail on the proposed quality standards, see Commission on the Future of Worker-Management Relations (1994b:29-33).

[8] The proposed system would not preclude court cases when management practices systematically discriminate against a group or potential group of employees. Particularly in such a setting, a majority of the existing work force may favor discrimination that favors incumbent workers; thus reliance on outside enforcement is called for.

At the same time, when management has practices in place that have been approved by the work force and that appear effective (such as education on sexual harassment and prompt and effective investigations of complaints), then the employer should not be held liable for the misdeeds of a single manager (Potter and Youngman 1995:352).

[9] In unionized settings, unions might retain their current right to stop certain grievances from being appealed all the way to outside arbitration. As under current law, in discrimination cases a worker should not need the union's permission to appeal a grievance.

[10] This section draws on Kamer, Abbot, and Salevitz (1994:4-48) and Sockell (1984:541-56).

[11] The current set of ESOP tax subsidies is quite complicated. See Blasi and Kruse (1991:23-4) for a short presentation.

[12] Richard Freeman (1990) has advocated works councils be required at companies enjoying the tax incentives for ESOP plans.

[13] See Levine (1995:Ch. 8) for a list of additional policies that remove barriers to employee involvement.

## References

Adler, Paul, Barbara Goldoftas, and David I. Levine. 1995. "Ergonomics, Employee Involvement, and the Toyota Production System: A Case Study of NUMMI's 1993 Model Change." Mimeo.

Bok, Derek, and John Dunlop. 1970. *Labor and the American Community.* New York: Simon and Schuster.

Bendick, Marc, et al. 1993. *Measuring Employment Discrimination through Controlled Experiments.* Washington, DC: Fair Employment Council of Greater Washington, Inc.

Bompey, Stuart H., and Andrea H. Stempel. 1995. "Four Years Later: A Look at Compulsory Arbitration of Employment Discrimination Claims after Gilmer v. Interstate/Johnson Lane Corp." *Employment Relations Law Journal*, Vol. 21, no. 2 (September 2).

Brown, Charles. 1980. "Equalizing Differences in Labor Markets." *Quarterly Journal of Economics*, Vol. 85.

Bureau of Labor Statistics. 1994. *Workplace Injuries and Illnesses in 1993.* Washington, DC: U.S. Department of Labor (USDL-94-600).

Commission on the Future of Worker-Management Relations. 1994a. *Fact-finding Report.* Washington, DC: U.S. Dept. of Labor and U.S. Dept. of Commerce.

_____. 1994b. *Report and Recommendations*. Washington, DC: U.S. Dept. of Labor and U.S. Dept. of Commerce.

Donahue, John J., III, and Peter Siegelman. 1991. "The Changing Nature of Employment Discrimination Litigation." *Stanford Law Review* (May).

Drago, Robert. 1988. "Quality Circle Survival." *Industrial Relations*, Vol. 27 (Fall), pp. 336-51.

Duffy, Shannon P. 1995. "Casellas: EEOC Suffering Backlash." *The Legal Intelligencer*, June 20, p. 1.

Equal Employment Opportunity Commission (EEOC). 1995. *Policy Statement on Alternative Dispute Resolution*. Reprinted in the *Daily Labor Reporter*, July 18, 1995, no. 137.

Freeman, Richard. 1991. "Employee Councils, Worker Participation, and Other Squishy Stuff." *Proceedings of the 43rd Annual Meeting* (Washington, DC). Madison, WI: Industrial Relations Research Association, pp. 328-37.

Freeman, Richard B., and Joel Rogers. 1993. "Who Speaks for Us? Employee Representation in a Nonunion Labor Market." In Bruce E. Kaufman and Morris M. Kleiner, eds., *Employee Representation: Alternatives and Future Directions*, Madison, WI, Industrial Relations Research Association.

General Accounting Office, U.S. (GAO). 1987. *ESOPs: Little Evidence of Effects on Corporate Performance*. Washington, DC: U.S. GAO, GAO-PEMD-88-1.

_____. 1992. "Workplace Safety and Health Programs Show Promise." Testimony before the House Committee on Education and Labor, GAO/T-HRD-92-15.

_____. 1994. *Report on Workplace Regulation*, June.

Glaster, George, Wendy Zimmerman, et al. 1994. *Sandwich Hiring Audit Pilot Program Report*. Washington, DC: Urban Institute.

Goldstein, Joseph. 1995. "Alternatives to High-Cost Litigation." *Cornell Hotel and Restaurant Administration Quarterly*, Vol. 36, no. 1 (February), p. 28 ff.

Gore, Al. 1995. *Common Sense Government*. New York: Random House.

Howard, Philip K. 1994. *The Death of Common Sense*. New York: Random House.

Kochan, Thomas A. 1995. "Using the Dunlop Report to Achieve Mutual Gains." *Industrial Relations*, Vol. 34, no. 3 (July), pp. 350-66.

Kochan, Thomas A., and Paul Osterman. 1994. *The Mutual Gains Enterprise*. Cambridge, MA: Harvard University Press.

Kahn, Shulamit, and Kevin Lang. 1992. "Constraints on the Choice of Hours of Work." *Journal of Human Resources*, Vol. 27, no. 4 (Fall), pp. 661-88.

Kamer, Gregory J., Scott M. Abbot, and Lisa G. Salevitz. 1994. "The New Legal Challenge to Participation." *Labor Law Journal* (January), pp. 41-48.

Levine, David I. 1991. "Just Cause Employment Policies in the Presence of Worker Adverse Selection." *Journal of Labor Economics*, Vol. 9, no. 3.

_____. 1995. *Reinventing the Workplace*. Washington, DC: Brookings Institute.

Lynch, Lisa. 1994. "Payoffs to Alternative Training Strategies at Work." In Richard B. Freeman, ed., *Working under Different Rules*. New York: Sage, pp. 63-96.

Neumark, David. 1995. "Employment Testers in Restaurants."

*New OSHA, The*. 1995. Department of Labor, URL http://www.osha-slc.gov/Reinventing/app_3.html.

*Occupational Safety and Health*. 1993. "Oregon Safety Committees Touted." September, pp. 26-27.

Occupational Safety and Health Administration (OSHA). 1995. "Review and Analysis of State-Mandated and Other Worker Protections Programs," June.

Potter, Edward E., and Judith A. Youngman. 1995. *Keeping America Competitive: Employment Policy for the Twenty-First Century*. Lakewood, CO: Glenbridge.

Quarrey, Michael. 1986. *Employment Ownership and Corporate Performance*. Oakland, CA: National Center for Employee Ownership.

*Regulatory Systems*. 1993. Accompanying Report of the National Performance Review. Washington, DC: Office of the Vice President, September.

Rowe, Mary P. 1990. "People Who Feel Harassed Need a Complaint System with Both Formal and Informal Options." *Negotiations Journal* (January), pp. 1-12

Sockell, Donna. 1984. "The Legality of Employee-Participation Programs in Unionized Firms." *Industrial and Labor Relations Review*, Vol. 37 (July), pp. 541-56.

Steiber, Jack. 1984. "Employment-at-Will: An Issue for the 1980s." *Proceedings of the 36th Annual Meeting* (San Francisco). Madison, WI: Industrial Relations Research Association, pp. 1-13.

Weil, David. 1991. "Enforcing OSHA: The Role of Labor Unions." *Industrial Relations*, Vol. 30, no. 1 (Winter), pp. 20-36.

Weiler, Paul. 1990. *Governing the Workplace: The Future of Labor and Employment Law*. Cambridge, MA: Harvard University Press.

# Chapter 14

# The Role of Management and Competitiveness Strategies in Occupational Safety and Health Standards

Ray Marshall
*University of Texas at Austin*

The basic hypothesis examined in this chapter is that improvements in safety and health have been impeded by deeply entrenched management practices and national economic policies, as well as inadequacies in OSHA's underlying assumptions and implementation.

The absence of reliable data makes it difficult to assess occupational safety and health policy in the United States. There are many reasons for the data inadequacies, including misclassification of industries for reporting purposes; confidentiality problems in collecting official data, which make it difficult to disaggregate; biases in data collection; falsification and underreporting by companies in order to avoid legal sanctions, increased OSHA surveillance, or higher insurance premiums; and failure to properly differentiate occupational safety and health problems from those occurring outside the workplace.

Despite these limitations, the evidence suggests that except for fatalities,[1] there was little improvement in U.S. occupational safety and health between 1984 and 1994. The Dunlop Commission, for example, reported that while fatalities declined, occupational injury rates during this period ranged from 7.6 to 8.7 incidents per 100 full-time workers and lost workday cases ranged from 3.4 to 4.0. Lost workdays per 100 full-time workers were much higher in the early 1990s (over 80) than in the 1970s (55) (CFWMR 1994:22-23, 121-23). And despite data and measurement problems, occupational deaths, injuries and illnesses undoubtedly inflict huge economic losses on the American economy, as well as much unnecessary human suffering and economic hardship on American workers.

The main assumptions of this chapter are:

1. Many occupational deaths, illnesses, and injuries can be prevented in cost-effective ways through state-of-the-art practices available in the United States and other countries.
2. The basic *rationale* for the 1970 Occupational Safety and Health Act (OSHA) is sound, but the act has never lived up to its promise. There are several components of OSHA's rationale:
   - Markets and market incentives will not protect workers' safety and health because employers who maximize short-run profits will shift the costs of injuries and deaths to workers and society. The main factor in the American environment that enables employers to shift these costs is the political and economic power of companies relative to workers. This power stems from weak labor organizations and a strong emphasis in the United States on individualism, private property, and laissez-faire economic policies.
   - OSHA internalizes the costs of occupational safety and health to companies, which are mainly responsible for the problems and thus have the greatest power to prevent them from occurring or to remedy those that do occur. There is almost universal agreement that properly structured preventive processes are the most humane and efficient way to address safety and health problems. We do not know how to cure cancer, but we do know how to prevent workers' on-the-job exposure to carcinogens.
   - OSHA has had limited success in protecting workers' safety and health, and progress seems to have stalled during the 1980s with little improvement seen in the 1990s.
3. A third basic assumption is that the best way to prevent occupational safety and health hazards is to strengthen management practices and internalize prevention to the workplace as much as possible. Indeed, the best predictors of sound safety and health practices are good management and industrial relations practices. Unfortunately, compared with other advanced industrial countries, relatively few American workplaces can be classified as high-performance organizations. The most complete comparative analysis was by the Commission on the Skills of the American Workforce (CSAW), which conducted 2,800 interviews in 560 companies in seven countries. The CSAW concluded that in 1990 only 5% of American companies could be classified as high performance (CSAW 1990). Other evidence confirms this estimate, but suggests that as many as 35% of American companies contain at least some elements of high-performance systems (Osterman 1993; Appelbaum and Batt 1993).

4. A major reason for the relative paucity of high-performance workplaces in the United States is our economic and policy environment which encourages the perpetuation of command-and-control management systems and low-wage economic policies. My basic orienting hypothesis is that measures to encourage companies to adopt a high-value added competitiveness strategy will improve safety and health outcomes, but a continuation of low-wage strategies will perpetuate inefficient processes and poor occupational safety and health outcomes that do not prevent problems and inflict unnecessary costs and suffering on workers, their families, and society.

## An Inadequate Concept

Despite the sound basic rationale of internalizing occupational safety and health costs to employers, the basic assumption for OSHA's implementation is inadequate. OSHA assumes, for example, that workers' safety and health can be protected mainly through safety and health standards and inspections. This approach has several major flaws. First, it is based on the theory that there is one best way to protect the safety and health of workers, that OSHA or company managers know what that is, and that they can develop process standards to protect workers by adapting that "one best way." This problem is particularly serious for numerous process standards that specify how companies should protect workers' safety and health. It is less true of outcome standards that specify minimum exposure levels for carcinogens, for example, and expect labor and management at the workplace to develop the best way to meet the standards. Process standards even create moral hazards, because the parties might assume that following the correct *processes* would prevent serious damage to the safety and health of workers, thus exposing them to catastrophes that are not likely to be prevented by process alone. Rather than being the rule, process standards should be restricted to those extremely hazardous cases where it is too risky to permit the parties to develop their own procedures to achieve desirable outcomes.

It is equally dangerous to assume that catastrophes and serious exposures can be prevented through inspections, because workplace inspections do not necessarily reduce the probability of negative outcomes. There are numerous examples of serious accidents occurring shortly after OSHA inspections. Moreover, there are gross disparities between OSHA's mandate and the resources it is given, or likely to be given, to implement a standards and inspection strategy. In 1995, when OSHA covered 93 million workers in 6.2 million worksites, it had only 1,120 inspectors; the states had another 1,280. At the current rate of inspections, the average worksite would be inspected once every 79 years.

Fines, along with the threat of inspections, are supposed to act as deterrents to violations, but the fines are too small and the penalties too weak to achieve this objective. Since OSHA was enacted, only one employer has been jailed for violating that act. And it is unlikely that OSHA will ever be given either the authority to impose fines high enough to act as deterrents or enough inspectors to succeed with an inspection strategy. Clearly, therefore, standards and inspections are inadequate to protect the safety and health of workers.

Even if OSHA had sufficient inspectors and authority to impose penalties, it is doubtful that this strategy would offer effective protection for workers. A standards-setting process is slow, ineffective for developing industry and firm-specific standards, and would be too punitive, reactive, and adversarial to achieve optimal results. Outcome standards and penalties must be components of effective occupational safety and health strategies but should be complemented by policies that give workers and managers the incentives, knowledge, and power to implement these strategies at the firm and industry levels.

## Administrative Problems

OSHA has been plagued with administrative problems from its inception, partly due to strong business opposition to OSHA. This opposition has led to adversarial relations between companies and their supporters on one side, and unions and safety and health advocates on the other. Adversarial relations make it more difficult to develop the kind of cooperative relationships needed to effectively protect the safety and health of workers—which should be OSHA's basic objective. The conflict surrounding OSHA often causes the parties to focus on the contest rather than on improving safety and health. Conflict also dissipates considerably more resources and energy in litigation than is the case in most other industrial countries. As a Japanese official put it, "When we have a problem we are more likely to hire engineers and hygienists to work it out; you are more likely to hire lawyers and fight it out." Adversarial processes are natural and serve the important function of providing mechanisms for resolving conflict. But when these relationships obscure common interests, they become functionless, making all parties worse off. Adversarial relations impede joint learning and information sharing and waste energy in blame casting. These relationships therefore cause the parties to focus on their differences, however trivial. Consensus processes, by contrast, facilitate information sharing and joint learning because they focus on the parties' common interests. I have found that two rules for effective consensus building are (1) let no one recommend anything until the parties agree on the facts, and (2) avoid blame casting and instead focus on problem solving to improve future outcomes for all parties.

Business opposition to OSHA not only has made it more difficult for OSHA to have adequate budgets but, in the early days, led to characterizations of OSHA designed to diminish public support and weaken the act's effectiveness. Republican-appointed administrators deliberately adopted nonsensical industrial consensus standards that politicians often cited as examples of ridiculous federal regulations. In 1976, for example, Gerald Ford made OSHA a major presidential campaign issue, saying, "We should throw OSHA in the ocean," even though OSHA was signed into law by President Nixon and had been administered by Republicans since its inception. Although the OSHA law was far from perfect, its main problem was in its administration, not in the provisions of the act.

During the 1980s, Republican administrators responded to business pressures by reducing OSHA's funding, weakening its administration, and blocking efforts to develop effective approaches for hazardous industries. A study of occupational safety and health problems in the petrochemical industry in the late 1980s, for which I served as an advisor, illustrates this problem (Wells and Smith 1991). The immediate cause of the study was an explosion at the Phillips 66 chemical complex in Pasadena, Texas, on October 23, 1989, which killed 23 workers and injured 314. This was not, however, an isolated case: in six years, 87 fires, leaks, and explosions in the oil refinery and chemical industry had killed 159 people and injured at least 2,200 others (Selcraig 1992). Ironically, the petrochemical industry was not high on OSHA's list of hazardous industries because official statistics found it to have a good safety record! We learned during the study that because of the use of contractors for the hazardous work in refineries and plants, injuries and accidents were reported in the construction rather than petrochemical industry. The study also revealed very poor statistics, either because records were not kept or because they were highly inaccurate. The main purpose of the study was to examine the impact of contract labor on occupational safety and health in the petrochemical industry, but it also provided a number of insights into the more general problems involved in implementing OSHA. First, it was very clear that contractors contributed to occupational safety and health problems because—except for unionized building trades contractors—they generally were not well trained or familiar with the worksite, factors that are known to contribute to occupational safety and health problems. In addition, petrochemical companies generally refused to take responsibility for either the practices or the safety and health training of contractors. In the one exceptional case where a company exercised unified management control, contract workers received the same training as regular employees, and this was reflected in superior safety and health records.

Another factor involved in the use of contractors was tension between the contractors and regular employees and deteriorating labor-management relations because of companies' increased use of contracting out of plant work in order to lower costs and increase flexibility. Relations were exacerbated by the fact that subcontracting was considered by the main union involved—the Oil, Chemical, and Atomic Workers (OCAW)—to be part of a union avoidance strategy. The worsening of labor relations reduced the effectiveness of safety and health programs in union plants. This was so because the use of contractors, cost-cutting strategies, and company emphasis on meeting production schedules caused the OCAW to distrust management motives. These conflicts reduced the parties' ability to cooperate on occupational safety and health matters. The union's mistrust even caused the OCAW to withdraw from the study's advisory committee, fearing that the project could not produce valid information because of management's hostility to the study as well as its attempts to use political influence with the Bush administration to weaken it.

Occupational safety and health programs in union companies were good, but because of adversarial relations, they were not as good as they could have been if the relationships had been more cooperative. Indeed, the best safety and health program, in the opinion of researchers and as measured by safety and health statistics, was in a nonunion company that integrated contractors into the company's training program and assumed full responsibility for the safety and health of all employees. Because the company considered prevention to be a sound business strategy, it had an exemplary, preventive safety and health program. The study also found that training in most companies resulted in lower injury rates for regular employees but not for contract employees.

Despite the effort by the OSHA-funded study group to work closely with industry and union representatives, industry representatives prevailed upon the Bush administration to try to prevent the study from being undertaken or published. The administration assigned a 25-year-old Republican campaign worker who had no OSHA experience and had formerly worked for a nonunion contractor to oversee the project for OSHA. The OMB sought to impose unrealistic requirements on the study and the OSHA representative assigned by the industry instigated an audit of the project, apparently for harassment purposes, which found nothing improper (Selcraig 1992:67). This study was completed and published mainly because of the tenacity of its director, John Calhoun Wells, director of the Federal Mediation and Conciliation Service in the Clinton administration, and close congressional oversight of the whole affair.

## Management Practices and Safety and Health Outcomes

There is fairly consistent evidence (which my experience confirms) that sound management practices are the best predictors of good occupational safety and health outcomes. Companies with the best occupational safety and health practices are likely to be well-managed enterprises that consider preventive safety and health programs sound investments yielding high returns, especially when embedded in effective management systems. The characteristics of well-managed companies that improve safety and health performance include lean, decentralized, participative management systems that include safety and health programs and give high priority to preventive safety and health practices, as well as to product quality, productivity, and flexibility; positive incentives for all workers and safety and health practices embedded in management reward systems; leading-edge technology that eliminates or "engineers out" occupational safety and health hazards; and continuous education and training for front-line workers, including safety and health training as an integral component of training.

Unfortunately, very few American companies can be classified as high performance (CSAW 1990). The Tayloristic organization of work that still characterizes most major American companies has components that discourage effective safety and health programs: they tend to be authoritarian command-and-control systems that give workers little responsibility for decision making about safety and health or other workplace activities; they stress short-term profit-maximizing processes that encourage them to attempt to shift the costs of safety and health to workers and society in order to minimize costs; if they are nonunion, they are likely to avoid giving workers effective participation in decision making; if unionized, the relationship is likely to be adversarial, which could diminish the effectiveness of safety and health processes; they give very little attention to the education and training of front-line workers, and as noted earlier, training is likely to be an effective determinant of positive safety and health outcomes; and they are likely to stress standardized (not leading-edge) technology, which is less likely to engineer out safety and health hazards.

## Economic Policies

Many aspects of U.S. economic policy tend to discourage the kind of high-performance management systems most likely to stress preventive safety and health processes: we provide workers very limited voice at work (Marshall 1987); our schools still educate mainly for mass production, not high-performance systems, and therefore do not provide most students with adequate thinking and learning skills; we do not have a very effective system to provide job training for workers who are not college bound (Marshall and Tucker 1992); we have weaker income support systems than most other industrial countries; and we are more likely to develop economic strategies that create incentives for low-wage strategies rather than encouraging companies to organize for high performance. Without strategies, we will automatically follow low-wage, cost-cutting strategies like those that aggravated the safety and health problems of the petrochemical industry in the 1980s.

The clash between standards to protect safety and health and economic policy is most apparent in international transactions, where bad standards can give companies an economic advantage and therefore drive out good standards. International transactions also clarify the relationships between labor standards and basic competitiveness policies. I say clarify because the same rationale applies to domestic as well as to international labor standards. Countries, individuals, states, or companies have two basic competitiveness choices: they can stress costs, mainly wages, or value-added. The cost-cutting strategy not only creates a bias against the maintenance of labor standards like occupational safety and health but also implies lower and more unequal wages—which is what most workers in the United States have experienced since the 1970s (Mishel and Bernstein 1994)—and also limits economic progress to working harder and using more physical resources, which also has been the U.S. experience since the 1970s. This choice is clearly self-limiting—there is a limit to how hard workers can work. A high-value-added strategy, by contrast, places greater emphasis on human resources and high-performance organizations, which is basically the substitution of ideas, skills, and knowledge for labor and physical resources. The high-value-added strategy therefore creates a bias for occupational safety and health standards as a way to reduce the long-run costs of worker protections through prevention measures.

High-value-added strategies therefore will embed occupational safety and health and other standards in international economic agreements, as the United States did with the North American Free Trade Agreement (NAFTA) and all other trade compacts during the 1980s. And in the Maastricht Agreement, the European Union has articulated a stronger rationale for a high-standards approach than that embodied in NAFTA. The basic rationale for trade-linked labor standards is to achieve equity and efficiency (Marshall 1994). Equity is achieved by a policy to close the gap between labor standards by raising the lower standards in developed and developing countries, not, as would be the case in a purely market-driven system, by reducing the higher standards. Efficiency is achieved by labor standards because they force companies to compete by increasing productivity and quality, not by reducing labor standards. By stressing high performance, the high-value-added strategy can create much steeper learning and earning curves.

Those who reject trade-linked labor standards frequently argue that trade automatically brings economic development which will improve labor standards. There is, of course, some merit to this "trickle down" approach to improving labor standards, but not much. It is true that economic development can provide more resources for occupational safety and health protections. But there is very little evidence that a laissez-faire, "trickle down" approach to labor standards will improve occupational safety and health and other standards in a reasonable time frame. The danger with the laissez-faire, low-standards option is that it can lead to degenerating systems or a "race to the bottom" with labor standards. There is, moreover, growing evidence that more equitable, bottom-up "shared growth" strategies like those followed in East Asia can lead to faster, equitably shared development and are therefore more sustainable (World Bank 1993; Marshall 1995). However, these strategies must be comprehensive in the sense of combining economic policies to increase the demand for skilled workers, human resource development programs, shared growth, and labor standards.

Some critics also believe that competitiveness strategies are incompatible with market forces, but a strong case can be made that market-friendly strategies improve market outcomes, which is essentially what drove East Asian industrial policies. It is not only naive but a misreading of the record to assume that industrial upgrading will take place without strategies to complement market forces. Indeed, it seems fairly clear that in the current economic climate, market forces alone will produce the low-wage outcome. In the occupational safety and health context, a market-friendly approach would set high outcome standards and leave it to the parties in the workplace to achieve the best outcomes. The alternative is a command-and-control approach typical of Tayloristic bureaucracies, which assume there is "one best way" to achieve an objective and mandate the methods and processes to achieve those objectives.

There is strong evidence that firms can find more cost-effective ways to meet standards than those specified by OSHA. This happened, for example, with OSHA's vinyl chloride and cotton dust standards with which I was involved, where the actual costs of implementation were much lower than either OSHA or the standards' opponents estimated in advance (Boroush 1993). For example, the study commissioned by OSHA stated unequivocally that a 1 part per million (ppm) permissible exposure level (PEL) for polyvinyl chloride (PVC) was simply not reachable with present technology and it would take many years to develop the necessary technology. However, most of the industry complied within eighteen months. Moreover, the actual cost of the vinyl chloride standard was only about a quarter of that estimated by the company commissioned by OSHA—or $243 million (1974 dollars) compared with the estimate of $1.1 billion. Similarly, a study commissioned by the Society for the Plastics Industry predicted that the standard would lead to a complete shutdown of the industry and a projected production loss of $65 to $90 billion (in 1974 dollars) and a loss of between 1.7 and 2.2 million jobs. The actual outcome was to strengthen the industry, not to weaken it as this dire forecast predicted.

The June 1978 cotton dust standard had similar dire predictions but actual positive outcomes for the industry. OSHA's final estimate of the cost of this standard was $820 million in capital costs (1982 dollars) or about $280 million a year; actual total costs were $245 million or almost $83 million a year. The impact on the industry of implementing the standard, which practically eliminated exposure to the very serious respiratory problem of "brown lung," was therefore a modest increase in textile prices of 0.3%, which was easily passed on to consumers. The improvement in productivity induced by the standard helped this part of the American textile industry become net exporters.

## Conclusions

OSHA has caused American workplaces to be more conscious of occupational safety and health hazards and undoubtedly has contributed to the long-run decline in occupational fatalities and occupational safety and health hazards. However, there is clearly room for better performance. And there has not been much improvement in the injury and health outcomes since the early 1980s.

Measures that might enhance OSHA's performance include:

1. Build consensus for a sustainable, high-value-added strategy that would give high priority to preventing safety and health problems. A sustainable strategy would internalize the costs of safety and health, as well as environmental protections, to the enterprise and would embed safety, health, and environmental standards in international economic agreements as well as in domestic labor laws. Such standards would enhance efficiency, equity, and sustainability.

2. With respect to OSHA:
   - Develop a preventive strategy that would induce as much self-regulation as possible. Process standards might be required in some cases where the risks are too great to rely exclusively on outcome standards, but a preventive strategy would have a bias against process standards in favor of allowing workers and managers to develop their own strategies to meet the standards. Such an approach clearly requires more trust between workers, managers, and government than currently exists.
   - Encourage the establishment of tripartite or bipartite industry occupational safety and health committees to develop comprehensive industry-specific occupational safety and health standards.

- Improve data collection. We are not likely to develop sound preventive strategies or adequate responses to occupational safety and health hazards without much more accurate data to identify problems, evaluate the outcomes of various interventions, and develop preventive measures, as well as responses to catastrophes. Adequate data require that all problems be reported—near misses and minor injuries as well as fatalities and serious injuries.

3. Encourage research and development to identify, model, and diffuse best practices by tripartite industry committees or bipartite committees working with OSHA.

4. Require joint labor-management safety and health committees. The evidence accumulated by the Dunlop Commission and others demonstrates that properly structured, joint safety and health committees can improve safety and health performance (CFWMR 1994:22-23, 122-23). The committees should give workers and managers the power to address safety and health problems in their workplace and to maintain complete and accurate safety and health data. Joint committees might ensure more accurate data than are likely if data are maintained by people and organizations with strong motives to falsify or underreport. The Dunlop Commission found that "the most effective [Joint Safety and Health Committee] programs offer technical training to committee members, have regularly scheduled meetings and well-defined internal procedures and responsibilities, conduct periodic on-site inspections to monitor compliance with safety regulations, and recommend (and usually secure) improvements in employee practices and equipment to avoid identifiable hazards. The best such committees are integrated with other employee participation and quality programs" (CFWMR 1994:122).

5. Develop safety and health training standards. There is abundant evidence that training helps give workers and managers the knowledge to prevent safety and health problems. Training standards might be coupled with a reintroduction of the New Directions Project developed by the Carter administration to fund research at universities and nonprofit organizations to strengthen occupational safety and health education and training.

6. Make it clear that plant managers have the legal responsibility for safety and health of all workers at the worksite, contract workers as well as permanent employees.

7. Strengthen enforcement as a component of a preventive strategy designed to give workers and managers in the workplace the knowledge, power, and incentives to understand and address their own health and safety hazards. OSHA resources should be used to strengthen industry and company safety and health practices and to target the most recalcitrant companies and worst cases.[2]

## Endnotes

[1] The National Safety Council reports 8,500 workers killed in 1992, down from 13,800 in 1970 and 14,300 in 1993 (Linder 1994:114). However, the BLS reports 6,083 "fatalities due to work injuries in 1992; about one-third of the fatalities from work injuries in 1992 resulted from highway accidents (18%) or homicides (17%). The highest fatality rates (per 100,000 workers) were in mining (27), agriculture (24), construction (14), and transportation and public utilities (13). The national average fatality rate was 5. Occupations with the highest fatality rates were forestry and logging (42), taxicab drivers (56), and construction laborers (34). Persons with fatality rates above the national average were self-employed and family members working in businesses (46), and workers 65 years of age or older (13).

[2] The Dunlop Commission recommended program elements for an effective joint safety and health program. These elements are similar to a workplace safety and health standard and includes: designation of responsibility, identification of hazards, setting priorities, safety rules and procedures, periodic internal inspection, accident investigations, safety and health training and communications, accident recordkeeping, first aid and medical care, and emergency preparedness care (CFWMR 1994:56).

## References

Appelbaum, Eileen, and Rosemary Batt. 1993. *High Performance Work Systems*. Washington, DC: Economic Policy Institute.

Boroush, M. A. 1993. "Forecasts versus Actual Outcomes: Three Historical Cases of OSHA Rulemaking." OTA Project Working Paper (May 3). Washington, DC: Office of Technical Assessment.

Commission on the Future of Worker-Management Relations (CFWMR). 1994. *Fact Finding Report*. Washington, DC: GPO.

Commission on the Skills of the American Workforce (CSAW). 1990. *America's Choice: High Skills or Low Wages!* Rochester, NY: National Center on Education and the Economy.

Linder, Marc. 1994. "Fatal Subtraction: Statistical MIAs on the Industrial Battlefield." *Journal of Legislation* (Notre Dame Law School), Vol. 20, no. 4.

Marshall, Ray. 1987. *Unheard Voices: Labor and Economic Policy in a Competitive World*. New York: Basic Books.

_____. 1994. "Importance of International Labor Standards in a More Competitive Global Economy." In Werner Sengenberger and Duncan Campbell, eds., *International Labor Standards and Economic Interdependence*. Geneva: International Institute for Labor Studies, pp. 65-79.

_____. 1995. "The Global Jobs Crisis." *Foreign Policy*, No. 100 (Fall), pp. 50-68.

Marshall, Ray, and Marc Tucker. 1992. *Thinking for a Living: Education and the Wealth of Nations*. New York: Basic Books.

Mishel, Lawrence, and Jared Bernstein. 1994. *The State of Working America 1994-95*. Armonk, NY: M.E. Sharpe.

Osterman, Paul. 1993. "How Common is Workforce Transformation and How Can We Explain Who Adopts It? Paper presented at Allied Social Science Association Meeting, Anaheim, California, January.

Selcraig, Bruce. 1992. "Bad Chemistry: How Reaganomics Has Fueled Plant Explosions." *Harper's Magazine* (April), pp. 62-68.

Wells, John Calhoun, and Michel Smith. 1991. *Managing Workplace Safety and Health: The Case of Contract Labor in the U.S. Petrochemical Industry*. Final Report to OSHA, USDL. Beaumont, Texas: John Gray Institute, Lamar University.

World Bank. 1993. *The East Asian Miracle: Economic Growth and Public Policy*. New York: Oxford University Press.

# Chapter 15

# The Myth of Deregulation in a Common Law System: Feudal Dreams

Robert J. Pleasure
*AFL-CIO*

Patricia A. Greenfield
*University of Massachusetts–Amherst*

> This is the Court of Chancery, . . . which gives to monied might the means abundantly of wearying out the right, which so exhausts finances, patience, courage, hope, so overthrows the brain and breaks the heart, that there is not an honorable man among its practitioners who would not give—who does not often give—the warning, "Suffer any wrong that can be done you rather than come here!"
> (Charles Dickens, *Bleak House*)

In common law countries like the U.S., Canada, England, and Australia, in the absence of legislation, disputed public and private matters are determined in courts through reference to precedent created by prior decisions of the courts. In the same countries, in the absence of legislation, regulation, or adequate common law remedies, disputed matters are decided in courts by reference to principles of equity (these remedies were originally available in special courts of equity or chancery and now are available in courts of general jurisdiction). Common law and equitable remedies have been used to regulate employment relations. For over eight hundred years common law and equity have been and will continue to be used whenever a vacuum is created by the absence or repeal of legislation and other forms of contemporary regulation.

Old common law and equitable principles pertaining to employment are to this day generally indexed under the heading "The Law of Master and Servant." This set of rules is not unfamiliar to students of industrial relations. A common equitable remedy is the labor injunction, and a well-known common law principle is the employment-at-will doctrine, which establishes the doctrine that in the absence of a contract, a worker can be fired for good reason, bad reason, or no reason. Although this rule has been modified by a number of state courts, it still exists as the basic rule in the United States. Dickens' world, described in *Bleak House*, was not an unregulated environment. He lived in a highly regulated world in which status in employment relationships were quite clearly prescribed.

John R. Commons' *The Legal Foundations of Capitalism* is an early American critique of the impact of the common law on employment, uncovering its bias against workers. Bruce Kaufman's survey of the ideas of the "old institutional economics" demonstrates the impact of that school of thought on modern employment regulation and its contribution to broad acceptance of government roles in social insurance, wage-hour, and safety regulation through legislation. Kaufman reminds us of the significant contribution made by Commons to the discussion of the role of modern legislative regulation. Like Senator Robert Wagner's observations a decade later as he authored and advocated for the passage of the National Labor Relations Act, Commons saw the real-life impact of laissez-faire capitalism and the dominance of capital's unilateral power on the lives of working people and the quality of society.

Commons and Wagner also shared another insight, often forgotten in today's debates over repeal of various forms of labor and employment regulation. It was their knowledge—from history, from law, and from experience—that the absence of statutory regulation did not mean the lack of legal regulation or the absence of state intervention in the employment relationship. In the absence of statutory regulation, they were well aware that the law of master and servant ruled. In fact, Atleson (1984) and others have made a persuasive argument that the law of master and servant is so powerful that its rules and accompanying assumptions survived the enactment of the National Labor Relations Act.

Underlying the call for repeal of various forms of labor and employment regulation is the assumption that the repeal of federal law accomplishes full deregulation—government is then out of the picture and the "market" rules. Conservative beliefs about deregulation constitute a replay of a very old debate among legal scholars. In the legal realm, proponents of deregulation essentially advance a notion that in the absence of statutory regulation (known as "public law"), the full range of private choice is realized and that private law litigation, i.e., litigation based not on a statute but on judicially created common law, does not involve an incident of state intervention and choice. Further, apart from pervasive common law rulings which fill voids, repeal of federal labor legislation uncovers otherwise preempted and often long-dormant state legislation.

The legal realists of the 1920s and 1930s, including Benjamin Cardozo and Karl Llewellyn, successfully challenged the notion that there was a sharp distinction between public and private law. Mensch (1982) cites Cohen's 1927 essay "Property and Sovereignty," in which he noted that property, traditionally assumed to be in the realm of private law rights, is in fact public, not private:

> Property means the legally granted power to withhold from others; as such it is created by the state and given its only content by legal decisions that limit or extend the property owner's power over others. Thus, property is really an (always conditional) delegation of sovereignty, and property law is simply a form of public law. Whereas the [pre-realist theorists] had drawn a bright line separating (private) property from (public) sovereignty, Cohen simply collapsed the two categories. (Mensch 1982:29)

Thus the legal realists argued that every decision involved moral and political choices and the implementation of ideology on either one side or another. Similarly, from his vantage point in the world of industrial relations, John R. Commons noted that the "lawgiver," be it judge or legislature, chooses between customs and lends the power of the state to the customs it deems "good" and penalizes those perceived by the lawgiver as "bad." And as a student and observer of the judicial decisions of the late 19th and early 20th century prior to the growth of public law in the 1930s, Commons noted that "it is the judge who believes in the law and custom of business and not the judge who believes in the law and custom of labor, that decides" (Commons 1959:298-300).

The historical evidence is clear and uncontrovertible. The National Labor Relations Act of 1935 was not the first time the labor and employment relationship had been regulated in this country. Even a casual student of U.S. labor history is well aware of government control over and intervention into the labor-management relationship that was not based on statutory or administrative law. From early in this country's history, workers' attempts to combine in order to use their economic strength to obtain higher wages from their employer were met with employer appeals to state and local courts. Until 1844, when the landmark Massachusetts case of *Commonwealth v. Hunt* turned the judicial tide, the courts regularly ruled that unions were illegal conspiracies. In 1917 the U.S. Supreme Court, basing its *Hitchman* decision on, among other justifications, the common law of contracts, ruled that "yellow dog contracts" (documents workers signed as a condition of employment guaranteeing that they would never join a union) were legal. Throughout the 19th and early 20th century, the courts regularly intervened in the labor-management relationship, issuing injunctions which enabled the executive branch on state and federal levels to send troops in to break strikes. It was only after statutory regulation in the form of the Norris-LaGuardia Act on the federal level followed by "little" Norris-LaGuardia Acts on the state level that the state stopped some of this sort of intervention.

In addition to the historical and legal theory aspects of the debate, we can also examine and critique the challenge to regulation from a process perspective. The federal Administrative Procedure Act of 1946, which "ushered in the modern era of administrative law" (Pierce et al. 1985:34) and is the basic federal regulation governing administrative law, sets up two decision-making processes: adjudication and rule making. Rule making by an administrative agency created by statute is conducted in the manner of a legislative hearing. Persons and institutions having an interest appear, usually through written submissions, but sometimes through oral testimony. Participation is not restricted to parties as in a controversy. Rather, participation is generally open in the manner of a legislative fact finding and the open solicitation of the views of the public is characteristic of rule making. The APA requires advance notice of a proposed rule prior to final rule making. The final rule must be published with a statement of purpose in order to provide the basis for judicial review. Adjudication by an administrative agency under the APA is conducted in the manner of a case or controversy in a court. Participation is restricted to parties having an interest in the particular case, and the record is adduced through testimony, documents, and the opportunity for cross examination. Unless otherwise restricted by statute, administrative agencies may choose to use either rule making, adjudication, or both to implement the enabling legislation.

Both processes are legitimate and are available for the implementation of legislatively enacted administrative laws. Each has advantages and disadvantages as governmental instruments. Adjudication is more flexible but less predictable than rule making; it often leaves out important stakeholders who do have a place in the development of rules and the original legislation. If one were to strip away all administrative law, you would still be left with adjudication in the courts, but the social norms adjudicated would be those based in private, or common, law and principles in equity. All the existing disadvantages of adjudication would still be present: unpredictability; the exclusion of important stakeholders; a slow, expensive process with decisions often made by inexpert decision makers. Why should we so disable our system in a manner that leaves adjudication as our only option?

Again, the critics of regulation reply with a set of arguments and assumptions, many of which are based upon a fundamental belief in the value and power of the market in effectuating private needs and choice. As we examine the current-day arguments for some significant degree of deregulation of the labor and employment law system in the United States, we see a number of assumptions presented as self-evident in this debate, many of which appear throughout this volume without any empirical support. Some of these assumptions are (1) firms vary infinitely in their character, purposes, and internal culture, and therefore, employment standards should vary to sustain the unique quality of each firm; (2) worker interests are contiguous with the interests of each individual employer, so it is inefficient and self-defeating for workers and their organizations to seek to maintain interfirm standards through collective bargaining, legislative enactment, and regulation; (3) the monopsony power of employers can be limited through their motivation to retain and encourage a loyal work force; (4) workers and their organizations can and should be persuaded to abandon maintenance of minimum employment standards with the alternative of firm-by-firm participation in creating unique and somehow more "appropriate" minima in each workplace; (5) the adoption of minimum employment standards (including safety and health regulation) is characteristic of "command and control" societies; and (6) the maintenance of employment standards across firms is monopolistic behavior and therefore should be limited by regulation!

The ideology reflected by these assumptions is a part of a very old American conservative tradition merely dressed up in new clothes. This approach purports to set the market free of regulation. The problems with an unrestricted free market are well argued elsewhere, most recently by Kuttner (1996). Most importantly, infinite variety in employment standards equals unilateral employer choice within each workplace. It is unnecessary to detail in this piece all the examples of the results of the impact of such unrestrained choice on workers for people to understand why unions and much of the American public want minimum standards which provide basic protections for individual workers and from which unions can negotiate even stronger protection in the collective bargaining agreement.

Regulation which establishes minimum standards is necessary because in our social, moral, and economic systems there needs to be a counterbalance to unregulated employer power. This need has, in fact, been recognized in one area of the common law where the courts have moved over the last 25 years to limit the scope of the employment-at-will rule, preventing employers in a number of circumstances from unilaterally dismissing workers for bad reason or no reason.

As the employment-at-will rule and its evolution illustrates, and as we have discussed above, in our common-law-based system there is no such thing as an unregulated free market in the area of labor and employment. Present-day proponents of deregulation are either naive about the common law or disingenuous about its impact. Without statutory regulation, employers maintain the upper hand, and their power advantage is generally backed up by the common law. Any attempt to try to equalize power through the organization of workers who then attempt to establish standards in collective bargaining or through statutory regulation is perceived as monopolistic, but that is not the case. As Willard Wirtz said about the NLRB's decisions in the area of employer speech,

> The cliche thinking about "equality" has caused perhaps the greatest difficulty here. . . . There is so much appeal in the warm language about treating employers and employees alike, letting them both say whatever they want to in their own promises, serving up a common sauce for goose and gander. It is hard, on the other hand, to persuade by the more intricate logic that the equal treatment of unequals produces only inequality. Denial that the rich and poor take equal advantage either from the right to beg or from tax exemptions on oil wells invariably invites more suspicion than understanding. (Wirtz, quoted in Gross 1985)

Far from the notion that the American public wants to reject or limit the scope of employment regulation, legislative bodies on federal, state, and local levels have most recently supported increased regulatory protection of workers and the need to establish higher minima in employment standards. Congressional bipartisan action in raising the minimum wage illustrates the societal desire and pressure for higher standards in the employment relationship than provided by either employers or the current regulatory environment. Going beyond the minimum wage, Baltimore and other municipalities have passed a living wage ordinance which requires employers to pay a minimum combination of wages and fringe benefits to achieve better than poverty conditions. Montana has a statute prohibiting employers from discharging workers without "good cause." Los Angeles and Washington, DC, have enacted worker retention laws requiring successor employers to retain the predecessor's work force (McCracken 1996).

Throughout the U.S., popular initiatives like these are being proposed and are passing, creating exciting experiments in the scope and impact of positive law and its power to change society for the better. At the very same time, opponents of a modern law of employment and labor relations would have labor go to the common law courts rather than the legislature. It is unlikely that the American public wants labor to go there any more than Charles Dickens wanted to go to the world of Bleak House.

## References

Atleson, James B. 1983. *Values and Assumptions in American Labor Law*. Amherst: University of Massachusetts Press.

Administrative Procedure Act of 1946, 60 Stat. 237, as amended at 5 U.S.C. Sec. 551-559.

Commons, John R. [1924] 1957. *The Legal Foundations of Capitalism*. Reprint. Madison, WI: The University of Wisconsin Press.

*Commonwealth v. Hunt*, 45 Mass 111 (1842).

Dickens, Charles. [1852] 1980. *Bleak House*. Reprint. New York: Penguin Press, p. 19.

Gross, James A. 1985. "Conflicting Statutory Purposes: Another Look at Fifty Years of NLRB Law Making." *Industrial and Labor Relations Review*, Vol. 39, no. 1, pp. 7-18.

*Hitchman Coal and Coke Co. v. Mitchell*, 245 U.S. 229 (1917).

Kuttner, Robert. 1997. *Everything for Sale: The Virtues and Limits of Markets*. New York: Knopf.

McCracken, Richard G. 1996. "Making State and Local Laws." Unpublished paper presented at the 1996 Lawyer's Coordinating Committee Conference, San Francisco, California.

Mensch, Elizabeth. 1982. "The History of Mainstream Legal Thought." In David Kairys, ed., *The Politics of Law: A Progressive Critique*. New York: Pantheon Books, pp. 18-39.

Pierce, Richard J., Jr., Sidney A. Shapiro, and Paul R. Verkuil. 1985. *Administrative Law and Process*. Mineola, NY: The Foundation Press.

# Chapter 16

# The Choice Is Simple: A Strong Independent Labor Movement or Federal Government Regulation

Thomas J. Schneider
*Restructuring Associates, Inc.*

The restructuring of the world economy has precipitated a restructuring in the workplaces of America, which in turn has generated calls for rethinking the system of laws regulating the workplace and the employment relationship. Examination of the current system of laws in the context of today's economy and future trends clearly reveals serious dysfunctional and suboptimal behaviors. Addressing these problems, however, requires coming to grips with and, as a society, reaching agreement on the fundamental objectives or desired outcomes of the regulatory system.

Sorting through the thicket of charges and countercharges in the debate over workplace regulation requires identifying what are real and pervasive problems in the economy and workplace and what are apparent or limited problems. In addition, the problems must be analyzed to determine whether they can be solved or whether they are caused by forces that can, at best, be managed over the long term.

We must remember that society, the economy, and the workplace, moreover, are all systems and are part of a larger worldwide system; the parts are interdependent. Changing one part has consequences for the other parts; therefore trying to remedy a problem in one area or trying to achieve a particular outcome requires addressing many different elements of the system simultaneously and recognizing the possibility of unanticipated consequences.

Finally, because we are not dealing with closed systems,[1] many of the problems we face may be caused by forces beyond the control of the U.S. government. In which case we must decide as a society how much cost we are willing to bear in order to ameliorate the consequences of the problem.

## Trends

Fundamental changes are transforming the world economic order and all of the parts therein. These changes first clearly appeared in the U.S. economy in the 1970s. The full impact of the changes was felt across the economy in the 1980s. Today, the dimensions of the changes are understood, and the long-term challenges that they pose for individuals, companies, unions, and the country as a whole are clear.

Successful strategies have emerged to meet some of the challenges, but tremendous anxiety and dislocation are rife throughout the U.S. economy, and many of the challenges and problems remain unsolved. New problems and consequences of the changing economic order are also appearing.

An analysis of government regulation of the workplace and the employment relationship must begin with an understanding of the changing economic order. Five basic trends are occurring in the economy that are driving the restructuring of companies, unions, and individuals' lives. All of the trends are beyond the control of the enterprise and individual governments. The trends are: (1) globalization of the economy, (2) the technological revolution, (3) deregulation of economic activity, (4) excess capacity and supply of basic goods, and (5) changing demographics and attitudes of people.

Together these trends confront individual economic units with ferocious competition from all directions and constant change. Analysis of the trends reveals a long-term—at least twenty-five to thirty years, if not forever—impact; there is no end in sight for the relentless competition and constant change. Understanding the trends explains the challenges facing employers and employees and frames the context for the regulatory system. In short, we are witnessing a continuous shift of resources and jobs from declining to expanding industries. Joseph Schumpeter described the process as "creative destruction." We have seen the process before with the advent of steam power, then railways, then electric power, and then the car (cheap oil).

The net result of these changes has been a sustained growth in the standard of living, quality of life, and overall employment. While the types of jobs offered, the location of the jobs, and the nature of the firms offering jobs have changed, the growth and benefits of the restructuring are clear. The process producing these benefits is far from painless and instantaneous. There are lags between the loss of old jobs and the creation of new ones, as well as mismatches between the skills required for the old jobs and their location and those required for new jobs.

One consequence of this employment shakeout is the call for government action. The call comes from all directions and makes contradictory demands. Some people call for the government to protect employees from market forces by limiting competition (e.g., restricting imports) or by insulating employees from market pressures by increasing regulatory protections (e.g., raising minimum wages, making terminations more difficult, limiting the right

to replace strikers) or by compensating employees when they suffer dislocation (e.g., extended unemployment benefits, trade displacement subsidies, job
retraining assistance). Others call for the government to facilitate the restructuring by reducing barriers to change (e.g., the Teamwork for Employees and
Management Act [TEAM Act] vetoed by President Clinton) and reducing the
costs and limitations on change (e.g., changing rules on computing base rates
in a performance-based pay system and overtime pay requirements); an unfettered marketplace with a highly flexible, mobile labor force is seen as key to
competing successfully in this dynamic, competitive world.

## The Interests in Regulating the Employment Relationship

The questions we face in light of this new world and the challenges it
poses concern the appropriate amount and type of regulation of the employment relationship. I believe an interest-based "gap" analysis can help provide
the answers. I do not have enough space here to fully use such an analysis, but
it is useful to frame the analysis in the context of satisfying interests.

Over the long term, the interests of society seem to be (1) a higher standard
of living for all its citizens (greater wealth), (2) the full exercise of the rights and
responsibilities delineated in the Declaration of Independence and Constitution, and (3) a more advanced civilization (the apex of human achievement).

The means to achieve these objectives are the source of different short-
term interests that must be satisfied. Some argue that economic growth is the
crucial engine to achieve the long-term interests of society. Others focus on
the rights and rising standards of civilization as either the critical forces or the
essence of society—without the free exercise of the rights and the higher
standard of civilization, wealth creation is worthless; wealth creation is merely
a means to achieving a freer, higher level of civilization.

Within this context, I believe that the proper governmental regulatory system should try to satisfy the following specific interests[2]: (1) maximize aggregate social wealth creation (economic competitiveness), (2) maximize labor
market efficiency (flexibility and mobility), (3) maximize productivity
improvements, (4) maximize individual freedom and choice, (5) maximize private or market-based decision making rather than public or government, (6)
protect individual rights, (7) maintain and improve social standards at a world-
class level (higher quality of life), and (8) maintain a strong independent labor
movement. I believe that only two interests need specific comment—protecting individual rights and maintaining a strong independent labor movement.

Individual rights are at the heart of the American experiment. So fundamental are individual rights in our society that our founding fathers preserved
many of the rights by adding them to the Constitution in the form of the Bill

of Rights. These rights have been supplemented and clarified over the years through amendment and Supreme Court decisions. Our founding fathers saw the need to add the Bill of Rights because they understood the threat of the majority to these essential rights. I believe that the civil rights and discrimination laws of this country (for example, the Civil Rights Act of 1964, as amended, and the Americans with Disabilities Act) are directly rooted in the First and Fourteenth Amendments and consequently rise to a higher level of societal interest. Although these laws regulate the workplace and the employment relationship, the compelling interest of society in preventing discrimination precludes letting private parties set the standards in this area. The poor history of employers and unions on these matters demonstrates the wisdom of our founding fathers about the tyranny of the majority and the need for the State to protect the rights of the individual. Some rights, therefore, require government regulation and cannot be left to the private parties to work out.

## A Strong Independent Labor Movement Is Needed

For many types of problems, however, private regulation is preferable to government regulation. The threshold question, therefore, is where to draw this line. For this to be a meaningful choice, a strong labor movement is imperative. Without one, the government must intercede and set the standards and rules, self-policing is a hoax, and economic interests will produce a race to the bottom among employers. History clearly demonstrates that the market does not set high standards for socially desirable behavior. One needs only to look at the current controversy about obscene and violent lyrics in contemporary music and movies; profit maximization is the yardstick of the market.

From the 1930s through the early 1970s, employees and management regulated the employment relationship through the collective bargaining process. Unions negotiated higher standards over time, and other companies within the same industry or community tended to adopt similar standards. Thus private regulation wound up creating the rules governing the employment relationship for society.

Organized labor's role has grown more difficult as its position in the economy has shrunk. If organized labor is truly going to act as a nongovernmental regulator, it must have sufficient weight. The existing labor law regulatory system has steadily and subtly shifted toward management so as to make union organizing very difficult. This must be remedied if we hope to rely on the bargaining table to negotiate workplace regulations rather than the halls of Congress.

The decline of organized labor that we have seen over the last twenty-five years, not surprisingly, has corresponded with society turning to the government to regulate the employment relationship. This, however, is contrary to the interests outlined above. Those interests are best maximized when the private parties closest to the market develop their own appropriate standards regulating the workplace. At the same time, in order for the individuals' interests and rights to be protected and for standards to rise commensurate with the rise of civilization, management power must be balanced.

For the private sector to set appropriate standards for issues such as plant closings and family leave, unions need to be far more pervasive in the economy than they have been in the last twenty years. Many significant sectors of the economy need the influence of union negotiations to set a labor market standard. However, the majority of businesses do not need to be organized for union standards to dominate. Unions simply need to have a critical mass in the economy in order for them to substantially affect the labor market standard. The experience of countries such as Canada and Australia indicates that a 30% market share should be sufficient.[3] With a higher level of labor market penetration, all of the businesses subject to the ripple effect of union negotiations will provide comparable benefits and work conditions in order to stay competitive in the labor market or to avoid unionization. When union presence is de minimus, as it is today in large parts of the economy, then management is free to set its own standards and the government must act if society wants to raise standards.

The regulatory system, therefore, should start by promoting and facilitating the growth of the labor movement. Without the private sector checks and balances of organized labor, government regulation is essential to protect individuals and raise standards. The rigidities and ill fit of those regulations (one rule does not fit all) will detract from maximizing many of the interests identified above.

## Unions Are Not Barriers to Change

Unions are often seen as inflexible and slow to change. The organizational changes proposed by companies in the 1980s and 1990s in response to the marketplace were often fiercely resisted by unions. Unions were seen as protecting wages, benefits, and rights that had been granted by companies over many years but which were inconsistent with current competitive challenges. Unions were seen as out of touch and barriers to change.

Close examination, however, reveals that this picture is only partially true and grossly distorts reality. Unions have resisted changes that took away hard-earned benefits when they saw no cuts by management and received nothing in return. What unions primarily saw was management trying to squeeze cost savings out of the workers without making comparable sacrifice or change.

Furthermore, while workers were asked to contribute to the success of the business through cuts and other changes, they were not asked to participate as equals in making the business successful or to share in the benefits of success if their efforts achieved the objectives.

Workers and unions have consistently shown flexibility and a willingness to change and have sustained performance at a superior level on a continuing basis when management has made the effort to (1) educate the work force and the union about the business, (2) work jointly to change operations in order to be competitive, (3) make changes throughout the business, (4) involve the work force as partners in the business, and (5) share the rewards of success. Examples of this type of change effort include: Rohm and Haas and the Oil Chemical and Atomic Workers (OCAW); General Mills and Quaker Oats and the American Federation of Grain Millers; Wesson Oil and Armour Swift Eckrich (both part of ConAgra) and the United Food and Commercial Workers (UFCW); Ford Motor Company and the United Automobile and Aerospace Workers; Allied Signal Aerospace and the International Association of Machinists; L-S Electrogalvinizing and the United Steelworkers of America; and Lever Brothers and OCAW and the International Chemical Workers Union (now part of the UFCW). The adage in industrial relations that "management gets the union it deserves" applies well to the view that unions are inflexible and slow to change. Upon careful analysis, in most cases the source of the problem can be found in the mirror.

Where change efforts are based on a mutual understanding of the challenges and a sharing of objectives and benefits, maximum results are achievable and can be sustained over the long term. The flexibility, responsiveness, and improvements in competitive position that have been demonstrated since the beginning of the 1980s (e.g., steel, autos, consumer products) clearly show the benefits of labor and management working within the enterprise to address the challenges raised by the marketplace.

The economic success of unions and companies that have developed partnerships and new systems of work also demonstrate that the conventional model of union power (i.e., taking wages out of competition) is overly simplistic and consequently inaccurate. These innovation organizations reveal that success for the business and for the workers can be achieved through much higher levels of productivity, innovative service, and quality. Economic power is thus achieved through superior performance. The dynamic pressure of the marketplace is recognized and accepted, but both labor and management recognize that success in the market is not likely to be sustainable by reducing wages and benefits. Market success depends on working smarter and better, but not for lower wages.

## The Appropriate Regulatory System Should Be Outcome Driven

The constant change and competitive pressures of the market require successful firms to be highly flexible and responsive and dogged in cutting costs and improving quality. In this environment, businesses are facing a unique set of challenges and are developing a unique set of answers.

Given these pressures and the fragmentation of the marketplace, the "one rule fits all" regulatory system is inappropriate. To allow firms and individuals to maximize their performance for their unique situations, the regulatory system should shift to outcome driven rather than process and procedure driven. The regulatory system should not focus on the type of ladder or container that is used but rather focus on the number and nature of accidents in the workplace. The regulatory system should set a high performance bar, then leave it to labor and management to develop their own unique methods of achieving the results while maximizing their performance.

To ensure that the inside-the-firm process has integrity there needs to be strong internal checks and balances. A labor union is usually sufficient to provide the balance. Thus a regulatory system designed around outcome-based standards and built around the presence of an independent labor union should both give the firm the freedom and flexibility to meet the demands of the marketplace and the standards of society while dramatically reducing the need for government micromanagement and policing.

The appropriate governmental regulatory system also needs to focus more on promoting labor market efficiency. The United States has one of the most efficient labor markets in the world, greatly facilitated by the general willingness of Americans to migrate to different places to find a good job. Europeans have many more regulations than Americans, which partially explains why job growth occurs in Europe much more slowly.[4] Nevertheless, the U.S. labor market has numerous barriers to mobility that produce rigidities which if reduced could improve the competitiveness of companies and make people's lives better. In 1996 Congress moved in the right direction when it made health care insurance portable.

Thus the appropriate regulatory system should do everything possible to encourage adjustment and movement of labor. Easing the pain for those hit hardest by change acts as a lubricant in the engine of change. Similarly, the more the government can do to improve the skills of the work force—both for children (i.e., future members of the work force) and existing workers—the more people will be able to take advantage of new opportunities.

In summary, the interests of society are maximized by a regulatory system that (1) is primarily driven by regulations developed jointly by labor and private firms, (2) is outcome focused and is routinely policed by unions (the government would focus on special or problem settings), and (3) emphasizes labor market fluidity. Such a framework would require substantial change in the current regulatory system. Let me describe several of the needed changes.

## Specific Regulatory System Changes

The starting point for regulatory reform must be, therefore, to foster the growth of a strong independent labor movement. Thirty years ago the U.S. labor movement was sufficient. Today it is not. The Commission on the Future of Worker-Management Relations (1995), or Dunlop Commission, defined the problem well in its report and recommendations when it proposed a coherent, thoughtful set of suggested regulatory changes to address the imbalance that has developed in the representation decision-making process. The nature and magnitude of the problem were succinctly described by the commission as follows:

> The Fact Finding Report revealed that in recent decades employer unfair labor practices during these campaigns have risen: both in terms of the ratio of unfair labor practice charges against employers to the number of elections and the percentage of such charges found to have merit. In particular, discharges of union activists are up: the data show that improper dismissals occur in one of every four elections. American workers are afraid of this prospect: 79% say it is likely that employees who seek union representation will lose their jobs, and 41% of nonunion workers say they think they might lose their own jobs if they tried to organize. This fear is no doubt one cause of the persistent unsatisfied demand for union representation on the part of a substantial minority of American workers. The Worker Representation and Participation Survey reported that 32% of nonunion workers would vote for a union and think their co-workers would too. (p. 19)

The modest changes the commission proposed would begin to give organized labor a level playing field in the representation decision-making process. Their recommended changes include:

> 1. Representation elections should be held before rather than after legal hearings about issues such as the scope of the bargaining unit. The elections should be conducted as promptly as administratively feasible, typically within two weeks.

> 2. The injunctions provided for in section 10(J) of the Act should be used to remedy discriminatory actions against employees that occur in organizing campaigns and first contract negotiations.

3. Employers and newly certified unions should be assisted in achieving first contracts by a substantially upgraded dispute resolution program. The program should feature mediation and a tripartite advisory board empowered to implement options ranging from self-help (strikes or lockouts) to binding arbitration for the relatively few disputes that warrant it . . .

4. Congress should reverse the Supreme Court's decision *Lechmere v. NLRB*, 112 S.Ct. 841 (1992) so that employees may have access to union organizers in privately owned, but publicly used spaces such as shopping malls.

Further revisions of the rules relating to access are best left to the considered judgment of the NLRB. We note that the Board has significant leeway in this area, and has not visited it in a fundamental way in three decades [General Electric Co., 156 NLRB 122 (1966)]. We encourage the Board to examine its current practice carefully to determine the extent to which it provides employees a fair opportunity to hear a balanced discussion of the relevant issues. . . . We urge the Board to strive to afford employees the most equal and democratic dialogue possible. (Commission on the Future of Worker-Management Relations 1994:18, 23-24)

The causes of the decline of organized labor are complex, and these proposed changes only address one set of causes. Nonetheless, the starting point for returning labor to a meaningful position in the economy would be the proposals of the Dunlop Commission.

The Dunlop Commission and many members of the business community have called for amending the National Labor Relations Act (NLRA) to "legalize" employee participation activities in nonunion settings. The TEAM Act, vetoed by President Clinton in 1996, embodied such an effort. Both sides in the argument about the TEAM Act recognized the legitimacy of concerns about employer-dominated labor organizations and the need for individuals to choose their representatives freely.

As both a consultant involved in developing new systems of work for over twenty years and as a practicing labor lawyer, I have reached the conclusion that good social science (and good organizational performance) coincide with good law as it stands today. In other words, there is no need to amend the NLRA to enable or promote legitimate and sound employee participation activities.

In short, the courts have recognized the legality of employee participation activities in nonunion settings[5] after assessing (1) the intent of the employer, (2) the desires of the employees, and (3) the actual domination activity of the employer.[6] In addition, the National Labor Relations Board has clearly recognized the legality of new systems of work in nonunion settings.[7] In effect, the workers in these organizations become managers. These new work systems are highly effective, truly empower and involve workers, and are legal; they are the best of social science and business performance. Only businesses that are trying to preserve control over their work forces need the law changed.

The occupational safety and health regulatory system should be revised on two fronts: (1) it should be rewritten to be results driven, and (2) the implementation process should center on joint employer and union safety committees. Again, the need for an independent and strong counterweight for management is needed. Employer-employee committees are insufficient without the presence of an independent voice at the table; the opportunity for standards to be compromised is too great without a union. Thus, under a revised regulatory system, the enforcement of standards in unionized settings and the means of determining how to achieve the results would be left to the private parties to work out themselves. The government would maintain its current regulatory and enforcement role in the absence of an independent union (although the focus would be on outcomes rather than the height of a railing) and in response to specific complaints in unionized settings. Under this system, private parties would have primary accountability for managing safety in the workplace without government intervention or direction.

The Fair Labor Standards Act must also be brought in line with the demands for flexibility of work, performance-based pay systems, and the blurring of lines between management and workers that arise within high-performance organizations. Flexibility must be written into the language of the occupational safety and health law, subject to private policing by independent unions. For unionized settings, the law should be drafted to allow discretion and flexibility in setting pay rates and hours of work. Nonunion settings should be subject to governmental standards. The law also needs to change so that performance-based bonuses are not built into subsequent-period base pay calculations for purposes of determining overtime rates. Finally, pension portability needs to follow health care portability. The fewer barriers to change, the more efficient the labor market.

In conclusion, the complexity of the challenge facing the U.S. economy makes answers to our problems difficult to find. The first step is to identify the desired outcomes: the interests that must be satisfied. From this point one can develop the basic structure of a regulatory system that is appropriate to satisfying the interests.

Experience over the last fifty years demonstrates that a private-sector-based system is likely to maximize overall interests and is therefore most desirable. However, for such a system to work, a strong, independent labor movement is critical; without one, a private-sector-based system is a hoax. Government must then fill the gap, and extensive government regulation is inconsistent with the demands of the modern marketplace.

## Endnotes

[1] It is not realistic to assume that the United States could (nor is it desirable that it should) erect meaningful barriers to isolate itself from the rest of the world. Moreover, technology development will not stop.

[2] I do not have the space to discuss how each of these interests was identified, but they seem to represent the different key interests in the current debate on government regulation of the workplace, if not the economy. These interests are not intended to be consensus societal interests. Different people and groups almost certainly will disagree with some or several of the interests, but substantial numbers of people see each interest as important and needing to be satisfied. Thus many people see appropriate government regulation as maximizing the satisfaction of all of these interests.

[3] This corresponds roughly with the level of interest of people, as expressed in various opinion polls, in joining a union under present conditions. One must ask, however, given the widespread negative press, the prevalence of intimidation and imbalance in the legal system, and the lack of exposure to unions in many parts of the country and economy, whether the number of people interested in joining unions might be larger if any of these conditions were to change. Logic would say that the numbers would go higher.

[4] See McKinsey Global Institute (1994). The power of the European unions is almost entirely political; labor parties impose more restrictions on employers, thus new startup businesses and high growth businesses are subject to extremely rigid employment regulations to the same extent as the heavily unionized, mature, large, basic industries. The enormous negative impact on job growth due to government regulations, in contrast to union power, is most clearly demonstrated in France which has one of the lowest levels of private sector union membership.

[5] My analysis is more completely laid out in an unpublished legal memorandum (Schneider 1982).

[6] See, for example, *NLRB v. Northeastern University*, 601 F.2d 1208 (1st Cir. 1979) and *Hertzka & Knowles v. NLRB*, 503 F.2d 625 (9th Cir. 1974), cert. denied, 423 U.S. 875 (1975).

[7] *General Foods Corp.*, 231 NLRB 1232 (1997).

## References

Commission on the Future of Worker-Management Relations. 1995. *Report and Recommendations*. Washington, DC: Government Printing Office (January 9).

McKinsey Global Institute. 1994. *Economic Performance*. New York: McKinsey & Company.

Schneider, Thomas J. 1982. "Sections 8(a)(2), 8(a)(5), and 2(5) of the National Labor Relations Act and Quality of Working Life Programs." Unpublished paper, Quasha Wessely & Schneider, Washington, DC.

CHAPTER 17

# Expanding Union Power by Comprehensive Corporate Campaigns and Manipulation of the Regulatory Process

HERBERT R. NORTHRUP
*University of Pennsylvania*

Union use of regulatory agencies, even those with no jurisdiction in labor matters, is widespread in the current labor relations scene. This practice is the result of the decline of union membership and power during the last fifty years and the concomitant increase in regulation of all types.

Union manipulation of the regulatory process is most egregious in corporate campaigns. The AFL-CIO Industrial Union Department (IUD) defines a corporate campaign as one which:

> applies pressure to many points of [corporate] vulnerability to convince the company to deal fairly and equitably [from the union's point of view] with the union. . . . It means vulnerabilities in all of the company's political and economic relationships—with other unions, shareholders, customers, creditors, and government agencies—to achieve union goals. (IUD 1985:1)

Originally, corporate campaigns concentrated pressures on personnel and institutions outside the targeted company facility. Comprehensive corporate campaigns add the "inside game" to the action. This is defined by the IUD as:

> the use of tactics within the workplace. . . . It is a guide to organizing workers to fight on their own behalf where they work—whether it's in a plant or a hospital, a retail store or an office, a construction site or an agency of government. (IUD 1986:foreword)

As a background, the reach of federal labor relations and employment regulatory policy should be noted. Such policy in the United States can be seen as a five-pronged approach. First, by means of the Federal Mediation and Conciliation Service, the government attempts to assist labor and management to achieve peaceful relations. Second, the National Labor Relations Act (NLRA), as amended, is designed to determine representation disputes peacefully and to sanction unfair labor practices committed by either party but, theoretically, does not control the terms and conditions of employment. Third, the Labor and Management Reporting and Disclosure Act (Landrum-Griffin) was passed primarily to force unions to conform more closely to democratic governance and proper financial practices. Fourth, came a series of laws concerning nondiscriminatory practices based upon race, national origin, religion, sex, age, Vietnam-era veteran status, and in some states, sexual orientation. Finally, adding to regulation of minimum wages and hours of work, other employment matters now regulated include safety and health performance and concern with the environment, plus numerous areas of doing business which are not directly employee oriented but which have impacted the labor-management relationship.

Government regulation of the employee-management relationship is thus today much more extensive than was the case fifty years ago when the IRRA was founded. After explaining why regulation is always likely to be utilized by unions as a key power tool and why I believe that this is socially undesirable, I shall then concentrate on how and why these regulatory endeavors have created serious questions of public policy during this period of increased emphasis by unions on comprehensive corporate campaigns in the private sector (Northrup 1994). Since the Railway Labor Act, which embodies several areas of labor-management regulation (and the failures of which I discussed in a paper presented at the IRRA's first meeting [Northrup 1949]), has been covered recently elsewhere (Northrup 1990), its reach and effect will not be included in this analysis.

## Regulation as a Significant Union Tool

Regulations force a variety of conduct changes both on unions and management. Concern here is not with obvious action, such as avoidance of unfair practices, filing reports, for unions holding conventions every five years, or for management having regular stockholders meetings, etc. Rather, the emphasis is how by its very nature, regulation usually, but not always, diminishes the power of the entity being regulated and, therefore, is a key weapon in unions' attack on management in comprehensive corporate campaigns. Regulation, to be sure, can affect both unions and companies, but the former seemingly much less than the latter under current laws and their administration and particularly as a result of a much wider use of regulation as a tactical weapon by unions.

*The Significance of Union Misuse of Regulation*

Today unions understand the impact that regulations have and, particularly in comprehensive corporate campaign activities, apply the whole panoply of regulatory potential against management. Often unions find regulators very much disposed to assist them:

> Labor unions and governmental regulatory agencies have much in common. Both have an economic purpose, but internally are political organizations. Both utilize political action to alter or to thwart the workings of the economic market. Perhaps most important, both are corporate management regulating devices that owe their existence to the political belief that corporate management must be regulated for an assumed public good which their staffs believe their organizations are uniquely qualified to achieve. As a result, it should come as no surprise that unions and regulatory agencies are natural allies and that unions quickly seek assistance from such agencies as a key aspect of comprehensive corporate campaigns. (Northrup 1996a:347)

What may be the bible of union comprehensive corporate campaigns has set forth succinctly why regulation is so significant in such union pressures:

> Both public institutions and private companies are subject to all sorts of laws and regulations, from the Securities and Exchange Commission to the Occupational Safety and Health Act, from the Civil Rights Act to the local fire codes. *Every law or regulation is a potential net in which management can be snared and entangled.* A complaint to a regulatory agency can cause the company managerial time, public embarrassment, potential fines, and the costs of compliance. One well-placed phone call can do a lot of damage. (La Botz 1991:127, emphasis in original)

Additionally, the regulatory agency can challenge and reduce the power of management for all to see. Since unions are a force for the same purpose, they naturally regard such management power decline as helping to gain employee support for their objectives. The Service Employees International Union (SEIU) advises that charges should be filed with regulatory agencies against management "even if the violations are completely unrelated to the bargaining issues" because it will harass management, add costs, and incur "damage to the employer's public image" (SEIU 1988:3-21).

*Philosophies of Regulation*

Many industrial relations academics see nothing wrong with this. Their reaction is likely to be, "That's great! I'm glad that unions do this and that regulators cooperate." Their reasoning is that unions have become so weak and the National Labor Relations Board (NLRB) allegedly so lacking in power that there is need for an affirmative action program to support unionism. Therefore, according to this view, it is sound public policy for regulators in all branches of government to support union policies regardless of the fact that this is not the purpose of the legislation.

Fundamental to such beliefs is a common philosophy that permeates academia and was most recently that underlying the recommendations of the Commission on the Future of Worker-Management Relations (Dunlop Commission). In this view, unions are an unmitigated good per se since they provide "voice," reduce exploitation, and offer increased worker bargaining power. Therefore, the federal government should do everything possible to ensure that workers are union represented even when they are either unaware or insufficiently intelligent to understand this alleged truism (Kochan 1993; Northrup 1996b).

There is, however, another and I believe, more accurate philosophy concerning unions—one that depicts them as necessary in the economy, although not in many industrial relations situations. If union representation means expensive dues, strikes over issues not of interest to employees and resultant loss of worker incomes, violent or other unsuitable tactics, use of dues money for political or other issues not pertinent to employee interests, unemployment if union power raises wage costs beyond market realities, or other negatives, then we have a different picture—one of neutrality—which needs voicing.

The union as a good per se viewpoint was the dominant philosophy underlying the 1935 National Labor Relations Act (NLRA-Wagner Act). Section 7 of this law guaranteed employees the right to organize and to join unions without management interference. Section 8 listed a series of unfair labor practices for management, but none for unions. National policy was clearly established as the encouragement of collective bargaining by means of the enhancement of union power.

Twelve years later, the Taft-Hartley amendments altered the NLRA and its philosophy. Section 7 not only retained the right of employees to organize and to join unions without management interference, but also guaranteed their right *to refrain therefrom*. Section 8 added an imposing list of union unfair labor practices to the Act which were enhanced by the Landrum-Griffin Act of 1959. Government labor relations policy was thus shifted from union enhancement to neutrality, a major change.

Since 1959, as already noted, a host of laws regulating primarily management conduct in such areas as discrimination, safety and health, environment, family leave, and other areas have been enacted. On the face, this legislation does not provide for union support and aggrandizement. Consequently, when the administrators of such legislation, as well as those charged with administration of the Taft-Hartley Act, use their positions to enhance union power rather than to enforce the law equally and without prejudice, they are going beyond the delicate balance prescribed in the purpose of the legislation. Of course, such balance is both difficult to define and to maintain. The examples provided later in the text, however, do demonstrate regulatory conduct that is certainly not evenhanded.

*Transferring and Enhancing Costs*

The misuse of regulatory action cannot be assigned a direct cost, at least without some detailed study, but it is undoubtedly considerable. It is quite clear that when it does occur, increased costs are incurred which burden the economy. Such costs may be threefold. The cost of operating the agency involved is either increased, or regulatory funding is transferred from objectively selected activity to union support activity. Concurrently with such action, costs are enhanced for the targeted company which must spend valuable management time, resources, and funds for legal and other outside assistance in order to defend itself and its policies, and usually the already overburdened courts end up with additional cases. Then if the union is successful in its aims, further costs are inflicted upon the public or the employees, since the higher costs can result in lower employment, higher wages and prices, and resource misallocation.

The agency's costs go directly to the taxpayers, thus reducing their ability to utilize their resources in economy bolstering ways; the company costs are passed along to the consumer, again reducing abilities to purchase goods and services, or resulting in unemployment, or both. Finally, after reviewing specific union tactics and regulatory cooperation therewith, we can raise a serious question of whether they do enhance union power and membership in the long run.

## Union Use of Regulatory Agencies for Power Enhancement

This section examines specific instances of union use of regulatory agencies to enhance their power and of agency assistance in this process. The agencies considered include the NLRB, the Occupational Safety and Health Administration (OSHA), the Environmental Protection Agency (EPA), and the Securities Exchange Commission (SEC), plus an examination of how unions utilize these and other agencies even where they have no representation rights or even no members in the targeted company.

*Corporate Campaign Use of NLRB*

Despite the 1947 Taft-Hartley amendments to the Wagner Act, complaints issued against companies by the NLRB far exceed those issued against unions. In fiscal 1994, for example, 26,058 charges were filed against employers, but only 8,674 against unions (NLRB 1995:92, Table 2). One reason is that unions, much more than managements, use charges of unfair labor practices as tactics in labor disputes (usually to be withdrawn when the dispute is settled) or even file such charges very frequently in any case. Thus in fiscal 1994, 35% of all charges were dismissed and 30.1% were withdrawn before the NLRB issued a complaint, and 30.5% were later settled or adjusted (NLRB 1995:5, Chart 3). Another reason for the lack of charges against unions may be a belief among some NLRB agents that although the Wagner Act philosophy was in effect legislated away by the 1947 Taft-Hartley amendments, the former law's proscriptions, which were confined solely to management's transgressions, remain the appropriate manner in which to administer the act.[1]

Currently, the NLRB is most responsive to unions' moves and of major assistance in corporate campaigns. For example, in the Caterpillar case, as of July 1996, 214 complaints have been issued by the Board since 1991 when the current dispute with the UAW resulted in the initial strike (BNA 1996a:A-1). Few of these cases involve monumental issues such as refusal to bargain or attempts to discriminate or undermine the union. For example, the Board has taken the position that the union should be permitted to place large signs with derogatory comments on the shopfloor, display hundreds of balloons there, and wear buttons and shirts with anticompany comments, as long as these disruptive demonstrations are related to the labor dispute. Complaints have been issued when the company has ordered such actions stopped and when the company has disciplined employees that take part therein. The NLRB has also issued complaints when (1) Caterpillar restricted yelling, screaming, chanting, and whistling on the shopfloor during work time; (2) a union committeeman filed more than 1,600 grievances in an eighteen-month period and was told to stop wasting time; (3) employees were told to cease marching through the plant during working hours; (4) an employee was discharged for posting a graphic cartoon of an identified supervisor and non-striker, both males, engaging in a sex act, another one was discharged for urinating in a tank of machine coolant; and (5) UAW personnel were trespassing on company property, etc. Such matters are regarded by the NLRB General Counsel and the Peoria regional director as union rights.

Not only are the disruptions, the impact on production, and the danger of injury because of the distractions ignored, but also not considered seriously has been the fact that the company takes visiting customers and potential customers on plant tours as part of its sales program. Moreover, for many of these incidents, the company offered arbitration which the UAW declined to accept (personal research; Gangemi and Torres 1996).

Given the NLRB's willingness to issue complaints on such flimsy charges, it should not be surprising that union tactical charges and NLRB resultant complaints magnify when a corporate campaign is undertaken, especially when it is accompanied by the inside game.

### Union Use of OSHA

Since no one is against improved safety and health, and since there is always the potential for improvement therein, OSHA is tailor-made for use in comprehensive corporate campaigns. It is particularly important in cases in which employees are still working and can point out or even develop situations where improvement is allegedly warranted. The effect is to provide the union with propaganda alleging that the employer disregards human safety, health, and decent values, thereby bolstering its charges that management is unfit.

The UAW has a pamphlet entitled *Health and Safety for Inside Strategies* and provides instructions to employees in plants where inside game activities have been instigated. Maintenance personnel whose jobs require them to work in several plant areas are especially instructed to work on safety charges (UAW, n.d.). The Oil, Chemical, and Atomic Workers Union (OCAW) published a magazine, *New Solutions*, with the same objectives that demonstrates how to utilize environmental as well as safety and health regulations for these purposes.

La Botz (1991:32) has a full chapter devoted to health and safety which stresses its value to organizing and urges the use of mass grievances, press releases and publicity, walkouts over safety, and other practices in which the inside game can be furthered by utilizing the health and safety issue. The chapter concludes by listing twelve "action questions" directed toward effective methods of organizing and utilizing health and safety for the inside game. Shostak's book (1991) also devotes a full chapter to health and safety, and it is likewise emphasized in the Eisenscher pamphlet (1990) and in the SEIU *Manual* (1988:3-10).

In mid-1996 OSHA announced that it would give special attention to injuries in nursing homes, particularly in seven states: New York, Pennsylvania, Illinois, Massachusetts, Missouri, Ohio, and Florida. Stories relating to the OSHA announcement also carried long comments from the SEIU, which with the United Food and Commercial Workers (UFCW) has long been conducting a corporate campaign against the country's largest operator of such establishments, Beverly Enterprises (King 1996:D1; BNA 1996d:A2; Perry 1987:115, 135). It is probably no coincidence that the seven states selected are those in which Beverly has a considerable number of facilities.

## Environmental Charges

Such charges are regularly used by unions in corporate campaigns to trap and to sully management and companies. Since the laws of thermodynamics guarantee that no industrial activity can be perfectly clean, no project exists that is not open to some degree of environmental criticism. The United Association of Journeymen and Apprentices of the Plumbing and Pipe Fitting Industry (UA) in California has made effective use of environmental actions to secure work. Union lawyers delay the issuance of permits to build by making all sorts of environmental charges and otherwise use legal and political efforts to harass owners who choose nonunion builders. If, however, a unionized contractor is retained, the union takes a pro-construction stance and urges that all obstacles, environmental and otherwise, be brushed aside and permits speedily granted. Such union policies have been successful in part because (1) delays in construction can be extremely costly, (2) the plethora of agencies in California are seemingly anxious to assert conflicting jurisdiction and views over environmental matters, and (3) the federal EPA has been very willing to enter a case after the state agencies have ruled and even overrule the state agencies without factual support for so doing—all examined in detail elsewhere (Northrup and White 1995:60).

Bayou Steel's experience provides another example of union use of environmental legislation. George Becker, president of the United Steelworkers (USW), in discussing the corporate campaign then being conducted against this small Louisiana mini-steel company, declared as reported by the union journal:

> There are other players in our society who can have and have had significant influence in helping resolve labor conflicts. . . . He cited Bayou's investors, creditors, customers and state and local governments as concerned groups that could bring pressure on the company. (*Steelabor* 1993:9)

True to its leader's word, the USW brought numerous NLRB, OSHA, EPA, and state environmental agency charges against Bayou. Many of these EPA charges were so flimsy that the state agency advised the local union that it "can no longer reasonably believe your unsupported allegations against" the company (Bordelson 1994). Nevertheless, the EPA then insisted on inspections of its own, thus subjecting this small company to further harassment.

After two inspections and numerous information requests over a ten-month period, EPA confirmed the findings of the state agency that there were no serious environmental violations at Bayou Steel (Hyman 1995:C-1).

## Union Use of the SEC

Although the SEC has no labor relations functions, it has become an almost standard stop for unions on the corporate campaign trail. Unions in such a campaign usually purchase a few shares of a company stock and then submit a resolution for the annual meeting of stockholders which criticizes the company for various reasons but particularly condemns its labor policy. Attempts are often made to take over the meeting for such actions, which are also frequently accompanied by picketing outside the meeting facility. International Paper experienced such activity for seven straight years beginning with the 1987 strikes and lockout at four of its plants.

Appeals to the SEC can be even more sophisticated. Complaints may be made by unions that the company has been issuing "misleading" reports (*Wall St. Journal* 1993:A4). Such charges may affect stock prices or otherwise damage the company, for example, by making it more difficult or more expensive to borrow money or to issue additional stock, as alleged in the Bayou Steel case.

According to the complaint of Bayou Steel in its RICO action against the Steelworkers, the union gave a report alleging environmental malpractice to the SEC. Although these charges were later refuted by the Louisiana environmental agency and the federal EPA, as noted above, Bayou claims that such "accusations before the SEC resulted in the company missing an important window in the credit markets and caused the [mortgage] notes to be priced at a yield higher than would otherwise have prevailed in a market free from the union's undue influence."[2]

## Union Use of Regulations without Representation

A local official of the UFCW has written that in order to conduct a comprehensive corporate campaign,

> you don't need a majority or even a 30% support among employees.
> A few people inside and outside are all that's necessary to be successful. (Note: Fired employees are a great source of information.
> They're not afraid and they're motivated!) (Crump 1991:43; parentheses in original)

For most cases when unions file charges with a regulatory agency, they either represent the employees of the target company or have a sizable inside following. Where union members are employed, unions can add the "inside game" to the corporate campaign. By a series of actions culminating in "work to rule" which is in fact a slowdown and an inside strike—and by massive appeals to regulatory bodies, union employee adherents can damage productivity and otherwise raise costs in attempting to force the company to agree to their demands (IUD 1986; Northrup 1994).

If, however, the union does not represent any employees of the company which is the target of its corporate campaign, it is at a disadvantage for utilizing regulatory agencies which require employee charges in order to act. Unions have overcome this problem by finding a disgruntled employee or former employee to file a lawsuit alleging a violation of a regulatory law. Then union-supplied attorneys request discovery in order to obtain lists of employees, purportedly to enlist other employees allegedly so treated, thereby attempting to convert the case into a class action. The union attorneys can circulate a letter to employees not only asking about similar alleged violations but also about a host of other matters, including working off the clock, a violation of the Fair Labor Standards Act (FLSA); alleged equal employment violations; and various company practices.

This is precisely what the UFCW has done in the Food Lion and Publix Markets situations. After failing to unionize employees of these major southeastern supermarkets, it has sought to damage their ability to enter markets in which they would be taking business from unionized competitors. This is in line with the views of the current president of the UFCW who has been preaching a "market share" concept of union organizing: "Over the long run," says President Dority, "we must either reduce these [nonunion] chains market share . . . or put them out of business" (Dority 1990; DiLorenzo 1996). Put clearly by a local UFCW official, this redefines successful organizing to mean either a company's destruction or unionization:

> My local, UFCW 951 in Michigan, subscribed to this policy by defining successful organizing in one of two ways: either a ratified, signed collective bargaining agreement with a previously nonunion employer or a significant curtailment of a nonunion operator's business, including shutting the business down. (Crump 1991:40)

## Concluding Remarks

Space limitations have permitted only the bare minimum recounting of the major role which regulatory agencies play in supporting union comprehensive corporate campaigns. The substantial role of the U.S. Department of Labor (DOL) in addition to its OSHA Department has not been recounted nor has the more minor role of the Food and Drug Administration, various state agencies, and other bodies. It is believed, however, that recounting the partisan activities of the NLRB, the OSHA, and the EPA clearly demonstrates the willingness of government agencies to adopt a union-assistance role.

Such partisanship is sometimes by bias, often by ignorance of the union's true purpose, and sometimes by the legislation involved. Even when the last is the case, there is little excuse for some regulatory action in the union behalf. For example, the NLRB's lopsided actions in the Caterpillar case challenge both common sense and common considerations of fair play. The EPA's role in rushing to the aid of unions when state agencies, after laborious examinations of the issues found no violations or impediments, calls loudly for congressional action. And OSHA's rush to inspect facilities where a labor dispute exists or to inaugurate a major drive aimed at one company that is a corporate campaign target needs to be rethought and revamped.

The attitude of regulators has been well illustrated by the comments of former Secretary of Labor Robert Reich after the DOL's regulations pertaining to the employment of foreign skilled employees were nullified by a federal court.[3] He promised to continue "efforts to reform a program . . ." declaring that this was a "broken program," but ignored the fact that industry regarded his efforts as "issuing an unrecognizable and unworkable final rule" (BNA 1996b:AA-3). What is needed, of course, is better drafted legislation, in some cases less legislation, and above all fewer regulatory rules and more understanding of the negative impact of government agency assistance to the inherently destructive union comprehensive corporate campaigns.

We have already noted the major social costs of union corporate campaigns, and the illustrations given above have emphasized the social inequities of government agencies supporting such activities. It should also be emphasized, however, that such union programs may well not be in the long-term best interests of the unions which engage in such activities. As David Lewin has stated:

> The difficulty with in-plant actions such as working to the rule . . . is that if the effort is successful, it will cause a decline in productivity and have a negative effect on the employer's business *just as a strike will. An action that "harms the company will harm the workers too, in the long run."* (BNA 1991:C-4; emphasis added)

The first two cases in which in-plant activity was tried as part of a corporate campaign involved the UAW and automobile parts companies, Moog of St. Louis and Schwitzer of Rolla, Missouri. In both cases the companies succumbed to the pressures and gave the union locals what they demanded. A

few years later, Moog had opened nonunion plants in Mississippi and Tennessee and halved its former 500 person labor force in St. Louis, while
Schwitzer shut down the Rolla plant and moved production to a nonunion
facility in Georgia (Northrup 1994:514). Recently, the long-closed Rolla plant
was purchased by Briggs & Stratton, the small motor manufacturer, to house
operations that are nonunion and were moved there after the Allied Industrial
Workers, now part of the United Papermakers International Union (UPIU),
conducted a costly work-to-rule slowdown in the company's major facility in
Milwaukee.

These are just examples of how corporate campaigns can do the opposite
of enhancing union membership. John J. Sweeney, President of the AFL-
CIO, has long been an advocate of corporate campaigns. He has claimed a
3,500 union membership increase has resulted from "Justice for Janitors," one
SEIU corporate campaign program begun when he was that union's president. It targets companies that retain nonunion janitorial services with agita-
tion, publicity, and boycotts, mass confrontations, and even in Washington,
D.C., blocked a main bridge into the city at rush hour (Ybarra 1994:A1).

Yet corporate campaigns have not stopped the decline of union membership which for 1996 stood at 14.5% of the total labor force but only 10.2% of
the private sector labor force (*Employment and Earnings*, Jan. issue, annually). Said Sweeney in July, 1996:

> We are still losing members as an absolute number, and as a per-
> centage of the workforce. We're running fewer [NLRB] elections
> than last year and last year [1995] was a disaster. (BNA 1996c:A-8)

Sweeney's remarks are affirmed by the data cited above and preliminary
data regarding NLRB representation elections for the first half of 1996. The
number of elections decreased from 1,424 during the first six months of 1995
to 1,374 in the same period of 1996. Unions won 652 elections by mid-1996 as
compared with 714 during the first half of 1995, and the union win rate
declined from 50.1% in the 1995 period to 47.5% of that in 1996 (BNA
1996e:C-1). Since NLRB representation elections are held almost always at
the request of unions with a showing that they have at least a 30% following
among the bargaining unit's employees, these data clearly demonstrate the
failure of unions to win support from the bulk of unorganized employees. One
can, therefore, predict a continued decline of unionization in the private sector. Of course, many factors are responsible for these lost members. Corporate campaigns aided by government agencies, however, do not seem to be an
offsetting factor in bolstering union membership and could well be destructive of a union membership resurgence.

## Endnotes

[1] There is a tendency of some to speak in terms as if the Wagner Act was still extant. Noteworthy was a conference in 1995 jointly sponsored by the NLRB and the Cornell School of Industrial and Labor Relations, entitled "Sixty Years of the Wagner Act," which would seem more of a yearning than a historical fact.

[2] *Bayou Steel Corporation v. United Steelworkers of America*, et al., U.S. Dis. Ct., Dis. Del., Civil Action No. 95-496-RRM, Plaintiff's Second Amended Complaint (October 12, 1995), p. 19.

[3] *National Association of Manufacturers v. U.S. Department of Labor*, 1996 WL [West Law] 420868 (July 22, 1996).

## References

AFL-CIO. 1985. *Developing New Tactics: Winning with Coordinated Corporate Campaigns*. Washington, DC: AFL-CIO Industrial Union Department.

_____. 1986. *The Inside Game: Winning with Workplace Strategies*. Washington: AFL-CIO, Industrial Union Department.

Bordelson, Filmore P., III. 1994. Letter from Deputy Secretary, Louisiana Department of Environmental Quality to Maurice Simoneaux, Chairman, Safety and Health, USW, Local 9121 (November 17).

Bureau of National Affairs (BNA). 1991. "Growing Numbers of Unions Adopting In-Plant Actions to Avoid Strikes." *Daily Labor Report*, No. 151 (August 6), pp. C-1-C-4.

_____. 1996a. "Judge Rules Caterpillar Illegally Removed Fliers from Bulletin Boards." *Daily Labor Report*, No. 134 (July 12), p. A-7.

_____. 1996b. "Court Sets Aside DOL Rules Setting Tougher Standards for H-1B Program." *Daily Labor Report*, No. 143 (July 25), p. AA-2, 3.

_____. 1996c. "Sweeney Calls on State Federations to 'Roll Out the Big Guns' for Organizing." *Daily Labor Report*, No. 148 (July 30), p. A-8.

_____. 1996d. "OSHA to Launch Nursing-Home Initiative in Seven States to Reduce Injuries, Costs." *Daily Labor Report*, No. 152 (August 7), pp. A-2, A-3.

_____. 1996e."Representation Elections." *Daily Labor Report*, No. 218 (November 12), pp. C-1, C-3.

Crump, Joe. 1991. "The Pressure Is on: Organizing without the NLRB." *Labor Research Review*, Vol. 18, pp. 33-43.

DiLorenzo, Thomas J. 1996. "The Corporate Campaign against Food Lion: A Study of Media Manipulation." *Journal of Labor Research*, Vol. 17, no. 3 (Summer), pp. 359-75.

Dority, Donald H. 1990. Speech before the UFCW Retail Food Conference, Tropicana Hotel, Las Vegas, NV (October 20).

Eisenscher, Michael. 1990. *Creative Persistence (CPR)*. San Francisco: The Author.

Gangemi, Columbus R., Jr., and Joseph J. Torres. 1996. "The Corporate Campaign at Caterpillar." *Journal of Labor Research*, Vol. 17, No. 3 (Summer), pp. 377-94.

Greenhouse, Steven. 1996. "Republicans Questioning Federal Deal with Union." *New York Times* (July 14), p. 14.

Hyman, Vicki. 1995. "Steel Mill Clean, EPA Probe Says." *Money* (April 26), p. C-1.

King, Sharon R. 1996. "Nursing Homes Draw Attention As Worker Safety Focus Shifts," *New York Times* (August 7), pp. D1, D5.

Kochan, Thomas A. 1993. "Trade Unionism and Industrial Relations: Notes on Theory and Practice for the 1990s." *Proceedings of the Forty-Fifth Annual Meeting* (Anaheim, CA, January 5-7). Madison, WI: Industrial Relations Research Association, pp. 185-95.

La Botz, Dan. 1991. *A Troublemaker's Handbook*. Detroit: A Labor Notes Book.

Miller, Edward B. 1980. *An Administrative Appraisal of the NLRB*. Labor Relations & Public Policy Series, No. 16. Philadelphia: The Wharton School Industrial Research Unit, University of Pennsylvania.

National Labor Relations Board. 1995. *Fifty-Ninth Annual Report for the Fiscal Year Ended September 30, 1994*. Washington: U.S. Government Printing Office.

Northrup, Herbert R. 1949. "Emergency Disputes under the Railway Labor Act." *Proceedings of the First Annual Meeting* (Cleveland, Dec. 29-30). Madison, WI: Industrial Relations Research Association, pp. 78-97.

_____. 1990. "The Railway Labor Act—Time for Repeal?" *Harvard Journal of Law & Public Policy*, Vol. 13, no. 2 (Spring), pp. 442-515.

_____. 1994. "Union Corporate Campaigns and Inside Games As a Strike Form." *Employee Relations Law Journal*, Vol. 19, No. 4 (Spring), pp. 507-49.

_____. 1996a. "Corporate Campaigns: The Perversion of the Regulatory Process." *Journal of Labor Research*, Vol. 17, no. 3 (Summer), pp. 346-58.

_____. 1996b. "The Dunlop Commission Report: Philosophy and Overview." *Journal of Labor Research*, Vol. 17, No. 1 (Winter), pp. 1-8.

Northrup, Herbert R., and Augustus T. White. 1995. "Construction Union Use of Environmental Regulation To Win Jobs." *Harvard Journal of Law and Public Policy*, Vol. 19, no. 1 (Fall), pp. 55-119.

Perry, Charles R. 1987. *Union Corporate Campaigns*. Philadelphia: Wharton School Industrial Research Unit, University of Pennsylvania.

Service Employees International Union (SEIU). 1988. *Contract Campaign Manual*. Washington: SEIU.

Shostak, Arthur. 1991. *Robust Unionism*. Ithaca: ILR Press.

Slovak, Patricia Costello, and Michael P. Posner. 1995. *The Developing Labor Law*. 3d ed., 1995 Cumulative Supp. Washington: The Bureau of National Affairs, Inc.

*Steelabor*. 1993. "USWA Widens Bayou Campaign" (July/August), p. 9.

United Auto Workers (UAW). Acquired in 1993. *Strategies for Union Health and Safety Programs*. Detroit: UAW.

*Wall Street Journal*. 1993. "Union Files SEC Complaint Alleging Misleading Report" (September 23), p. A4.

Ybarra, Michael. 1994. "Janitors' Union Uses Pressure and Threats to Expand Its Ranks." *Wall Street Journal* (March 3), p. A1.

# CHAPTER 18

# Employee Relations Law Reform

JOHN NEIL RAUDABAUGH°

*Partner, Matkov, Salzman, Madoff & Gunn, Chicago, Illinois*

Eighty years ago, John R. Commons wrote in his introduction to *History of Labor in the United States*, that labor movements in America are explained by "the interaction of economic, industrial, and political conditions, with many varieties of individualistic, socialistic, and protectionistic philosophies. The labor history of the country is . . . a part of its industrial and political history."[1] In his conclusions, Commons noted that "[t]o the American labor movement a conquest of the right to exist was ever its paramount problem . . . [and] to American employers unionism has always remained the invader and usurper to be expelled at the first opportunity" (Commons 1918, Vol. 1:3). Commons argued that for American employers, the institution of private property was and remains central, absolute and the bulwark against union incursions. In his final paragraph, he opined that "the verdict is that the general plan of labor's campaign through the forty years shows an appreciation of realities, but that several critical defeats came from lack of neutral coordination of labor's fighting armies" (Commons 1918, Vol. 4:621).

Commons' assessments remain applicable. Organized labor is fighting its demise more than ever. Property rights are still honored and continue under attack. (See Sweeney 1996.) Between political disinterest and checkmate, employee relations law and policy is moribund.

Some 66 years later, in studying U.S. trade unionism, Richard Freeman and James Medoff concluded that "[i]n a well-functioning labor market, there should be a sufficient number of union and of nonunion firms to offer alternative work environments to workers, innovation in workplace rules and conditions, and competition in the market. Such competition will, on the one hand, limit union monopoly power and on the other, management's power over workers."[2] They observed "[t]hat the paradox of American unionism is that it is at one and the same time a plus on the overall social balance sheet (in most though not all circumstances) and a minus on the corporate balance sheet (again, in most though not all circumstances)." Freeman and Medoff (1984)

°Member, National Labor Relations Board, 1990-93.

assessed the role of unions against benchmarks of efficiency, income distribution, and social organization. They focused the policy argument well:

> What policies might better enable society to benefit from the pluses of unionism and to reduce the minuses of the institution?

> How should society deal with the paradox of an institution that is socially valuable but that conflicts with the private interests of firms? (p. 248)

Commons' "job conscious unionists" undoubtedly would rebel against the economists' recognition of the need for and benefits of alternatives in optimizing socioeconomic outcomes. If ever we get our policymakers focused, will it be capital, labor, sideline observer, consumer, or a new coalition which calls the shots in overhauling workplace law and policy? Without pushing a particular agenda for reform, where do we go from here? Surely no one debates that industrial conditions have changed substantially over the century. The nature of work is different today than in 1918, 1935, or even 1984. Technological progress has and will continue to supplant specific jobs, tasks, processes, and indeed whole industries while creating new work systems and industries. No one can debate that economic conditions over the long view have improved substantially, yet the income distribution issue remains a problem and must be addressed.

Political fortunes come and go as well. Fitting workplace legislation on the national legislative agenda continues to be difficult. Labor law "reform" seems to be never more than an issue or two in any single Congress, taking backseat to budget battles and other national debates where the alleged injuries apparently seem more poignant, more systemic or just more voter sensitive. Perhaps the Beltway purveyors of bits of biennial ballyhoo should sit out a Congress and work toward an honest and comprehensive employment law reform proposal rather than push their single item proprietary agenda despite the membership marketing bonanza.

The most recent effort at thorough legislative reform began with much potential but ended without fanfare. The Commission on the Future of Worker-Management Relations could have been the vehicle for future legislative change. Unfortunately, the Commission quickly was tainted by politics, perhaps by the selection of Commission appointees, the characterization of issues for study, and the manipulation of selecting presenters (Commission on the Future of Worker-Management Relations 1994). Ultimately, of course, it was doomed by the November 1994 political sea change.

The three questions presented to the Commission for study could not then and cannot now be fairly and adequately answered without considering the questions posed by Freeman and Medoff. Exactly what are the pluses and minuses of unionism? If unionism is indeed socially valuable, to a greater or lesser extent, and if the quantifiable conflicts with business are significant, how should we draw the line between rights and responsibilities? Employment law reform must consider the full array of workplace laws and regulations. And policymakers must also grapple with adjusting remedial deficiencies, jurisdictional prerequisites, differing proof burdens and evidentiary standards as well as the multiplicity of forums.

Many voices have called attention to problems, inconsistencies, and downright injustices in our present "system" (or patchwork approach) to the law of the workplace (Raudabaugh 1995). Some parties openly flout the law. Others announce that they choose to ignore the existing statutory forums designed to protect their very interests. Undoubtedly, the current state of affairs is due not only to the passage of time, the structural changes in work, and the vastly more differentiated work force, but also to the frailties of the process—the manner of selection of political appointees, the actions or inactions of the political appointees, entrenched and out-of-touch bureaucracies, statutory design, interested parties' rhetoric, inaction and/or ineptitude, congressional inattention or, at least, inaction in holding agencies accountable by turning a blind eye, cutting deals, rhetorical extremism or lack of follow-through, to name just a few. Something is terribly wrong when the only way Congress prompts action against administrative agency excess is to threaten to cut agency budgets.

Consider the National Labor Relations Board. The selection process for political appointees is byzantine. Because there is no formal process, and because selection of appointees is indeed political, the "process" often but understandably defaults to an "inside the Beltway" fraternity, many of whom are not sitting at bargaining tables, arbitrating cases, or otherwise engaged "in the trenches." Occasionally, candidates surface from other parts of the country by serendipity. Sometimes vacancies are awarded to Hill staffers or other Washington players seen as deserving for one extraneous reason or another. In any case, concern for a candidate's real-world practice and experience seems secondary to meeting political litmus tests. Political appointees with specific experience in labor relations matters sometimes are viewed as biased because they necessarily come from either the union or management side. Those without specific, hands-on experience tend to come from quasi policy-making backgrounds that routinely favor a results-oriented disposition of cases and the seizure of nonexistent opportunities to announce new principles instead of the less exciting task of applying precedent to facts and reserving important policy articulation for a few deserving cases.

The agency bureaucracy is a significant force because it outlasts the comings and goings of political appointees. While staff members are generally diligent and true to the statute, the problems of agency management, productivity standards, resource allocation, bias and the like remain. For example, something as simple as analyzing case intake statistics would suggest adjustments in the number of regional offices and staffing assignments, especially considering the Board's huge investment in computer technology. Despite repeated congressional inquiries, next to nothing has been done largely due to the public sector's lack of access to strategic management consulting expertise, the bureaucracy's natural self-protection and instinctive resistance to change and the lack of congressional persistence in forcing agency accountability.

Current criticism of political appointees, while intense and sometimes deserved, mimics that directed at previous Boards. It is true that appointees often build voting or prosecutorial records, casting doubt on their neutrality. Some conduct is truly reprehensible whether it's a board member who "never saw an injunction request they didn't like" or a general counsel who exercises prosecutorial discretion with a questionable purpose, or the board member or general counsel who communicates behind the scenes with labor, management or their affiliated Beltway interest groups or coordinates agendas between the general counsel's office and the Board. But it is the statute and its enforcement structure that should be the real focus of correction. What should be our national employee relations policy and what changes must be made to get it?

In his 1990 book, *Governing the Workplace*, Paul Weiler seemingly agreed with Freeman and Medoff, noting that "the value of unionism consists in its capacity to meld and discharge the dual roles of participation and protection. . . . A new labor law should expand beyond traditional unionism the range of choices available to satisfy these needs. . . . In that new environment unionism as we know it now would likely reveal considerable flaws as well as attractions."[3] Weiler (1990) seems to supplement the Freeman-Medoff macro policy identification by advancing a practical process for selecting promising proposals for statutory change:

> There are two dimensions to this selection process. The first is pragmatic. How significant is the particular problem? How likely is the proposed reform measure to ameliorate our concerns? How much leverage would success at this pressure point exert on the performance of the entire system? The second dimension is one of principle. How does any specific proposal accord with the values that animate the general body of labor law and the objectives that led us to adopt the system of labor law in the first place? (p. 226)

Unless collectively we decide to "throw the baby out with the bath water" and start from scratch, there is an array of specific issues that must be studied with input from all interested parties, prioritized and measured against our national values. The starting point is to confront and clearly address, once and for all, the real intentions of employee relations law and policy (Weiler 1990:227). Is it intended that the National Labor Relations Act, as amended, 29 U.C.C. §§ 151 *et seq.*, ("Act") protect employee choice to join or not join a labor organization and if employees so choose, only then to encourage and facilitate bargaining? Or is it intended to encourage and facilitate employee organizing, since collective bargaining presumably requires the existence of a labor organization? While the academic community often argues the latter, the statute is unclear.

Section 1 of the Act seems to suggest that the professors are right since the language emphasizes "the right of employees to organize," "[t]he inequality of bargaining power between employees who do not possess full freedom of association or actual liberty of contract," "the protection by law of the right of employees to organize and bargain collectively safeguards commerce," and "the policy of the United States [is] to eliminate the causes of certain substantial obstructions to the free flow of commerce . . . by encouraging the practice and procedure of collective bargaining and by protecting the exercise by workers of full freedom of association, self-organization and designation of representatives of their own choosing, for the purpose of negotiating the terms and conditions of their employment or other mutual aid or protection" (Weiler 1990:118-24).

On the other hand, Section 7 declares that while "[e]mployees shall have the right to self-organization, to form, join, or assist labor organizations, to bargain collectively through representatives of their own choosing . . . [employees] shall also have the right to refrain from any or all of such activities. . . ."[4] In other words, is it national labor policy to ensure that the salutary process of collective bargaining thrives, in part, due to a less than neutral federal preference for choosing the process or is it national labor policy to view collective bargaining, albeit beneficial, as but one choice among many?[5]

Making this policy choice after a full debate will do much to assist the adjudication of disputes. The current wiggle room enabling political ebbs and flows in statutory interpretation would be substantially reduced. Parties and the public would benefit from clearer guidance and less built-in interpretative discretion which for years has made fashioning behavior a litigation lottery.

Another critical issue concerns the enforcement model and attendant remedial scheme. For some time, many have decried the absence of meaningful remedies. The Act is viewed as an aging, toothless tiger (Raudabaugh

1994b). Should there be tort-like remedies? Should employee relations policy be administered by an adjudicatory agency or by an Article III court? (See Gould and Weiler 1990:247-49.) Enhanced remedies invariably bring more sophisticated litigation opportunities. To move from the mere remedial to more punitive relief calls for serious debate whether enforcement should remain with what is essentially a political institution and whether adjudication of disputes should continue to eschew discovery in favor of "trial by ambush." Perhaps with longer appointment terms, some fears could be ameliorated. Unfortunately, under Sections 3, 9, and 10 of the Act, political appointees have incredible discretion to pursue selective enforcement, turn a blind eye to advancing new issues, and tolerate or even encourage variability in statutory application from region to region.

Another source of concern is Section 6 of the Act which confers authority to engage in rulemaking, an avenue rarely traveled by the Board. If the current enforcement scheme were changed to create a specialized court or to channel cases to federal district courts, the role of rulemaking should be reconsidered. On the other hand, if the choice is to retain the adjudicatory model, the potential for rulemaking as a rarely used supplement to a 63-year history of case adjudication should be re-examined toward providing affected parties something other than an appropriations rider as the only effective means for checking the agency's flex of political muscle.

Specific statutory provisions must be refined and parity restored at least as to certain fundamental statutory rights/responsibilities. There are many suggestions regarding statutory overhaul and all ideas should be given the light of day. In Section 2 of the Act, there is a need for balance and parity in the treatment of agency, holding an employer or a labor organization responsible for acts performed on their behalf (Raudabaugh 1994b; Yager 1996). All manner of activities are undertaken with impunity by persons encouraged by a party, yet often it is difficult or impossible to hold a party responsible. In terms of the shopworn adage "level playing field," and considering Congress' perception that the world of labor relations is unique—where a wink and a nod excuses heightened emotions, vandalism, and threats—something must be done to shield a party from unlawful actions by persons encouraged, aided and abetted in conducting large-scale corporate campaigns while holding the other side responsible for every sneeze of any first line supervisor.

Section 2(2) should be clarified to end the *Rescare, Inc.–Management Training Corp.*, debate regarding the statutory reach over government contractors.[6] In Section 2(3) the definition of independent contractor status and the questions regarding the contingent work force must be resolved.[7] The "salting" issue should be examined and language added to state clearly the policy choice.[8]

The continuing *Electromation* debate, the proposed TEAM Act, and the issues of employee involvement concern not only Section 8(a)(2) but also Section 2(5). If the labor organization definition were amended to mean any representative organization in which employees participate, such would limit unlawful employer overreaching only to representative groups and would protect many employee participation programs. The Labor Management Reporting and Disclosure Act defines "labor organization" similarly which, if left alone, may facilitate collateral challenges to the employee participation issue despite the proposed Section 8(a)(2) –TEAM Act "fix."[79]

The Section 2(11) definition of "supervisor" needs attention. Despite 63 years of adjudication and interpretation, we still see the Board "struggle" in individual cases while parties decry manipulative outcomes. The definitional factor, "independent judgment," facilitates interpretive abuse. All too often, individuals who clearly exercise supervisory functions are treated as employees and allowed to vote in elections where the Board views the exercise of supervisory functions as merely "routine" rather than embracing "judgment." Likewise, persons are deprived of the franchise by adjudicatory fiat for possessing such "judgment" even though the decisions are less than clear and consistent in explaining the concept.

Sections 3 and 4 present concerns regarding internal Board administration. Perhaps one solution to depoliticizing the agency is to extend the length of terms and/or prohibit reappointment. Out of an abundance of caution, perhaps the statute should be amended to prohibit the executive secretary from assigning cases to board members on any basis other than random, prohibiting any board member from opting off an assigned case for any reason other than a previously reported conflict, defining the parameters for and placing limits on the practice of "icing" cases (batching cases with the same or similar issues while waiting for a best, lead case—or dodging a politically hot potato?), and establishing limits on the "one member only" phenomenon (institutionalizing and apparently condoning a practice of waiting for the last Board member on a panel to "act" or signoff on a decision—or delay taking a position on a sensitive issue?). In Section 5, Congress may wish to consider amending the statute to permit the relocation of the Board's principal office to other than the District of Columbia for purposes of cost savings and to limit the number of regional and subregional offices, a number to be determined by oversight hearings and a review of historic case intake and personnel staffing. Presently, there is no limitation on the number of field offices and political and bureaucratic infighting resists change. Section 7 should be clarified to define "concerted" activities to eliminate the possibility of further adjudicatory redefinition.

Parity should be considered in aligning the prohibited restrictions in Section 8(a)(1) with Section 8(b)(1) to add "interference" as an additional source of potential union unfair labor practices. Section 8(a)(2) should be amended to delete references to "interference" and "formation" as variables in determining employer control of employee participation activities. The subsection should also reflect that minimal levels of employer financial or other forms of support are lawful.

The language of Section 8(a)(3) should be adjusted to reflect the series of Supreme Court decisions regarding an employee's limited financial obligation.[10]

Section 8(b) should be expanded to add a section correlative to Section 8(a)(4) to specifically prohibit unions from discriminating against employees who file charges or give testimony under the Act.

Certainly one of the most intractable problems, especially in representation case matters, is the issue of free speech. Section 8(c) refers to unfair labor practice issues and does not address speech other than threats or promises. What is lacking is good definition of free speech and that which can be regulated by the Board. The Board's discretion in this area is unacceptable.

Section 8(d) is short of the mark. Current statutory guidance for parties is woefully lacking. What we do know is that good faith requires the mutual obligation to meet and intention to work toward an agreement even though there is no statutory obligation to make a concession. Much has been said about the problems of first-time contract negotiations considering the difficulties of hammering out language within the one-year protected certification bar. It is argued that employers can engage in stalling tactics and hard or surface bargaining. Yet with the advent of sophisticated union corporate campaigns, much can be said of union tactics. In a large, multi-facility, nationwide campaign, unions may have little reason to pursue negotiations in timely fashion if there are remaining facilities to organize. And, for any negotiations—first time or renewal—surely no party can be held hostage to bargain forever. The statute needs to incorporate additional factors to guide the parties and the Board. Too much discretion lies with the political appointees and staff, many of whom have never experienced collective bargaining or managing against a financial bottom line. Surely there should be some concept of a minimum efficiency requirement to preclude opportunities for deliberate delay and endless information requests which, admittedly, may be metaphysically relevant to the bargaining process but add nothing on the margin to the efficiency of negotiations and maximizing a bargained outcome. Additionally, the concept of impasse is not addressed and there is no statutory guidance to the parties as to the mysteries or art of reaching impasse. While one cannot draft language that would resolve all circumstances, the clear fact is that this statutory section needs work.

Sections 9(b) and 9(c)(5) should be deleted. If we continue to opt for "an" appropriate unit rather than "the most" appropriate unit, then Section 9(c)(5)'s dictate must be honored and not in the breach. The Board has historically manipulated unit determinations and ignored this statutory provision. It is common knowledge that in almost every case, unions get whatever unit they petition for. This is not a small problem. To ignore the employer's business and its organizational structure while assisting the union in the short-term considerations of ensuring an election victory, ignores long-term structural problems created if the union wins and bargaining and contract administration are in the cards. If employee relations policy favors constructive relationships between employers and unions then, at the least, the employer's industry and organizational structure should weigh heavily in considering appropriate bargaining units to help the parties succeed in their possible, future relationships.

Consideration also should be directed to amending Section 9(c) to state minimum and/or maximum time limits for the critical period to ensure that all interested parties have an opportunity to exercise their rights of expression. Of course, this raises another major issue—whether the employer should have any role to play in a representation election and further, should mere card majorities supplant elections. If the policy choice is made that employers have an interest and right to express opinions concerning employee organization, then some statutory minimum statement is necessary to avoid politicized Boards from attempting to eliminate any opportunity for employer expression as a further assist to union organizing.

Section 9(e)(1) should be amended in several ways. The statute should provide guidance for testing good faith majority status. The vexing problem of the Board's treatment of blocking charges must be addressed. The simple process of impounding ballots with certifications withheld until unfair labor practices are resolved would suffice. This would eliminate a party's ability to play games with the election date scheduling by last minute filing of often questionable unfair labor practice charges.

Section 10(b) should be amended to require minimal specifications regarding Board investigation prior to the issuance of a complaint and bargaining order standards should be codified. Section 10(j) should be amended to permit any named party to an injunction the opportunity to present oral argument before the Board prior to the Board's determination whether to authorize such injunction requests. The named party should be given the opportunity to review any general counsel memorandum in support of an injunction request. Board authorization should require unanimous approval considering the extraordinary purpose, especially if remedies are made tort-like. Consideration should be given to permitting only Senate-confirmed members to vote on such extraordinary remedies. The standard for Board approval of any such injunction request should be statutorily defined and based on traditional equitable criteria. Of course, the debate must be resolved over whether Board remedies are remedial or punitive and whether interest arbitration should be specifically prohibited.

In the end, all parties have certain ghosts to confront. There is the reality of global market competition. If economic competitors do not share the same social values and legal parameters, to what extent will we be willing to endure economic costs to advance and protect our national values. Protections ultimately inflict costs on a society in competition with others who do not share the same legal prescriptions. And, if we are willing to accept such costs, how do we go about paying for them.

The present system of nonpunitive remedies and the time involved in getting "relief" reduces the effectiveness of advancing stated federal policy goals. Should we continue to rely on political appointees and cloistered bureaucracies to make these decisions or do we need to toss in the towel and turn to the courts?

> At bottom, the Board's difficulties arise from the fact that Congress and the President have asked it to resolve something they can't decide themselves: how—and perhaps even whether—to promote workplace democracy in the bewildering new economic order.[11]

Congress has an obligation to be engaged and, ultimately, to act. The workplace has changed dramatically, just in this century. The politics of some administrations have worked hard to ignore the need for change, while results-oriented politics of other administrations ultimately failed in their efforts to recommend future employee relations policies. Rather than set a time certain for completing a review, the process must be single-minded in its non-partisanship, open to many voices—not just those selected by insiders— and daring enough to act.

### Endnotes

[1] *United Food and Commercial Workers Local No. 880 v. NLRB*, 60 F.3d 855 (DC Cir. 1996); *Riesbeck Food Markets, Inc. v. NLRB*, 91 F.3d 132 (4th Cir. 1996). See also Raudabaugh (1994a).

[2] See Commons (1918 Vol. 4:636).

[3] See Epstein and Paul (1985); Finkin (1994); Gould (1993); Kochan, Katz, and McKersie (1986); Freeman and Medoff (1984); Weiler (1990); Harry (1968); Yager (1996).

[4] 29 U.S.C. § 151.

[5] 29 U.S.C. § 157

[6] See e.g., *Coastal Stevedoring*, 323 NLRB No. 178 (1997) (Chairman Gould, dissenting); *Westwood Horizons Hotel*, 270 NLRB 802 (1984); *NLRB v. Herbert Halperin Distrib. Corp.*, 826 F.2d 287 (4th Cir. 1987).

[7] *Res-Care, Inc.*, 280 NLRB 670 (1986) rev'd, *Management Training Corp.*, 317 NLRB 1355 (1995), aff'd, *Teledyne Economic Development v. NLRB*, 108 F.3d 56 (4th Cir. 1997).

[8] See e.g., *Roadway Package System, Inc.*, NLRB Case Nos. 31-RC-7267, 31-RC-7277; *Dial-A-Mattress Operating Corp.*, NLRB Case No. 29-RC-8442; *M.B. Sturgis, Inc.*, NLRB Case No. 14-RC-11572; *Jeffboat Div.*, American Commercial and Marine Services Co., NLRB Case No. 9-UC-406; *Value Recycle, Inc.*, NLRB Case No. 33-RC-4042.

[9] *Architectural Glass and Metal Co., Inc. v. NLRB*, 107 F.3d 426 (6th Cir. 1997).

[10] Compare, 29 USC § 152(5) and 29 USC § 402(i), (j). See also Raudabaugh (1996).

[11] *Communication Workers v. Beck*, 487 US 735 (1988); *California Saw and Knife Works*, 320 NLRB 224 (1995).

## References

Commission on the Future of Worker-Management Relations. 1994. *Report and Recommendations*. Washington, DC: U.S. Departments of Labor and Commerce.

Commons, John R. 1918. Vols. 1 & 4. *History of Labor in the United States*. New York: The MacMillan Company.

Epstein, Richard A., and Jeffrey Paul, eds. 1985. *Labor Law and the Employment Market*. New Brunswick, NJ: Transaction Books.

Finkin, Matthew W., ed. 1994. *The Legal Future of Employee Representation*. Ithaca, NY: ILR Press.

Freeman, Richard B., and James L. Medoff. 1984. *What Do Unions Do?* New York: Basic Books.

Gould, William B. IV. 1993. *Agenda for Reform*. Cambridge, MA: The MIT Press.

Kochan, Thomas A., Harry C. Katz, and Robert B. McKersie. 1986. *The Transformation of American Industrial Relations*. New York: Basic Books.

Raudabaugh, John N. 1994a. "Access to Private Property: Jurisprudence or Realpolitik." Toronto: American Conference Institute.

_____. 1994b. "Perspectives on Labor Law Reform." *Proceedings of the 1994 Spring Meeting* (Philadelphia). Madison, WI: Industrial Relations Research Association, pp. 470-75.

_____. 1995. "A Critique of the 15 Key Resolutions." Washington, DC: Business Research Publications.

_____. 1996. "Employee Participation Programs and Federal Labor Policy." Stetson University: Eleventh Annual National Conference.

Sweeney, John J. 1996. *America Needs a Raise*. New York: Houghton Mifflin Co.

Weiler, Paul C. 1990. *Governing the Workplace*. Cambridge: Harvard University Press.

Wellington, Harry H. 1968. *Labor and the Legal Process*. New Haven: Yale University Press.

Yager, Daniel V. 1996. *NLRB Agency in Crisis*. Washington, DC: LPA.